Vauxhall Astra and Belmont Owners Workshop Manual

Matthew Minter

Models covered
Vauxhall Astra Hatchback and Estate models, including GTE
Vauxhall Belmont Saloon models, including GLSi
1196 cc, 1297 cc, 1598 cc and 1796 cc petrol engines

Covers most features of the Bedford Astra & Astramax Vans
Does not cover Diesel engine or revised range introduced October 1986

(1136 - 10M1)

ABCDE
FGHIJ
KLMNO
PQR

Haynes Publishing Group
Sparkford Nr Yeovil
Somerset BA22 7JJ England

Haynes Publications, Inc
861 Lawrence Drive
Newbury Park
California 91320 USA

Acknowledgements
Thanks are due to the Champion Sparking Plug Company who supplied the illustrations showing the spark plug conditions. Certain other illustrations are the copyright of Vauxhall Motors Ltd, and are used with their permission. Thanks are also due to Vauxhall Motors for the supply of technical information and for the loan of a project vehicle, to Sykes-Pickavant who provided some of the workshop tools, and to all those people at Sparkford who helped in the production of this manual

A book in the **Haynes Owners Workshop Manual Series**

Printed by J. H. Haynes & Co. Ltd, Sparkford, Nr Yeovil, Somerset BA22 7JJ, England

ISBN 1 85010 320 8

British Library Cataloguing in Publication Data
Minter, Matthew
Vauxhall Astra & Belmont owners workshop manual.–2nd ed.–(Owners Workshop Manual)
1. Vauxhall Astra automobile 2. Vauxhall Belmont automobile
I. Title II. Minter, Matthew. Vauxhall Astra owners workshop manual III. Series
629.28'722 TL215.V3
ISBN 1-85010-320-8

Contents

Vauxhall Astra GTE

About this manual

Its aim

The aim of this manual is to help you get the best value from your vehicle. It can do so in several ways. It can help you decide what work must be done (even should you choose to get it done by a garage), provide information on routine maintenance and servicing, and give a logical course of action and diagnosis when random faults occur. However, it is hoped that you will use the manual by tackling the work yourself. On simpler jobs it may even be quicker than booking the car into a garage and going there twice, to leave and collect it. Perhaps most important, a lot of money can be saved by avoiding the costs a garage must charge to cover its labour and overheads.

The manual has drawings and descriptions to show the function of the various components so that their layout can be understood. Then the tasks are described and photographed in a step-by-step sequence so that even a novice can do the work.

Its arrangement

The manual is divided into thirteen Chapters, each covering a logical sub-division of the vehicle. The Chapters are each divided into Sections, numbered with single figures, eg 5; and the Sections into paragraphs (or sub-sections), with decimal numbers following on from the Section they are in, eg 5.1, 5.2, 5.3 etc.

It is freely illustrated, especially in those parts where there is a detailed sequence of operations to be carried out. There are two forms of illustration: figures and photographs. The figures are numbered in sequence with decimal numbers, according to their position in the Chapter – eg Fig. 6.4 is the fourth drawing/illustration in Chapter 6. Photographs carry the same number (either individually or in related groups) as the Section or sub-section to which they relate.

There is an alphabetical index at the back of the manual as well as a contents list at the front. Each Chapter is also preceded by its own individual contents list.

References to the 'left' or 'right' of the vehicle are in the sense of a person in the driver's seat facing forwards.

Unless otherwise stated, nuts and bolts are removed by turning anti-clockwise, and tightened by turning clockwise.

Vehicle manufacturers continually make changes to specifications and recommendations, and these, when notified, are incorporated into our manuals at the earliest opportunity.

Introduction to the Vauxhall Astra and Belmont

The 'new' Astra was introduced to the UK market in October 1984. Mechanically it is very similar to its predecessor, although the body has been completely redesigned and numerous improvements have been made in other areas.

The Belmont was introduced in January 1986, and is mechanically identical to the Astra, only the rear end body styling being different; this aspect being dealt with in the Supplement to this manual.

Four petrol engines are available: 1.2 OHV (Astra only) and 1.3, 1.6 and 1.8 OHC (Astra and Belmont models). The 1.8 engined versions (Astra GTE and Belmont GLSi) are fitted with fuel injection. A 1.6 diesel engine is also available, but is not dealt with in this manual. Both OHV and OHC engines are well proven designs and, provided regular maintenance is carried out, are unlikely to give trouble.

The Astra Estate is only fitted with the 1.3 or 1.6 engine. An Astra Van is sold under the Bedford label, and with the exception of the Astramax, which has leaf spring rear suspension, the Vans closely resemble the passenger car range.

Transmission and running gear follow established Vauxhall front-wheel-drive practice. Manual transmission is either four or five-speed; automatic transmission is available on most models.

Both the Astra and Belmont are attractive, comfortable, well-equipped vehicles, requiring minimal maintenance, with most service and repair tasks being straightforward.

General dimensions, weights and capacities

For modifications, and information applicable to later models, see Supplement at end of manual

Dimensions

Overall height:	
Hatchback (except GTE)	1.400 m (55.1 in)
Hatchback (GTE)	1.395 m (54.9 in)
Estate	1.430 m (56.3 in)
Van	1.440 m (56.7 in)
Overall width:	
Hatchback	1.663 m (65.5 in)
Estate and Van	1.666 m (65.6 in)
Overall length:	
Hatchback	3.998 m (157.4 in)
Estate and Van	4.228 m (166.5 in)
Wheelbase	2.520 m (99.2 in)
Ground clearance (unladen):	
Hatchback	133 mm (5.2 in)
Estate	135 mm (5.3 in)
Van	130 mm (5.1 in)

Weights*

Kerb weights:	
1.2 Hatchback	830 to 865 kg (1830 to 1907 lb)
1.3 Hatchback	845 to 915 kg (1863 to 2018 lb)
1.6 Hatchback	925 to 975 kg (2040 to 2150 lb)
1.8 GTE	950 kg (2095 lb)
1.3 Estate	900 to 1000 kg (1985 to 2205 lb)
1.6 Estate	965 to 1045 kg (2128 to 2304 lb)
1.3 Van	880 to 920 kg (1940 to 2029 lb)
1.6 Van	945 to 970 kg (2084 to 2139 lb)
Payload:	
1.2 Hatchback	490 to 505 kg (1081 to 1114 lb)
1.3 Hatchback	475 to 495 kg (1047 to 1092 lb)
1.6 Hatchback	480 to 500 kg (1058 to 1103 lb)
1.8 GTE	485 kg (1069 lb)
1.3 Estate	460 to 535 kg (1014 to 1180 lb)
1.6 Estate	540 to 595 kg (1191 to 1312 lb)
1.3 Van	600 to 605 kg (1323 to 1334 lb)
1.6 Van	610 to 615 kg (1345 to 1356 lb)
Gross vehicle weight:	
1.2 Hatchback	1335 kg (2944 lb)
1.3 Hatchback	1335 to 1400 kg (2944 to 3087 lb)
1.6 Hatchback	1415 to 1455 kg (3120 to 3208 lb)
1.8 GTE	1435 kg (3164 lb)
1.3 Estate	1420 to 1475 kg (3131 to 3252 lb)
1.6 Estate	1560 to 1585 kg (3439 to 3494 lb)
1.3 Van	1480 to 1525 kg (3263 to 3362 lb)
1.6 Van	1560 to 1580 kg (3439 to 3483 lb)

Gross train weight:	
1.3 Van	2075 to 2330 kg (4575 to 5137 lb)
1.6 Van	2560 to 2580 kg (5644 to 5688 lb)
Caravan/trailer weight limit – unbraked:	
1.2 and 1.3	400 kg (882 lb)
1.6 and 1.8	450 kg (992 lb)
Caravan/trailer weight limit – braked:	
1.2 Hatchback, 4-speed	600 kg (1323 lb)
1.2 Hatchback, 5-speed	650 kg (1433 lb)
1.3 Hatchback, 4-speed	900 kg (1985 lb)
1.3 Hatchback, 5-speed	950 kg (2095 lb)
1.3 Hatchback, automatic	750 kg (1654 lb)
1.3 Estate, 4 or 5-speed	850 kg (1874 lb)
1.3 Estate, automatic	650 kg (1433 lb)
1.6, Hatchback or Estate, manual or automatic	1000 kg (2205 lb)
1.8 GTE	1000 kg (2205 lb)
Towing hitch downward load	50 kg (110 lb) max
Roof load (including rack)	100 kg (221 lb) max

** Kerb weights are approximate and vary according to equipment fitted, Payload, GVW, GTW and trailer weight limits may be subject to current legislation.*

Capacities (approx)

Cooling system:	
1.2	1.7 litres (3.0 pints)
1.3 (manual)	1.8 litres (3.2 pints)
1.3 (automatic)	7.1 litres (12.5 pints)
1.6 (manual)	7.8 litres (13.7 pints)
1.6 (automatic)	7.6 litres (13.4 pints)
1.8	7.6 litres (13.4 pints)
Fuel tank:	
Hatchback	42 litres (9.3 gallons)
Estate and Van	50 litres (11.0 gallons)
Engine oil (drain and refill, including filter):	
1.2	2.75 litres (4.8 pints)
1.3	3.00 litres (5.3 pints)
1.6 and 1.8	3.25 litres (5.7 pints)
Manual gearbox oil:	
F10/4	1.7 litres (3.0 pints)
F10/5	1.8 litres (3.2 pints)
F16/4	2.0 litres (3.5 pints)
F16/5	2.1 litres (3.7 pints)
Automatic transmission (drain and refill)	6.3 litres (11.1 pints)
Brake hydraulic system	0.4 litre (0.7 pint)
Screen washer reservoir	2.5 litres (4.4 pints)
Headlamp washer reservoir	8.0 litres (14.1 pints)

Jacking, towing and wheel changing

Jacking

Use the jack supplied with the vehicle only for wheel changing during roadside emergencies (photo). Chock the wheel diagonally opposite the one being removed.

When raising the vehicle for repair or maintenance, preferably use a trolley or hydraulic jack with a wooden block as an insulator to prevent damage to the underbody. Place the jack under a structural member at the points indicated, never raise the vehicle by jacking up under the engine sump, transmission casing or rear axle. If both front or both rear wheels are to be raised, jack up one side first and securely support it on an axle stand before raising the other side.

To avoid repetition, the procedures for raising the vehicle in order to carry out work under it is not included before each relevant operation described in this manual.

It is to be preferred and is certainly recommended that the vehicle is positioned over an inspection pit of raised on a lift. When such equipment is not available, use ramps or jack up the vehicle as previously described, but always supplement the lifting device with axle stands.

Towing

Towing hooks are welded to the front and rear of the vehicle. If a front spoiler is fitted, a towing shackle and pin are provided which must be inserted through the access cover in the spoiler (photos). The

Tool kit jack in use

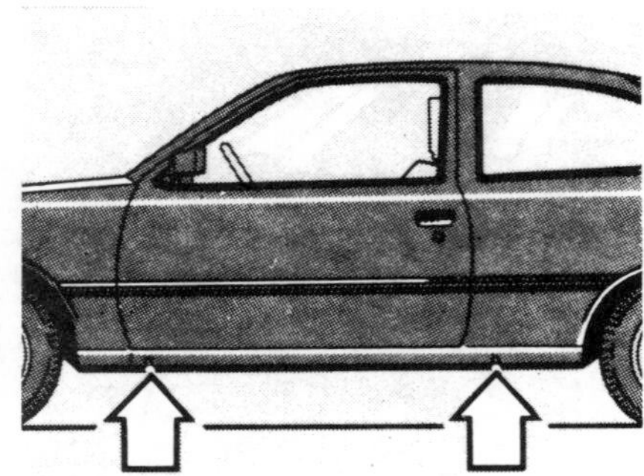

Jacking points (arrowed) for tool kit jack

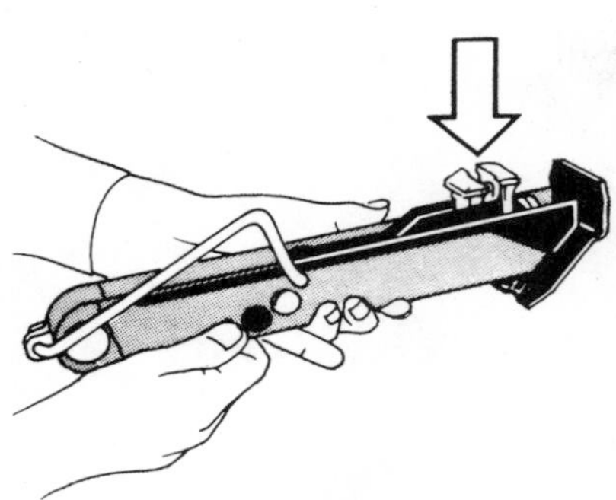

Groove in jack head (arrowed) must engage with seam on sill

Workshop jack location – front

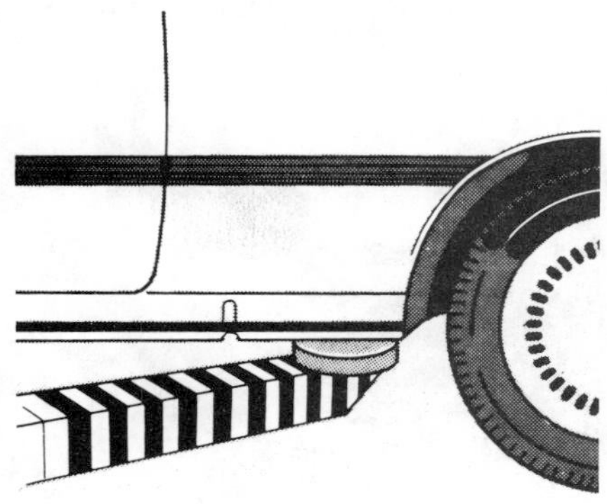

Workshop jack location – rear

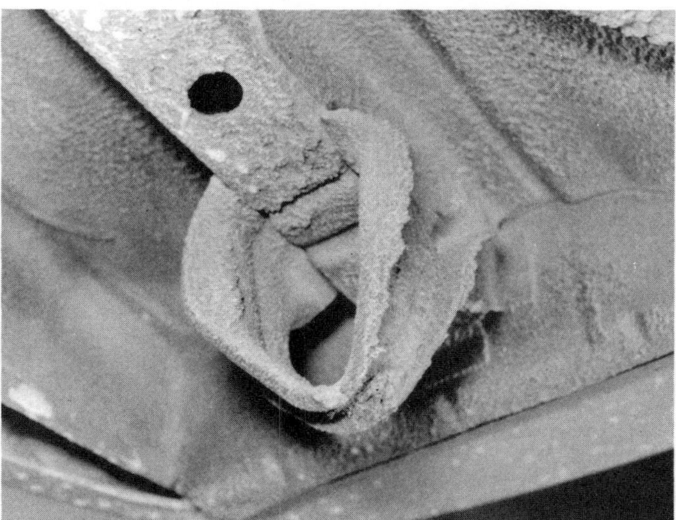

Rear towing eye

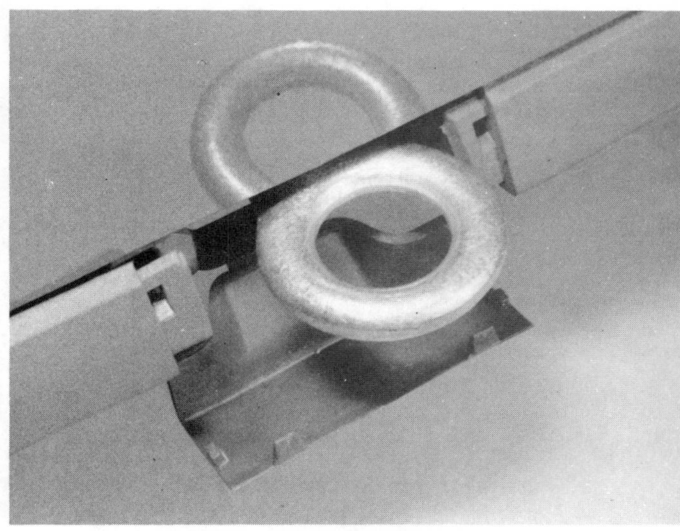

Front towing shackle (GTE)

Towing shackle fixing details (GTE)

rear towing hook should only be used for emergency towing of another vehicle; for trailer towing a properly fitted towing bracket should be installed.

Vehicles with automatic transmission should not be towed further than 60 miles (100 km) or faster than 50 mph (80 km/h). If these conditions cannot be met, or if transmission damage has already occurred, the vehicle must be towed with its front wheels off the ground.

When being towed, remember to insert the ignition key and turn it to Position 1. Expect to apply greater pressure to the footbrake, as servo assistance will not be available after the first few brake applications.

Wheel changing

To change a roadwheel, first park on a firm flat surface if possible. Prise off the wheel trim or lever off the wheel bolt caps, as applicable (photo). Apply the handbrake and engage reverse gear (or P on automatic).

If the car is fairly new, the wheels and tires will have been balanced on the vehicle during production. To maintain this relationship, mark the position of the wheel relative to the hub. (This is not necessary if the tyre is to be removed for repair or renewal, since the balance will inevitably be altered.)

Removing the wheel trim

Undoing a wheel bolt

Slacken the wheel bolts by half a turn each (photo). Chock the wheel diagonally opposite the one being removed, then raise the vehicle with the jack. When the wheel is clear of the ground, remove the wheel bolts and take off the wheel.

Fit the new wheel and secure it with the bolts. Tighten the bolts until they are snug, but do not try to tighten them fully yet. Lower the vehicle and remove the jack, then tighten the wheel bolts in criss-cross sequence. The use of a torque wrench is strongly recommended, especially when alloy wheels are fitted; see Chapter 10 Specifications for the recommended tightening torque.

Refit the wheel trim or bolt caps and stow the tools. If a new wheel has been brought into service, have it balanced on the vehicle if necessary.

Buying spare parts and vehicle identification numbers

Buying spare parts

Spare parts are available from many sources, for example: Vauxhall garages, other garages and accessory shops, and motor factors. Our advice regarding spare part sources is as follows:

Officially appointed Vauxhall garages – This is the best source for parts which are peculiar to your vehicle and are otherwise not generally available (eg, complete cylinder heads, internal gearbox components, badges, interior trim etc). It is also the only place you should buy parts if your vehicle is still under warranty; non-Vauxhall components may invalidate the warranty. To be sure of obtaining the correct parts it will always be necessary to give the storeman your vehicle's engine and chassis number, and if possible, to take the 'old' part along for positive identification. Remember that some parts are available on a factory exchange scheme – any parts returned should always be clean. It obviously makes good sense to go straight to the specialists on your vehicle for this type of part, for they are best equipped to supply you.

Other garages and accessory shops – These are often very good places to buy materials and components needed for the maintenance of your vehicle (eg, spark plugs, bulbs, drivebelts, oils and greases, touch-up paint, filler paste etc.) They also sell general accessories, usually have convenient opening hours, charge lower prices and can often be found not far from home.

Motor factors – Good factors will stock all the more important components which wear out relatively quickly (eg, clutch components, pistons, valves, exhaust systems, brake cylinders/pipes/hoses/seals/shoes and pads etc). Motor factors will often provide new or reconditioned components on a part exchange basis – this can save a considerable amount of money.

Vehicle identification numbers

The *Vehicle Identification Number* is located inside the engine compartment on top of the front end panel. The plate is marked with the vehicle chassis and designation number and the colour code. Also shown is the maximum gross weight for the car (photo).

The *engine number* is stamped on a flat machined on the engine cylinder block.

The *chassis number* is stamped on the body floor panel between the driver's seat and the door sill.

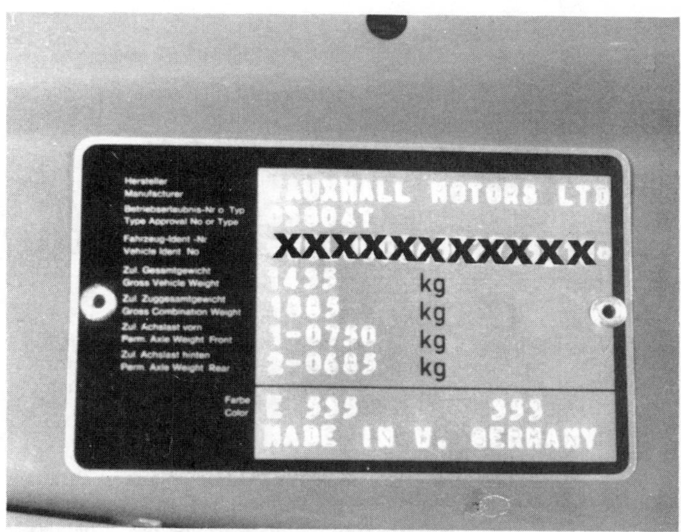

Vehicle identification plate

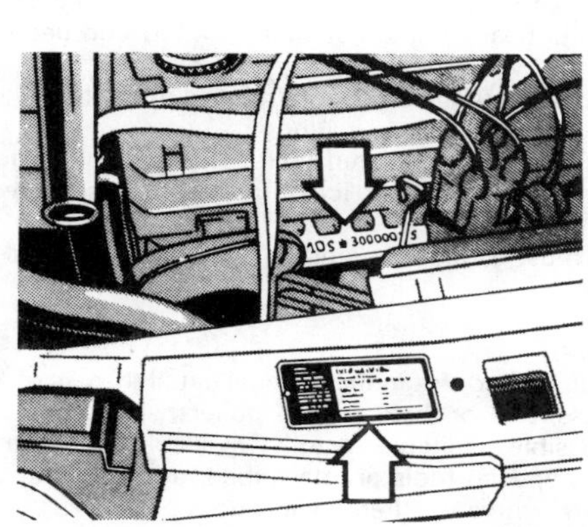

Engine number and VIN plate locations (arrowed)

Chassis number location (arrowed)

General repair procedures

Whenever servicing, repair or overhaul work is carried out on the car or its components, it is necessary to observe the following procedures and instructions. This will assist in carrying out the operation efficiently and to a professional standard of workmanship.

Joint mating faces and gaskets

Where a gasket is used between the mating faces of two components, ensure that it is renewed on reassembly, and fit it dry unless otherwise stated in the repair procedure. Make sure that the mating faces are clean and dry with all traces of old gasket removed. When cleaning a joint face, use a tool which is not likely to score or damage the face, and remove any burrs or nicks with an oilstone or fine file.

Make sure that tapped holes are cleaned with a pipe cleaner, and keep them free of jointing compound if this is being used unless specifically instructed otherwise.

Ensure that all orifices, channels or pipes are clear and blow through them, preferably using compressed air.

Oil seals

Whenever an oil seal is removed from its working location, either individually or as part of an assembly, it should be renewed.

The very fine sealing lip of the seal is easily damaged and will not seal if the surface it contacts is not completely clean and free from scratches, nicks or grooves. If the original sealing surface of the component cannot be restored, the component should be renewed.

Protect the lips of the seal from any surface which may damage them in the course of fitting. Use tape or a conical sleeve where possible. Lubricate the seal lips with oil before fitting and, on dual lipped seals, fill the space between the lips with grease.

Unless otherwise stated, oil seals must be fitted with their sealing lips toward the lubricant to be sealed.

Use a tubular drift or block of wood of the appropriate size to install the seal and, if the seal housing is shouldered, drive the seal down to the shoulder. If the seal housing is unshouldered, the seal should be fitted with its face flush with the housing top face.

Screw threads and fastenings

Always ensure that a blind tapped hole is completely free from oil, grease, water or other fluid before installing the bolt or stud. Failure to do this could cause the housing to crack due to the hydraulic action of the bolt or stud as it is screwed in.

When tightening a castellated nut to accept a split pin, tighten the nut to the specified torque, where applicable, and then tighten further to the next split pin hole. Never slacken the nut to align a split pin hole unless stated in the repair procedure.

When checking or retightening a nut or bolt to a specified torque setting, slacken the nut or bolt by a quarter of a turn, and then retighten to the specified setting.

Locknuts, locktabs and washers

Any fastening which will rotate against a component or housing in the course of tightening should always have a washer between it and the relevant component or housing.

Spring or split washers should always be renewed when they are used to lock a critical component such as a big-end bearing retaining nut or bolt.

Locktabs which are folded over to retain a nut or bolt should always be renewed.

Self-locking nuts can be reused in non-critical areas, providing resistance can be felt when the locking portion passes over the bolt or stud thread.

Split pins must always be replaced with new ones of the correct size for the hole.

Special tools

Some repair procedures in this manual entail the use of special tools such as a press, two or three-legged pullers, spring compressors etc. Wherever possible, suitable readily available alternatives to the manufacturer's special tools are described, and are shown in use. In some instances, where no alternative is possible, it has been necessary to resort to the use of a manufacturer's tool and this has been done for reasons of safety as well as the efficient completion of the repair operation. Unless you are highly skilled and have a thorough understanding of the procedure described, never attempt to bypass the use of any special tool when the procedure described specifies its use. Not only is there a very great risk of personal injury, but expensive damage could be caused to the components involved.

Tools and working facilities

Introduction

A selection of good tools is a fundamental requirement for anyone contemplating the maintenance and repair of a motor vehicle. For the owner who does not possess any, their purchase will prove a considerable expense, offsetting some of the savings made by doing-it-yourself. However, provided that the tools purchased are of good quality, they will last for many years and prove an extremely worthwhile investment.

To help the average owner to decide which tools are needed to carry out the various tasks detailed in this manual, we have compiled three lists of tools under the following headings: *Maintenance and minor repair, Repair and overhaul,* and *Special.* The newcomer to practical mechanics should start off with the *Maintenance and minor repair* tool kit and confine himself to the simpler jobs around the vehicle. Then, as his confidence and experience grow, he can undertake more difficult tasks, buying extra tools as, and when, they are needed. In this way, a *Maintenance and minor repair* tool kit can be built-up into a *Repair and overhaul* tool kit over a considerable period of time without any major cash outlays. The experienced do-it-yourselfer will have a tool kit good enough for most repair and overhaul procedures and will add tools from the *Special* category when he feels the expense is justified by the amount of use to which these tools will be put.

It is obviously not possible to cover the subject of tools fully here. For those who wish to learn more about tools and their use there is a book entitled *How to Choose and Use Car Tools* available from the publishers of this manual.

Maintenance and minor repair tool kit

The tools given in this list should be considered as a minimum requirement if routine maintenance, servicing and minor repair operations are to be undertaken. We recommend the purchase of combination spanners (ring one end, open-ended the other); although more expensive than open-ended ones, they do give the advantages of both types of spanner.

Combination spanners - 10, 11, 12, 13, 14 & 17 mm
Adjustable spanner - 9 inch
Spark plug spanner (with rubber insert)
Spark plug gap adjustment tool
Set of feeler gauges
Brake bleed nipple spanner
Screwdriver - 4 in long x 1/4 in dia (flat blade)
Screwdriver - 4 in long x 1/4 in dia (cross blade)
Combination pliers - 6 inch
Hacksaw (junior)
Tyre pump
Tyre pressure gauge
Oil can
Fine emery cloth (1 sheet)
Wire brush (small)
Funnel (medium size)

Repair and overhaul tool kit

These tools are virtually essential for anyone undertaking any major repairs to a motor vehicle, and are additional to those given in the *Maintenance and minor repair* list. Included in this list is a comprehensive set of sockets. Although these are expensive they will be found invaluable as they are so versatile - particularly if various drives are included in the set. We recommend the 1/2 in square-drive type, as this can be used with most proprietary torque wrenches. If you cannot afford a socket set, even bought piecemeal, then inexpensive tubular box spanners are a useful alternative.

The tools in this list will occasionally need to be supplemented by tools from the *Special* list.

Sockets (or box spanners) to cover range in previous list
Reversible ratchet drive (for use with sockets)
Extension piece, 10 inch (for use with sockets)
Universal joint (for use with sockets)
Torque wrench (for use with sockets)
'Mole' wrench - 8 inch
Ball pein hammer
Soft-faced hammer, plastic or rubber
Screwdriver - 6 in long x 5/16 in dia (flat blade)
Screwdriver - 2 in long x 5/16 in square (flat blade)
Screwdriver - 1 1/2 in long x 1/4 in dia (cross blade)
Screwdriver - 3 in long x 1/8 in dia (electricians)
Pliers - electricians side cutters
Pliers - needle nosed
Pliers - circlip (internal and external)
Cold chisel - 1/2 inch
Scriber
Scraper
Centre punch
Pin punch
Hacksaw
Valve grinding tool
Steel rule/straight-edge
Allen keys
Torx splined keys
Selection of files
Wire brush (large)
Axle-stands
Jack (strong scissor or hydraulic type)

Special tools

The tools in this list are those which are not used regularly, are expensive to buy, or which need to be used in accordance with their manufacturers' instructions. Unless relatively difficult mechanical jobs are undertaken frequently, it will not be economic to buy many of these tools. Where this is the case, you could consider clubbing together with friends (or joining a motorists' club) to make a joint purchase, or borrowing the tools against a deposit from a local garage or tool hire specialist.

The following list contains only those tools and instruments freely available to the public, and not those special tools produced by the vehicle manufacturer specifically for its dealer network. You will find occasional references to these manufacturers' special tools in the text of this manual. Generally, an alternative method of doing the job without the vehicle manufacturers' special tool is given. However, sometimes, there is no alternative to using them. Where this is the case and the relevant tool cannot be bought or borrowed, you will have to entrust the work to a franchised garage.

Valve spring compressor
Piston ring compressor
Balljoint separator
Universal hub/bearing puller
Impact screwdriver
Micrometer and/or vernier gauge
Dial gauge
Stroboscopic timing light
Dwell angle meter/tachometer
Universal electrical multi-meter
Cylinder compression gauge
Lifting tackle
Trolley jack
Light with extension lead

Buying tools

For practically all tools, a tool factor is the best source since he will have a very comprehensive range compared with the average garage or accessory shop. Having said that, accessory shops often offer excellent quality tools at discount prices, so it pays to shop around.

Remember, you don't have to buy the most expensive items on the shelf, but it is always advisable to steer clear of the very cheap tools. There are plenty of good tools around at reasonable prices, so ask the proprietor or manager of the shop for advice before making a purchase.

Care and maintenance of tools

Having purchased a reasonable tool kit, it is necessary to keep the tools in a clean serviceable condition. After use, always wipe off any dirt, grease and metal particles using a clean, dry cloth, before putting the tools away. Never leave them lying around after they have been used. A simple tool rack on the garage or workshop wall, for items such as screwdrivers and pliers is a good idea. Store all normal wrenches and sockets in a metal box. Any measuring instruments, gauges, meters, etc, must be carefully stored where they cannot be damaged or become rusty.

Take a little care when tools are used. Hammer heads inevitably become marked and screwdrivers lose the keen edge on their blades from time to time. A little timely attention with emery cloth or a file will soon restore items like this to a good serviceable finish.

Working facilities

Not to be forgotten when discussing tools, is the workshop itself. If anything more than routine maintenance is to be carried out, some form of suitable working area becomes essential.

It is appreciated that many an owner mechanic is forced by circumstances to remove an engine or similar item, without the benefit of a garage or workshop. Having done this, any repairs should always be done under the cover of a roof.

Wherever possible, any dismantling should be done on a clean, flat workbench or table at a suitable working height.

Any workbench needs a vice: one with a jaw opening of 4 in (100 mm) is suitable for most jobs. As mentioned previously, some clean dry storage space is also required for tools, as well as for lubricants, cleaning fluids, touch-up paints and so on, which become necessary.

Another item which may be required, and which has a much more general usage, is an electric drill with a chuck capacity of at least 56 in (8 mm). This, together with a good range of twist drills, is virtually essential for fitting accessories such as mirrors and reversing lights.

Last, but not least, always keep a supply of old newspapers and clean, lint-free rags available, and try to keep any working area as clean as possible.

Spanner jaw gap comparison table

Jaw gap (in)	Spanner size
0.250	1/4 in AF
0.276	7 mm
0.313	5/16 in AF
0.315	8 mm
0.344	11/32 in AF; 1/8 in Whitworth
0.354	9 mm
0.375	3/8 in AF
0.394	10 mm
0.433	11 mm
0.438	7/16 in AF
0.445	3/16 in Whitworth; 1/4 in BSF
0.472	12 mm
0.500	1/2 in AF
0.512	13 mm
0.525	1/4 in Whitworth; 5/16 in BSF
0.551	14 mm
0.563	9/16 in AF
0.591	15 mm
0.600	5/16 in Whitworth; 3/8 in BSF
0.625	5/8 in AF
0.630	16 mm
0.669	17 mm
0.686	11/16 in AF
0.709	18 mm
0.710	3/8 in Whitworth; 7/16 in BSF
0.748	19 mm
0.750	3/4 in AF
0.813	13/16 in AF
0.820	7/16 in Whitworth; 1/2 in BSF
0.866	22 mm
0.875	7/8 in AF
0.920	1/2 in Whitworth; 9/16 in BSF
0.938	15/16 in AF
0.945	24 mm
1.000	1 in AF
1.010	9/16 in Whitworth; 5/8 in BSF
1.024	26 mm
1.063	1 1/16 in AF; 27 mm
1.100	5/8 in Whitworth; 11/16 in BSF
1.125	1 1/8 in AF
1.181	30 mm
1.200	11/16 in Whitworth; 3/4 in BSF
1.250	1 1/4 in AF
1.260	32 mm
1.300	3/4 in Whitworth; 7/8 in BSF
1.313	1 5/16 in AF
1.390	13/16 in Whitworth; 15/16 in BSF
1.417	36 mm
1.438	1 7/16 in AF
1.480	7/8 in Whitworth; 1 in BSF
1.500	1 1/2 in AF
1.575	40 mm; 15/16 in Whitworth
1.614	41 mm
1.625	1 5/8 in AF
1.670	1 in Whitworth; 1 1/8 in BSF
1.688	1 11/16 in AF
1.811	46 mm
1.813	1 13/16 in AF
1.860	1 1/8 in Whitworth; 1 1/4 in BSF
1.875	1 7/8 in AF
1.969	50 mm
2.000	2 in AF
2.050	1 1/4 in Whitworth; 1 3/8 in BSF
2.165	55 mm
2.362	60 mm

Conversion factors

Length (distance)					
Inches (in)	X	25.4	= Millimetres (mm)	X	0.0394	= Inches (in)
Feet (ft)	X	0.305	= Metres (m)	X	3.281	= Feet (ft)
Miles	X	1.609	= Kilometres (km)	X	0.621	= Miles

Volume (capacity)						
Cubic inches (cu in; in^3)	X	16.387	= Cubic centimetres (cc; cm^3)	X	0.061	= Cubic inches (cu in; in^3)
Imperial pints (Imp pt)	X	0.568	= Litres (l)	X	1.76	= Imperial pints (Imp pt)
Imperial quarts (Imp qt)	X	1.137	= Litres (l)	X	0.88	= Imperial quarts (Imp qt)
Imperial quarts (Imp qt)	X	1.201	= US quarts (US qt)	X	0.833	= Imperial quarts (Imp qt)
US quarts (US qt)	X	0.946	= Litres (l)	X	1.057	= US quarts (US qt)
Imperial gallons (Imp gal)	X	4.546	= Litres (l)	X	0.22	= Imperial gallons (Imp gal)
Imperial gallons (Imp gal)	X	1.201	= US gallons (US gal)	X	0.833	= Imperial gallons (Imp gal)
US gallons (US gal)	X	3.785	= Litres (l)	X	0.264	= US gallons (US gal)

Mass (weight)						
Ounces (oz)	X	28.35	= Grams (g)	X	0.035	= Ounces (oz)
Pounds (lb)	X	0.454	= Kilograms (kg)	X	2.205	= Pounds (lb)

Force						
Ounces-force (ozf; oz)	X	0.278	= Newtons (N)	X	3.6	= Ounces-force (ozf; oz)
Pounds-force (lbf; lb)	X	4.448	= Newtons (N)	X	0.225	= Pounds-force (lbf; lb)
Newtons (N)	X	0.1	= Kilograms-force (kgf; kg)	X	9.81	= Newtons (N)

Pressure						
Pounds-force per square inch (psi; lbf/in^2; lb/in^2)	X	0.070	= Kilograms-force per square centimetre (kgf/cm^2; kg/cm^2)	X	14.223	= Pounds-force per square inch (psi; lbf/in^2; lb/in^2)
Pounds-force per square inch (psi; lbf/in^2; lb/in^2)	X	0.068	= Atmospheres (atm)	X	14.696	= Pounds-force per square inch (psi; lbf/in^2; lb/in^2)
Pounds-force per square inch (psi; lbf/in^2; lb/in^2)	X	0.069	= Bars	X	14.5	= Pounds-force per square inch (psi; lbf/in^2; lb/in^2)
Pounds-force per square inch (psi; lbf/in^2; lb/in^2)	X	6.895	= Kilopascals (kPa)	X	0.145	= Pounds-force per square inch (psi; lbf/in^2; lb/in^2)
Kilopascals (kPa)	X	0.01	= Kilograms-force per square centimetre (kgf/cm^2; kg/cm^2)	X	98.1	= Kilopascals (kPa)

Torque (moment of force)						
Pounds-force inches (lbf in; lb in)	X	1.152	= Kilograms-force centimetre (kgf cm; kg cm)	X	0.868	= Pounds-force inches (lbf in; lb in)
Pounds-force inches (lbf in; lb in)	X	0.113	= Newton metres (Nm)	X	8.85	= Pounds-force inches (lbf in; lb in)
Pounds-force inches (lbf in; lb in)	X	0.083	= Pounds-force feet (lbf ft; lb ft)	X	12	= Pounds-force inches (lbf in; lb in)
Pounds-force feet (lbf ft; lb ft)	X	0.138	= Kilograms-force metres (kgf m; kg m)	X	7.233	= Pounds-force feet (lbf ft; lb ft)
Pounds-force feet (lbf ft; lb ft)	X	1.356	= Newton metres (Nm)	X	0.738	= Pounds-force feet (lbf ft; lb ft)
Newton metres (Nm)	X	0.102	= Kilograms-force metres (kgf m; kg m)	X	9.804	= Newton metres (Nm)

Power						
Horsepower (hp)	X	745.7	= Watts (W)	X	0.0013	= Horsepower (hp)

Velocity (speed)						
Miles per hour (miles/hr; mph)	X	1.609	= Kilometres per hour (km/hr; kph)	X	0.621	= Miles per hour (miles/hr; mph)

*Fuel consumption**						
Miles per gallon, Imperial (mpg)	X	0.354	= Kilometres per litre (km/l)	X	2.825	= Miles per gallon, Imperial (mpg)
Miles per gallon, US (mpg)	X	0.425	= Kilometres per litre (km/l)	X	2.352	= Miles per gallon, US (mpg)

Temperature

Degrees Fahrenheit = (°C x 1.8) + 32

Degrees Celsius (Degrees Centigrade; °C) = (°F - 32) x 0.56

**It is common practice to convert from miles per gallon (mpg) to litres/100 kilometres (l/100km), where mpg (Imperial) x l/100 km = 282 and mpg (US) x l/100 km = 235*

Safety first!

Professional motor mechanics are trained in safe working procedures. However enthusiastic you may be about getting on with the job in hand, do take the time to ensure that your safety is not put at risk. A moment's lack of attention can result in an accident, as can failure to observe certain elementary precautions.

There will always be new ways of having accidents, and the following points do not pretend to be a comprehensive list of all dangers; they are intended rather to make you aware of the risks and to encourage a safety-conscious approach to all work you carry out on your vehicle.

Essential DOs and DON'Ts

DON'T rely on a single jack when working underneath the vehicle. Always use reliable additional means of support, such as axle stands, securely placed under a part of the vehicle that you know will not give way.
DON'T attempt to loosen or tighten high-torque nuts (e.g. wheel hub nuts) while the vehicle is on a jack; it may be pulled off.
DON'T start the engine without first ascertaining that the transmission is in neutral (or 'Park' where applicable) and the parking brake applied.
DON'T suddenly remove the filler cap from a hot cooling system – cover it with a cloth and release the pressure gradually first, or you may get scalded by escaping coolant.
DON'T attempt to drain oil until you are sure it has cooled sufficiently to avoid scalding you.
DON'T grasp any part of the engine, exhaust or catalytic converter without first ascertaining that it is sufficiently cool to avoid burning you.
DON'T allow brake fluid or antifreeze to contact vehicle paintwork.
DON'T syphon toxic liquids such as fuel, brake fluid or antifreeze by mouth, or allow them to remain on your skin.
DON'T inhale dust – it may be injurious to health (see *Asbestos* below).
DON'T allow any spilt oil or grease to remain on the floor – wipe it up straight away, before someone slips on it.
DON'T use ill-fitting spanners or other tools which may slip and cause injury.
DON'T attempt to lift a heavy component which may be beyond your capability – get assistance.
DON'T rush to finish a job, or take unverified short cuts.
DON'T allow children or animals in or around an unattended vehicle.
DO wear eye protection when using power tools such as drill, sander, bench grinder etc, and when working under the vehicle.
DO use a barrier cream on your hands prior to undertaking dirty jobs – it will protect your skin from infection as well as making the dirt easier to remove afterwards; but make sure your hands aren't left slippery.
DO keep loose clothing (cuffs, tie etc) and long hair well out of the way of moving mechanical parts.
DO remove rings, wristwatch etc, before working on the vehicle – especially the electrical system.
DO ensure that any lifting tackle used has a safe working load rating adequate for the job.
DO keep your work area tidy – it is only too easy to fall over articles left lying around.
DO get someone to check periodically that all is well, when working alone on the vehicle.
DO carry out work in a logical sequence and check that everything is correctly assembled and tightened afterwards.
DO remember that your vehicle's safety affects that of yourself and others. If in doubt on any point, get specialist advice.
IF, in spite of following these precautions, you are unfortunate enough to injure yourself, seek medical attention as soon as possible.

Asbestos

Certain friction, insulating, sealing, and other products – such as brake linings, brake bands, clutch linings, torque converters, gaskets, etc – contain asbestos. *Extreme care must be taken to avoid inhalation of dust from such products since it is hazardous to health.* If in doubt, assume that they *do* contain asbestos.

Fire

Remember at all times that petrol (gasoline) is highly flammable. Never smoke, or have any kind of naked flame around, when working on the vehicle. But the risk does not end there – a spark caused by an electrical short-circuit, by two metal surfaces contacting each other, by careless use of tools, or even by static electricity built up in your body under certain conditions, can ignite petrol vapour, which in a confined space is highly explosive.

Always disconnect the battery earth (ground) terminal before working on any part of the fuel or electrical system, and never risk spilling fuel on to a hot engine or exhaust.

It is recommended that a fire extinguisher of a type suitable for fuel and electrical fires is kept handy in the garage or workplace at all times. Never try to extinguish a fuel or electrical fire with water.

Fumes

Certain fumes are highly toxic and can quickly cause unconsciousness and even death if inhaled to any extent. Petrol (gasoline) vapour comes into this category, as do the vapours from certain solvents such as trichloroethylene. Any draining or pouring of such volatile fluids should be done in a well ventilated area.

When using cleaning fluids and solvents, read the instructions carefully. Never use materials from unmarked containers – they may give off poisonous vapours.

Never run the engine of a motor vehicle in an enclosed space such as a garage. Exhaust fumes contain carbon monoxide which is extremely poisonous; if you need to run the engine, always do so in the open air or at least have the rear of the vehicle outside the workplace.

If you are fortunate enough to have the use of an inspection pit, never drain or pour petrol, and never run the engine, while the vehicle is standing over it; the fumes, being heavier than air, will concentrate in the pit with possibly lethal results.

The battery

Never cause a spark, or allow a naked light, near the vehicle's battery. It will normally be giving off a certain amount of hydrogen gas, which is highly explosive.

Always disconnect the battery earth (ground) terminal before working on the fuel or electrical systems.

If possible, loosen the filler plugs or cover when charging the battery from an external source. Do not charge at an excessive rate or the battery may burst.

Take care when topping up and when carrying the battery. The acid electrolyte, even when diluted, is very corrosive and should not be allowed to contact the eyes or skin.

If you ever need to prepare electrolyte yourself, always add the acid slowly to the water, and never the other way round. Protect against splashes by wearing rubber gloves and goggles.

When jump starting a car using a booster battery, for negative earth (ground) vehicles, connect the jump leads in the following sequence: First connect one jump lead between the positive (+) terminals of the two batteries. Then connect the other jump lead first to the negative (–) terminal of the booster battery, and then to a good earthing (ground) point on the vehicle to be started, at least 18 in (45 cm) from the battery if possible. Ensure that hands and jump leads are clear of any moving parts, and that the two vehicles do not touch. Disconnect the leads in the reverse order.

Mains electricity

When using an electric power tool, inspection light etc, which works from the mains, always ensure that the appliance is correctly connected to its plug and that, where necessary, it is properly earthed (grounded). Do not use such appliances in damp conditions and, again, beware of creating a spark or applying excessive heat in the vicinity of fuel or fuel vapour.

Ignition HT voltage

A severe electric shock can result from touching certain parts of the ignition system, such as the HT leads, when the engine is running or being cranked, particularly if components are damp or the insulation is defective. Where an electronic ignition system is fitted, the HT voltage is much higher and could prove fatal.

Routine maintenance

Maintenance is essential for ensuring safety, and desirable for the purpose of getting the best in terms of performance and economy from your car. Over the years the need for periodic lubrication has been greatly reduced if not totally eliminated. This has unfortunately tended to lead some owners to think that, because no such action is required, the items either no longer exist, or will last forever. This is certainly not the case; it is essential to carry out regular visual examination as comprehensively as possible in order to spot any possible defects at an early stage before they develop into major expensive repairs.

The following service schedules are a list of the maintenance requirements and the intervals at which they should be carried out, as recommended by the manufacturers. Where applicable these procedures are covered in greater detail throughout this manual, near the beginning of each Chapter.

Where a vehicle covers a low annual mileage, follow the time intervals to determine when maintenance is due. Some fluids and components deteriorate with age as well as with use.

Vehicles which operate under adverse conditions (eg in extremes of temperature, or full-time trailer towing, or mainly on short journeys) may benefit from more frequent maintenance than specified. If in doubt consult a GM dealer.

Under-bonnet view of a 1.6 Astra – air cleaner, wind deflector and water deflector removed

1 Wiper motor
2 Heater blower
3 Heater blower resistor
4 Windscreen washer tube
5 Screen washer reservoir
6 Suspension turrets
7 Coolant expansion tank filler
8 Ignition coil
9 Battery
10 Coolant hose
11 Radiator fan
12 Distributor cover
13 Engine oil filler
14 Bonnet catch
15 Radiator
16 VIN plate
17 Engine breather
18 Air cleaner hot air pick-up
19 Thermostat housing
20 Fuel hoses
21 Fuel pump
22 Alternator
23 Accelerator cable
24 Carburettor
25 Choke cable
26 Servo non-return valve
27 Steering rack bellows
28 Air cleaner breather hose
29 Brake fluid reservoir
30 Brake servo

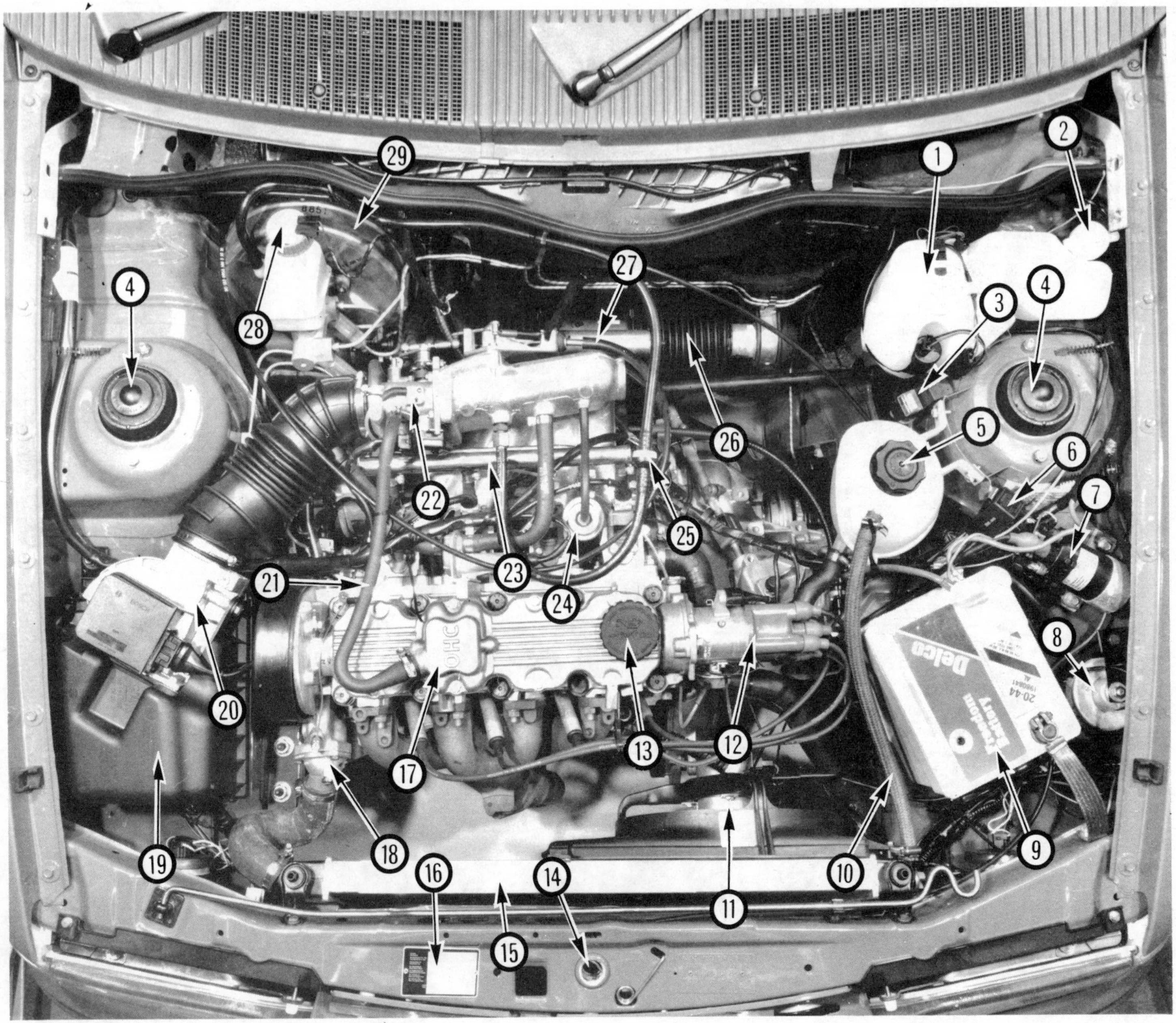

Under-bonnet view of a 1.8 Astra

1 Screen washer reservoir
2 Headlamp washer filler cap
3 Headlamp washer relay and fuse
4 Suspension turrets
5 Coolant expansion tank filler
6 Control relay (fuel injection system)
7 Ignition coil
8 Horn
9 Battery
10 Coolant hose
11 Radiator fan
12 Distributor
13 Engine oil filler
14 Bonnet catch
15 Radiator
16 VIN plate
17 Engine breather
18 Thermostat housing
19 Air cleaner
20 Airflow meter
21 Breather hose
22 Throttle valve housing
23 Fuel rail
24 Fuel pressure regulator
25 Servo non-return valve
26 Steering rack bellows
27 Accelerator cable
28 Brake fluid reservoir
29 Brake servo

Underside front view of a 1.8 Astra – other models similar

1 *Control arm rear bush*
2 *Control arm*
3 *Anti-roll bar link*
4 *Driveshaft damper weight*
5 *Engine oil filter*
6 *Oil cooler hose*
7 *Air induction trunking*
8 *Radiator*
9 *Exhaust downpipes*
10 *Sump drain plug*
11 *Radiator fan*
12 *Gearbox sump*
13 *Driveshaft bellows*
14 *Brake hose*
15 *Steering balljoint attachment*
16 *Engine/transmission rear mounting*
17 *Gearchange tube*
18 *Exhaust pipe*
19 *Brake pipe*
20 *Brake and fuel pipes*

Underside rear view of a 1.8 Astra – other models similar

1 Centre silencer
2 Handbrake adjuster
3 Handbrake cables
4 Fuel tank
5 Brake pipe
6 Brake and fuel pipes
7 Brake hoses
8 Axle beam
9 Axle mountings
10 Spring
11 Shock absorber mounting
12 Fuel filler pipe
13 Fuel gauge sender/fuel tank outlet
14 Fuel tank breather
15 Fuel filter
16 Fuel pressure regulator
17 Fuel pump
18 Towing eye
19 Rear silencer
20 Rear brake pipes

Weekly or before a long journey

Check engine oil level (see Chapter 1, Section 2 or 26)
Check coolant level (see Chapter 2, Section 2)
Check brake fluid level (see Chapter 9, Section 2)
Check operation of lights, indicators, wipers, washers, horn etc
Top up washer reservoir(s) (see Chapter 12, Section 48 to 50)
Check tyre pressures (cold), including the spare (see Chapter 10, Section 18)

Every 9000 miles (15 000 km) or six months, whichever comes first

Renew engine oil and filter (see Chapter 1, Section 2 or 26)

Every 9000 miles (15 000 km) or 12 months, whichever comes first

Renew engine oil and filter (see Chapter 1, Section 2 or 26)
Check valve clearances (1.2 only – see Chapter 1, Section 7)
Adjust or renew contact breaker points (1.2 only – see Chapter 4, Section 3)
Inspect spark plugs. Clean and gap or renew as necessary (see Chapter 4, Section 12)
Check ignition timing (1.2 only – see Chapter 4, Section 11)
Check idle speed and mixture (see Chapter 3, Section 14 or 27)
Check fuel system hoses for security and good condition
Check accessory drivebelt(s) for correct tension and good condition (see Chapter 2, Section 9)
Lubricate throttle and manual choke linkages
Check coolant level and inspect cooling system hoses and hose clips
Inspect brake pads and renew if necessary (see Chapter 9, Section 3)
Check automatic transmission fluid level (see Chapter 6, Section 24)
Lubricate hinges, locks, catches etc
Check headlamp beam alignment (see Chapter 12, Section 38)
Inspect brake pipes and hoses (see Chapter 9, Section 16)
Check brake pressure regulating valve (Estate and Van only) for correct spring adjustment and lever movement (see Chapter 9, Section 15)
Inspect and lubricate handbrake cable, adjust if necessary (see Chapter 9, Section 22)
Check exhaust system for security and good condition (see Chapter 3, Section 33)
Check driveshaft joint bellows (see Chapter 7, Section 2)
Check steering tie-end balljoints, rubber covers and steering rack bellows. Also check the steering column flexible coupling (see Chapter 8, Section 2)
Check suspension bushes, shock absorbers etc (see Chapter 10, Section 2)
Check tightness of wheel bolts (see Chapter 10, Section 2)
Check rear wheel bearing adjustment (see Chapter 10, Section 2)
Inspect tyres thoroughly (see Chapter 10, Section 18)
Road test and check operation of seat belts, steering, brakes controls etc

Every 18 000 miles (30 000 km) or two years, whichever comes first

In addition to the work previously specified
Renew air cleaner element (see Chapter 3, Section 6)
Renew spark plugs (see Chapter 4, Section 12)
Renew contact breaker points (1.2 only – see Chapter 4, Section 4)
Clean or renew carburettor fuel inlet strainer, or renew fuel filter on fuel injection models (see Chapter 3, Section 2 or 30)
Inspect brake shoes (see Chapter 9, Section 8)
Check power steering fluid level, when fitted (see Chapter 8, Section 2)
Check manual gearbox oil level (see Chapter 6, Section 2)
Check clutch pedal stroke (see Chapter 5, Section 2)
Check front wheel alignment (see Chapter 8, Section 18)

Every 36 000 miles (60 000 km) or four years, whichever comes first

Renew automatic transmission fluid (see Chapter 6, Section 24)
Renew camshaft drivebelt (not 1.2) if wished (see Chapter 1, Section 26)

Every 54 000 miles (90 000 km) or three years, whichever comes first

Renew braking system seals and hoses if wished (see Chapter 9, Section 2)

Seasonal maintenance

Adjust air cleaner intake on 1.2 models to suit prevailing temperatures (see Chapter 3, Section 5)
On all models, have antifreeze concentration checked in the autumn (see Chapter 2, Section 2)

Annually, regardless of mileage

Renew brake fluid (see Chapter 9, Section 17)

Every two years, regardless of mileage

Renew cooling system antifreeze (see Chapter 2, Section 13)

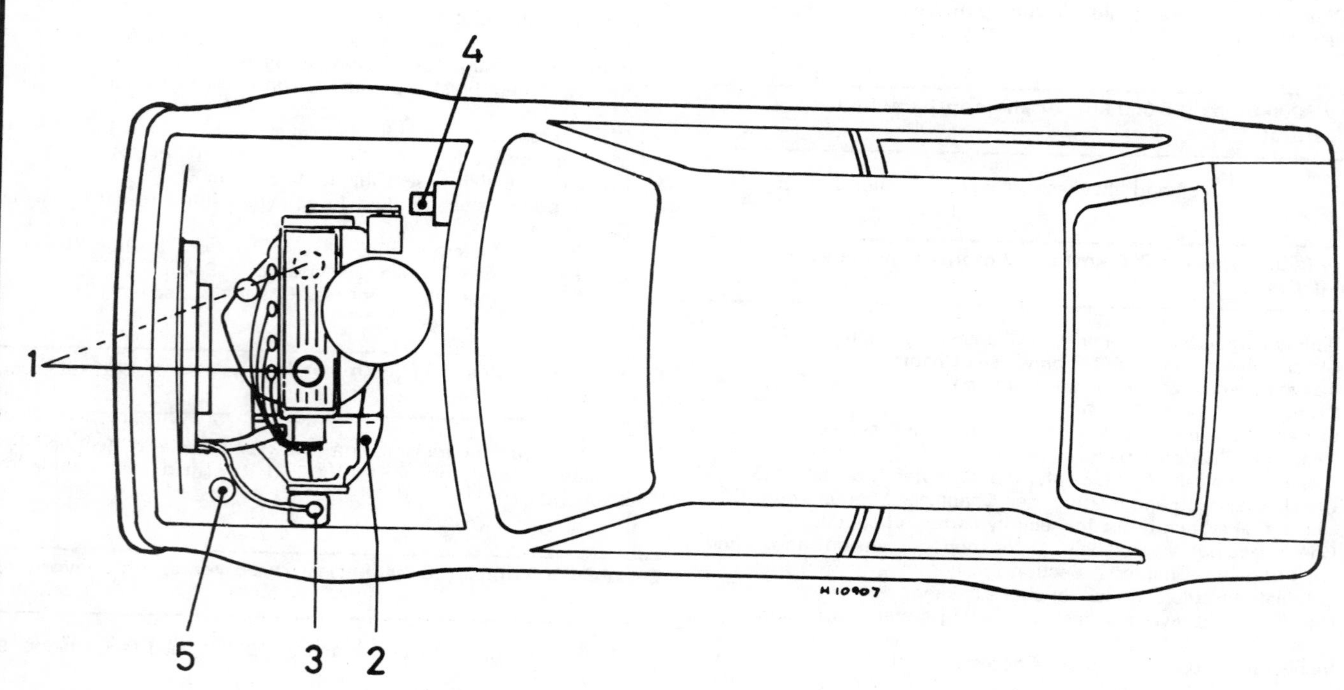

Recommended lubricants and fluids

Component or system	Lubricant type or specification
Engine (1)	Multigrade engine oil, viscosity in the range 10W-40 to 20W-50, to API SE/CC or better
Manual transmission (2)	
All except GTE	SAE 80 gear oil to API GL3 or GL4
GTE (and others if wished)	Special transmission fluid, GM part No 90 188 629
Automatic transmission	Dexron® II ATF
Cooling system (3)	Ethylene glycol based antifreeze (to GME 13368) and soft water
Brake hydraulic system (4)	Hydraulic fluid to FMVSS 571, 116 DOT3/DOT4, or SAE J1703
Power steering fluid (5)	Dexron® II ATF

Fault diagnosis

Introduction

The vehicle owner who does his or her own maintenance according to the recommended schedules should not have to use this section of the manual very often. Modern component reliability is such that, provided those items subject to wear or deterioration are inspected or renewed at the specified intervals, sudden failure is comparatively rare. Faults do not usually just happen as a result of sudden failure, but develop over a period of time. Major mechanical failures in particular are usually preceded by characteristic symptoms over hundreds or even thousands of miles. Those components which do occasionally fail without warning are often small and easily carried in the vehicle.

With any fault finding, the first step is to decide where to begin investigations. Sometimes this is obvious, but on other occasions a little detective work will be necessary. The owner who makes half a dozen haphazard adjustments or replacements may be successful in curing a fault (or its symptoms), but he will be none the wiser if the fault recurs and he may well have spent more time and money than was necessary. A calm and logical approach will be found to be more satisfactory in the long run. Always take into account any warning signs or abnormalities that may have been noticed in the period preceding the fault – power loss, high or low gauge readings, unusual noises or smells, etc – and remember that failure of components such as fuses or spark plugs may only be pointers to some underlying fault.

The pages which follow here are intended to help in cases of failure to start or breakdown on the road. There is also a Fault Diagnosis Section at the end of each Chapter which should be consulted if the preliminary checks prove unfruitful. Whatever the fault, certain basic principles apply. These are as follows:

Verify the fault. This is simply a matter of being sure that you know what the symptoms are before starting work. This is particularly important if you are investigating a fault for someone else who may not have described it very accurately.

Don't overlook the obvious. For example, if the vehicle won't start, is there petrol in the tank? (Don't take anyone else's word on this particular point, and don't trust the fuel gauge either!) If an electrical fault is indicated, look for loose or broken wires before digging out the test gear.

Cure the disease, not the symptom. Substituting a flat battery with a fully charged one will get you off the hard shoulder, but if the underlying cause is not attended to, the new battery will go the same way. Similarly, changing oil-fouled spark plugs for a new set will get you moving again, but remember that the reason for the fouling (if it wasn't simply an incorrect grade of plug) will have to be established and corrected.

Don't take anything for granted. Particularly, don't forget that a 'new' component may itself be defective (especially if it's been rattling round in the boot for months), and don't leave components out of a fault diagnosis sequence just because they are new or recently fitted. When you do finally diagnose a difficult fault, you'll probably realise that all the evidence was there from the start.

Electrical faults

Electrical faults can be more puzzling than straightforward mechanical failures, but they are no less susceptible to logical analysis if the basic principles of operation are understood. Vehicle electrical wiring exists in extremely unfavourable conditions – heat, vibration and chemical attack – and the first things to look for are loose or corroded connections and broken or chafed wires, especially where the wires pass through holes in the bodywork or are subject to vibration.

All metal-bodied vehicles in current production have one pole of the battery 'earthed', ie connected to the vehicle bodywork, and in nearly all modern vehicles it is the negative (–) terminal. The various electrical components – motors, bulb holders etc – are also connected to earth, either by means of a lead or directly by their mountings. Electric current flows through the component and then back to the battery via the bodywork. If the component mounting is loose or corroded, or if a good path back to the battery is not available, the circuit will be incomplete and malfunction will result. The engine and/or gearbox are also earthed by means of flexible metal straps to the body or subframe; if these straps are loose or missing, starter motor, generator and ignition trouble may result.

Assuming the earth return to be satisfactory, electrical faults will be due either to component malfunction or to defects in the current supply. Individual components are dealt with in Chapter 12. If supply wires are broken or cracked internally this results in an open-circuit, and the easiest way to check for this is to bypass the suspect wire temporarily with a length of wire having a crocodile clip or suitable connector at each end. Alternatively, a 12V test lamp can be used to verify the presence of supply voltage at various points along the wire and the break can be thus isolated.

If a bare portion of a live wire touches the bodywork or other earthed metal part, the electricity will take the low-resistance path thus formed back to the battery: this is known as a short-circuit. Hopefully a short-circuit will blow a fuse, but otherwise it may cause burning of the insulation (and possibly further short-circuits) or even a fire. This is why it is inadvisable to bypass persistently blowing fuses with silver foil or wire.

Spares and tool kit

Most vehicles are supplied only with sufficient tools for wheel changing; the *Maintenance and minor repair* tool kit detailed in *Tools and working facilities*, with the addition of a hammer, is probably sufficient for those repairs that most motorists would consider attempting at the roadside. In addition a few items which can be fitted

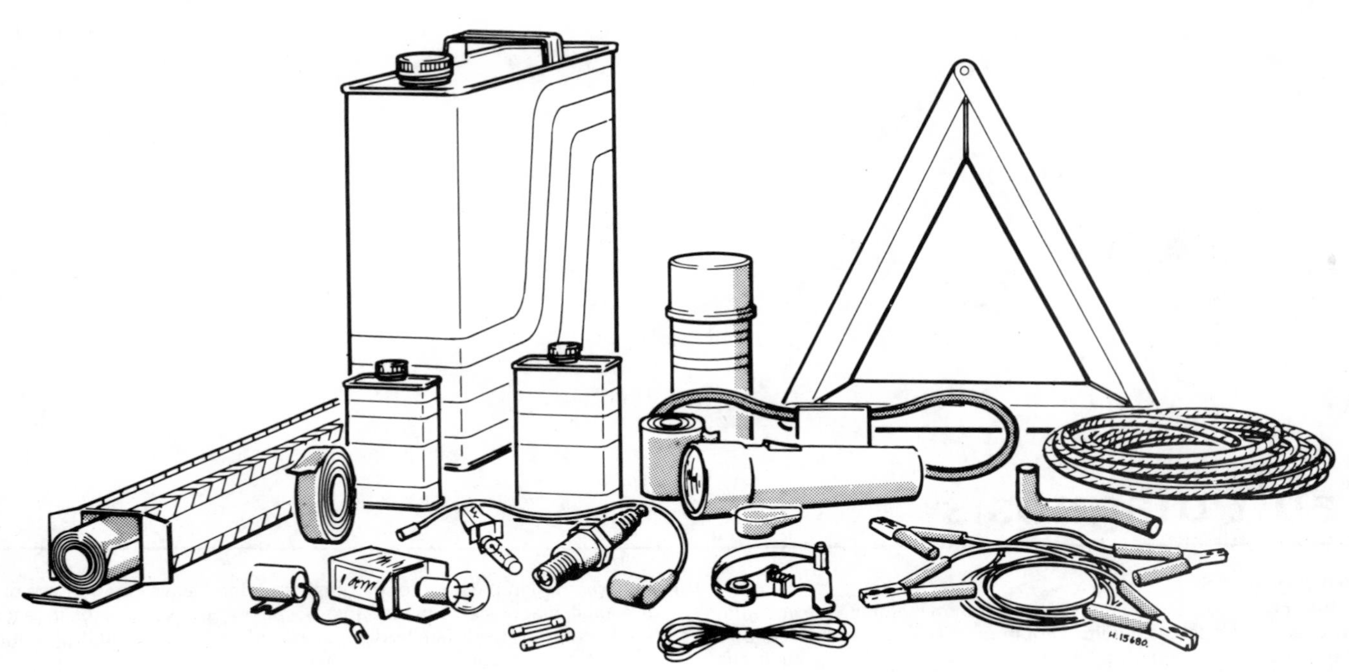

Carrying a few spares can save a long walk

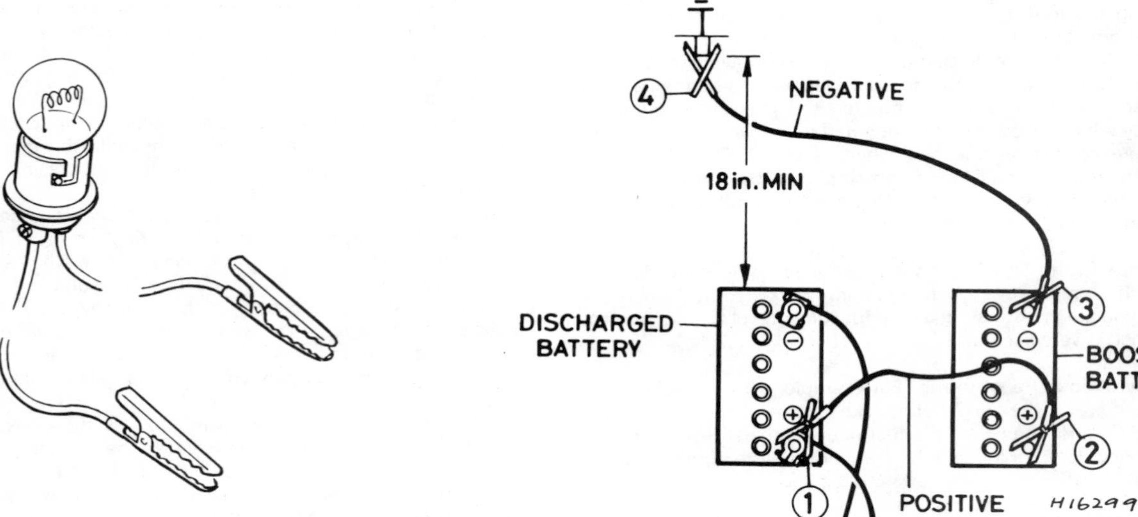

Simple test lamp is useful for tracing electrical faults

Jump start lead connections for negative earth vehicles – connect leads in order shown

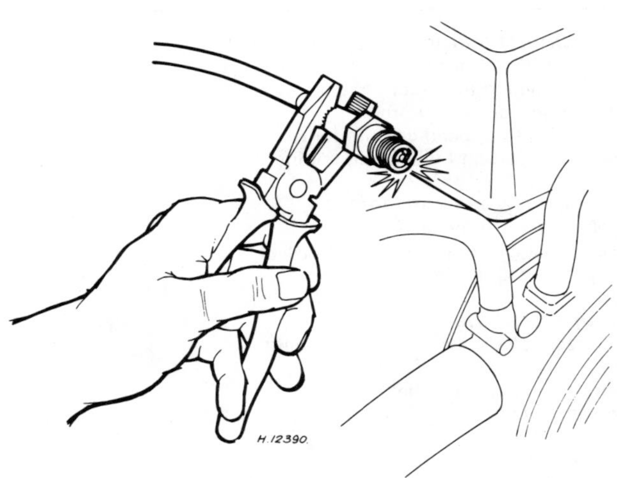

Crank engine and check for a spark. Note use of insulated tool

without too much trouble in the event of a breakdown should be carried. Experience and available space will modify the list below, but the following may save having to call on professional assistance:

Spark plugs, clean and correctly gapped
HT lead and plug cap – long enough to reach the plug furthest from the distributor
Distributor rotor, condenser and contact breaker points (as applicable)
Drivebelt(s) – emergency type may suffice
Spare fuses
Set of principal light bulbs
Tin of radiator sealer and hose bandage
Exhaust bandage
Roll of insulating tape
Length of soft iron wire
Length of electrical flex
Torch or inspection lamp (can double as test lamp)
Battery jump leads
Tow-rope
Ignition waterproofing aerosol
Litre of engine oil
Sealed can of hydraulic fluid
'Jubilee' clips
Tube of filler paste

If spare fuel is carried, a can designed for the purpose should be used to minimise risks of leakage and collision damage. A first aid kit and a warning triangle, whilst not at present compulsory in the UK, are obviously sensible items to carry in addition to the above.

When touring abroad it may be advisable to carry additional spares which, even if you cannot fit them yourself, could save having to wait while parts are obtained. The items below may be worth considering:

Clutch and throttle cables
Cylinder head gasket
Alternator brushes
Tyre valve core

One of the motoring organisations will be able to advise on availability of fuel etc in foreign countries.

Engine will not start

Engine fails to turn when starter operated

Flat battery (recharge, use jump leads, or push start)
Battery terminals loose or corroded
Battery earth to body defective
Engine earth strap loose or broken
Starter motor (or solenoid) wiring loose or broken
Automatic transmission selector in wrong position, or inhibitor switch faulty
Ignition/starter switch faulty
Major mechanical failure (seizure)
Starter or solenoid internal fault (see Chapter 12)

Starter motor turns engine slowly

Partially discharged battery (recharge, use jump leads, or push start)
Battery terminals loose or corroded
Battery earth to body defective
Engine earth strap loose
Starter motor (or solenoid) wiring loose
Starter motor internal fault (see Chapter 12)

Starter motor spins without turning engine

Flywheel gear teeth damaged or worn
Starter motor mounting bolts loose

Engine turns normally but fails to start

Damp or dirty HT leads and distributor cap (crank engine and check for spark)
Dirty or incorrectly gapped distributor points (if applicable)
No fuel in tank (check for delivery at carburettor)
Excessive choke (hot engine) or insufficient choke (cold engine)
Fouled or incorrectly gapped spark plugs (remove, clean and regap)
Other ignition system fault (see Chapter 4)
Other fuel system fault (see Chapter 3)
Poor compression
Major mechanical failure (eg camshaft drive)

Engine fires but will not run

Insufficient choke (cold engine)
Air leaks at carburettor or inlet manifold
Fuel starvation (see Chapter 3)
Ballast resistor defective, or other ignition fault (see Chapter 4)

Engine cuts out and will not restart

Engine cuts out suddenly – ignition fault

Loose or disconnected LT wires
Wet HT leads or distributor cap (after traversing water splash)
Coil or condenser failure (check for spark)
Other ignition fault (see Chapter 4)

Engine misfires before cutting out – fuel fault

Fuel tank empty
Fuel pump defective or filter blocked (check for delivery)
Fuel tank filler vent blocked (suction will be evident on releasing cap)
Carburettor needle valve sticking
Carburettor jets blocked (fuel contaminated)
Other fuel system fault (see Chapter 3)

Engine cuts out – other causes

Serious overheating
Major mechanical failure (eg camshaft drive)

Engine overheats

Ignition (no-charge) warning light illuminated – OHV only

Slack or broken drivebelt – retension or renew (Chapter 2)

Ignition warning light not illuminated

Coolant loss due to internal or external leakage (see Chapter 2)
Thermostat defective
Low oil level

Brakes binding
Radiator clogged externally or internally
Electric cooling fan not operating correctly
Engine waterways clogged
Ignition timing incorrect or automatic advance malfunctioning
Mixture too weak

Note: *Do not add cold water to an overheated engine or damage may result*

Low engine oil pressure

Gauge reads low or warning light illuminated with engine running

Oil level low or incorrect grade
Defective gauge or sender unit
Wire to sender unit earthed
Engine overheating
Oil filter clogged or bypass valve defective
Oil pressure relief valve defective
Oil pick-up strainer clogged
Oil pump worn or mountings loose
Worn main or big-end bearings

Note: *Low oil pressure in a high-mileage engine at tickover is not necessarily a cause for concern. Sudden pressure loss at speed is far more significant. In any event, check the gauge or warning light sender before condemning the engine.*

Engine noises

Pre-ignition (pinking) on acceleration

Incorrect grade of fuel
Ignition timing incorrect
Distributor faulty or worn
Worn or maladjusted carburettor
Excessive carbon build-up in engine

Whistling or wheezing noises

Leaking vacuum hose
Leaking carburettor or manifold gasket
Blowing head gasket

Tapping or rattling

Incorrect valve clearances (OHV only)
Worn valve gear
Worn timing chain or belt
Broken piston ring (ticking noise)

Knocking or thumping

Unintentional mechanical contact (eg fan blades)
Worn drivebelt
Peripheral component fault (generator, water pump etc)
Worn big-end bearings (regular heavy knocking, perhaps less under load)
Worn main bearings (rumbling and knocking, perhaps worsening under load)
Piston slap (most noticeable when cold)

Chapter 1 Engine

For modifications, and information applicable to later models, see Supplement at end of manual

Contents

Specifications

Part A: OHV engine

General

Maker's designation	12 SC
Bore x stroke	79.0 x 61.0 mm (3.11 x 2.40 in)
Cubic capacity	1196 cc (73.0 cu in)
Compression ratio	9.0 : 1
Maximum power	40 kW (54 bhp) @ 5600 rpm
Maximum torque	84 Nm (62 lbf ft) @ 3600 rpm

Valve clearances (warm)

Inlet	0.15 mm (0.006 in)
Exhaust	0.25 mm (0.010 in)

Cylinder head

Identification mark	E
Valve seat width:	
Inlet	1.25 to 1.50 mm (0.049 to 0.059 in)
Exhaust	1.60 to 1.85 mm (0.063 to 0.073 in)
Overall height	81 ± 0.25 mm (3.1890 ± 0.0098 in)

Valves and guides

	Inlet	Exhaust
Overall length	99.3 mm (3.909 in)	101.1 mm (3.980 in)
Head diameter	32 mm (1.260 in)	29 mm (1.142 in)
Stem diameter (nominal, ± 0.005 mm/0.0002 in):		
Standard	7.005 mm (0.2758 in)	6.995 mm (0.2754 in)
Oversize 1	7.080 mm (0.2787 in)	7.060 mm (0.2780 in)
Oversize 2	7.155 mm (0.2817 in)	7.135 mm (0.2809 in)
Oversize A	7.255 mm (0.2856 in)	7.235 mm (0.2848 in)
Valve guide bore (± 0.01 mm/0.0004 in):		
Standard	7.035 mm (0.2770 in)	
Oversize 1	7.110 mm (0.2799 in)	
Oversize 2	7.185 mm (0.2829 in)	
Oversize A	7.285 mm (0.2868 in)	
Valve clearance in guide:		
Inlet	0.015 to 0.045 mm (0.0006 to 0.0018 in)	
Exhaust	0.035 to 0.065 mm (0.0014 to 0.0026 in)	
Sealing face angle	44°	

Camshaft

Radial run-out	0.03 mm (0.0012 in) max
Endfloat	0.17 to 0.43 mm (0.006 to 0.017 in)
Cam lift	6.45 mm (0.254 in)

Pistons and bores

	Diameters (nominal)	Marking
Production size 1	78.95 mm (3.1083 in)	5
	78.96 mm (3.1087 in)	6
	78.97 mm (3.1091 in)	7
	78.98 mm (3.1094 in)	8
Production size 2	78.99 mm (3.1098 in)	99
	79.00 mm (3.1102 in)	00
	79.01 mm (3.1106 in)	01
	79.02 mm (3.1110 in)	02
Production size 3	79.03 mm (3.1114 in)	03
	79.04 mm (3.1118 in)	04
	79.05 mm (3.1122 in)	05
	79.06 mm (3.1126 in)	06
Production size 4	79.07 mm (3.1130 in)	07
	79.08 mm (3.1134 in)	08
	79.09 mm (3.1138 in)	09
	79.10 mm (3.1142 in)	1
Oversize (+0.5 mm/0.020 nominal)	79.47 mm (3.1287 in)	79.47/7 +0.5
	79.48 mm (3.1291 in)	79.48/8 +0.5
	79.49 mm (3.1295 in)	79.49/9 +0.5
	79.50 mm (3.1299 in)	79.50/0 +0.5
Pistons clearance in bore	0.1 to 0.3 mm (0.004 to 0.012 in) estimated	
Bore out-of-round and taper	0.013 mm (0.0005 in) max	

Piston rings

Quantity (per piston)	2 compression, 1 oil control (scraper)
Thickness:	
Compression	2.0 mm (0.079 in)
Oil control	5.0 mm (0.197 in)
End gap:	
Compression	0.30 to 0.45 mm (0.012 to 0.018 in)
Oil control	0.40 to 1.40 mm (0.016 to 0.055 in)
Ring gap offset	180° (see text)
Ring vertical clearance in groove	Not specified – typically 0.06 mm (0.002 in)

Gudgeon pins

Length	65 mm (2.559 in)
Diameter	20 mm (0.787 in)
Clearance in piston	0.0015 to 0.0195 mm (0.00006 to 0.00077 in)
Clearance in connecting rod	None (interference fit)

Crankshaft and bearings

Number of main bearings	3	
Main bearing journal diameters – standard:		
Front	53.997 to 54.010 mm (2.1259 to 2.1264 in)	
Centre and rear	54.007 to 54.020 mm (2.1263 to 2.1268 in)	
Centre journal width – standard	29.000 to 29.052 mm (1.1417 to 1.1438 in)	
Main bearing shell identification – standard:	**Colour code**	**Embossed code**
Front, top	Brown	1 ON or 701-N
Front, bottom	Brown	1 UN or 702-N
Centre, top	Brown	20+UN or 705-N
Centre, bottom	Green	20+UN or 725-N
Rear, top	Green	631-N
Rear, bottom	Green	635-N

Main bearing shell identification – standard journal, oversize housing:	
Front, top	U1-0B
Front, bottom	U1-U
Centre, top and bottom	U
Rear, top	U3-0B
Rear, bottom	U3-U
Big-end bearing journal diameter – standard	44.971 to 44.987 mm (1.7705 to 1.7711 in)
Big-end bearing shell identification – standard	None
Main and big-end bearing undersizes	0.25 mm (0.0098 in) production and service; 0.50 mm (0.0197 in) service only

	Colour code	Embossed code
Main bearing shell identification – 0.25 undersize:		
Front, top	Brown-blue	1 OA or 006-A
Front, bottom	Brown-blue	1 UA or 008-A
Centre, top	Brown-blue	20+UA or 014-A
Centre, bottom	Brown	20+UA or 034-A
Rear, top	Green-blue	632-A
Rear, bottom	Green-blue	636-A
Main bearing shell identification – 0.50 undersize:		
Front, top	Brown-black	1 OB or 027 B
Front, bottom	Brown-black	1 U or 029 B
Centre, top	Brown-black	2 OB 0.35 B
Centre, bottom	Green-black	2 UB 035 B
Rear, top	None	3 OB 0,50
Rear, bottom	None	3 U 0,50

Big-end bearing shell identification:	
0.25 undersize	A
0.50 undersize	B
Main and big-end bearing journal out-of-round	0.006 mm (0.0002 in) max
Main and big-end bearing journal taper	0.01 mm (0.0004 in) max
Crankshaft endfloat	0.09 to 0.20 mm (0.0035 to 0.0079 in)
Connecting rod endfloat	0.02 to 0.06 mm (0.0008 to 0.0024 in)
Main bearing running clearance:	
Front	0.020 to 0.046 mm (0.0008 to 0.0018 in)
Centre	0.010 to 0.036 mm (0.0004 to 0.0014 in)
Rear	0.010 to 0.032 mm (0.0004 to 0.0013 in) estimated
Big-end bearing running clearance	0.11 to 0.24 mm (0.0043 to 0.0095 in)
Crankshaft radial run-out (at centre journal, shaft in block)	0.03 mm (0.0012 in) max

Flywheel

Ring gear run-out	0.5 mm (0.02 in) max
Refinishing limit – depth of material which may be removed from clutch friction surface	0.3 mm (0.012 in) max

Lubrication system

Lubricant type	Multigrade engine oil, viscosity range 10W-40 to 20W-50, to API SE/CC or better
Lubricant capacity (drain and refill, including filter)	2.75 litre (4.8 pints) approx
Oil pump tolerances:	
Teeth backlash	0.1 to 0.2 mm (0.004 to 0.008 in)
Teeth projection	0.04 to 0.10 mm (0.0016 to 0.0039 in)
Oil pressure at idle (engine warm)	1.5 bar (22 lbf/in²)

Torque wrench settings

	Nm	lbf ft
Flywheel bolts	35	26
Main bearing caps	62	46
Oil filter	20	15
Water pump	8	6
Big-end bearing caps	27	20
Sump bolts (with locking compound)	5	4
Cylinder head bolts (use **new** bolts every time):		
Stage 1	25	18
Stage 2	Further 60°	
Stage 3	Further 60°	
Stage 4	Further 60°	
Camshaft sprocket	40	30
Crankshaft pulley	40	30
Inlet manifold	23	17
Engine mounting bracket, RH:		
To block (use sealant on lower bolt)	20	15
To damping pad	40	30
Engine mountings to body:		
LH rear	65	48
RH rear	40	30
Sump drain plug	45	33
Oil pump mounting bolts	20	15

Part B: OHC engine

General

Maker's designation:	
1.3	13 N or 13 S
1.6	16 SH
1.8	18 E
Bore x stroke:	
13 N and 13 S	75.0 x 73.4 mm (2.95 x 2.89 in)
16 SH	80.0 x 79.5 mm (3.15 x 3.13 in)
18 E	84.8 x 79.5 mm (3.34 x 3.13 in)
Cubic capacity:	
13 N and 13 S	1297 cc (79 cu in)
16 SH	1598 cc (98 cu in)
18 E	1796 cc (110 cu in)
Compression ratio:	
13 N	8.2 : 1
13 S and 16 SH	9.2 : 1
18 E	9.5 : 1
Maximum power:	
13 N	44 kW (60 bhp) @ 5800 rpm
13 S	55 kW (75 bhp) @ 5800 rpm
16 SH	66 kW (90 bhp) @ 5800 rpm
18 E	85 kW (115 bhp) @ 5800 rpm
Maximum torque:	
13 N	94 Nm (69 lbf ft) @ 3400 to 3800 rpm
13 S	101 Nm (75 lbf ft) @ 4200 rpm
16 SH	126 Nm (93 lbf ft) @ 3800 to 4200 rpm
18 E	151 Nm (111 lbf ft) @ 4800 rpm

Valve clearances

Inlet and exhaust	Automatic adjustment by hydraulic lifters

Camshaft toothed belt

Tension (using gauge KM-510-A):	**1.3**	**1.5 and 1.8**
New belt, cold	6.0	3.0
New belt, warm	8.0	8.0
Used belt, cold	5.0	3.0
Used belt, warm	7.5	8.0

Cylinder head

Valve seat width:	
Inlet	1.3 to 1.4 mm (0.051 to 0.055 in)
Exhaust	1.7 to 1.8 mm (0.067 to 0.071 in)
Overall height	96.00 ± 0.25 mm (3.7795 ± 0.0098 in)

Valves and guides

	Inlet	**Exhaust**
Overall length – production:		
1.3	105.3 ± 0.5 mm (4.146 ± 0.02 in)	105.3 ± 0.5 mm (4.146 ± 0.02 in)
1.6 and 1.8	106.5 mm (4.193 in)	106.5 mm (4.193 in)
Overall length – service:		
1.3	102.6 mm (4.039 in)	102.6 mm (4.039 in)
1.6 and 1.8	106.1 mm (4.177 in)	106.1 mm (4.177 in)
Head diameter:		
1.3	33 mm (1.30 in)	29 mm (1.14 in)
1.6	35 mm (1.38 in)	32 mm (1.26 in)
1.8	41 mm (1.61 in)	35 mm (1.38 in)
Stem diameter (nominal, ± 0.005 mm/0.0002 in):		
Standard, 1.3	7.005 mm (0.2758 in)	6.985 mm (0.2750 in)
Standard, 1.6 and 1.8	7.980 mm (0.3142 in)	7.965 mm (0.3136 in)
Oversize 1, 1.3	7.080 mm (0.2787 in)	7.060 mm (0.2780 in)
Oversize 1, 1.6 and 1.8	8.055 mm (0.3171 in)	8.040 mm (0.3165 in)
Oversize 2, 1.3	7.155 mm (0.2817 in)	7.135 mm (0.2809 in)
Oversize 2, 1.6 and 1.8	8.130 mm (0.3201 in)	8.115 mm (0.3195 in)
Oversize A, 1.3	7.255 mm (0.2856 in)	7.235 mm (0.2848 in)
Oversize A, 1.6 and 1.8	8.230 mm (0.3240 in)	8.215 mm (0.3234 in)
Valve guide bore (± 0.01 mm/0.0004 in):		
Standard, 1.3	7.040 mm (0.2772 in)	
Standard, 1.6 and 1.8	8.010 mm (0.3154 in)	
Oversize 1, 1.3	7.115 mm (0.2801 in)	
Oversize 1, 1.6 and 1.8	8.085 mm (0.3183 in)	
Oversize 2, 1.3	7.180 mm (0.2831 in)	
Oversize 2, 1.6 and 1.8	8.160 mm (0.3213 in)	
Oversize A, 1.3	7.290 mm (0.2870 in)	
Oversize A, 1.6 and 1.8	8.260 mm (0.3252 in)	

Valve clearance in guide:	
Inlet, 1.3	0.02 to 0.05 mm (0.0008 to 0.0020 in)
Inlet, 1.6 and 1.8	0.015 to 0.042 mm (0.0006 to 0.0017 in)
Exhaust, 1.3	0.04 to 0.07 mm (0.0016 to 0.0028 in)
Exhaust, 1.3 and 1.8	0.03 to 0.06 mm (0.0012 to 0.0024 in)
Sealing face angle	44°

Camshaft

Radial run-out	0.03 mm (0.0012 in) max	
Endfloat	0.09 to 0.21 mm (0.004 to 0.008 in)	
Cam lift:		
13 N	5.54 mm (0.2181 in)	
13 S	6.00 mm (0.2362 in)	
16 SH	6.12 mm (0.2409 in)	
18 E	6.95 mm (0.2736 in)	
	1.3	**1.6 and 1.8**
Camshaft journal diameter (nominal, tolerance – 0.015 mm/0.0006 in):		
No 1	39.450 mm (1.5532 in)	42.470 mm (1.6720 in)
No 2	39.700 mm (1.5630 in)	42.720 mm (1.6819 in)
No 3	39.950 mm (1.5728 in)	42.970 mm (1.6917 in)
No 4	40.200 mm (1.5827 in)	43.220 mm (1.7016 in)
No 5	40.450 mm (1.5925 in)	43.470 mm (1.7114 in)
Corresponding housing diameters (nominal, tolerance +0.025 mm/0.0010 in):		
No 1	39.500 mm (1.5551 in)	42.500 mm (1.6732 in)
No 2	39.750 mm (1.5650 in)	42.750 mm (1.6831 in)
No 3	40.000 mm (1.5748 in)	43.000 mm (1.6929 in)
No 4	40.250 mm (1.5846 in)	43.250 mm (1.7028 in)
No 5	40.500 mm (1.5945 in)	43.500 mm (1.7126 in)
Camshaft journal and housing production undersize (not 1.3)	–0.1 mm (0.004 in)	

Pistons and bores

	Diameter (nominal)*	Marking
1.3:		
Production size 1	74.95 mm (2.9508 in)	5
	74.96 mm (2.9512 in)	6
	74.97 mm (2.9516 in)	7
	74.98 mm (2.9520 in)	8
Production size 2	74.99 mm (2.9524 in)	99
	75.00 mm (2.9528 in)	00
	75.01 mm (2.9531 in)	01
	75.02 mm (2.9535 in)	02
Production size 3	75.03 mm (2.9539 in)	03
	75.04 mm (2.9543 in)	04
	75.05 mm (2.9547 in)	05
	75.06 mm (2.9551 in)	06
Production size 4	75.07 mm (2.9555 in)	07
	75.08 mm (2.9559 in)	08
	75.09 mm (2.9563 in)	09
	75.10 mm (2.9567 in)	10
Oversize (+0.5 mm/0.020 in)	75.47 mm (2.9713 in)	75.47/7 +0.5
	75.48 mm (2.9717 in)	75.48/8 +0.5
	75.49 mm (2.9720 in)	75.49/9 +0.5
	75.50 mm (2.9724 in)	75.50/0 +0.5
1.6:		
Production size 1	79.95 mm (3.1476 in)	5
	79.96 mm (3.1480 in)	6
	79.97 mm (3.1484 in)	7
	79.98 mm (3.1488 in)	8
Production size 2	79.99 mm (3.1492 in)	99
	80.00 mm (3.1496 in)	00
	80.01 mm (3.1500 in)	01
	80.02 mm (3.1504 in)	02
Production size 3	80.03 mm (3.1508 in)	03
	80.04 mm (3.1512 in)	04
	80.05 mm (3.1516 in)	05
	80.06 mm (3.1520 in)	06
Production size 4	80.07 mm (3.1524 in)	07
	80.08 mm (3.1528 in)	08
	80.09 mm (3.1531 in)	09
	80.10 mm (3.1535 in)	1
Oversize (+0.5 mm/0.020 in)	80.47 mm (3.1681 in)	7 +0.5
	80.48 mm (3.1685 in)	8 +0.5
	80.49 mm (3.1689 in)	9 +0.5
	80.50 mm (3.1693 in)	0 +0.5

1.8:		
Production size 1	84.75 mm (3.3366 in)	5
	84.76 mm (3.3370 in)	6
	84.77 mm (3.3374 in)	7
	84.78 mm (3.3378 in)	8
Production size 2	84.79 mm (3.3382 in)	99
	84.80 mm (3.3386 in)	00
	84.81 mm (3.3390 in)	01
	84.82 mm (3.3394 in)	02
Production size 3	84.83 mm (3.3398 in)	03
	84.84 mm (3.3402 in)	04
	84.85 mm (3.3406 in)	05
	84.86 mm (3.3409 in)	06
Production size 4	84.87 mm (3.3413 in)	07
	84.88 mm (3.3417 in)	08
	84.89 mm (3.3421 in)	09
	84.90 mm (3.3425 in)	1
Oversize (+0.5 mm/0.020 in)	85.27 mm (3.3571 in)	7 +0.5
	85.28 mm (3.3575 in)	8 +0.5
	85.29 mm (3.3579 in)	9 +0.5
	85.30 mm (3.3583 in)	0 +0.5

* *Actual bore size ± 0.005 mm (0.0002 in); actual piston size – 0.005 mm to – 0.015 mm (0.0002 to 0.0006 in)*

Piston clearance in bore:	
New	0.02 mm (0.0008 in)
After rebore – 1.3	0.01 to 0.03 mm (0.0004 to 0.0012 in)
After rebore – 1.6 and 1.8	0.02 to 0.04 mm (0.0008 to 0.0016 in)
Bore out-of-round and taper	0.013 mm (0.0005 in) max

Piston rings

Quantity (per piston)	2 compression, 1 oil control (scraper)
Thickness:	
Top (square) compression – 1.3	1.75 mm (0.069 in)
Top (square) compression – 1.6 and 1.8	1.50 mm (0.059 in)
Second (tapered) compression – 1.3	2.00 mm (0.079 in)
Second (tapered) compression – 1.6 and 1.8	1.75 mm (0.069 in)
Scraper	4.0 mm (0.158 in)
End gap:	
Compression	0.3 to 0.5 mm (0.012 to 0.020 in)
Scraper	0.4 to 1.4 mm (0.016 to 0.055 in)
Ring gap offset	180° (see text)
Ring vertical clearance in groove	Not specified

Gudgeon pins

Length:	
1.3	65 mm (2.559 in)
1.6 and 1.8	70 mm (2.756 in)
Diameter:	
1.3	20 mm (0.787 in)
1.6 and 1.8	23 mm (0.906 in)
Clearance in piston:	
1.3	0.007 to 0.010 mm (0.0003 to 0.0004 in)
1.6 and 1.8	0.011 to 0.014 mm (0.0004 to 0.0006 in)
Clearance in connecting rod	None (interference fit)

Crankshaft and bearings – 1.3

Number of main bearings	5	
Main bearing journal diameter – standard	54.972 to 54.985 mm (2.1643 to 2.1648 in)	
Centre journal width – standard	26.000 to 26.052 mm (1.0236 to 1.0257 in)	
Main bearing shell identification – standard:	**Colour code**	**Embossed code**
Centre, top	Brown	GM-400 225 N
Centre, bottom	Green	GM-400 205 N
All others, top	Brown	GM-400 221 N
All others, bottom	Green	GM-400 201 N
Big-end bearing journal diameter – standard	42.971 to 42.987 mm (1.6918 to 1.6924 in)	
Big-end bearing shell identification – standard	GM-400 529 N	
Main and big-end bearing undersizes	0.25 mm (0.0098 in) production and service; 0.50 mm (0.0197 in) service only	
Main bearing shell identification – 0.25 undersize:	**Colour code**	**Embossed code**
Centre, top	Brown-blue	226 A
Centre, bottom	Green-blue	206 A
All others, top	Brown-blue	GM-400 222 A
All others, bottom	Green-blue	GM-400 202 A
Main bearing shell identification – 0.50 undersize:		
Centre, top	Brown-white	227 B

Centre, bottom	Green-white	207 B
All others, top	Brown-white	GM-400 223 B
All others, bottom	Green-white	GM-400 203 B
Big-end bearing shell identification:		
0.25 undersize	Blue	GM-400 530 A
0.50 undersize	White	GM-400 531 B
Main and big-end bearing journal out-of-round	0.04 mm (0.0016 in) max	
Crankshaft radial run-out (at centre journal, shaft in block)	0.03 mm (0.0012 in) max	
Crankshaft endfloat	0.1 to 0.2 mm (0.004 to 0.008 in)	
Main bearing running clearance	0.025 to 0.050 mm (0.0010 to 0.0020 in)	
Big-end bearing running clearance	0.019 to 0.071 mm (0.0008 to 0.0028 in)	
Connecting rod endfloat	0.11 to 0.24 mm (0.0043 to 0.0095 in)	

Crankshaft and bearings – 1.6 and 1.8

Number of main bearings	5	
Main bearing journal diameter – standard	57.982 to 57.995 mm (2.2828 to 2.2833 in)	
Centre journal width – standard	25.950 to 26.002 mm (1.0217 to 1.0237 in)	
Main bearing shell identification – standard:	**Colour code**	**Embossed code**
Centre, top	Brown	400 N, 675 N or 657 N
Centre, bottom	Green	401 N, 667 N or 658 N
All others, top	Brown	GM-400 413 N, A-200 668N, or A-770 650 N
All others, bottom	Green	GM-400 414 N, A-200 669 N, or A-770 651 N
Big-end bearing journal diameter – standard	48.971 to 48.987 mm (1.9280 to 1.9286 in)	
Big-end bearing shell identification – standard	GM-400 419 N, A-200 682 N, or R-770 664 N	
Main and big-end bearing undersizes	0.25 mm (0.098 in) production and service; 0.50 mm (0.0197 in) service only	
Main bearing shell identification – 0.25 undersize:	**Colour code**	**Embossed code**
Centre, top	Brown-blue	402 A, 677 A or 659 A
Centre, bottom	Green-blue	403 A, 678 A or 660 A
All others, top	Brown-blue	GM-400 415 A, A-200 670 A, or R-770 652 A
All others, bottom	Green-blue	GM-400 416 A, A-200 671 A, or R-770 653 A
Big-end bearing shell identification – 0.25 undersize	Blue	GM-400 420 A, A-200 638 A, or R-770 665 A
Main bearing shell identification – 0.50 undersize:		
Centre, top	Brown-white	238 B or 414 B
Centre, bottom	Green-white	239 B or 415 B
All others, top	Brown-white	GM-400 236 B, or GM-400 407
All others, bottom	Green-white	GM-400 237 B, or GM-400 408
Big-end bearing shell identification – 0.50 undersize	White	GM-400 421 B
Main and big-end bearing journal out-of-round	0.04 mm (0.0016 in) max	
Crankshaft radial run-out (at centre journal, shaft in block)	0.03 mm (0.0012 in) max	
Crankshaft endfloat	0.07 to 0.30 mm (0.0028 to 0.0118 in)	
Main bearing running clearance	0.015 to 0.040 mm (0.0006 to 0.0016 in)	
Big-end bearing running clearance	0.019 to 0.063 mm (0.0008 to 0.0025 in)	
Connecting rod endfloat	0.07 to 0.24 mm (0.0028 to 0.0095 in)	

Flywheel

Ring gear run-out	0.5 mm (0.02 in) max
Refinishing limit – depth of material which may be removed from clutch friction surface	0.3 mm (0.012 in) max

Lubrication system

Lubricant type	Multigrade engine oil, viscosity range 10W-40 to 20W-50, to API SE/CC or better
Lubricant capacity (drain and refill, including filter):	
1.3	3.00 litres (5.3 pints) approx
1.6 and 1.8	3.25 litres (5.7 pints) approx
Oil pump tolerances:	
Teeth backlash	0.1 to 0.2 mm (0.004 to 0.008 in)
Gear-to-housing clearance (endfloat)	
1.3	0.08 to 0.15 mm (0.003 to 0.006 in)
1.6 and 1.8	0.03 to 0.10 mm (0.001 to 0.004 in)
Oil pressure at idle (engine warm)	1.5 bar (22 lbf/in²)

Torque wrench settings

	Nm	lbf ft
Flywheel or driveplate bolts	60	44
Main bearing caps	70	52
Oil pump cover	6	4
Oil pressure relief valve plug	30	22
Oil filter	15	11

Torque wrench settings

	Nm	lbf ft
Water pump:		
1.3	8	6
1.6 and 1.8	25	18
Big-end bearing caps:		
1.3	25	18
1.6 and 1.8	50	37
Sump bolts (use sealing compound)	5	4
Cylinder head bolts (use **new** bolts every time):		
Stage 1	25	18
Stage 2	Further 60°	
Stage 3	Further 60°	
Stage 4:		
1.3	Further 30°	
1.6 and 1.8	Further 60°	
Stage 5 (after warm-up)	Further 30°	
Camshaft sprocket bolt	45	33
Crankshaft pulley bolt (use locking compound):		
1.3	55	41
1.6 and 1.8	60	44
Inlet manifold:		
1.3	20	15
1.6 and 1.8	22	16
Engine mounting bracket, RH:		
To cylinder block	50	37
To mounting pad	40	30
Other engine mountings	40	30
Oil pressure switch	30	22
Sump drain plug	45	33

PART A: OHV ENGINE

1 General description

The engine is of four-cylinder, in-line overhead valve type, mounted transversely at the front of the car.

The crankshaft is supported in three shell type main bearings. Thrust washers are incorporated in the centre main bearing to control crankshaft endfloat.

The connecting rods are attached to the crankshaft by horizontally split shell type big-end bearings, and to the pistons by gudgeon pins which are an interference fit in the connecting rod small-end bore. The aluminium alloy pistons are of the slipper type and are fitted with three piston rings: two compression rings and an oil control ring.

The camshaft is chain driven from the crankshaft and operates the rocker arms via tappets and short pushrods. The inlet and exhaust valves are each closed by a single valve spring and operates in guides, integral with the cylinder head. The valves are actuated directly by the rocker arms.

Engine lubrication is by a gear type oil pump. The pump is mounted beneath the crankcase and is driven by a camshaft, as are the distributor and fuel pump.

Many of the engine component retaining bolts are of the socket-headed type and require the use of special Torx type multi-tooth keys or socket bits for removal. These are readily available from retail outlets and should be obtained if major dismantling or repair work is to be carried out on the engine.

2 Maintenance and inspection

1 The engine oil should be checked weekly or before a long run, and topped up if necessary. At the same time it is wise to inspect the engine joint faces for coolant or oil leaks, especially around the rocker cover, sump, cylinder head and timing cover. Rectify leaks as described in the appropriate Sections of this Chapter.

2 At the major service intervals (see Routine Maintenance), carry out the following work.

3 Carefully inspect the condition of the engine breather hoses and renew them if there are any signs of cracking or deterioration of the rubber.

4 The engine oil should ideally be drained just after a run. Place a suitable container beneath the oil drain plug at the rear of the sump. Unscrew the plug (photo) and allow the oil to drain. Inspect the condition of the drain plug sealing washer and renew it if necessary, refit and tighten the plug after draining.

5 Refill the engine using the correct grade of oil through the filter orifice on the rocker cover. Fill until the level reaches the MAX mark on the dipstick (photo).

6 Move the bowl to the front of the engine under the oil filter.

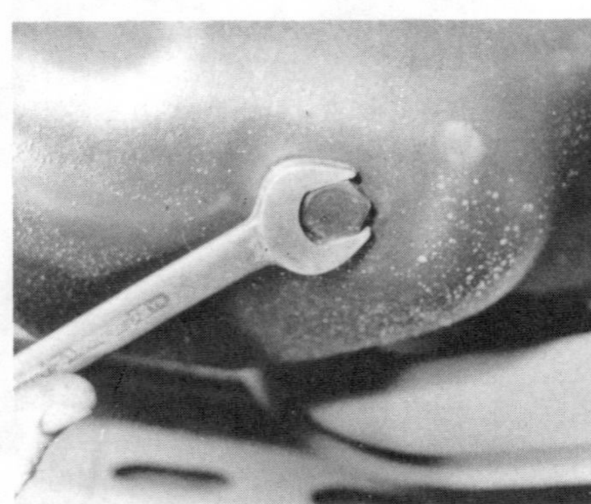

2.4 Engine oil drain plug

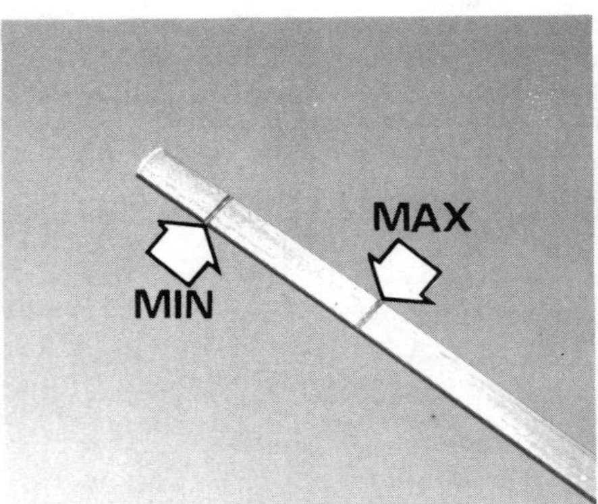

2.5 Dipstick MAX and MIN marks

2.6 Engine oil filter (typical)

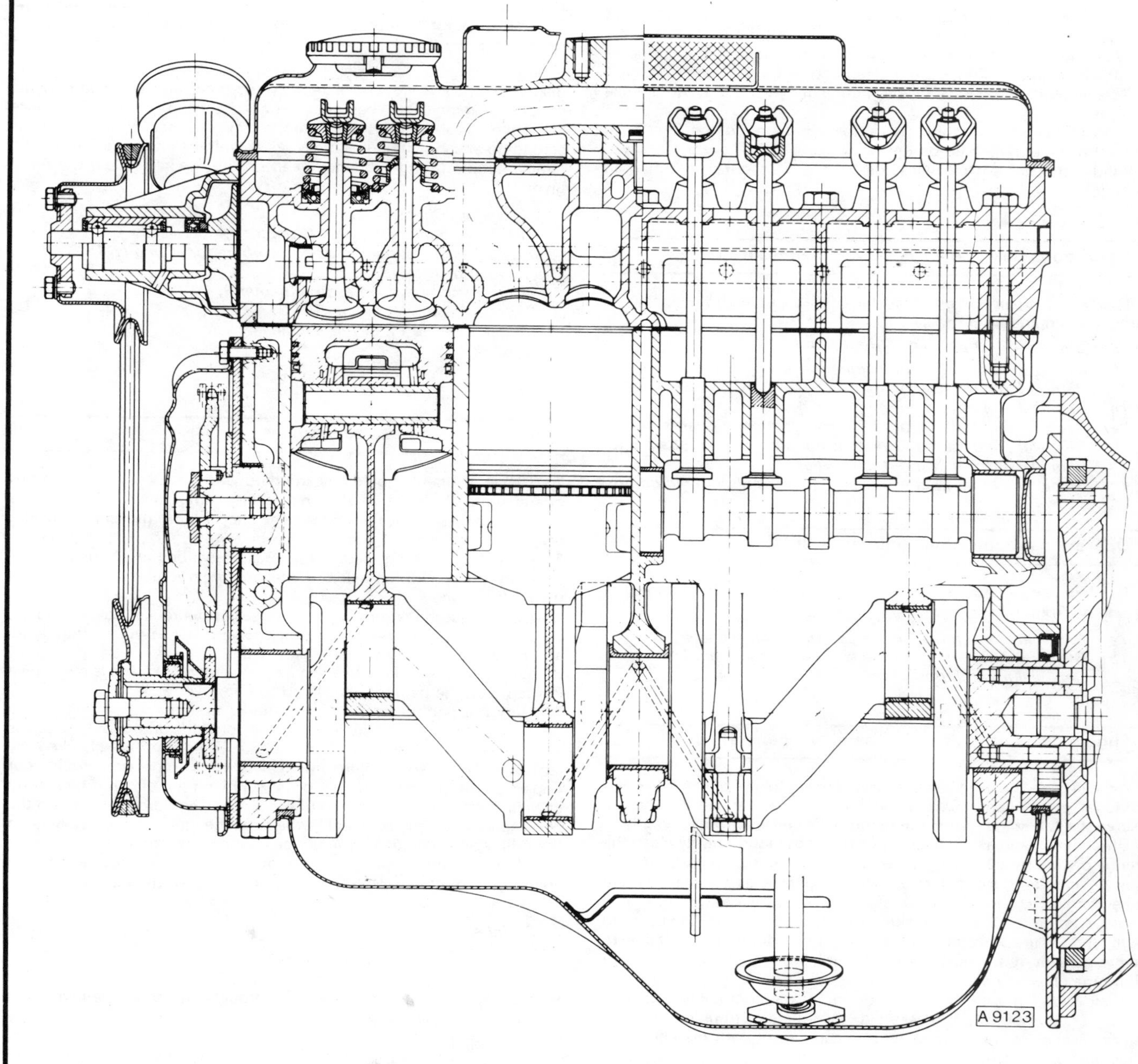

Fig. 1.1 Longitudinal section of OHV engine (Sec 1)

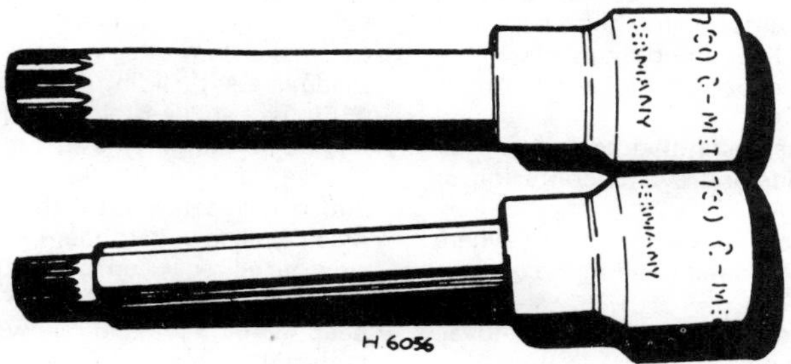

Fig. 1.2 Typical multi-tooth socket bits (Sec 1)

7 Using a strap wrench or filter removal tool, slacken the filter and then unscrew it from the housing and discard it (photo).
8 Wipe the mating face on the housing with a rag and then lubricate the rubber seal on the filter using clean engine oil.
9 Screw the filter into position and tighten it by hand only, do not use any tools.
10 With the engine running, check for leaks around the filter seal. Switch off the engine and top up the oil level.
11 Adjust the valve clearances, using the procedure described in Section 7.

3 Operations possible with the engine in the car

The following operations may be carried out without having to remove the engine from the car:

(a) Adjustment of the valve clearances
(b) Removal and refitting of cylinder head
(c) Removal and refitting of sump
(d) Removal and refitting of oil pump
(e) Removal and refitting of the timing gear components
(f) Removal and refitting of pistons and connecting rods
(g) Removal and refitting of the flywheel
(h) Removal and refitting of the engine/transmission mountings

4 Operations requiring engine removal

The following operations can only be carried out after removal of the engine from the car:

(a) Removal and refitting of the camshaft and tappets
(b) Removal and refitting of the crankshaft and main bearings
(c) Removal and refitting of the crankshaft rear oil seal

5 Engine dismantling and reassembly – general

1 If the engine has been removed from the car for major overhaul, or if individual components have been removed for repair or renewal, observe the following general hints on dismantling and reassembly.
2 Drain the oil into a suitable container and then thoroughly clean the exterior of the engine using a degreasing solvent or paraffin. Clean away as much of the external dirt and grease as possible before dismantling.
3 As parts are removed, clean them in a paraffin bath. However, do not immerse parts with internal oilways in paraffin as it is difficult to remove, usually requiring a high pressure hose. Clean oilways with nylon pipe cleaners.
4 Avoid working with the engine or any of the components directly on a concrete floor, as grit presents a real source of trouble.
5 Wherever possible, work should be carried out with the engine or individual components on a strong bench. If the work must be done on the floor, cover it with a board or sheets of newspaper.
6 Have plenty of clean, lint-free rags available and also some containers or trays to hold small items. This will help during reassembly and also prevent possible losses.
7 Always obtain a complete set of gaskets if the engine is being completely dismantled, or all those necessary for the individual component or assembly being worked on. Keep the old gaskets with a view to using them as a pattern to make a replacement if a new one is not available.
8 When possible refit nuts, bolts and washers in their locations after removal as this helps to protect the threads and avoids confusion or loss.
9 During reassembly thoroughly lubricate all the components, where this is applicable, with engine oil, but avoid contaminating the gaskets and joint mating faces.
10 Where applicable, the following Sections describe the removal, refitting and adjustment of components with the engine in the car. If the engine has been removed from the car, the procedures described are the same except for the disconnection of hoses, cables and linkages, and the removal of components necessary for access, which will already have been done.

6 Ancillary components – removal and refitting

If the engine has been removed from the car for complete dismantling, the following externally mounted ancillary components should be removed. When the engine has been reassembled these components can be refitted before the engine is installed in the car, as setting up and adjustment is often easier with the engine removed. The removal and refitting sequence need not necessarily follow the order given:

Alternator (Chapter 12)
Distributor and spark plugs (Chapter 4)
Inlet and exhaust manifolds and carburettor (Chapter 3)
Fuel pump (Chapter 3)
Water pump and thermostat (Chapter 2)
Clutch assembly (Chapter 5)
Oil filler (Section 2 of this Chapter)
Dipstick

7 Valve clearances – adjustment

1 This adjustment should be carried out with the engine at its normal operating temperature. If it is being done after overhaul when the engine is cold, repeat the adjustment after the car has been driven a few miles when the engine will then be hot.
2 Begin by removing the air cleaner, as described in Chapter 3.
3 Mark the spark plug leads to ensure correct refitting and then pull them off the spark plugs.
4 Disconnect the engine breather hoses at the rocker cover (photo).
5 Undo the four bolts securing the rocker cover to the cylinder head and lift off the shaped spreader washers.
6 Withdraw the rocker cover from the cylinder head. If it is stuck give it a tap with the palm of your hand to free it.
7 Turn the engine by means of the crankshaft pulley bolt, or by engaging top gear and pulling the car forward, until No 1 piston is approaching TDC on the firing stroke. This can be checked by removing No 1 spark plug and feeling for compression with your fingers as the engine is turned, or by removing the distributor cap and checking the position of the rotor arm which should be pointing to the No 1 spark plug lead segment in the cap. The ignition timing marks on the pulley and timing cover must be aligned (photo).
8 With the engine in this position the following valves can be adjusted – counting from the timing cover end of the engine.

1 exhaust
2 inlet
3 inlet
5 exhaust

9 Now turn the engine crankshaft through one complete revolution and adjust the following remaining valves:

4 exhaust
6 inlet
7 inlet
8 exhaust

10 As each clearance is being checked, slide a feeler blade of the appropriate size, as given in the Specifications, between the end of the valve stem and the rocker arm (photo). Adjust the clearance by turning the rocker arm retaining nut using a socket or ring spanner until the blade is a stiff sliding fit.
11 It is also possible to check and adjust the clearances with the engine running. This is done in the same way, but each valve is checked in turn. It will of course be necessary to refit the plug leads and No 1 spark plug if this method is adopted. To reduce oil splash place a piece of cardboard, suitably cut to shape, between the pushrod side of the rocker arms and the edge of the cylinder head.
12 After adjustment remove all traces of old gasket from the cylinder head mating face and renew the rocker cover gasket if it is cracked or perished.
13 Refit the rocker cover and secure with the retaining bolts and shaped spreader washers.
14 Refit the spark plug and plug leads, reconnect the engine breather hoses and refit the air cleaner, as described in Chapter 3.

7.4 Removing the breather hose from the rocker cover

7.7 Ignition timing marks (arrowed) in alignment

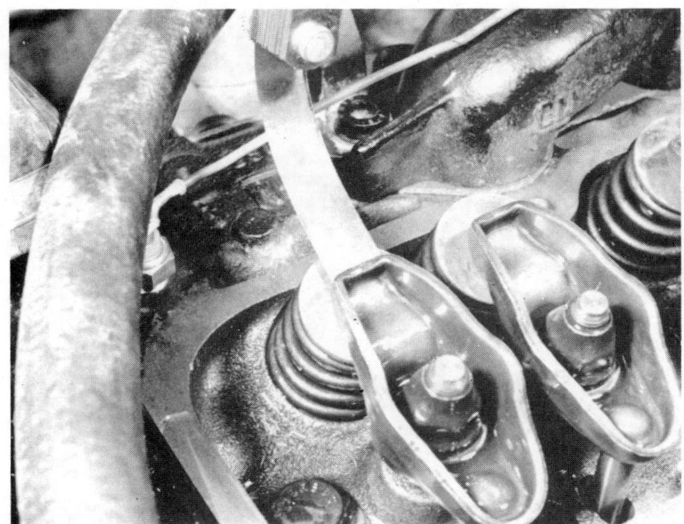
7.10 Checking a valve clearance

8 Cylinder head – removal and refitting

1 Make sure that the engine is cold before commencing operations to avoid any chance of the head distorting.
2 Disconnect the battery negative terminal.
3 Drain the cooling system, as described in Chapter 2, and remove the air cleaner, as described in Chapter 3.
4 From behind the engine, undo the two bolts securing the exhaust front pipe to the manifold. Remove the bolts and tension springs; then separate the pipe joint from the manifold.
5 Slacken the retaining clip and disconnect the radiator top hose from the thermostat housing in the water pump.
6 Slacken the alternator mounting and adjustment arm bolts, move the alternator towards the engine and slip the drivebelt off the pulleys.
7 Slacken the retaining clips and disconnect the heater hose and radiator bottom hose from the water pump.
8 Disconnect the other heater hose at the cylinder head outlet after slackening the retaining clip.
9 Undo the union nut and disconnect the brake servo vacuum hose from the inlet manifold.
10 Note the location of the plug leads to aid refitting and pull them off the spark plugs. Disconnect the HT lead at the coil, undo the distributor cap retaining screws and remove the cap and leads.
11 Refer to Chapter 3 and disconnect the choke and accelerator cables from the carburettor. Detach the distributor vacuum advance pipe.
12 Disconnect the fuel hose from the carburettor and plug its end after removal.
13 Disconnect the engine breather hoses from the rocker cover.
14 Undo the three socket-headed screws securing the inlet manifold to the cylinder head. Note the spark plug lead support brackets fitted to the two end retaining bolts.
15 Lift the inlet manifold complete with carburettor from the cylinder head and recover the gasket.
16 Undo the four bolts and shaped spreader washers and lift off the rocker cover.
17 Slacken the rocker arm retaining nuts, move the rocker arms to one side and lift out the pushrods (photo). Keep the pushrods in order after removal.
18 Undo the cylinder head retaining bolts, half a turn at a time in the reverse sequence to that shown in photo 8.26. Unscrew the bolts fully and remove them. Obtain **new** bolts for use when refitting.
19 Lift the cylinder head from the block. If it is stuck, tap it free with a soft-faced mallet. Do not insert a lever into the gasket joint – you may damage the mating surfaces.
20 With the cylinder head removed, recover the gasket.
21 If the cylinder head has been removed for decarbonising or for attention to the valves or springs, reference should be made to Sections 9 and 10.
22 Before refitting the cylinder head, ensure that the cylinder block

7.17 Removing the pushrods

Fig. 1.3 Cylinder head guide studs made from old head retaining bolts (Sec 8)

and head mating faces are spotlessly clean and dry with all traces of old gasket removed. Use a scraper and wire brush to do this, but take care to cover the water passages and other openings with masking tape or rag to prevent dirt and carbon falling in. Remove all traces of oil and water from the bolt holes, otherwise hydraulic pressure created by the bolts being screwed in could crack the block or give inaccurate torque settings. Ensure that the bolt threads are clean and dry.

23 When all is clean, screw two guide studs into the cylinder block. These can be made from the two old cylinder head bolts by cutting off their heads and sawing a screwdriver slot in their ends.

24 Locate a **new** gasket in position on the block as shown (photo). *Do not use any jointing compound on the gasket*

25 Lower the cylinder head carefully into position. Screw in **new** bolts finger tight, remove the guide pins and screw in the two remaining bolts.

26 Tighten the cylinder head bolts in the order shown (photo) to the first stage specified torque. Now tighten the bolts through three further stages as given in the Specifications. No further retightening will be required.

27 Refit the pushrods, making quite sure that each one is located in its tappet.

28 Reposition the rocker arms over the ends of the pushrods and then adjust the valve clearances, as described in Section 7.

29 Place a new gasket in position and refit the inlet manifold and carburettor (photo).

30 Refit the rocker cover, using a new gasket, and secure with the four bolts and spreader washers.

31 Refit the heater hoses and radiator hoses to the outlets on the water pump and cylinder head.

32 Refit the fuel hose to the carburettor, the vacuum advance pipe to the distributor and the breather hoses to the rocker cover.

33 Refit and adjust the accelerator and choke cables, as described in Chapter 3.

34 Refit the brake servo vacuum hose to the inlet manifold.

35 Refit the distributor cap and reconnect the plug leads and coil lead.

36 Slip the drivebelt over the pulleys and adjust its tension, as described in Chapter 2.

37 Reconnect the exhaust front pipe to the manifold and tighten the bolts to compress the tension springs.

38 Refill the cooling system as described in Chapter 2, refit the air cleaner as described in Chapter 3 and connect the battery negative terminal.

9 Cylinder head – overhaul

1 Unscrew the rocker arm retaining/adjustment nuts and withdraw the rocker arms from the studs. Keep them in order as they are removed.

8.24 Fitting a cylinder head gasket

8.26 Cylinder head bolt tightening sequence

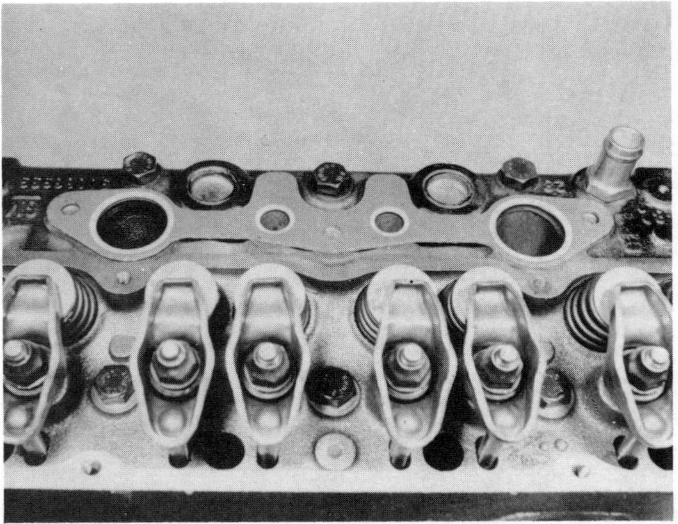

8.29 Inlet manifold gasket in position

2 To remove the valves, the springs will have to be compressed to allow the split collets to be released from the groove in the upper section of the valve stems. A valve spring compressor will therefore be necessary.
3 Locate the compressor to enable the forked end of the arm to be positioned over the valve spring collar whilst the screw part of the clamp is situated squarely on the face of the valve.
4 Screw up the clamp to compress the spring and release the pressure of the collar acting on the collets. If the collar sticks, support the head and clamp frame and give the end of the clamp a light tap with a hammer to help release it.
5 Extract the two collets and then release the tension of the clamp. Remove the clamp, withdraw the collar and spring and extract the valve. Remove the valve stem seals and the exhaust valve rotators.
6 As they are released and removed, keep the valves in order so that if they are to be refitted they will be replaced in their original positions in the cylinder head. A piece of stiff card with eight holes punched in it is a sure method of keeping the valves in order.
7 Examine the head of the valves for pitting and burning, especially the heads of the exhaust valves. The valve seatings should be examined at the same time. If the pitting on valve and seat is very slight, the marks can be removed by grinding the seats and valves together with coarse, and then fine, valve grinding paste.
8 Where bad pitting has occurred to the valve seats it will be necessary to recut them and fit new valves. The latter job should be entrusted to the local agent or engineering works. In practice it is very seldom that the seats are so badly worn. Normally it is the valve that is too badly worn for refitting, and the owner can easily purchase a new set of valves and match them to the seats by valve grinding.
9 Valve grinding is carried out as follows. Smear a trace of coarse carborundum paste on the seat face and apply a suction grinder tool to the valve head. With a semi-rotary motion, grind the valve head to its seat, lifting the valve occasionally to redistribute the grinding paste. When a dull matt even surface is produced on both the valve seat and the valve, wipe off the paste and repeat the process with fine carborundum paste, lifting and turning the valve to redistribute the paste as before. A light spring placed under the valve head will greatly ease this operation. When a smooth unbroken ring of light grey matt finish is produced, on both valve and valve seat faces, the grinding operation is complete.
10 Scrape away all carbon from the valve head and the valve stem. Carefully clean away every trace of grinding compound; take great care to leave none in the ports or in the valve guides. Clean the valves and valve seats with a paraffin-soaked rag, then with a clean rag and finally, if an air line is available, blow the valves, valve guides and valve ports clean.
11 Check that all valve springs are intact. If any one is broken, all should be renewed. Check the free height of the springs against new ones. If some springs are not within specification, replace them all. Springs suffer from fatigue and it is a good idea to renew them even if they look serviceable.
12 Check that the oil supply holes in the rocker arm studs are clear.
13 The cylinder head can be checked for warping either by placing it on a piece of plate glass or using a straight-edge and feeler blades. Slight distortion may be corrected by having the head machined to remove metal from the mating face.
14 Valve guide renewal is necessary if the valve stem clearance in the guide exceeds that specified. Renewal, or reaming to accept oversize valves, should be left to a GM dealer.
15 Commence reassembly by lubricating a valve stem and inserting it into its guide (photo).
16 Fit the valve stem oil seal, using the protective sleeve supplied with the new seals over the valve stem to avoid damage. Lubricate the sleeve and push on the seal, ring downwards. Recover the sleeve.
17 On exhaust valves, fit the valve rotator (photo).
18 Fit the valve spring and collar, with the recessed part of the collar inside the spring (photos).
19 Place the end of the spring compressor over the collar and valve stem and, with the screw head of the compressor over the valve head, screw up the clamp until the spring is compressed past the groove in the valve stem. Then put a little grease round the groove.
20 Place the two halves of the split collar (collets) into the groove with the narrow ends pointing towards the spring (photo). The grease will hold them in the groove.
21 Release the clamp slowly and carefully, making sure that the collets are not dislodged from the groove. When the clamp is fully released the

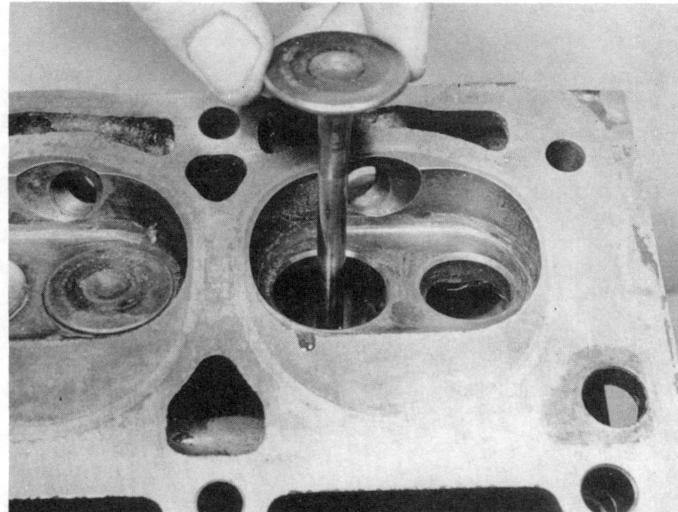
9.15 Fitting a valve to its guide

Fig. 1.4 Use a protective sleeve when fitting the valve stem oil seals (Sec 9)

9.17 Fitting an exhaust valve rotator

9.18A Fit the valve spring ...

9.18B ... followed by the spring collar

9.20 Compress the spring and fit the collets

9.24A Fitting a rocker arm ...

9.24B ... and its pivot ball

9.25 Fit the nut with the self-locking collar uppermost

top edges of the collets should be in line with each other. Give the top of each spring a smart tap with a soft-faced mallet when assembly is complete to ensure that the collets are properly settled.
22 Repeat the above procedure for the other 7 valves.
23 The rocker gear can be refitted with the head either on or off the engine. The only part of the procedure to watch is that the rocker nuts must not be screwed down too far or it will not be possible to refit the pushrods.
24 Next put the rocker arm over the stud followed by the pivot ball (photos). Make sure that the spring fits snugly round the rocker arm centre section and that the two bearing surfaces of the interior of the arm and the ball face, are clean and lubricated with engine oil.
25 Oil the stud thread and fit the nut with the self-locking collar uppermost (photo). Screw it down until the locking collar is on the stud.

10 Cylinder head and pistons – decarbonising

1 This can be carried out with the engine either in or out of the car. With the cylinder head removed, carefully use a wire brush and blunt scraper to clean all traces of carbon deposits from the combustion spaces and the ports. The valve head stems and valve guides should also be freed from any carbon deposits. Wash the combustion spaces and ports down with petrol and scrape the cylinder head surface free of any foreign matter with the side of a steel rule or a similar article.
2 If the engine is installed in the car, clean the pistons and the top of the cylinder bores. If the pistons are still in the block, then it is essential that great care is taken to ensure that no carbon gets into the cylinder bores as this could scratch the cylinder walls or cause damage to the piston and rings. To ensure this does not happen, first turn the crankshaft so that two of the pistons are at the top of their bores. Stuff rag into the other two bores or seal them off with paper and masking tape. The waterways should also be covered with small pieces of masking tape to prevent particles of carbon entering the cooling system and damaging the water pump.
3 Press a little grease into the gap between the cylinder walls and the two pistons which are to be worked on. With a blunt scraper carefully scrape away the carbon from the piston crown, taking great care not to scratch the aluminium. Also scrape away the carbon from the surrounding lip of the cylinder wall. When all carbon has been removed, scrape away the grease which will now be contaminated with carbon particles, taking care not to press any into the bores. To assist prevention of carbon build-up the piston crown can be polished with a metal polish. Remove the rags or masking tape from the other two cylinders and turn the crankshaft so that the two pistons which were at the bottom are now at the top. Place rag or masking tape in the cylinders which have been decarbonised and proceed as just described. Decarbonising is now complete.

11 Sump – removal and refitting

1 Jack up the front of the car and securely support it on axle stands.
2 Drain the engine oil into a suitable container (Section 2) and refit the plug after draining.
3 Undo the bolts securing the flywheel cover plate and side support braces and remove the cover.
4 Undo the retaining bolts and lift away the sump. It will probably be necessary to tap the sump from side to side with a hide or plastic mallet to release the joint face.
5 Thoroughly clean the sump in paraffin or a suitable solvent and remove all traces of external dirt and internal sludge. Scrape away all traces of old gasket from the sump and crankcase faces and ensure that they are clean and dry. Also clean the bearing cap grooves.
6 Apply a thick bead of jointing compound to the crankcase flange and at the joints of the front and rear main bearng caps

Fig. 1.5 Apply jointing compound to the four gasket/main bearing cap joints before fitting the sump (Sec 11)

7 Position the cork side gaskets on the crankcase flanges and then insert the cork and sealing strips to the main bearing cap grooves (photo).
8 Apply a further bead of jointing compound to the gasket faces and to the gasket joints at the bearing caps.
9 Refit the sump (photo) and secure it in place with the retaining bolts which should be progressively tightened in a diagonal sequence.
10 Refit the flywheel cover plate, lower the car and fill the engine with oil.

12 Oil pump – removal and refitting

1 Remove the sump, as described in the previous Section.
2 Undo the two socket-headed bolts and withdraw the pump from the crankcase (photos).
3 Refitting the pump is the reverse sequence to removal, but engage the pump shaft in the distributor driveshaft slot, and tighten the retaining bolts to the specified torque.

11.7 Insert the cork strips in the main bearing cap grooves

11.9 Refitting the sump

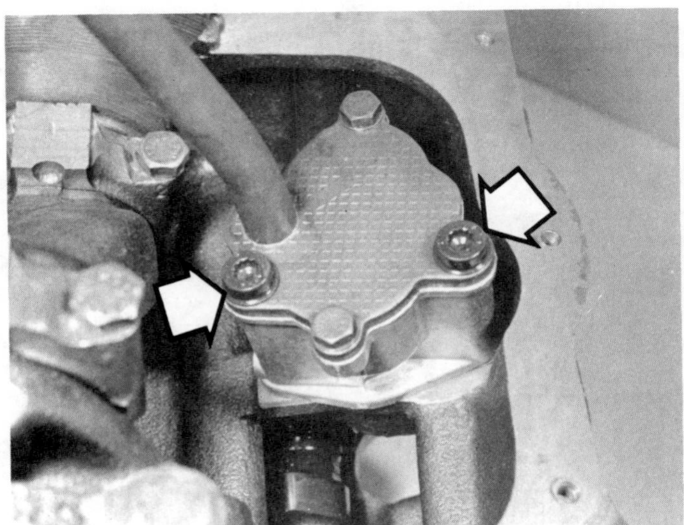

12.2A Undo the two socket-headed bolts (arrowed) ...

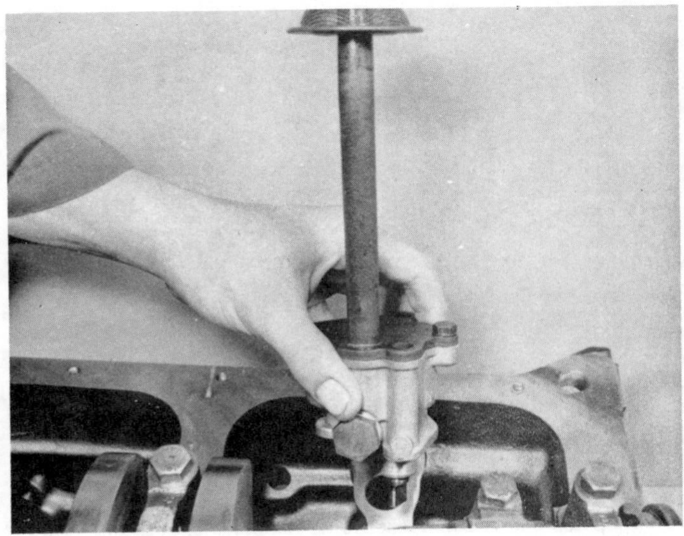

12.2B ... and remove the oil pump

13 Oil pump – overhaul

1 Remove the pump, as described in the previous Section.
2 Undo the two pump cover bolts and lift off the cover and oil pick-up tube. Remove the cover gasket.
3 Take out the driving gear and driven gear (photos).
4 Undo the large nut on the side of the housing and remove the sealing washer and oil pressure relief spring and ball valve (photo).
5 Clean all the parts in paraffin and dry with a lint-free cloth.
6 Inspect the pump gears, housing, cover and relief valve ball for scoring, scuff marks or other signs of wear and renew the pump if evident.
7 If the pump condition is satisfactory, check the pump clearances as follows.
8 Using a feeler gauge, check the backlash between the gear teeth. Place a straight-edge across the top edge of the gears and check their projection. If any of the clearances exceeds the tolerances given in the Specifications, renew the pump (photo).
9 If the clearances are satisfactory, refit the relief valve assembly and assemble the pump gears. Fill the pump with oil and refit the cover using a new gasket. Tighten the cover securing bolts and refit the pump.

14 Timing gear components – removal and refitting

1 For greater access remove the front right-hand wheel trim and slacken the wheel bolts. Jack up the front of the car, support it securely on axle stands and remove the roadwheel.
2 Undo the four retaining bolts and remove the clutch access plate at the base of the bellhousing (photo).
3 Slacken the alternator mounting and adjustment arm bolts, move the alternators towards the engine and slip the drivebelt off the pulleys.
4 Lock the flywheel by wedging a screwdriver between the ring gear teeth and the side of the bellhousing.
5 Using a socket or spanner undo the crankshaft pulley retaining bolt and withdraw the pulley.
6 Undo the bolts securing the timing cover to the front of the engine and lift off the cover.
7 Withdraw the oil slinger from the crankshaft, noting which way round it is fitted (photo).
8 Temporarily refit the pulley and turn the crankshaft until the crankshaft sprocket keyway is uppermost and the timing marks on the two sprockets are in alignment (photo). Remove the pulley.
9 Undo the two retaining bolts and remove the timing chain tensioner. One of two types of tensioner may be fitted: simple

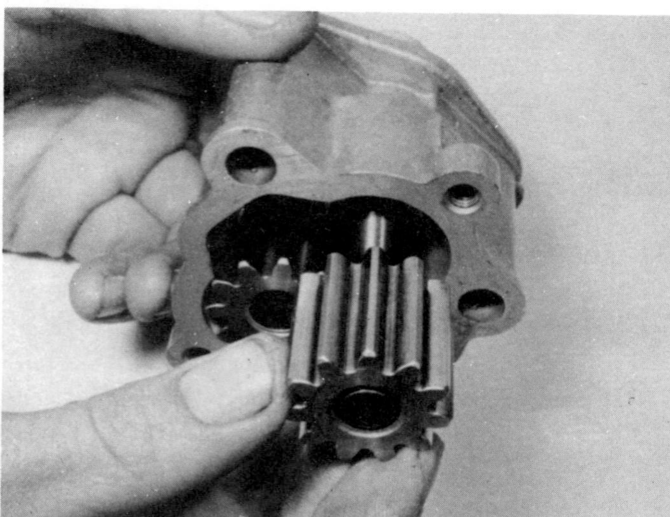
13.3A Removing the oil pump driving gear ...

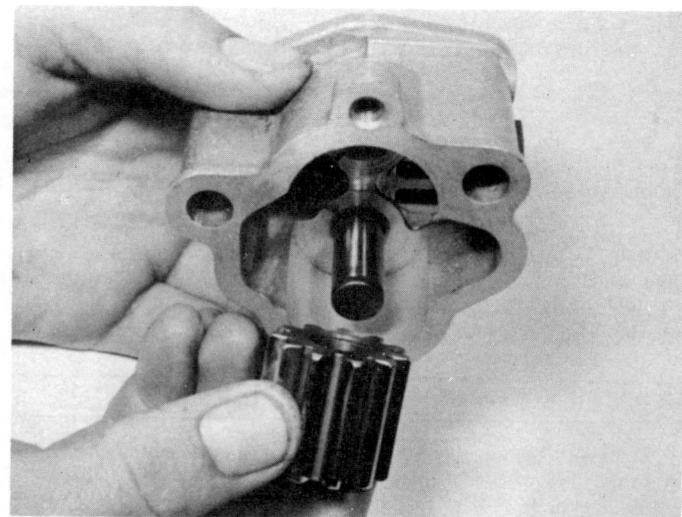
13.3B ... and the driven gear

13.4 Oil pump and pressure relief valve components

13.8 Check the pump gear teeth backlash

14.2 Clutch access plate

14.7 Crankshaft oil slinger

14.8 Crankshaft sprocket keyway (A) and sprocket timing marks (B)

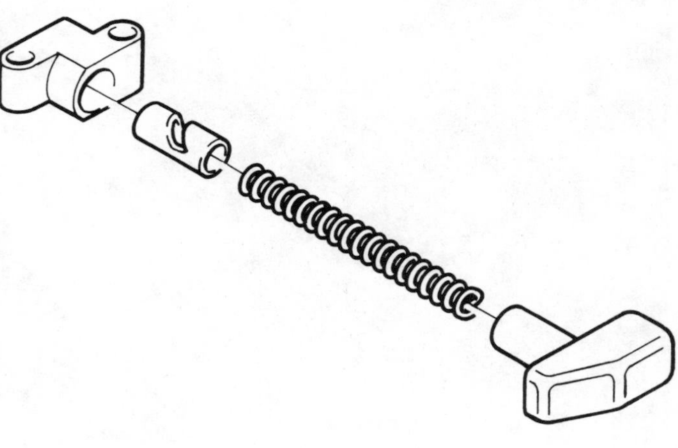
Fig. 1.6 Timing chain tensioner – oil pressure assisted type (Sec 14)

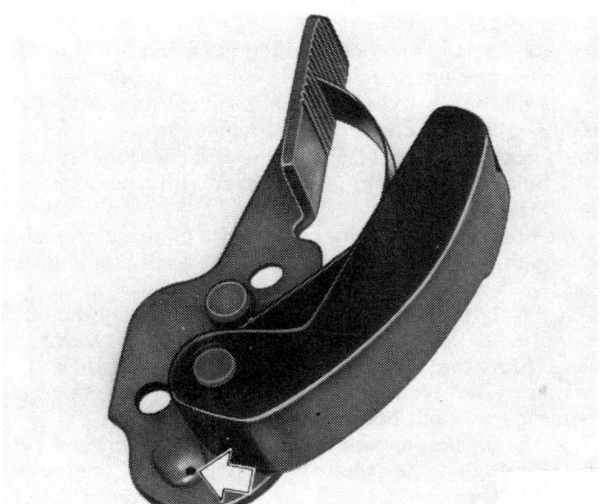
Fig. 1.7 Timing chain tensioner – spring-operated type. Oil hole (arrowed) must not be blocked (Sec 14)

spring-operated, or oil pressure assisted. With the oil pressure assisted type, restrain the thrust pad to prevent premature ejection of the tensioner components.

10 Undo the camshaft sprocket retaining bolt and remove the bolt and washer (photo). Place a screwdriver through one of the sprocket holes and in contact with the camshaft retaining plate behind the sprocket to stop it turning as the bolt is undone.

11 Withdraw the camshaft sprocket and crankshaft sprocket from their respective locations, using a screwdriver as a lever if necessary, then remove the sprockets complete with chain (photo).

12 Thoroughly clean all the components in paraffin and dry them with a lint-free cloth. Remove all traces of old gasket from the faces of the timing cover and engine.

13 To renew the oil seal in the timing cover, place the cover outer face downwards over two blocks of wood and drive out the old seal and holder using a hammer and drift (photo).

14 Place the new seal, which must be soaked in engine oil for 24 hours, in the holder (photo) and then tap the holder into the cover using a block of wood (photo). The seal holder must be fitted flush with the outer edge of the timing cover.

14.10 Camshaft sprocket retaining bolt and washer

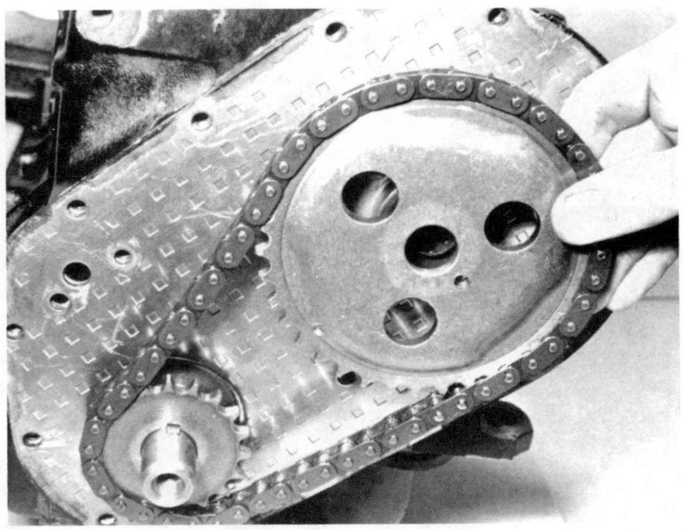
14.11 Removing the sprockets and timing chain

14.13 Using a drift to remove the timing cover oil seal

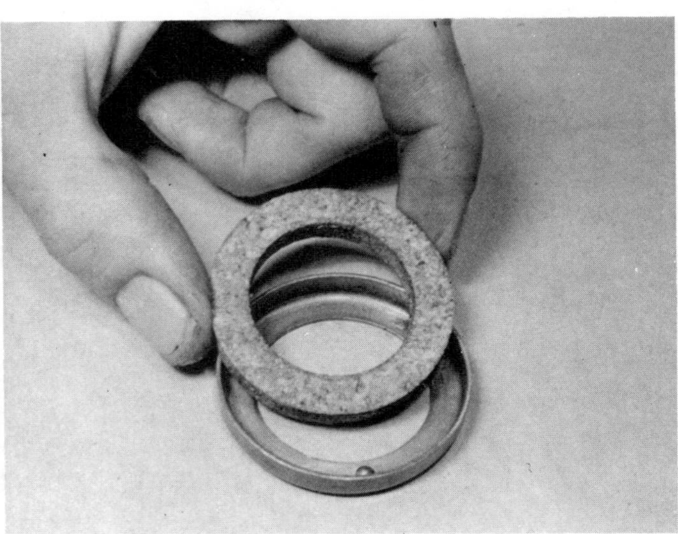
14.14A Fit the new seal to the holder ...

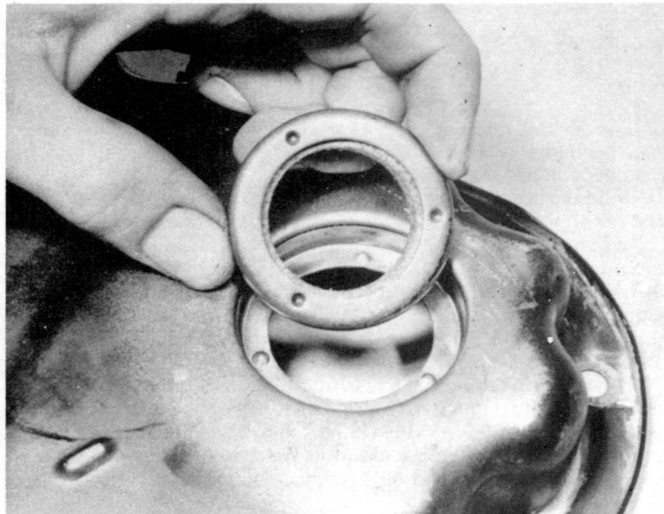
14.14B ... and refit the holder and seal to the timing cover

15 Commence reassembly by engaging the chain around the crankshaft sprocket.

16 Engage the camshaft sprocket within the loop of the chain so that it can be fitted to the camshaft and will have its timing mark in alignment with the one on the crankshaft sprocket. Adjust the camshaft sprocket as necessary within the chain loop to achieve this.

17 Fit the sprocket to the camshaft, screw in the bolt and washer and tighten the bolt while holding the sprocket with a screwdriver, as was done during removal.

18 Refit the timing chain tensioner. With the oil pressure assisted type, compress the thrust pad by hand, secure the tensioner and release the thrust pad.

19 To refit the spring-operated chain tensioner, place the tensioner in position and fit the lower retaining bolt finger tight. Move the spring blade away from the tensioner body with a screwdriver, pivot the tensioner into position and fit the upper retaining bolt, then release the springs and tighten both bolts (photos).

20 Position the oil slinger over the crankshaft and place a new gasket on the front of the engine (photo). Apply jointing compound to both sides of the gasket.

21 Refit the cover (photo) and the retaining bolts, but only screw the bolts in two or three turns. Position the crankshaft pulley on the crankshaft to centralise the cover and then tighten the bolts progressively in a diagonal sequence.

14.19A Fit the tensioner lower bolt ...

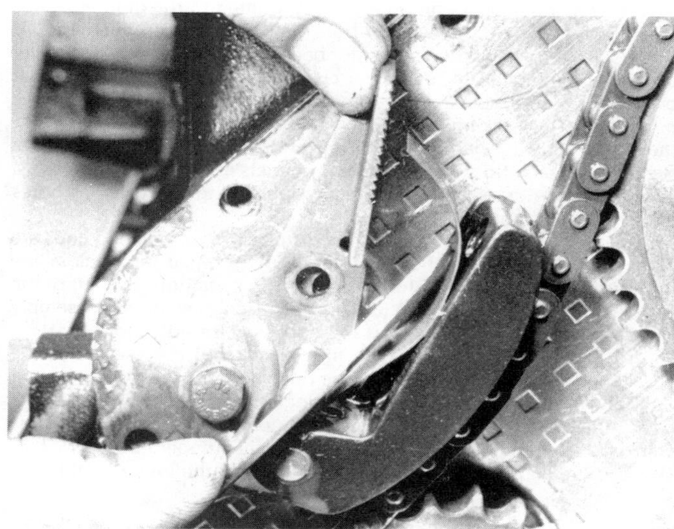
14.19B ... then push back the spring, pivot the tensioner and fit the upper bolt

14.20 Fitting a new timing cover gasket

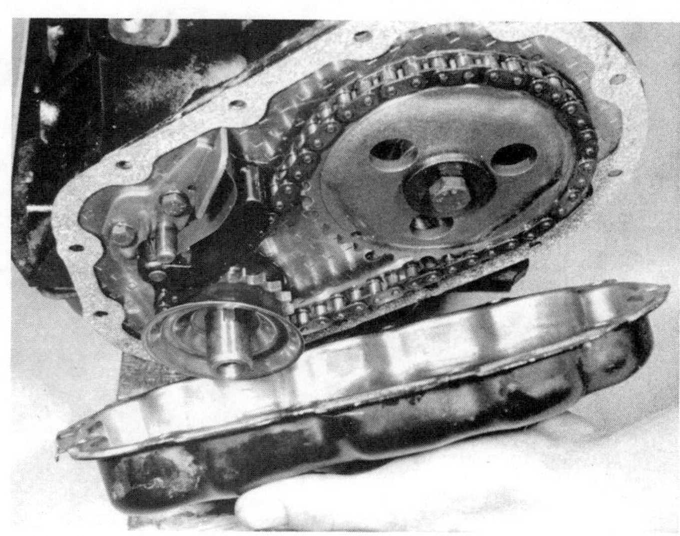
14.21 Refitting the timing cover

22 Refit the pulley retaining bolt and tighten to the specified torque.
23 Refit the drivebelt and adjust its tension, as described in Chapter 2.
24 Refit the roadwheel and lower the car to the ground. Tighten the wheel bolts.

15 Pistons and connecting rods – removal and refitting

1 Remove the cylinder head, the sump and the oil pump, as described in earlier Sections.
2 The connecting rod big-end caps and rods may not be marked numerically for location when new and therefore they must be inspected for identification marks before dismantling. If no marks are evident, punch, scribe or file identification marks on the caps and rods starting with No 1 at the timing cover end. Mark them all on the same side to avoid confusion during reassembly. If they have already been marked then this will not, of course, be necessary.
3 Undo and remove the big-end cap retaining bolts and keep them in order for correct refitting.
4 Detach the big-end bearing caps. If they are stuck, lightly tap them free using a soft-faced mallet.
5 To remove the bearing shells for inspection and/or renewal, press the bearing end opposite the groove in both connecting rod and bearing cap and the shells will slide out. Again keep the shells in order of removal.
6 The piston rod assemblies are removed through the top of each cylinder bore, being pushed upwards from underneath using a wooden hammer handle which is pushed against the connecting rod. Rotate the crankshaft accordingly to gain suitable access to each rod assembly. Note that, if there is a pronounced wear ridge at the top of the cylinder bore, there is a risk of piston ring damage unless the ridge is first removed using a suitable ridge reaming tool, or scraper.
7 The pistons should not be separated from their connecting rods unless they or the gudgeon pins are to be renewed. The gudgeon pin is a press fit and special tools are required for removing and installation. This task should therefore be entrusted to your local agent or automotive machine shop.
8 If for any reason the pistons are separated from their rods, mark them numerically on the same side as the rod markings to ensure correct refitting.

9 If new pistons or piston rings are being fitted to the old bores, it is essential to roughen the cylinder bore walls slightly with medium grit emery cloth to allow the rings to bed in. Do this with a circular up-and-down action to produce a criss-cross pattern on the cylinder bore walls. Make sure that the bearing journal on the crankshaft is protected with masking tape during this operation. Thoroughly clean the bores with a paraffin-soaked rag and dry with a lint-free cloth. Remove the tape from the crankshaft journals and clean them also.
10 Commence reassembly by liberally lubricating the cylinder bores and crankshaft journals.
11 Space the piston rings around the pistons so that their end gaps are 180° apart. In the case of the oil scraper ring, offset the gaps in the upper and lower rails by 25 to 50 mm (1 to 2 in) to right and left of the end gap of the central section. Offer a piston/connecting rod assembly to its bore, making sure that it is the right way round (photo).
12 Oil the piston and rings, then fit a piston ring compressor to the piston and tighten it to compress the rings (photo).
13 Gently tap the piston through the ring compressor and into its bore using the hammer handle. Guide the connecting rod near to its crankshaft journal and then fit the bearing shell upper half.
14 Ease the connecting rod onto the journal, fit the lower shell to the cap and fit the cap to the rod (photo). Refit and tighten the retaining bolts to the specified torque (photo).
15 Repeat the sequence described for the remaining three piston/connecting rod assemblies.
16 Refit the cylinder head, oil pump and sump, as described in earlier Sections.

16 Flywheel – removal and refitting

1 Remove the clutch assembly and the release bearing, as described in Chapter 5.
2 Undo the three bolts and remove the release bearing guide tube.
3 Mark the position of the flywheel in relation to the crankshaft mounting flange or pulley.
4 Wedge a screwdriver between the ring gear teeth and transmission casing and then undo the socket-headed retaining bolts using a multi-tooth key or socket bit (photo). Remove the bolts and withdraw the flywheel.
5 Refitting is the reverse sequence to removal. Tighten the flywheel retaining bolts to the specified torque.

15.11 Offering the piston to the bore

15.12 Piston ring compressor fitted

15.14A Fitting a big-end bearing cap

15.14B Tightening a big-end bearing cap bolt

16.4 Flywheel retaining bolts are socket-headed

18.4A Camshaft retaining plate bolts (arrowed)

17 Engine/transmission mountings – removal and refitting

1 The engine/transmission assembly is supported in a triangular arrangement of three mountings: one on the right-hand side supporting the engine, one on the left-hand side supporting the transmission and a third centrally sited mount supporting the complete assembly at the rear.

2 To remove either of the front mountings position a jack under the engine or transmission adjacent to the mounting and just take the weight of the engine or transmission.

3 Undo the bolts securing the support bracket to the engine or gearbox and the bolts securing the mounting to the bodyframe. Lift off the bracket and remove the relevant mounting.

4 To remove the rear mounting jack up the front of the car and support it on axle stands.

5 Support the engine/transmission assembly under the differential cover plate using a jack and interposed block of wood.

6 Undo the two bolts securing the mounting to the underbody and the through-bolt and nut securing the mounting to the support bracket. Slide the mounting rearwards out of the bracket and remove it from under the car.

7 In all cases refitting is the reverse sequence to removal, but tighten the retaining bolts to the specified torque. Where thread locking compound was evident on the old bolts, clean out the bolt holes using a tap (or an old bolt with a slot cut in its threads); clean the bolt threads and re-apply thread locking compound.

8 If there is an arrow stamped on the rear mounting, it should point to the front when the mounting is fitted.

18.4B Removing the engine front plate

18 Camshaft and tappets – removal and refitting

1 Remove the engine from the car, as described in Section 23, and then remove the sump and timing gear components, as described in earlier Sections.

2 If the cylinder head is still in place, slacken the rocker arm nuts, move the rocker arms to one side and lift out the pushrods, keeping them in order.

3 Invert the engine or, if the cylinder head is still in place, lay the engine on its side.

4 Undo the two bolts securing the camshaft retaining plate in position and lift off the plate (photos). The engine front plate should also be removed as all the bolts securing it in place have now been undone.

5 Carefully withdraw the camshaft from the cylinder block, taking care not to scratch the bearing journals with the sharp edges of the cam lobes (photo).

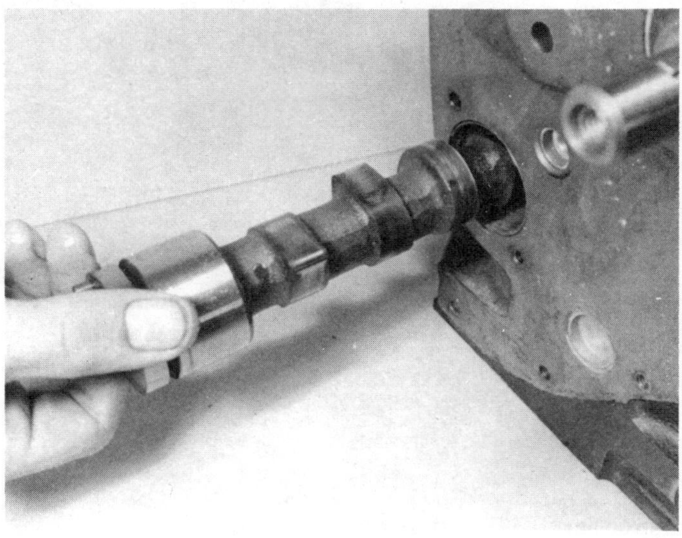
18.5 Removing the camshaft

6 From within the crankcase withdraw each tappet from its bore and keep them in order for refitting (photo).
7 Scrape away all traces of old gasket from the engine front plate and cylinder block. Make sure that both mating faces are clean and dry.
8 Lubricate the tappet bores in the crankcase and insert each tappet into its respective bore.
9 Lubricate the camshaft bearing journals and carefully insert the camshaft.
10 Place a new gasket in position (photo) and then locate the front plate, patterned side outward, over the gasket. Temporarily refit two or three of the timing cover bolts to act as alignment guides, but only tighten them finger tight.
11 Now position the camshaft retaining plate with its forks located into the groove in the boss on the end of the camshaft. Note that the fork section faces upwards. Secure the retaining plate with the two bolts.
12 Check that the camshaft is free to turn.
13 Refit the timing gear components and the sump, as described in earlier Sections. If the cylinder head is in place, refit the pushrods and adjust the valve clearances.
14 Refit the engine to the car.

18.6 Removing a tappet

18.10 Fitting a new front plate gasket

19 Crankshaft rear oil seal – removal and refitting

1 Remove the engine from the car, as described in Section 23, and then remove the sump and flywheel, as described in earlier Sections.
2 Slacken the rear main bearing cap bolts slightly and withdraw the oil seal from its location.
3 Lubricate the lips of a new oil seal and carefully ease it over the crankshaft boss and into position. Make sure that the seal is fully entered into its location so that its outer face is flush with the edge of the bearing cap and cylinder block.
4 Apply jointing compound to the contact edges of the main bearing cap and then tighten the retaining bolts to the specified torque.
5 Refit the sump and flywheel, as described earlier, and then refit the engine to the car, as described in Section 23.

20 Crankshaft and main bearings – removal and refitting

1 With the engine removed from the car, as described in Section 23, and all the components removed from it, as described in earlier Sections, the crankshaft can be removed as follows.
2 Invert the engine. The three main bearing caps are all different so note their locations.
3 Undo the retaining bolts and remove the bearing caps.
4 Lift out the crankshaft and remove the rear oil seal from the crankshaft boss.
5 Remove the main bearing shells from the crankcase and bearing caps and identify them for location.
6 Commence reassembly as follows.
7 Ensure that the crankcase and crankshaft are thoroughly clean and that all oilways are clear. If possible blow the drillings out with compressed air, and then inject clean engine oil through them to ensure they are clear.
8 Avoid using old bearing shells; wipe the shell seats in the crankcase clean and then fit the upper halves of the main bearing shells into their seats.
9 Note that there is a tab on the back of each bearing which engages with a groove in the shell seating (in both crankcase and bearing cap) (photo).
10 Wipe away all traces of protective grease on the new shells.
11 The central bearing shell also takes up the crankshaft endfloat. Note that the half-shells fitted to the cylinder block all have oil duct holes, while only the centre main bearing cap half-shells has an oil duct hole.
12 When the shells are fully located in the crankcase and bearing caps, lubricate them with clean engine oil (photo).

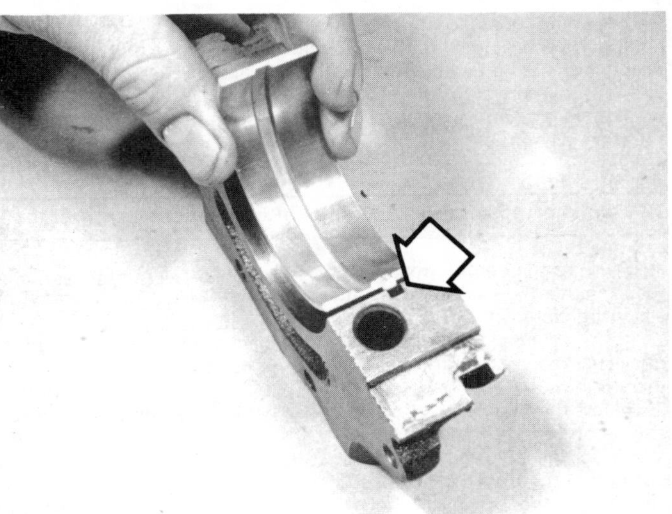
20.9 Bearing shell tab engages with groove (arrowed)

20.12 Lubricate the bearing shells

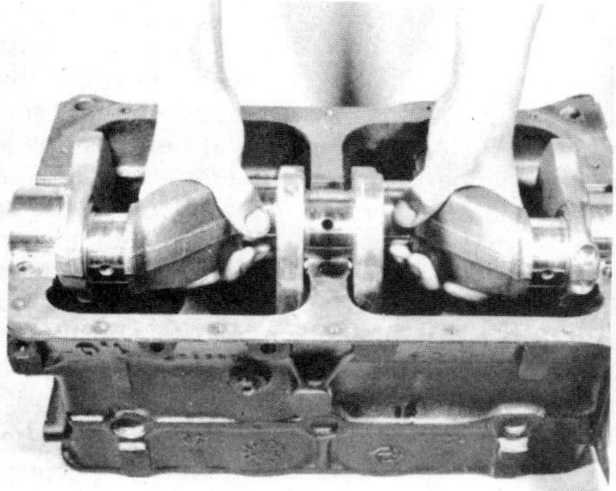
20.13 Fitting the crankshaft

20.14 Fitting the centre main bearing cap

20.15 Crankshaft rear oil seal

20.16 Fitting the rear main bearing cap

20.18 Checking the crankshaft endfloat

13 Carefully install the crankshaft into position in the crankcase (photo).
14 Lubricate the crankshaft main bearing journals and then refit the centre main bearing cap (photo). Tighten the retaining bolts to the specified torque wrench setting.
15 Locate the new oil seal onto the rear end of the crankshaft (photo), and apply jointing compound to the block mating flange. Also fill the grooves on both sides of the rear main bearing cap with sealant (Fig. 1.8).
16 Fit the rear main bearing cap (photo) and tighten the retaining bolts to the specified torque.
17 Fit the front main bearing cap, but before fitting the retaining bolts smear them with jointing compound and then tighten to the specified torque wrench setting. Check that the bearing cap is exactly flush with the end face of the crankcase as it is tightened.
18 Now rotate the crankshaft and check that it turns freely, and shows no signs of binding or tight spots. Check that the crankshaft endfloat is within the limits specified using a feeler gauge as shown (photo). No provision is made for adjusting crankshaft endfloat; if it is outside the specified limits, the most likely reasons are wear or incorrect regrinding (assuming that the correct shells have been fitted).

Fig. 1.8 Fill the rear main bearing cap grooves with sealant (Sec 20)

21 Engine components – examination and renovation

Crankshaft

1 Examine the crankpin and main journal surfaces for signs of scoring or scratches, and check the ovality and taper of the crankpins and main journals. If the bearing surface dimensions do not fall within the tolerance ranges given in the Specifications at the beginning of this Chapter, the crankpins and/or main journals will have to be reground.
2 Big-end and crankpin wear is accompanied by distinct metallic knocking, particularly noticed when the engine is pulling from low revs, and some loss of oil pressure.
3 Main bearing and main journal wear is accompanied by severe engine vibration rumble – getting progressively worse as engine revs increase – and again by loss of oil pressure.
4 If the crankshaft requires regrinding take it to an engine reconditioning specialist, who will machine it for you and supply the correct undersize bearing shells.

5 On some engines, the crankshaft journal diameters are machined undersize in production to allow for greater manufacturing tolerances.

Big-end and main bearing shells

6 Inspect the big-end and main bearing shells for signs of general wear, scoring, pitting and scratches. The bearings should be matt grey in colour. With lead-indium bearings, should a trace of copper colour be noticed, the bearings are badly worn as the lead bearing material has worn away to expose the indium underlay. Renew the bearings if they are in this condition or if there are any signs of scoring or pitting. **You are strongly advised to renew the bearings – regardless of their condition – at time of major overhaul. Refitting used bearings is a false economy.**

7 The undersizes available are designed to correspond with crankshaft regrind sizes. The bearings are in fact, slightly more than the stated undersize as running clearances have been allowed for during their manufacture.

Cylinder bores

8 The cylinder bores must be examined for taper, ovality, scoring and scratches. Start by carefully examining the top of the cylinder bores. If they are at all worn a very slight ridge will be found on the thrust side. This marks the top of the piston travel. The owner will have a good indication of the bore wear prior to dismantling the engine, or removing the cylinder head. Excessive oil consumption accompanied by blue smoke from the exhaust can be caused by worn cylinder bores and piston rings.

9 Measure the bore diameter across the block and just below any ridge. This can be done with an internal micrometer or a dial gauge. Compare this with the diameter of the bottom of the bore, which is not subject to wear. If no measuring instruments are available, use a piston from which the rings have been removed and measure the gap between it and the cylinder wall with a feeler gauge.

10 Refer to the Specifications. If the cylinder wear exceeds the permitted tolerances then the cylinders will need reboring.

11 If the cylinders have already been bored out to their maximum it may be possible to have liners fitted. This situation will not often be encountered.

Connecting rods

12 Examine the mating faces of the big-end caps to see if they have ever been filed in a mistaken attempt to take up wear. If so, the offending rods must be renewed.

13 Check the alignment of the rods visually, and if all is not well, take the rods to your local agent for checking on a special jig.

Pistons and piston rings

14 If the pistons and/or rings are to be re-used, remove the rings from the pistons. Three strips of tin or 0.38 mm (0.015 in) feeler gauges should be prepared and the top ring then sprung open just sufficiently to allow them to be slipped behind the ring. The ring can then be slid off the piston upwards without scoring or scratching the piston lands.

15 Repeat the process for the second and third rings.

16 Mark the rings or keep them in order so they may be refitted in their original locations.

17 Inspect the pistons to ensure that they are suitable for re-use. Check for cracks, damage to the piston ring grooves and lands, and scores or signs of picking-up the piston walls.

18 Clean the ring grooves using a piece of old piston ring ground to a suitable width and scrape the deposits out of the grooves, taking care not to remove any metal or score the piston lands. Protect your fingers – piston rings are sharp.

19 Check the rings in their respective bores. Press the ring down to the unworn lower section of the bore (use a piston to do this, and keep the ring square in the bore). Measure the ring end gap and check that it is within the tolerance allowed (see Specifications). Also check the ring's side clearance in its groove. If these measurements exceed the specified tolerances the rings will have to be renewed, and if the ring grooves in the pistons are worn new pistons may be needed.

20 Proprietary piston rings are available which are reputed to reduce oil consumption due to bore wear without the expense of a rebore. Depending on the degree of wear, the improvement produced by fitting such rings may be short-lived.

21 If new rings (or pistons and rings) are to be fitted to an existing bore the top ring must be stepped to clear the wear ridge at the top of the bore, or the bore must be de-ridged.

22 Check the clearance and end gap of any new rings, as described in paragraph 19. If a ring is slightly tight in its groove it may be rubbed down using an oilstone or a sheet of carborundum paper laid on a sheet of glass. If the end gap is inadequate the ring can be carefully ground until the specified clearance is achieved.

23 If new pistons are to be installed they will be selected from the grades available (see Specifications), after measuring the bores as described in paragraph 9. Normally the appropriate oversize pistons are supplied by the repairer when the block is rebored.

24 Removing and refitting pistons on the connecting rod is a job for your dealer or specialist repairer. Press equipment and a means of accurately heating the connecting rod will be required for removal and insertion of the gudgeon pin.

Camshaft and bearings

25 With the camshaft removed, examine the bearings for signs of obvious wear and pitting. If there are signs, then the three bearings will need renewal. This is not a common requirement and to have to do so is indicative of severe engine neglect at some time. As special tools are necessary to do this work properly, it is recommended that it is done by your dealer. Check that the bearings are located properly so that the oilways from the bearing housings are not obstructed.

26 The camshaft itself should show no marks on either the bearing journals or the profiles. If it does, it should be renewed.

27 Examine the skew gear for signs of wear or damage. If this is badly worn it will mean renewing the camshaft.

28 The thrust plate (which also acts as the locating plate) should not be ridged or worn in any way. If it is, renew it.

Timing chain sprockets and tensioner

29 Examine the teeth of both sprockets for wear. Each tooth is the shape of an inverted V and if the driving (or driven) side is concave in shape, the tooth is worn and the sprocket should be renewed. The chain should also be renewed if the sprocket teeth are worn. It is sensible practice to renew the chain anyway.

30 Inspect the chain tensioner, which is automatic in operation. The most important item to check is the shoe which wears against the chain. If it is obviously worn, scratched or damaged in any way, then it must be renewed. Check the spring for signs of wear and renew the unit if generally worn or defective, or when a new chain is being fitted.

Valve rocker arms, pushrods and tappets

31 Each rocker arm has three wearing surfaces, namely the pushrod recess, the valve stem contact, and the centre pivot recess. If any of these surfaces appear severely grooved or worn the arm should be renewed. If only the valve stem contact area is worn it is possible to clean it up with a fine file.

32 If the rocker ball is pitted, or has flats in it, this should also be renewed.

33 The nut on the rocker stud is a self-locking type. If it has been removed or adjusted many times, the self-locking ring may have become ineffective and the nut may be slack enough to turn involuntarily and alter the tappet clearance.

34 The rocker studs should be examined to ensure that the threads are undamaged and that the oil delivery hole in the side of the stud at the base of the thread is clear. Place a straight-edge along the top of all the studs to ensure that none is standing higher than the rest. If any are, it means that they have pulled out of the head some distance. They should be removed and replaced with an oversize stud. As this involves reaming out the stud hole to an exact size to provide an interference fit for the replacement stud, you should seek professional advice and assistance to ensure that the new oversize stud is securely fitted at the correct angle.

35 Any pushrods which are bent should be renewed. On no account attempt to straighten them. They are easily checked by rolling over a perfectly flat surface such as a sheet of glass.

36 Examine the bearing surfaces of the tappets which lie on the camshaft. Any indentation in these surfaces or any cracks indicate serious wear and the tappets should be renewed. Thoroughly clean them out, removing all traces of sludge. It is most unlikely that the sides of the tappets will prove worn but, if they are a very loose fit in their bores and can readily be rocked, they should be exchanged for new ones. It is very unusual to find any wear in the tappets, and any wear present is likely to occur at very high mileages, or in cases or neglect. If the tappets are worn, examine the camshaft carefully as well.

Flywheel

37 If the teeth on the flywheel starter ring are badly worn, or if some are missing, then it will be necessary to remove the ring and fit a new one.

38 Either split the ring with a cold chisel after making a cut with a hacksaw blade between two teeth, or use a soft-headed hammer (not steel) to knock the ring off, striking it evenly and alternately at equally spaced points. Take great care not to damage the flywheel during this process, and protect your eyes from flying fragments.

39 Clean and polish with emery cloth four evenly spaced areas on the outside face of the new starter ring.

40 Heat the ring evenly with a flame until the polished portions turn dark blue. Alternatively heat the ring in a bath of oil to a temperature of 200°C. (If a naked flame is used take adequate fire precautions.) Hold the ring at this temperature for five minutes and then quickly fit it to the flywheel, so the chamfered portion of the teeth faces the gearbox side of the flywheel. Wipe all oil off the ring before fitting it.

41 The ring should be tapped gently down onto its register and left to cool naturally when the contraction of the metal on cooling will ensure that it is a secure and permanent fit. Great care must be taken not to overheat the ring, indicated by it turning light metallic blue. If this happens the temper of the ring will be lost.

42 If the driven plate contact surface of the flywheel is scored or on close inspection shows evidence of small hair cracks, caused by overheating, it may be possible to have the flywheel surface ground provided the overall thickness of the flywheel is not reduced too much. Consult a specialist engine repairer and if it is not possible, renew the flywheel complete.

43 If the needle bearing in the centre of the crankshaft flange is worn, fill it with grease and tap in a close-fitting rod. Hydraulic pressure will remove it. Tap the new bearing into position and apply a little grease.

22 Engine lubrication system – general description

The engine lubrication system is quite conventional. A gear type oil pump draws oil up from the sump, via the suction pipe and strainer, and pumps the oil under pressure in the cartridge oil filter. From the oil filter the oil flows into galleries drilled in the engine block to feed the main bearings on the crankshaft and the moving components of the cylinder head. Oil is bled from the main bearing journals in the crankshaft to supply the big-end bearings.

Therefore, the bearings which receive pressure lubrication are the main crankshaft bearings, the big-end bearings, the camshaft bearings, and the rocker arms.

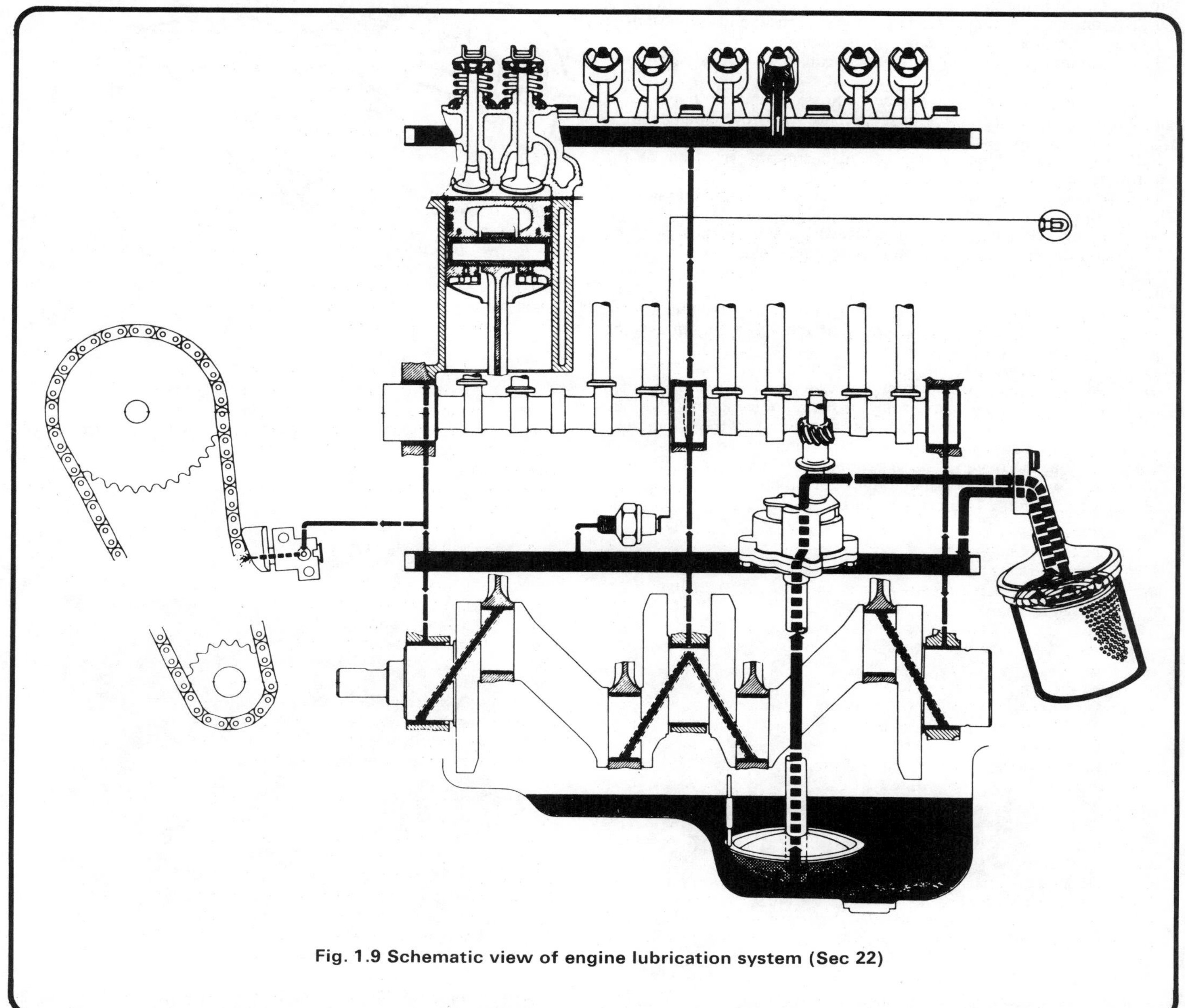

Fig. 1.9 Schematic view of engine lubrication system (Sec 22)

The remaining moving parts receive oil by splash or drip feed and these include the timing chain and associated items, the distributor and fuel pump drive, the tappets, the valve stems and to a certain extent the pistons.

The lubrication system incorporates two safeguards. The first is a pressure operated ball valve situated in the gallery between the oil and oil filter. This is in effect a filter bypass valve and allows oil to pass directly into the engine block gallery, downstream of the filter, when the filter is clogged up and resists the flow of oil.

The second system is an oil pressure relief valve, located in the oil pump casing, which controls the oil pressure to the specified maximum.

23 Engine – removal and refitting

1 The makers recommend that the engine be removed from above, leaving the gearbox in the vehicle.
2 Disconnect the battery positive and negative terminals.
3 Remove the air cleaner (Chapter 3).
4 Drain the cooling system (Chapter 2). Disconnect the coolant hoses from the water pump, thermostat housing and cylinder head. not forgetting the heater hoses.
5 Disconnect and plug the fuel pump feed hose, and (when fitted) the fuel return hose. Be prepared for fuel spillage.
6 Disconnect the throttle and choke cables from the carburettor (Chapter 3).
7 Disconnect the brake servo vacuum hose, either from the servo or from the manifold. Secure the hose so that it will not be damaged.
8 Release the electrical connectors for the oil pressure switch and the coil LT terminals. Unplug the coil-to-distributor HT lead at the distributor cap.
9 Disconnect the engine wiring harness multi-plug, pressing its locking device to release it.
10 Withdraw the clutch input shaft (see Chapter 5, Section 5).
11 Unbolt the exhaust downpipe from the manifold.
12 Remove the three flywheel cover plate bolts, which are accessible from below.
13 Secure the lifting tackle to the engine and take its weight.
14 Support the gearbox with a jack or blocks, then remove the right-hand mounting completely.
15 Remove the remaining engine-to-clutch housing bolts.
16 Make sure that no attachments have been overlooked, then carefully draw the engine away from the clutch housing and lift it out.
17 Refit in the reverse order to removal, referring to the appropriate Chapters for guidance if necessary. If the clutch has been disturbed, make sure that the driven plate is centralised (Chapter 5, Section 5), otherwise it will not be possible to refit the clutch input shaft.
18 Refer to Section 24 before starting the engine.

24 Engine – initial start-up after overhaul

1 Make sure the battery is fully charged and that all lubricants, coolant and fuel are replenished.
2 If the fuel system has been dismantled it will require several revolutions of the engine on the starter motor to pump the petrol up to the carburettor.
3 As soon as the engine fires and runs, keep it going at a fast tickover only (no faster) and bring it up to the normal working temperature.
4 As the engine warms up there will be odd smells and some smoke from parts getting hot and burning off oil deposits. The signs to look for are leaks of water or oil which will be obvious if serious. Check also the exhaust pipe and manifold connections, as these do not always

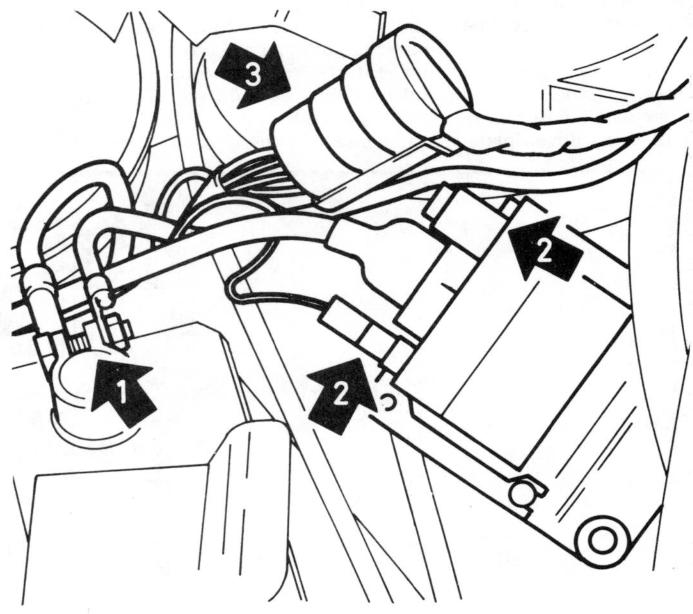

Fig. 1.10 Electrical connection near the battery (Sec 23)

1 Battery positive terminal
2 Coil LT terminals
3 Engine wiring multi-plug

Fig. 1.11 Flywheel cover plate bolts (arrowed) (Sec 23)

Fig. 1.12 Engine-to-clutch housing bolts (arrowed) (Sec 23)

'find' their exact gastight position until the warmth and vibration have acted on them, and it is almost certain that they will need tightening further. This should be done, of course, with the engine stopped.

5 When normal running temperature has been reached adjust the engine idling speed, as described in Chapter 3, and check the valve clearances, as described in Section 7 of this Chapter.

6 Stop the engine and wait a few minutes to see if any lubricant or coolant is dripping out when the engine is stationary.

7 Road test the car to check that the timing is correct and that the engine is giving the necessary smoothness and power. Do not race the engine – if new bearings and/or pistons have been fitted it should be treated as a new engine and run in at a reduced speed for the first 500 miles (800 km).

8 If many new internal components have been fitted, it will be beneficial to change the engine oil and oil filter after the first 1000 miles (1600 km) or so.

PART B: OHC ENGINE

25 General description

The engine is of four-cylinder, in-line overhead camshaft type, mounted transversely at the front of the car.

The crankcase is supported in five shell type main bearings. Thrust washers are incorporated in the centre main bearing to control crankshaft endfloat.

The connecting rods are attached to the crankshaft by horizontally split shell type main bearings, and to the pistons by gudgeon pins which are an interference fit in the connecting rod small-end bore. The aluminium alloy pistons are fitted with three piston rings: two compression rings and an oil control ring.

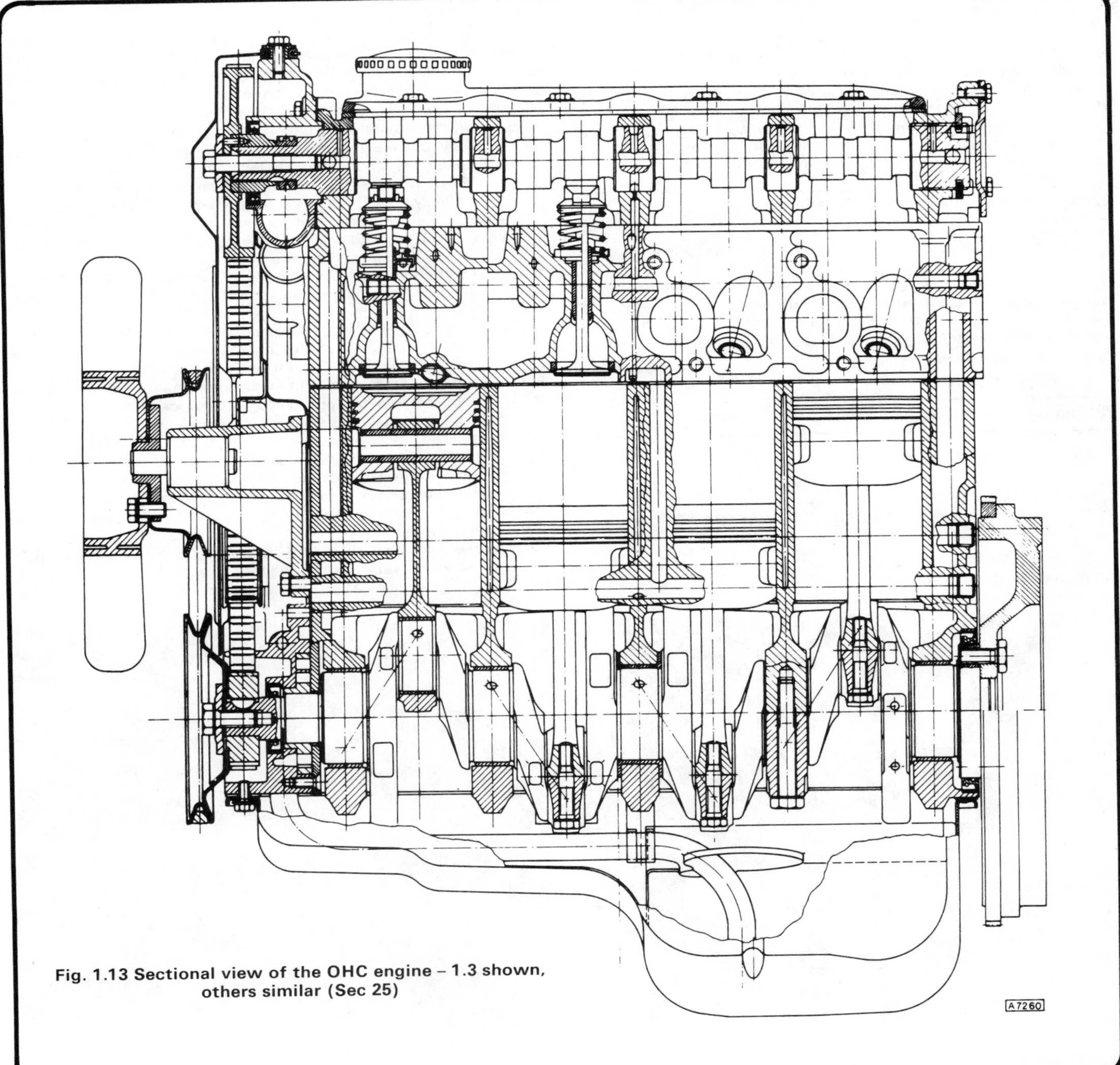

Fig. 1.13 Sectional view of the OHC engine – 1.3 shown, others similar (Sec 25)

The camshaft is driven by a toothed rubber belt from the crankshaft and operates the valves via rocker arms. The rocker arms are supported at their pivot end by hydraulic self-adjusting valve lifters (tappets) which automatically take up any clearance between the camshaft, rocker arm and valve stems. The inlet and exhaust valves are each closed by a single spring and operate in guides pressed into the cylinder head.

Engine lubrication is by a gear type pump located in a housing attached to the front of the cylinder block. The oil pump is driven by the crankshaft, while the fuel pump (on carburettor models) and the distributor are driven by the camshaft.

26 Maintenance and inspection

Refer to Section 2, but disregard the reference to valve clearance adjustment, as on these engines no adjustment is necessary.

Note that although a maximum service life for the camshaft toothed belt is not specified by the manufacturers, it is recommended that renewal should be carried out at 36 000 miles (60 000 km). Renewal procedures are contained in Section 31.

For maintenance of the crankcase ventilation system, see Section 46.

If a dipstick incorporating an oil level sensor is fitted, treat it carefully: it is fragile.

27 Operations requiring engine removal

The design of the engine is such that great accessibility is afforded and it is only necessary to remove the engine for attention to the crankshaft and main bearings. It is possible to renew the crankshaft rear oil seal with the engine in the car, but this entails the use of the manufacturer's special tools and it is quite a difficult operation due to lack of working clearance. For this reason this operation is described with the engine removed.

28 Engine dismantling and reassembly – general

Refer to Section 5.

29 Ancillary components – removal and refitting

Refer to Section 6. For fuel injection models, refer to the appropriate Sections of Chapter 3.

30 Oil pressure regulator valve – removal and refitting

1 From just to the rear of the crankshaft pulley, unscrew the pressure regulator valve and extract the spring and plunger.
2 Renew the spring if it is distorted or weak (compare it with a new one if possible).
3 If the plunger is scored, renew it.
4 Clean out the plunger hole and reassemble using a new plug sealing washer.

31 Camshaft toothed belt – removal, refitting and adjustment

1 Undo the belt cover retaining bolts (5 on 1.3 engines, 3 on larger engines) and remove the cover.
2 Use a socket or spanner on the crankshaft pulley to turn the crankshaft until No 1 piston is at its firing point. This is indicated by the notch on the crankshaft pulley being in line with the pointer on the oil pump housing, and the mark on the camshaft sprocket being in line with the rib on the camshaft housing (photos).
3 Slacken the alternator mounting and adjustment bolts, move the alternator towards the engine and remove its drivebelt.
4 Release the crankshaft pulley central bolt without disturbing the set position of the crankshaft. To prevent the crankshaft turning as the bolt is undone, it may be sufficient to engage a gear (manual gearbox only) and apply the handbrake; a better way is to remove the flywheel bottom cover plate and jam the flywheel ring gear with a large screwdriver or a tyre lever (photo).
5 Remove the pulley central bolt. On all except 1.3 models, remove the four Allen screws which secure the pulley to the sprocket. Remove the pulley.
6 Drain the cooling system, as described in Chapter 2.
7 Slacken the three bolts which secure the water pump. The bolts are accessible through holes in the belt backplate (photo).
8 Swivel the pump to release the tension on the toothed belt. There are flats behind the pump sprocket for this purpose (photo).
9 Note the belt's running direction if it is to be used again, then slip it off the sprockets.
10 A new belt, or one which is to be re-used, must not be kinked or be contaminated with oil, grease etc
11 Fit the new belt without disturbing the set position of the crankshaft and camshaft sprockets. Apply some tension by moving the water pump.
12 Refit the crankshaft pulley and check that the pulley and camshaft sprocket marks are still correctly aligned (paragraph 2). If not, release the belt tension and align the sprockets correctly. Tighten the

31.2A Crankshaft pulley notch and oil pump pointer in alignment (arrowed)

31.2B Camshaft sprocket mark and housing rib (both arrowed) should be aligned

31.4 Jamming the flywheel ring gear

31.7 Slackening a water pump bolt

31.8 Swivelling the water pump using a spanner on the flats

crankshaft pulley bolt to the specified torque, using locking compound on the bolt threads.

13 To adjust the tension of the belt, ideally the tension gauge specified by the makers (KM-510-A) should be used. If this is available, proceed as follows.

14 Turn the crankshaft through at least half a turn in the normal direction of rotation. Set the tension gauge, apply it to the 'slack' side of the belt (above the alternator) and release it. Read the gauge and compare the figure with that given in the Specifications.

15 If adjustment is necessary, move the water pump to increase or decrease belt tension, rotate the crankshaft through one full turn and take another gauge reading. Repeat as necessary until the desired tension is achieved.

16 In the absence of the belt tension gauge, an approximation to the correct tension can be judged by twisting the belt in the middle of its 'tight' side (photo). It should just be possible to twist the belt through 90° (a quarter turn) by hand. A belt which is too tight will normally be heard to hum or honk when running.

17 When adjustment is correct, tighten the water pump bolts to the specified torque. Refit and secure the belt cover.

18 Refit and tension the alternator drivebelt and refill the cooling system, both as described in Chapter 2. Refit the flywheel bottom cover if it was removed.

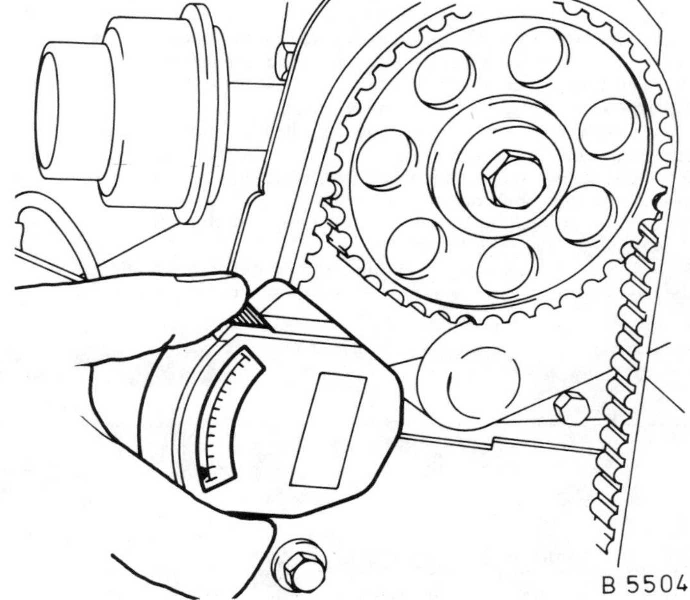

Fig. 1.14 Checking the camshaft toothed belt tension with gauge KM-510-A (Sec 31)

32 Cylinder head – removal and refitting

The procedure given here is for carburettor models. The procedure for fuel injection models is similar; refer to Chapter 3 for details of fuel injection component removal.

1 The cylinder head may only be removed when the engine is cold, otherwise there is a risk of distortion.

2 Disconnect the battery earth lead.

3 Remove the air cleaner, as described in Chapter 3.

4 Drain the cooling system, as described in Chapter 2.

5 Disconnect the radiator and heater hoses from the cylinder head and inlet manifold.

6 Disconnect and plug the fuel lines and unbolt the fuel pump. Also disconnect the fuel return line from the T-piece or carburettor. Be prepared for fuel spillage.

7 Unbolt and remove the camshaft cover, noting the location of the clips which secure the HT leads and fuel lines. Also disconnect the breather hose (when fitted). Recover the gasket.

8 Disconnect the control cables and electrical cables (as applicable) from the carburettor, referring to Chapter 3 if necessary.

9 Release the coolant pipe bracket at the inlet manifold.

10 Disconnect the brake servo vacuum hose from the inlet manifold.

11 Slacken the alternator pivot bolt, remove the adjusting strap bolt at the engine end and remove the alternator drivebelt.

12 Align the timing marks, slacken the camshaft toothed belt and remove it from the camshaft sprocket, as described in Section 31. Unless it is wished to remove the belt entirely, there is no need to remove the crankshaft pulley.

13 Disconnect the HT leads, identifying them if necessary. Remove the distributor cap and the distributor itself, as described in Chapter 4.

31.16 Checking the belt tension by twisting it

14 Disconnect the temperature gauge wire from the sender on the thermostat housing or inlet manifold.
15 Unbolt the exhaust downpipe(s) from the exhaust manifold.
16 Working in a spiral pattern from outside to inside, slacken each cylinder head bolt by a quarter turn. Follow the same order and slacken the bolts a further half turn, then remove them completely. Obtain **new** bolts for use when refitting.
17 Lift off the camshaft housing and camshaft, disconnecting any breather hoses which are connected to the housing.
18 Lift off the cylinder head, using the manifolds as handles if it is stuck. Do not prise between the head and block or damage may result.
19 Remove the rocker arms, thrust pads and hydraulic tappets from the cylinder head, keeping them in order if they are to be refitted (photo).
20 If the cylinder head has been removed for decarbonising or for attention to the valves and springs, reference should be made to Sections 34 and 35.
21 Before refitting the cylinder head, ensure that the block and head mating faces are spotlessly clean and dry with all traces of old gasket removed. Use a scraper to do this, but take care to cover the water passages and other openings with masking tape or rag to prevent dirt and carbon falling in. Remove all traces of oil and water from the bolt holes otherwise hydraulic pressure created by the bolts being screwed in could crack the block or give inaccurate torque settings. Ensure that the bolt threads are clean and dry.
22 When all is clean locate a **new** gasket on the block so that the worn OBEN can be read from above (photo). Do not use any jointing compound on the gasket.
23 Refit the hydraulic tappets, thrust pads and rocker arms to the cylinder head in their original positions.
24 Locate the cylinder head on the block so that the positioning dowels engage in their holes.
25 Apply a uniform bead of jointing compound to the mating face of the cylinder head and lower the camshaft housing into place. Position the sprocket with the timing marks aligned.
26 Fit the **new** cylinder head bolts and tighten them in a spiral pattern, starting at the centre and working outwards, in the stages given in the Specifications. The required angular measurement can be marked on a card and then placed over the bolt as a guide to the movement of the bolt (photo).
27 Refit the distributor, as described in Chapter 4.
28 Refit and secure the exhaust downpipe(s). Apply a little anti-seize compound to the bolts.
29 Refit the camshaft cover, using a new gasket. Tighten the bolts in diagonal sequence, remembering to fit the HT lead and fuel line brackets (photos).
30 Reconnect the HT leads and refit the distributor cap.
31 Refit the fuel pump, using new gaskets on each side of the spacer. Reconnect the fuel supply and return lines.
32 Refit and tension the camshaft toothed belt, as described in Section 31, then refit the belt cover.
33 Refit and tension the alternator drivebelt, as described in Chapter 2.
34 Refit the coolant hoses and refill the cooling system, as described in Chapter 2. Secure the coolant pipe bracket to the inlet manifold.
35 Reconnect the throttle and choke cables to the carburettor, as described in Chapter 3. On models with automatic choke, reconnect the electrical lead to the choke.
36 Refit the brake servo vacuum hose, the temperature gauge wire and the crankcase breather hose(s).
37 Check that nothing has been overlooked, then refit the air cleaner.
38 Reconnect the battery and start the engine. There may be considerable valvegear noise until the hydraulic tappets fill with oil.
39 Run the engine until it reaches normal operating temperature, then check the ignition timing, as described in Chapter 4.
40 Switch off the engine, immediately remove the air cleaner and tighten the cylinder head bolts through the final specified angle, following the outward spiral pattern previously used. No further tightening is necessary.

32.19 Removing a rocker arm

32.22 Head gasket must be fitted with the word OBEN uppermost

32.26 Using a marked card to measure angular rotation when tightening cylinder head bolts

32.29A Fitting a new camshaft cover gasket

32.29B HT lead bracket is secured by one of the camshaft cover bolts

33 Camshaft – removal and refitting

1 The camshaft can only be removed without disturbing the housing if special tool 603 850, or equivalent, is available to depress the cam followers whilst the camshaft is withdrawn.
2 Assuming that the special tool is not available, the camshaft housing must be removed. Since the cylinder head bolts will be removed, it would certainly be good practice to fit a new cylinder head gasket; however, if the cooling system is drained and the housing is removed gently, there is a good chance that the head gasket seal will not be broken. It is the reader's choice whether to undertake the extra work of renewing the head gasket as a precaution, or to risk the vexation of finding that the old gasket has 'blown' after reassembly.
3 With the camshaft housing removed, as described in Section 32, clamp the cylinder head with four head bolts and some spacers if the head is not to be disturbed (photo).
4 Undo the camshaft sprocket bolt, using an open-ended spanner on the flats of the camshaft to stop the shaft turning. Remove the bolt, washer and sprocket.
5 At the other end of the housing, remove the two Allen screws which secure the thrust plate. Push the camshaft rearwards and extract the plate (photos).
6 Carefully withdraw the camshaft from the distributor end of the housing. Be careful not to damage the bearing surfaces in the housing (photo).
7 On 1.3 models, undo the bolts which secure the belt cover backplate and remove the plate (photo).
8 Prise out the oil seal with a screwdriver. Drive in a new seal until it is flush with the housing, using a piece of wood or a suitably sized socket (photos).
9 Liberally lubricate the camshaft bearings and the oil seal lip. (If special lubricant has been supplied with a new crankshaft, use it; otherwise use clean engine oil, perhaps with a molybdenum disulphide additive.) Carefully insert the camshaft.
10 Refit the thrust plate and tighten its screws. Check the camshaft endfloat using a feeler blade (photo). If the endfloat exceeds that specified, renew the thrust plate.
11 On 1.3 models, refit the belt backplate.
12 Refit the camshaft sprocket, engaging the peg on the shaft with the hole in the sprocket. Tighten the sprocket bolt to the specified torque, holding the camshaft as before (photos).
13 Refit the camshaft housing, as described in Section 32.
14 If a new camshaft has been fitted, it is most important to observe

33.3 Cylinder head bolt, with nuts and washers for spacers, used to clamp head down

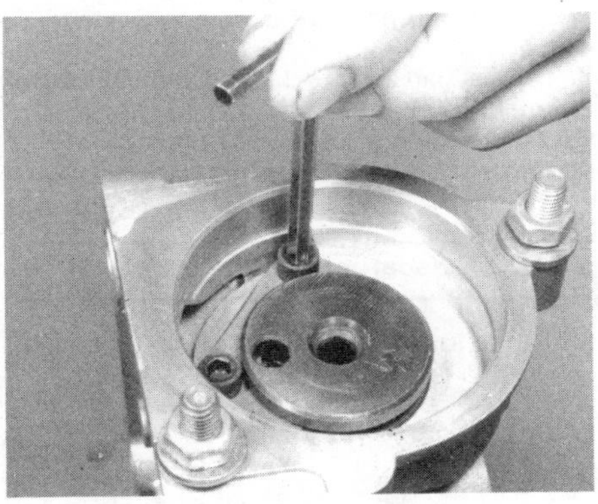

33.5A Removing the Allen screws which secure the camshaft thrust plate

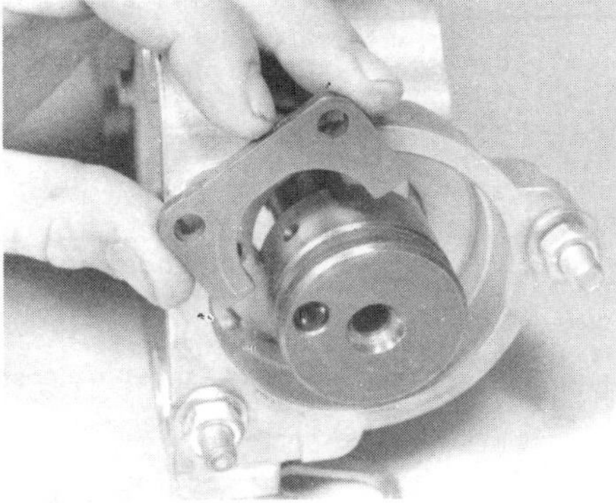

33.5B Removing the camshaft thrust plate

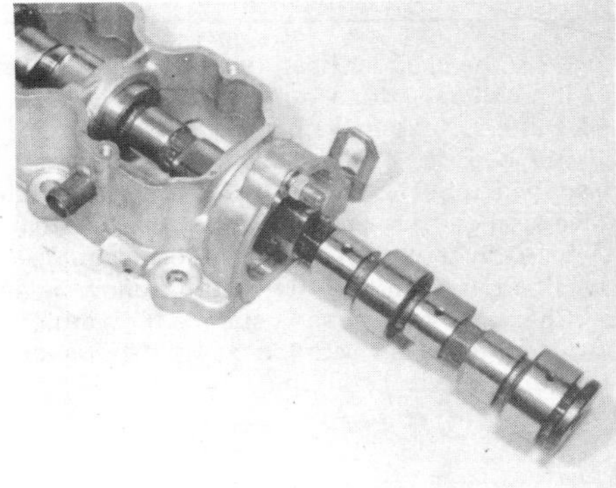

33.6 Removing the camshaft from the housing

33.7 Camshaft belt cover backplate (1.3 only)

33.8A Prising out the camshaft housing oil seal

33.8B Fitting a new camshaft housing oil seal

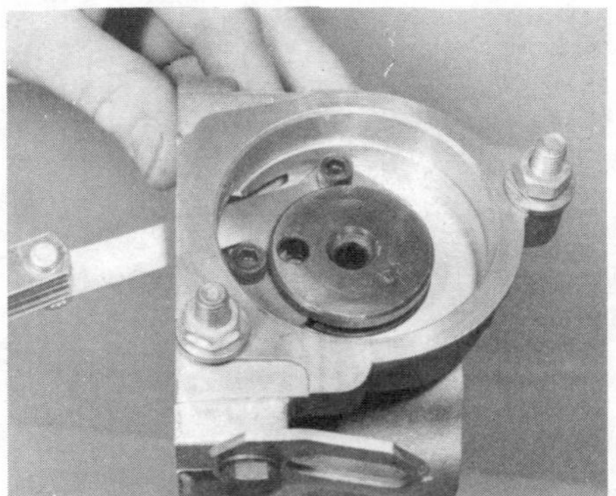

33.10 Checking the camshaft endfloat

33.12A Fitting the camshaft sprocket. Peg locating hole is arrowed

33.12B Tightening the camshaft sprocket bolt. The rag will protect the housing if the spanner slips

the following running-in schedule (unless otherwise specified by the manufacturer) immediately after start-up:

One minute at 2000 rpm
One minute at 1500 rpm
One minute at 3000 rpm
One minute at 2000 rpm

15 Change the engine oil (but not the filter, unless due in any case) approximately 600 miles/1000 km after fitting a new camshaft.

34 Cylinder head – overhaul

1 With the cylinder head removed, clean away external dirt.
2 If not already done, remove the rocker arms, the thrust pads and the valve lifters. Keep these components in order if they are to be re-used.
3 Remove the valves, springs and associated components, as described in Section 9 of this Chapter. Note that both inlet and exhaust valve springs have seats, but they are different (photo).
4 Inspect the valves, valve seats, guides and springs, also as described in Section 9. Regrind or renew as necessary.
5 Check the head sealing surface for warping by placing it on a piece of plate glass, or using a straight-edge and feeler blades. Slight distortion, or corrosion, may be corrected by machining. Seek expert advice if this is necessary: the removal of too much metal will render the head useless.
6 The hydraulic valve lifters should be renewed if there is a history of noisy operation of if they are obviously damaged or defective.
7 An oil pressure regulating valve in the head stabilises the oil pressure applied to the valve lifters (photo). To renew the valve, access is gained via the circular plug covering the end of the valve. The old valve must be crushed and its remains extracted, and a thread (M10) cut in the valve seat to allow removal using a suitable bolt. A new valve and plug can then be driven into position. Care must be taken to keep foreign matter and swarf out of the oilways; it is probably best to have the valve renewed by a GM dealer if necessary.
8 Refit the valves, springs etc, as described in Section 9. Remember to fit new valve stem seals.
9 Lubricate the valve lifters, thrust pads and rocker arm and refit them to their original position (if applicable).
10 On 1.6 and 1.8 engines, take the opportunity to renew the thermostat housing sealing ring whilst the head is removed.

35 Cylinder head and pistons – decarbonising

Refer to Section 10 of this Chapter; bear in mind also that the head is of light alloy construction and is easily damaged.

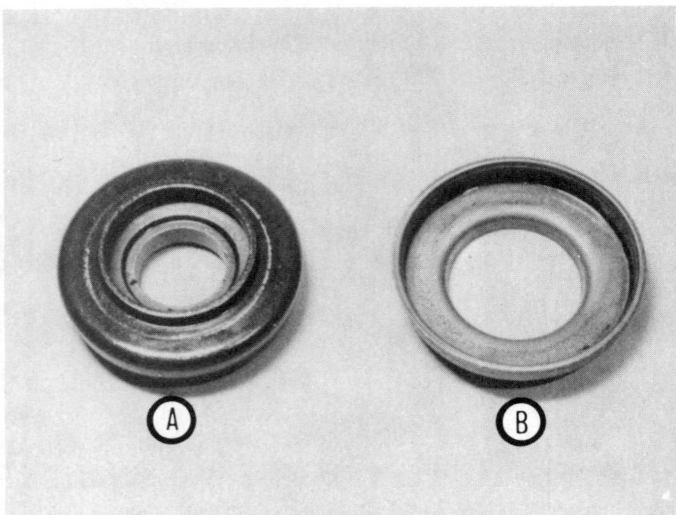

34.3 Exhaust valve spring rotator seat (A) and inlet valve spring seat (B)

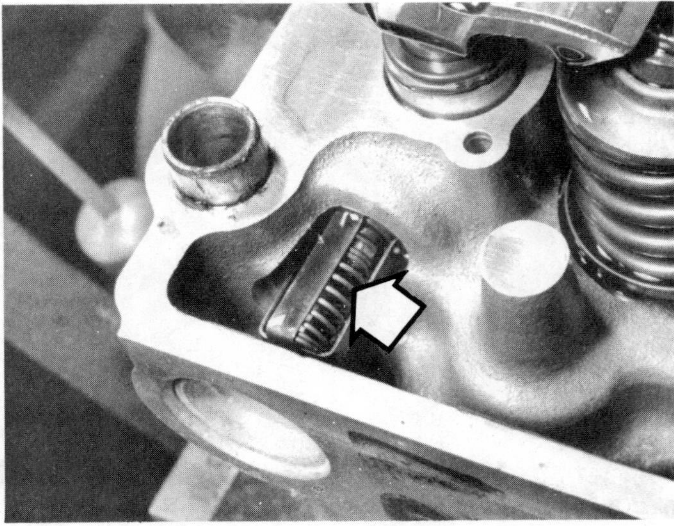

34.7 Cylinder head oil pressure regulating valve (arrowed)

36 Sump – removal and refitting

1 Jack up the front of the car and support it on axle stands.
2 Drain the engine oil into a suitable container and refit the plug after draining.
3 Unbolt the exhaust downpipe(s) from the exhaust manifold.
4 Undo the bolts securing the flywheel cover plate to the transmission bellhousing and remove the plate.
5 Undo the retaining bolts and lift away the sump. It will probably be necessary to tap the sump from side to side with a hide or plastic mallet to release the joint face.
6 Thoroughly clean the sump in paraffin or a suitable solvent and remove all traces of external dirt and internal sludge. Scrape away the remains of the old gasket from the sump and crankcase faces and ensure that they are clean and dry.
7 Apply jointing compound to the oil pump housing joint, the crankcase mating face and the rear main bearing cap joint, then place a new gasket in position.
8 Apply jointing compound to the sump face and retaining bolt threads, place the sump in position and refit the bolts. Progressively tighten the bolts in a diagonal sequence.
9 Refit the exhaust downpipe(s) and flywheel cover plate, lower the car to the ground and fill the engine with oil.

37 Oil pump – removal and refitting

1 Remove the camshaft toothed belt and the sump, as described in earlier Sections of this Chapter.
2 Undo the retaining bolts and remove the toothed belt cover backplate.
3 Using two screwdrivers, lever off the crankshaft sprocket. Extract the Woodruff key (photos).
4 Undo the two bolts securing the oil pick-up pipe to the oil pump housing and the bolt securing the support bracket to the centre main bearing cap (photo). Remove the pick-up pipe.
5 Undo the retaining bolts and withdraw the oil pump housing from the front of the engine.
6 To refit the pump housing assembly, ensure that all mating faces are clean and place a new gasket which is smeared with jointing compound on both sides in position.
7 Before refitting the oil pump, steps must be taken to protect the seal lips from damage or turning back on the shoulder at the front end of the crankshaft. To do this, grease the seal lips and then bind tape around the crankshaft to form a gentle taper (photo).
8 Refit the oil pump and unwind and remove the tape.
9 Tighten the bolts to the specified torque. Refit the Woodruff key and the belt sprocket.

37.3A Removing the crankshaft sprocket

37.3B Woodruff key (arrowed) in crankshaft nose

37.4 Oil pick-up pipe retaining bolts (arrowed)

37.7 Tape the crankshaft nose

10 Refit the oil pick-up pipe using a new gasket.
11 Refit the sump, then refit and adjust the camshaft toothed belt, as described in previous Sections.

38 Oil pump – overhaul

1 With the oil pump removed from the vehicle, withdraw the rear cover. The cross-head fixing screws are very tight and an impact driver will be required to remove them (photo).
2 Check the backlash between the inner and outer gear teeth (photo).
3 Check the endfloat between the gear outer faces and the housing (photo).
4 If any of the clearances are outside the specified tolerance, renew the components as necessary. Note that the outer gear face is marked for position (photo).
5 The pressure regulator valve can be unscrewed from the oil pump housing and the components cleaned and examined (photo).
6 Always renew the oil seal; a socket is useful to remove and install it (photo).

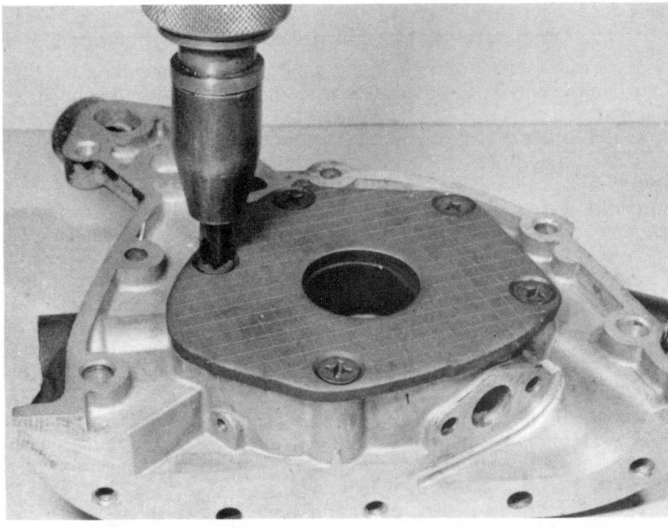

38.1 Using an impact screwdriver to undo the oil pump rear cover screws

38.2 Checking oil pump gear teeth backlash

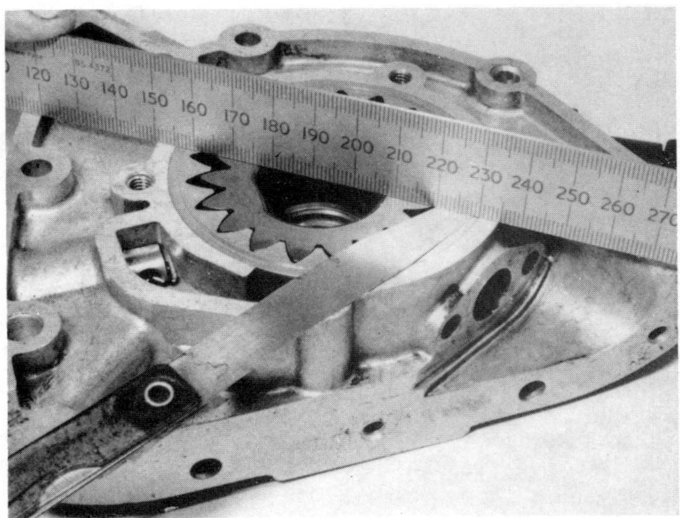

38.3 Checking oil pump gear endfloat

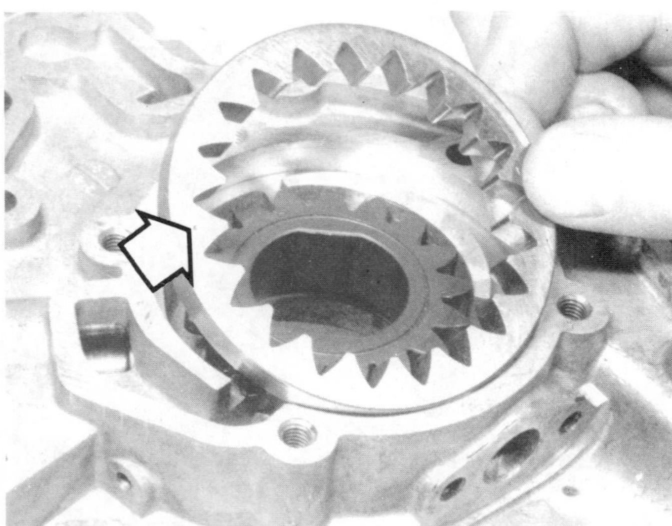

38.4 Gear outer face identification mark (arrowed)

38.5 Oil pressure regulator valve components

38.6 Fitting a new front oil seal

39.1 Piston orientation: large land (arrowed) faces the flywheel end of the engine

39 Pistons and connecting rods – removal and refitting

Proceed as described in Section 15 of this Chapter; note also that the piston crowns are not marked to show their direction of fitting, but the underside of the piston is (photo).

40 Flywheel – removal and refitting

1 The procedure is as described in Section 16, but the flywheel securing bolts are hexagon-headed. Because the bolt heads are rather shallow, it may be necessary to grind the chamfer off the mouth of the socket used to undo them in order to get a better grip.
2 Use thread locking compound when refitting the flywheel bolts and tighten them to the specified torque.

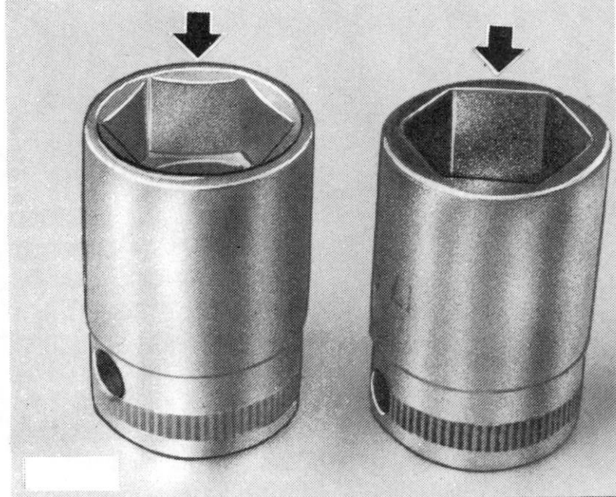
Fig. 1.15 Chamfer (arrowed, left) should be ground square (arrowed, right) to undo flywheel bolts (Sec 40)

41 Crankshaft front oil seal – removal and refitting

1 Remove the camshaft toothed belt, as described in Section 31.
2 Remove the crankshaft sprocket, using two screwdrivers to lever it off if it is tight. Remove the Woodruff key.
3 Punch or drill a small hole in the metal face of the oil seal, screw in a self-tapping screw and use this to lever out the seal. Several attempts may be necessary. Be careful not to damage the sealing face of the crankshaft.
4 Apply PVC tape to the step on the crankshaft nose to protect the seal lip as it is fitted.
5 Lubricate the lip of the seal and, using a suitable tube, tap the seal into its location. Remove the masking tape.
6 Refit the Woodruff key and sprocket.
7 Refit and adjust the toothed belt, as previously described.

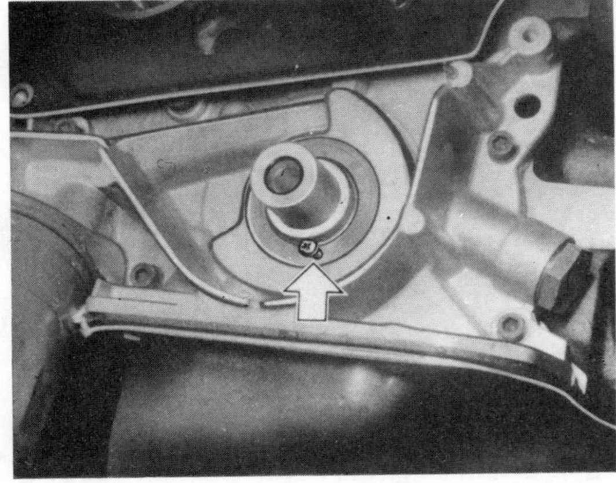
Fig. 1.16 Self-tapping screw (arrowed) in oil seal ready for extraction (Sec 41)

42 Engine/transmission mountings – removal and refitting

Refer to Section 17.

43 Crankshaft rear oil seal – removal and refitting

1 Remove the engine from the car, as described in Section 47.
2 Renew the oil seal, as described in Section 19.

44 Crankshaft and main bearings – removal and refitting

1 With the engine removed from the car, as described in Section 47, and all the components removed from it, as described in earlier Sections, the crankshaft can be removed as follows.
2 Invert the engine so that it is standing on the top surface of the cylinder block.
3 The main bearing caps are numbered 1 to 4 from the toothed belt end of the engine. The rear cap is not marked. To ensure that the caps are fitted the correct way round, note that the numbers are read from the water pump side when the crankcase is inverted (photo).
4 Unscrew and remove the main bearing cap bolts and tap off the caps. If the bearing shells are to be used again, keep them with their respective caps. The original shells are colour-coded and if used again must be returned to their original locations.
5 Note that the centre bearing shell incorporates thrust flanges to control crankshaft endfloat.
6 Lift the crankshaft from the crankcase. Extract the upper half shells and again identify their position in the crankcase if they are to be used again.
7 The rubber plug location adjacent to the bellhousing flange on the crankcase covers the aperture for installation of a TDC sensor. This sensor when connected to a suitable monitoring unit, indicates TDC from the position of the contact pins set in the crankshaft counter-balance weight (photo).
8 Ensure that the crankcase and crankshaft are thoroughly clean and that all oilways are clear. If possible blow the drillings out with compressed air, and then inject clean engine oil through them to ensure they are clear.
9 Wipe the shell seats in the crankcase and bearing caps clean and then fit the upper halves of the main bearing shells into their seats.
10 Note that there is a tag on the back of each bearing which engages with a groove in the shell seating in both crankcase and bearing cap (photo).
11 Wipe away all traces of protective grease on the new shells.
12 The central bearing shell also takes up the crankshaft endfloat (photo). Note that the half shells fitted to the cylinder block all have oil duct holes, while only the centre main bearing cap half shell has an oil duct hole.
13 When the shells are fully located in the crankcase and bearing caps, lubricate them with clean engine oil.

44.3 Identification number on No 3 main bearing cap

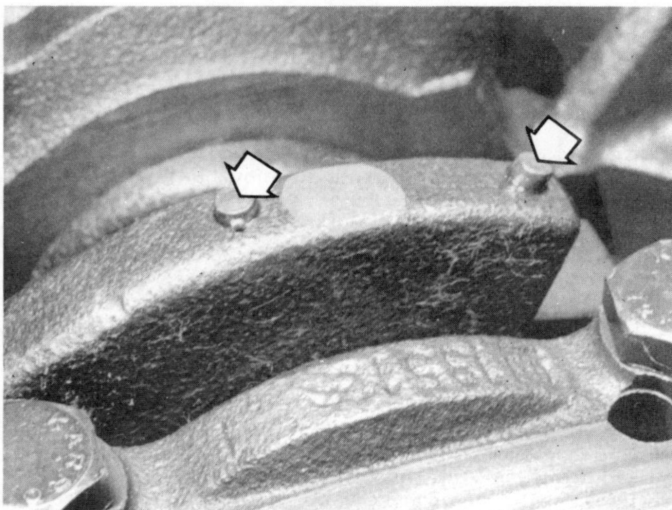
44.7 TDC sensor contact pins (arrowed) in crankshaft web

44.10 Main bearing shell correctly fitted, with tag and groove (arrowed) engaged

44.12 Centre main bearing shell, showing thrust flanges

44.14 Crankshaft rear oil seal

44.15 Fitting the crankshaft

44.16A Fitting a main bearing cap

44.16B Tightening a main bearing cap bolt

44.17 Inject jointing compound into the cap side grooves

44.19 Checking crankshaft endfloat

14 Fill the lips of a new crankshaft oil seal with grease and fit it to the end of the crankshaft (photo).
15 Carefully install the crankshaft into position in the crankcase (photo).
16 Lubricate the crankshaft main bearing journals and then refit the centre and intermediate main bearing caps (photo). Tighten the retaining bolts to the specified torque wrench setting (photo).
17 Coat the inner surfaces of the rear main bearing cap with sealant to GM spec 15 04 200/8 983 368. (This sealant is available in 200 ml tubes from GM parts departments.) Fill the side grooves of the bearing cap with RTV jointing compound. After fitting the bearing cap and tightening its securing bolts, inject further RTV jointing compound into the side grooves until it is certain that they are full (photo).
18 Fit the front main bearing cap, but before fitting the retaining bolts, smear them with jointing compound, and then tighten to the specified torque wrench setting. Check that the bearing cap is exactly flush with the end face of the crankcase as it is tightened.
19 Now rotate the crankshaft and check that it turns freely, and shows no signs of binding or tight spots. Check that the crankshaft endfloat is within the limits specified, using a dial gauge or with feeler blades inserted between the flange of the centre bearing shell and the machined surface of the crankshaft (photo). Before measuring, make sure that the crankshaft has been forced fully towards one end of the crankcase to give the widest gap at the measuring location. Incorrect endfloat will most likely be due to wear or to incorrect regrinding (assuming that the correct shells have been fitted).

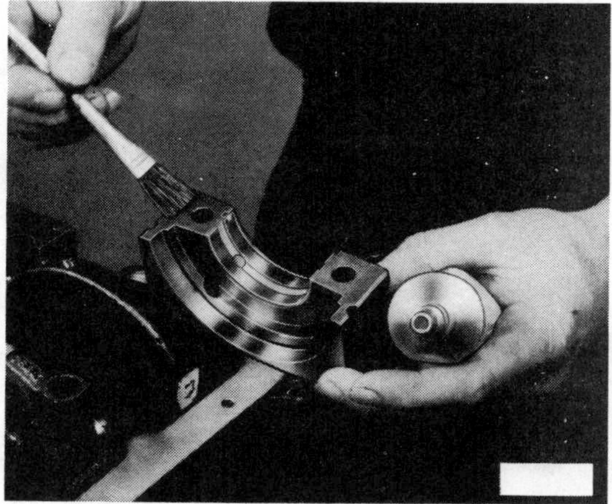
Fig. 1.17 Applying sealant to the main bearing cap inner surfaces (Sec 44)

45 Engine components – examination and renovation

1 Refer to Section 21, but note the following additional information.

Camshaft

2 With the camshaft removed, examine the bearings for signs of obvious wear and pitting. If evident, a new camshaft housing will probably be required.
3 The camshaft itself should show no marks or scoring on the journal or cam lobe surfaces. If evident, renew the camshaft.
4 The retaining plate should appear unworn and without grooves. In any event, check the camshaft endfloat and fit a new plate where necessary.
5 The housing front oil seal should always be renewed at major overhaul.

Camshaft toothed belt

6 Closely inspect the belt for cracking, fraying or tooth deformation. Where evident, renew the belt.

7 If the belt has been in use for 30 000 miles (48 000 km) or more, it is recommended that it is renewed even if it appears in good condition.

8 Whenever the original belt is to be removed, but is going to be used again, always note its running direction before removing it. It is even worthwhile marking the tooth engagement points on each sprocket. As the belt will have worn in a set position, refitting it in exactly the same way will prevent any increase in noise which might otherwise occur when the engine is running.

Valve lifters, rockers and thrust pads

9 Any signs of wear in a hydraulic valve lifter can only be rectified by renewal, the unit cannot be dismantled.

10 Inspect the rockers and thrust pads for wear or grooving. Again, renew if evident.

Piston/bore grade marks

11 The number or code denoting the piston and bore grade (see Specifications) will be found on the sump sealing surface of the 1.3 engine, and near the engine number on the larger engines.

46 Engine lubrication and crankcase ventilation systems – general description

1 Oil pressure for all moving components is provided by a gear type oil pump which is driven from the front end of the crankshaft. The crankshaft has flats for this purpose.

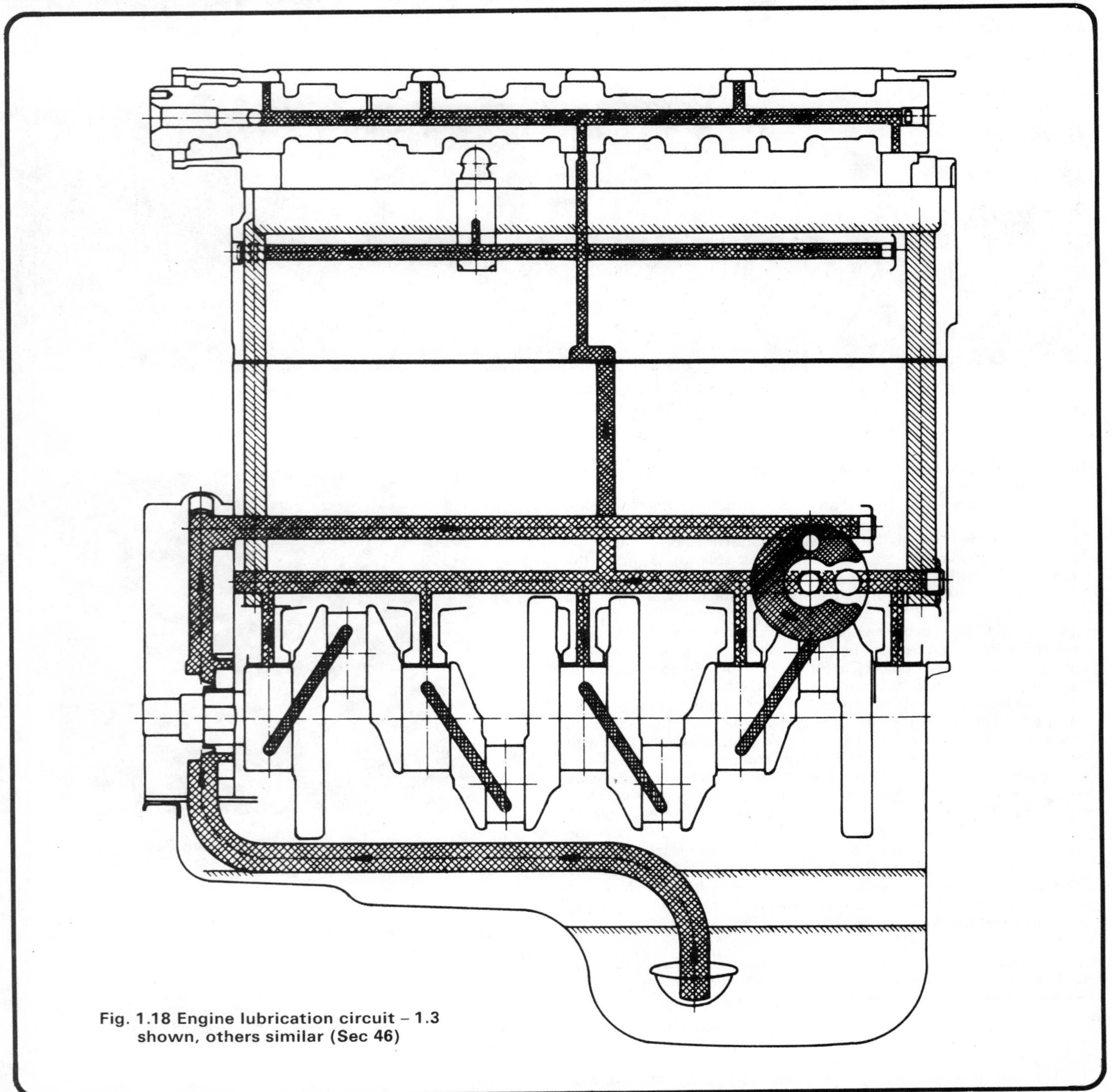

Fig. 1.18 Engine lubrication circuit – 1.3 shown, others similar (Sec 46)

2 The pump draws oil from the sump through a pick-up pipe and strainer and pumps it through the oil filter and oil galleries to the engine friction surfaces.
3 A pressure regulator valve is screwed into the body of the oil pump. A relief valve, located in the oil filter mounting base, opens should the filter block due to clogging caused by neglected servicing. An oil pressure switch is screwed into the pump casing.
4 The cylinder bores are lubricated by oil splash from the sump.
5 The hydraulic valve lifters are pressurised with oil to maintain optimum valve clearance at all times.
6 The crankcase ventilation system is designed to draw oil fumes and blow-by gas (combustion gas which has passed the piston rings) from the crankcase into the air cleaner, whence they are drawn into the engine and burnt during the normal combustion cycle.
7 On 1.6 and 1.8 engines, one of the crankcase ventilation hoses is attached to the camshaft cover (photo). Inside the cover is a filter which should be cleaned in paraffin periodically.
8 On the 1.3 engine, the ventilation system incorporates an oil separator bolted to the block. Although it is not a specified maintenance task, the separator can be removed for cleaning (photo).
9 On all engines, the breather hoses should be cleaned out periodically and renewed if necessary. Investigate the cause of any build-up of "mayonnaise" – sometimes this indicates a cooling system fault or a blown head gasket, although it may simply mean that the engine is not reaching operating tempertature (eg short runs in winter).
10 The lubrication system on the 1.8 engine incorporates an oil cooler. Oil leaves and returns via an adaptor mounted between the oil filter and its housing (photo). The adaptor contains a thermostatic valve which prevents the oil from circulating in the cooling circuit until it has warmed up. The oil cooler itself is mounted in front of the radiator.
11 The oil cooler pipes and hoses should be inspected regularly for signs of deterioration or leakage. The oil cooler fins will benefit from an occasional cleaning with solvent, followed if possible by blowing through the fins with compressed air.
12 At time of engine overhaul, consideration should be given to renewing the oil cooler, especially if major mechanical failure has occurred. If the old cooler is to be re-used it should be flushed with several changes of clean oil in an attempt to remove metal particles and other contaminants.
13 Access to the oil cooler is gained by removing the radiator (Chapter 2) or the front trim panel (Chapter 11).

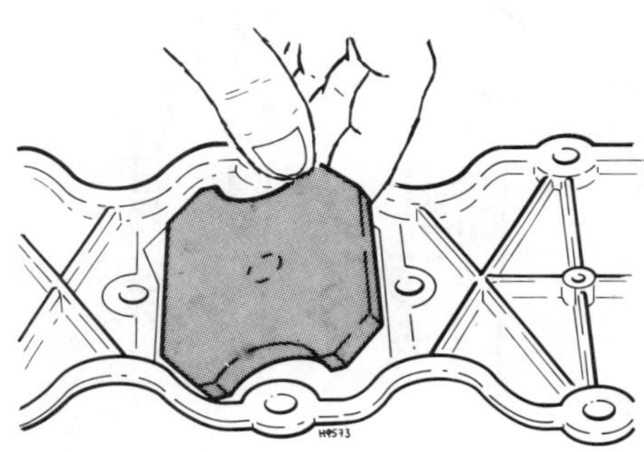

Fig. 1.19 Camshaft housing filter (Sec 46)

46.7 Crankcase ventilation hose attached to camshaft cover (1.6/1.8)

46.8 Crankcase ventilation system oil separator (1.3)

46.10 Oil cooler adaptor (arrowed) above oil filter

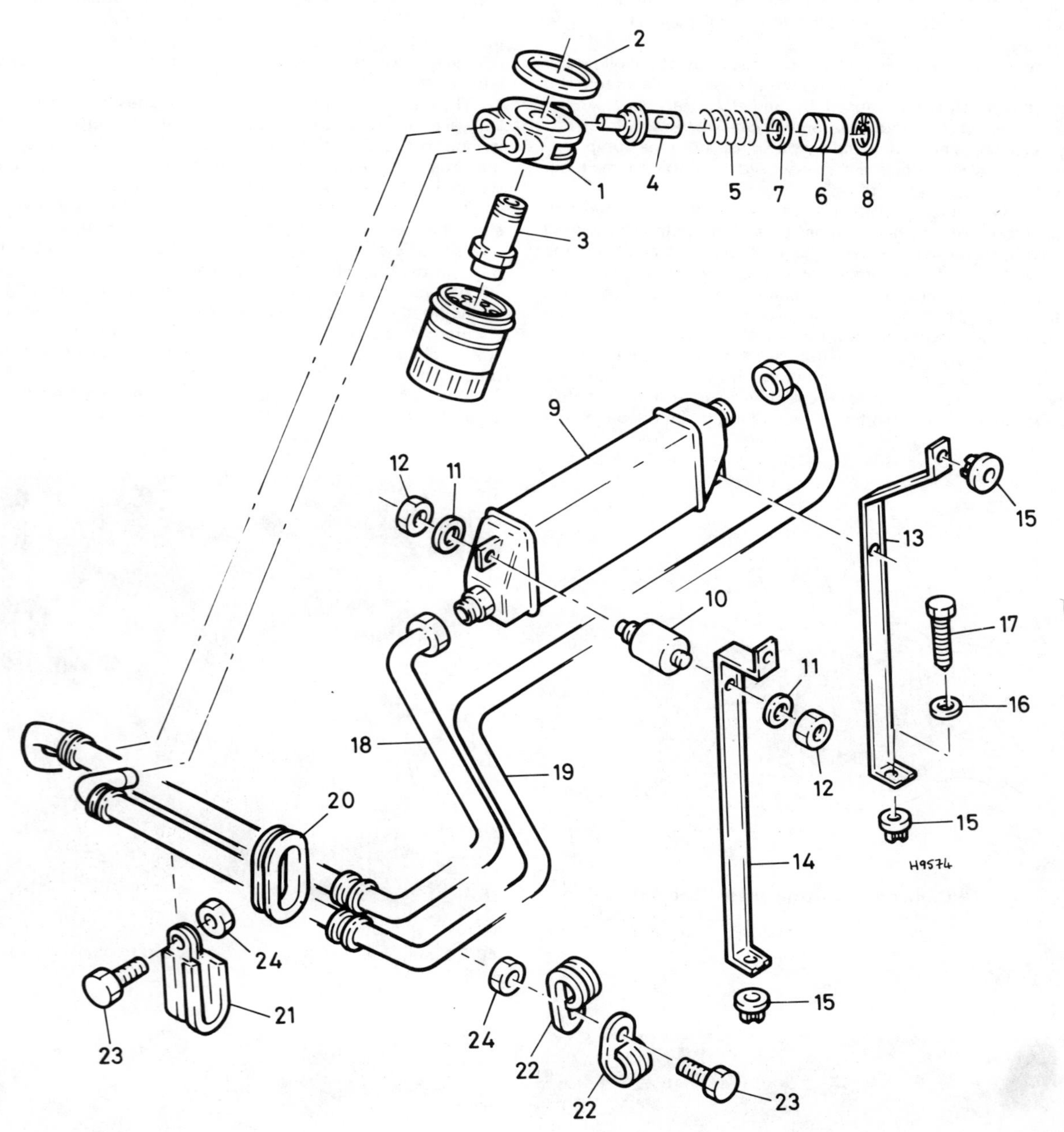

Fig. 1.20 Oil cooler and associated components (Sec 46)

1 Adaptor
2 Sealing ring
3 Hollow screw
4 Thermostatic valve
5 Spring
6 Plug
7 Seal
8 Circlip
9 Oil cooler
10 Mounting rubber
11 Washer
12 Nut
13 Bracket
14 Bracket
15 Nuts
16 Washer
17 Screw
18 Flow pipe
19 Return pipe
20 Grommet
21 Clamp
22 Clamps
23 Screws
24 Nuts

47 Engine – removal and refitting

1 The OHC engines may be removed either with or without the manual gearbox. To remove the engine alone, proceed as described in Section 23, making allowances for differences in the attachment of components such as the carburettor or fuel injection items.
2 Removal of the engine and automatic transmission together may be possible, but it is not recommended because of the weight and unwieldiness of the combined units.
3 To remove the engine and manual gearbox together, first disconnect both battery terminals.
4 Remove the air cleaner, as described in Chapter 3.
5 Drain the cooling system as described in Chapter 2. Disconnect all coolant hoses from the engine, not forgetting the heater hoses and (if fitted) the inlet manifold/carburettor heating hoses.
6 Disconnect the throttle cable and (if fitted) the choke cable, as described in Chapter 3.
7 Disconnect the brake servo vacuum hose. Either remove the hose completely, or secure it so that it will not be damaged.
8 Disconnect and plug the fuel feed and return lines. Be prepared for some fuel spillage.
9 Disconnect the engine wiring harness plug (photo). On models so equipped, disconnect the dipstick sensor wiring also (photo).
10 Disconnect the HT lead, LT leads and multi-plug from the ignition coil and module.
11 Disconnect the gearchange remote control rod at the pinch-bolt.
12 Disconnect the speedometer cable at the gearbox end.
13 Disconnect the clutch cable, as described in Chapter 5.
14 Slacken the front wheel bolts, raise and securely support the front of the car and remove the front wheels.
15 Unbolt and remove the exhaust downpipe(s). Also disconnect the earth strap from the gearbox.
16 On 1.8 models, disconnect and plug the oil cooler hoses. Be prepared for some oil spillage.
17 Separate the control arm balljoints from the steering knuckles. See Chapter 10 for details.
18 Separate the driveshafts from the final drive housing, as described in Chapter 7. Be prepared for some oil spillage; plug the driveshaft holes and tie the shafts up out of the way.
19 Attach the lifting tackle to the engine and gearbox and take the weight of the assembly.
20 Unbolt the engine/transmission mountings from the body members (photos).
21 Carefully lower the assembly through the engine bay to the ground. Depending on the type and reach of the vehicle lifting gear, it may be necessary to lift the vehicle off the engine to enable it to be withdrawn.

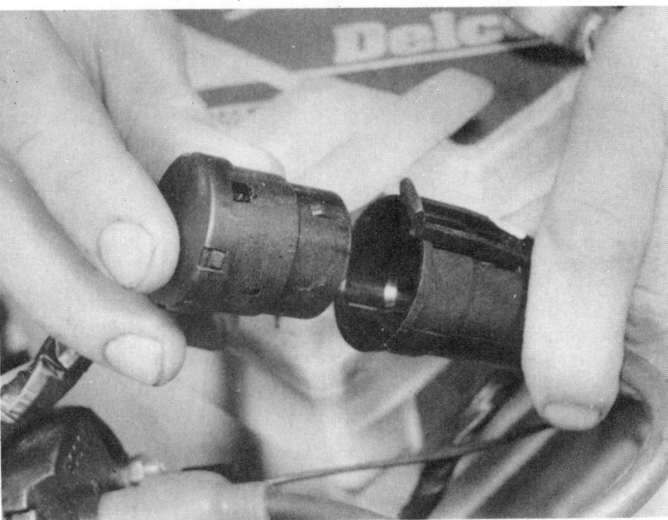
47.9A Engine wiring harness plug

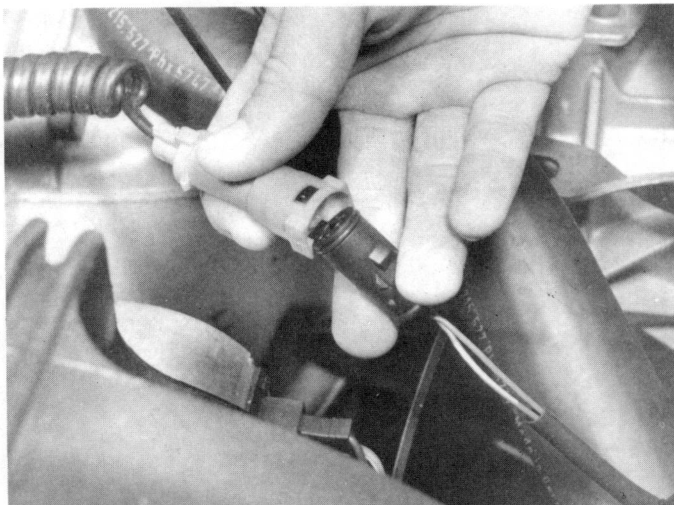
47.9B Dipstick sensor plug

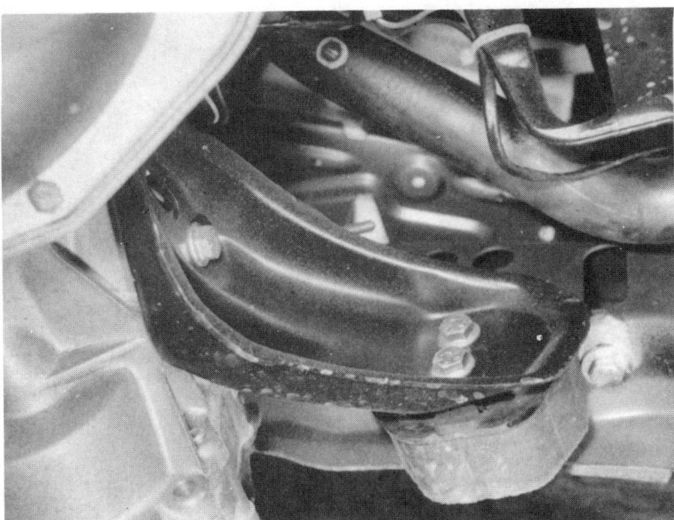
47.20A Engine/transmission left-hand mounting

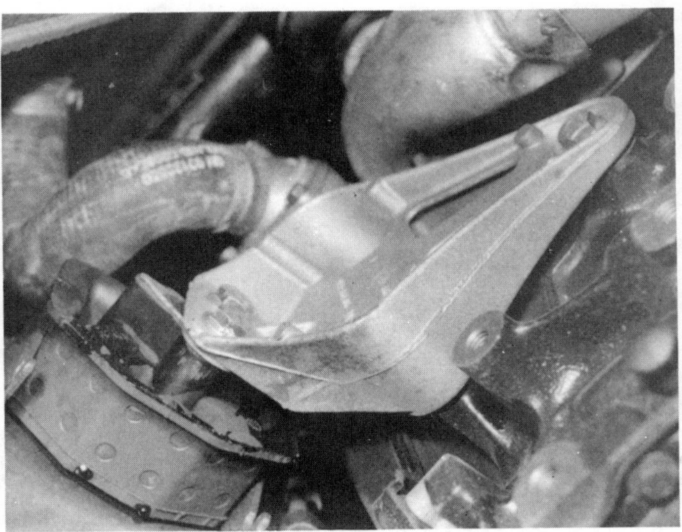
47.20B Engine/transmission right-hand mounting

22 To separate the engine and gearbox, support the latter and unbolt the starter motor and flywheel bottom cover. Remove the remaining engine-to-bellhousing bolts and carefully withdraw the gearbox from the engine. Do not allow the weight of the gearbox to hang on the clutch input shaft.
23 When refitting, tighten the engine/transmission mounting bolts finger tight at first, then to the specified torque, in the following order:

(a) RH front mounting
(b) LH front mounting
(c) Rear mounting

24 The remainder of the refitting process follows the reverse order to removal. Refer to the appropriate Chapters for guidance if necessary.
25 Remember to replenish the gearbox oil after refitting.

48 Engine – initial start-up after overhaul

Refer to Section 24. There is no need to adjust the valve clearances, but remember to tighten the head bolts (Section 32) if the head has been disturbed.

PART C: ALL ENGINES

49 Fault diagnosis – engine

Symptom	Reason(s)
Engine fails to start	Discharged battery Loose battery connection Loose or broken ignition leads Moisture on spark plugs, distributor cap, or HT leads Incorrect spark plug gaps Cracked distributor cap or rotor Other ignition system fault Dirt or water in fuel Empty fuel tank Faulty fuel pump Other fuel system fault Faulty starter motor Low cylinder compressions
Engine idles erratically	Intake manifold air leak Leaking system head gasket Worn rocker arms, timing chain, and gears (where applicable) Worn camshaft lobes Faulty fuel pump Loose crankcase ventilation hoses Idle adjustment incorrect Uneven cylinder compressions
Engine misfires	Spark plugs or worn or incorrectly gapped Dirt or water in fuel Carburettor adjustment incorrect Burnt out valve Leaking cylinder head gasket Distributor cap cracked Incorrect valve clearances Uneven cylinder compressions Worn carburettor Other ignition system fault
Engine stalls	Idle adjustment incorrect Intake manifold air leak Ignition timing incorrect
Excessive oil consumption	Worn pistons, cylinder bores or piston rings Valve guides and valve stem seals worn Oil leaks
Engine backfires	Carburettor adjustment incorrect Ignition timing incorrect Incorrect valve clearances Intake manifold air leak Sticking valve

Chapter 2 Cooling system

Contents

Specifications

General

System type	Water-based coolant, pump-assisted circulation pressurized and thermostatically controlled
Blow-off pressure	1.20 to 1.35 bar (17.4 to 19.6 lbf/in²)
Nominal boiling temperature	125°C (257°F)

Coolant

Type	Ethylene glycol based antifreeze (to GM spec GME 13368) and soft water
Capacity:	
1.2	5.9 litres (10.4 pints)
1.3 (manual)	6.3 litres (11.1 pints)
1.3 (automatic)	7.1 litres (12.5 pints)
1.6 (manual)	7.8 litres (13.7 pints)
1.6 (automatic)	7.6 litres (13.4 pints)
1.8	7.6 litres (13.4 pints)

Thermostat

Opening commences:	
1.2, 1.6 and 1.8	91°C (196°F)
1.3	92°C (198°F)
Fully open:	
1.2 and 1.3	107°C (225°F)
1.6 and 1.8	103°C (217°F)

Radiator fan thermoswitch

Cuts in at	97°C (207°F)
Cuts out at	93°C (199°F)

Torque wrench settings

	Nm	lbf ft
Water pump bolts:		
OHV	8	6
OHC – 1.3	8	6
OHC – 1.6 and 1.8	25	18
Thermostat housing (OHC):		
1.3	10	7
1.6 and 1.8	15	11
Temperature sensor in manifold	10	7
Temperature sensor in thermostat housing	8	6

1 General description

Engine cooling is achieved by a conventional thermo-syphon, pump-assisted system in which the cooling water is pressurised. The system consists of a radiator, water pump, electric fan, thermostat expansion tank and associated hoses.

The system functions as follows. Cold water from one side of the radiator, which is mounted at the front of the engine compartment, is directed to the inlet side of the water pump where it is then forced round the cooling passages in the engine cylinder block and cylinder head. The cooling water, now hot, is returned to the other side of the radiator where it flows across and cools before repeating the cycle.

To enable the engine to warm up quickly when starting from cold the thermostat prevents cooling water returning to the radiator until a predetermined temperature is reached. Instead the same water is recirculated around the passages in the cylinder block and cylinder head. When hot the thermostat opens, allowing the water to return to the radiator.

Air flows through the radiator to cool the water as a result of the car's forward motion. However, if the temperature of the cooling water exceeds a given figure, a temperature switch in the radiator switches on an electrical fan to assist and increase the airflow through the radiator.

An expansion tank is incorporated in the system to accommodate expansion of the cooling water. The system is topped up through a filler cap on this tank.

2 Maintenance and inspection

1 Weekly or before a long journey check the level of cooling water in the expansion tank, with the engine cold, and top up to just above the KALT mark if necessary (photo). Under normal operating conditions coolant loss should be negligible and any need for frequent topping-up should be investigated.

2.1 Topping-up the cooling system expansion tank

2 Every 9000 miles (15 000 km) or 12 months, whichever comes first, carefully inspect the drivebelt for signs of cracks, fraying or incorrect tension. Renew and/or adjust the belt tension, as described in Section 9.

3 At the same service intervals check the condition and security of all hoses and hose clips. Also inspect the joint faces of the water pump, thermostat housing, cylinder head etc for any sign of coolant seepage.

4 Every autumn, have the concentration of antifreeze in the cooling system checked and if necessary add fresh antifreeze to maintain the required stength, as described in Section 13. To provide adequate protection against corrosion in the cooling system renew the antifreeze completely every two years.

3 Cooling system – draining

Note: *Take care to protect the hands from escaping steam when removing the expansion tank filler cap if the system is hot.*

1 With the car parked on level ground, move the heater control to the full heat position and then unscrew the expansion tank filler cap. If the system is hot unscrew the cap slowly and allow the pressure in the system to be released before completely removing the cap.

2 Position a clean container beneath the bottom hose connection on the left-hand side of the radiator. Slacken the hose clip, ease the hose off the outlet and allow the water to drain into the container.

3 On OHV models a cylinder block drain plug is provided and is located on the side of the engine beneath the exhaust manifold. Reposition the container beneath the engine and unscrew the plug using a suitable Allen key. Refit and tighten the plug after draining.

4 No drain plug is provided on OHC engines, so complete draining of the coolant is not possible.

5 On completion, remove the container to a safe place and cover it to prevent contamination of the coolant if it is to be re-used.

4 Cooling system – flushing

1 If coolant renewal has been neglected, or if the antifreeze mixture has become diluted, then in time the cooling system will gradually lose efficiency as the cooling passages become choked with rust, scale deposits and other sediment. To restore cooling system efficiency it is necessary to flush the system clean.

2 First drain the system, as described in the previous Section, and then remove the thermostat, as decribed in Section 7. Temporarily refit the thermostat housing and reconnect the hose.

3 Insert a garden hose into the disconnected radiator bottom hose and secure it in place with rags. Turn on the supply and allow clean water to flow through the system and out of the radiator bottom outlet. Continue flushing for ten to fifteen minutes or until clean rust-free water emerges from the radiator.

4 If the contamination is particularly bad, reverse flush the system by inserting the garden hose in the radiator bottom outlet and allow the water to flow through the system and out of the radiator bottom hose. This should dislodge deposits that were not moved by conventional flushing. If any doubt exists about the cleanliness of the radiator after flushing, it should be removed, as described in Section 6, so that it can be flushed and agitated at the same time. After reverse flushing carry out a normal flow flush before refitting the thermostat and reconnecting the system hoses.

5 In extreme cases the use of a proprietary de-scaling compound may be necessary. If such a compound is used, adhere to the manufacturer's instructions and satisfy yourself that no damage will be caused to the engine or cooling system components.

6 If the coolant is renewed regularly, flushing will not normally be required, simply drain the old coolant and refill with a fresh mixture.

5 Cooling system – filling

1 Before filling the cooling system make sure that all the hoses and hose clips are in good condition and that the clips are tight. On OHV models ensure that the cylinder block drain plug is fully tightened.

2 To ensure adequate protection against corrosion, as well as the effects of winter weather, a proportion of antifreeze must be maintained in the cooling system at all times. *Never fill the system with water only, even in summer.* Refer to Section 13 for details of the required antifreeze strength. In areas where the lime content of the mains water supply is high it is advantageous to use rainwater in the system, as this will reduce the build-up of scale in the radiator.

3 Check that the heater control is in the hot position and then remove the filler cap from the expansion tank. To allow air to escape from the system as it is being filled, slacken the clip and remove the heater hose at the cylinder head on OHV models (photo), or disconnect the lead and unscrew the temperature gauge transmitter from the inlet manifold or thermostat housing (photo). If there is a bleed screw on the thermostat cover, this may be used instead.

4 Pour the required quantity of antifreeze into the expansion tank and

5.3A Bleed the cooling system through the heater hose outlet (OHV engine)

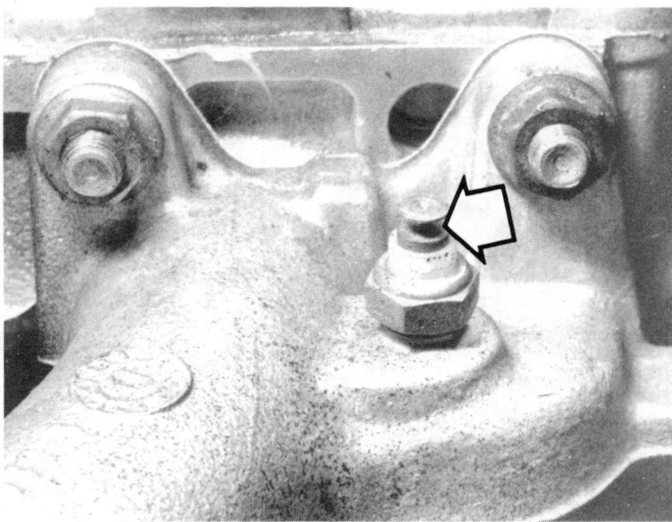

5.3B Bleed the cooling system by unscrewing the temperature gauge transmitter (arrowed) – OHC engine, 1.3 shown

then add the water. When coolant emerges from the heater hose outlet or temperature gauge transmitter orifice, refit the hose or transmitter and ensure that it is secure.

5 Continue adding water until the level in the expansion tank is just above the KALT mark. Repeated squeezing of the large coolant hoses will induce surging of the mixture in the system which will help to dislodge any air bubbles. Refit the expansion tank filler cap and wipe up any spilt coolant.

6 Run the engine at a fast tickover until the cooling fan motor engages and, particularly if the system has been disturbed in any way, examine carefully for leaks. Stop the engine and allow it to cool before topping-up the level in the expansion tank if necessary. Remember that the system must be cold before an accurate level is indicated in the expansion tank.

6 Radiator – removal, inspection and refitting

Note: *The radiator can be removed with the cooling fan still attached, but due to the limited space available care must be taken to avoid damaging the radiator. If preferred, the cooling fan may be removed first, as described in Section 10, to provide greater access.*

1 Drain the cooling system, as described in Section 3, and disconnect the battery earth terminal.

2 Slacken the retaining clips and detach the radiator top and bottom hoses and also the smaller diameter expansion tank vent hose.

3 Disconnect the two electrical leads at the thermal switch on the side of the radiator.

4 If the cooling fan is still in position, disconnect the electrical leads at the multi-plug adjacent to the fan motor. Release the cable clips securing the wiring harness to the fan cowl bracket and move the harness to one side.

5 On automatic transmission models equipped with a fluid cooler, disconnect and plug the cooler lines at the radiator side tank. Be prepared for fluid spillage, and take care not to allow dirt to enter the cooler lines.

6 Remove the radiator mounting bolts (one on each side at the top). Carefully lift out the radiator, with fan and shroud if not previously removed.

7 With the radiator assembly removed it is easier to examine for leaks which will show up as corroded or stained areas. No permanent repairs are possible with this type of radiator which is made of light alloy and plastic and, although proprietary leak stopping compounds can be tried, it is far better to renew a defective assembly.

8 Clean out the inside of the radiator by flushing, as described in Section 4, and also clean the matrix, removing all the dead flies and bugs which reduce the radiator's efficiency. Take this opportunity to inspect the hoses and clips, making sure that all are fit for further use.

9 Refitting the radiator is the reverse of the removal procedure. Check that the rubber mountings are in good condition and ensure that the bottom location pegs fit correctly on installation. Refer to Section 5 for refilling the system.

10 On automatic transmission models, remember to check the transmission fluid level and top up if necessary. See Chapter 6 for details.

7 Thermostat – removal, testing and refitting

1 Drain the cooling system, saving the coolant if it is fit for re-use. Disconnect the battery earth lead.

OHV engine

2 After draining the coolant, disconnect the radiator top hose from the outlet connection at the top of the water pump. This will expose the thermostat and it will be seen that it is retained in position by a snap-ring.

3 Prise the snap-ring free using a suitable screwdriver blade and then remove the thermostat from the pump outlet (photos).

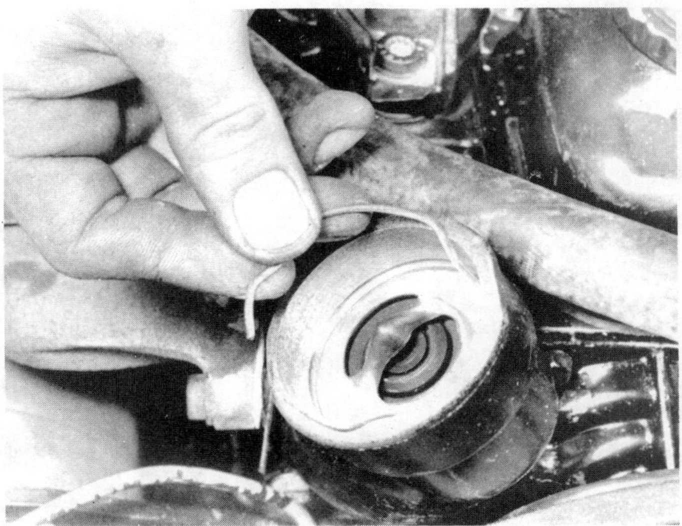

7.3A Removing the thermostat retaining snap-ring

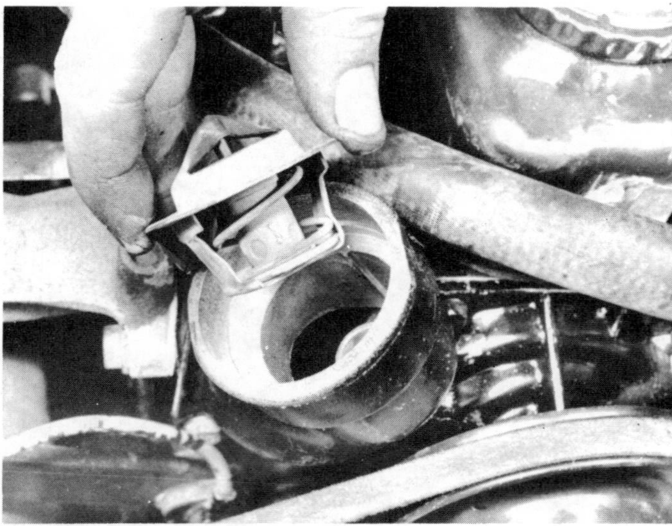
7.3B Removing the thermostat (OHV)

4 The thermostat can be tested easily for correct functioning if this should be in doubt. Boil a pan of water and suspend the thermostat on a piece of cord. Lower the thermostat into the hot water and it should be seen to open on immersion. Remove the thermostat from the water and it should be seen to close. This is only a simple functional test but it will identify a failed thermostat. With a thermometer you can check the correct opening temperature, see Specifications, but the full open temperature will be difficult to check as it is above the boiling point of water. When renewing this component make sure that the replacement item is the correct one for your car, as a wide range of thermostats are made for different models and conditions.
5 Refitting the thermostat is the reverse sequence to removal, but use a new rubber seal and install the thermostat with the arrow on the web pointing upwards. Refill the cooling system, as described in Section 5.

1.3 OHC engine

6 Remove the camshaft toothed belt cover, which is secured by five screws.
7 Slacken the clip and detach the radiator top hose from the thermostat housing.
8 Remove the two bolts and detach the thermostat housing (photo).
9 Remove the thermostat from its recess, noting how the projections on the thermostat fit in cut-outs in the recess (photo).
10 Testing the thermostat is as described in paragraph 4.
11 Refit in the reverse order to removal; use a new rubber seal on the thermostat (photo). Refill the cooling system, as described in Section 5.

1.6 and 1.8 OHC engines

12 Slacken the clip and detach the radiator top hose from the thermostat housing (photo).
13 Unbolt and remove the thermostat cover and extract the thermostat (photo).
14 Testing the thermostat is as described in paragraph 4.
15 Refit in the reverse order to removal; use a new rubber seal on the thermostat. Refill the cooling system, as described in Section 5.

8 Water pump – removal and refitting

Note: *Water pump failure is indicated by water leaking from the front of the pump, or by rough and noisy operation. This is usually*

7.8 Removing the thermostat housing (1.3 OHC)

7.9 Removing the thermostat from its recess (1.3 OHC)

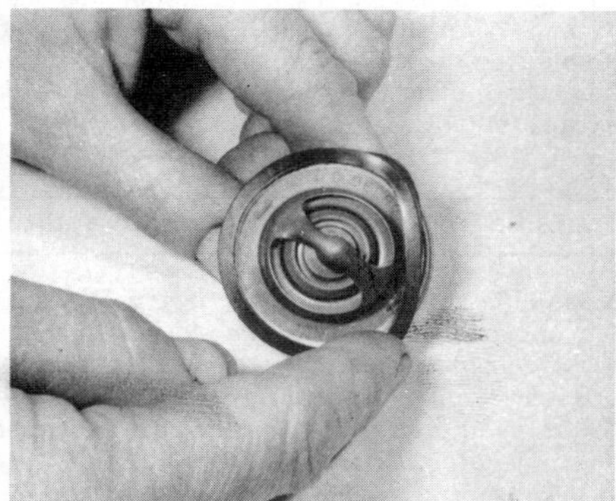
7.11 Fitting a new seal to the thermostat

7.12 Slackening the hose clip at the thermostat housing (1.6/1.8 OHC)

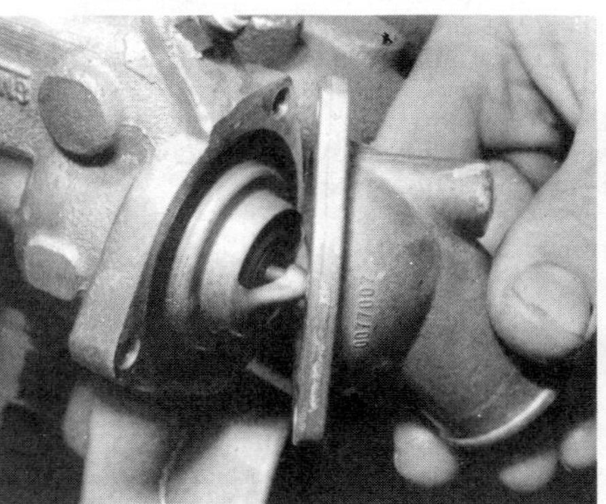
7.13A Removing the thermostat cover ...

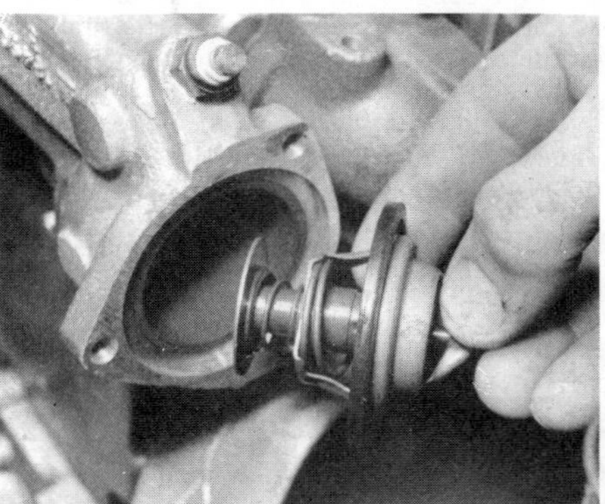
7.13B ... and the thermostat itself (1.6/1.8 OHC)

accompanied by excessive play of the pump spindle which can be checked by moving the pulley or sprocket from side to side. Should the pump prove to be defective a factory exchange unit should be obtained as repair of the old unit is not a practical proposition.

OHV engine

1 Drain the cooling system (Section 3) and disconnect the battery earth lead.

2 Remove the alternator/water pump drivebelt, as described in Section 9.

3 Slacken the hose clips and disconnect the three hoses from the pump.

4 Remove the six retaining bolts and carefully pull the pump off the head (photo). Recover the gasket.

5 If a new pump is being fitted, unbolt and transfer the pump pulley. Transfer the thermostat also, or fit a new one if the old one has seen much service.

6 Before refitting the water pump clean away all traces of old gasket from the pump and cylinder head mating faces.

7 Apply a little grease to a new gasket and place it in position on the pump. Refit the pump and secure the unit with the six bolts tightened progressively to the specified torque.

8 Refit the three hoses and tighten the clips securely. Refit the drivebelt and adjust the tension, as described in Section 9. Finally, refill the cooling system, as described in Section 5, and reconnect the battery.

OHC engine

9 Remove the camshaft toothed belt, as described in Chapter 1, Section 31.

10 Remove the toothed belt backplate.

11 Remove the three securing bolts and withdraw the water pump (photo). It may be necessary to remove the alternator completely, as described in Chapter 12, to provide enough room to remove the pump from the engine bay.

12 Before refitting the pump, clean its recess in the block. Always fit a new sealing ring to the pump (photo). Renew the camshaft toothed belt if it is well used.

13 Refit in the reverse order to removal. Only tighten the pump bolts lightly until the toothed belt has been adjusted (Chapter 1, Section 31), then tighten them to the specified torque.

14 Remember to refill the cooling system and adjust the alternator drivebelt on completion.

8.4 Removing the water pump (OHV)

8.11 Removing the water pump (OHC)

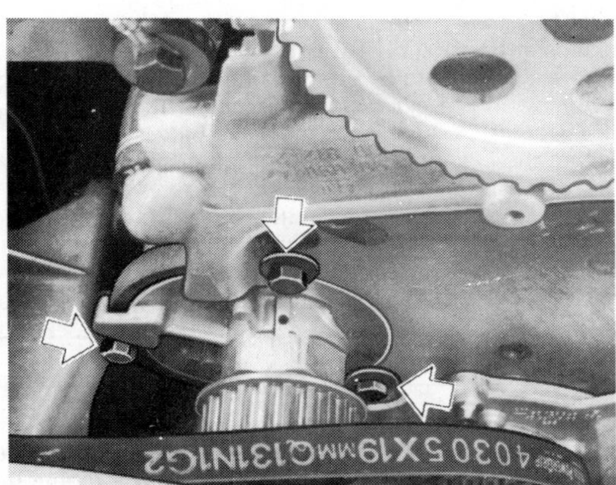

Fig. 2.1 Water pump securing bolts (arrowed) (Sec 8)

8.12 Fitting a new sealing ring to the pump

9 Drivebelt – removal, refitting and adjustment

Note: *On OHV models the drivebelt runs in the crankshaft, water pump and alternator pulleys. On OHC models the belt only runs in the crankshaft and alternator pulleys as the water pump is driven by the toothed camshaft belt. However, the removal, refitting and adjustment procedures on all models are similar.*

1 Correct tensioning of the drivebelt will ensure that it has a long and useful life. Beware, however, of overtightening as this can cause excessive wear in the alternator and/or water pump bearings.

2 A regular inspection of the belt should be made and if it is found to be overstretched, worn, frayed or cracked it should be renewed before it breaks in service. To insure against such an event arising it is a good idea to carry a spare belt, of the correct type, in the car at all times.

3 On models with power-assisted steering, the pump drivebelt must be removed before the alternator/water pump drivebelt, and refitting and tensioned afterwards. See Chapter 8, Section 15.

4 To remove an old belt, loosen the alternator mounting bolts and nuts just sufficiently to allow the unit to be pivoted in towards the engine. This will release all tension from the belt which can now be slipped off the respective pulleys. Fit a new belt after checking that it is of the correct type and take up the slack in the belt by swinging the alternator away from the engine and lightly tightening the bolts just to hold it in that position.

5 Although special tools are available for measuring the belt tension, a good approximation can be achieved if the belt is tensioned so that there is 13 mm (0.5 in) of lateral movement at the mid-point position on the longest run of belt between pulleys. With the alternator bolts just holding the unit firm, lever away from the engine using a wooden lever at the mounting bracket end until the correct tension in the belt is reached and then tighten the alternator bolts. On no account apply any loads at the free end of the alternator as serious damage can be caused internally.

6 When a new belt has been fitted it will probably stretch slightly to start with and the tension should be rechecked, and if necessary adjusted, after about 250 miles (400 km).

10 Radiator electric cooling fan – removal and refitting

1 Disconnect the battery negative terminal.

2 Disconnect the fan motor electrical leads at the multi-plug adjacent to the motor. Release the wiring harness cable ties at the fan cowl bracket and move the harness to one side.

3 Undo and remove the two small bolts securing the fan cowl to the top of the radiator. Lift the fan and cowl assembly upwards to release the lower mounting lugs and remove the unit from the car.

4 To separate the fan motor from the cowl unscrew the three nuts. The fan blades may be withdrawn from the motor spindle after removal of the retaining clip.

5 Further dismantling of the assembly depends on the extent of the problem. If the motor is defective it would be better to have it overhauled by a specialist, as spare parts may be difficult to obtain. The alternative is to renew the motor which may prove cheaper and quicker in the long run.

6 Reassembly, if the unit was dismantled, and refitting to the car are the reverse of the dismantling and removal sequences. On completion run the engine up to normal operating temperature and check the fan for correct functioning.

11 Cooling fan thermal switch – testing, removal and refitting

1 The radiator cooling fan is controlled by a thermal switch which is screwed into one of the radiator side tanks. During normal driving in temperate climates the fan will probably not be switched on very often.

2 If the fan fails to switch on at high engine temperatures, disconnect the two leads from the thermal switch and join the leads with a paper clip or a short piece of wire. (Do not allow the link to touch other metal on the car.) Switch on the ignition and the fan should operate, showing that the switch was at fault. If the fan still fails to operate then either a fuse has blown, there is a break in the wiring, or the fan meter is defective.

3 To remove the thermal switch, first drain the cooling system (Section 3) and disconnect the battery earth lead. (If a new switch is available for immediate fitting, and some coolant spillage can be tolerated, there is no need to drain the cooling system – just depressurize it by removing the expansion tank cap.)

4 Disconnect the leads from the switch and unscrew it from the radiator (photo).

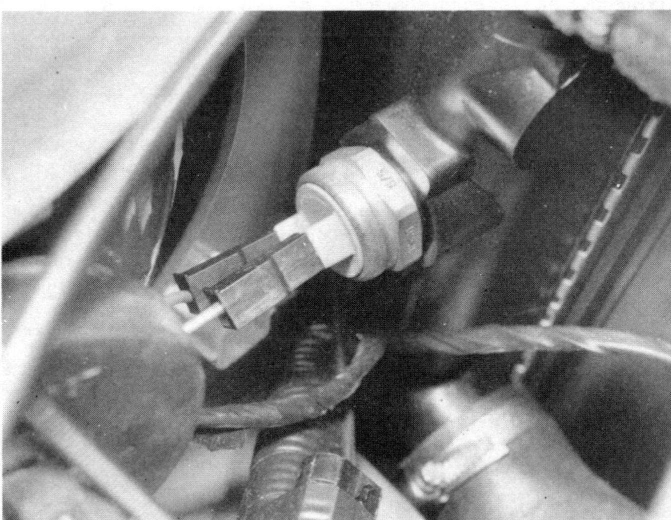

11.4 Thermal switch screwed into side of radiator

5 The thermal switch may be tested in the same way as the thermostat (Section 7), using a torch bulb and battery across the switch terminals to determine when the contacts close. If the contacts do not close in boiling water (100°C/212°F) the switch is certainly defective.

6 Refit the switch in the reverse order to removal; apply a little sealant to the switch threads. Top up or refill the cooling system on completion, reconnect the battery and run the engine until the fan cuts in to prove the switch is functioning correctly.

12 Temperature gauge transmitter – removal and refitting

1 The transmitter unit is located in the cylinder head behind the water pump on OHV engines, on the inlet manifold on 1.3 OHC engines, and on the thermostat housing on 1.6 and 1.8 OHC engines.

2 If a new transmitter is to be fitted at once, depressurize the cooling system by removing the expansion tank cap. Otherwise, partly drain the system (Section 3). Also disconnect the battery earth terminal.

3 Disconnect the electrical lead from the transmitter and unscrew it (photo).

4 Apply a little sealant to the transmitter threads before refitting, then screw it into its location and reconnect the electrical lead. Refill or top up the cooling system and reconnect the battery.

13 Antifreeze mixture

1 It is essential that an antifreeze mixture is retained in the cooling system at all times to act as a corrosion inhibitor and to protect the engine against freezing in winter months. The mixture should be made up from clean water with a low lime content (preferably rainwater) and a good quality ethylene glycol based antifreeze which contains a corrosion inhibitor and is suitable for use in aluminium engines.

2 The proportions of antifreeze to water required will depend on the maker's recommendations, but the mixture must be adequate to give protection down to approximately -30°C (-22°F).

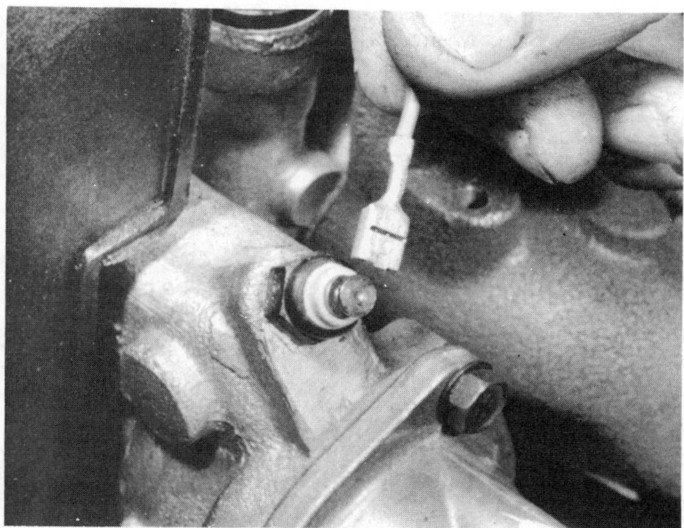

12.3 Disconnecting the temperature gauge transmitter (1.6/1.8 OHC)

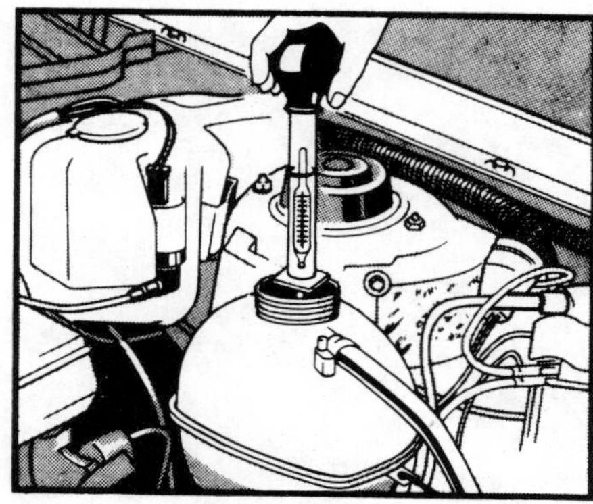

Fig. 2.2 Checking the antifreeze concentration (Sec 13)

3 Before filling with fresh antifreeze drain, and if necessary flush, the cooling system, as described in Section 3 and 4. Check that all hoses are in good condition and that all clips are secure, then fill the system, as described in Section 5.

4 The antifreeze should be renewed every two years to maintain adequate corrosion protection. Do not use engine coolant antifreeze in the windscreen or tailgate wash systems; it will damage the car's paintwork and smear the glass. *Finally remember that antifreeze is poisonous and must be handled with due care.*

5 The strength of the antifreeze already in the cooling system can be checked with an instrument similar to a battery hydrometer. Most garages should possess such an instrument, or one may be purchased from an accessory shop.

14 Fault diagnosis – cooling system

Symptom	Reason(s)
Overheating	Insufficient coolant in system Pump ineffective due to slack drivebelt (OHV) Radiator blocked either internally of externally Kinked or collapsed hose causing coolant flow restriction Thermostat not working properly Faulty electric fan Faulty fan thermal switch Engine out of tune Ignition timing retarded or auto advance malfunction Cylinder head gasket blown Engine not yet run-in Exhaust system partially blocked Engine oil level too low Brakes binding
Engine running too cool	Faulty, incorrect or missing thermostat
Loss of coolant	Loose hose clips Hoses perished or leaking Radiator leaking Filler/pressure cap defective Blown cylinder head gasket Cracked cylinder block or head

Chapter 3 Fuel and exhaust systems

Contents

Specifications

General

System type:

All except 1.8	Rear fuel tank, mechanical fuel pump, downdraught carburettor
1.8	Rear fuel tank, electric fuel pump, Bosch LE Jetronic fuel injection

Idle adjustment data

Idle speed:

All models with manual gearbox	900 to 950 rpm
All models with automatic transmission	800 to 850 rpm (in P)
CO level at idle (carburettor)	1.0 to 1.5%
CO level at idle (fuel injection)	0.5% max

Carburettor application

32 TL	12 SC
35 PDSI	13 N
2E3	13 SC
Varajet II	16 SH

Fuel tank capacity

Hatchback	42 litres (9.3 gallons)
Estate and Van	50 litres (11.0 gallons)

Fuel grade

All engines except 13 N	98 octane (UK 4-star)
13 N engine	91 octane (UK 2-star)

Carburettor calibration – 32 TL

Needle valve	1.75 mm
Venturi diameter	25 mm
Main jet	117
Mixture outlet	2.5 mm
Air correction jet	75
Mixture tube	F96
Idle fuel jet	47
Idle air jet	90
Idle mixture jet	210
Auxiliary mixture fuel jet	35
Auxiliary mixture air jet	170
Auxiliary mixture jet	100
Full load enrichment jet	65
Partial load enrichment jet (idle)	40
Partial load enrichment jet (main)	40
Accelerator pump jet	45
Accelerator pump return jet	30
Accelerator pump delivery	6.5 to 9.5 cc per 10 strokes
Pull-down reduction jet	35
Pull-down adjustment (choke valve gap)	4.3 to 4.8 mm (0.17 to 0.19 in)
Throttle valve gaps:	
Fast idle	0.6 to 0.7 mm (0.02 to 0.03 in)
Mechanical pull-down	0.8 to 0.9 mm (0.03 to 0.04 in)
Fast idle speed	3600 to 4000 rpm
Float level	23.5 to 24.0 mm (0.93 to 0.95 in)
Vacuum at idle speed	1 to 20 mbar (0.03 to 0.59 in Hg)

Carburettor calibration – 35 PDSI

Needle valve	1.75 mm
Needle valve sealing ring	2.5 mm
Venturi diameter	26 mm
Mixture outlet	2.4 mm
Accelerator pump delivery:	
Manual gearbox	10 ± 1.0 cc per 10 strokes
Automatic transmission	7 ± 1.0 cc per 10 strokes
Accelerator pump arm	Throttle valve shaft
Main jet	X 122.5
Air correction jet	80
Idle cut-off jet	50
Pump injector tube	50
Enrichment jet in float chamber:	
Manual gearbox	50
Automatic transmission	70
Enrichment jet in cover:	
Manual gearbox	100
Automatic transmission	80
Auxiliary fuel jet	35
Auxiliary mixture jet	5.0

Carburettor calibration – 2E3

	Primary	Secondary
Venturi diameter	20 mm	24 mm
Main jet	X97.5	X112.5
Air correction jet	80	100
Emulsion tube code number	88	60
Partial load enrichment orifice	0.5 mm	–
Pre-atomizer diameter	8 mm	7 mm
Mixture outlet orifice	2.5 mm	3.0 mm
Idle fuel jet	37.5	–
Idle air jet	130	–
Full load enrichment jet	–	85 to 105
Automatic choke adjustment data:		
Choke valve pull-down gap	2.1 to 2.5 mm (0.08 to 0.10 in)	
Fast idle speed	2400 to 2800 rpm	
Throttle valve fast idle gap	1.1 to 1.2 mm (0.04 to 0.05 in)	
Accelerator pump delivery:		
Manual transmission	10.3 to 12.7 cc per 10 strokes	
Automatic transmission	7.8 to 10.2 cc per 10 strokes	
Float level	29 to 30 mm (1.14 to 1.18 in)	

Carburettor calibration – Varajet II

Fast idle speed:	
Manual gearbox	2050 to 2150 rpm
Automatic transmission	2250 to 2350 rpm
Choke valve gaps (see text):	
A	2.8 to 3.4 mm (0.11 to 0.13 in)
B	2.3 to 2.8 mm (0.09 to 0.11 in)
C	9.5 to 10.5 mm (0.37 to 0.41 in)
Automatic choke cover adjustment	1 mark towards L
Float level	4.5 to 6.5 mm (0.18 to 0.26 in)
Idle jet	0.65 mm
Primary main jet	2.04 mm (marked 204)
Primary main jet needle	1.51 mm (marked 151)
Secondary main jet	3.20 mm
Secondary main jet needle	2.20 mm (marked G)
Float needle valve diameter	1.93 mm

Fuel injection system test data

Airflow sensor resistance (at 20°C/68°F):	
Terminals 8 and 9	160 to 300 Ω
Terminals 7 and 8	60 to 1000 Ω
Throttle valve switch condition at idle:	
Terminals 2 and 18	Closed (zero resistance)
Terminals 3 and 18	Open (infinite resistance)
Temperature sensor II resistance (terminals 10 and 33):	
0°C (32°F)	4.8 to 6.6 kΩ
20°C (68°F)	2.2 to 2.8 kΩ
40°C (104°F)	1.0 to 1.4 kΩ
80°C (176°F)	0.27 to 0.38 kΩ
Injector winding resistance	15 to 19 Ω
Fuel pump delivery	0.8 to 1.0 litre (1.4 to 1.8 pints) per minute
Regulated fuel pressure (inlet manifold at atmospheric pressure)	2.5 bar (36 lbf/in²)

Torque wrench settings

	Nm	lbf ft
Inlet manifold-to-head nuts or bolts:		
1.2	23	17
1.3	20	15
1.6 and 1.8	22	16
Carburettor securing nuts:		
1.2	18	13
1.3	20	15
1.6	15	11
Fuel pump to camshaft housing (OHC):		
1.3	20	15
1.6	15	11
Exhaust manifold nuts or bolts	Not specified. Use inlet manifold values as a guide	

1 General description

All carburettor models are fitted with a rear-mounted fuel tank, a mechanical fuel pump and a downdraught carburettor. A disposable element air cleaner is fitted to all models; on all but 1.2 models, preheating of incoming air is automatically regulated.

The exhaust system is in two or three sections, and incorporates a spring-loaded joint at one end or other of the front section to allow for engine movement. Twin downpipes are used on most models.

The fuel injection system fitted to 1.8 models is described in Section 25.

Warning: *Many of the procedures in this Chapter entail the removal of fuel pipes and connections which may result in some fuel spillage. Before carrying out any operation on the fuel system refer to the precautions given in Safety First! at the beginning of this manual and follow them implicitly. Petrol is a highly dangerous and volatile liquid and the precautions necessary when handling it cannot be overstressed.*

2 Maintenance and inspection

1 At every major service interval, remove the air cleaner, as described in Section 6. Remove the element and wipe clean inside the housing.
2 Renew the air cleaner element at least every 18 000 miles or 2 years, or earlier if it is obviously clogged, torn, wet or oil-soaked.
3 At every major service, check the exhaust system for good condition, freedom from leaks and security of mountings. Repair or renew as necessary (Section 33).
4 At the same interval, check the idle speed and mixture adjustments (Section 14 or 27) and correct as necessary.
5 Although not specified as a routine operation, it is wise to remove the fuel pump filter screen for cleaning at alternate major services. This is only possible on some mechanical pumps – see Section 3.
6 Clean or renew the carburettor inlet filter at alternate major services. When fitted, this will be found by removing the fuel inlet union. On fuel injection models, renew the in-line fuel filter at the same interval.
7 At every major service, or whenever a fuel leak is suspected, carry out the following work.
8 With the car over a pit, raised on a vehicle hoist or securely supported on axle stands carefully inspect the fuel pipes, hoses and unions for chafing, leaks and corrosion. Renew any pipes that are severely pitted with corrosion or in any way damaged. Renew any hoses that show signs of cracking or other deterioration.
9 Examine the fuel tank for leaks, particularly around the fuel gauge sender unit, and for signs of corrosion or damage.
10 From within the engine compartment check the security of all fuel hose attachments and inspect the fuel hoses and vacuum hoses for kinks, chafing or deterioration.
11 Check the operation of the accelerator and choke controls and lubricate the linkage, cables and pivots with a few drops of engine oil.
12 On 1.2 models, change the position of the intake air preheating control according to climatic conditions – see Section 5.

3 Fuel pump – description and maintenance

Carburettor models

1 On OHV models the fuel pump is located on the side of the engine which faces the front of the car. It is driven by a camshaft lobe which bears on the pump rocker arm.

2 On OHC models the fuel pump is mounted on the timing gear end of the camshaft housing. Again it is driven by a camshaft lobe, this time via a pushrod.

3 One of two types of pump may be fitted; a semi-sealed unit or a completely sealed type. The completely sealed type of pump is easily identifiable by the position of the hose nozzles, one of which is horizontal with respect to the pump body and the other vertical. This type of pump cannot be dismantled for overhaul or repair and no maintenance is required.

4 The semi-sealed pump can also be identified by the position of the hose nozzles which are both horizontal in relation to the pump body. Also on these pumps a screw will be found in the centre of the top cover. As with the completely sealed type, dismantling and overhaul is not possible; however, the top cover can be removed to allow access to the gauze filter which can be cleaned or renewed.

5 To clean the filter, undo the retaining screw and lift off the top cover complete with hose. Be prepared for some fuel spillage and ensure adequate ventilation.

6 Lift off the filter gauze and clean it by blowing through it or by using an air line (photo).

7 Check the condition of the rubber seal in the top cover and renew it if it is in any way damaged, cracked or deformed.

8 Refit the filter, cover and retaining screw, but take care not to overtighten the screw.

Fuel injection models

9 The fuel pump is located under the car near the fuel tank, and is electrically operated; periodic maintenance is not required.

3.6 Fuel pump cover, filter gauze and rubber seal

4 Fuel pump – testing, removal and refitting

Carburettor models

1 Disconnect the battery earth lead.

2 Identify the fuel inlet and outlet hoses, then slacken their clips and disconnect them from the pump (photo). Plug the hoses with rods or bolts to prevent fuel leakage.

3 Remove the pump retaining nuts or bolts and washers and withdraw the pump from the engine. Recover the spacer and (on OHV engines) the gaskets on either side of it (photo).

4 To test the pump operation, refit the fuel inlet hose to the pump inlet nozzle and hold a rag near the outlet. Operate the pump lever by hand and if the pump is in a satisfactory condition a strong jet of fuel should be ejected from the outlet as the lever is released. If this is not the case, check that fuel will flow from the inlet hose when it is held below tank level; if so the pump is faulty and renewal is necessary.

5 Before refitting the pump, clean all traces of old gasket from the pump and engine mating faces. If necessary use a new gasket on each side of the spacer and refit the pump using the reverse sequence to removal.

Fuel injection models

6 To check the fuel pump delivery, disconnect the fuel feed hose at the injector rail and lead it into a calibrated container of at least 3 litres (over 5 pints) capacity.

7 Disconnect the wiring plug from the control relay. Bridge terminals 28 and 59 of the plug. Do not allow the bridge to touch earth.

8 Switch on the ignition for one minute exactly, then switch it off again and measure the quantity of fuel delivered. If it is less than the amount given in the Specifications, renew the fuel filter (Section 30) and test again. If the delivery is still low, renew the pump.

9 For removal and refitting of the pump see Section 30.

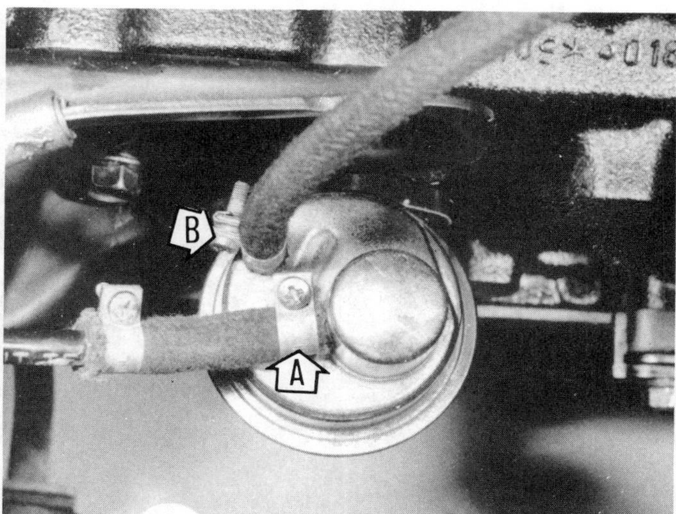

4.2 Fuel inlet (A) and outlet (B) hose connections – typical

4.3 Removing the fuel pump (OHC engine)

5 Air cleaner – description

1 The air cleaner on all models provides clean air for combustion, excluding airborne dust and grit which could damage the engine, carburettor or fuel injection system.
2 On carburettor models, arrangements are made to warm the incoming air in cold weather. These arrangements vary as follows.

OHV models

3 Intake air pre-heating is controlled manually by a flap valve located in the side of air cleaner casing. The valve can be set in any one of three positions according to seasonal operating temperature as shown in the following table.

Summer position	–	*above 10°C (50°F)*
Intermediate position	–	*10°C to –5° (50°F to 23°F)*
Winter position	–	*below –5°C (23°F)*

4 In terms of fuel economy the engine will run most efficiently with the valve set in the summer position and least efficiently in the winter position. Providing the engine is running smoothly, and accelerates evenly, the summer position may be retained down to 0°C (32°F). If roughness or hesitation occurs, move the flap valve to the next position.
5 The three positions are shown on the air cleaner cover. In the winter position only hot air from the hot air box on the exhaust manifold enters the air cleaner. In the summer position only cold from the air cleaner intake spout enters. In the intermediate position a blended supply from both sources enters the air cleaner.

OHC models

6 A thermostatically controlled air cleaner is used to regulate the temperature of the air entering the carburettor according to ambient temperatures and engine load. The air cleaner has two sources of supply, through the normal intake spout (cold air) or from a hot air box mounted on the exhaust manifold (hot air).
7 The airflow through the air cleaner is controlled by a flap valve in the air cleaner spout, which covers or exposes the hot or cold air ports according to temperature and manifold vacuum.
8 A vacuum motor operates the flap valve and holds it fully open when the temperature in the air cleaner is below a predetermined level. As the air intake temperature rises the vacuum motor opens or closes the flap valve dependent entirely on manifold vacuum. Thus, during light or constant throttle applications, the flap valve will remain open, supplying the carburettor with hot air, and will close under heavy throttle application so that only cold air enters the carburettor.
9 As the temperature in the air cleaner rises further the vacuum motor closes the flap valve therefore allowing only cold air to enter the carburettor under all operating conditions.
10 The vacuum motor is operated by vacuum created in the inlet manifold and is controlled by a temperature sensing unit located inside the air cleaner.

Fig. 3.1 Air cleaner seasonal adjustment control (arrowed) – OHV only (Sec 5)

6 Air cleaner – servicing, removal and refitting

Servicing

Carburettor models

1 To remove the air cleaner element, remove the cover (secured by one or more nuts or screws near the centre, and/or spring clips round the edge). Lift out the element (photo). If the element is not symmetrical, note which way up it is fitted.
2 Wipe clean inside the air cleaner, being careful not to introduce dirt into the carburettor throat. It is preferable to remove the air cleaner completely. Remember to clean the inside of the cover.
3 Fit the new element and refit and secure the cover. Observe any cover-to-body alignment lugs or slots (photo).

Fuel injection models

4 Release the locking clip and disconnect the plug from the airflow meter (photos). Disconnect the air trunking.

6.1 Removing an air cleaner element – carburettor model

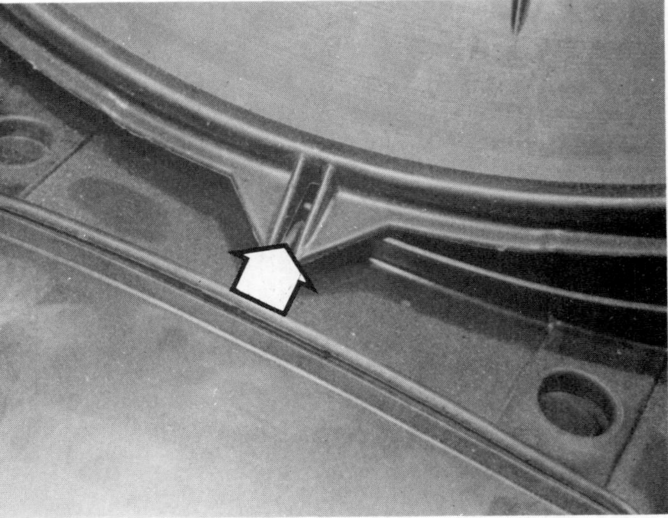

6.3 Air cleaner cover-to-body alignment slot and lug (arrowed)

5 Release the spring clips and lift off the air cleaner cover with airflow meter attached. The element will probably come away with the cover (photos). Do not drop or jar the airflow meter.
6 Remove and discard the element. Wipe clean inside the cover and housing.
7 Fit a new element to the cover, engaging the element seal in the cover recess (photo). Refit and secure the cover and reconnect the airflow meter plug. Refit the air trunking.

Removal and refitting

Carburettor models

8 Remove the central nut or screws from the air cleaner cover.
9 Lift the air cleaner off the carburettor, disengaging the hot air pick-up from the manifold shroud and (when applicable) disconnecting the vacuum and breather hoses (photos).
10 Refit in the reverse order to removal, making sure that the gasket or sealing ring is in place on the carburettor.

Fuel injection models

11 Remove the air cleaner element, as previously described, then undo the four screws and remove the housing, disconnect it from the air inlet tube.
12 Refit in the reverse order to removal.

7 Fuel tank – removal and refitting

Note: *Refer to the warning note in Section 1 before proceeding.*
1 Disconnect the battery negative lead. Remove the fuel tank filler cap.

6.4A Releasing the airflow meter plug locking clip

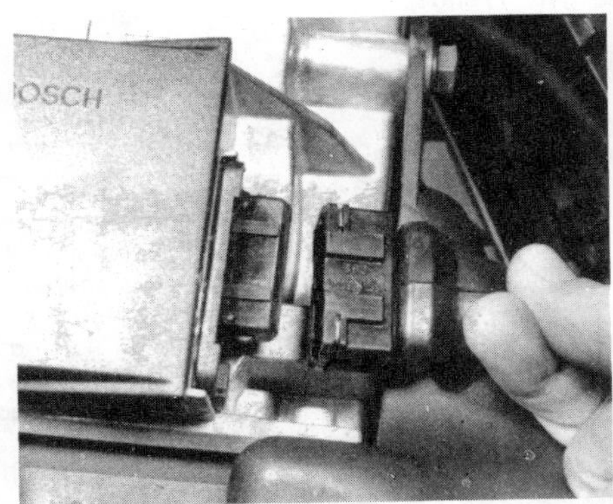

6.4B Disconnecting the airflow meter plug

6.5A Air cleaner cover spring clip

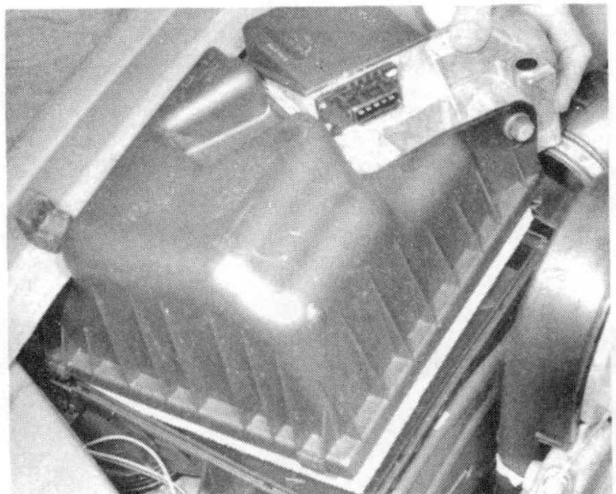
6.5B Removing the air cleaner cover, element and airflow meter

6.7 Fitting a new element to the air cleaner cover

6.9A Hot air pick-up tube (arrowed) engages with air cleaner

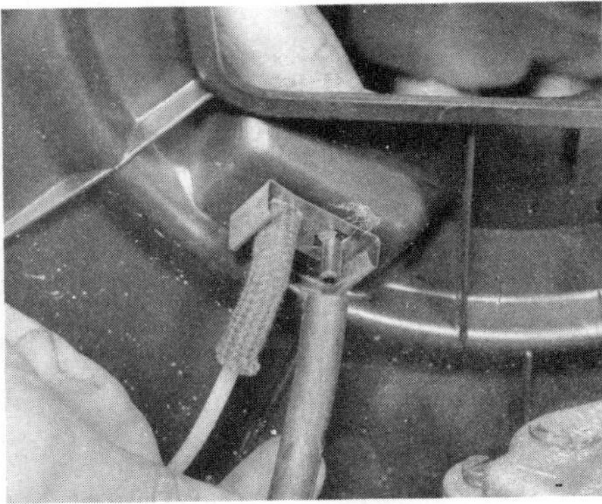
6.9B Air cleaner vacuum hose connection

6.9C Air cleaner breather hose connection

2 A drain plug is not provided and it will therefore be necessary to syphon or hand pump all the fuel from the tank before removal.
3 Having emptied the tank, jack up the rear of the car and support it on axle stands.

Hatchback

4 Refer to Section 33 and remove the exhaust system.
5 Measure and record the length of exposed thread protruding through the handbrake cable adjusting locknut at the compensating yoke on the rear axle.
6 Hold the cable with pliers or a spanner, unscrew the adjusting nut and remove the cable end from the yoke.
7 Remove the retainer and detach the cable from the connecting link located just to the rear of the handbrake lever rod.
8 Detach the cable from its retainers on the fuel tank and underbody and move it clear of the tank.
9 Disconnect the two electrical leads from the fuel gauge sender unit.
10 Remove the single bolt which secures the fuel filler pipe to the underbody.
11 Slacken the hose clips and disconnect the filler pipe from the tank neck (photo). Unclip the vent hose.
12 Support the tank with a jack and suitable blocks of wood, or have an assistant hold it up, then undo the two retaining strap nuts (photo). Pivot the straps out of the way of the tank.

7.11 Fuel tank filler pipe-to-neck junction

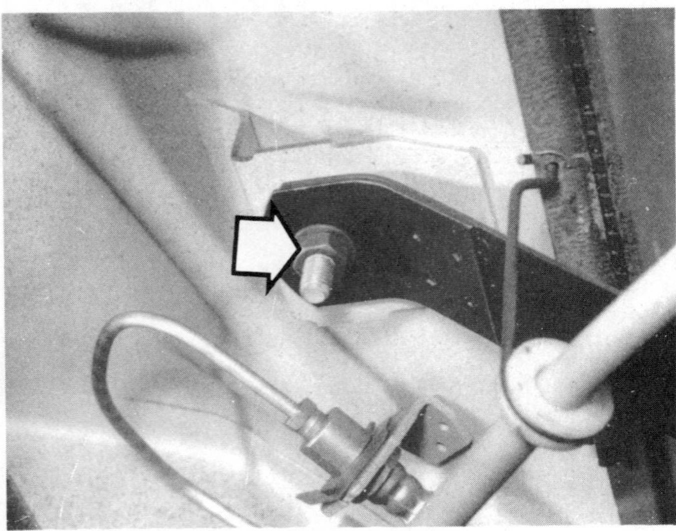

7.12 One of the fuel tank retaining strap nuts (arrowed)

13 Lower the tank slightly and, when sufficient clearance exists, disconnect the overflow and vent hoses from the top of the tank.
14 Lower the tank fully and slide it out from under the car.
15 If the tank is contaminated with sediment or water, remove the sender unit and swill out the tank with clean fuel. If the tank is damaged, or leaks, it should be repaired by a competent specialist or renewed. **Do not** attempt to solder or weld a fuel tank yourself.
16 Refit in the reverse order to removal. Renew hoses, clips etc as necessary, and adjust the handbrake on completion, as described in Chapter 9.

Estate and Van

17 The procedure is similar to that just described, but note the following points:

(a) *The fuel filler pipe must be unscrewed from the rear quarter panel (Fig. 3.2)*
(b) *There is no need to disconnect the handbrake cable or to remove the exhaust system*

8 Fuel gauge sender unit – removal and refitting

1 Proceed as described in Section 7. paragraphs 1 to 3.
2 Disconnect the electrical leads from the sender unit (photo). On fuel injection models, also disconnect the fuel supply hose.
3 On carburettor models, release the sender unit by engaging a flat bar between two of the raised tabs on the unit and turning it anti-clockwise. Apply a releasing agent around the unit if it is reluctant to move. On fuel injection models, remove the securing bolts (photo).
4 Withdraw the sender unit carefully to avoid bending the float arm. Recover the sealing ring.
5 A defective sender unit must be renewed.
6 Refit in the reverse order to removal, using a new sealing ring if necessary.

9 Accelerator cable – removal, refitting and adjustment

Carburettor models

1 Remove the air cleaner as described in Section 6.
2 Extract the spring clip (when fitted) and disconnect the cable ball end from the carburettor throttle lever (photo).

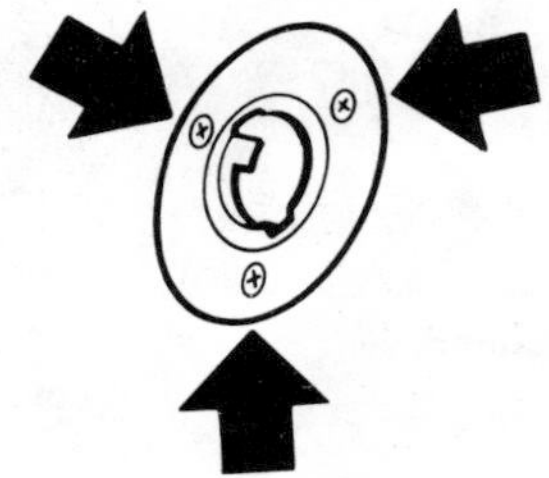

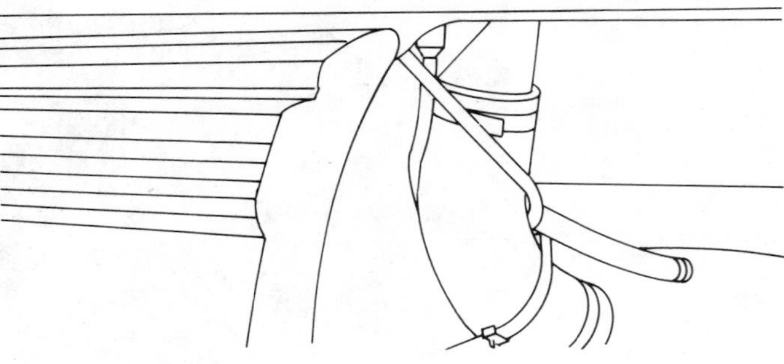

Fig. 3.2 Fuel filler pipe securing screws – Estate (Sec 7)

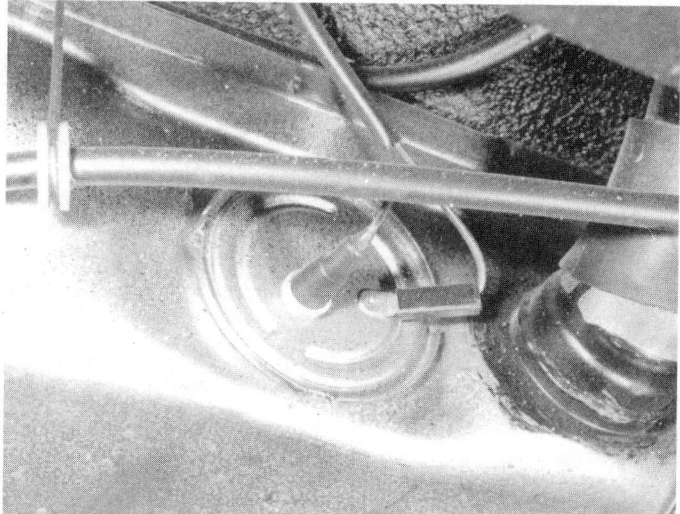
8.2 Fuel gauge sender unit (carburettor models)

8.3 Fuel gauge sender unit (fuel injection model) secured by bolts

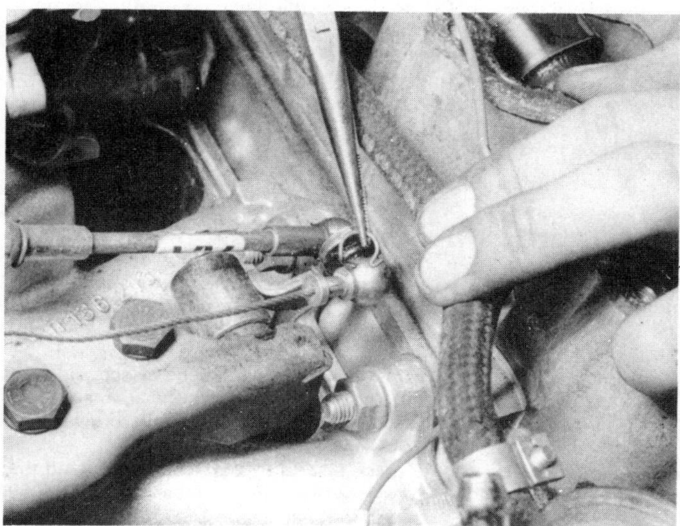
9.2 Accelerator cable ball and spring clip

9.3 Accelerator cable bracket and bush

3 Slide the cable outer bush out of the support bracket on the carburettor (photo).
4 Inside the car, release the cable from the 'keyhole' fitting on the pedal by easing back the spring and prising the cable end out of the slot.
5 Release the grommet from the bulkhead and pull the cable into the engine compartment.
6 Refit in the reverse order to removal. Adjust the cable, by selecting the appropriate position of the spring clip behind the cable outer bush, to give a small amount of free play in the inner cable when the pedal is released.

Fuel injection models

7 The procedure is similar to that just described, but there is no need to remove the air cleaner.
8 Adjust the position of the cable outer securing clip when refitting so that, with the pedal released, there is a barely perceptible amount of slack in the inner.

10 Accelerator pedal – removal and refitting

1 If necessary, remove the under-dash trim on the driver's side to improve access.
2 Disconnect the accelerator cable from the pedal, as described in Section 9.
3 Prise the spring clip off the end of the accelerator pivot. Remove the pedal, recovering any spacers, washers, bushes etc, and unhooking the pedal return spring.
4 Refit in the reverse order to removal. Adjust the accelerator cable if necessary on completion, as described in Section 9.

11 Choke cable – removal, refitting and adjustment

1 Disconnnect the battery earth lead.
2 Tap out the small pin which secures the choke control knob to the cable end fitting. Unscrew and remove the knob.

3 Undo the retaining ring or nut which secures the choke control to the facia. Push the control into the facia and disconnect the warning light switch (when fitted).
4 Remove the air cleaner, as described in Section 6.
5 Disconnect the choke inner and outer cable from the carburettor (photo). On some carburettors the inner cable is secured by a grub screw which must be undone with an Allen key.
6 Release the bulkhead grommet and remove the cable.
7 Refit in the reverse order to removal. Adjust the positions of the inner and outer cables at the carburettor so that, with the control knob pushed home, there is a small amount of slack in the inner cable.

11.5 Choke cable inner clamp screw (arrowed) – Varajet carburettor

12 Carburettor – description

Several types and makes of carburettor are fitted to the vehicles covered by this manual. All are of the downdraught type.

The 32 TL carburettor fitted to the 1.2 engine is a fixed jet, single barrel instrument. The 35 PDSI fitted to low compression versions of the 1.3 engine is similar.

The 2E3 carburettor fitted to normal compression versions of the 1.3 engine is a fixed jet, twin barrel instrument. Opening of the throttle valves is sequential; the primary throttle valve is opened mechanically, but the secondary throttle valve is opened by vacuum developed in both venturis. Primary and secondary transition systems, and a part load enrichment valve, ensure efficient operation under all speed and load conditions.

The GM Varajet II carburettor fitted to 1.6 models is also a twin barrel type, but the main fuel jet is controlled by a tapered needle valve. The design is well proven and has been used on several earlier models.

All carburettors have a bypass system for providing idle mixture, and an accelerator pump for mixture enrichment when the throttle is opened rapidly.

When an automatic choke is fitted, the choke cover is heated electrically when the engine is running; as the cover warms up, the choke is released. On the 2E3 carburettor the choke cover is also heated by engine coolant. Both types of automatic choke need to be 'primed' by depressing and releasing the accelerator pedal before starting the engine from cold.

13 Carburettor adjustments – general

1 Before attempting to adjust the carburettor, make sure that the ignition system is in good order, the air cleaner element is clean and that the engine itself is in good mechanical condition.
2 Some adjustment screws or orifices may be protected by 'tamperproof' plugs, caps or seals. The purpose of tamperproofing is to discourage, and to detect, adjustment by unqualified operators. In some EEC countries (though not yet in the UK) it is an offence to drive a vehicle without the necessary tamperproof devices fitted. Satisfy yourself that current leglislation permits the removal of tamperproof devices before making adjustments, and fit new devices on completion when this is required. Note that removal of tamperproof devices may also invalidate any warranty, when applicable.

14 Carburettor – idle speed and mixture adjustments

1 An adequate tachometer (rev counter) and an exhaust gas analyser (CO meter), or other proprietary mixture indicating device, will be needed for accurate adjustment.
2 Refer to Section 13. Make sure also that the engine is at operating temperature, that the choke is fully off and that the accelerator cable is correctly adjusted.
3 Adjustment should be made with the air cleaner fitted, although this has been removed for clarity in the accompanying illustrations.
4 Connect the tachometer and exhaust gas analyser as instructed by the instrument makers. Start the engine and allow it to idle.
5 Read the idle speed on the tachometer and compare it with the value given in the Specifications. If adjustment is necessary, turn the idle speed adjustment screw until the speed is correct. Refer to Fig. 3.3, or to the appropriate photo, for the location of the screw.
6 If the idle mixture (CO level) is within limits, no further action is necessary. If the mixture is outside the specified limits, turn the idle mixture adjustment screw until it is correct (photos).
7 When the mixture is correctly adjusted, readjust the idle speed if necessary, then recheck the mixture adjustment.
8 When both adjustments are correct, switch off the engine and disconnect the test gear. Fit a new tamperproof seal to the mixture adjustment screw where this is required by law.

Basic idle setting

9 If, on 32 TL and Varajet II carburettors, the specified idle speed and mixture cannot be achieved, as just described, the basic idle setting should be checked. This is not a routine operation and should only be necessary when setting up a carburettor from scratch.
10 Connect a vacuum gauge to the distributor vacuum take-off point on the carburettor.
11 Allow the engine to idle and reduce the idle speed by screwing the idle sped adjusting screw fully home. Do not force the screw onto its seat or it may be damaged. Adjust the idle mixture screw to give a CO level of 1 to 2%.
12 At this point the engine speed should be 550 to 650 rpm, and the vacuum gauge should indicate between 1 and 20 mbar (0.03 and 0.59 in Hg). If not, break the tamperproof valve stop screw and adjust the

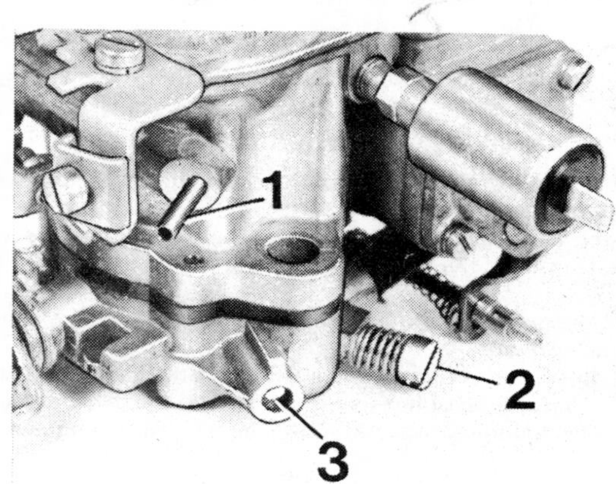

Fig. 3.3 Idle adjustment points – 35 PDSI carburettor (Sec 14)

1 Distributor vacuum take-off
2 Idle speed adjustment screw
3 Idle mixture adjustment screw

14.5A Idle speed adjustment screw (arrowed) – 32 TL carburettor

14.5B Idle speed adjustment screw (arrowed) – 2E3 carburettor

14.5C Adjusting the idle speed – Varajet carburettor

14.6A Idle mixture adjustment screw (arrowed) – 32 TL carburettor

14.6B Idle mixture adjustment screw under tamperproof plug (arrowed) – 2E3 carburettor

14.6C Adjusting the idle mixture – Varajet carburettor

14.12A Throttle valve stop screw (arrowed) – 32 TL carburettor

14.12B Throttle valve stop screw under tamperproof cap (arrowed) – Varajet carburettor

screw, aiming for 600 rpm and 10 mbar (0.3 in Hg) (photos).

13 Disconnect the vacuum gauge and reconnect the distributor pipe.

14 Repeat the normal idle adjustments described earlier in this Section to bring the speed and mixture back within specified limits.

15 Disconnect the test gear and fit new tamperproof caps, where required.

15 32 TL carburettor – other adjustments

Note: *Under normal operating conditions only the carburettor idle adjustments described in Section 14 will need attention. Checking and adjustment of the following settings is not a routine operation and should only be necessary after carburettor overhaul or if the operation of the carburettor is suspect.*

Fast idle

1 This operation may be carried out with the carburettor installed or removed.

2 If the carburettor is removed, rotate the choke linkage on the side of the carburettor until the linkage arm is against its stop and the choke valve is fully closed.

3 With the linkage held in this position a small drill bit, of diameter equal to the fast idle valve gap given in the Specifications, should just slide between the throttle valve and the carburettor barrel (photo).

4 If adjustment is necessary slacken the locknut on the fast idle

15.3 Using a drill bit to check the fast idle gap

15.4 Fast idle adjusting screw (arrowed)

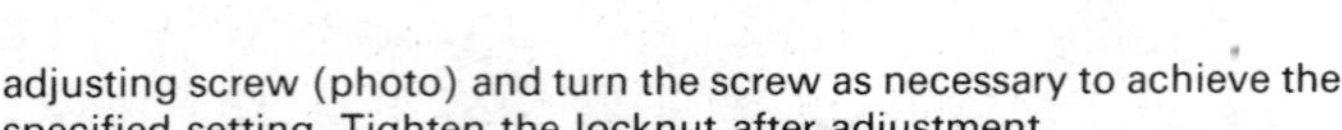

adjusting screw (photo) and turn the screw as necessary to achieve the specified setting. Tighten the locknut after adjustment.

5 If the carburettor is in the car, first allow the engine to reach normal operating temperature and then if necessary adjust the idle speed, as described in Section 14. Also make sure that, when the choke knob is pulled fully out, the linkage rotates to the fully closed position with the linkage arm against its stop. If necessary adjust the choke cable, as described in Section 11.

6 Connect a tachometer to the engine in accordance with the manufacturer's instructions.

7 Start the engine and, with the choke knob pulled fully out, compare the engine speed with the fast idle speed setting given in the Specifications. If adjustment is necessary slacken the locknut and turn the fast idle adjusting screw to achieve the specified speed. Tighten the locknut after adjustment.

8 Switch off the engine and disconnect the tachometer.

Choke valve gap

9 Run the engine until normal operating temperature is reached and then switch off and remove the air cleaner.

10 Pull the choke knob fully out and check that the linkage rotates to the fully closed position with the linkage arm against its stop. If necessary adjust the choke cable, as described in Section 11.

11 With the choke knob still pulled out, start the engine and check that a drill of diameter equal to the choke valve gap dimension will just slide between the valve and choke barrel (photo). If necessary slacken the locknut and turn the adjusting screw above the vacuum unit until the correct gap is achieved (photo).

12 Switch off the engine, tighten the locknut and refit the air cleaner.

Accelerator pump delivery

13 With the carburettor installed, and the air cleaner removed, start the engine and allow it to idle for a few seconds, then switch it off.

14 Look down the carburettor barrel and open the throttle by hand. As the throttle is opened, a squirt of petrol should emerge from the accelerator pump jet. If no petrol is delivered, the pump is faulty or the jet is blocked.

15 The above check only serves to show whether or not the pump is working. For an accurate check, the carburettor must be removed.

16 With the carburettor assembled and the float chamber full of fuel, place the carburettor over a measuring cylinder. Take appropriate fire precautions.

17 Operate the throttle over its full stroke 10 times, taking about 3 seconds per stroke. Catch the fuel delivered by the pump in the measuring cylinder. The desired delivery is given in the Specifications. No adjustment is possible: cleaning or renewal of the pump components will be necessary if the delivery is incorrect.

15.11A Using a drill bit to check the choke valve gap

15.11B Choke valve gap adjusting screw (arrowed)

16 35 PDSI carburettor – other adjustments

1 Refer to the note at the beginning of Section 15.

Fast idle

2 The fast idle system comes into play when the choke control is operated. It is adjusted by a screw which acts on the throttle spindle lever ((Fig. 3.4).

3 Adjustment is correct when, with the choke control pushed in and the throttle released, the end of the screw is just in contact with the lever.

Accelerator pump delivery

4 The stroke of the accelerator pump can be adjusted by turning a nut on the end of the pump operating rod (Fig. 3.5). The desired delivery is given in the Specifications.

5 Apart from the above points, the procedure is as described in Section 15, paragraphs 13 to 17.

6 Check that the stream of fuel ejected from the accelerator pump delivery tube hits the throttle valve shaft. Adjust if necessary by careful bending of the delivery tube.

Fig. 3.4 Fast idle adjustment screw (arrowed) – 35 PDSI carburettor (Sec 16)

17 2E3 carburettor – other adjustments

1 Refer to the note at the beginning of Section 15.

Adjustments with carburettor fitted

Fast idle

2 The engine must be at operating temperature and the idle speed and mixture must be correctly adjusted. Remove the air cleaner to improve access.

3 Position the fast idle adjustment screw on the second highest step of the fast idle cam. Connect a tachometer to the engine. Make sure that the choke plate is fully open.

4 Start the engine without touching the throttle pedal and compare the engine speed with that given in Specifications. If adjustment is necessary, remove the tamperproof cap from the head of the fast idle screw by crushing it with pliers and adjust by means of the screw (photo).

5 When adjustment is correct, stop the engine and disconnect the tachometer. Fit a new tamperproof cap where this is required by law.

Choke pull-down

6 Remove the air cleaner.

7 Remove the choke cover by removing the three screws and the securing ring. There is no need to disconnect the coolant hoses, just

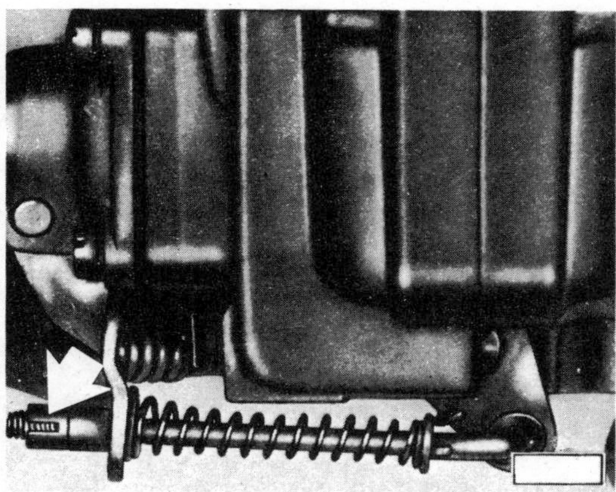

Fig. 3.5 Accelerator pump rod and adjusting nut (arrowed) – 35 PDSI carburettor (Sec 16)

17.4 Fast idle adjustment screw under tamperproof cap (arrowed)

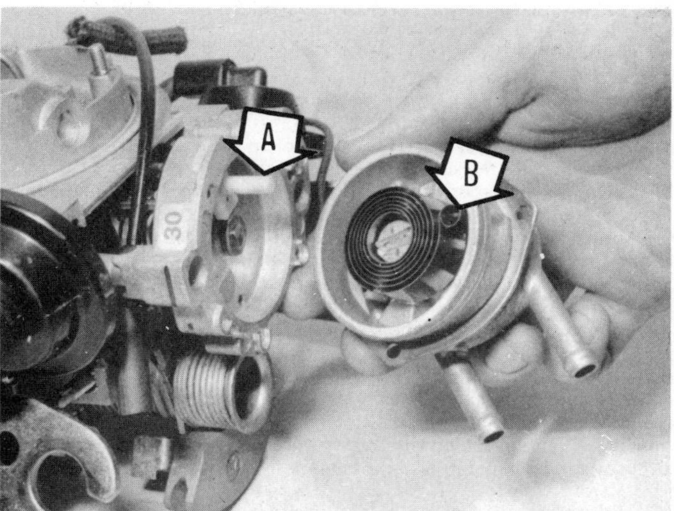

17.7 Choke drive lever (A) engages with loop (B)

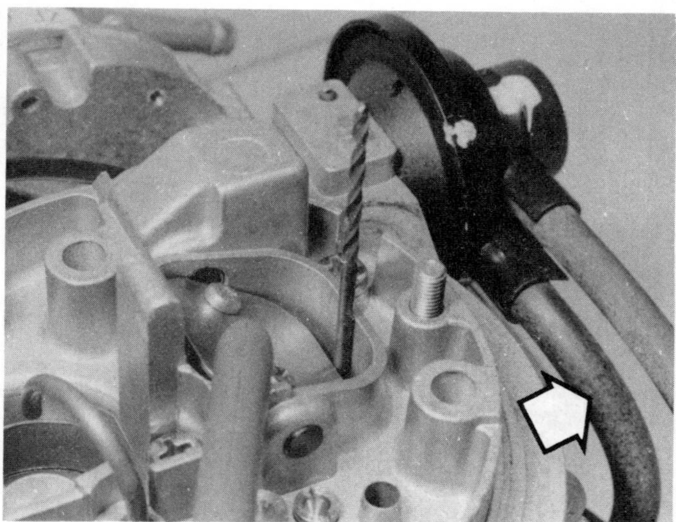
17.9 Checking the choke pull-down gap with a twist drill. Apply vacuum to hose arrowed

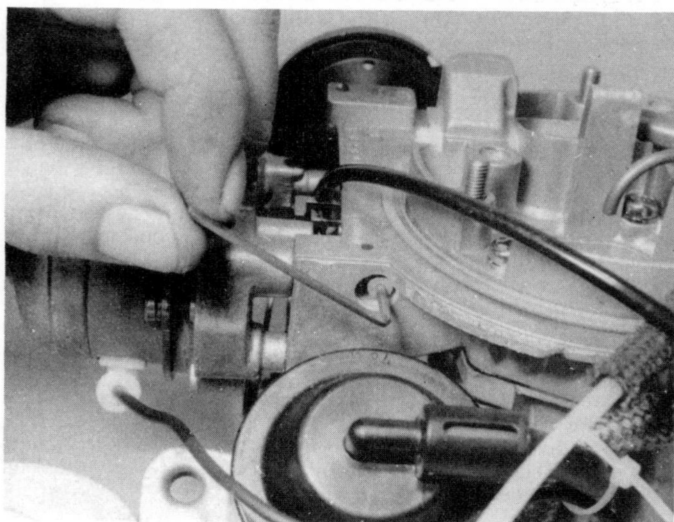
17.10 Choke pull-down adjusting screw

17.11 Choke cover alignment marks (arrowed)

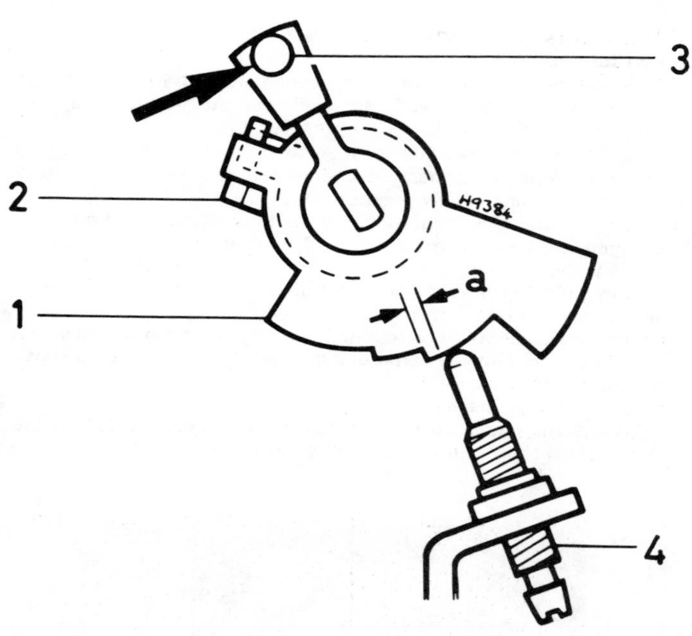

Fig. 3.6 Fast idle cam adjustment – 2E3 carburettor (Sec 17)

1 *Fast idle cam*
2 *Adjustment lever*
3 *Choke drive lever (press in direction arrowed)*
4 *Fast idle adjustment screw*
a *= 0.2 to 0.8 mm (0.008 to 0.032 in)*

move the cover aside. Notice how the loop in the end of the bi-metallic spring engages in the choke drive lever (photo).
8 Move the choke drive lever to close the choke valve completely. Position the fast idle screw on the highest step of the cam.
9 Apply vacuum to the choke pull-down unit (at the hose nearest the carburettor body) using a modified bicycle pump or similar item. Apply light pressure to the choke drive lever in a clockwise direction (as if to close the choke valve) and check the choke valve gap by inserting a gauge rod or twist drill of the specified size (photo).
10 If adjustment is necessary, turn the adjusting screw on the side of the choke housing (photo).
11 Refit the choke cover, making sure that the spring loop engages in the choke drive lever. Align the notches in the choke cover and choke housing when tightening the screws (photo).
12 This adjustment can also be done with the carburettor removed.

Adjustments with carburettor removed

Fast idle cam position

13 The choke pull-down adjustment previously described must be correct.
14 If not already done, remove the choke cover.
15 Open the throttle, then close the choke valve by light finger pressure on the choke drive lever. Release the throttle.
16 Check that the fast idle adjustment screw is resting on the second highest step of the fast idle cam, in the position shown in Fig. 3.6. If not, first check that the choke return spring is correctly positioned, then adjust by bending the lever 2 (Fig. 3.6).
17 Refit and secure the choke cover, observing the alignment marks.

Throttle valve fast idle gap

18 Position the fast idle adjustment screw on the highest step of the fast idle cam.

19 Use a gauge rod or twist drill of the specified diameter to measure the opening of the primary throttle valve. Adjust if necessary at the fast idle adjustment screw. (This is a preliminary adjustment; final adjustment of the fast idle speed should take place with the engine running.)

Accelerator pump delivery

20 It will be necessary to feed the float chamber with fuel from a small reservoir during this test. Take all necessary fire precautions when dealing with fuel and fuel vapour.

21 Position the primary barrel over an accurate measuring glass. Fully open and close the throttle ten times, taking approximately one second for each opening and pausing for three seconds after each return stroke. Make sure that the fast idle cam is not restricting throttle travel at either end.

22 Measure the quantity of fuel delivered and compare it with the specified value.

23 If adjustment is necessary, release the clamp screw and turn the cam plate in the desired direction (photo). Tighten the clamp screw and recheck the pump delivery.

17.23 Accelerator pump delivery adjustment: '+' to increase, '–' to decrease

18 Varajet II carburettor – other adjustments

1 Refer to the note at the beginning of Section 15.

Automatic choke carburettor

Fast idle speed

2 The engine must be at operating temperature and normal idle adjustments must be correct. The air cleaner must be removed and its vacuum hose plugged.

3 Connect a tachometer to the engine.

4 Slightly open the throttle valve plate so that the fast idle adjusting screw can be positioned on the second step of the cam (Fig. 3.7).

5 Start the engine without touching the accelerator. The engine speed should be as specified; if not, turn the fast idle adjusting screw as necessary.

Choke pull-down (gap A)

6 In order to be able to carry out this adjustment, a suitable vacuum pump must be available. It is possible to create sufficient vacuum using a modified hand pump or by making a connection with a rubber hose or plastic tube between the choke vacuum unit of the carburettor and the inlet manifold of another vehicle (engine running).

7 Remove the air cleaner.

8 Position the fast idle screw on the uppermost step of the cam. Check that the choke valve plate is fully closed. This may not be the case if the choke cover is still warm, in which case use a rubber band to close it.

9 Apply vacuum to the choke vacuum unit as described in paragraph 6.

10 Refer to Fig. 3.9. Measure the gap A between the edge of the choke valve plate and the wall of the carburettor. Measure at the flatter side of the valve plate. A twist drill or similar should be used as a gauge. The gap should be as specified.

11 If necessary, turn the screw B to bring the gap to the specified clearance. If the gap was found to be too small, it will probably be necessary to bend the pullrod slightly to provide sufficient clearance for movement of the adjustment screw.

12 On completion of adjustment, lock the adjustment screw with a drop of suitable sealant.

Fig. 3.7 Fast idle screw (arrowed) positioned on cam second highest step (Sec 18)

Fig. 3.8 Using a rubber band to close the choke valve plate (Sec 18)

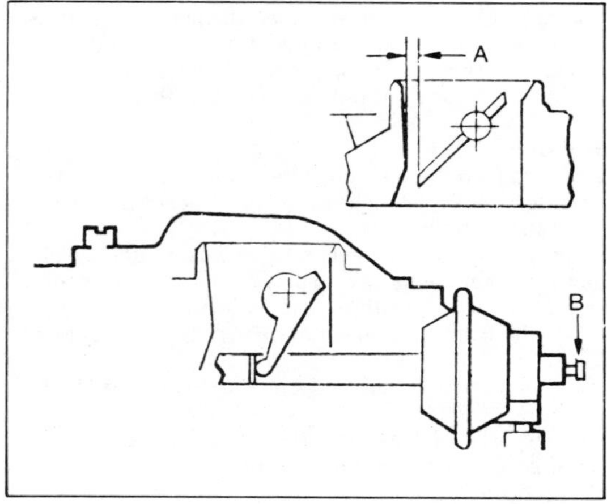

Fig. 3.9 Choke pull-down measurement – Varajet carburettor (Sec 18)

A See Specifications (choke valve gap A) *B Adjustment screw*

13 Now check the play between the baffle flap lever and the pullrod with the vacuum source still connected so that the pullrod is in the fully extended position (Fig. 3.10). The clearance A must be as shown. Where necessary, bend the end of the pullrod to bring the clearance within tolerance.

Choke fast idle (gap B)

14 Close the choke valve with a rubber band.

15 Open the throttle and position the fast idle screw on the second highest step of the fast idle cam. Release the throttle and check that the screw stays on the step.

16 Open the choke valve slightly and release it in order to let it find its correct position. Check the choke valve gap B by the same method as when checking the pull-down gap.

17 If adjustment is necessary, remove the carburettor and take off the choke cover. Bend the rod which connects the fast idle cam to the choke valve lever until the gap is correct.

18 If adjustment has been necessary, recheck the pull-down gap after refitting the carburettor.

Full throttle opening

19 Close the choke valve with a rubber band.

20 Open the throttle fully and hold it open while measuring the choke valve gap C.

21 If adjustment is necessary, carefully bend that part of the linkage shown in Fig. 3.11. Bend the tag to the right to increase the gap, to the left to decrease it.

Automatic choke cover

22 The pointer on the choke housing cover should be set against the mark given in the Specifications. If there is a tendency to stall or hesitate during warm-up, it is permissible to turn the cover through one or two divisions towards R (rich). The clamp ring screws must be slackened to do this.

23 If the ignition is switched on with the engine cold (approx 20°C/68°F), the choke valve should open fully in three to four minutes. If a longer time is required, check the choke valve for free movement; renew the choke cover if the valve is free.

Accelerator pump

24 With the engine at operating temperature and the accelerator released, no clearance should exist between the pump operating lever and the pump plunger.

25 Have an assistant depress the accelerator to its full extent and hold it there. Press the pump plunger with a screwdriver and check that it will move further downwards before resistance is encountered.

26 Bend the pump operating lever as necessary to achieve these conditions.

27 Check that when the pump plunger is depressed, a jet of fuel is delivered towards the inner venturi. If not, dismantle the carburettor and clean or renew the pump components.

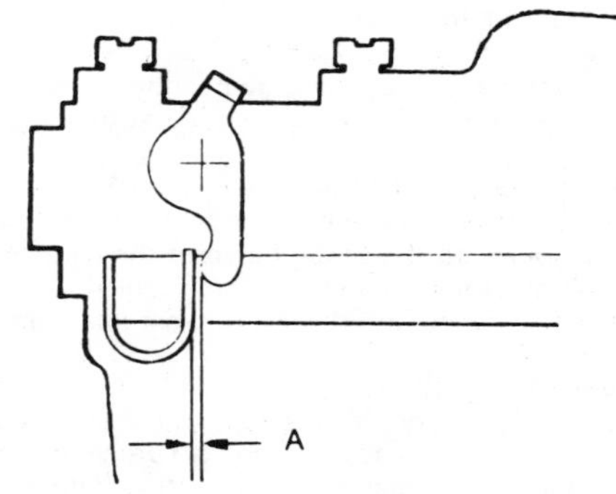

Fig. 3.10 Baffle flap lever-to-pullrod clearance (Sec 18)

A = 0.1 to 0.3 mm (0.004 to 0.012 in)

Fig. 3.11 Varajet carburettor adjustment: bend tag G to adjust choke gap C (not shown) (Sec 18)

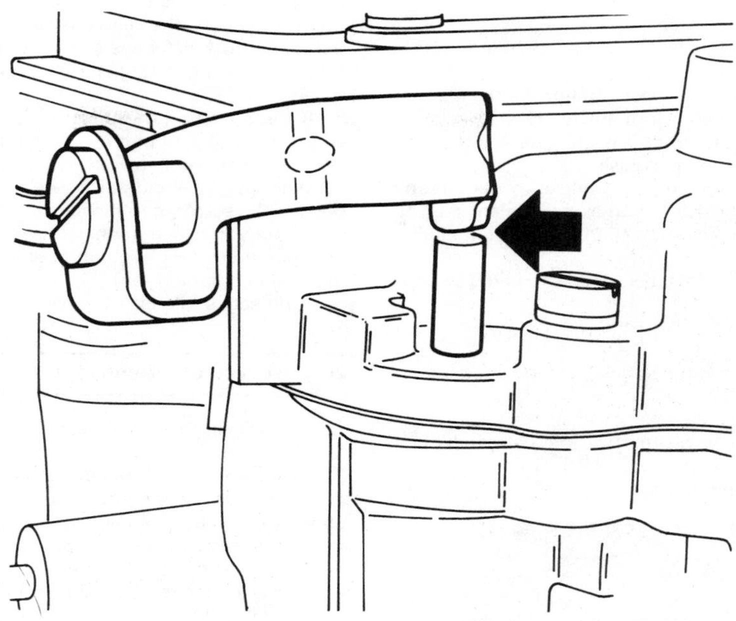

Fig. 3.12 Varajet carburettor accelerator pump operating lever and plunger (arrowed) (Sec 18)

Throttle damper adjustment (automatic transmission only)

28 Automatic transmission models are equipped with a throttle linkage damper, the purpose of which is to stop the throttle snapping shut suddenly when the pedal is released.

29 Correct adjustment of the damper is carried out as follows. Release the damper locknut and unscrew the damper until the damper pin is only just touching the throttle lever. From this position, screw the damper back in between 3 and 4 complete turns, then secure with the locknut.

Part load regulator screw adjustment

30 Problems such as jerking or hesitation at light throttle openings, or excessive fuel consumption despite moderate driving habits, may be due to incorrect adjustment of the part load regulator screw.

31 It is emphasised that this adjustment should not be attempted until

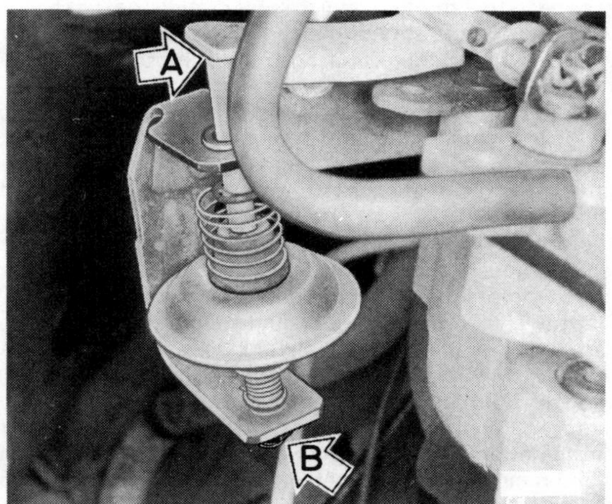

Fig. 3.13 Varajet carburettor throttle damper (Sec 18)

A Damper pin *B Locknut*

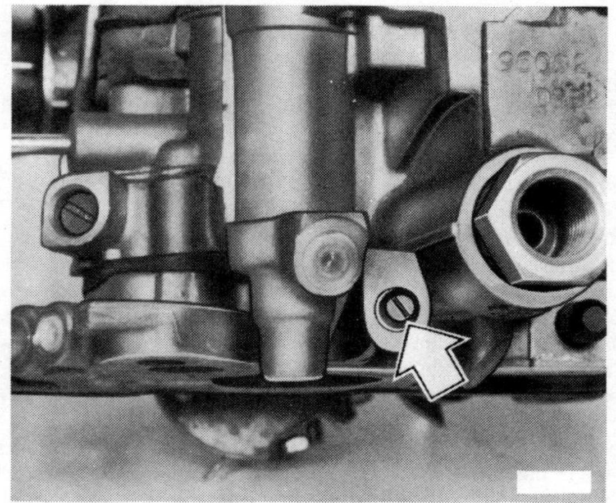

Fig. 3.14 Varajet carburettor: part load regulator screw (arrowed) (Sec 18)

all other possible causes of the problems mentioned have been investigated.
32 Remove the carburettor from the vehicle.
33 Prise out the metal plug covering the part load regulator screw (adjacent to the fuel inlet union).
34 If stalling or hesitation is the reason for adjustment – ie the mixture is too weak – turn the screw one-quarter turn anti-clockwise.
35 If excessive fuel consumption is the problem – ie the mixture is too rich – turn the screw one-quarter turn clockwise.
36 Refit the carburettor and test drive the vehicle to see if any improvement has occurred. If necessary a further adjustment can be made, but **do not** deviate from the original setting by more than half a turn of the screw.
37 Fit a new metal plug on completion, where this is required by law.

Manual choke carburettor

Fast idle speed

38 The idle speed must be correct and the engine must be at operating temperature.
39 Remove the air cleaner and plug its vacuum hose.
40 Pull out the choke until the mark on the fast idle cam is aligned with the tip of the fast idle adjustment screw (Fig. 3.15). Hold the choke valve plate open with a rubber band.

Fig. 3.15 Mark on fast idle cam (arrowed) must be aligned with tip of screw (Sec 18)

41 Connect a tachometer to the engine.
42 Start the engine and check the fast idle speed against that given in the Specifications. If adjustment is necessary, turn the fast idle adjustment screw; the tamperproof cap over the screw head may be removed by crushing it with pliers.
43 Switch off the engine when adjustment is correct. Fit a new tamperproof cap where this is required by law.

Choke pull-down (gap A)

44 Remove the air cleaner.
45 Pull the choke control out fully. Apply vacuum to the choke vacuum unit, as described in paragraph 6. With the vacuum applied, measure gap A (see Fig. 3.9 and Specifications). Correct if necessary by means of the adjusting screw on the vacuum unit.
46 Check the clearance between the baffle flap lever and the pullrod, as described in paragraph 13.

Other adjustments

47 Accelerator pump and part load regulator screw adjustments are as previously described for the automatic choke carburettor. This completes the range of adjustments applicable to the manual choke carburettor.

19 Idle cut-off solenoid – description and testing

1 Some of the carburettors described in this Chapter are fitted with an idle cut-off solenoid. This is an electrically-operated valve which interrupts the idle mixture circuit when the ignition is switched off, thus preventing the engine from running-on.
2 The idle cut-off solenoid is energised all the time that the ignition is switched on. A defective solenoid, or a break in its power supply, will cause the engine to stall or idle roughly, although it will run normally at speed.
3 If the operation of the solenoid is suspect, first check (using a 12 volt test lamp) that battery voltage is present at the solenoid terminal when the ignition is on.
4 With the solenoid unscrewed from the carburettor, connect the body of the solenoid to the negative terminal of a 12 volt battery. When the battery positive terminal is connected to the solenoid centre terminal, there should be an audible click and the needle at the tip of the solenoid should retract.
5 A defective idle cut-off solenoid must be renewed.

20 Carburettor – removal and refitting

1 Disconnect the battery earth lead.
2 Remove the air cleaner, as described in Section 6.
3 Disconnect the choke cable (manual choke models) or the automatic choke electrical and/or coolant connections. Plug the coolant hoses to avoid spillage.
4 Disconnect the fuel supply hose from the carburettor or vapour separator. Be prepared for fuel spillage. On carburettors with a fuel return hose attached, disconnect that too. Plug the fuel hoses.
5 Disconnect the accelerator cable, as described in Section 9.
6 Disconnect the distributor vacuum hose.
7 Disconnect the idle cut-off solenoid wire (when fitted).
8 Disconnect any remaining hoses or wires, then remove the securing nuts and lift the carburettor off its studs. Recover the gasket.
9 Refit in the reverse order to removal. Use a new gasket if the old one was damaged.
10 Adjust the accelerator cable and (when fitted) the choke cable, as described in Sections 9 and 11.
11 If coolant hoses were disturbed, check the coolant level after running the engine and top up if necessary.
12 Adjust the idle speed and mixture, as described in Section 14.

21 32 TL carburettor – overhaul

1 Remove the carburettor from the engine.
2 Clean the carburettor externally using a suitable cleaning solvent, or petrol in a well ventilated area. Wipe the carburettor dry with a lint-free cloth and prepare a clean uncluttered working area.
3 Disconnect the throttle return spring from the linkage and the support bracket on the side of the carburettor (photo).
4 Disconnect the vacuum unit hose from the outlet on the throttle valve housing (photo).
5 Undo the four retaining screws and separate the carburettor cover from the float chamber housing (photos).
6 At the base of the carburettor undo the single securing the throttle valve housing to the float chamber housing (photo). Separate the two housings.
7 Undo the screw securing the choke cable support bracket to the throttle valve housing and lift off the bracket. Undo the blanking plug and remove the seal ring from the housing (photo).
8 As a guide to refitting, count and record the number of turns necessary to screw the auxiliary idle mixture screw and the basic idle mixture screw fully into the housing. Now remove the two screws.
9 Undo the four screws and remove the accelerator pump cover, diaphragm, and spring from the float chamber housing (photo).
10 From the other side of the float chamber housing, undo the three screws and remove the enrichment valve cover, diaphragm and spring (photo).
11 Carefully withdraw the fuel discharge nozzle from the housing (photo).
12 Tap the float pivot pin out of the pivot posts and withdraw the pin using long-nosed pliers (photo).
13 Lift out the float and then remove the gasket from the carburettor top cover (photo).
14 Lift out the float needle valve and then unscrew the main jet (photo).

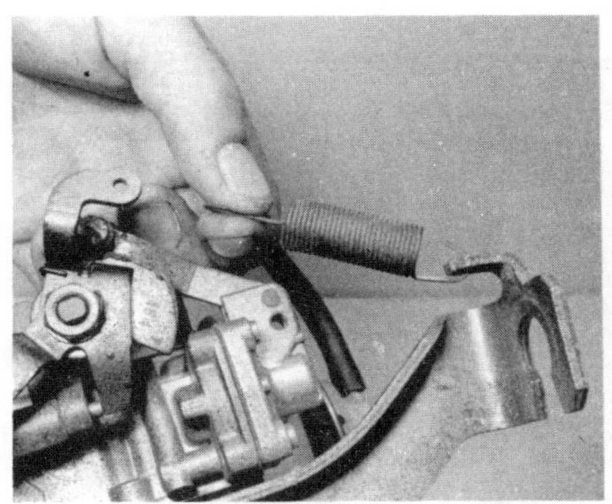
21.3 Removing the throttle return spring

21.4 Disconnecting the vacuum hose

21.5A Four screws (arrowed) securing the carburettor cover to the float chamber housing

21.5B Separating the cover from the float chamber housing

21.6 Undo the screw (arrowed) to separate the throttle valve and float chamber housings

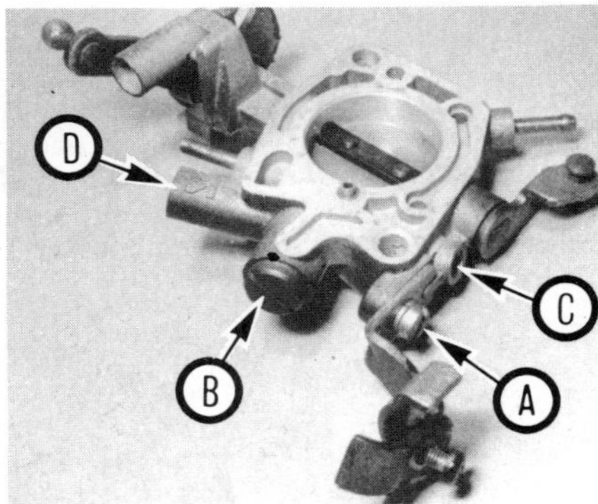

21.7 Throttle valve housing components – support bracket screw (A), blanking plug (B), idle mixture screw (C) and idle speed screw (D)

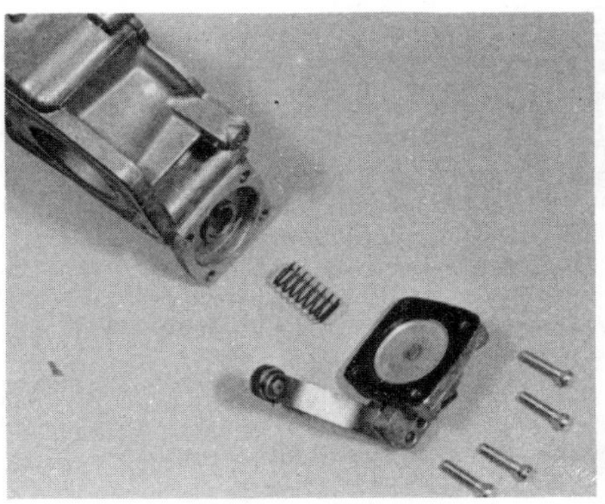
21.9 Accelerator pump components

21.10 Enrichment valve components

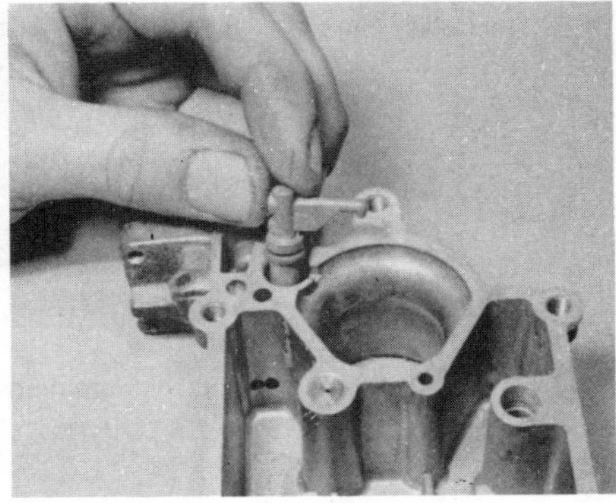
21.11 Removing the fuel discharge nozzle

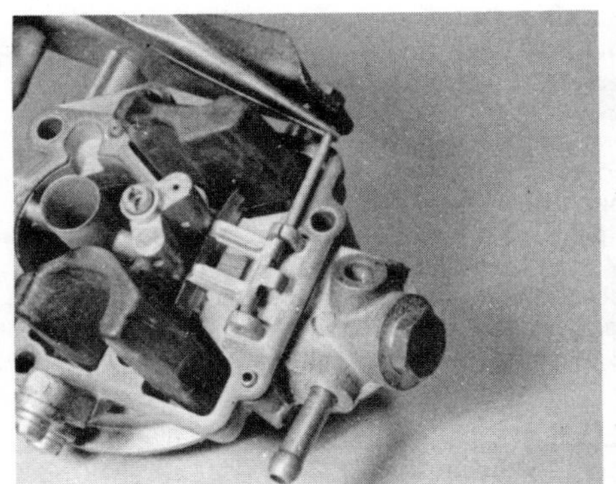
21.12 Extracting the float pivot pin

21.13 Lift off the gasket

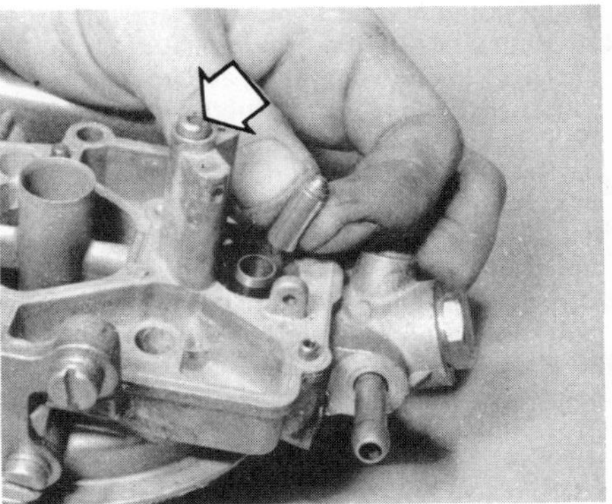
21.14 Removing the float needle valve. Main jet is arrowed

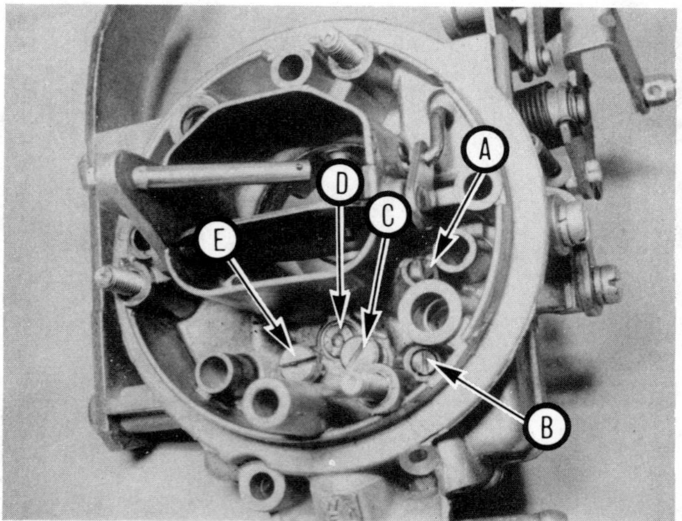

21.15 Plugs (A and B), idle jet (C), air correction jet (D) and auxiliary fuel/air jet (E) in carburettor cover

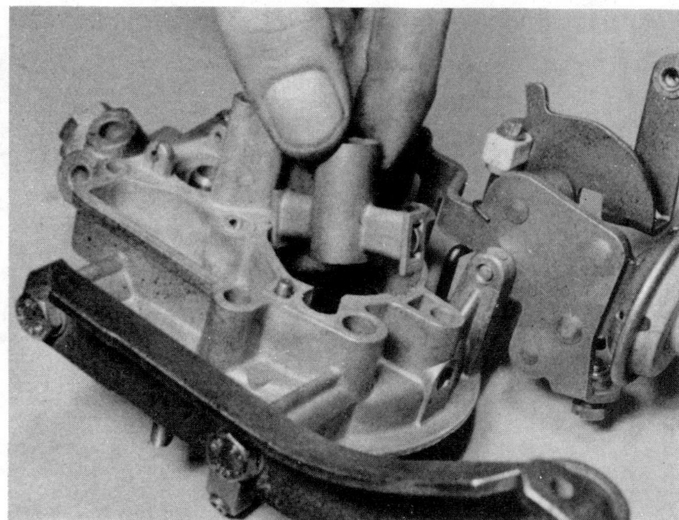
21.16 Removing the pre-atomizer

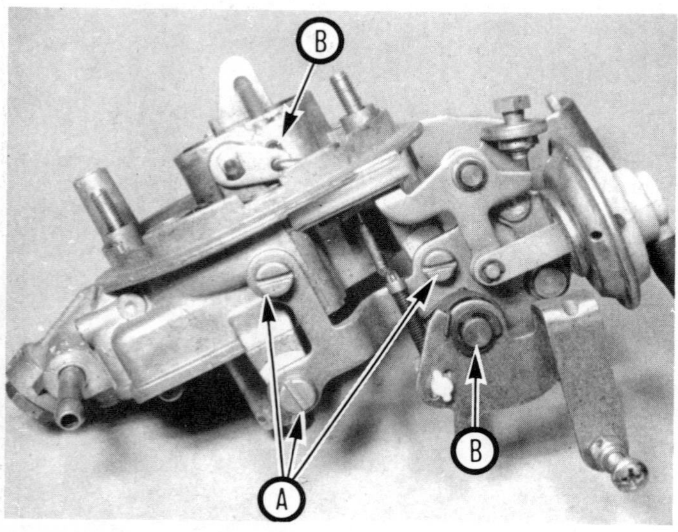

21.18 Choke linkage screws (A) and retaining clips (B)

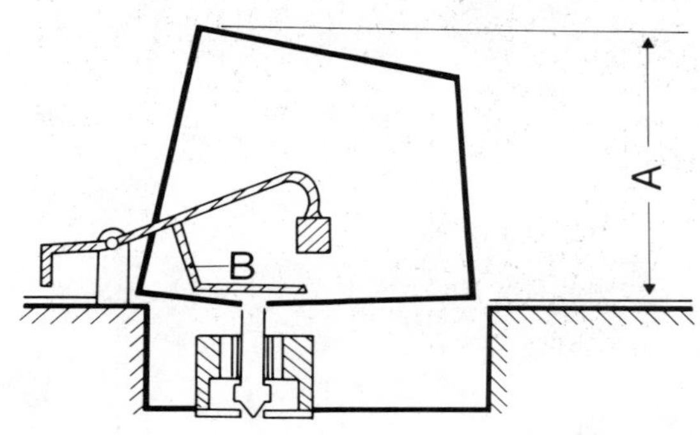

Fig. 3.16 Float level measurement – 32 TL carburettor (Sec 21)

A Measurement point *B Bend here to adjust*

15 Unscrew all the jets and plugs from the carburettor cover, making a careful note of their locations (photo). Remove the mixture tube from the air correction jet bore.
16 Withdraw the pre-atomizer from the top cover venturi (photo).
17 Undo the retaining plug and withdraw the fuel filter adjacent to the inlet hose connection on the top cover.
18 If necessary the choke valve operating linkage and vacuum unit can be removed from the top cover. Undo the three retaining screws and the retaining clips for the operating cam and choke valve rod. Remove the cam and spring, disengage the operating rod from the cam and choke valve lever and withdraw the assembly (photo).
19 With the carburettor now dismantled, clean the components in petrol in a well ventilated area. Allow the parts to air dry.
20 Blow out all the jets and the passages in the housings using compressed air or a tyre foot pump. Never probe with wire.
21 Examine the choke and throttle valve spindles and linkages for wear or excessive side-play. If wear is apparent in these areas it is advisable to obtain an exchange carburettor.
22 Check the diaphragms and renew them if they are punctured or show signs of deterioration.
23 Examine the float for signs of deterioration and shake it, listening for fuel inside. If so renew it, as it is leaking and will give an incorrect float level height causing flooding.
24 Blow through the float needle valve assembly while holding the needle valve closed, then open. Renew the valve if faulty, or as a matter of course if high mileages have been covered.
25 Obtain the new parts as necessary and also a carburettor repair kit which will contain a complete set of gaskets, washers and seals.
26 Reassembly the carburettor using the reverse of the dismantling procedures, but carry out the settings and adjustments described in Section 15 as the work progresses.
27 Check the float level as shown (Fig. 3.16) after refitting the float. Bend the float arm if necessary to achieve the specified level.
28 After refitting the carburettor, carry out the basic idle adjustment described in the second part of Section 14.

22 35 PDSI carburettor – overhaul

1 Major carburettor overhaul is not a routine operation and should only be carried out when components are obviously worn. Removing

of the cover and mopping out the fuel and any sediment from the fuel bowl, and clearing the jets with compressed air is usually sufficient to keep a carburettor in good working order. When a unit has covered a very high mileage, it will probably be more economical to renew it with a new or exchange rebuilt carburettor rather than to renew individual components.
2 With the carburettor removed from the engine and cleaned externally, remove the clip which retains the fast idle rod to the lever on the choke valve plate spindle.
3 Extract the six screws and remove the cover.
4 Use a socket wrench to unscrew the fuel inlet needle valve.
5 Extract the screw plug and withdraw the metering pin.
6 Extract the spring clip and withdraw the float from the carburettor bowl.
7 The part load enrichment valve is screwed into the base of the float bowl.
8 The main jet can be unscrewed if the plug in the float bowl is extracted and a screwdriver inserted through the hole.
9 The throttle valve housing is held to the main body of the carburettor by two securing screws. To remove the housing, first disconnect the accelerator pump link and then extract the screws.
10 The accelerator pump housing can be dismantled by extracting the four pump housing screws.
11 Clean all components and examine for wear or damage.
12 Blow through all jets and passages with air from a tyre pump; never probe them with wire in an attempt to clean them or their calibration will be ruined.
13 Renew all seals, gaskets, diaphragms etc; these will be available in the form of an overhaul kit.
14 No provision is made for float level adjustment, nor is any checking procedure or dimension specified.
15 Reassemble the carburettor in the reverse order to dismantling, observing the settings and adjustments described in Section 16.

Fig. 3.17 Fast idle rod connecting clip (arrowed) – 35 PDSI (Sec 22)

Fig. 3.18 Fuel inlet needle valve (arrowed) – 35 PDSI (Sec 22)

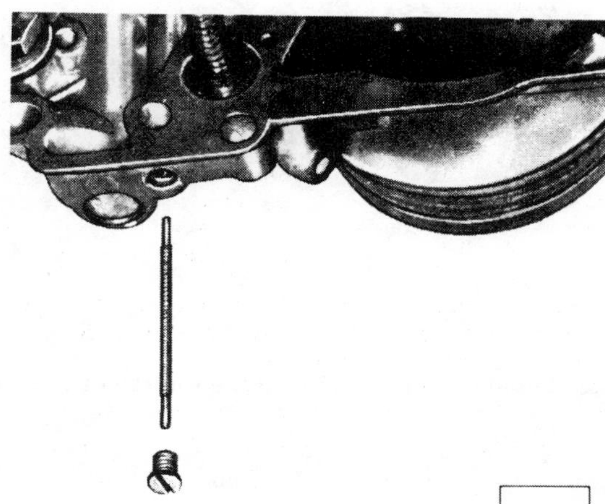

Fig. 3.19 Metering pin and plug – 35 PDSI (Sec 22)

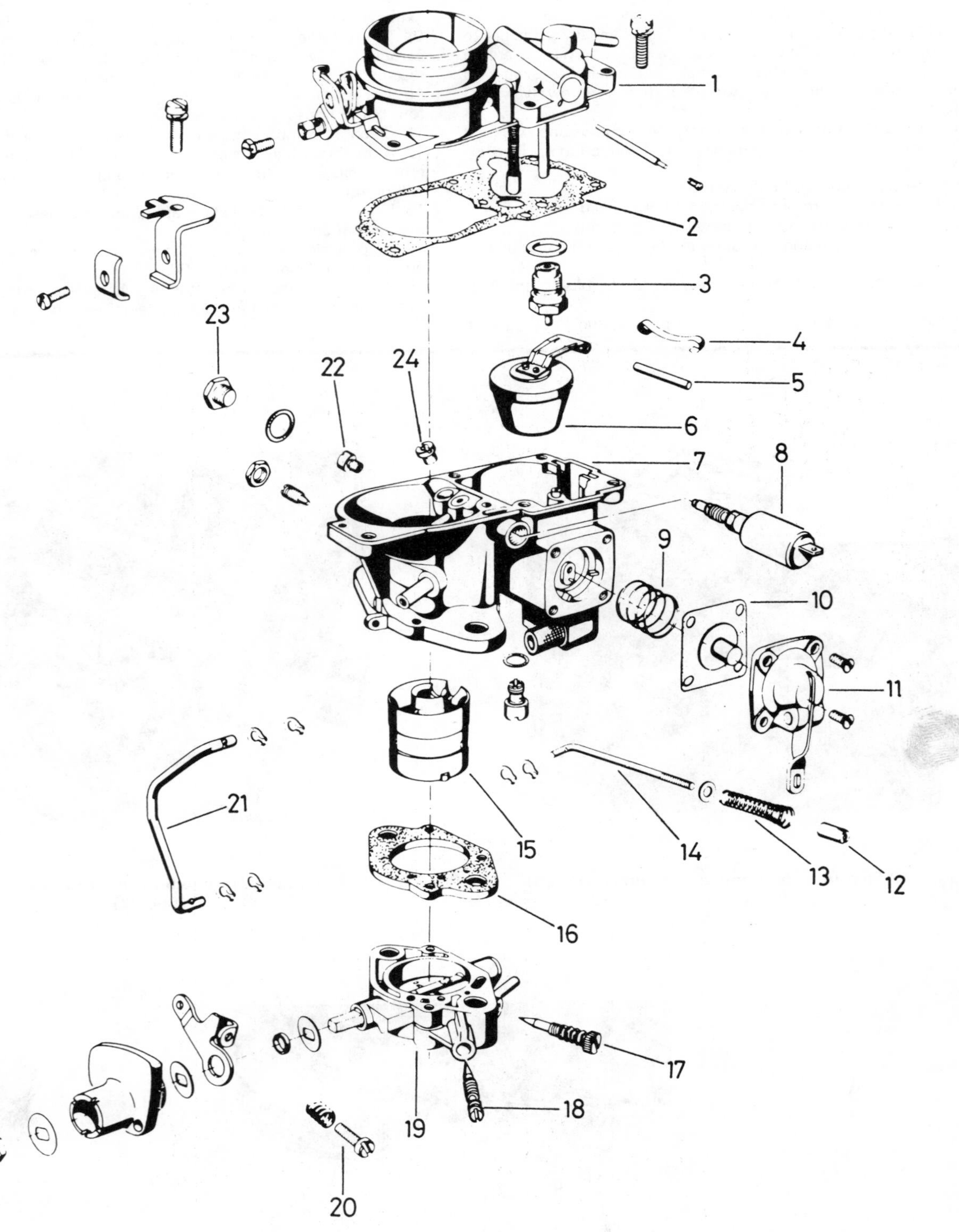

Fig. 3.20 Exploded view of 35 PDSI carburettor (Sec 22)

1 Cover
2 Gasket
3 Fuel inlet needle valve
4 Float pivot pin clip
5 Float pivot pin
6 Float
7 Body
8 Fuel cut-off solenoid valve
9 Accelerator pump diaphragm spring
10 Diaphragm
11 Diaphragm housing cover
12 Accelerator pump rod nut
13 Spring
14 Accelerator pump rod
15 Venturi
16 Gasket
17 Idle speed adjustment screw
18 Idle mixture adjustment screw
19 Throttle valve block
20 Fast idle adjustment screw
21 Fast idle link rod
22 Main jet
23 Main jet plug
24 Part load enrichment valve

23 2E3 carburettor – overhaul

1 With the carburettor removed from the vehicle, drain the fuel from the float chamber and vapour separator. Clean the outside of the carburettor.
2 Remove the hoses and wires from the carburettor, making identifying marks or notes to avoid confusion on reassembly (photos).
3 Access to the jets and float chamber is obtained by removing the top half of the carburettor, which is secured by five screws. Blow through the jets and drillings with compressed air, or air from a foot pump – do not probe them with wire. If it is wished to remove the jets, unscrew them carefully with well-fitting tools.
4 Remove the fuel strainer from the inlet pipe by hooking it out with a small screwdriver, or by snaring it with a long thin screw. Renew the strainer (photo).
5 Clean any foreign matter from the float chamber. Renew the inlet needle valve and seat if wear is evident, or if a high mileage has been covered. Renew the float if it is punctured or otherwise damaged.
6 No procedure has been specified for float level adjustment. Simply check that the inlet needle valve is closed completely before the float reaches the top of its stroke.
7 Renew the diaphragms in the part load enrichment valve and in the accelerator pump. If additional pump or valve parts are supplied in the overhaul kit, renew these parts also.
8 Further dismantling is not recommended. Pay particular attention to the throttle opening mechanism if it is decided to dismantle it: the interlocking arrangement is important.
9 Reassemble in the reverse order to dismantling. Use new gaskets and seals throughout; lubricate linkages with a smear of molybdenum-based grease.
10 Before refitting the carburettor, carry out the checks and adjustments described in Section 17.

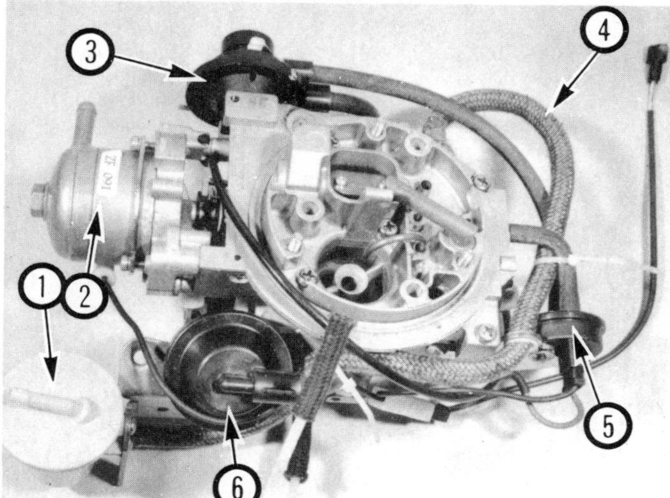

23.2A Top view of 2E3 carburettor

1 Vapour separator
2 Choke cover
3 Choke pull-down unit
4 Fuel hose
5 Thermotime valve
6 Secondary throttle vacuum unit

23.2B 2E3 carburettor – choke cover side view

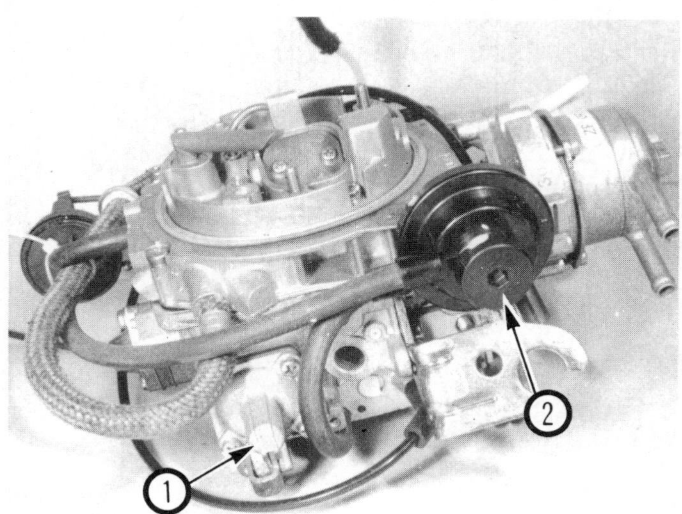

23.2C 2E3 carburettor – side view showing accelerator pump (1) and choke pull-down unit (2)

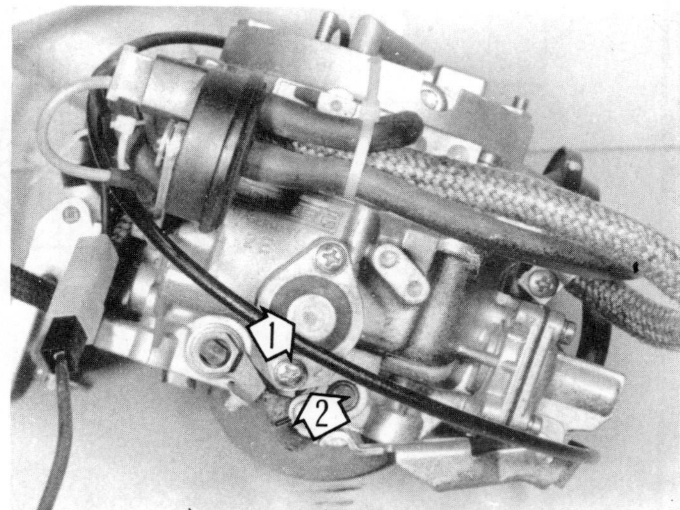

23.2D 2E3 carburettor – side view showing part load enrichment valve (1) and accelerator pump cam (2)

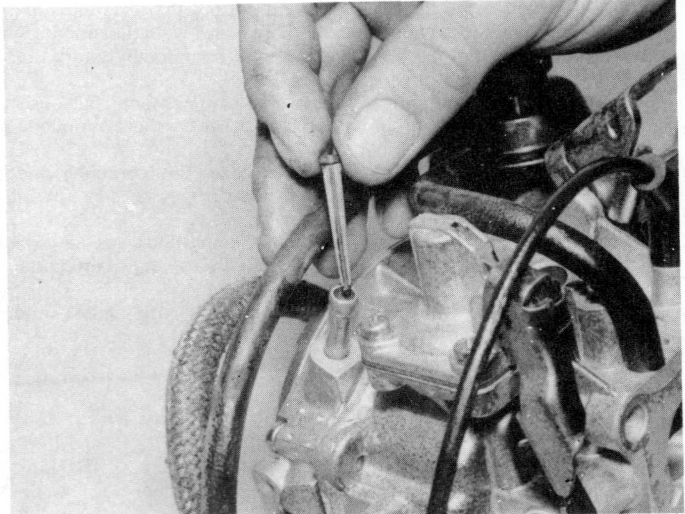

23.4 Fuel inlet fuel strainer – 2E3 carburettor

Fig. 3.21 Sectional view of 2E3 carburettor (Sec 23)

1 Primary throttle valve
2 Idle mixture outlet
3 Idle mixture adjustment screw
4 Transition louvre
5 Not used
6 Not used
7 Not used
8 Carburettor body
9 Gasket
10 Carburettor cover
11 Primary pre-atomizer
12 Choke valve
13 Idle fuel and air jet
14 Primary air correction jet and emulsion tube
15 Secondary air correction jet and emulsion tube
16 Riser tube (secondary full load enrichment)
17 Discharge beak (secondary full load enrichment)
18 Riser tube (secondary transition)
19 Secondary pre-atomizer
20 Secondary transition vent
21 Secondary transition louvre
22 Choke pull-down vacuum take-off
23 Secondary throttle valve
24 Secondary transition jet
25 Secondary main jet
26 Primary main jet

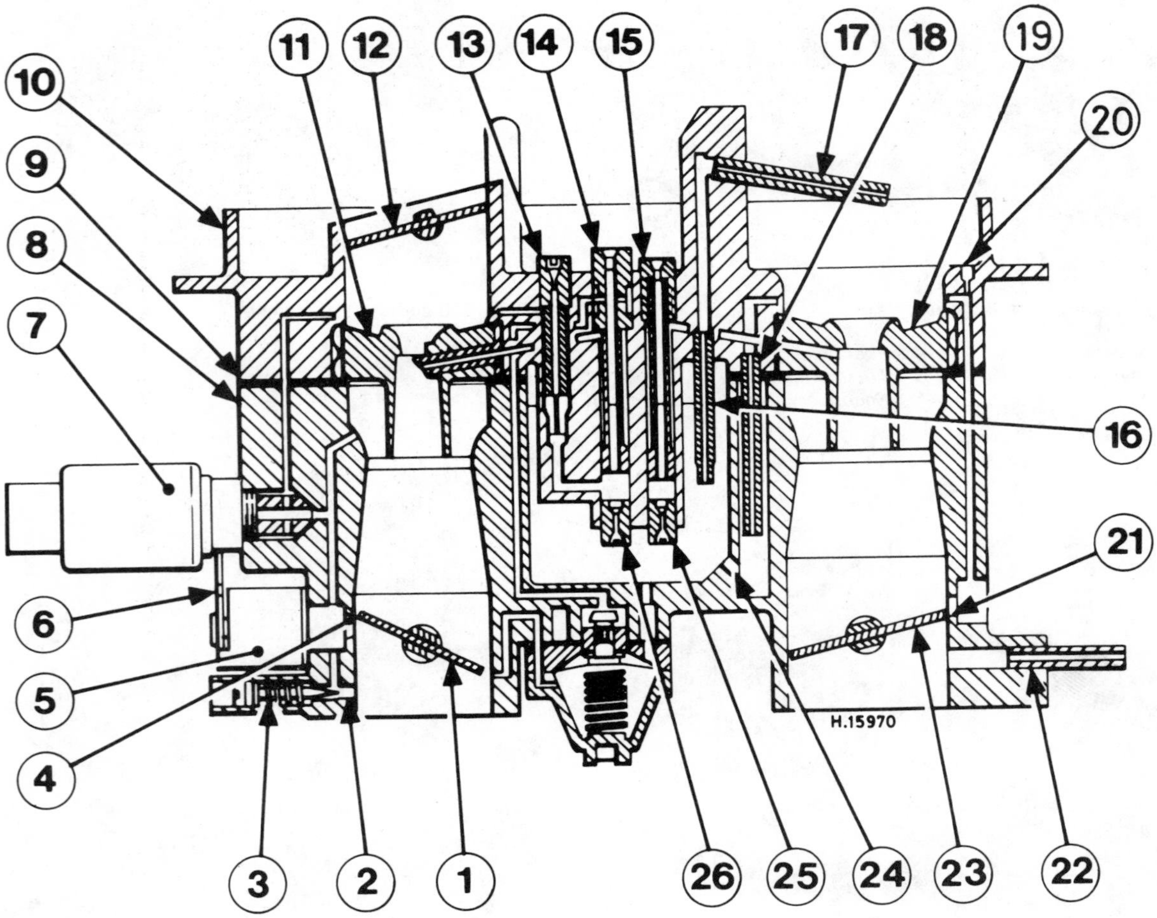

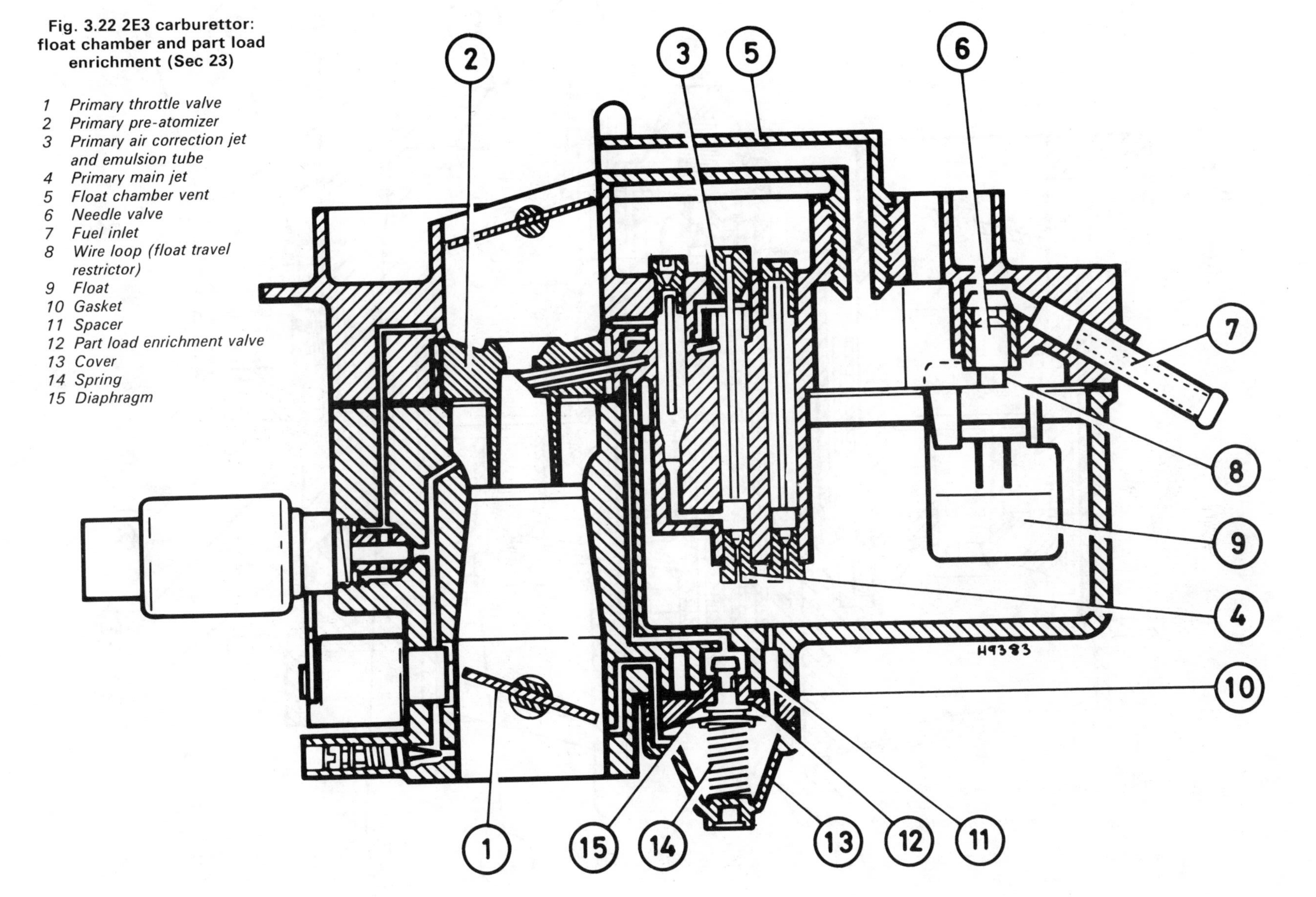

Fig. 3.22 2E3 carburettor: float chamber and part load enrichment (Sec 23)

1 *Primary throttle valve*
2 *Primary pre-atomizer*
3 *Primary air correction jet and emulsion tube*
4 *Primary main jet*
5 *Float chamber vent*
6 *Needle valve*
7 *Fuel inlet*
8 *Wire loop (float travel restrictor)*
9 *Float*
10 *Gasket*
11 *Spacer*
12 *Part load enrichment valve*
13 *Cover*
14 *Spring*
15 *Diaphragm*

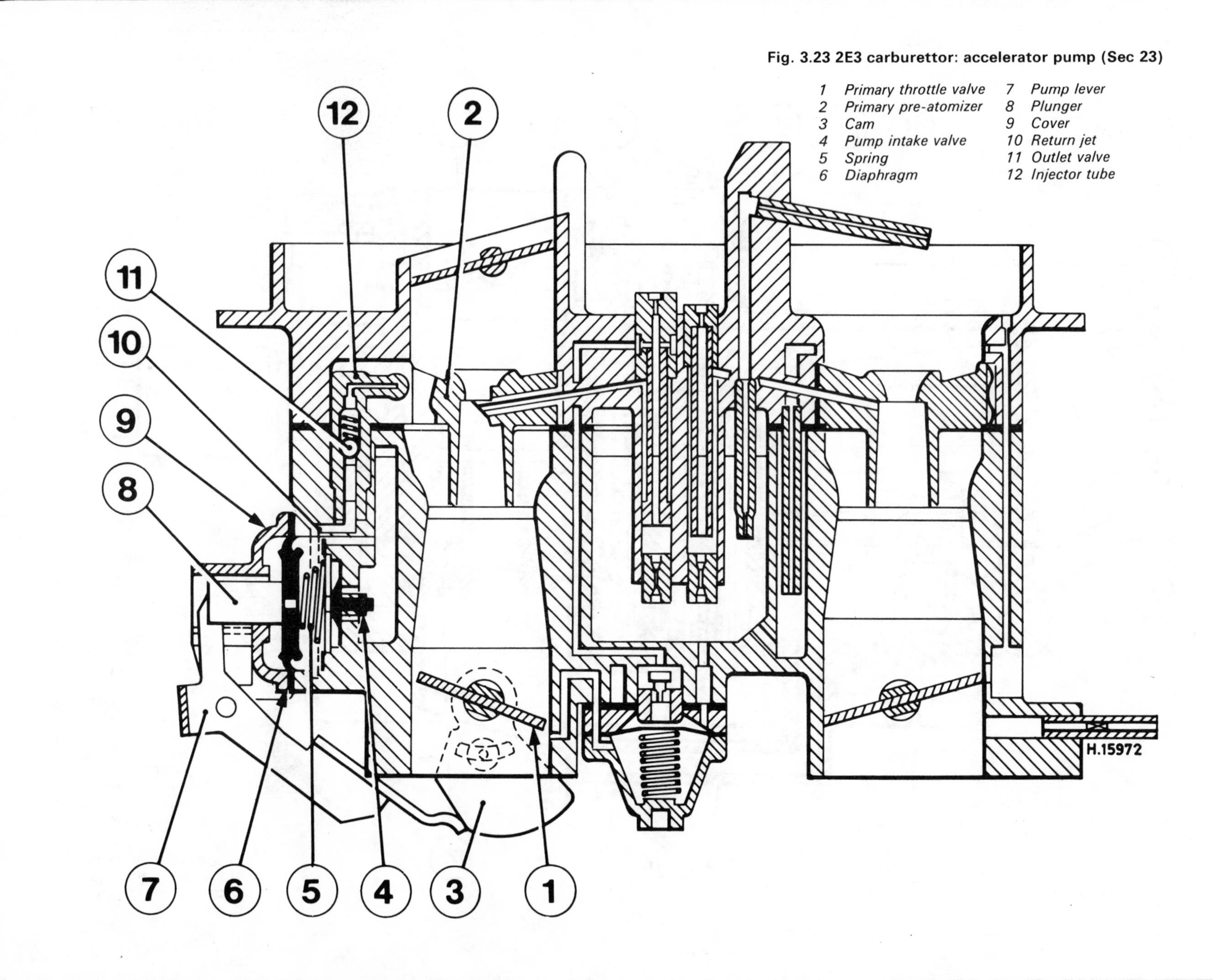

Fig. 3.23 2E3 carburettor: accelerator pump (Sec 23)

1 *Primary throttle valve*
2 *Primary pre-atomizer*
3 *Cam*
4 *Pump intake valve*
5 *Spring*
6 *Diaphragm*
7 *Pump lever*
8 *Plunger*
9 *Cover*
10 *Return jet*
11 *Outlet valve*
12 *Injector tube*

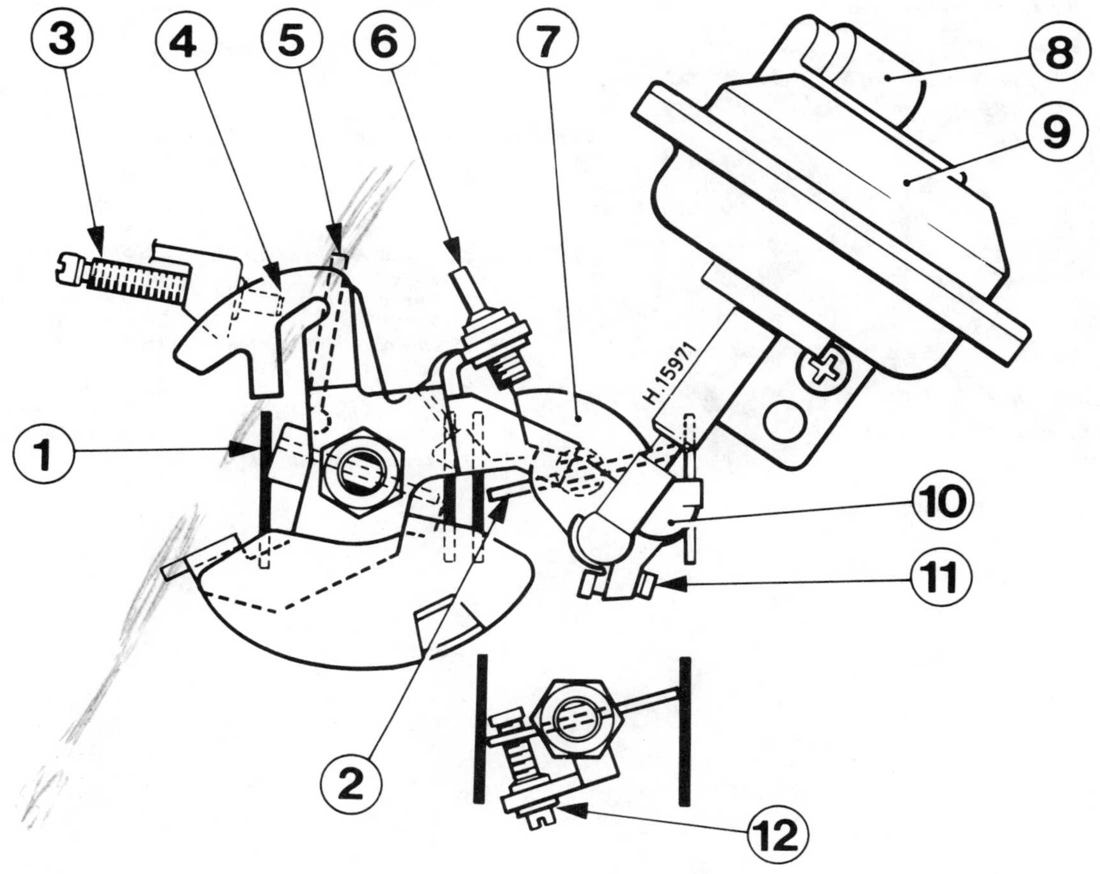

Fig. 3.24 2E3 carburettor: throttle linkage (Sec 23)

1 Primary throttle valve
2 Secondary throttle valve
3 Throttle stop screw
4 Segment lever
5 Throttle lever
6 Fast idle adjustment screw
7 Secondary interlock lever
8 Mounting bracket
9 Vacuum unit
10 Spring
11 Fork lever
12 Secondary stop screw

24 Varajet II carburettor – overhaul

Automatic choke type

1 It is rare for the carburettor to require complete dismantling; indeed, normally where this is required then it would probably be more economical to renew the complete unit.

2 It will usually be found that the first few operations described in the following paragraphs to remove the cover will be sufficient to enable cleaning of the jets and carburettor float chamber to be carried out.

3 With the carburettor removed and external dirt cleaned away, pull off the vacuum hose from the choke vacuum unit.

4 Extract the three screws from the automatic choke retaining ring and withdraw the assembly.

5 Extract the split pin and disconnect the accelerator pump rod from the lever.

6 Unscrew the fuel inlet nozzle and extract the gauze filter from inside it (photo).

7 Extract the retaining clip and disconnect the choke connecting rod from the cam.

8 Extract the three short and four long carburettor cover retaining screws (photo).

9 Remove the cover making sure that, as it is withdrawn, the gasket remains behind on the flange of the float chamber. Remember that the accelerator pump plunger is under spring tension.

24.6 Fuel inlet union and gauze – Varajet carburettor

24.8 Varajet carburettor top cover

Fig. 3.25 Exploded view of Varajet II carburettor (Sec 24)

1 Cover
2 Gasket
3 Packing piece
4 Float pin
5 Accelerator pump piston
6 Spring
7 Float
8 Fuel inlet needle valve
9 Check ball (accelerator pump)
10 Fuel inlet union
11 Fuel filter
12 Idle speed adjustment screw
13 Link rod
14 Idle mixture adjustment screw
15 Throttle valve block
16 Fast idle screw and spring
17 Gasket
18 Fast idle cam
19 Fast idle link rod
20 Vacuum hose
21 Part load needle valve and piston
22 Spring
23 Suction valve and check ball
24 Choke vacuum unit
25 Choke housing cover
26 Cover retainer
27 Choke valve plate (primary barrel)
28 Baffle flap (secondary barrel)
29 Full load needle valve

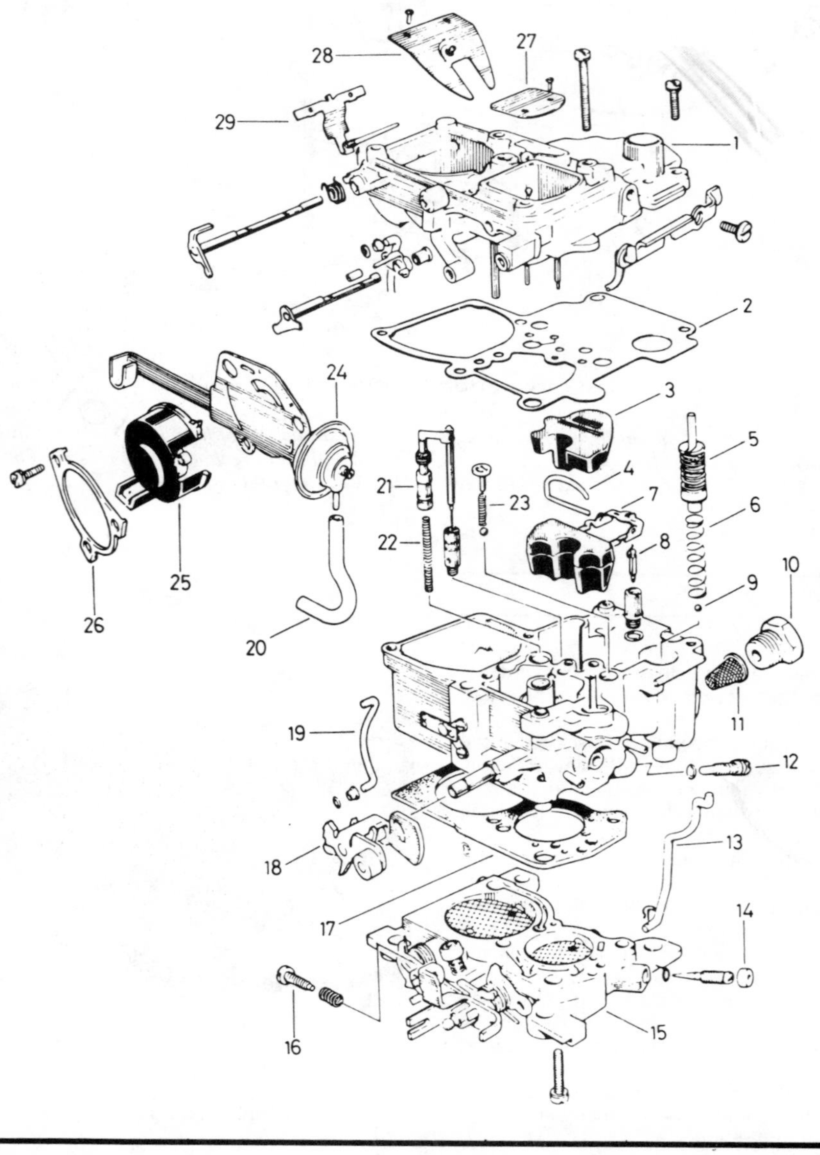

Fig. 3.26 Choke rod-to-cam connection (arrowed) (Sec 24)

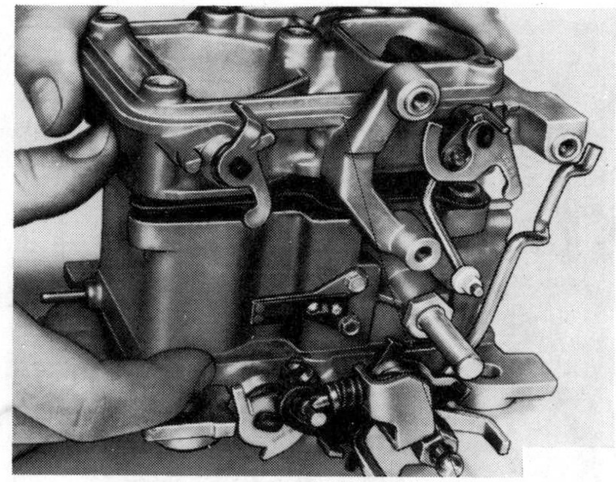

Fig. 3.27 Removing the carburettor cover (Sec 24)

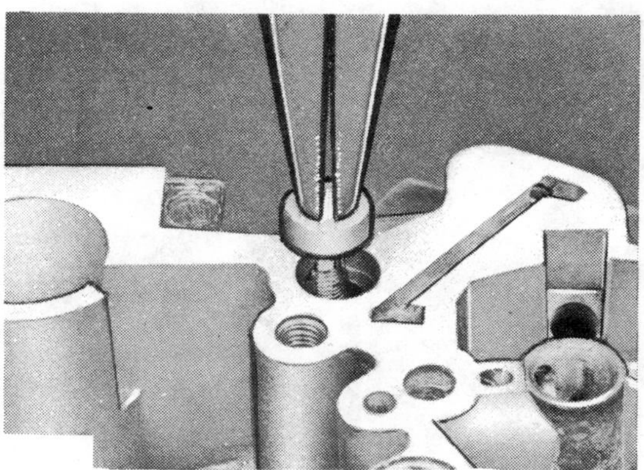

Fig. 3.28 Removing the pump suction valve spring retainer (Sec 24)

10 Remove the accelerator pump plunger and spring and carefully peel off the cover gasket. Remove the pump suction valve spring retainer (photo).

11 Pull or twist out the vacuum piston spring and needle of the carburettor first stage. Take care not to bend the retaining bracket or partial load needle.

12 If necessary, the partial load plunger may be withdrawn by gripping its rod with a pair of pliers.

13 Remove the packing piece, float and needle from the float chamber. Empty the fuel from the chamber (photo).

14 Note their location and unscrew the jets.

15 Extract the four retaining screws and remove the throttle valve plate block.

16 Further dismantling is not recommended.

17 Clean all components and renew any that are worn or damaged. If the throttle valve plate spindle is worn then the complete throttle block must be renewed. Clean jets and passages with air pressure only; never probe with wire or their calibration will be ruined.

18 Obtain a repair kit which will contain all the necessary renewable items, including gaskets.

19 Reassembly is a reversal of dismantling, but observe the following points.

20 When assembling the accelerator pump, ensure that the check ball is correctly located.

21 Check that the needle valve spring is correctly located on the float arm bracket. There should be approximately 0.2 mm (0.008 in) free

24.10 Accelerator pump plunger and spring

24.13 Float and needle valve

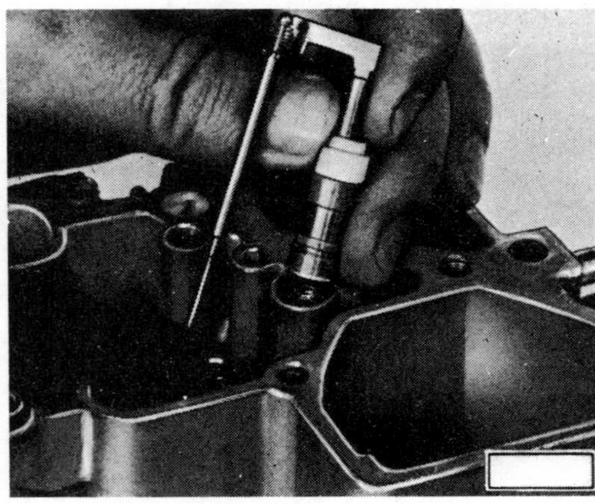

Fig. 3.29 Withdrawing the part load needle valve (Sec 24)

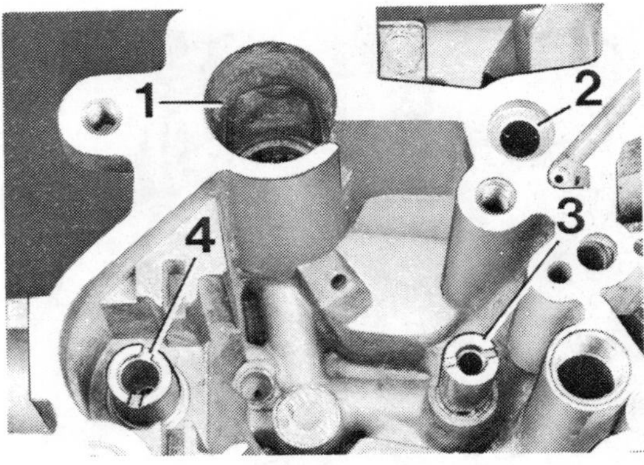

Fig. 3.30 Jet and bore identification – Varajet II carburettor (Sec 24)

1 Accelerator pump bore
2 Vacuum valve spring drilling
3 Main jet
4 Fuel inlet valve seat

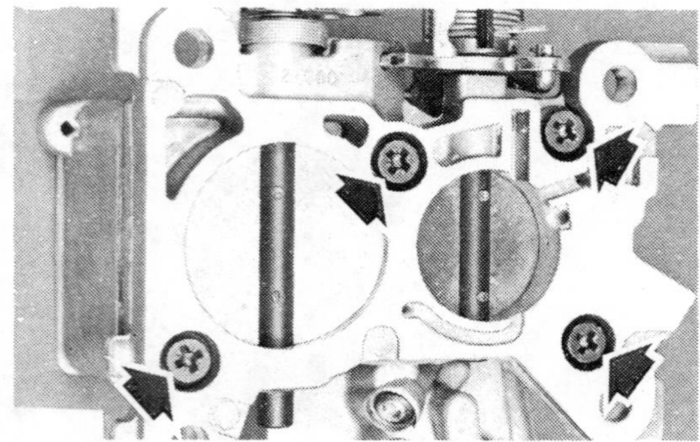

Fig. 3.31 Throttle block securing screws (arrowed) (Sec 24)

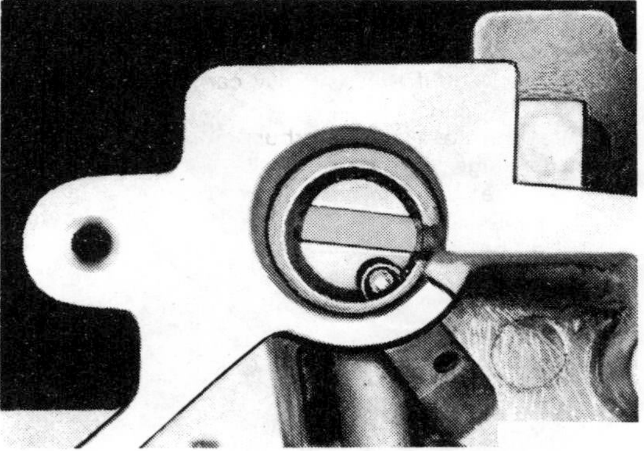

Fig. 3.32 Accelerator pump check ball location (Sec 24)

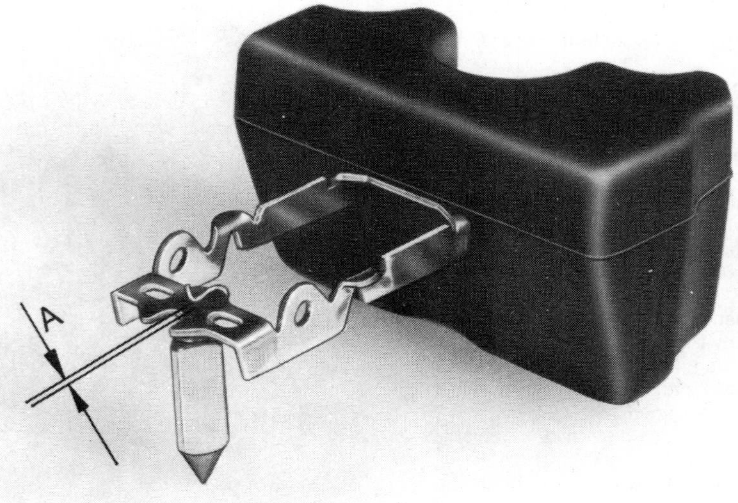

Fig. 3.33 Check the free play (A) between the needle valve spring and the bracket (Sec 24)

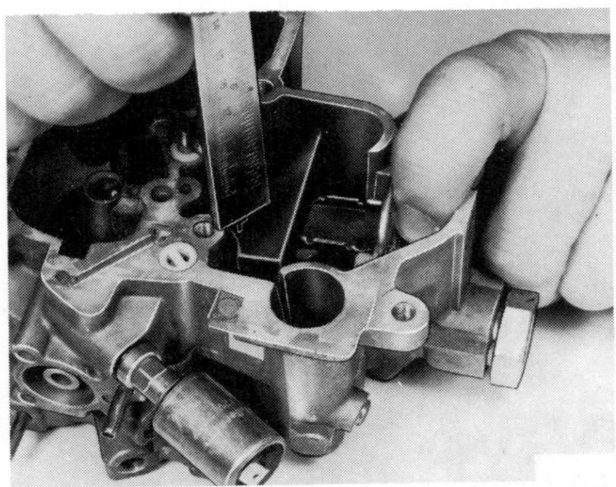

Fig. 3.34 Measuring the float level – Varajet II carburettor (Sec 24)

Fig. 3.35 Float adjustment points (arrowed) – Varajet II carburettor (Sec 24)

play between the spring and the bracket (Fig. 3.33). Correct if necessary by carefully bending one item or the other.
22 Refit the float, needle valve and pivot clips. Check the float level, with the gasket fitted, by applying moderate finger pressure to the float arms and pivot clip to close the needle valve. The top surface of the float should be the specified distance below the carburettor top flange.
23 Correct the float level if necessary by carefully bending the float arms at the points shown (Fig. 3.35).
24 When installing the cover to the carburettor body, take care that the accelerator pump plunger does not become wedged.
25 Make sure that the breather screen is in position.
26 Check that the bi-metallic spring of the automatic choke engages positively with the choke valve plate spindle arm.
27 Check the operation of the throttle valve plate lever. Remember that the secondary valve plate does not open until the primary valve plate has opened by two-thirds of its travel. The secondary throttle valve plate will not open until the choke valve plate is fully open after the engine has reached operating temperature.
28 Carry out those checks and adjustments in Section 18 which can be performed with the carburettor on the bench.
29 After refitting, set the idle speed and mixture, as described in Section 14, then carry out any adjustments outstanding from Section 18.

Manual choke type

30 The operations are very similar to those described in the preceding paragraphs, but the references to automatic choke components should be ignored.

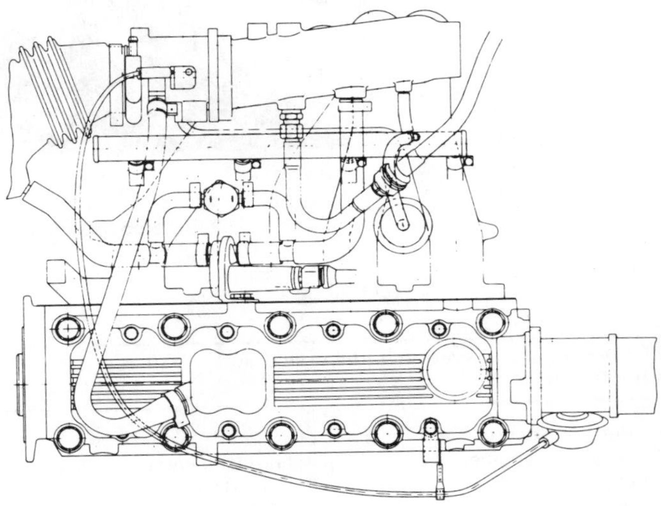

Fig. 3.36 Plan view of 1.8 fuel injection engine, showing hose connections (Sec 25)

25 Fuel injection system – description

1 A Bosch LE Jetronic fuel injection system is fitted to 1.8 models.
2 This system is designed to ensure minimum exhaust emission levels throughout the engine speed range, as the fuel is metered precisely according to engine speed and load.
3 The main components of the system are:

- (a) *A* **control unit** *which incorporates an overrun cut-off, triggered by the throttle valve switch. This device further reduces fuel consumption. A cold start booster eliminates the need for a separate cold start valve and a thermotime switch*
- (b) **Injection valves,** *one to each cylinder, ensure precise metering of the fuel*
- (c) **Airflow meter**. *This incorporates the air temperature sensor*
- (d) **Control relay.** *This comprises an electronic timing element and a switch relay which cuts off the fuel supply immediately after the engine stops*
- (e) *An electrically-operated* **fuel pump**

4 In addition and essential to the system are a fuel filter, a throttle valve switch, an auxiliary air valve, a pressure regulator, and temperature sensors to monitor both intake air and coolant.

26 Fuel injection system – precautions

1 The fuel injection system is normally trouble-free. Avoid damage to the electrical components by observing the following precautions:

- (a) *Do not run the engine unless the battery terminals are securely connected*
- (b) *Do not use a boost charger as a starting aid*
- (c) *Do not disconnect the battery with the engine running*
- (d) *Disconnect the battery before using a battery charger*
- (e) *Do not pull the plug out of the control unit, or plug it back in, with the ignition switched on*
- (f) *Remove the control unit if the temperature will exceed 80°C (176°F) – eg in a paint drying oven*
- (g) *Before performing a cylinder compression test, unplug the control relay*

2 When working on the fuel side of the system, observe scrupulous cleanliness. Dirt entering the fuel lines may damage components.
3 When tracing wiring faults, do not 'flash' wires to earth or use a test lamp to check for voltage. Use a good quality multi-meter.
4 Observe normal safety precautions when handling fuel – see Section 1.

Fig. 3.37 Idle speed adjusting screw and locknut (Sec 27)

27 Fuel injection system – idle speed and mixture adjustment

1 Refer to Section 13: the same applies.
2 With the engine at normal operating temperature, connect an accurate tachometer (rev counter) in accordanace with its maker's instructions.
3 Allow the engine to idle and compare the idle speed with that given in the Specifications. If adjustment is necessary, act on the adjusting screw after slackening its locknut. The adjusting screw is on the rear of the throttle valve housing (Fig. 3.37). Tighten the locknut on completion.
4 To check the mixture (CO level), connect an exhaust gas analyser or other proprietary mixture analysis device in accordance with its maker's instructions. With the engine idling at the specified speed, read the CO level and compare it with that specified.
5 If adjustment of the mixture is necessary, remove the tamperproof cap from the adjusting screw on the airflow sensor (photo). Turn the screw clockwise to enrich the mixture, anti-clockwise to weaken it.
6 Readjust the idle speed if necessary, then fit a new tamperproof cap over the mixture adjusting screw if required.
7 Failure to bring the CO level within the specified range indicates a fault in the injection system, or a well worn (oil burning) engine.

27.5 Tamperproof cap (arrowed) covering mixture adjusting screw

28 Fuel injection system throttle valve – adjustment

1 Make sure that the throttle valve plate is closed. Refer to Fig. 3.38.
2 Release the locknut and unscrew the throttle valve stop screw until the screw is clear of the cam, then screw it back in until it just contacts the cam. Screw it in a further quarter turn, then tighten the locknut without altering the position of the screw (photo).
3 Release the locknuts on the connecting rod and adjust its length by rotating it until dimension X is as shown in Fig. 3.38. Tighten the locknuts on completion.

29 Fuel injection system throttle valve switch – adjustment

1 Release the switch mounting screws and rotate the switch in an anti-clockwise direction until resistance is felt. Tighten the screws (photo).
2 Have an assistant open the throttle valve slightly by depressing the accelerator pedal. A click should be heard from the switch as the throttle opens; another click should be heard when the pedal is released.

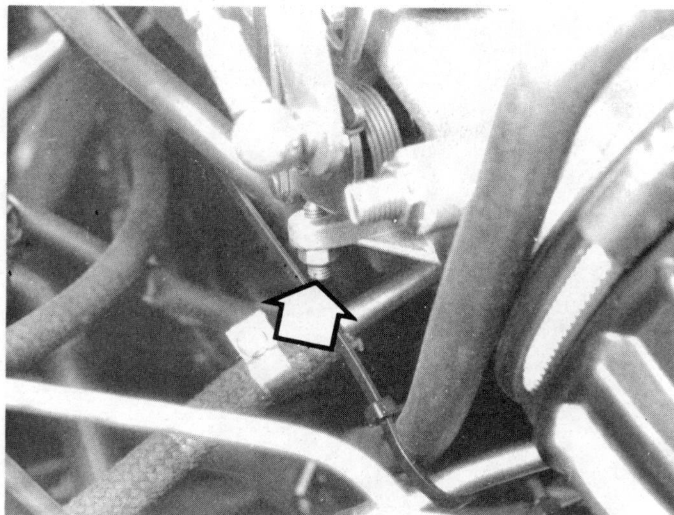

28.2 Throttle valve stop screw (arrowed) – idle speed adjustment screw is in foreground

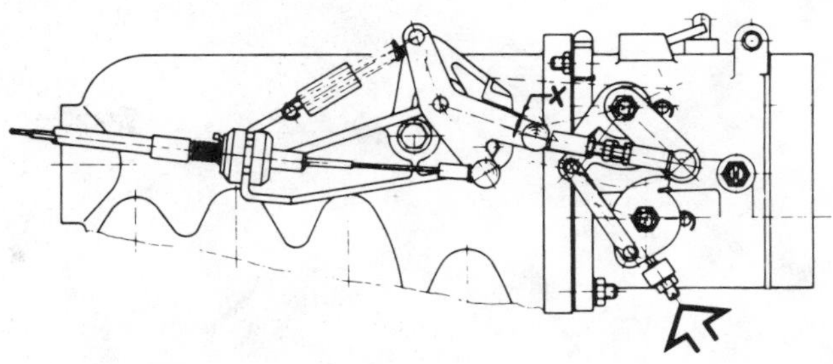

Fig. 3.38 Throttle valve linkage – stop screw is arrowed (Sec 28)

X = 0.5 mm (0.02 in)

29.1 Tightening a throttle valve switch screw

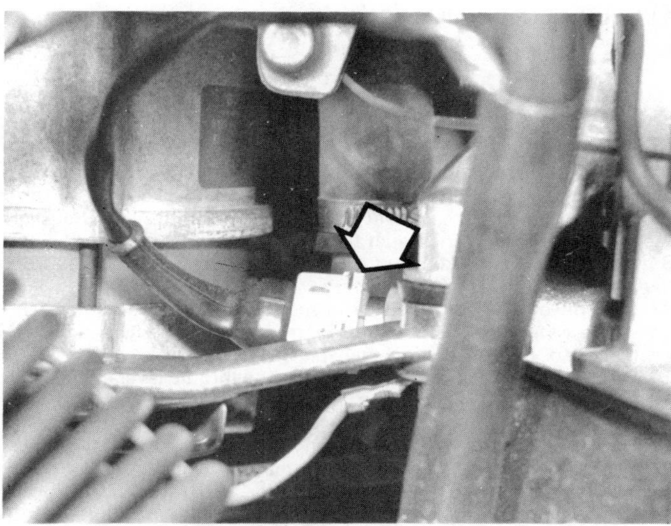

30.4A Coolant temperature sensor plug (arrowed)

30 Fuel injection system components – removal and refitting

1 It is not possible to repair the main components of the fuel injection system. In the event of a fault, it is best to have the fault isolated by a GM dealer or other competent specialist who will have the necessary test equipment. With the problem diagnosed, there is no reason why the defective component cannot be renewed by following the instructions in this Section.

Throttle valve housing

2 The throttle valve housing is removed complete with injectors, fuel pressure regulator and inlet manifold.
3 Disconnect the battery earth lead.
4 Disconnect the injection wiring harness plugs and earth connections as follows:

(a) Airflow meter plug
(b) Coolant temperature sensor (photo)
(c) Fuel injectors (photo)
(d) Throttle valve switch (photo)
(e) Auxiliary air valve (photo)
(f) Cam cover earth tags

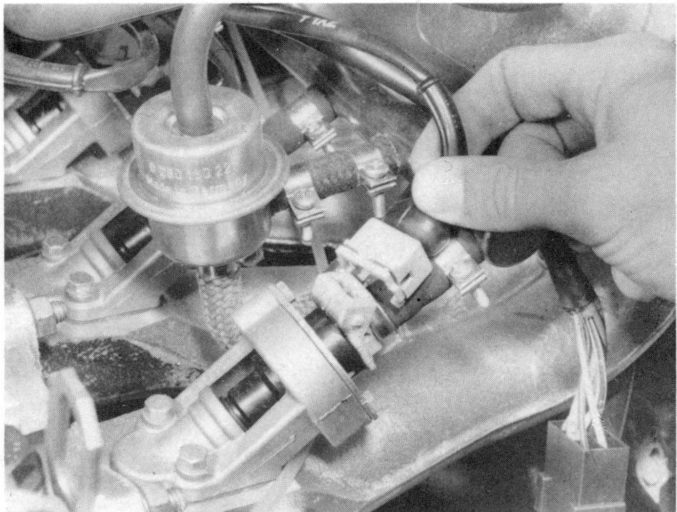

30.4B Disconnecting a fuel injector plug

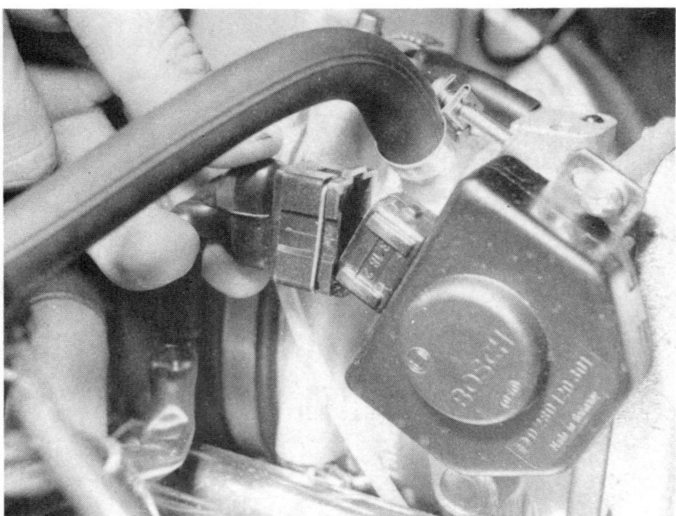

30.4C Unplugging the throttle valve switch

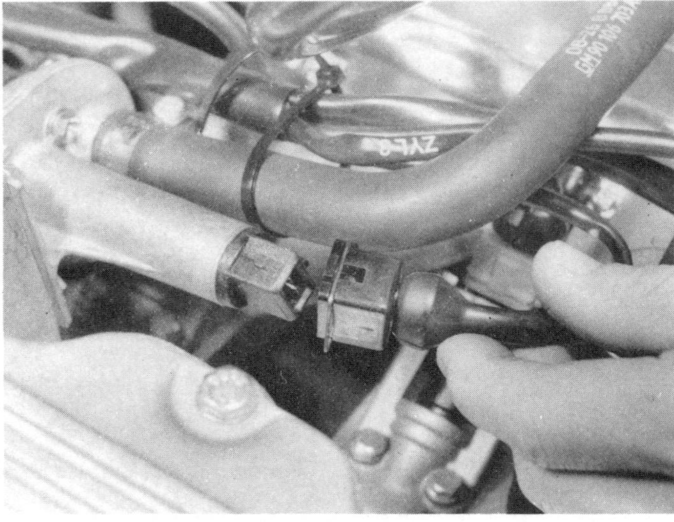

30.4D Unplugging the auxiliary air valve

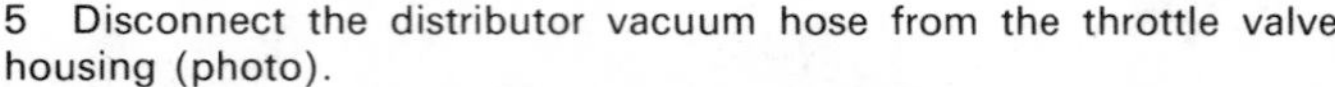

5 Disconnect the distributor vacuum hose from the throttle valve housing (photo).
6 Depressurize the cooling system by unscrewing the expansion tank cap, taking precautions against scalding if the system is hot. Disconnect and plug the coolant hoses from the throttle valve housing.
7 Disconnect the air inlet duct from the housing.
8 Disconnect the brake servo and crankcase ventilation hoses from the housing.
9 Disconnect and plug the fuel hoses from the fuel rail stubs. The hoses are different sizes and one of them carries a white band for identification. Be prepared for fuel spillage.
10 Disconnect the accelerator cable from the throttle levers. The cable inner is secured by a wire clip, and the outer is retained in its bracket by an E-clip (photo).
11 Unscrew the nuts which secure the inlet manifold to the cylinder head. The lower nuts are different to reach: a small socket or ring spanner will be needed.
12 Lift away the throttle valve housing with manifold etc and recover the gasket (photos).
13 Refit in the reverse order to removal, using new gaskets, hose clips etc as necessary. Note the wiring harness connections: No 4 injector is at the flywheel end (photo).

30.5 Distributor vacuum hose (A) and coolant hoses (B) on throttle valve housing

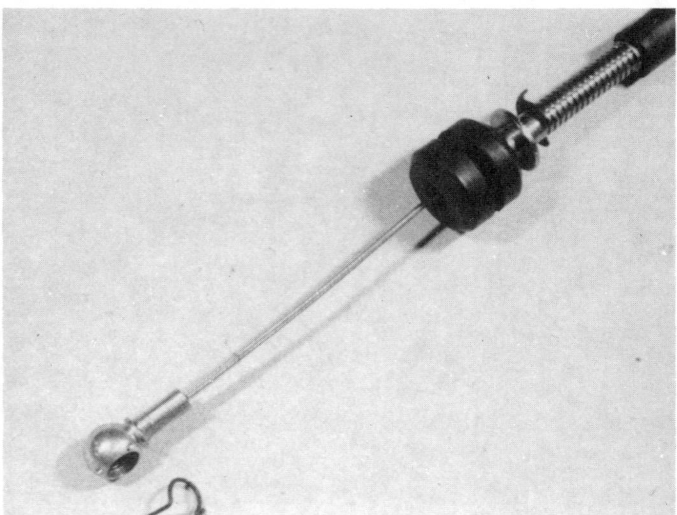

30.10 Accelerator cable at engine end

30.12A Removing the throttle valve housing

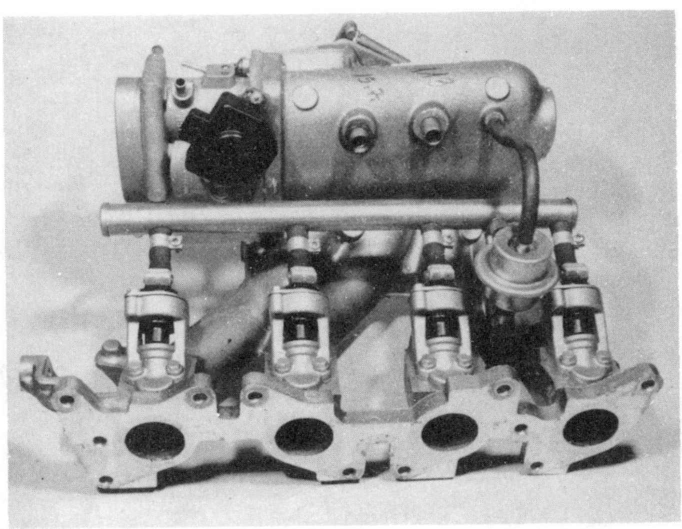

30.12B Throttle valve housing removed

30.12C Throttle valve housing showing control linkage

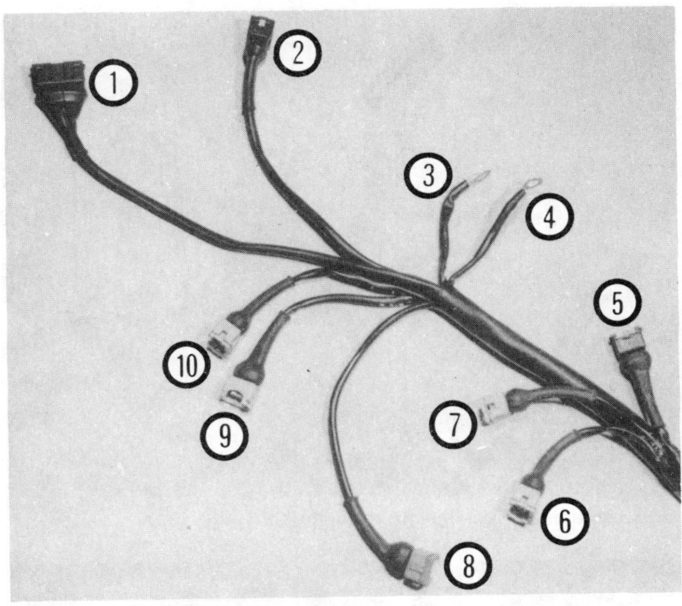

30.13 Fuel injection wiring harness

1	*Airflow sensor*	6	*No 4 injector*
2	*Throttle valve switch*	7	*No 3 injector*
3	*Earth to cam cover*	8	*Coolant temperature sensor*
4	*Earth to cam cover*	9	*No 2 injector*
5	*Auxiliary air valve*	10	*No 1 injector*

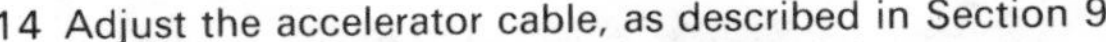

30.19 Fuel pump, damper and filter

14 Adjust the accelerator cable, as described in Section 9.

15 Check the coolant level after the engine is next run and top up if necessary.

Throttle valve switch

16 Disconnect the wiring plug from the switch.

17 Remove the two mounting screws and pull the switch off the throttle valve spindle.

18 Refit in the reverse order to removal, adjusting the switch as described in Section 29.

Fuel pump

19 The fuel pump is located just forward of the fuel tank, along with the fuel filter and a damper (photo).

20 Disconnect the battery earth lead.

21 Clamp the hoses on either side of the pump to minimise fuel loss. Self-locking grips, with suitably protected jaws, are useful for this. Disconnect the hoses.

22 Release the pump mounting clamp and withdraw the pump from its flexible insulator, disconnecting the electrical plug as the pump is withdrawn.

23 Alternatively, the pump can be removed complete with filter and damper unit. To do this, release the mounting strap nuts and remove the assembly from its flexible mountings.

24 Refit in the reverse order to removal, using new hose clips if necessary.

Fuel filter

25 The fuel filter is mounted next to the fuel pump.

26 Disconnect the battery earth lead.

27 Clamp the hoses on either side of the filter to minimise fuel loss. Disconnect the hoses.

28 Release the mounting clamp and withdraw the filter. Dispose of it carefully: remember it is full of fuel.

29 Fit the new filter in the reverse order to removal. Observe the AUS (out) marking on the filter showing the direction of fuel flow (photo).

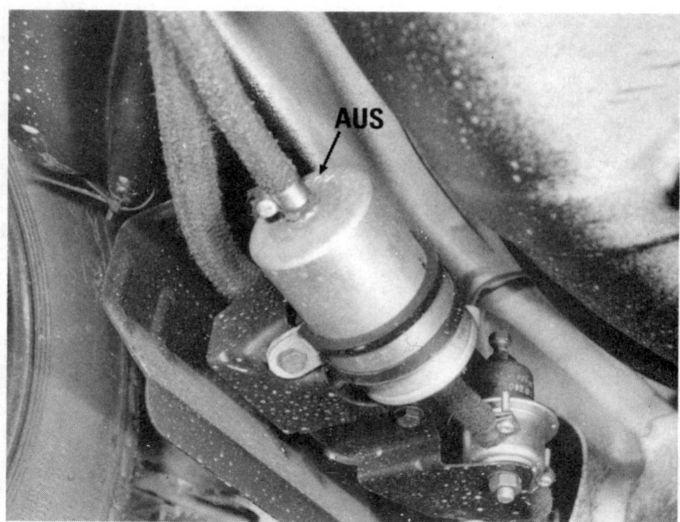

30.29 Fuel filter – note AUS marking

30.31 Slackening a fuel rail hose clamp

Fuel injectors

30 Make sure that the engine is cool, and that all sources of external ignition (eg pilot lights) have been extinguished. Disconnect the battery earth lead.

31 Release the hose clamps and withdraw the fuel rail from the injectors (photo). Catch as much fuel as possible.

32 Disconnect the wiring plugs from the injectors.

33 Unscrew the retaining bolts (two per injector) and withdraw the injectors from their holders, being careful not to damage the needle valves (photo).

34 Refit in the reverse order to removal; renew the injector sealing rings if their condition is at all doubtful.

Airflow meter

35 The airflow meter is located between the air cleaner and the throttle valve housing.

36 Disconnect the wiring harness plug from the airflow meter. Release the securing band and remove the rubber trunking (photo).

37 Release the spring clips and remove the airflow meter with the upper part of the air cleaner housing.

38 Unbolt the airflow meter from the air cleaner housing (photo).

30.33 Undoing a fuel injector retaining bolt

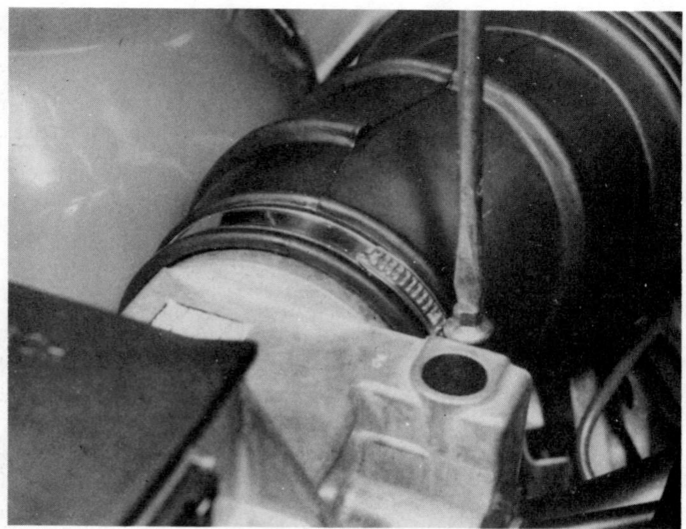
30.36 Disconnecting the airflow meter trunking

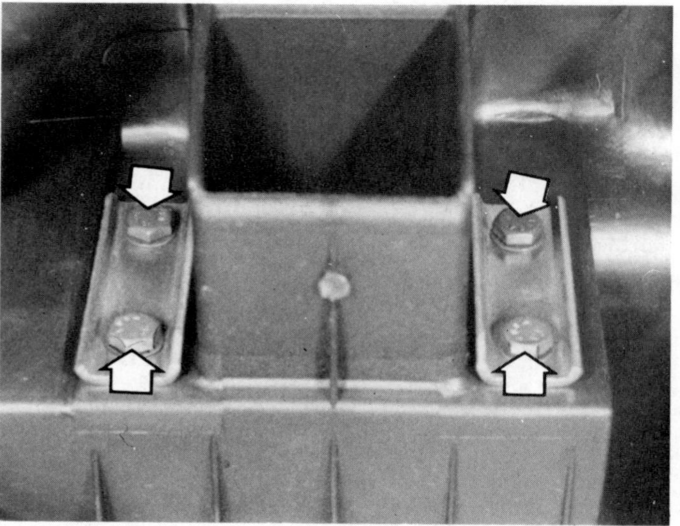
30.38 Airflow meter securing bolts (arrowed)

39 Check the meter flap for free movement, without any jerkiness. If necessary, clean away any dirt in the area of the flap using a clean lint-free rag.
40 Refit in the reverse order to removal.

Control unit

41 The control unit is located at the side of the front footwell, on the passenger side.
42 Remove the footwell trim panel.
43 Make sure that the ignition is switched off, then release the multi-plug spring clip and disconnect the multi-plug.
44 Remove the three securing screws and withdraw the control unit.
45 Refit in the reverse order to removal, but make sure that the ignition is switched off before reconnecting the multi-plug.

Coolant temperature sensor

46 The coolant temperature sensor for the fuel injection system is located near the alternator. Because it is additional to the temperature gauge sensor, it is known as temperature sensor II.
47 Partially drain the cooling system – about 3 litres (5 pints) should be sufficient.
48 Disconnect the electrical lead and unscrew the sensor.
49 If a multi-meter is available, the resistance across the sensor terminals at various temperatures can be checked against the values given in the Specifications.
50 Refit in the reverse order to removal. Use a little sealant on the sensor threads, and refill the cooling system on completion.

Fig. 3.39 Control unit mounting screws (arrowed) – LHD shown, RHD similar (Sec 30)

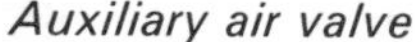

Auxiliary air valve

51 The auxiliary air valve is bolted to the side of the camshaft housing.
52 Disconnect the wiring plug from the valve.
53 Release the hose clips and disconnect the air hoses from the valve.
54 Unbolt and remove the valve.
55 The function of the valve may be checked by looking through the hose connecting stubs. A clear passage should exist between the stubs when the valve is cold. As the valve is heated (achieved by connecting its terminals to a 12 volt battery) the regulator disc should move round and block the hole.
56 Refit in the reverse order to removal, using new hose clips if necessary. An air leak on the intake side of the valve will raise the idle speed.

Control relay

57 The control relay is located on the front suspension strut turret. Unplugging the relay disables the fuel pump – this is necessary when performing a compression test.
58 Slacken the securing bolt, remove the relay and its bracket from the turret, and withdraw the relay from the plug (photos).
59 Refit in the reverse order to removal.

Fuel pressure regulator

60 The fuel pressure regulator is located between injectors 3 and 4 (photo).

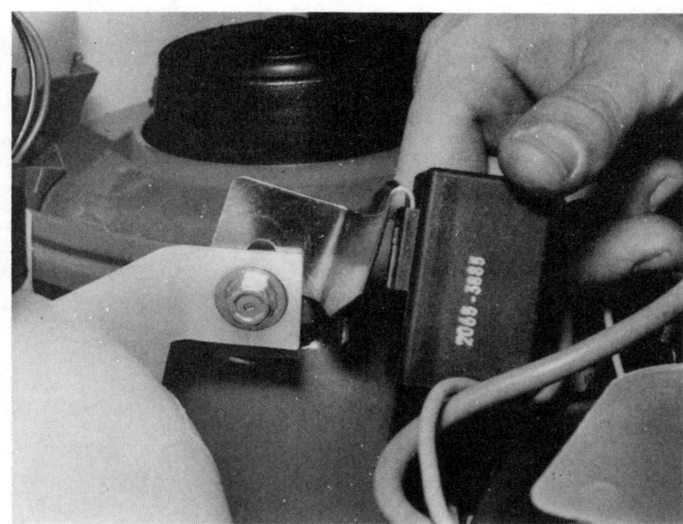

30.58A Removing the control relay and bracket

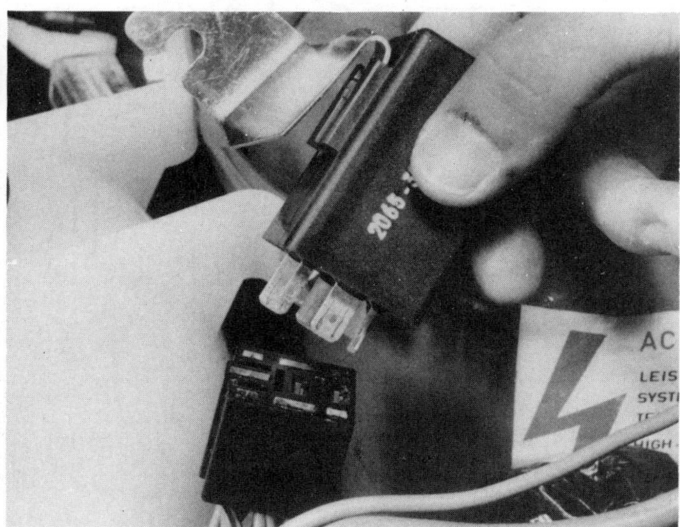

30.58B Unplugging the control relay

30.60 Fuel pressure regulator

61 Disconnect the battery earth lead and take appropriate fire precautions.
62 Clamp the fuel hoses to minimise fuel loss, using self-locking grips with suitably protected jaws.
63 Disconnect the fuel and vacuum hoses form the pressure regulator and remove it. Be prepared for fuel spillage.
64 Refit in the reverse order to removal.

31 Inlet manifold – removal and refitting

OHV engine

1 The manifold may be removed with or without the carburettor. In either case, refer to Section 20 and follow the steps preparing for carburettor removal.
2 Disconnect the brake servo vacuum hose.
3 Remove the three screws which secure the manifold to the cylinder head.
4 Remove the manifold and recover the gasket.
5 Refit in the reverse order to removal, but use a new gasket and tighten the retaining screws to the specified torque.

OHC carburettor engine

6 Drain the cooling system, as described in Chapter 2.
7 Remove the alternator, as described in Chapter 12.
8 Release the coolant pipe from the inlet manifold and clutch housing.
9 On 1.3 models, disconnect the coolant temperature gauge lead.
10 Refer to Section 20 and either remove the carburettor, or follow the steps preparing for carburettor removal.
11 Disconnect the brake servo vacuum hose.
12 Remove the securing nuts and withdraw the manifold. Recover the gasket.

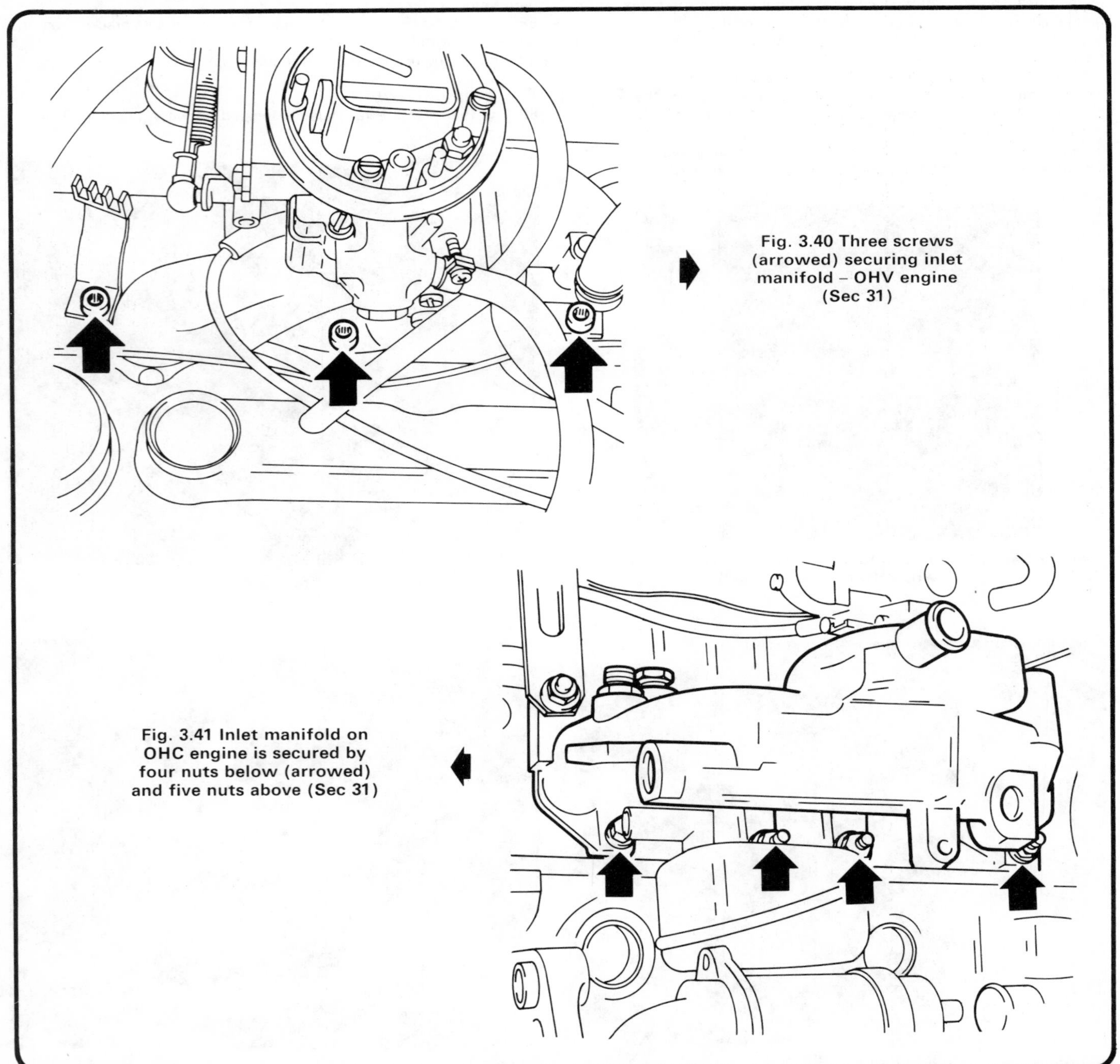

Fig. 3.40 Three screws (arrowed) securing inlet manifold – OHV engine (Sec 31)

Fig. 3.41 Inlet manifold on OHC engine is secured by four nuts below (arrowed) and five nuts above (Sec 31)

13 Refit in the reverse order to removal, using a new gasket. Tighten the manifold nuts progressively to the specified torque.
14 Refill the cooling system and adjust the alternator drivebelt, as described in Chapter 2.

OHC fuel injection engine

15 Removal of the inlet manifold is covered in Section 30, paragraphs 2 to 15.

32 Exhaust manifold – removal and refitting

OHV engine

1 Raise and securely support the front of the car.
2 From under the car, separate the manifold-to-downpipe joint by removing the two bolts and recovering the tension springs.
3 Remove the air cleaner, as described in Section 6.
4 Remove the six bolts which secure the exhaust manifold to the cylinder head. Remove the manifold and recover the gasket.
5 Refit in the reverse order to removal, using a new gasket. Tighten the manifold securing bolts progressively, starting in the middle and working towards the ends, to avoid destructive stresses. Use a little anti-seize compound on the downpipe joint, and a new seal if necessary.

OHC engine

6 On carburettor models, remove the air cleaner, as described in Section 6. Also remove the hot air shroud; noting how its sections fit over the manifold.
7 Remove the securing nuts or bolts from the manifold-to-downpipe joint.
8 Remove the manifold securing nuts and withdraw the manifold from the studs. Recover the gaskets.
9 Refit in the reverse order to removal. Use a new gasket and tighten the nuts as described in paragraph 5. Also renew the gasket or seal at the downpipe joint.

33 Exhaust system – inspection, removal and refitting

1 The exhaust system should be examined for leaks, damage and security at the intervals given in Routine Maintenance. To do this, apply the handbrake and allow the engine to idle. Lie down on each side of the car in turn, and check the full length of the exhaust system for leaks while an assistant temporarily places a wad of cloth over the end of the tailpipe. If a leak is evident repairs may be made using a proprietary exhaust repair kit; however, if the leak is excessive, or damage is evident, the relevant section should be renewed. Check the rubber moutings for condition and security and renew them if necessary.
2 To remove the exhaust system, jack up the front and/or rear of the car and support it securely on axle stands. Alternatively drive the front or rear wheels up on ramps, over a pit, or on a hoist.
3 The system is made up of three or four sections. The front and rear sections can be removed independently, but to remove a middle section it will be necessary to remove an adjacent end section also. it is certainly easier to free stubborn joints with the complete system removed from the car.
4 To remove a front or rear section, remove the U-bolt clamps which hold the section together. Unhook the section from its rubber mounting rings, and for the front section unbolt the manifold or downpipe (photos). Free the joints and remove the section concerned. The application of penetrating oil will be of assistance in freeing seized joints. Heat from a blowlamp can also be helpful, but take great care to shield the fuel tank, fuel lines and other vulnerable or inflammable areas.
5 Use a little exhaust jointing compound, or (preferably) copper-based anti-seize compound, when assembling sliding joints. Renew clamps, rubber rings, seals and gaskets as a matter of course unless they are in perfect condition (photo).
6 When refitting the complete exhaust system, position it so that the mountings are evenly loaded before tightening the U-bolt clamps.

33.4A Exhaust system flexible joint

33.4B Exhaust system rubber mounting ring

33.5 Graphite sealing ring fitted at the flexible joint

34 Fault diagnosis – fuel and exhaust systems

Unsatisfactory engine performance, bad starting and excessive fuel consumption are not necessarily the fault of the fuel system or carburettor. In fact they more commonly occur as a result of ignition system faults. Before acting on the following it is necessary to check the ignition system first. Even though a fault may lie in the fuel system, it will be difficult to trace unless the ignition system is correct. The faults below therefore assume that, where applicable, this has been attended to first.

Diagnosis of fuel injection system faults should be left to an expert.

Symptom	Reason(s)
Difficult starting when cold	Choke cable incorrectly adjusted Choke valve gap incorrect Automatic choke defective Fuel starvation (see below) Air leak in induction system Float needle valve sticking Poor compression
Difficult starting when hot	Choke cable incorrectly adjusted Choke linkage sticking Automatic choke defective Pedal pumped before starting Dirty or clogged air cleaner Fuel starvation (see below) Float chamber flooding Idle settings incorrect
Fuel starvation	Leak on suction side of pump Fuel pump faulty Fuel tank breather blocked Fuel pipes or hoses kinked Incorrect float level Blocked carburettor jets Clogged fuel pump or carburettor filter (when applicable)
Engine will not idle	Idle settings incorrect Air leak in induction system Idle jet blocked Idle cut-off solenoid (when fitted) defective or disconnected
Poor performance, hesitation or erratic running	Air cleaner temperature control defective or wrongly set Faulty accelerator pump or enrichment valve Blocked carburettor jet(s) Wrong jet(s) fitted at overhaul Carburettor vacuum unit(s) leaking Air leak on induction side Fuel starvation (see above)
Backfiring in exhaust	Air leak in exhaust system Weak mixture (fuel starvation or induction leak) Exhaust valve(s) burnt or incorrectly adjusted

Chapter 4 Ignition system

For modifications, and information applicable to later models, see Supplement at end of manual

Contents

Specifications

General

System type:

1.2	Contact breaker and coil
All other models	Breakerless (electronic) distributor
Firing order	1-3-4-2 (No 1 at pulley end)

Distributor (contact breaker gap)

Contact breaker gap	0.4 mm (0.016 in) minimum
Dwell angle (percentage)	50 ± 3° (56 ± 3%)
Direction of rotation	Clockwise (viewed from cap)

Distributor (breakerless type)

Make	Delco-Remy or Bosch
Direction of rotation	Anti-clockwise (viewed from cap)

Ignition timing

Static or idle (all models)	10° BTDC
Timing marks	Notch on crankshaft pulley, pointer or rib on engine

Ignition coil

Make	Delco-Remy or Bosch
Primary resistance:	
Contact breaker type	1.2 to 1.6Ω
Breakerless type – 1.3	0.3 to 0.6Ω
Breakerless type – 1.6 and 1.8	0.6 to 0.9Ω

Spark plugs

Make and type:	
1.2	ACR 42 6FS, Champion RL82YC or equivalent
1.3, 1.6 and 1.8	ACR 42 XLS, Champion RN7YC or equivalent
Electrode gap (all models):	
ACR	0.7 to 0.8 mm (0.028 to 0.032 in)
Champion	1.0 mm (0.039 in)

Torque wrench settings

	Nm	lbf ft
Spark plugs:		
1.2	40	30
1.3, 1.6 and 1.8	20	15

1 General description

In order that the engine can run correctly, it is necessary for an electrical spark to ignite the fuel/air mixture in the combustion chamber at exactly the right moment in relation to engine speed and load.

The ignition system is divided into two circuits, low tension and high tension. On 1.2 models with conventional ignition, the low tension circuit consists of the battery, ignition switch, coil primary windings and the contact breaker points and condenser, both located at the distributor. On other models, with electronic ignition, an electronic module controlled by an induction sensor, permanent magnets and a pulse generator wheel performs the same function electronically as the mechanical contact breaker points in the conventional system. In both the conventional and electronic systems the high tension circuit consists of the coil secondary windings, the heavy ignition lead from the centre of the coil to the distributor cap, the rotor arm and the spark plugs and leads. The ignition system is based on feeding low tension voltage from the battery to the coil where it is converted to high tension voltage. The high tension voltage is powerful enough to jump the spark plug gap in the cylinders many times a second under high compression pressures, providing the system is in good order and all adjustments are correct.

The wiring harness on conventional systems includes a ballast resistor wire in the coil feed circuit. During starting this resistor wire is bypassed allowing full battery voltage to be fed to the coil. This ensures that during cold starting when the starter motor current consumption would be high, sufficient voltage is still available at the coil to produce a powerful spark. Under normal running, battery voltage is directed through the resistor cable before reaching the coil.

The ignition advance is controlled both mechanically and by vacuum to ensure that the spark occurs at just the right instant for the particular engine load and speed. The mechanical governor comprises two weights, which move out from the distributor shaft as the engine speed rises due to centrifugal force. The vacuum control consists of a diaphragm, one side of which is connected via a small bore tube to the carburettor, and the other side to the distributor baseplate. Depression in the inlet manifold and carburettor, which varies with engine speed and throttle opening, causes the diaphragm to move, so moving the baseplate and advancing or retarding the spark.

Warning: *The voltages produced by the electronic ignition system are considerably higher than those produced by the conventional system. Extreme care must be used when working on the system with the ignition switched on, particularly by persons fitted with a cardiac pacemaker.*

2 Maintenance and inspection

1 At the specified service intervals, carry out the following operations on the ignition system.

2 Remove, clean and regap the spark plugs, as described in Section 12. Renew all four plugs if any are in poor condition (electrodes worn or eroded, insulator damaged). Renew the plugs in any case at alternate service intervals, even if they appear to be still in good condition.

3 Check the HT leads for corrosion of the end fittings; if any is found, clean it off and apply a little petroleum jelly or silicone grease. Wipe the HT leads clean and inspect them for cracks or other damage: renew if necessary. Wipe clean inside and outside the distributor cap, and around the top of the ignition coil.

4 On 1.2 models check the condition of the contact breaker points, as described in Section 3, and if necessary renew them, as described in Section 4. After resetting the contact breaker points gap, refer to Section 11 and adjust the ignition timing. Although not a specific service requirement on electronic ignition systems, it is desirable to check the ignition timing on other models at this time also.

5 Check the condition and security of all leads and wiring associated with the ignition system. Make sure that no chafing is occurring on any of the wires and that all connections are secure, clean and free of corrosion.

3 Contact breaker points (1.2 models) – adjustments

1 To adjust the contact breaker points so that the correct gap is obtained, first undo the two distributor cap retaining screws, lift off the cap and withdraw the rotor arm from the distributor shaft. At this stage it is a good idea to clean the inside and outside of the cap and inspect its condition. It is unlikely that the four segments inside the cap will be badly burned or corroded, but if they are the cap must be renewed. If only a small deposit is on the segments, it may be scraped away using a small screwdriver.

2 Push in the carbon brush located in the centre of the cap several times to ensure that it moves freely. The brush should protrude by at least 6.3 mm (1/4 in).

3 Gently prise the contact breaker points open to examine the condition of their faces. If they are rough, pitted or dirty it will be necessary to remove them to enable new points to be fitted.

4 Assuming that the points are in a satisfactory condition, or that they have been renewed, the gap between the two faces should be measured using feeler gauges as follows.

5 Pull off the plug leads, after marking them to ensure correct refitment, and then remove the spark plugs.

6 With the transmission in gear and the handbrake released, slowly pull the car forward, while at the same time watching the distributor, until the heel of the contact breaker arm is on the peak of one of the four cam lobes. A feeler blade equal to the contact breaker points gap, as given in the Specifications, should now just fit between the contact

3.6 Checking the contact breaker points gap using a feeler gauge

faces (photo). Make sure that the feeler blade is clean – if the contact faces are contaminated with oil or grease, the LT current will be greatly reduced and malfunction will result.
7 If the gap varies from this amount, slacken the contact breaker plate retaining screw and move the breaker plate in or out to achieve the desired gap. The plate can be easily moved with a screwdriver inserted between the notch in the breaker plate and the two adjacent pips in the distributor baseplate.
8 When the gap is correct, tighten the retaining screw and then recheck the gap.
9 Refit the rotor arm, distributor cap, spark plugs and leads.
10 If a dwell meter is available, a far more accurate method of setting the contact breaker points gap is by measuring and setting the distributor dwell angle.
11 The dwell angle is the number of degrees of distributor cam rotation during which the contact breaker points are closed, ie the period from when the points close after being opened by one cam lobe until they are opened again by the next cam lobe. The advantages of setting the points by this method are that any wear of the distributor shaft or cam lobes is taken into account, and also the inaccuracies of using a feeler gauge are eliminated. In general, a dwell meter should be used in accordance with the manufacturer's instructions. However, the use of one type of meter is outlined as follows.
12 To set the dwell angle, remove the distributor cap and rotor arm and connect one lead of the dwell meter to the '+' terminal (15) on the coil and the other lead to the '-' terminal (1) on the coil.
13 Whilst an assistant turns on the ignition and operates the starter, observe the reading on the dwell meter scale. With the engine turning on the starter the reading should be as stated in the Specifications.
Note: *Fluctuation of the dwell meter needle indicates that the engine is not turning over fast enough to give a steady reading. If this is the case, remove the spark plugs and repeat the checks.*
14 If the dwell angle is too small, the contact breaker point gap is too wide, and if the dwell angle is excessive the gap is too small.
15 Adjust the contact breaker points gap, using the method described in paragraph 7, until the correct dwell angle is obtained.
16 When the dwell angle is satisfactory, disconnect the meter and refit the rotor arm, distributor cap and, if removed, the spark plugs and leads.
17 Check the ignition timing, as described in Section 11.

4 Contact breaker points (1.2 models) – renewal

1 When significant pitting or burning of the contact faces has occurred, the contact set should be renewed. It is not an expensive item and is worth renewing as a preventive measure at alternate service intervals, even if apparently still in good condition.
2 Undo the two distributor cap retaining screws, lift off the cap and withdraw the rotor arm from the distributor shaft (photo).
3 Move the contact breaker arm spring blade away from the plastic insulator and slip the low tension and condenser lead terminals off the insulator (photo).
4 Undo the retaining screw securing the contact breaker plate to the distributor baseplate (photo) and lift off the contact set.
5 Locate the new contact set on the baseplate and refit the retaining screw.
6 Move the contact breaker spring blade away from the insulator, fit the low tension and condenser leads and allow the spring blade to slip back into place. Make sure that the leads and the blade locate squarely in the insulator.
7 Check and adjust the contact breaker points gap or dwell angle, as described in Section 3, then refit the rotor arm and distributor cap.

5 Condenser (1.2 models) – removal and refitting

1 The purpose of the condenser (sometimes known as a capacitor) is to prevent excessive arcing of the contact breaker points, and to ensure that a rapid collapse of the magnetic field, created in the coil and necessary if a healthy spark is to be produced at the plugs, is allowed to occur.
2 The condenser is fitted in parallel with the contact breaker points. If it becomes faulty it will cause ignition failure, as the points will be prevented from cleanly interrupting the low tension circuit.

4.2 Removing the rotor arm

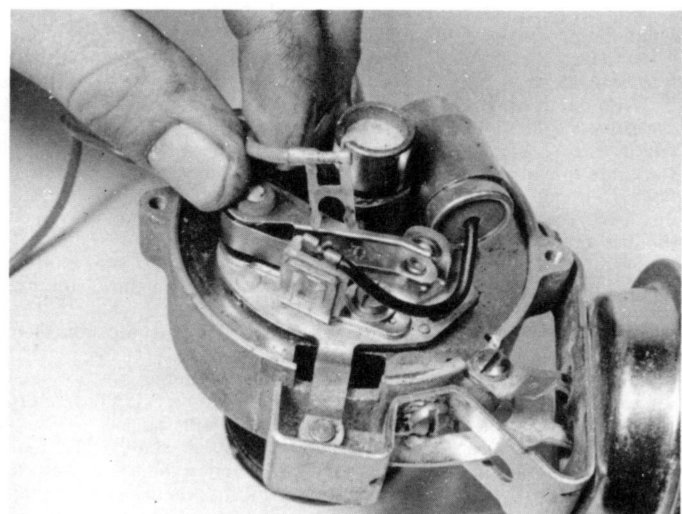
4.3 Slip the low tension and condenser leads out of the insulator

4.4 Undoing the points retaining screw

3 If the engine becomes very difficult to start, or begins to miss after several miles of running, and the contact breaker points show signs of excessive burning, then the condition of the condenser must be suspect. A further test can be made by separating the points by hand, with the ignition switched on. If this is accomplished by an excessively strong flash, it indicates that the condenser has failed.
4 Without special test equipment, the only reliable way to diagnose condenser trouble is to renew the suspect unit and note if there is any improvement in performance. It is not an expensive component and it is worth considering periodic renewal on a preventive basis, to avoid the inconvenience entailed by failure in use.
5 To remove the condenser from its location in the distributor, undo the distributor cap retaining screws, lift off the cap and withdraw the rotor arm from the distributor shaft.
6 Move the contact breaker arm spring blade away from the plastic insulator and withdraw the condenser lead.
7 Undo the screw securing the condenser to the distributor baseplate and lift the condenser off.
8 Refitting is the reverse sequence to removal, but make sure that the condenser and low tension leads are securely located in the insulator behind the contact breaker arm spring blade.

6 Distributor (1.2 models) – removal and refitting

1 Pull off the spark plug leads, after marking them to ensure correct refitment, and remove the spark plugs.
2 Undo the distributor cap retaining screws, lift off the cap and place it to one side.
3 With the transmission in gear and the handbrake released, pull the car forward until, with a finger over the plug hole, compression can be felt in No 1 cylinder (the cylinder nearest the crankshaft pulley). Continue moving the car forwards until the notch on the crankshaft pulley is in line with the raised mark on the timing cover (photo). The distributor rotor arm should now be pointing to the notch on the rim on the distributor body.
4 Disconnect the distributor low tension lead at the harness connector and detach the vacuum advance pipe from the distributor vacuum unit.
5 Undo the distributor clamp retaining bolt, lift off the clamp plate and withdraw the distributor from its location.
6 Before refitting the distributor, check that the engine has not been inadvertently turned whilst the distributor was removed; if it has, return it to the original position, as described in paragraph 3.
7 As the distributor is refitted, the distributor shaft will rotate anti-clockwise slightly due to the meshing action of the skew gears on the distributor shaft and camshaft. To ensure that the distributor shaft is in the correct position after fitting, ie with the rotor arm pointing towards the notch in the rim of the distributor body, set the shaft so that the rotor arm is pointing towards the low tension lead grommet in the side of the distributor body (photo), prior to fitting. As the skew gears mesh, the shaft will turn back to the correct position.
8 It is also necessary to position the oil pump driveshaft so that it engages with the slot in the distributor shaft as the distributor is inserted. The shaft should be positioned so that it is at approximately 90° to the crankshaft centreline (photo).
9 Make sure that the O-ring seal is in position at the base of the distributor and, with the shafts set as previously described, insert the distributor into its location. It may take two or three attempts to engage the oil pump driveshaft, and finish with the rotor arm pointing to the notch. If necessary move the distributor shaft very slightly one way or the other, until the correct position is achieved.
10 With the distributor in place, turn the distributor body clockwise a few degrees so that the contact breaker points are closed, and then slowly turn it anti-clockwise until they just open with the rotor arm once more pointing towards the notch in the distributor body rim. Hold the distributor in this position and refit the clamp plate and clamp bolt. Tighten the bolt securely.

6.3 Ignition timing marks (arrowed) in alignment – 1.2 models

6.7 Distributor rotor position prior to refitting
A LT lead grommet B No 1 reference mark

6.8 Correct position of oil pump driveshaft prior to fitting distributor

11 Reconnect the low tension lead and the vacuum advance pipe. Refit the spark plugs, distributor cap and leads.
12 Refer to Section 11 and adjust the ignition timing.

7 Distributor (1.2 models) – dismantling, inspection and reassembly

1 Remove the distributor from the engine, as described in the previous Section, and then prepare a clean uncluttered working area.
2 Remove the rotor arm, ease the contact breaker arm spring blade away from the plastic insulator and slip the low tension and condenser leads off the insulator.
3 Withdraw the low tension lead grommet from the slot in the side of the distributor body (photo) and remove the lead.
4 Undo the retaining screw and lift off the contact set.
5 Undo the retaining screw and lift off the condenser (photo).
6 On the side of the distributor body, undo the two vacuum unit securing screws (photo). Withdraw the vacuum unit and at the same time disengage the operating arm from the peg on the side of the baseplate (photo).
7 Undo the two baseplate securing screws, noting the earth tag

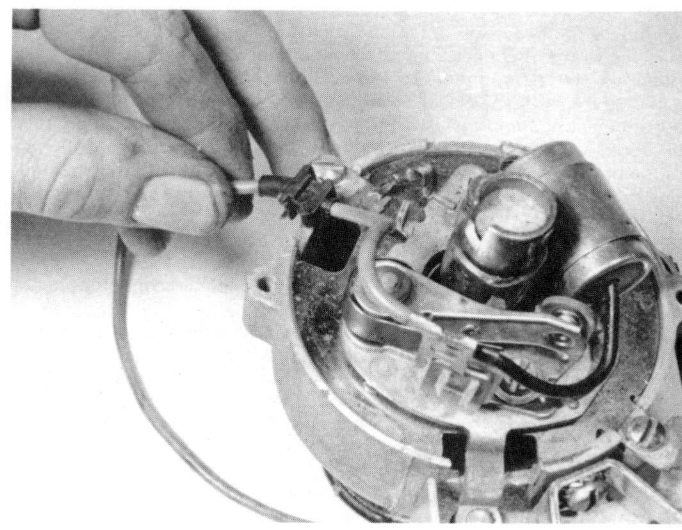
7.3 Removing the LT lead

7.5 Undoing the condenser retaining screw

7.6A Remove the vacuum unit retaining screws (arrowed) ...

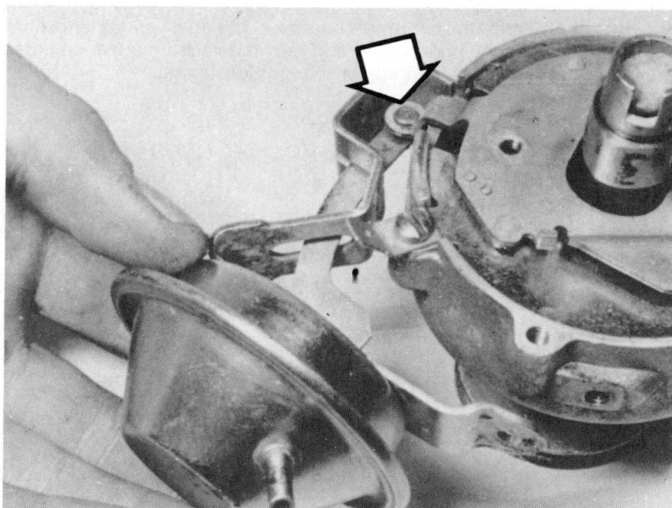
7.6B ... and disengage the operating arm (arrowed) while withdrawing the unit

7.7 Undo the baseplate retaining screws (arrowed)

under one screw and the spade terminal under the other (photo). Withdraw the baseplate assembly from the distributor body.

8 This is the practical limit of dismantling of these distributors, as none of the components below the baseplate are renewable as separate items. If, however, it is necessary to remove the centrifugal advance springs and weights for cleaning or inspection, this can now be done. Mark each spring and its associated locating post with a dab of paint for identification and then carefully hook off the springs. Ensure that the springs and weights are refitted in the same positions otherwise the ignition advance characteristics of the engine will be altered. The weights can be withdrawn after extracting the small retaining clips (photo).

9 With the distributor dismantled, clean the mechanical components in paraffin and dry with a lint-free cloth.

10 Check the condition of the contact breaker points, as described in Section 3. Check the distributor cap for corrosion of the segments and for signs of tracking, indicated by a thin black line between the segments. Make sure that the carbon brush in the centre of the cap moves freely and stands proud by at least 6.3 mm (1/4 in). Renew the cap if necessary.

11 If the metal portion of the rotor arm is badly burned or loose renew the arm. If slightly burnt, clean the arm with a fine file.

12 Check that the plates of the baseplate assembly move freely, but without excessive slackness. If defective the baseplate assembly must be renewed.

13 Suck on the end of the vacuum unit outlet and check that the operating arm moves in as the suction is applied. Release the suction and check that the arm returns to its original position. If this is not the case, renew the vacuum unit.

14 Inspect the distributor body and shaft assembly for excessive side movement of the shaft in its bushes. With the advance weights and springs in position, hold the skew gear at the base of the shaft with one hand, and with the other hand turn the upper shaft clockwise as far as it will go and then release it. Check as this is done, that the advance weights move out and then return under the action of the springs. Finally check the drivegear for wear, chips or pitting of the teeth. It will be necessary to renew the complete distributor if the body, shafts, weights, springs or drivegear are worn or are in any way unsatisfactory.

15 Reassembly of the distributor is a direct reversal of the removal seqence, but apply a few drops of engine oil to the locating pivot posts of the advance weights and to the felt pad at the top of the distributor shaft. After reassembly adjust the contact breaker points, as described in Section 3, and then refit the distributor to the car, as described in Section 6.

8 Distributor (1.3, 1.6 and 1.8 models) – removal and refitting

1.3 models

1 Remove the spark plugs, as described in Section 12.

2 Release the distributor cap cover and undo the cap retaining screws. Lift off the cap and place it to one side.

3 With the transmission in gear and the handbrake released, pull the car forward until, with a finger over the plug hole, compression can be felt in No 1 cylinder (the cylinder nearest the crankshaft pulley). Continue moving the car forward until the notch on the crankshaft pulley is aligned with the timing pointer (photo). (On automatic transmission models, turn the engine by means of a spanner on the crankshaft pulley bolt.) If the distributor cap is temporarily placed in position, the distributor rotor contact should be pointing towards the No 1 spark plug lead segment in the cap.

4 Disconnect the distributor wiring connector at the ignition coil (photo) and detach the vacuum advance pipe from the distributor vacuum unit.

5 Undo the distributor clamp retaining bolt, lift off the clamp plate and withdraw the distributor from the camshaft housing (photo).

6 Before refitting the distributor check that the engine has not been inadvertently turned whilst the distributor was removed; if it has, return it to the original position, as described in paragraph 3.

7 Position the distributor rotor so that the rotor contact is in line with the arrow or notch on the distributor body (photo). In this position the offset lug on the distributor drive coupling will be in the correct position to engage the similarly offset slot in the end of the camshaft (photos).

8 Check that the O-ring seal is in place on the distributor body and then insert the distributor into its camshaft housing location. With the rotor contact and arrow on the distributor body still in line, refit the distributor clamp and clamp bolt. Tighten the clamp bolt securely.

9 Refit the distributor cap and cap cover, the spark plugs and plug leads. Reconnect the wiring plug and refit the vacuum advance pipe.

10 Refer to Section 11 and adjust the ignition timing.

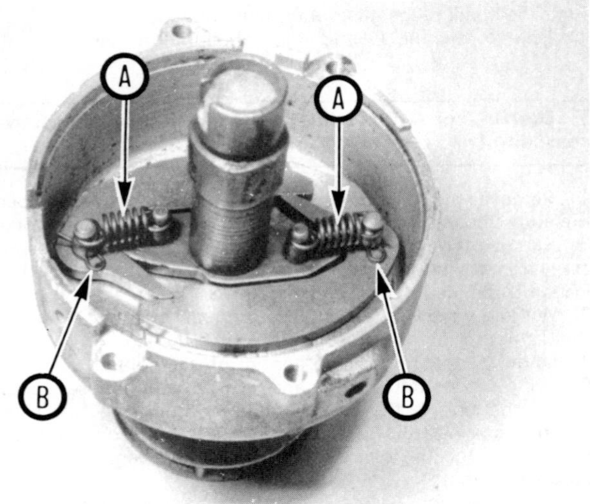

7.8 Centrifugal advance springs (A) and advance weight retaining clips (B)

8.3 Ignition timing marks (arrowed) – 1.3 shown, 1.6 and 1.8 similar

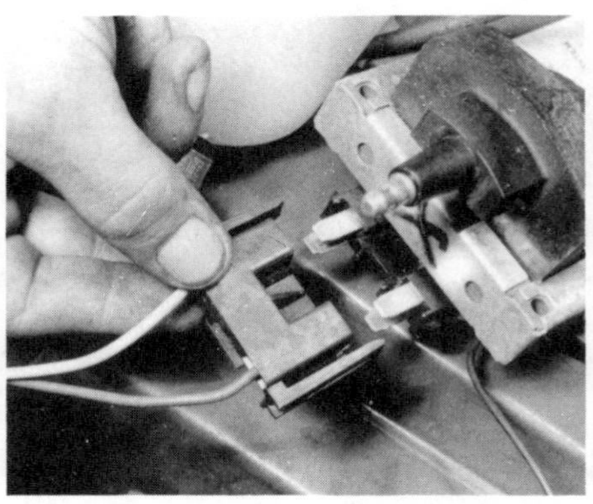

8.4 Disconnecting the distributor wiring connector at the ignition coil

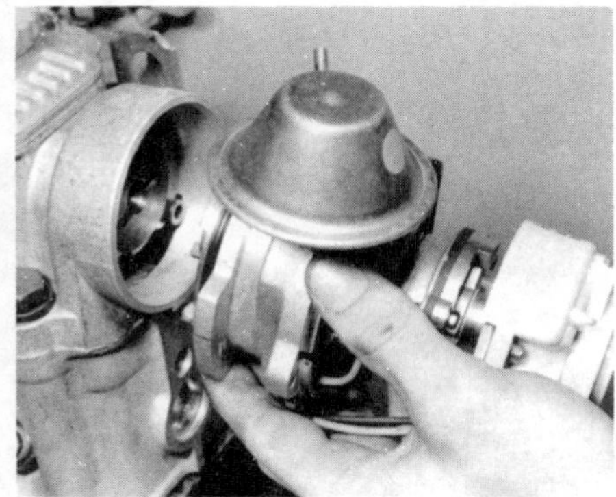

8.5 Removing the distributor from the camshaft housing

8.7A Distributor rotor contact and arrow on distributor body (circled) in alignment ...

8.7B ... causing the drive coupling to be aligned like this ...

8.7C ... to engage the offset slot in the camshaft

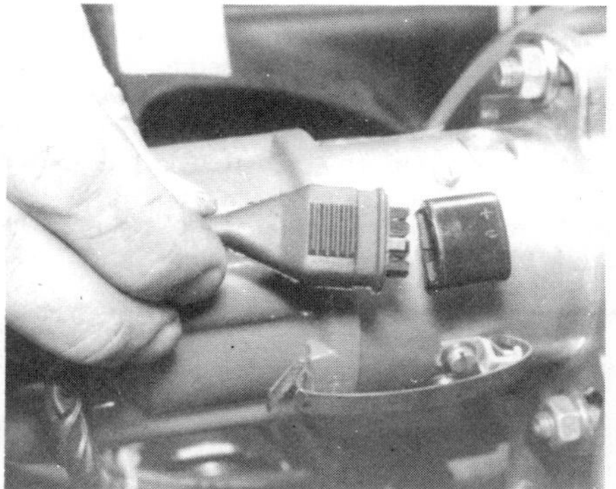
8.12 Unplugging the distributor LT connector (1.6/1.8)

8.13 Removing the distributor cap (1.6/1.8)

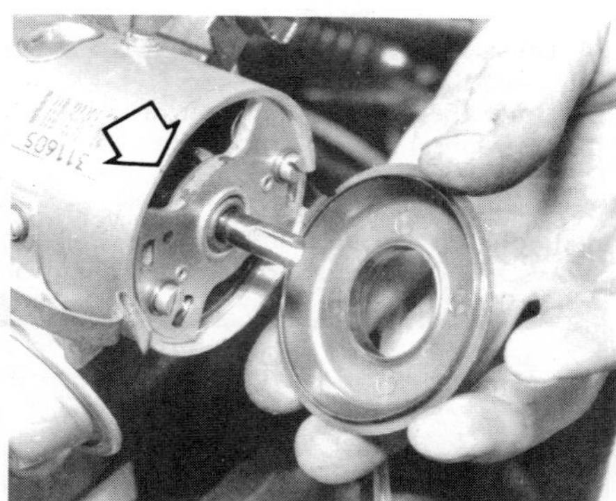
8.14 Removing the flash shield to expose the No 1 reference mark (arrowed)

8.15 Removing the distributor top securing nut (1.6/1.8)

8.16 Removing the distributor (1.6/1.8) – note peg and hole drive

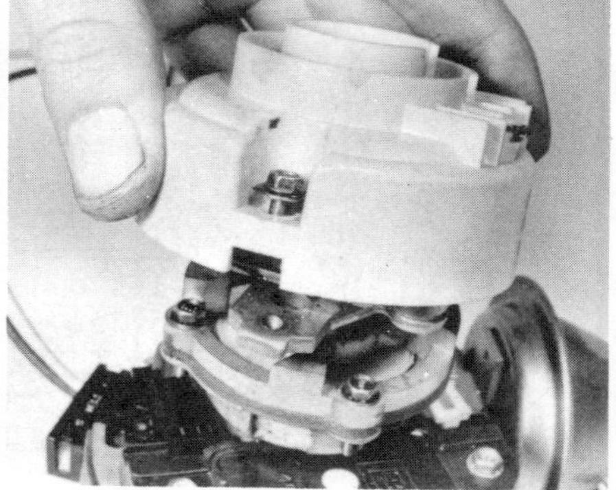
9.2 Removing the distributor rotor (1.3)

1.6 and 1.8 models

11 The procedure is similar to that just described for 1.3 models, with the following differences.

12 The wiring connector must be unplugged from the distributor, not from the coil (photo).

13 The distributor cap is secured by two spring clips, not by screws (photo).

14 There is a mark on the edge of the distributor body to indicate the rotor contact position for No 1 cylinder firing, but the rotor and flash shield must be removed to expose it (photo). The rotor can then be refitted to confirm the alignment.

15 The distributor is secured by two nuts, not by a clamp plate (photo).

16 The distributor drive is by means of an offset peg and hole, not a slot and dogs (photo).

9 Distributor (1.3 models) – dismantling, inspection and reassembly

1 Remove the distributor from the engine, as described in the previous Section.

2 Undo the two retaining screws and lift off the rotor (photo).

3 Disconnect the two electrical plugs, one at each end, from the ignition module (photo).

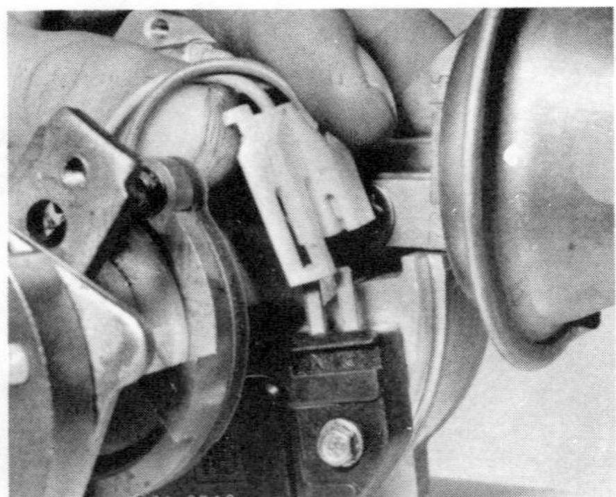

9.3 Disconnecting an electrical plug from the ignition module

9.4 Ignition module securing screws (arrowed)

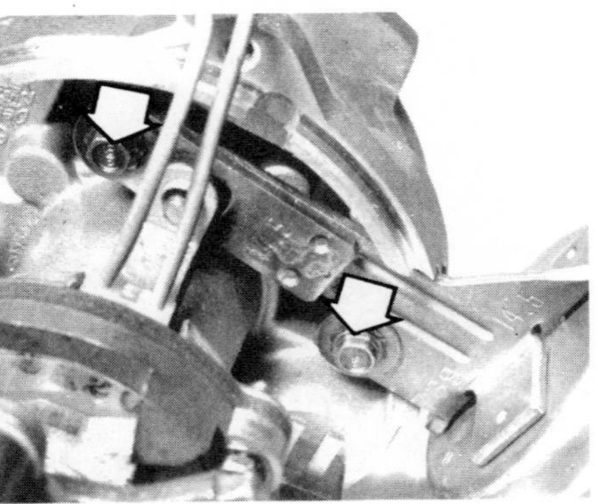

9.5 Vacuum unit retaining screws (arrowed)

4 Undo the two module retaining screws (photo) and withdraw the unit from the distributor.

5 Undo the two vacuum unit retaining screws (photo), disengage the operating rod and remove the vacuum unit.

6 Due to its design and construction, this is the limit of dismantling possible on this distributor. It is possible to renew the rotor, vacuum unit, ignition module and distributor cap separately, but if inspection shows any of the components remaining on the distributor to be in need of attention the complete distributor assembly must be renewed.

7 Check the distributor cap for corrosion of the segments and for signs of tracking, indicated by a thin black line between the segments. Make sure that the carbon brush in the centre of the cap moves freely and stands proud by at least 6.3 mm (1/4 in). Renew the cap if necessary.

8 If the metal portion of the rotor is badly burned or loose, renew the rotor. If slightly burnt it may be cleaned with a fine file.

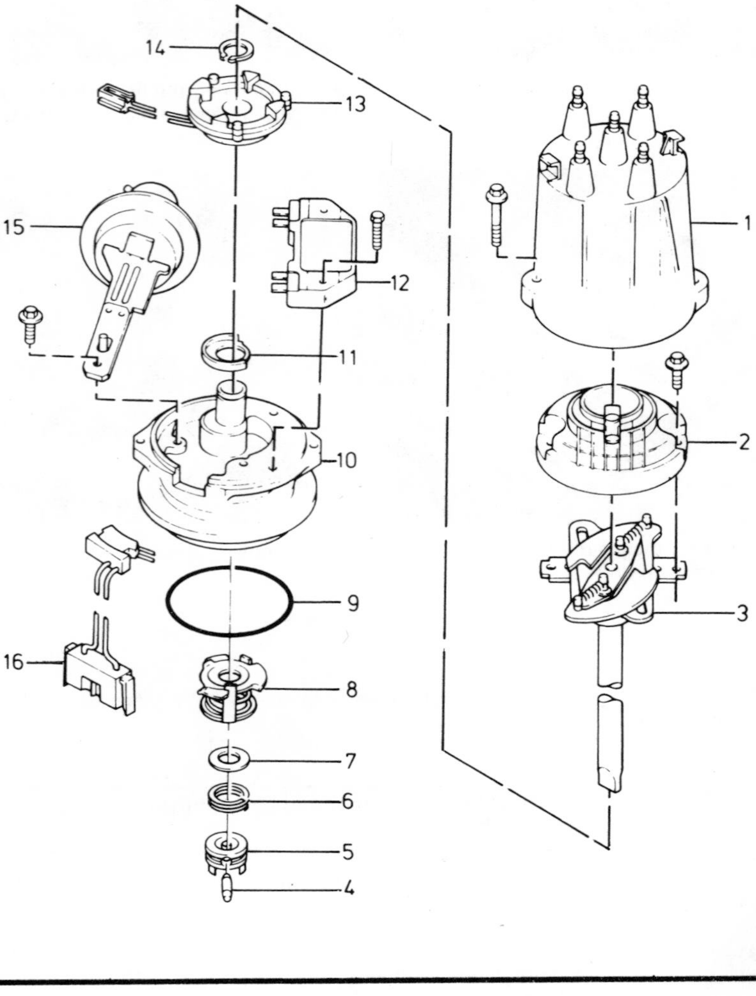

Fig. 4.1 Exploded view of breakerless distributor fitted to 1.3 models (Sec 9)

1 *Distributor cap*
2 *Rotor*
3 *Shaft and centrifugal weights*
4 *Pin*
5 *Dog*
6 *Spring*
7 *Washer*
8 *Spring*
9 *O-ring*
10 *Body*
11 *Seal*
12 *Module*
13 *Induction sensor*
14 *Circlip*
15 *Vacuum unit*
16 *Connector*

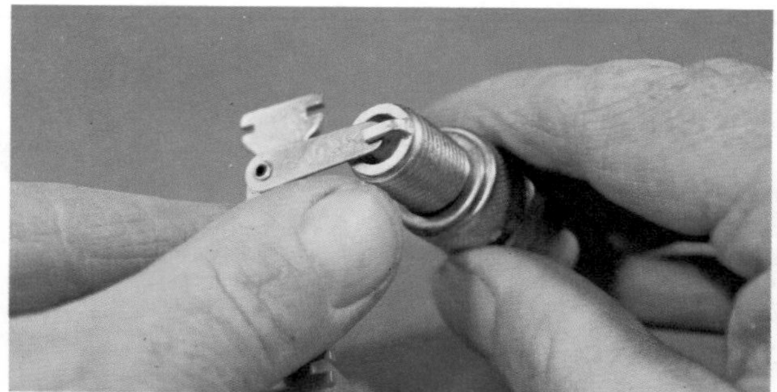

Measuring plug gap. A feeler gauge of the correct size (see ignition system specifications) should have a slight 'drag' when slid between the electrodes. Adjust gap if necessary

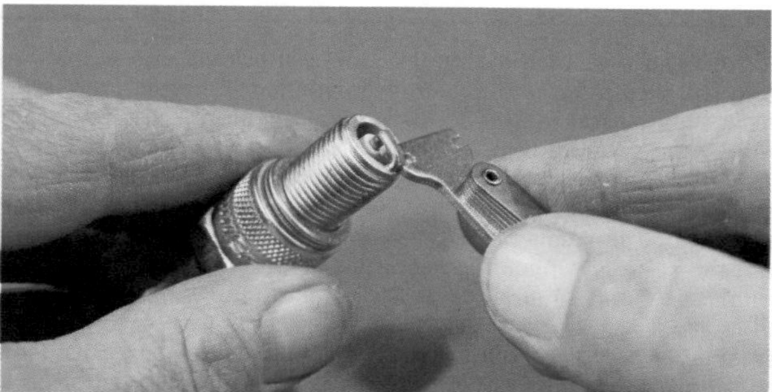

Adjusting plug gap. The plug gap is adjusted by bending the earth electrode inwards, or outwards, as necessary until the correct clearance is obtained. Note the use of the correct tool

Normal. Grey-brown deposits, lightly coated core nose. Gap increasing by around 0.001 in (0.025 mm) per 1000 miles (1600 km). Plugs ideally suited to engine, and engine in good condition

Carbon fouling. Dry, black, sooty deposits. Will cause weak spark and eventually misfire. Fault: over-rich fuel mixture. Check: carburettor mixture settings, float level and jet sizes; choke operation and cleanliness of air filter. Plugs can be re-used after cleaning

Oil fouling. Wet, oily deposits. Will cause weak spark and eventually misfire. Fault: worn bores/piston rings or valve guides; sometimes occurs (temporarily) during running-in period. Plugs can be re-used after thorough cleaning

Overheating. Electrodes have glazed appearance, core nose very white – few deposits. Fault: plug overheating. Check: plug value, ignition timing, fuel octane rating (too low) and fuel mixture (too weak). Discard plugs and cure fault immediately

Electrode damage. Electrodes burned away; core nose has burned, glazed appearance. Fault: pre-ignition. Check: as for 'Overheating' but may be more severe. Discard plugs and remedy fault before piston or valve damage occurs

Split core nose (may appear initially as a crack). Damage is self-evident, but cracks will only show after cleaning. Fault: pre-ignition or wrong gap-setting technique. Check: ignition timing, cooling system, fuel octane rating (too low) and fuel mixture (too weak). Discard plugs, rectify fault immediately

9 Suck on the end of the vacuum unit outlet and check that the operating rod moves in as the suction is applied. Release the suction and check that the rod returns to its original position. If this is not the case, renew the vacuum unit.
10 Inspect the distributor body and shaft assembly for excessive side movement of the shaft in its bushes. Check that the advance weights are free to move on their pivot posts and that they return under the action of the springs. Check the security of all the components on the distributor shaft and finally check for wear of the lug on the drive coupling.
11 Reassembly of the distributor is the reverse sequence to dismantling, but apply a few drops of engine oil to the advance weight pivot posts before refitting the rotor. If a new ignition module is being fitted the new module will be applied between the module and its housing to improve heat dissipation.
12 Refit the distributor, as described in Section 8, after reassembly.

10 Distributor (1.6 and 1.8 models) – dismantling, inspection and reassembly

1 Remove the distributor, as described in Section 8.
2 Pull off the rotor arm and unclip the flash shield.
3 Although the top bearing plate can be removed after undoing its retaining screws, this is of academic interest since no spare parts are available, neither are there any items requiring adjustment.
4 The vacuum unit can be renewed separately if required. Remove it by undoing the two retaining screws and unhooking the operating arm from the baseplate (photos). Note that the screws are not of equal length: the longer screw also secures one of the distributor cap clips.
5 Test the vacuum unit as described in Section 9, paragraph 9.
6 Inspect the distributor cap and rotor, as described in Section 9, paragraphs 7 and 8.
7 Reassemble the distributor in the reverse order to that followed when dismantling. Make sure that the vacuum unit operating arm is correctly engaged with the peg on the baseplate: several attempts may be needed to reconnect it.
8 Refit the distributor, as described in Section 8.

10.4A Removing a vacuum unit retaining screw (1.6/1.8)

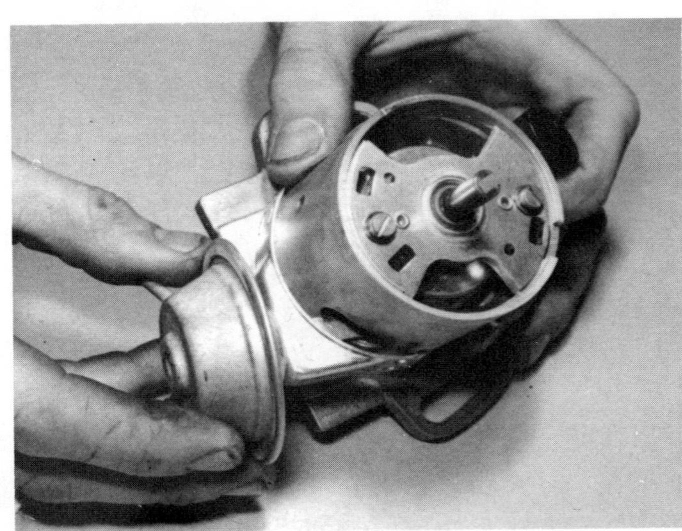
10.4B Removing the vacuum unit (1.6/1.8)

11 Ignition timing – adjustment

1 For prolonged engine life, efficient running performance and economy it is essential for the fuel/air mixture in the combustion chambers to be ignited by the spark plugs at precisely the right moment in relation to engine speed and load. For this to occur the ignition timing must be set accurately and should be checked at the intervals given in Section 2 or wherever the position of the distributor has been altered. To make an accurate check of the ignition timing it is necessary to use a stroboscopic timing light, whereby the timing is checked with the engine running at idling speed.
2 If the distributor has been removed, or if for any reason its position on the engine has been altered, obtain an initial setting to enable the engine to be run, as described in Section 6 for 1.2 models or Section 8 for larger models. Also, on 1.2 models, make sure that the contact breaker points gap or dwell angle is correctly set, as described in Section 3.
3 To check the timing, first highlight the timing marks using white chalk or quick-drying paint. On 1.2 models the marks are a notch on the crankshaft pulley and a raised mark on the timing cover (photo 6.3). On larger models the marks consist of a notch on the crankshaft pulley and a pointer on the oil pump housing (photo 8.3). In both cases the engine is at the specified number of degrees BTDC when the marks are aligned, **not** TDC.
4 Run the engine up to its normal operating temperature and then switch off.
5 Connect a timing light to the spark plug lead of No 1 cylinder, following the manufacturer's instructions.
6 With the engine idling, point the timing light at the timing marks. The marks will appear stationary, and if the timing is correct, they will be aligned.
7 If the marks are not aligned, slacken the distributor clamp bolts or retaining nuts and move the distributor body slowly in one direction or the other until the marks line up. Tighten the clamp bolt or retaining nuts and check that the setting has not altered.
8 Open the throttle slightly and note the movement of the timing marks. If the centrifugal advance in the distributor is working correctly the marks should appear to move away from each other as the engine speed increases. The same should happen if suction is applied to the vacuum advance pipe after disconnecting it from the carburettor, indicating that the distributor vacuum unit is satisfactory.
9 After checking the timing, switch off the engine and disconnect the timing light, if removed, refit the vacuum pipe to the carburettor.

12 Spark plugs and HT leads – general

1 The correct functioning of the spark plugs is vital for the correct running and efficiency of the engine.
2 At the intervals specified in Section 2, the spark plugs should be removed, cleaned and regapped, or renewed.
3 To remove the spark plugs, open the bonnet and, on 1.2 models, remove the air cleaner assembly, as described in Chapter 3. Grip the rubber end fittings and pull the HT leads from the plugs. On larger models a heat shield adaptor is fitted between the end of each spark

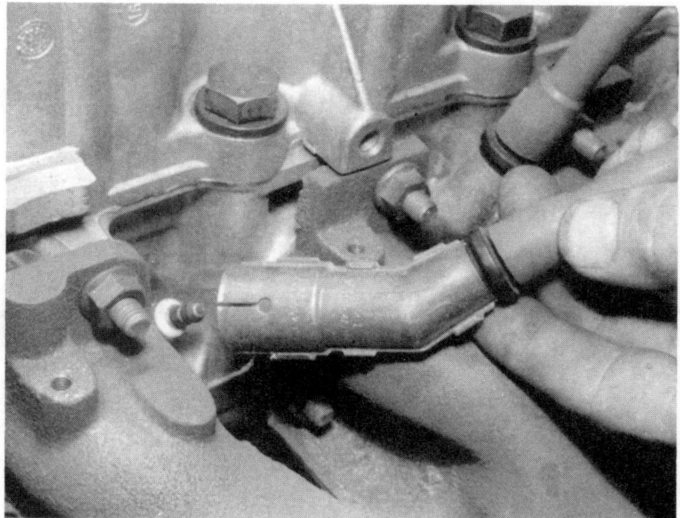

12.3 Removing a plug heat shield adaptor

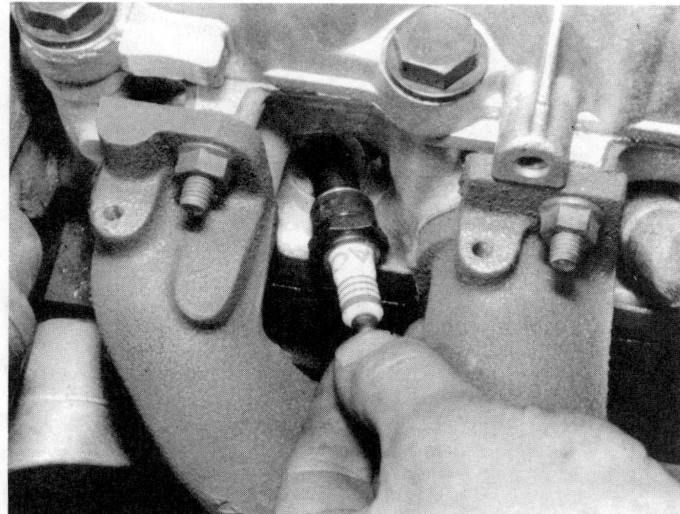

12.14 Refitting a spark plug

plug and the HT lead (photo). To remove these, pull off the HT lead and then withdraw the heat shield using pliers. The shield will be quite tight and require a good pull to remove it, but be careful not to damage the plug.

4 Brush out any accumulated dirt or grit from the spark plug recess in the cylinder head, otherwise it may drop into the combustion chamber when the plug is removed.

5 Unscrew the spark plugs with a deep socket or box spanner. Do not allow the tool to tilt, otherwise the ceramic insulator may be cracked or broken.

6 Examination of the spark plugs will give a good indication of the condition of the engine.

7 If the insulator nose of the spark plug is clean and white, with no deposits, this is indicative of a weak mixture, or too hot a plug (a hot plug transfers heat away from the electrode slowly – a cold plug transfers heat away quickly). The plugs fitted as standard are detailed in the Specifications at the beginning of this Chapter.

8 If the top and insulator nose is covered with hard black-looking deposits, then this is indicative that the mixture is too rich. Should the plug be black and oily, then it is likely that the engine is fairly worn, as well as the mixture being too rich.

9 If the insulator nose is covered with light tan to greyish brown deposits, then the mixture is correct, and it is likely that the engine is in good condition.

10 If there are any traces of long brown tapering stains on the outside of the white portion of the plug, then the plug will have to be renewed, as this shows that there is a faulty joint between the plug body and the insulator and compression is being allowed to leak away.

11 Plugs should preferably be cleaned by a sand-blasting machine, which will free them from carbon better than cleaning by hand. The machine will also test the condition of the plugs under compression. Any plug that fails to spark at the recommended pressure should be renewed.

12 The spark plug gap is of considerable importance, because if it is either too large or too small the size of the spark and its efficiency will be seriously impaired. The spark plug gap should be set to the figure given in the Specifications.

13 To set it, measure the gap with a feeler gauge and then bend open, or close, the outer plug electrode until the correct gap is achieved. The centre electrode should never be bent as this may crack the insulation and cause plug failure, if nothing worse.

14 To refit the plugs, ensure that the thread is clean and dry and then screw each plug in by hand (photo). Tighten the plugs to the specified torque. If a torque wrench is not available tighten them hand tight onto their seating and then tighten further by approximately 1/8 of a turn.

15 When reconnecting the HT leads, make sure that they are refitted in their correct order.

16 The plug leads themselves require no routine attention other than being kept clean and wiped over regularly. When attending to the spark plugs it is a good idea to remove each plug lead in turn from the distributor cap. Water can seep down into the joints giving rise to a white corrosive deposit which must be carefully removed from the end of each cable.

17 The HT leads fitted as original equipment are of the resistive type. If a multi-meter is available, the resistance of each lead can be checked: it should not exceed 20 000 Ω.

13 Coil – general

1 The coil is an auto-transformer, having two sets of windings wound around a core of soft iron wires or laminations. It is located on the left-hand inner wing (photo).

2 If the coil is suspect, the surest test is by substitution of a known good unit. If suitable equipment is available, the winding resistances can be checked. The primary winding resistance is given in the

13.1 Ignition coil location (1.3)

13.3A Disconnecting a coil LT lead (1.6/1.8)

13.3B Ignition module wiring plug (1.6/1.8)

13.3C Removing a coil securing bolt

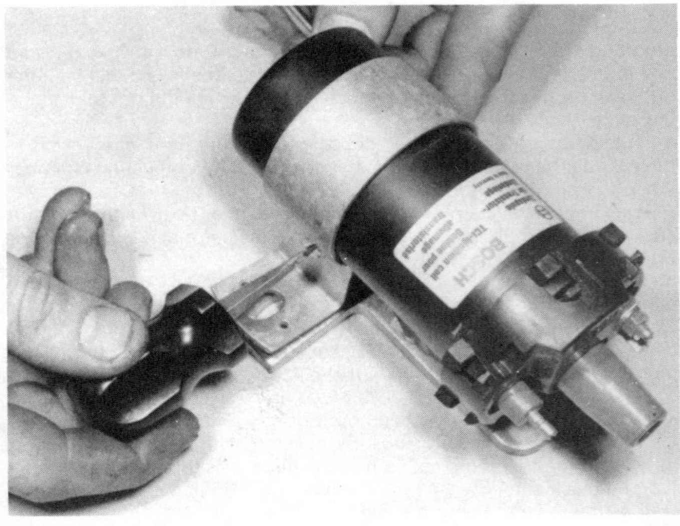

13.4 Undoing the coil clamp screw and nut

Specifications; secondary resistance is not specified, but is typically in the range 4000 to 12 000 Ω.

3 To remove the coil, disconnect its LT and HT leads and remove the securing bolts. On 1.6 and 1.8 models, also unplug the ignition module (photo).

4 The cylindrical type of coil can be removed from its clamp by slackening the clamp screw and nut (photo).

5 Some coils have a safety plug: in the event of overheating the plug will come out and oil or other insulating material will be discharged. Should this happen, renew the coil and the ignition module.

6 The different types of coil used with the different ignition systems are not interchangeable.

7 When refitting the coil, note that the LT connectors are of different size and shape, thus preventing incorrect fitting.

14 Ignition module (breakerless system) – removal and refitting

1 On 1.3 models the ignition module is located in the distributor. See Section 9 for details.

2 On 1.6 and 1.8 models the module is located on the coil mounting plate. To gain access, first remove the coil, as described in Section 13.

3 With the coil removed from its bracket, the module can be unbolted from the mounting plate (photo).

4 If a new module is being fitted, it should be supplied with a small quantity of silicone grease which must be applied to the mounting plate to improve heat dissipation (photo). Similar heat sink compounds can also be obtained from shops selling radio and electronic components.

5 Refit the ignition module in the reverse order to removal. Make sure the locating pins engage with the holes in the mounting plate.

15 TDC sensor – general

1 All OHC engines in this range incorporate a facility for connecting a TDC sensor, necessary for the use of certain diagnostic equipment.

2 A brass sleeve is located in the crankcase to accept the sensor which in turn monitors the position of the two pins which are fitted to the crankshaft counterweights.

3 Without a suitable ignition tester it is unlikely that this device will

14.3 Unbolting the ignition module (1.6/1.8)

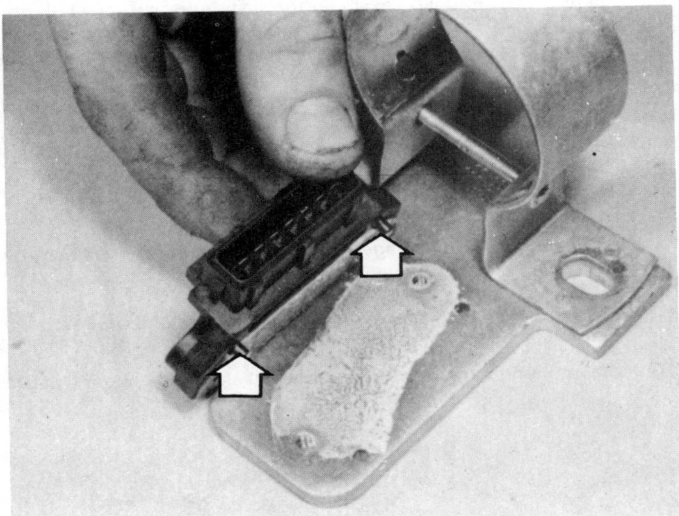

14.4 Ignition module and mounting plate – note locating pins (arrowed), and heat sink compound on baseplate

be of use to the home mechanic, only to garages or service stations.
4 No 1 piston is at TDC when the notch in the crankshaft pulley is 10° past the timing pointer, the pulley having been turned in the normal direction of crankshaft rotation.

16 Fault diagnosis – conventional ignition system

1 By far the majority of breakdown and running troubles are caused by faults in the ignition system either in the low tension or high tension circuits.
2 There are two main symptoms indicating faults. Either the engine will not start or fire, or the engine is difficult to start and misfires. If it is a regular misfire (ie the engine is running on only two or three cylinders), the fault is almost sure to be in the secondary or high tension circuit. If the misfiring is intermittent the fault could be in either the high or low tension circuits. If the car stops suddenly, or will not start at all, it is likely that the fault is in the low tension circuit. Loss of power and overheating, apart from faulty carburation settings, are normally due to faults in the distributor or to incorrect ignition timing.

Engine fails to start

3 If the engine fails to start and the car was running normally when it was last used, first check that there is fuel in the petrol tank. If the engine turns over normally on the starter motor and the battery is evidently well charged, then the fault may be in either the high or low tension circuits. First check the HT circuit.
4 One of the commonest reasons for bad starting is wet or damp spark plug leads and distributor. Remove the distributor cap. If condensation is visible internally, dry the cap with a rag and also wipe over the leads. Refit the cap.
5 If the engine still fails to start, check that voltage is reaching the plugs by disconnecting each plug lead in turn at the spark plug end and holding the end of the cable with rubber or an insulated tool about 6 mm (1/4 in) away from the cylinder block. Spin the engine on the starter motor.
6 Sparking between the end of the cable and the block should be fairly strong with a regular blue spark. If voltage is reaching the plugs, then remove them and clean and regap them. The engine should now start.
7 If there is no spark at the plug leads, take off the HT lead from the centre of the distributor cap and hold it to the block as before. Spin the engine on the starter once more. A rapid succession of blue sparks between the end of the lead and the block indicates that the coil is in order and that the distributor cap is cracked, the rotor arm is faulty or the carbon brush in the top of the distributor cap is not making good contact with the rotor arm.
8 If there are no sparks from the end of the lead from the coil, check the connections at the coil end of the lead. If it is in order start checking the low tension circuit. Possibly, the points are in bad condition. Clean and reset them as described in this Chapter, Section 3.
9 Use a 12V voltmeter or a 12V bulb and two lengths of wire. With the ignition switch on and the points open, test between the low tension wire to the coil and earth. No reading indicates a break in the supply from the ignition switch. Check the connections at the switch to see if any are loose. Refit them and the engine should run. A reading shows a faulty coil or condenser, or broken lead between the coil and the distributor.
10 Take the condenser wire off the points assembly and with the points open test between the moving point and earth. If there is now a reading then the fault is in the condenser. Fit a new one and the fault is cleared.
11 With no reading from the moving point to earth, take a reading between earth and the distributor terminal of the coil. A reading here shows a broken wire between the coil and the distributor. No reading confirms that the coil had failed and must be renewed, after which the engine will run once more. Remember to refit the condenser wire to the points assembly. For these tests it is sufficient to separate the points with a piece of dry paper while testing with the points open.
12 Note that if a 12V bulb is used for these tests, full brilliance cannot be expected because of the ballast resistor in the coil feed (see Section 1). If the resistor fails, the engine will fire when the starter motor is operated but it will not run. Do not bypass the resistor wire with ordinary wire, or the coil may overheat and points life will be very short.

Engine misfires

13 If the engine misfires regularly run it at a fast idling speed. Pull off each of the plug caps in turn and listen to the note of the engine. Hold the plug cap in a dry cloth or with a rubber glove as additional protection against a shock from the HT supply.
14 No difference in engine running will be noticed when the lead from the defective circuit is removed. Removing the lead from one of the good cylinders will accentuate the misfire.
15 Remove the plug lead from the plug which is not firing and hold it about 6 mm (1/4 in) away from the block. Restart the engine. If the sparking is fairly strong and regular, the fault must lie in the spark plug.
16 The plug may be loose, the insulation may be cracked, or the points may have burnt away giving too wide a gap for the spark to jump. Worse still, one of the points may have broken off. Either renew the plug or clean it, reset the gap, and then test it.
17 If there is no spark at the end of the plug lead, or if it is weak and intermittent, check the ignition lead from the distributor to the plug. If the insulation is cracked or perished, renew the lead. Check the connections at the distributor cap.

18 If there is still no spark, examine the distributor cap carefully for tracking. This can be recognised by a very thin black line running between two or more electrodes, or between an electrode and some other part of the distributor. These lines are paths which now conduct electricity across the cap thus letting it run to earth. The only answer is a new distributor cap.
19 Apart from the ignition timing being incorrect, other causes of misfiring have already been dealt with when considering the failure of the engine to start. To recap, these are that

(a) *The coil may be faulty giving an intermittent misfire*
(b) *There may be a damaged wire or loose connection in the low tension circuit*
(c) *The condenser may be faulty*
(d) *There may be a mechanical fault in the distributor (broken driving spindle or contact breaker spring)*

20 If the ignition timing is too far retarded, it should be noted that the engine will tend to overheat, and there will be a quite noticeable drop in power. If the engine is overheating and the power is down, and the ignition timing is correct, then the carburettor should be checked, as it is likely that this is where the fault lies.

17 Fault diagnosis – breakerless ignition system

1 Fault diagnosis on the HT side of the ignition system follows the same pattern as that described for the conventional system in the previous Section. Take great care to avoid receiving personal electric shocks, since the voltage is appreciably higher.
2 Fault diagnosis on the LT side of the system should be left to a GM dealer or other competent specialist. Do not embark on a course of haphazard substitution of components, since a fault in one component can cause damage to others.

Chapter 5 Clutch

Contents

Specifications

General

Clutch type	Single dry plate, diaphragm spring pressure plate
Actuation	Cable
Disc (driven plate) diameter (nominal):	
1.2 and 1.3	190 mm (7.5 in)
1.6	203 mm (8.0 in)
1.8	216 mm (8.5 in)

Adjustment

Free play at pedal	Nil
Pedal stroke:	
Desired value	138 mm (5.4 in)
Permitted	Up to 145 mm (5.7 in)
Adjustment point	Nut on release lever

Torque wrench settings

Torque wrench settings	Nm	lbf ft
Clutch cover to transmission casing	7	5
Clutch pressure plate to flywheel	15	11
Release fork clamp bolt	35	26
Transmission end cover plug:		
4-speed	50	37
5-speed	30	22

1 General description

All models with manual transmission have a single plate diaphragm spring clutch. The clutch pressure plate is bolted to the flywheel. The gearbox input shaft projects through the clutch assembly.

The clutch driven plate is located between the flywheel and the clutch pressure plate and slides on splines on the gearbox input shaft. When the clutch is engaged, the diaphragm spring forces the pressure plate to grip the driven plate against the flywheel and drive is transmitted from the crankshaft, through the driven plate, to the gearbox input shaft. On disengaging the clutch the pressure plate is lifted to release the driven plate with the result that the drive to the gearbox is disconnected.

The clutch is operated by a foot pedal suspended under the facia, and a cable connected to the clutch release lever mounted on the transmission casing. Depressing the pedal causes the release lever to move the release bearing against the fingers of the diaphragm spring in the pressure plate assembly. The spring is sandwiched between two rings which act as fulcrums. As the centre of the spring is moved in, the periphery moves out to lift the pressure plate and disengage the clutch. The reverse takes place when the pedal is released.

As wear occurs on the driven plate with usage, the foot pedal will rise progressively relative to its original position. Periodic adjustment is not required.

An unusual feature of the design of this particular clutch is that the driven plate, pressure plate and release bearing assembly can be renewed without having to remove either the engine or transmission from the car.

Fig. 5.1 Clutch pedal released measurement – A (Sec 2)

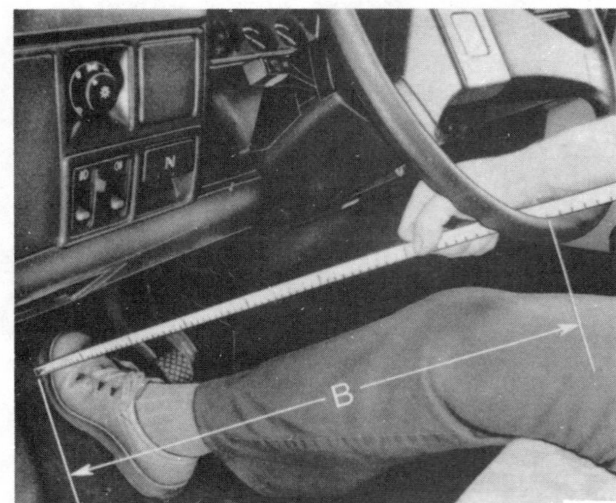

Fig. 5.2 Clutch pedal depressed measurement – B (Sec 2)

2 Clutch – adjustment

1 Clutch adjustment is not a routine operation; it should only be necessary after the cable or pressure plate has been renewed. In use the clutch pedal will rise relative to the brake pedal as the clutch linings wear: this is normal and is not a reason for adjustment as long as the pedal stroke remains correct.
2 To perform the initial adjustment after component renewal, proceed as follows.
3 With the clutch pedal released, take a measurement from the outer edge of the steering wheel to the centre of the clutch pedal pad and record the dimension. Now take a second measurement with the clutch pedal fully depressed. These measurements can be taken using a suitable strip of wood or metal as the important figure is the difference between the two measurements, that is the movement (stroke) of the pedal itself. This should be within the limits given in the Specifications. If adjustment is necessary, it is done at the release lever end.
4 To carry out the adjustment, first remove the spring clip from the threaded end of the cable at the release lever. Pull the end of the cable to gain some slack and turn the adjuster as necessary until the desired pedal stroke is obtained. Refit the spring clip when adjustment is correct (photo).
5 Note that when correctly adjusted the clutch pedal will be slightly higher than the brake pedal and it is incorrect for the two pedals to be in alignment. Note also that there should be no play in the clutch pedal of these vehicles.

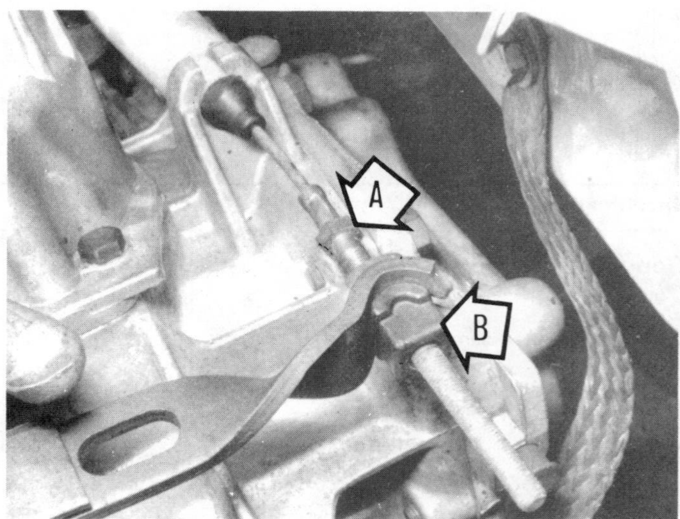

2.4 Clutch adjuster nut (A) and spring clip (B)

3 Clutch cable – removal and refitting

1 Before disturbing the clutch cable installation, take a measurement of the length of the threaded end of the cable protruding through the cable adjuster at the clutch release lever. This will enable an initial adjustment setting to be made when refitting the cable.
2 Remove the spring clip, slacken the cable adjuster and slip the cable out of the release lever slot. Move the cable assembly rearwards and withdraw it from the lug on the transmission casing.
3 Remove the cable from the support bracket behind the engine and, where applicable, release any clips or ties securing the engine wiring harness to the clutch cable.
4 If necessary to improve access, remove under-facia trim on the driver's side.
5 Unhook the return spring from the clutch pedal and disconnect the cable from the pedal lever.
6 The cable can now be withdrawn into the engine compartment by pulling it through the bulkhead.
7 Refitting the clutch cable is the reverse sequence to removal. Position the cable adjuster initially so that the same amount of cable protrudes through the adjuster as noted during removal, then adjust the clutch, as described in Section 2.

Fig. 5.3 Clutch cable attachment to pedal (arrowed) (Sec 3)

4 Clutch pedal – removal and refitting

1 Disconnect the clutch cable from the release lever and from the pedal, as described in the previous Section.
2 Remove the wire locking clip from the pedal shaft retaining nut. Remove the nut and washers from the shaft.
3 Push the pedal shaft nut out of the pedal bush. Recover the return spring and remove the pedal.
4 When refitting, coat the pedal shaft with a 'dry' lubricant (molybdenum disulphide paste, copper-based anti-seize compound, or equivalent).
5 Refit the pedal and spring and secure the shaft. Reconnect the clutch cable and check the adjustment, as described in the previous Sections.

5 Clutch assembly – removal and refitting (engine and transmission in car)

1 Prise off the wheel trim from the left-hand front roadwheel and slacken the wheel bolts. Jack up the car and support it securely on axle stands. Remove the roadwheel.
2 Working under the left-hand wheel arch, unscrew the large plug from the transmission end cover (photos).
3 Extract the circlip, now exposed, from the centre of the input shaft using circlip pliers (photo).
4 Underneath the circlip is a socket-headed screw which will require a twelve-sided splined key or socket bit to extract it. Motor accessory shops can usually supply this type of key (photo). Undo and remove the screw from the input shaft (photo).
5 Mark the input shaft position relative to its gear cluster with two dots of paint. The shaft can now be withdrawn to allow the clutch driven plate to be removed. To do this, screw a suitable bolt into the end of the input shaft and withdraw it using a self-locking wrench (photo). One of the bolts securing the gearchange mechanism cover to the top of the transmission casing can be used for this purpose if no other suitable bolt can be found. *Don't forget to refit it to the cover after withdrawing the input shaft.* If the shaft is tight, use a long screwdriver or suitable bar and lever between the wrench jaws and the end cover. The makers specify the use of a puller to withdraw the shaft, and this or a slide hammer may be needed if the shaft is really tight. Note that the input shaft cannot be removed completely and it is only necessary to withdraw it about half way, until it reaches its stop, to allow removal of the clutch.
6 Working underneath the car unscrew the four bolts securing the clutch access plate to the transmission casing (photo) and lift off the plate.
7 Before the clutch can be removed the pressure plate must be compressed against the tension of the diaphragm spring, otherwise the clutch assembly will be too thick to pass through the space between the flywheel and the edge of the casing.
8 Three special clamps are available from the manufacturer for this operation, but suitable alternatives can be made up from strips of metal. The clamps should be U-shaped and conform to the following dimensions (photo):

Thickness of metal strip = 3.0 mm (0.12 in)
Distance between U legs = 15.0 mm (0.6 in)

9 Bevel the edges of the clamps to make them easier to fit and file or cut a notch in one side to clear the pressure plate rivets.
10 To fit the clamps, have an assistant depress the clutch pedal fully and then fit each clamp securely over the edge of the cover/pressure plate assembly (photos). Ensure that they engage in the apertures spaced around the rim of the clutch cover. Turn the crankshaft by means of a socket on the pulley bolt to bring each aperture into an accessible position.

5.2A Removing the transmission end cover plug – 4-speed

5.2B Transmission end cover plug – 5-speed

5.3 Using circlip pliers to extract the input shaft circlip

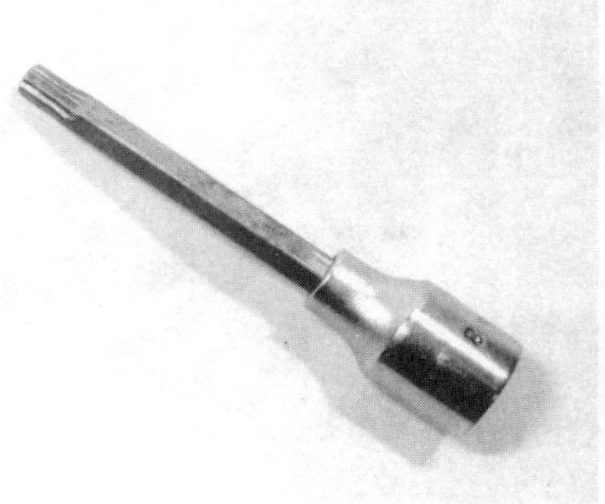
5.4A A splined bit for socket-headed screw

5.4B Input shaft socket-headed screw

5.5 Using a self-locking wrench and a bolt to withdraw the input shaft

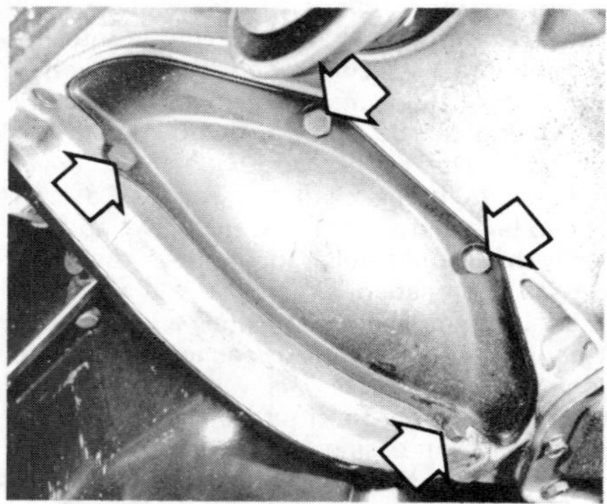

5.6 Clutch access plate retaining bolts (arrowed)

5.8 Clutch pressure plate retaining clamp – see text for dimensions

5.10A Retaining clamp in position – gearbox side

5.10B Retaining clip in position – flywheel side

5.12A Removing a pressure plate retaining bolt

5.12B Withdrawing the clutch assembly through the aperture in the transmission casing

11 When all three clamps are in position and secure, the clutch pedal can be released.

12 Progressively slacken and remove each of the six bolts securing the pressure plate to the flywheel (photo). Withdraw the clutch assembly downwards and out through the aperture in the transmission casing (photo).

13 If necessary, the three clamps can be removed from the cover/pressure plate by compressing the assembly in a vice between blocks of wood, one across the flywheel side of the cover and one against the diaphragm spring. A proprietary tool is also available for this purpose.

14 It is important that no grease or oil is allowed to come into contact with the driven plate friction linings, or the pressure plate and flywheel faces. It is advisable to handle the parts with clean hands and to wipe off the pressure plate and flywheel faces with a clean, dry rag before inspection or refitting commences.

15 Inspect the clutch components, as described in Section 7.

16 Commence refitting by clamping the driven plate to the pressure plate, using the procedure described in paragraph 13. Make sure that the driven plate is the right way round: the greater projecting part of the hub faces away from the flywheel.

17 Apply a thin smear of grease to the driven plate hub splines, then offer the clutch assembly to the flywheel. Turn the flywheel as necessary until the paint mark on the flywheel and the V mark on the cover are aligned (Fig. 5.4).

18 Hold the clutch up with one hand and push the input shaft in with the other, so that the input shaft and driven plate hub splines engage. Only use hand pressure on the input shaft, and observe the alignment marks made when dismantling (paragraph 5).

19 Insert the pressure plate-to-flywheel bolts, turning the flywheel to bring the bolt holes into view. Tighten the bolts progressively to the specified torque.

20 Refit the socket-headed screw to the input shaft, then press the shaft home. **Do not** use hammer blows to move the shaft: if necessary use a screw or hydraulic pusher similar to that shown in Fig. 5.5.

21 Refit the circlip to the input shaft.

22 Apply PTFE tape or sealant to the threads of the end cover plug (photo). Refit the plug and tighten it to the specified torque. The plug should not protrude more than 4 mm (0.16 in) from the face of the cover when it is fitted, otherwise its sealing properties may be impaired.

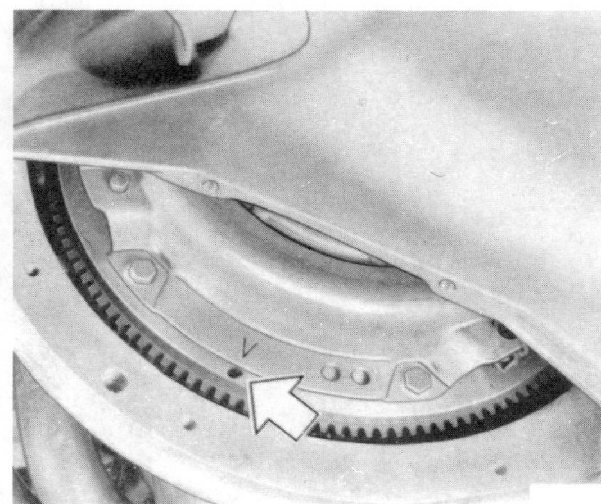

Fig. 5.4 Clutch cover and flywheel alignment marks (arrowed) (Sec 5)

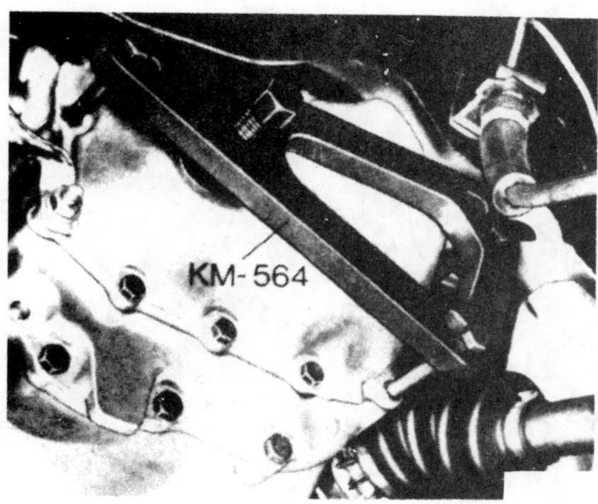

Fig. 5.5 Pusher tool KM-564 used for pressing home the input shaft (Sec 5)

23 Have an assistant depress the clutch pedal. Turn the flywheel and remove the clutch plate clamps.
24 Refit the clutch access plate.
25 Adjust the clutch, as described in Section 2.
26 Refit the roadwheel, lower the vehicle and tighten the wheel bolts.

6 Clutch assembly – removal and refitting (engine or transmission removed from car)

1 With the engine or transmission removed from the car, as described in Chapter 1 or 6, proceed as follows.
2 Progressively slacken the bolts which secure the clutch pressure plate to the flywheel. Lift off the pressure plate and recover the driven plate (photo).
3 It is important that no grease or oil is allowed to contact the driven plate friction linings, or the flywheel and pressure plate friction surfaces. Handle the parts with clean hands, and wipe them with a clean rag before inspection or refitting commences
4 Inspect the clutch components, as described in Section 3.

5.22 Applying PTFE tape to the threads of the end cover plug – 4-speed shown

5 Commence refitting by placing the driven plate against the flywheel so that the greater projecting part of the hub faces away from the flywheel.
6 Fit the pressure plate over the driven plate, aligning the V mark on the cover with the paint mark on the flywheel. Refit the pressure plate retaining bolts and tighten them finger tight so that the driven plate is just gripped, but can still be moved.
7 The driven plate must now be centralised so that, when the engine and transmission are mated, the input shaft splines will pass through the splines in the driven plate hub.
8 Centralisation can be carried out by inserting a round bar or long screwdriver through the the driven plate hub so that it rests in the hole in the end of the crankshaft. Moving the bar sideways or up and down will move the driven plate as necessary, to achieve centralisation.
9 Centralisation can be checked by removing the bar and checking that the hole in the end of the crankshaft is exactly in the centre of the driven plate hub. If a universal clutch aligning tool is available, this will enable precise centralisation to be achieved at the first attempt (photo).
10 When centralisation is perfect, tighten the pressure plate retaining bolts progressively to the specified torque. Refit the engine or transmission, as described in Chapter 1 or 6.

6.2 Removing the clutch assembly with the engine out of the car

6.9 Universal clutch aligning tool in use while pressure plate bolts are tightened

7 Clutch components – inspection

1 With the clutch assembly removed, examine the driven plate friction linings for wear and loose rivets, and the hub for distortion, cracks, broken or weak cushioning springs and worn splines, but as long as the friction material pattern can be clearly seen, this is acceptable. If the friction material is worn down to the level of the rivet heads, the driven plate must be renewed. The plate must also be renewed if there is any sign of oil contamination of the friction material caused by a leaking transmission input shaft oil seal or crankshaft rear oil seal. If oil contamination is evident the cause of the trouble must be rectified immediately, as described in Chapter 1 or Chapter 6.
2 Check the machined faces of the flywheel and pressure plate. If either is grooved or heavily scored, renewal is necessary. If the pressure plate is cracked or split, or if the diaphragm spring is damaged or its pressure suspect, a new unit must be fitted.
3 Check the release bearing for smoothness of operation. There should be no harshness or slackness in it and it should spin freely without tight spots.
4 When considering renewing clutch components individually, bear in mind that new parts (or parts from different manufacturers) do not always bed into old ones satisfactorily. A clutch cover assembly or driven plate renewed separately may sometimes cause judder or snatch. Although expensive, the clutch cover assembly, driven plate and release bearing should be renewed together wherever possible.

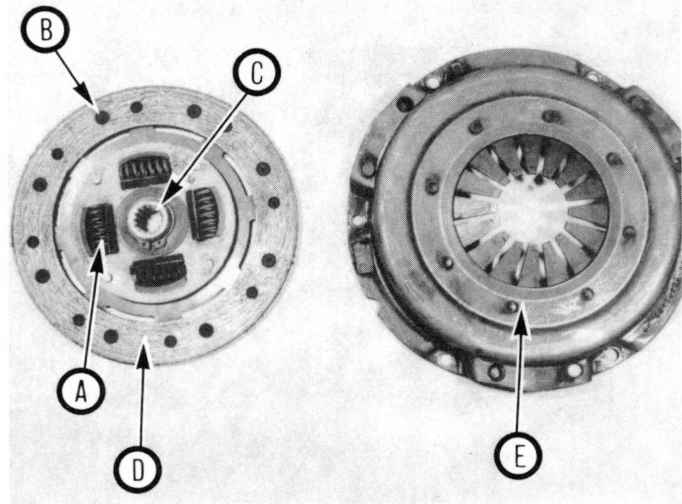

7.1 Items requiring careful inspection when checking the clutch components for wear
A Cushioning springs *D Lining material*
B Rivets *E Diaphragm spring*
C Hub splines

8 Clutch release bearing – removal and refitting

Note: *If this operation is being carried out with the engine/transmission in the car, it will first be necessary to remove the clutch assembly, as described in Section 5.*
1 With the clutch assembly removed, undo the clamp bolt securing the release fork to the release lever pivot shaft (photo).
2 Referring to Section 3 if necessary, disconnect the clutch cable from the release lever.
3 Pull the release lever upwards out of the transmission casing, lift out the release fork and slide the release bearing off the guide tube (photo).
4 Before refitting, smear the guide tube and the fingers of the release fork with molybdenum disulphide grease.
5 Slide the release bearing onto the guide tube, engage the release fork and push the pivot shaft down into engagement with the fork.
6 Align the clamp bolt hole in the fork with the machined groove on the pivot shaft (photo) and refit the clamp bolt. Tighten the clamp bolt to the specified torque.
7 Refit the clutch assembly, as described in Section 5.

8.1 Removing the release fork clamp bolt

8.3 Removing the release fork and release bearing

8.6 Groove in pivot shaft (arrowed) must align with release fork clamp bolt hole

9 Fault diagnosis – clutch

Symptom	Reason(s)
Judder when taking up drive	Loose or worn engine or transmission mountings Oil contamination of driven plate friction linings Excessive wear of driven plate friction linings Broken or weak driven plate cushioning springs Distorted or damaged pressure plate or diaphragm spring Clutch cable binding
Clutch spin (failure to disengage so that gears are difficult to engage)	Incorrect clutch adjustment Driven plate sticking to flywheel face due to corrosion or oil contamination Input shaft seized in crankshaft spigot bearing
Clutch slip (increase in engine speed does not result in increase in road speed – particularly on gradients)	Incorrect clutch adjustment Oil contamination of driven plate friction linings Excessive wear of driven plate friction linings Weak or broken diaphragm spring
Noise evident on depressing clutch pedal	Worn or damaged release bearing Damaged or broken diaphragm spring Incorrect clutch adjustment
Noise evident as clutch pedal is released	Broken or weak driven plate cushioning springs Damaged or broken diaphragm spring Worn gearbox bearings or internal components (see Chapter 6)

Chapter 6 Transmission

For modifications, and information applicable to later models, see Supplement at end of manual

Contents

Specifications

Part A: Manual transmission

General

Transmission type ... Four or five forward speeds and one reverse, synchromesh on all forward gears. Integral final drive

Maker's designation:
- 1.2 and 1.3 ... F10/4W (4-speed) or F10/5W (5-speed)
- 1.6 ... F16/4W (4-speed) or F16/5W (5-speed)
- 1.8 ... F16/5W (wide ratio 5-speed) or F16/5C (close ratio 5-speed)

Gear ratio (:1)

	F10/4W and /5W	F16/4W and /5W	F16/5C
1st	3.55	3.42	3.42
2nd	1.96	1.95	2.16
3rd	1.30	1.28	1.48
4th	0.89	0.89	1.12
5th	0.71	0.71	0.89
Reverse	3.18	3.33	3.33

Final drive ratios (:1)

	Hatchback	Estate and Van
F10/4W	3.94	4.18
F10/5W	4.18	4.18
F16/4W	3.74	3.74
F16/5W	3.94	3.94
F16/5C	3.74	–

Lubrication

Lubricant type:	
All except GTE (F16/5C)	SAE 80 gear oil to API GL3 or GL4
GTE (F16/5C)	Special transmission fluid, GM part No 90 188 629
Lubricant capacity:	
F10/4W	1.7 litres (3.0 pints)
F10/5W	1.8 litres (3.2 pints)
F16/4W	2.0 litres (3.5 pints)
F16/5W and F16/5C	2.1 litres (3.7 pints)

Torque wrench settings

	Nm	lbf ft
Transmission casing to engine	75	55
End cover to casing	22	16
Selector cover bolts	15	11
Selector cover screw plug:		
4-speed	50	37
5-speed	30	22
5th gear fork pivot socket screws	22	16
Input shaft socket screw	15	11
Selector rod clamp bolt	14	10
Differential cover to casing	30	22
Differential-to-crownwheel bolts	85	63
Differential bearing flange to casing (F16)	25	18
Reversing lamp switch	20	15
Mounting to casing	65	48
Mounting to body or side-member	75	55
Interlock pin bridge piece screws (5-speed)	5	4
Selector interlock pawl screws (5-speed)	9	6

Part B: Automatic transmission

General

Transmission type	Fully automatic, 3 forward speeds and 1 reverse
Maker's designation	125 THM

Ratios (:1)

1st	2.84
2nd	1.60
3rd	1.00
Reverse	2.07
Primary drive chain	1.12
Final drive:	
1.3	3.33
1.6 and 1.8	3.06
Torque converter:	
1.3	2.4 max
1.6 and 1.8	2.0 max

Transmission fluid

Fluid type	Dexron ® II ATF
Fluid capacity:	
From dry	9.0 litre (15.9 pints) approx
Drain and refill	6.3 litres (11.1 pints) approx

Torque wrench settings

	Nm	lbf ft
Fluid pan screws	10	7
Fluid cooler connections to transmission	38	28
Fluid pipe bracket	24	18
Kickdown cable bracket	10	7
Torque converter housing to engine	75	55
Selector lever to shaft	27	20
Transmission mounting:		
To transmission	22	16
To engine	40	30
Fluid cooler connections to cooler	22	16
Torque converter to flexplate:		
1.3	65	48
All other models	60	44

PART A: MANUAL TRANSMISSION

1 General description

A four- or five-speed manual transmission may be fitted, depending on engine size and options specified. 1.2 and 1.3 models are fitted with the F10 series transmission; larger-engined models have the heavier duty F16 range. All types of transmission have synchromesh on all forward gears.

Drive is transmitted through the transmission and the integral final drive/differential assembly to the driveshafts. Gear selection is by a floor-mounted lever and a remote control linkage.

If transmission overhaul is necessary, careful consideration should be given to the likely cost. If is often more economical, and certainly quicker, to obtain a factory exchange or good second-hand unit rather then to fit new parts to the existing transmission.

Fig. 6.1 Oil level checking plug (arrowed) – F10 transmission (Sec 2)

2 Maintenance and inspection

1 At every major service interval, inspect the transmission joint faces and oil seals for damage, deterioration or oil leakage. Repair or renew as necessary.

2 At alternate services, or if leakage has occurred, check the transmission oil level and top up if necessary. The level checking plug is located on the side of the transmission casing, near the left-hand driveshaft joint on F10 series transmissions (Fig. 6.1) or near the right-hand joint on F16 series transmissions (photo). With the car on level ground, the oil should be up to the bottom of the level plug hole. If topping-up is necessary, this is done through the breather/filler plug on top of the transmission until oil runs out of the level plug hole (photo).

3 Renewal of the transmission oil is not specified by the manufacturer. Should the diligent home mechanic wish to renew the oil as a precautionary measure, the old oil may be drained by unbolting the differential cover plate. No drain plug is provided.

4 The special gear oil specified for GTE transmission is supposed to reduce transmission noise. It may be used in the transmission of other models if wished. For supplies of this oil, consult your GM dealer.

5 If problems are experienced with the gearchange, check the adjustment of the linkage, as described in Section 3. Also check for wear in the linkage joints and bushes, and renew as necessary (Chapter 4).

2.2A Removing the oil level plug – F16 transmission

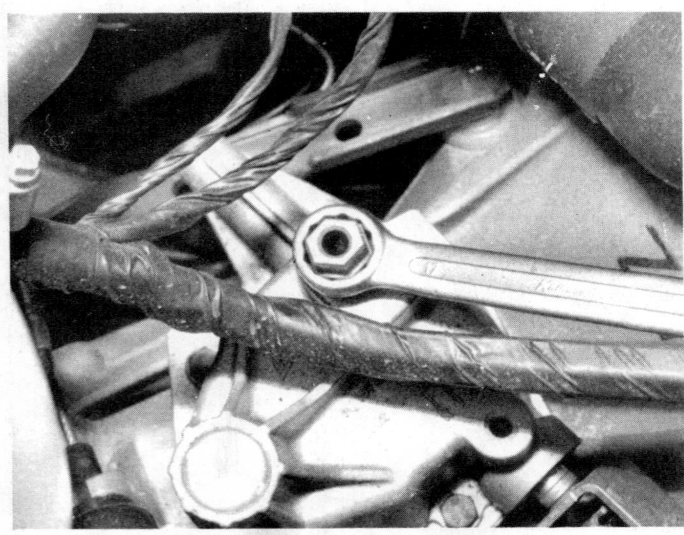

2.2B Removing the transmission breather/filler plug

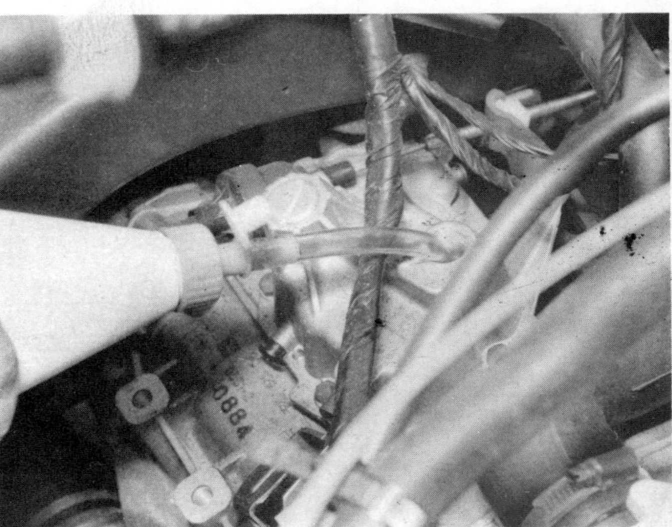

2.2C Topping-up the transmission oil

3 Gearchange linkage – adjustment

1 Remove the centre console, if fitted, as described in Chapter 11. Put the gear lever in the neutral position.
2 Working in the engine bay, prise out the adjuster hole plug and slacken the pinch-bolt on the gearchange rod coupling (Fig. 6.2).
3 Turn the selector rod protruding from the selector cover in an anti-clockwise direction (looking towards the front of the car) until a twist drill of diameter 4.5 mm (3/16 in approx) can be inserted into the adjuster hole and into the correspondence hole in the selector lever (photo).
4 Pull the rubber boot up from the base of the gear lever and move the lever, still in neutral, to the 1st/2nd gear plane. In this position the reference marks on the stop sleeve and lever housing will be aligned (photo).
5 Have an assistant hold the gear lever in this position. Tighten the gearchange coupling pinch-bolt.
6 Remove the drill from the adjuster hole. Check that all gears can be engaged satisfactorily, then fit a new adjuster hole plug.
7 Refit the gear lever boot and (if applicable) the centre console.

3.3 Using a drill to set the gearchange linkage – casing removed for clarity

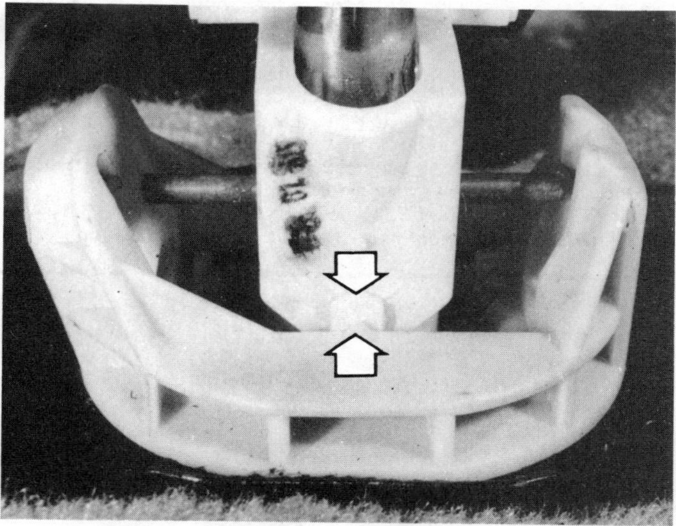

3.4 Gear lever reference marks (arrowed) – 5-speed

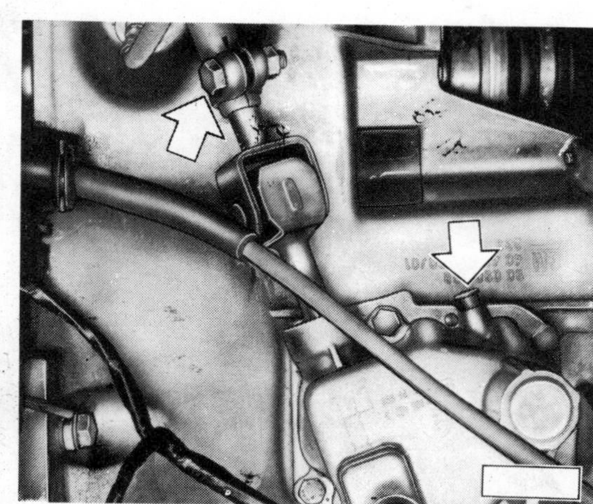

Fig. 6.2 Adjuster hole plug and gearchange coupling pinch-bolt (arrowed) (Sec 3)

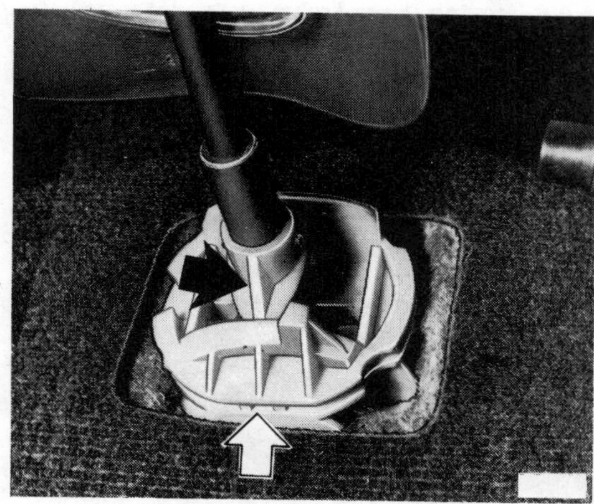

Fig. 6.3 Gear lever reference marks (arrowed) – 4-speed (Sec 3)

4 Gearchange linkage – removal and refitting

1 Slacken the pinch-bolt on the gearchange rod coupling.
2 Remove the screws which hold the gearchange rod protective tube to the underbody. Pull back the rubber cover and disgage the eye in the intermediate lever from the base of the gearchange lever (photo).
3 Withdraw the linkage from the vehicle. Remove the rubber cover and bellows from the protective tube.
4 To dismantle the linkage, drive out the roll pin which secures the intermediate lever to the rod, then tap the rod out of the lever. The rod can then be removed from the protective tube.
5 The universal joint may be dismantled by grinding or filing off the rivet heads. Special pins and spring clips should be available for reassembly from your GM dealer, but check that this is so before destroying the rivets.
6 The bushes can be removed from the protective tube by driving them out with a rod.
7 When reassembling, fill the grooves in the tube bushes with silicone grease before fitting.
8 Use a new roll pin to secure the intermediate lever to the rod, making sure it is aligned as shown in Fig. 6.7.
9 Fit the rubber cover and the bellows, applying silicone grease to their inner surfaces. Do not twist the bellows after installation.

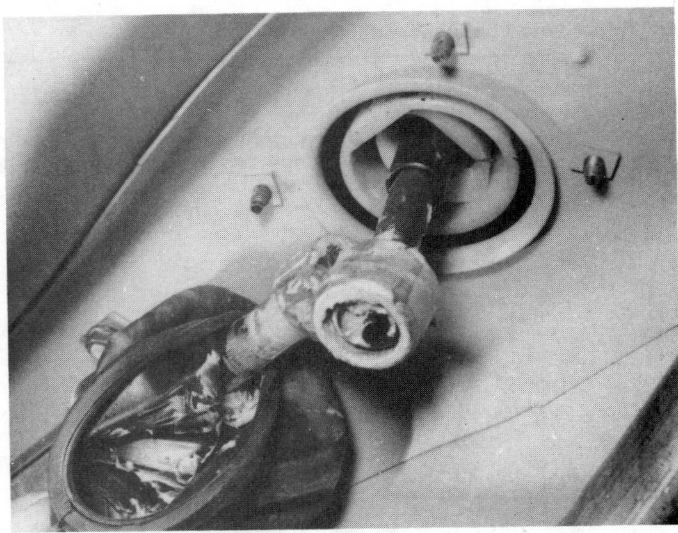

4.2 Removing the gearchange rod rubber cover

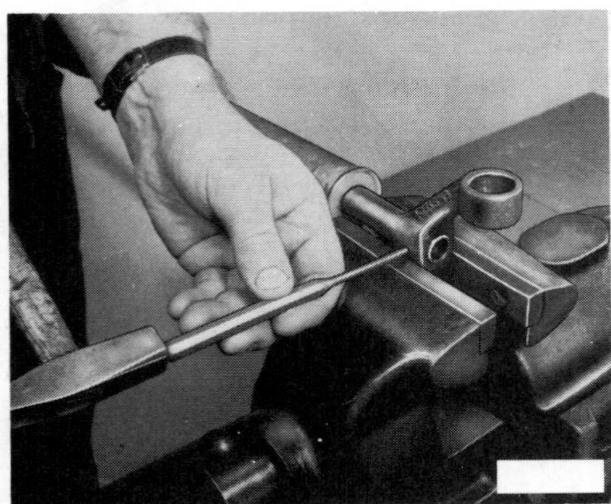

Fig. 6.4 Removing the gearchange rod intermediate lever roll pin (Sec 4)

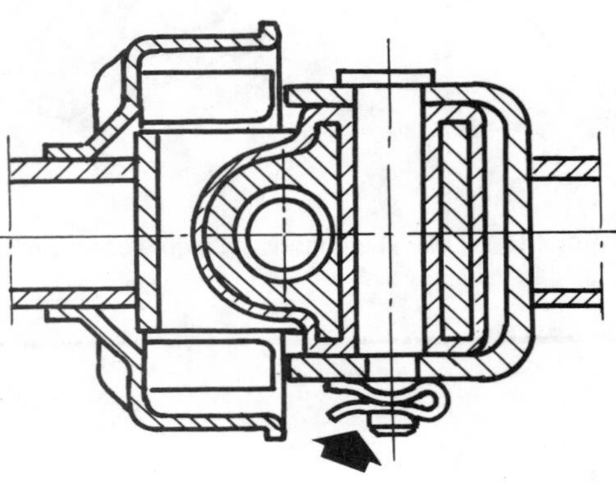

Fig. 6.5 Pin and spring clip (arrowed) used for UJ reassembly (Sec 4)

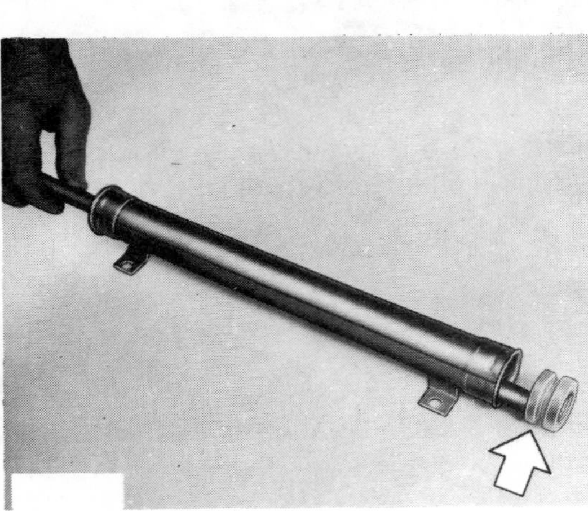

Fig. 6.6 Driving a bush (arrowed) from the protective tube (Sec 4)

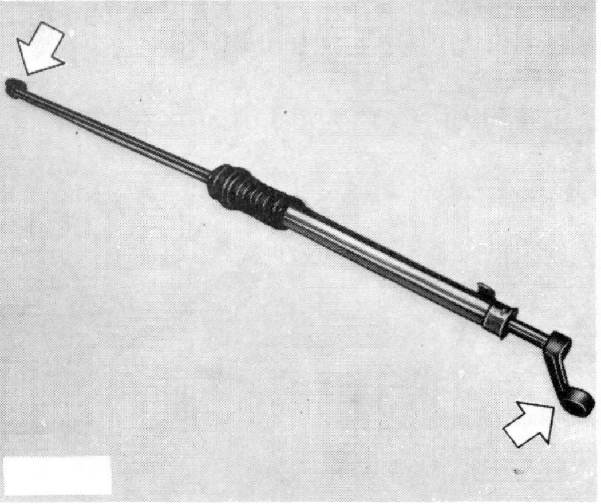

Fig. 6.7 Intermediate lever and clamp (both arrowed) correctly aligned (Sec 4)

10 Offer the linkage to the car, engaging the intermediate lever with the gearchang lever, and secure it with the screws. Refit the rubber cover around the base of the lever.
11 Adjust the linkage, as described in Section 3.

5 Gear lever – removal and refitting

1 Remove the centre console, when fitted, as described in Chapter 11. Put the gear lever in neutral.
2 Peel back the rubber boot from the base of the gear lever.
3 On 4-speed models, remove the circlip from the gear lever. Push the lever to the left and remove it.
4 On 5-speed models, it is probably best to remove the four screws which hold the gear lever housing to the floor, then remove the lever and housing complete. Check that spares are available before attempting to separate the housing components.
5 Refit in the reverse order to removal, lubricating the contact surfaces with silicone grease.

6 Gear lever reverse blocker cable – removal and refitting

1 The reverse blocker mechanism prevents inadvertent selection of reverse gear. It is released by lifting the collar under the gear lever knob: this collar is connected to the top of a cable, the bottom end of which is attached to a finger or rod. If the cable breaks it may be renewed as follows, but check first that spare parts are available.
2 Remove the gear lever, as described in Section 5, and the gear lever knob, as described in Section 7. Recover the spring from below the knob.
3 Remove the grub screw from the top of the gear lever. These may have a plain slotted head or a recessed hexagon head (photo).
4 Drive out the roll pins which secure the plastic coupling and shift finger to the base of the gear lever (photo). It is likely that the plastic coupling will be damaged. Remove the cable and its end fitting.
5 Refit in the reverse order to removal. No adjustment procedure is laid down for the cable: experiment with the grub screws which clamp the top of the cable until a satisfactory result is obtained.

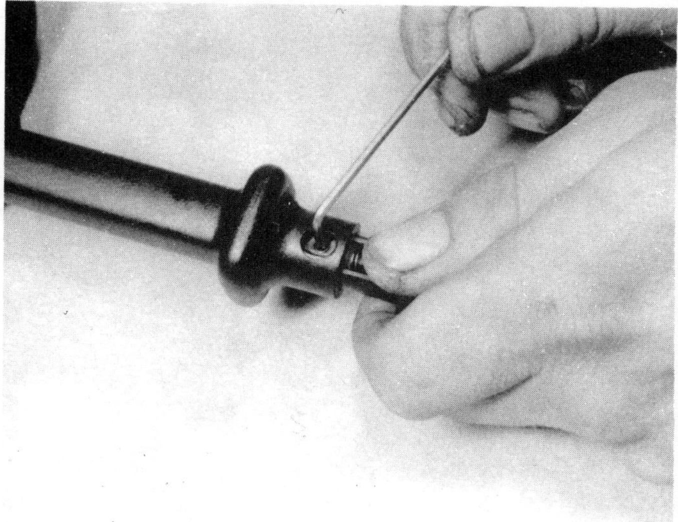

6.3 Removing a grub screw from the reverse blocker collar

6.4 Drive out the roll pins

7 Gear lever rubber boot – removal and refitting

1 Remove the gear lever, as described in Section 5.
2 Immerse the gear lever knob in hot water (approximately 80°C/176°F) for a few minutes, then twist and tap it off the lever. There is a good chance of destroying the knob.
3 Slide the old rubber boot off the lever and fit the new one. Use a little liquid detergent as a lubricant, if necessary. The arrow or triangular mark at the base of the boot should face the front of the vehicle.
4 Refit the knob, preheating it in hot water and driving it on with a mallet. Make sure it is the right way round.
5 Refit the gear lever, as described in Section 5.

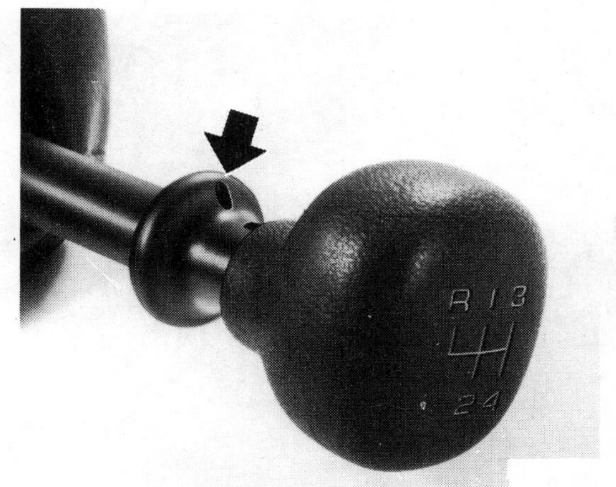

Fig. 6.8 Gear lever knob should be aligned as shown relative to hole (arrowed) (Sec 7)

8 Manual transmission – removal and refitting

1 Disconnect the battery earth lead.
2 Disconnect the clutch cable from the release lever (Chapter 5, Section 3).
3 Disconnect the leads from the reversing lamp switch.
4 Disconnect the speedometer cable, or sender unit, at the transmission (photo).
5 Slacken the gearchange rod coupling pinch-bolt and separate the coupling.
6 Remove the three bolts which secure the top of the transmission casing to the engine.
7 Slacken the front wheel bolts, raise and securely support the front of the vehicle, and remove the front wheels.
8 It is now necessary to support the engine from above, either with a bar and hook braced across the engine bay, or with a crane or similar engine lifting tackle. Attach the tackle and adjust it to take the weight of the engine.

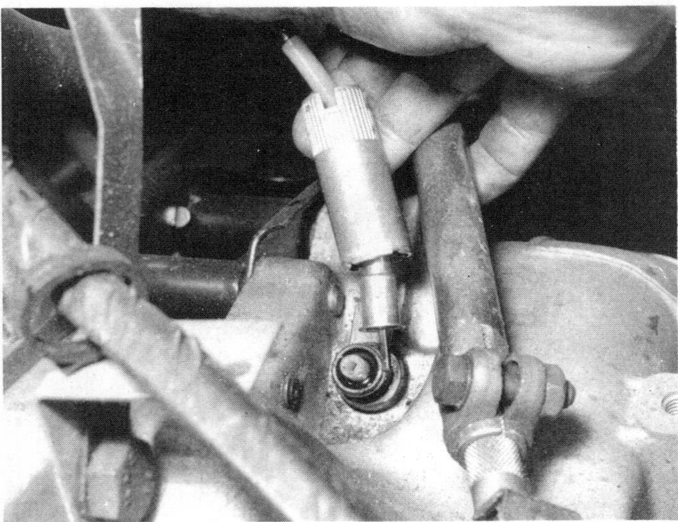
8.4 Disconnecting the speedometer cable

9 Unbolt the earth strap from the transmission end cover.
10 Disconnect the central arm balljoints on both sides.
11 Separate the driveshafts from the transmission, as described in Chapter 7. Be prepared for oil spillage. Plug the driveshaft apertures to reduce spillage and to keep out dirt.
12 Withdraw the clutch input shaft, as described in Chapter 5, Section 5.
13 Remove the engine/transmission left-hand mounting completely.
14 Unbolt the engine/transmission rear mounting from the underframe. Also unbolt the exhaust pipe bracket.
15 Unbolt the clutch access plate, then remove the remaining engine-to-transmission bolts.
16 Withdraw the transmission from its dowels on the engine and lower it to the ground. Ideally a cradle and hydraulic jack should be used.
17 Take care not to damage projecting components when setting the transmission down. It should be stored in the same position it assumes in use.
18 Commence refitting by offering the transmission to the engine, engaging the dowels and fitting the retaining bolts. Tighten the bolts to the specified torque.
19 Clean out the rear mounting bolt holes with a tap, or an old bolt with a slot nut in its threads. Fasten the rear mounting using new bolts coated with thread locking compound. Tighten the bolts to the specified torque.
20 Refit the left-hand mounting bracket and tighten its fastenings to the specified torque.
21 Refit the driveshafts, as described in Chapter 7.
22 Reconnect the control arm balljoints, tightening their securing nuts to the specified torque – see Chapter 10.
23 Refit the clutch input shaft, as described in Chapter 5, Section 5. Fit and tighten the end cover plug.
24 Secure the earth strap to the end cover.
25 Disconnect the engine support tackle, refit the roadwheels and lower the car to the ground. Tighten the wheel bolts.
26 Reconnect the speedometer cable, the reversing lamp switch and the clutch cable. Adjust the clutch cable, as described in Chapter 5, Section 2.
27 Reconnect the gearchange rod coupling. Adjust the linkage, as described in Section 3, and tighten the pinch-bolt.
28 Refill the transmission with oil, as described in Section 2.

9 Transmission overhaul – general

The overhaul of the transmission requires certain special tools and the ability to carry out some critical adjustments if the work is to be successful. Readers should study the procedures and satisfy themselves that they have the tools and skills required. It is relatively simple to dismantle the transmission into its major assemblies.

Before starting work on the transmission, drain the oil by removing the differential cover plate. Thoroughly clean the outside of the transmission with paraffin or a suitable solvent, then dry it with a lint-free rag. Prepare an uncluttered working area, with plenty of small containers and trays handy to store the various parts. Label everything as it is removed.

Before starting reassembly all components must be absolutely clean. Lubricate components with clean gear oil during reassembly.

10 F10/4 transmission – dismantling into major assemblies

Gearbox

1 With the transmission removed from the car and on the bench, proceed as follows.
2 Unbolt and remove the selector cover from the transmission casing (photos).
3 Unbolt the retaining plate and withdraw the speedometer driven gear (photos).
4 Unscrew and remove the reversing lamp switch (photo).

10.2A Undo the retaining bolts ...

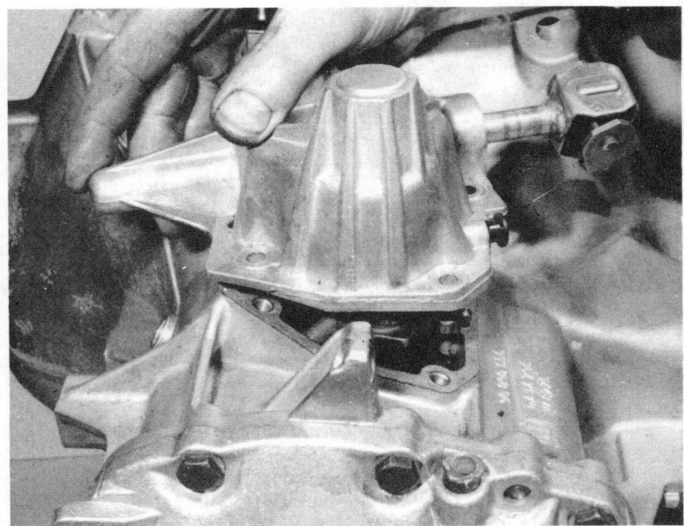
10.2B ... and remove the selector cover

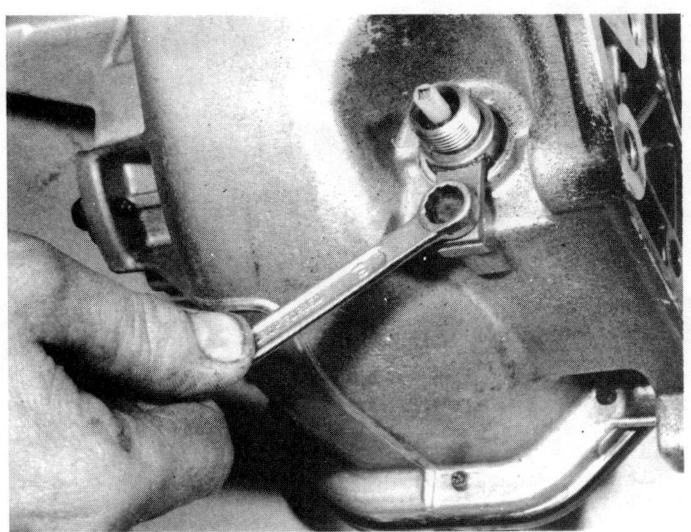

10.3A Unbolt the retaining plate ...

10.3B ... and withdraw the speedometer driven gear

10.4 Removing the reversing lamp switch

10.7 Removing the casing from the end cover

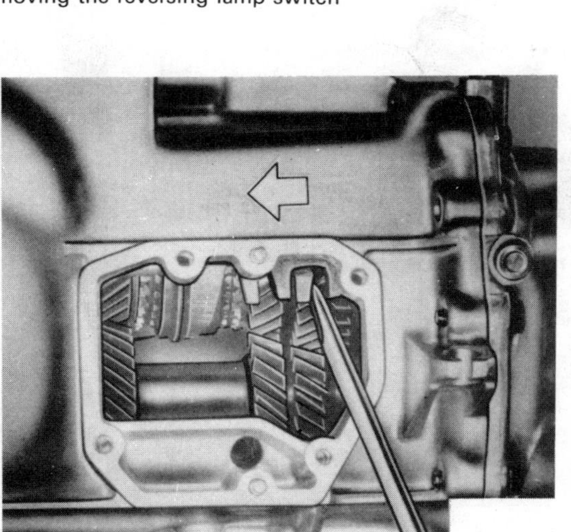

Fig. 6.9 Using a screwdriver to engage 2nd gear (Sec 10)

5 Using a screwdriver as a lever, engage 2nd gear by moving the selector fork nearest the end cover.

6 Unscrew and remove the end cover bolts and nuts.

7 Withdraw the main casing from the end cover and geartrains (photo).

8 Prise out the detent plugs from the end cover and extract the springs and detent plungers (photos).

9 Drive out the roll pins which secure the selector forks to the selector rods.

10 Move the synchro sleeve back to the neutral position and then withdraw 3rd/4th and reverse selector forks and their rods from the end cover.

11 Extract the circlips which retain the mainshaft and input shaft gear trains. Extract the swarf collecting magnet (photos).

12 Remove the geartrain assemblies, together with the 1st/2nd selector fork and rod, simultaneously.

13 Extract the selector rod interlock pins from the end cover.

14 Remove the reverse idler shaft from the end cover. To do this, grip the shaft in the jaws of a vice fitted with soft metal protectors and using a brass drift, gently tap the cover off the shaft. Take care not to lose the locking ball (photo).

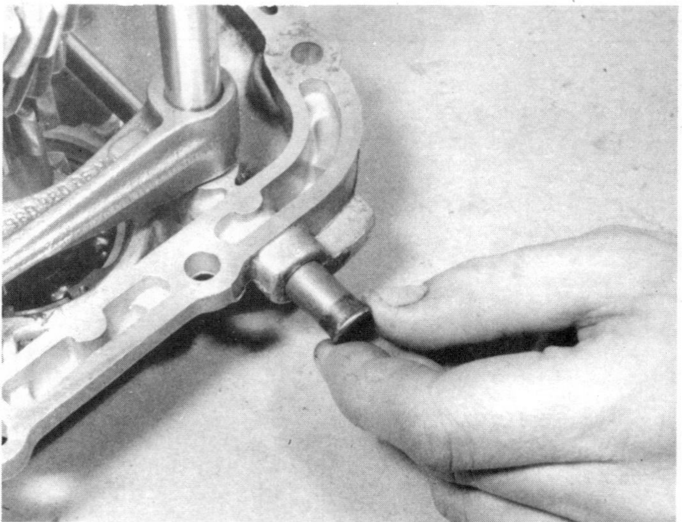

10.8A Removing a detent plug

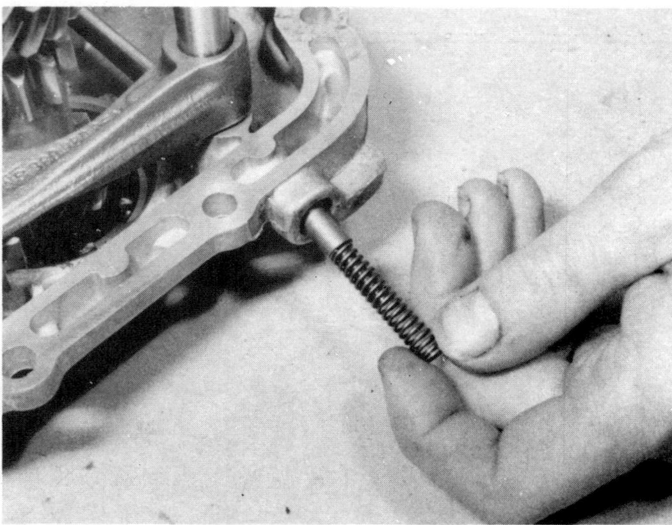

10.8B Detent spring and plunger

10.11A Mainshaft bearing retaining circlip

10.11B Removing the swarf-collecting magnet

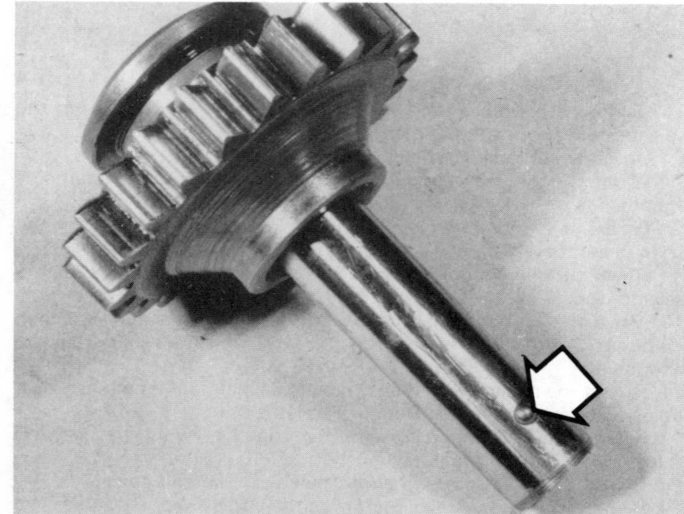

10.14 Reverse idler shaft locking ball (arrowed)

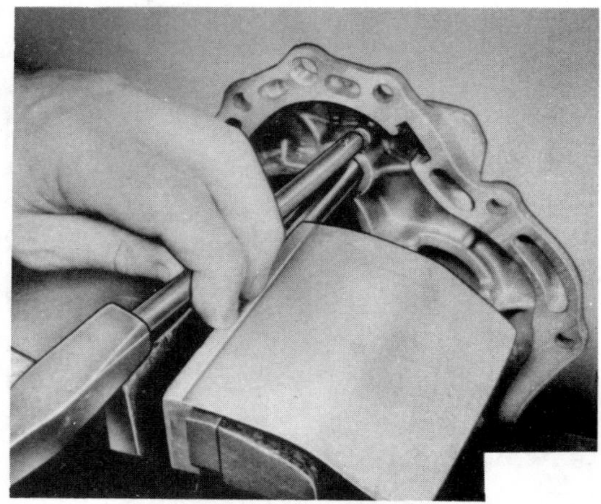

Fig. 6.10 Tapping the end cover off the reverse idler shaft (Sec 10)

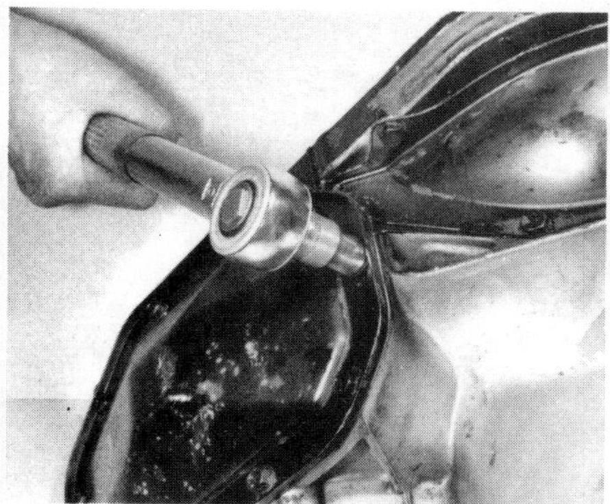
10.15 Removing the differential cover plate

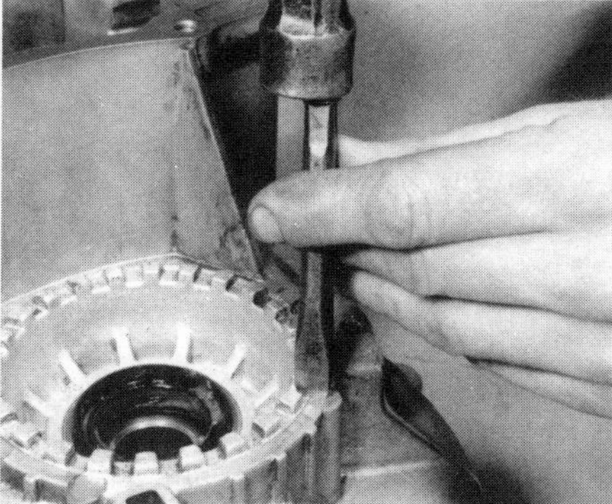
10.16A Marking the position of the differential bearing adjuster ring

10.16B Unbolting the ring lock

10.17A Unscrewing the adjuster ring with a flat steel bar

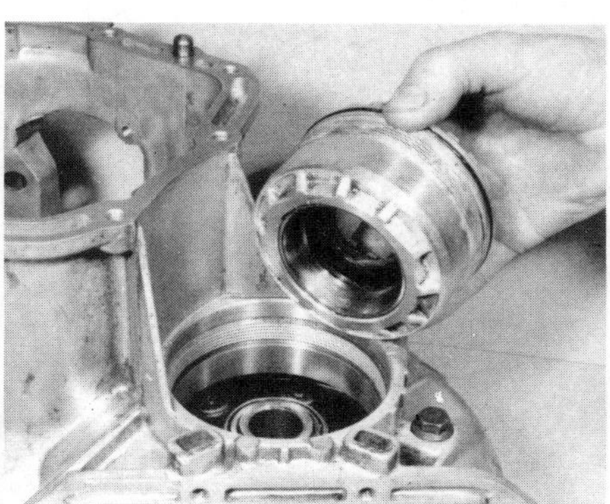
10.17B Removing the adjuster ring from the casing

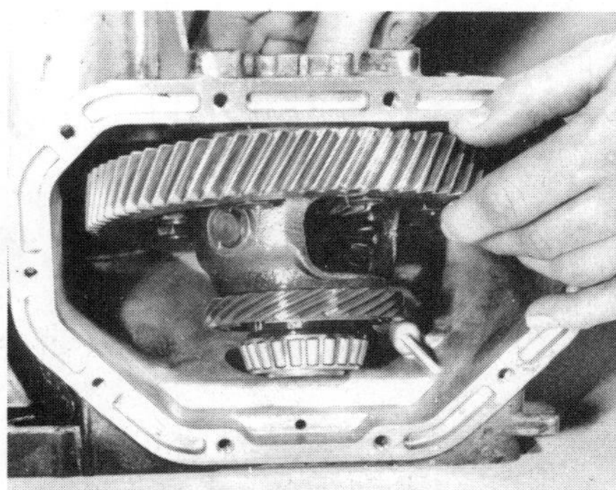
10.18 Removing the differential/crownwheel assembly

Differential

15 Unbolt and remove the pressed-steel cover from the transmission casing at the base of the differential (photo).
16 Mark the position of the bearing adjuster ring in relation to the transmission casing (photo). Unbolt the ring lock (photo).
17 Unscrew the bearing adjuster ring. A piece of flat steel bar will act as a suitable wrench (photos).
18 Withdraw the differential/crownwheel assembly (photo).
19 Depending upon the need for further dismantling due to leaking oil seals or worn bearings, proceed in the following way.
20 Renew the oil seals and bearings in the adjuster ring and transmission casing using a piece of tubing to remove the old components and to install the new (photos).
21 Using a sutiable puller remove the tapered roller bearings from the differential.
22 Unbolt the crownwheel and tap it from its register using a brass

10.20A Renewing the oil seal in the adjuster ring ...

10.20B ... and in the transmission casing

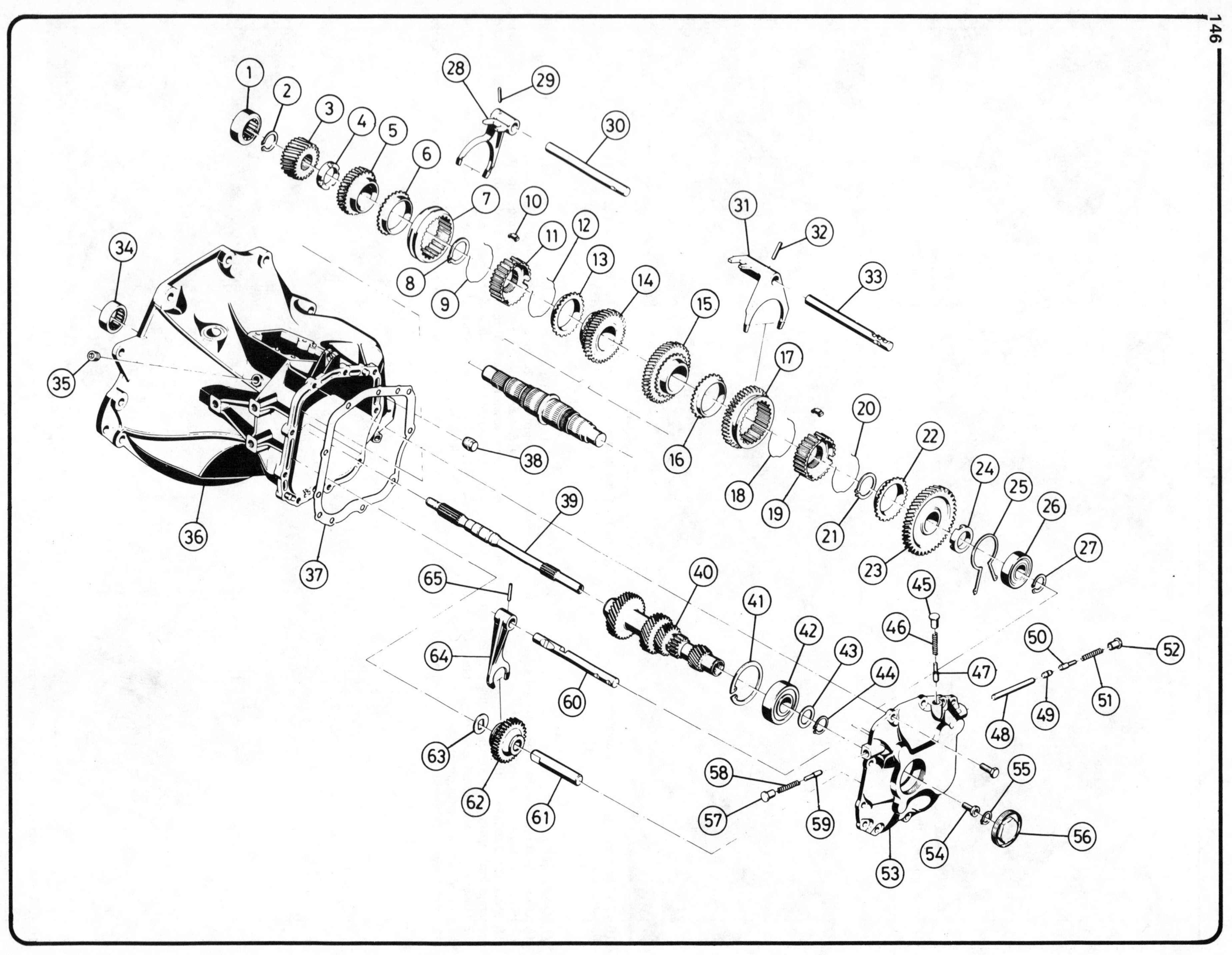
1
2
3
4
5
6
7
8
9
10
11
12
13
14
15
16
17
18
19
20
21
22
23
24
25
26
27
28
29
30
31
32
33
34
35
36
37
38
39
40
41
42
43
44
45
46
47
48
49
50
51
52
53
54
55
56
57
58
59
60
61
62
63
64
65

Fig. 6.11 Exploded view of F10/4 transmission components (Sec 10)

1 Mainshaft roller bearing (in casing)
2 Circlip
3 Pinion gear
4 Spacer
5 4th gear
6 Baulk ring
7 Synchro sleeve (3rd/4th)
8 Circlip
9 Synchro spring
10 Sliding key
11 Synchro-hub (3rd/4th)
12 Synchro spring
13 Baulk ring
14 3rd gear
15 2nd gear
16 Baulk ring
17 1st/2nd synchro sleeve with reverse gear
18 Synchro spring
19 Synchro-hub (1st/2nd)
20 Synchro spring
21 Circlip
22 Baulk ring
23 1st gear
24 Spacer
25 Mainshaft securing circlip
26 Bearing
27 Circlip
28 3rd/4th selector fork
29 Roll pin
30 Selector rod
31 1st/2nd selector fork
32 Roll pin
33 Selector rod
34 Input shaft roller bearing (in casing)
35 Plug
36 Transmission casing
37 Gasket
38 Plug
39 Input shaft
40 Input geartrain
41 Input geartrain retaining circlip
42 Bearing
43 Thrust washer
44 Circlip
45 Detent plug
46 Detent spring
47 Detent plunger
48 Long interlock plunger
49 Short interlock plunger
50 Detent plunger
51 Detent spring
52 Detent plug
53 End cover
54 Input shaft screw
55 Circlip
56 End cover screw plug
57 Detent plug
58 Detent spring
59 Detent plunger
60 Reverse selector rod
61 Reverse idler shaft
62 Reverse idler gear
63 Thrust washer
64 Reverse selector fork
65 Roll pin

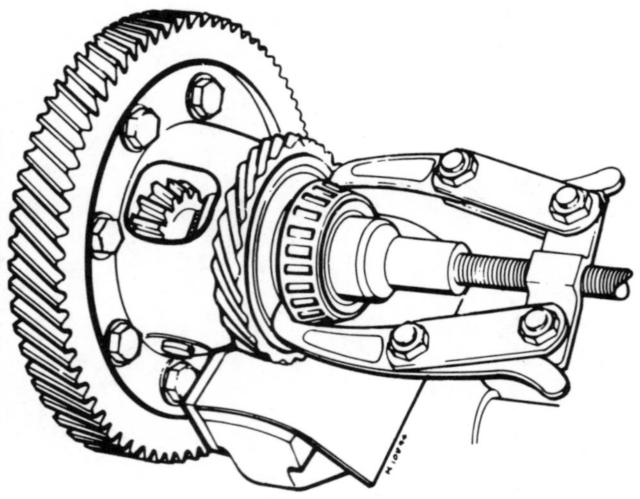

Fig. 6.12 Differential bearing removal (Sec 10)

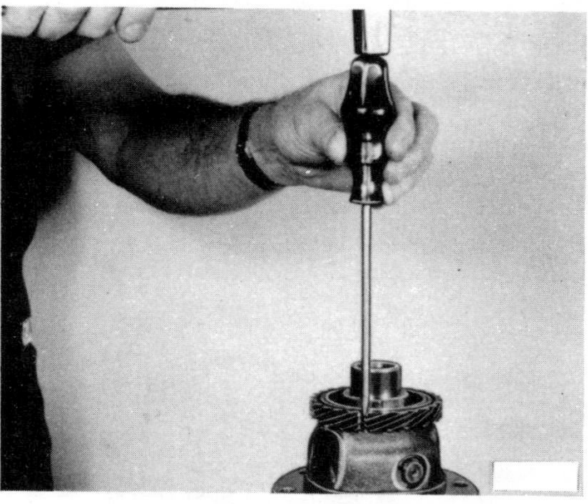

Fig. 6.13 Splitting the speedometer drivegear (Sec 10)

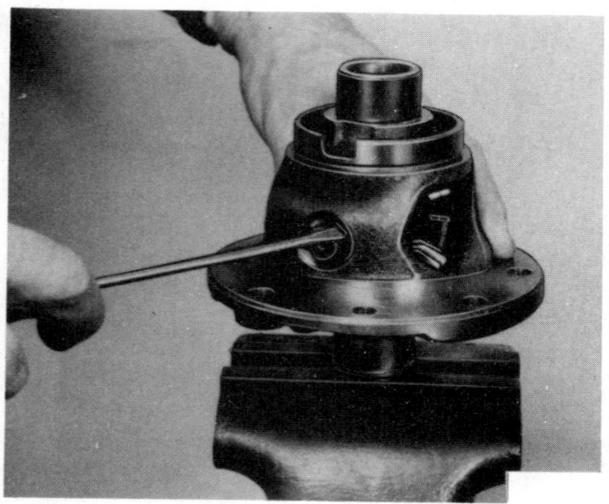

Fig. 6.14 Removing the pinion shaft circlips (Sec 10)

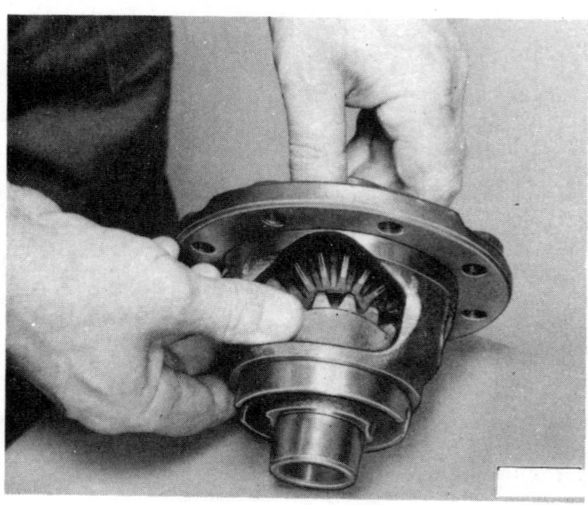

Fig. 6.15 Differential pinion and side gear removal (Sec 10)

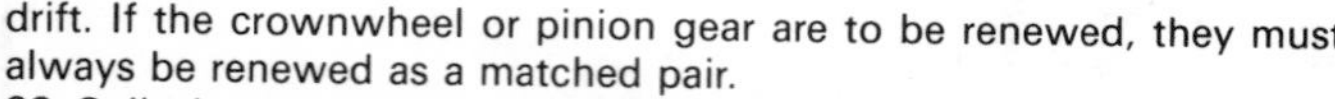

drift. If the crownwheel or pinion gear are to be renewed, they must always be renewed as a matched pair.
23 Split the speedometer drivegear and discard it.
24 Extract the circlips from the differential pinion shaft.
25 Use a drift to remove the pinion shaft from the differential case.
26 Slide the differential pinions and side gears out of the differential case. Remove the spring discs.

11 Selector housing cover – overhaul

1 Unscrew and remove the oil filler/breather plug.
2 Remove the circlip from the top of the guide pin (photo).
3 Take off the retainer, coil spring and intermediate selector lever (photos).
4 Drive out the retaining pin to release the selector finger from the rod and withdraw both components from the cover.
5 If the universal joint on the selector rod is worn, grind off the rivet to dismantle it and fit new components (if available). A pin and spring clip are available for reassembly.
6 Renew the oil seal in the selector cover.

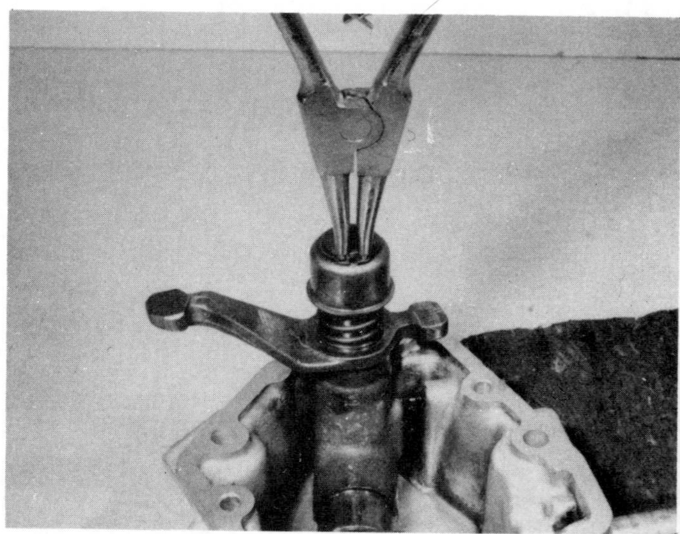

11.2 Removing the circlip from the guide pin

11.3A Removing the retainer and spring ...

11.3B ... followed by the intermediate selector lever

12 Transmission casing – overhaul

1 Undo the clamp bolt securing the clutch release fork to the release lever pivot shaft. Pull the release lever upwards out of the transmission casing and withdraw the release fork.
2 Undo the three retaining bolts and remove the release bearing guide tube and input shaft oil seal (photo). Recover the O-ring seal.
3 Prise the old seal out of the guide tube and tap in a new seal using a tube of suitable diameter (photo). Fill the space between the lips with general purpose grease.
4 The release lever bushes in the casing can be removed by tapping them out with a suitable drift. Install the new bushes with their locating tongues engaged in the slots in the casing. Coat the bush inner surfaces with molybdenum disulphide grease.
5 Prise out the speedometer driven gear and its guide. Renew the O-ring and small oil seal before refitting (photos).
6 Inspect the roller bearing in the casing and renew if necessary by drifting it out with a tube of suitable diameter. Refit a new bearing in the same way.
7 With a new O-ring in place (photo), refit the release bearing guide tube and release lever and fork using the reverse procedure to removal.

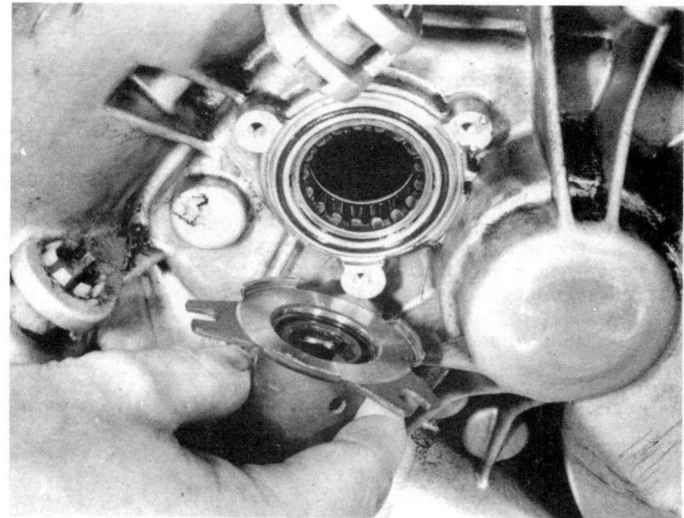
12.2 Removing the release bearing guide tube and input shaft oil seal

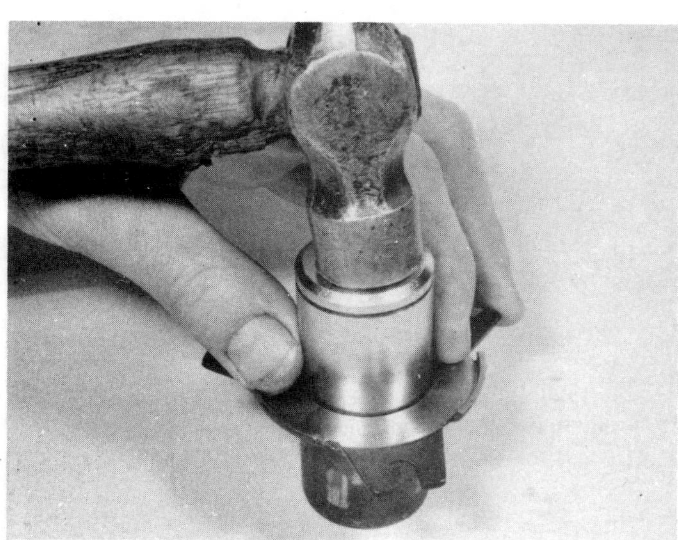
12.3 Fitting a new input shaft oil seal

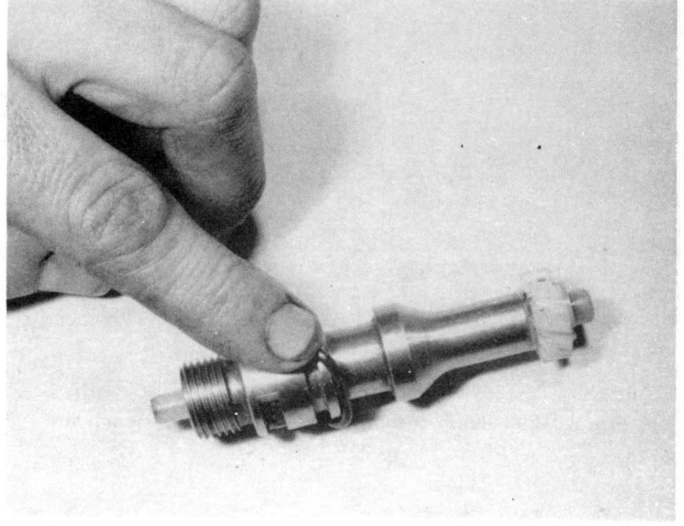
12.5A Speedometer driven gear O-ring ...

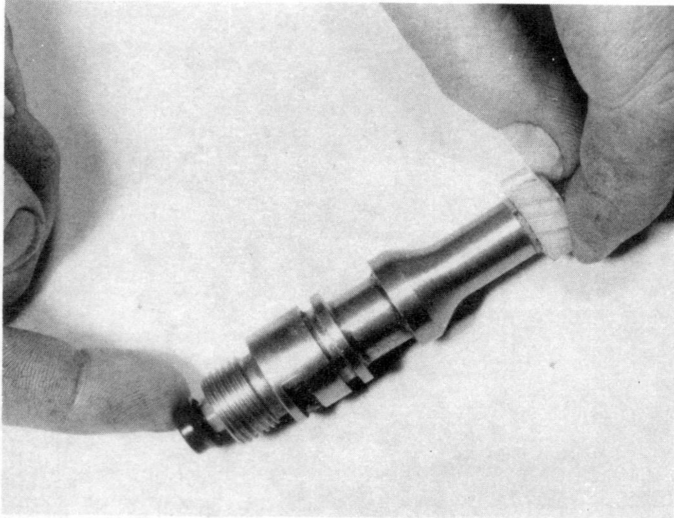

12.5B ... and small oil seal

12.7 Fit a new O-ring under the release bearing guide tube

13 Input shaft – overhaul

1 Support the end of the geartrain and tap or press the shaft from it.
2 Extract the circlip which secures the bearing to the end of the shaft (photo). Take off the washer.
3 Using a piece of tubing, drive the geartrain out of the bearing.
4 If any of the gears are damaged, the geartrain complete will have to be renewed. This will mean that the matching gears on the mainshaft will also have to be renewed.
5 Reassembly is a reversal of dismantling, but note that the sealed side of the bearing is away from the gear.
6 Remember to locate the geartrain securing circlip ready for installation in its transmission casing groove.

14 Mainshaft – overhaul (F10/4 transmission)

1 Extract the retaining circlip from the bearing at the end of the shaft (photo).
2 Support the 1st gear and drive the shaft out of the bearing and gear. note the spacer washer between the bearing and gears (photos).
3 Support 2nd gear and then extract the circlip which secures the 1st/2nd synchro (photo).
4 Take the synchro baulk ring from the shaft (photo).
5 Take the 1st/2nd synchro unit from the shaft. Note the reverse gearteeth on the sleeve (photo).
6 Remove the next baulk ring (photo).
7 Remove the 2nd gear (photo).

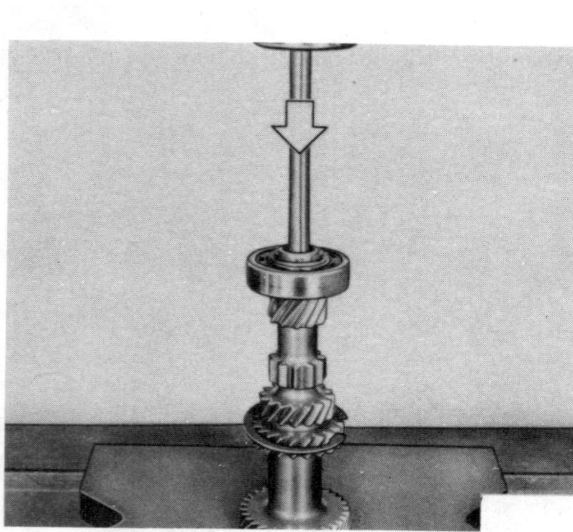

Fig. 6.16 Pressing the input shaft out of its geartrain (Sec 13)

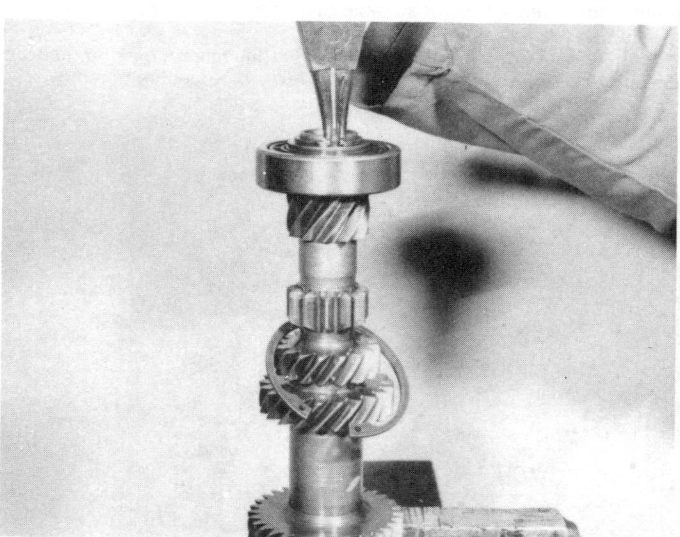

13.2 Removing the input shaft bearing retaining circlip

14.1 Removing the mainshaft bearing retaining circlip

14.2A Removing the mainshaft bearing ...

14.2B ... the spacer washer ...

14.2C ... and 1st gear itself

14.3 Extract the circlip which retains 1st/2nd synchro unit

14.4 Lift off the baulk ring

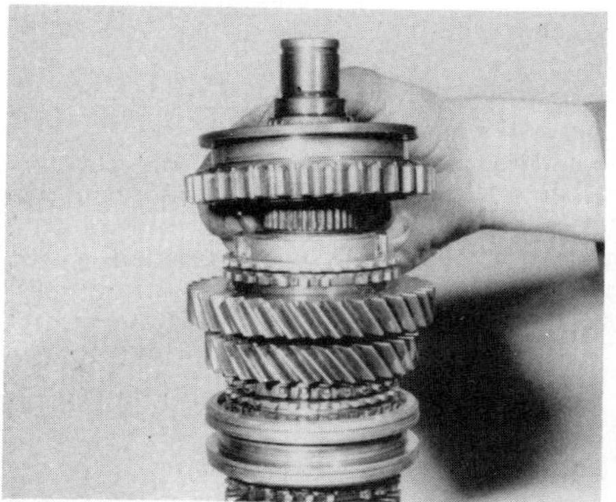
14.5 Removing 1st/2nd synchro unit

14.6 Removing 2nd gear baulk ring

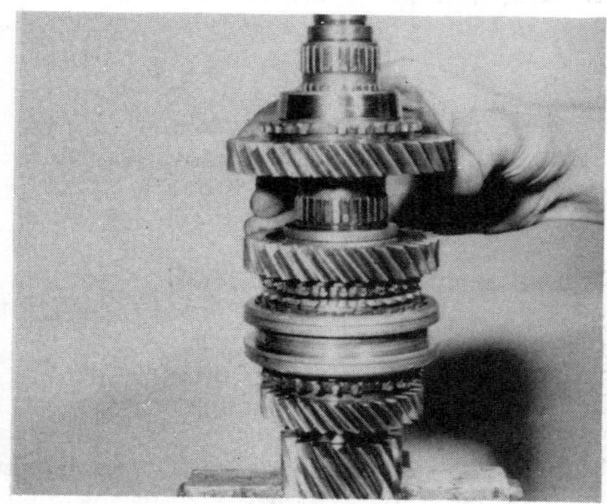
14.7 Removing 2nd gear

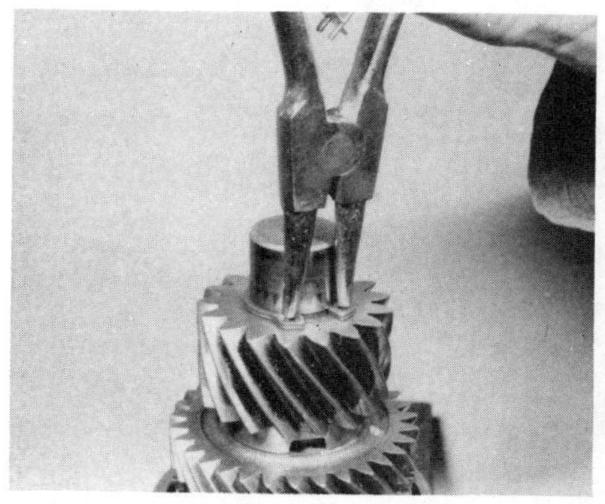
14.8 Removing the pinion gear retaining circlip

14.9 Removing the pinion gear

14.10 Removing the spacer washer

14.11 Removing 4th gear

14.12 Removing 4th gear baulk ring

14.13 Extracting 3rd/4th synchro retaining circlip

14.14 Removing 3rd/4th synchro unit

14.15 Removing 3rd gear baulk ring

14.23 Using a tube to press on 3rd/4th synchro unit

8 Now turn your attention to the opposite end of the mainshaft. Extract the circlip which secures the pinion gear to the shaft (photo).
9 Remove the pinion gear (photo).
10 Remove the spacer washer (photo).
11 Remove 4th gear (photo).
12 Remove the baulk ring (photo).
13 Extract the circlip which secures the 3rd/4th synchro unit to the mainshaft (photo).
14 Remove the 3rd/4th synchro unit (photo).
15 Remove the next baulk ring (photo).
16 Remove 3rd gear
17 If any of the foregoing components cannot be removed from the shaft by hand, use a puller or press, or drive the shaft out of them provided the gear is adequately supported at its lower face.
18 With the mainshaft completely dismantled, examine the gears for chipped or worn teeth and the shaft for deformation of splines. Renew all circlips.
19 If there has been a history of noisy gear changing or if the synchromesh could be easily beaten during changes, renew the synchro units complete or overhaul, as described in the next Section.
20 With all parts clean and oiled, reassemble in the following sequence.
21 Fit 3rd gear to the pinion gear end of the mainshaft.
22 Place the baulk ring on the cone of 3rd gear.
23 Fit the 3rd/4th synchro unit, applying pressure to the hub (photo). Preheating the synchro unit to 100°C (212°F) is recommended.
24 Secure the synchro unit with a new circlip.
25 Fit the baulk ring and 4th gear.
26 Fit the spacer washer and the pinion gear. Preheating of both these components to 100°C (212°F) is recommended.
27 Secure the pinion gear with a new circlip.
28 Working at the other end of the mainshaft, fit 2nd gear.
29 Fit the baulk ring to the cone of 2nd gear.
30 Preheat 1st/2nd synchro unit to 100°C (212°F), then press it onto the shaft with the reverse gear teeth nearer 2nd gear (photo).
31 Secure the synchro unit with a new circlip.
32 Fit 1st gear baulk ring and 1st gear.
33 Preheat the spacer washer to 100°C (212°F), then press it onto the shaft; grooves towards 1st gear (photo).
34 Locate a new long-eared circlip ready for installation in its transmission casing groove.
35 Fit the bearing and secure it with a new circlip.

14.30 Fitting 1st/2nd synchro unit – note correct orientation of reverse gear teeth

14.33 Spacer washer grooves (arrowed) face 1st gear

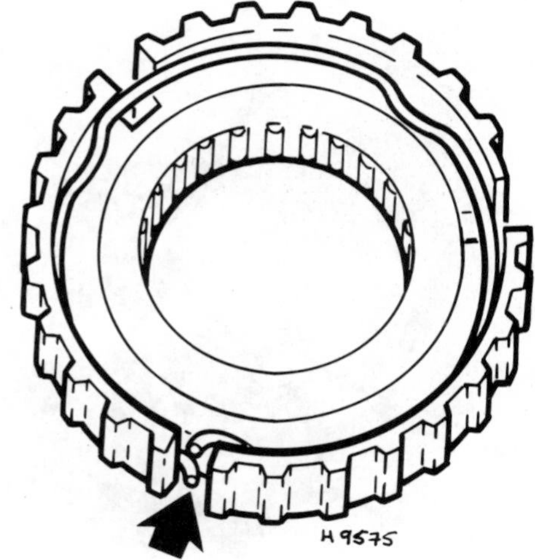

Fig. 6.17 Synchro spring ends (arrowed) (Sec 15)

15 Synchro units – overhaul

1 Components of 1st/2nd and 3rd/4th synchro units are interchangeable.
2 It is not good practice, however, to mix parts which have been in use for a high mileage and which have run-in together.
3 If either the hub or sleeve show signs of wear in their teeth, the individual part may be renewed, but general wear is best rectified by complete renewal of the unit.
4 To dismantle, push the sleeve off the hub, taking care not to allow the sliding keys to fly out.
5 Extract the circular springs and keys.
6 Reassembly is a reversal of dismantling. Make sure that the hooked ends of the springs engage in the same sliding key but run in opposite directions in relation to each other (photos).
7 To check the baulk rings for wear, twist them onto the gear cones. The ring should 'stick' to the cone and show a definite clearance between the ring and the gear shoulder. If these conditions are not met, renew the baulk rings.

15.6A Fitting the synchro sleeve to the hub

15.6B Fitting a sliding key in its groove

15.6C Fitting a synchro unit spring

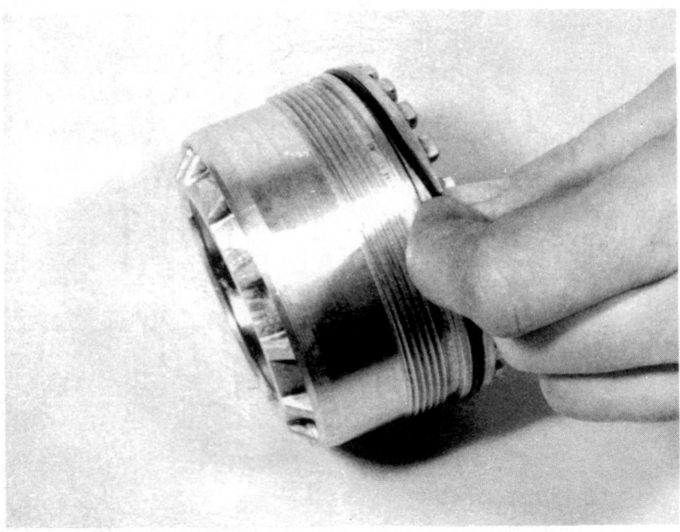
16.10A Fitting a new O-ring to the bearing adjuster ring

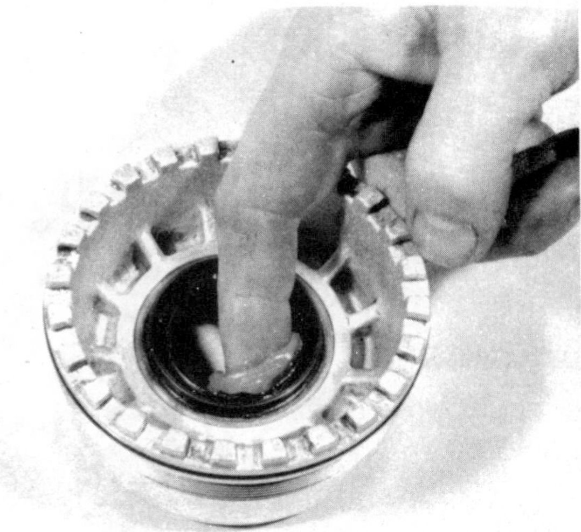
16.10B Fill the space between the oil seal lips with grease

16 F10/4 transmission – reassembly

1 Liberally lubricate the differential components with the recommended grade of oil.
2 Install the side gears and pinions, the spring discs and the pinion shaft into the differential case.
3 Fit new retaining circlips.
4 If the speedometer drivegear was removed, warm the new gear in hot water at 80°C (176°F) and tap it onto the differential case with a piece of tubing until it snaps into position. Make sure that the lugs on the gear are aligned with the cut-outs in the differential case.
5 Warm the crownwheel to 80°C (176°F) and locate it on the differential case. Use new bolts and tighten them to the specified torque.
6 Fit the tapered roller bearings to the differential case (if removed at dismantling).
7 If not already done, fit the bearing outer tracks to the transmission casing.
8 Fit new driveshaft seals into the transmission casing (if not already done) and fill the lips with grease.
9 Lower the differential into the transmission casing.
10 Fit a new O-ring and oil seal to the bearing adjuster ring (photo). Apply grease to the seal lips and to the screw threads (photo).
11 Screw the adjuster ring into the transmission casing, hand tight at this stage.
12 Adjust the bearing in one of the following ways, depending upon whether the original bearings have been refitted or new ones installed.
13 **Original bearing:** Simply screw in the adjuster ring until the alignment marks made before dismantling are opposite to each other. Should any axial play exist, the ring may be further adjusted to give a turning torque of between 6.1 and 10.3 kgf cm (5.3 and 8.9 lbf in) as described for new bearings in the following paragraph.
14 **New bearings:** The bearing preload must be adjusted by means of the adjuster ring so that a torque of 15.3 to 18.3 kgf cm (13.3 to 15.9 lbf in) is required to keep the crownwheel and bearings turning at approximately 1 revolution per second. Unless a special torsion or friction gauge is available, push a softwood rod of suitable diameter into the splined side gear, wrap a cord around it and attach the end of the cord to a spring balance. Pull on the spring balance until the crownwheel is turning at the set speed and note the force required (in kg or lb) to achieve this. Multiply the force by the radius of the rod (in cm or in) to find the turning torque. Adjust the ring until the turning torque is within the specified range.
15 Refit and secure the adjuster lock without moving the position of the adjuster ring. The ring lock fixing hole is elongated to allow this.
16 Refit the differential cover plate, using a new gasket, and tighten the bolts to the specified torque (photo).

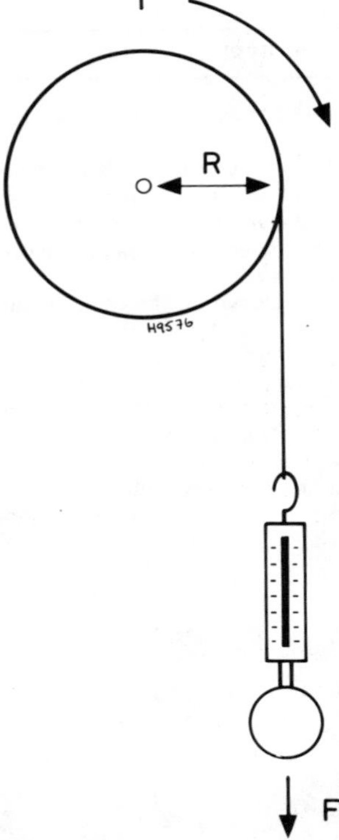

Fig. 6.18 Calculation of differential turning torque. Do not mix metric and Imperial units (Sec 16)

F = Force (kg or lb) read on spring balance
R = Radius (cm or in) of rod
T = F x R (kgf cm or lbf in)

17 Fit the reverse idler shaft to the transmission end cover, making sure that the locking ball is in position.
18 Pin the 1st/2nd selector fork to its rod, but leave the pin projecting by approximately 2.0 mm (0.08 in)
19 Hold the mainshaft, input shaft and reverse geartrains meshed

together, with the 1st/2nd selector fork and rod engaged in the groove of 1st/2nd synchro.

20 Locate the assembly into the end cover. The help of an assistant will facilitate the work. Fit the selector rod interlock plungers (photos).

21 Fit the circlips which retain the mainshaft and input shaft assemblies to the transmission casing (photo). Make sure that they engage positively in their grooves. Fit the thrust washer to the reverse idler gear (photo), also the swarf collecting magnet.

22 Check that the sleeve on 1st/2nd synchro is in neutral, then fit the 3rd/4th and reverse selector forks and rods (photos).

23 Pin the forks to the rods (photo). Support the rods when driving in the pins so as not to overload the rods or their guides.

24 Refit the detent plungers and springs. If the sealing plugs are not a really tight fit, oversize ones should be obtained and driven in.

25 Using a screwdriver, move the sleeve of the appropriate synchro unit to engage 2nd gear.

26 Stick a new gasket, with grease, to the transmission casing (photo) and then insert the geartrains with end cover into the casing until the fixing bolts and nuts can be screwed in to the specified torque.

27 Fit the speedometer driven gear and bolt on its retainer plate.

28 Screw in the reversing lamp switch to the specified torque.

29 Set the transmission in neutral and stick a new selector cover gasket in position with a smear of grease.

30 Bolt on the selector cover, tightening the bolts to the specified torque.

31 The transmission can be filled with oil now, as described in Section 2, provided it is held in the in-vehicle attitude, otherwise wait until it has been refitted to the vehicle.

16.16 Refitting the differential cover plate, using a new gasket

16.20A Locating the short interlock plunger ...

16.20B ... and the long interlock plunger

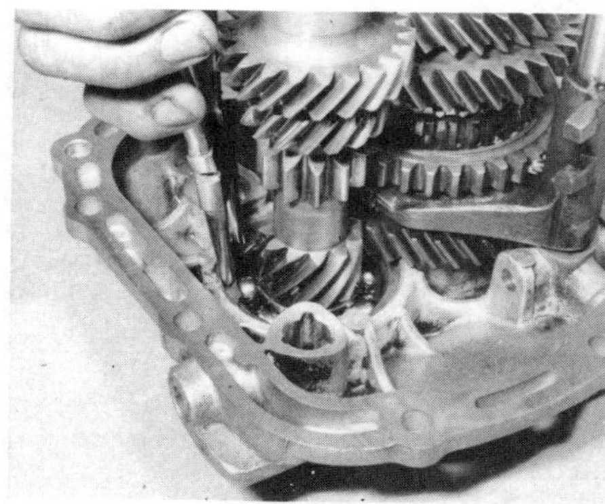
16.21A Engaging the input shaft circlip in its groove

16.21B Reverse idler gear thrust washer

16.22A Fitting 3rd/4th selector fork and rod ...

16.22B ... and reverse selector fork and rod

16.23 Pinning a fork to its rod

16.26 Fitting a new gasket to the casing

17 F10/5 transmission – dismantling, overhaul and reassembly

1 The small five-speed transmission is essentially the same as the four-speed one, with the addition of the 5th gear and its synchro unit, and modifications to the selector mechanism. Follow the dismantling, overhaul and reassembly procedures given for the four-speed transmission in conjunction with the following supplementary information.

2 Undo the bolts securing the end cover shield to the end cover and then proceed with the dismantling, as described in Section 10, paragraphs 2 to 7 inclusive.

3 Using a suitable Allen key undo the two socket-headed screws and remove the bearing support with selector fork from the end cover.

4 Engage 3rd and reverse gear by moving the selector forks.

5 Extract the 5th gear synchroniser retaining circlip and then remove the synchroniser using a two-legged puller. Recover the baulk ring.

6 Lift off the mainshaft 5th gear, needle roller bearing, the two thrust washer halves and the thrust washer retaining ring.

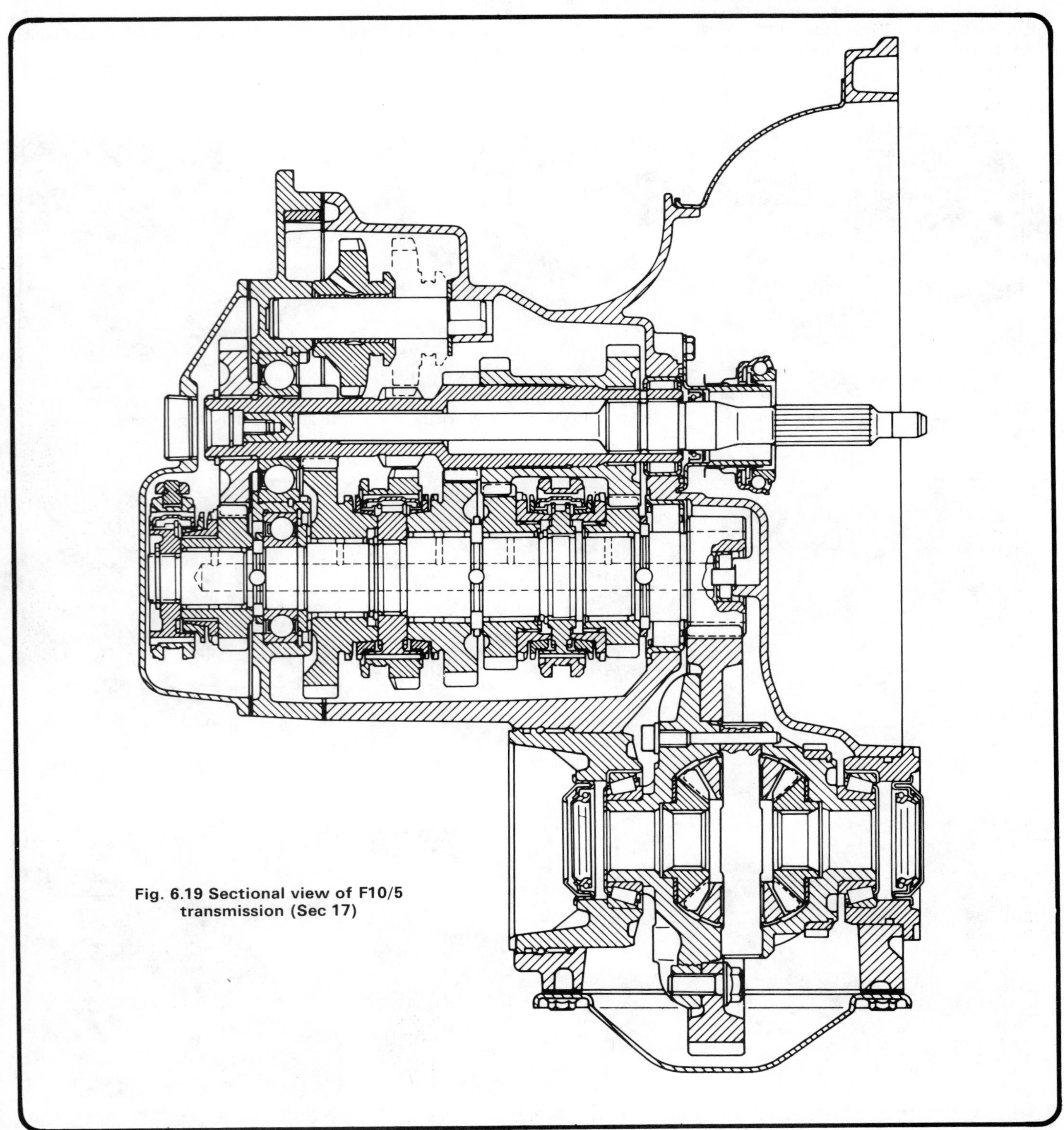

Fig. 6.19 Sectional view of F10/5 transmission (Sec 17)

7 Extract the input shaft 5th gear retaining circlip and then draw off the gear using a large puller. Use a tubular distance piece for the puller centre screw so that it bears against the input geartrain and not directly on the input shaft itself.
8 Using an Allen key, unscrew the socket-headed screws which secure the 5th gear selector interlock pawl to the end cover.
9 Using a forked tool as a lever, extract the four detent plugs from the edge of the end cover. Be prepared to catch the coil spring which will be ejected. Pull out the detent plungers. Renew the detent plugs if they were damaged during removal.
10 Move 5th gear selector rod to its engaged position and also move the 2nd gear selector fork to engage the gear.
11 Again using an Allen key, unscrew the socket-headed bolts and remove the interlock pin bridge piece.
12 Return all the gears and selector rods to neutral.
13 Drive out the securing roll pin and remove the selector shaft and fork for 3rd/4th gears. Remove the reverse shaft and fork in the same way.
14 Pull the 5th gear selector driver from the end cover.
15 The remainder of the dismantling sequence now follows the procedure described in Section 10, paragraphs 11 to 26 inclusive.
16 Overhaul of the selector housing cover, transmission casing, input shaft, mainshaft and synchronisers also follows the procedures previously described.
17 To reassemble the transmission, begin by following the procedure described in Section 16, paragraphs 1 to 21 inclusive.
18 Refit the reverse, and 3rd/4th gear selector shafts and forks, and the 5th gear selector driver to the end cover. Secure the forks with the roll pins.
19 Refit the interlock pin bridge piece and secure it in position, using thread locking compound and new screws tightened to the specified torque.
20 Refit the 5th gear selector interlock pawl to the end cover, noting that the slot in the 3rd/4th selector shaft must align with the pawl. Secure the assembly with new socket-headed screws tightened to the specified torque, using thread locking compound.

Fig. 6.20 5th gear selector fork and (arrowed) its socket-headed retaining screws (Sec 17)

Fig. 6.21 Mainshaft 5th gear components (Sec 17)

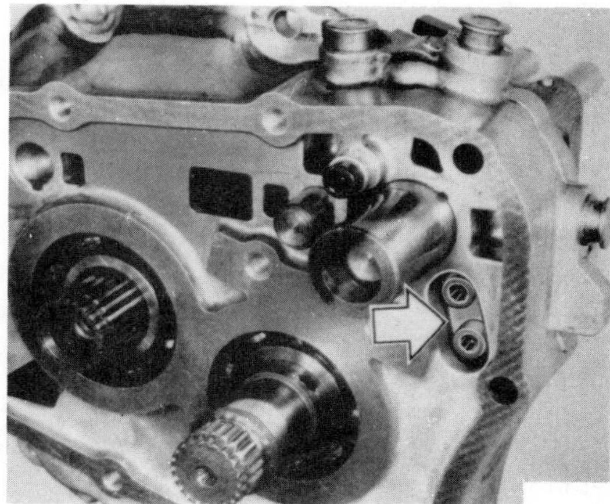

Fig. 6.22 5th gear interlock pawl screws (arrowed) (Sec 17)

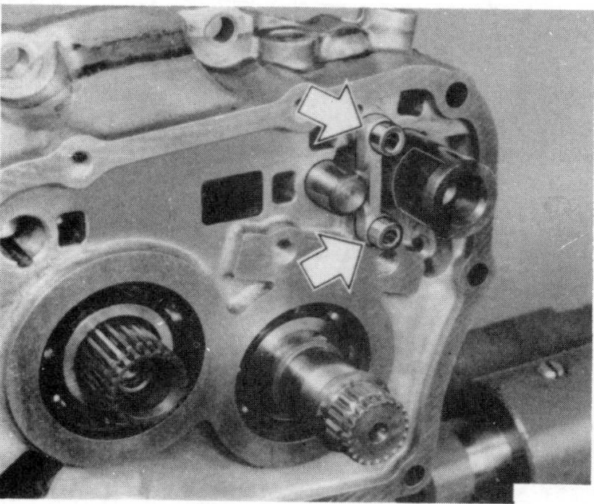

Fig. 6.23 Interlock pin bridge piece retaining screws (arrowed) (Sec 17)

21 Refit the detent plungers and springs and drive in the detent plugs, noting that the long plug is for the 3rd/4th selector shaft.
22 Press the input shaft 5th gear onto the geartrain with the longer hub toward the bearing.
23 Refit the retaining circlip.
24 Refit the two thrust washer halves, retaining ring, needle roller bearing and 5th gear to the mainshaft.
25 Place the baulk ring in position over 5th gear.
26 Heat the 5th gear synchroniser assembly to 100°C (212°F) and then position it over the mainshaft. Press or drive it into place using a suitable tube, ensuring that the slots in the baulk ring engage with the sliding keys.
27 Refit the retaining circlip.
28 Refit the bearing support and selector fork to the end cover and secure with two new socket-headed screws tightened to the specified torque, using thread locking compound.
29 The remainder of the reassembly procedure is now as described in Section 16, paragraphs 26 to 31 inclusive. Refit the end cover shield using a new gasket before refilling the transmission with oil.

18 F16/4 transmission – dismantling, overhaul and reassembly

1 The operations are mostly identical to those described in previous Sections for the F10/4 transmission. The main difference is in the design of the mainshaft, resulting in the following changes:

(a) *Needle roller thrust washer against 1st gear*
(b) *Needle roller bearings for 1st, 2nd, 3rd and 4th gears*
(c) *Semi-circular thrust washers between 2nd and 3rd gears complete with washer retaining ring*
(d) *3rd/4th synchro retaining circlip*
(e) *Composite mainshaft with pinion gear*
(f) *Roller bearing, semi-circular thrust washers and washer retaining ring next to pinion gear*

2 If either the crownwheel or pinion (part of mainshaft) is being renewed then the pair must be renewed as a matching set.

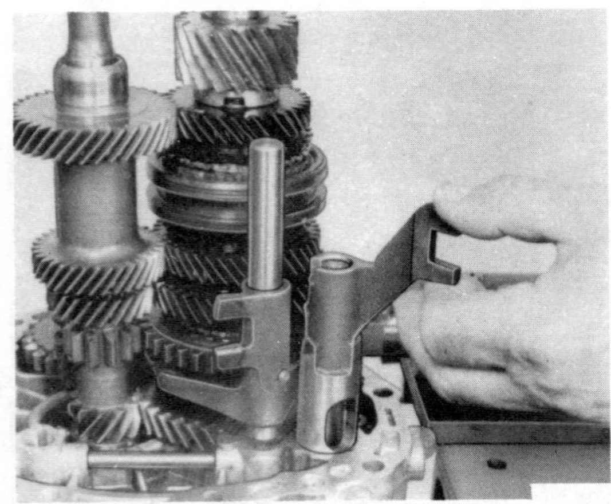

Fig. 6.24 Removing 5th gear selector driver (Sec 17)

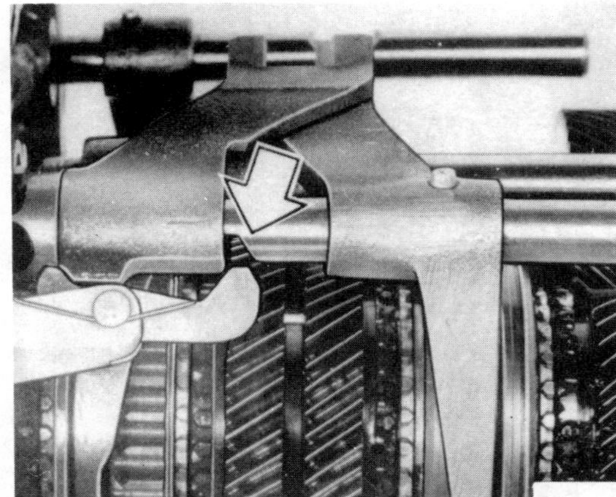

Fig. 6.25 Alignment of 3rd/4th selector shaft slot (arrowed) with 5th gear interlock pawl (Sec 17)

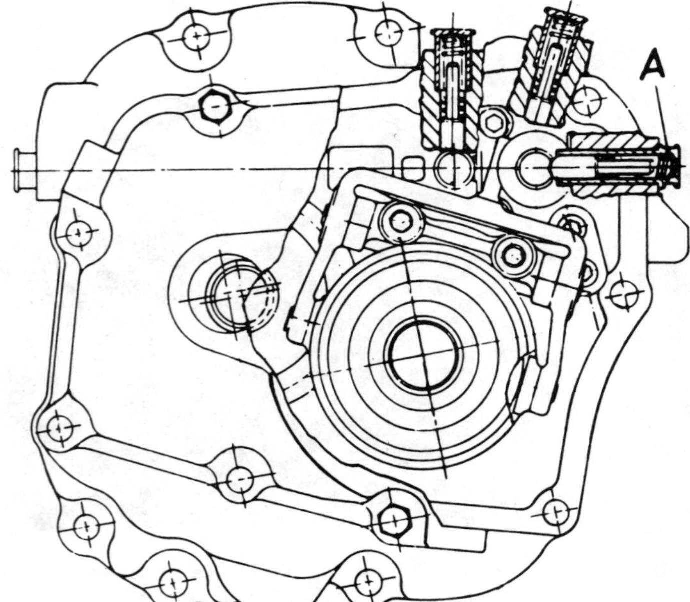

Fig. 6.26 3rd/4th detent plug (A) is longer than the rest (Sec 17)

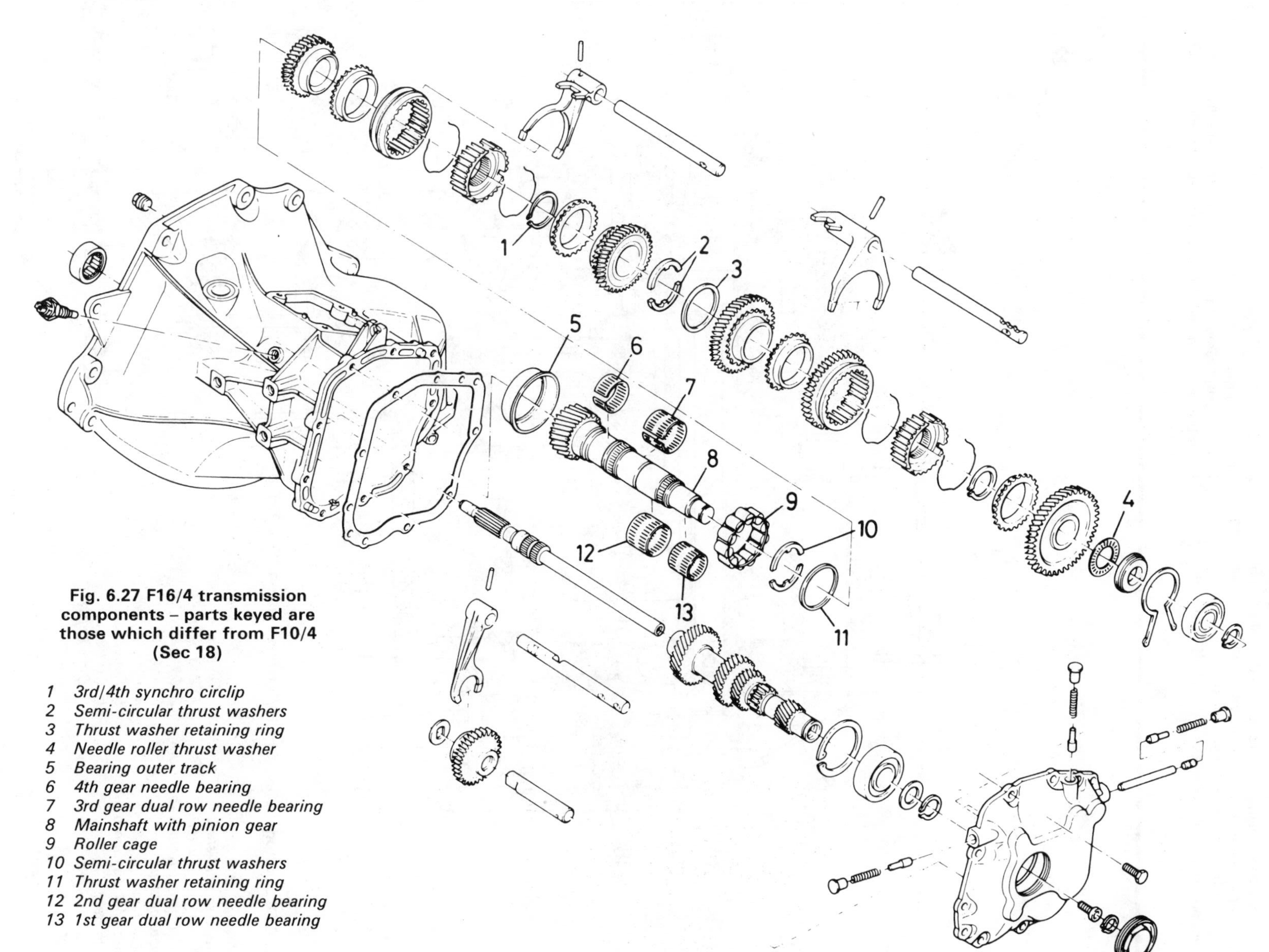

Fig. 6.27 F16/4 transmission components – parts keyed are those which differ from F10/4 (Sec 18)

1 *3rd/4th synchro circlip*
2 *Semi-circular thrust washers*
3 *Thrust washer retaining ring*
4 *Needle roller thrust washer*
5 *Bearing outer track*
6 *4th gear needle bearing*
7 *3rd gear dual row needle bearing*
8 *Mainshaft with pinion gear*
9 *Roller cage*
10 *Semi-circular thrust washers*
11 *Thrust washer retaining ring*
12 *2nd gear dual row needle bearing*
13 *1st gear dual row needle bearing*

3 All the synchromesh sleeves are interchangeable. Do not interchange part-worn sleeves though, since wear patterns are unlikely to be identical.
4 When reassembling the mainshaft, proceed as described in Section 20 for the F16/5 transmission. Remember also to fit the circlip securing the ball-bearing (not fitted to 5-speed versions).
5 Refer to Section 20 also for details of input shaft selection.

19 F16/5 transmission – dismantling into major assemblies

1 Unbolt the cover plate from the final drive housing and allow the lubricant to drain.
2 Unbolt and remove the cover plate from the flywheel housing.
3 Unbolt and remove the selector housing and peel off the flange gasket.

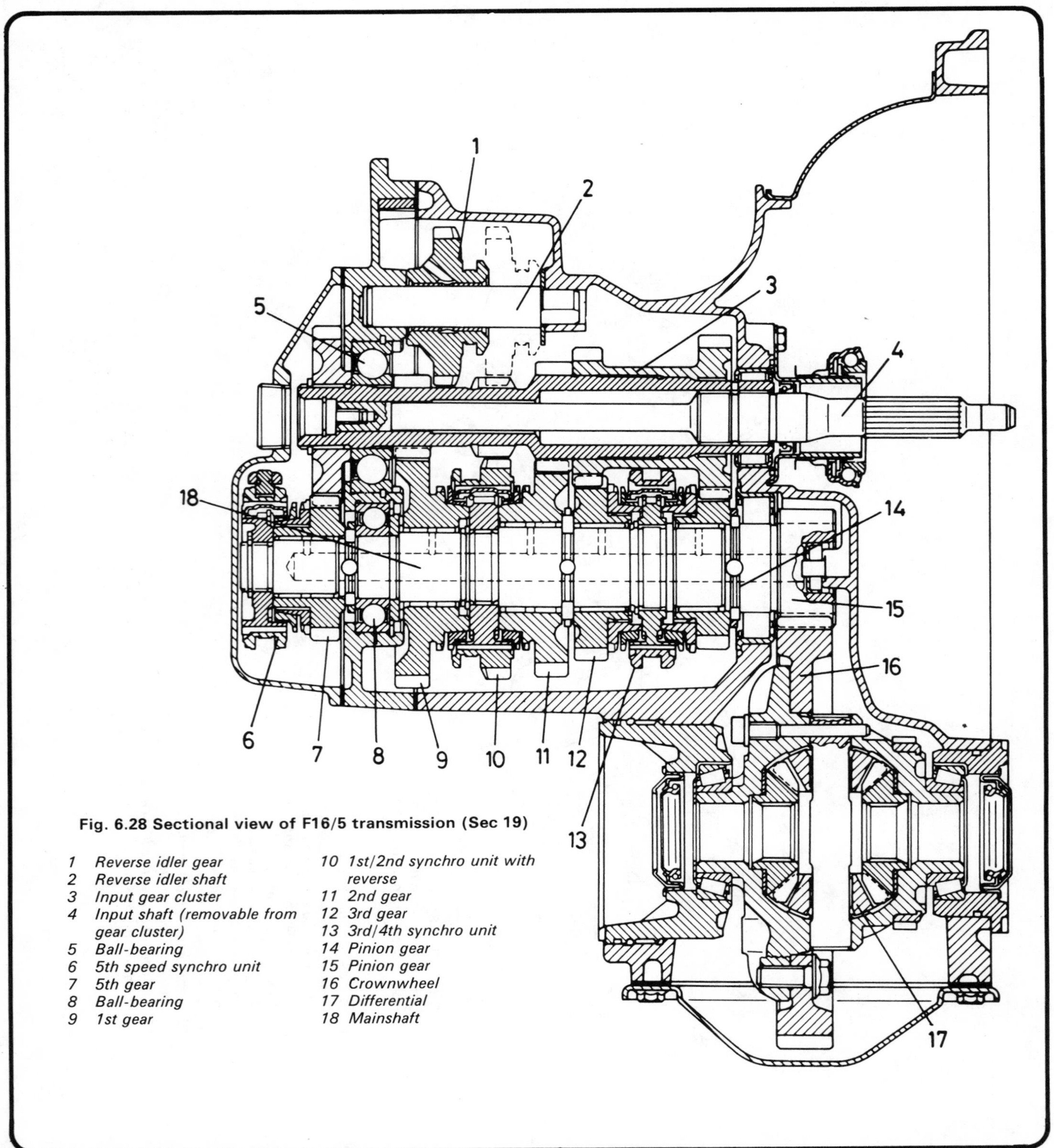

Fig. 6.28 Sectional view of F16/5 transmission (Sec 19)

1 Reverse idler gear
2 Reverse idler shaft
3 Input gear cluster
4 Input shaft (removable from gear cluster)
5 Ball-bearing
6 5th speed synchro unit
7 5th gear
8 Ball-bearing
9 1st gear
10 1st/2nd synchro unit with reverse
11 2nd gear
12 3rd gear
13 3rd/4th synchro unit
14 Pinion gear
15 Pinion gear
16 Crownwheel
17 Differential
18 Mainshaft

19.10A Extracting the circlip from the input shaft

19.10B Levering off 5th gear

19.12A Levering out a detent plug

19.12B Detent plug extraction tool suitable for attachment to a slide hammer

19.22 Circlip retaining clip

19.23 Expanding the input shaft circlip

4 Unbolt and remove the end cover with gasket.
5 Extract the circlip from the end of the input shaft now exposed. This circlip is located deep in the shaft recess and a pair of long-nosed pliers will be needed to extract it.
6 Unscrew and remove the socket-headed screw from the shaft recess. This will require the use of a special key or socket bit which are available from motor accessory shops.
7 Unbolt and remove the transmission main casing from the intermediate plate
8 Using an Allen key, unbolt the 5th gear selector fork. It will facilitate removal of the socket-headed screws if 5th gear synchro unit is first moved by hand to its engaged position.
9 Extract the circlip from the end of the mainshaft and then, using a two-legged puller, draw 5th gear and 5th gear synchro unit from the mainshaft. Locate the puller claws under 5th gear.
10 Extract the circlip from the end of the input shaft and withdraw 5th gear from the shaft. Two tyre levers placed under the gear will remove it quite easily (photos).
11 Using an Allen key, unscrew the socket-headed screws which hold the 5th gear selector interlock pawl to the intermediate plate.
12 Using a forked lever or slide hammer with suitable attachment, withdraw the detent plugs from the edge of the intermediate plate (photos). Be prepared to catch the coil springs which will be ejected. Pull out the detent plungers.
13 If you have damaged the detent caps during removal, they should be renewed.
14 Move 5th gear selector rod to its engaged position.
15 Push 2nd gear selector fork to engage the gear.
16 Again using the Allen key unscrew the socket headed screws and remove the interlock pin bridge piece.
17 Return all gears to neutral.
18 Drive out the securing roll pin and remove the selector shaft and fork for 3rd/4th gears. Remove reverse selector in a similar way.
19 Withdraw the interlock rod from the intermediate plate.
20 Pull the 5th gear selector driver from the intermediate plate.
21 Drive out the roll pin and remove the 1st/2nd selector rod and fork.
22 Squeeze together the ends of the large circlip which hold the mainshaft bearing into the intermediate plate. A piece of thin rod should be made up to form a retaining clip to keep the circlip contracted (photo).
23 Now expand the legs of the circlip which holds the input shaft bearing in the intermediate plate (photo).
24 With the help of an assistant, withdraw the geartrains complete with reverse idler gear. The shafts and bearings may require a little gentle tapping with a plastic-faced hammer to eject them from the intermediate plate. Note the thrust washer on the reverse idler.
25 To remove the differential components, refer to Section 10, paragraph 15 onwards.

20 F16/5 transmission – overhaul

Selector housing cover
1 Refer to Section 11.

Transmission casing
2 Refer to Section 12.

Input shaft
3 Refer to Section 13, but note that two sizes of input shaft are available. With the shaft pushed into the geartrain by hand, measure dimension A (Fig. 6.29). If A is greater than 5 mm (0.2 in), renew the geartrain. If A is less than zero – ie the shaft is recessed in the geartrain – fit a group 2 shaft. If A is between zero and 5 mm (0.2 in), the fit of the shaft in the geartrain is satisfactory. Consult a GM dealer for shaft identification.

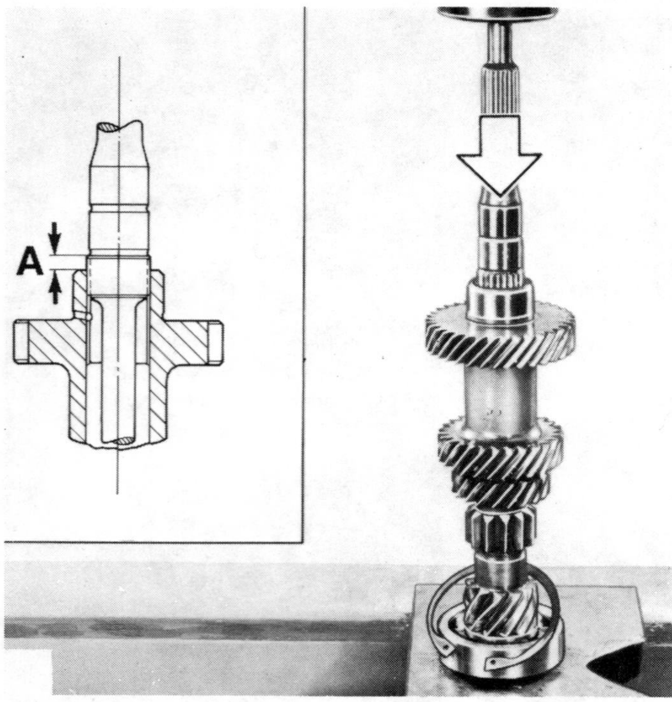

Fig. 6.29 Input shaft selection – push shaft into geartrain by hand. For dimensions A see text (Sec 20)

Mainshaft

4 Place the claws of a two-legged puller under the 1st gear and draw the gear and shaft ball-bearing from the mainshaft (photo).

5 Extract the circlip, remove the plain thrust washer and then the needle type thrust washer.

6 Remove 1st gear baulk ring.

7 Remove the split type needle roller bearing.

8 Extract the circlip.

9 Take off the plain thrust washer

10 Place the claws of a puller under 2nd gear and withdraw 1st/2nd synchro unit (with reverse), the baulk ring and 2nd gear all together from the mainshaft. Note that the reverse gear teeth on the synchro sleeve are towards the pinion gear on the end of the shaft.

11 Remove the semi-circular thrust washers and their retaining ring.

12 Remove 3rd gear.

13 Remove 3rd gear baulk ring.

14 Take off the split type needle roller bearing.

15 Extract the circlip which retains the 3rd/4th synchro unit.

16 Take off the thrust washer.

17 Place the claws of a puller behind 4th gear and draw off 3rd/4th synchro unit, 4th gear baulk ring and 4th gear all together from the mainshaft.

18 Take off the split type needle roller bearing.

19 Remove the semi-circular thrust washers with their retaining ring.

20 Remove the roller race from the shaft. The pinion gear cannot be removed.

21 Examine the gears for chipped or worn teeth, and the shaft for deformation of splines. Renew as necessary.

22 Renew or overhaul the synchro units – see Section 15.

23 Renew all circlips as a matter of course, and the bearings unless their condition is known to be perfect.

24 With all parts clean and well oiled, reassemble as follows.

25 Apply thick grease to retain the rollers to their cage and fit the bearing assembly up against the mainshaft pinion gear.

26 Locate the semi-circular thrust washers so that their keys engage in the holes in the shaft and then fit the retaining ring.

27 Fit the split type needle roller bearing.

28 Fit 4th gear.

29 Fit 4th gear baulk ring (photo).

30 Fit 3rd/4th synchro unit, preheated to 100°C (212°F), so that the thin groove in the sleeve is furthest from the shaft pinion (photo). Drive the synchro-hub down the shaft using a bearing puller or by applying a length of tubing to the synchro hub.

31 Fit the thrust washer (photo).

32 Fit the circlip (photo).

33 Fit 3rd gear baulk ring (photo).

34 Fit the split type needle roller bearing (photo).

35 Fit 3rd gear (photo).

36 Fit the semi-circular thrust washers and their retaining ring. Fit the needle roller bearing (photos).

37 Fit 2nd gear (phtoo).

38 Fit 2nd gear baulk ring (photo).

39 Fit 1st/2nd synchro, preheated to 100°C (212°F), with reverse gear teeth nearest the pinion gear (photo).

40 Fit the plain thrust washer and circlip (photos).

41 Fit the split needle bearing, 1st gear baulk ring and 1st gear (photos).

42 Fit the needle roller thrust washer (photo).

43 Preheat the plain thrust washer to 100°C (212°F) and fit it, step upwards. Place the long-eared circlip on the shaft (photos).

20.4 Pulling off 1st gear and the bearing from the mainshaft

20.29 Mainshaft assembled as far as 4th gear baulk ring

20.30 3rd/4th synchro is fitted with thin groove upwards

20.31 Fit the thrust washer ...

20.32 ... and 3rd/4th synchro circlip

20.33 Fitting 3rd gear baulk ring

20.34 3rd gear needle roller bearing

20.35 Fitting 3rd gear

20.36A Fit the semi-circular thrust washers ...

20.36B ... and their retaining ring

20.36C 2nd gear needle roller bearing

20.37 Fitting 2nd gear

20.38 2nd gear baulk ring

20.39 Fitting 1st/2nd synchro unit – note orientation of reverse gear teeth

20.40A Fit the plain thrust washer ...

20.40B ... and the 1st/2nd synchro circlip

20.41A Fit 1st gear baulk ring ...

20.41B ... and 1st gear

20.42 Needle roller type thrust washer

20.43A Fit the plain thrust washer, step upwards ...

20.43B ... and upon it place the long-eared circlip

20.44 Fitting the mainshaft ball-bearing

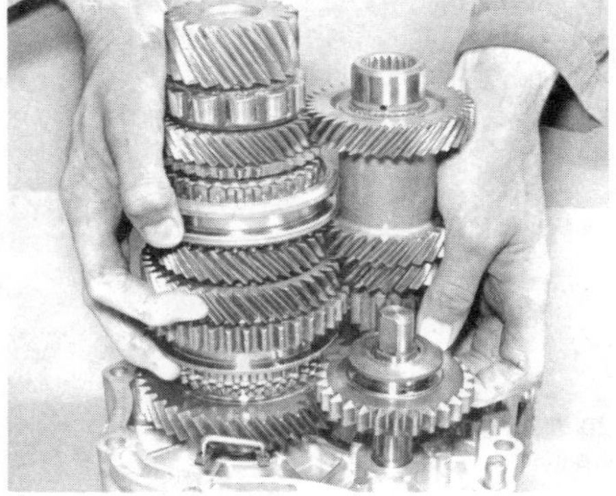
21.2 Offering the geartrain to the intermediate plate

44 Fit the ball-bearing to the mainshaft so that the sealed side is visible when fitted (photo).
45 Locate the long-eared circlip in the thrust washer step. compress it and fit a retaining clip (see photo 19.22).

21 F16/5 transmission – reassembly

1 Expand the input shaft circlip in the intermediate plate.
2 With the help of an assistant, mesh the input and output shaft geartrain together with the reverse idler gear. The reverse idler selector fork groove must be nearer the pinion gear. Offer the geartrains to the intermediate plate (photo).
3 Release the input shaft bearing circlip and remove the mainshaft circlip retaining clip.
4 Refit 1st/2nd selector rod and fork. Secure with a new roll pin, supporting the rod as the pin is driven in. Leave about 2 mm (0.08 in) of the pin protruding (photos).
5 Fit reverse selector rod and fork and drive in a new roll pin (photo).
6 Fit 5th gear selector driver into the intermediate plate.
7 Locate 5th gear selector driver and 3rd/4th selector fork and insert the selector rod through them (photo).
8 Fix 3rd/4th selector fork to its rod with a new roll pin.
9 Insert the interlock rod into the hole in the intermediate plate (photo).
10 Fit the interlock pin bridge piece. The screws will only be able to be screwed in if 2nd gear and then 5th gear driver are moved to the

21.4A Fitting 1st/2nd selector rod and fork

21.4B Selector fork roll pin

21.5 Remove selector rod and fork

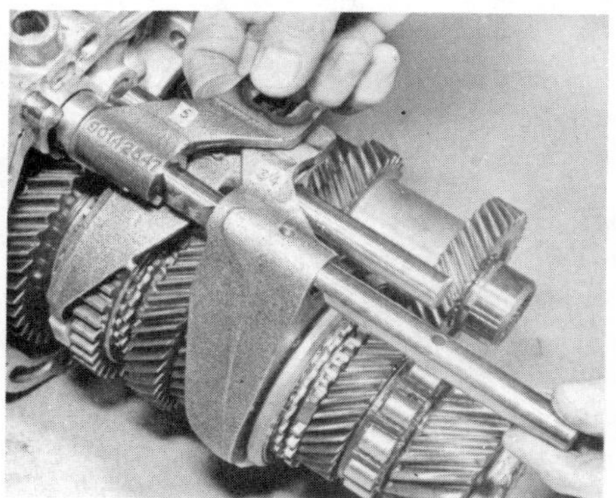
21.7 Passing the selector rod through 3rd/4th fork and 5th driver

21.9 Interlock rod in intermediate plate

21.10A Fitting the interlock pin bridge piece

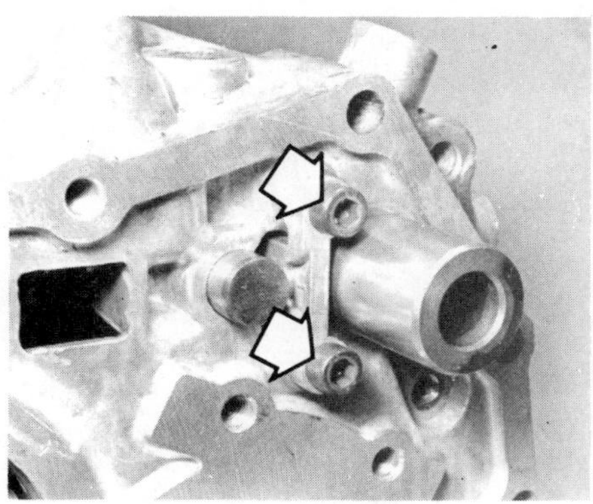
21.10B Bridge piece fixing screws (arrowed)

21.11A Fitting 5th gear interlock pawl

21.11B Tightening a pawl securing screw

engaged position (photos). Use new screws and thread locking compound, and tighten them to the specified torque.

11 Engage the 5th gear interlock pawl in the cut-out of the driver. Using new screws, coated with thread locking compound, secure the pawl to the plate (photos). Tighten the screws to the specified torque.

12 Insert the detent plungers and their coil springs in their holes in the intermediate plate (photo).

13 Tap in the plugs, noting that the one for 3rd/4th selector is longer than the rest (photos).

14 Locate the thrust washer (which has the centre hole with flat sides) on the reverse idler shaft. Retain it with thick grease (photo).

15 Fit the magnet (clean) into its slot in the intermediate plate (photo).

16 Place a new gasket on the transmission casing flange and lower the geartrains with intermediate plate into the casing (photo).

17 Mesh the pinion and crownwheel teeth as the geartrains are lowered.

18 Screw in the securing bolts.

19 If the input shaft was removed, now is the time to refit it into the input shaft gear cluster (photo).

20 Fit the 5th gear to the end of the input shaft. Secure it with the circlip (photo).

21 To the end of the mainshaft fit the semi-circular thrust washers and retaining ring (photos).

22 Fit the split type needle roller bearing to the mainshaft (photo).

23 Fit 5th gear to the mainshaft (photo).

21.12 Inserting detent components into the intermediate plate

21.13A Detent plug identification

21.13B Reverse detent plug

21.14 Reverse gear thrust washer

21.15 Fitting the swarf-collecting magnet

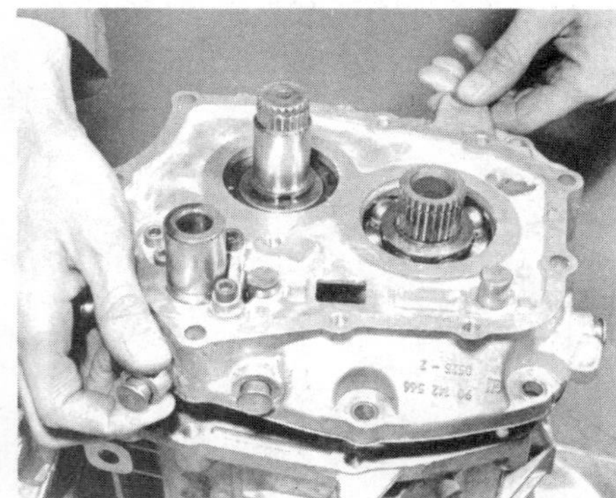

21.16 Lowering the geartrain into the casing

21.19 Fitting the input shaft

21.20 Fitting 5th gear to the input shaft

21.21A Fit the last two semi-circular thrust washers ...

21.21B ... and their retaining ring

21.22 5th gear mainshaft needle roller bearing

21.23 Fitting 5th gear to the mainshaft

21.24 Fitting 5th gear baulk ring

21.25 Fitting 5th gear synchro unit

21.26 Fitting the mainshaft circlip

24 Fit 5th gear baulk ring (photo).
25 Fit 5th gear synchro unit so that the side where the movable keys are visible is towards 5th gear (photo).
26 Fit the retaining circlip (photo).
27 Move 5th gear to its engaged position and fit the selector fork/pivot assembly. Fit new socket-headed screws, using thread locking compound, and tighten them to the specified torque (photo).
28 If the gearbox is to be refitted to the engine in the car, the input shaft screw, circlip and end cover plug should not be fitted yet, as the input shaft must be withdrawn during refitting. If engine and transmission are both removed, proceed as follows.
29 Fit the screw and the circlip to the end of the input shaft (photos).
30 Using a new gasket bolt on the end cover (photo).
31 Screw the threaded plug (if removed) into the end cover (photo).
32 Using a new gasket, locate the selector cover so that the selector fingers engage in the dogs (gears in neutral). Insert and tighten the fixing bolts (photo).
33 Bolt on the final drive cover plate.
34 Bolt on the flywheel housing cover plate.
35 Check that the selection of all gears is smooth and positive.
36 Fill the transmission with lubricant after it has been refitted to the vehicle.

21.27 Tightening a 5th gear selector fork pivot screw

21.29A Input shaft socket-headed screw (arrowed)

21.29B Fitting the circlip to the input shaft recess

21.30 Fitting the end cover

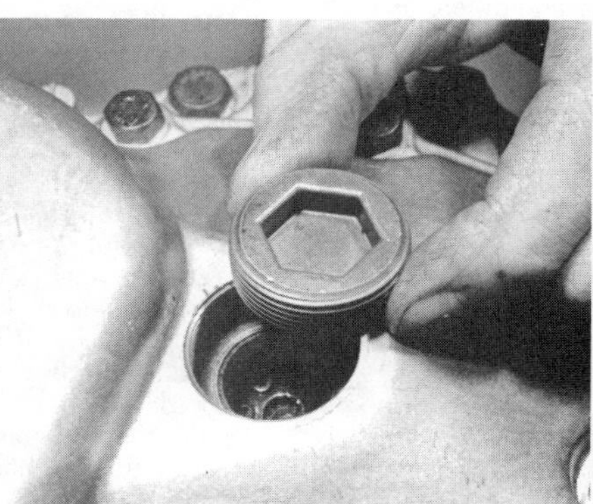
21.31 Screw in the end plug

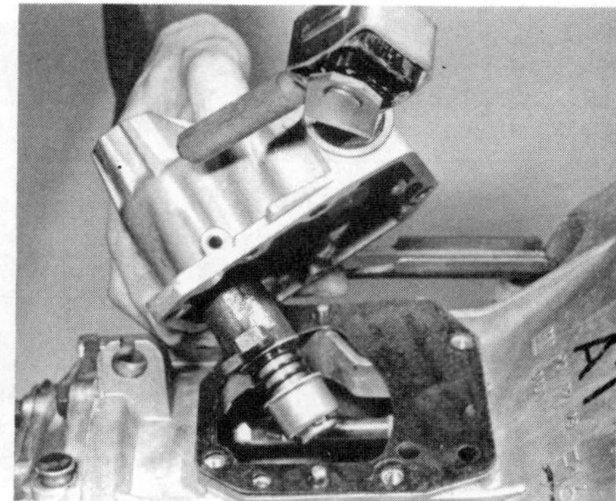
21.32 Fitting the selector cover

22 Fault diagnosis – manual transmission

Note: *It is sometimes difficult to decide whether it is worthwhile removing and dismantling the gearbox for a fault which may be nothing more than a minor irritant. Gearboxes which howl, or where the synchromesh can be beaten by a quick gearchange, may continue to perform a long time in this state. A worn gearbox usually needs a complete rebuild to eliminate noise because the various gears, if re-aligned on new bearings, will continue to howl when different wearing surfaces are presented to each other. The decision to overhaul, therefore, must be considered with regard to time and money available, relative to the degree of noise or malfunction that the driver has to suffer.*

Symptom	Reason(s)
Transmission noisy in neutral	Input shaft bearings worn
Transmission noisy in all gears	Oil level low, or incorrect grade (also refer to Section 2) Mainshaft or differential bearings worn Crownwheel and pinion worn Differential bearing adjustment incorrect
Transmission noisy in one gear	Worn, damaged or chipped gearteeth
Transmission jumps out of gear	Worn synchro unit Worn selector forks Worn detent plunger or springs
Ineffective synchromesh	Oil level low, or incorrect grade Synchro units or baulk rings worn
Difficulty in engaging gears*	Gear linkage adjustment incorrect Worn selector forks or selector mechanism Clutch fault (see Chapter 5)

* *Before being able to engage reverse gear, it is normal to have to wait a couple of seconds with the clutch pedal fully depressed, the engine idling and the vehicle stationary. This is not a fault.*

PART B: AUTOMATIC TRANSMISSION

23 General description

The automatic transmission is of General Motors construction, and is available as an option on certain models. The unit provides three forward speeds and one reverse. Gearchanging between the three forward ratios is normally fully automatic, the transmission responding to engine speed and load. A 'kickdown' facility gives an immediate downchange (subject to speed limitations) when the throttle is floored. The driver also has the option of locking out top and intermediate gears, although the transmission will not change into 1st gear until speed is sufficiently low.

Drive from the engine is transmitted via a torque converter, which provides fluid drive with a variable torque multiplication ratio, and a chain.

As with the manual transmission, the final drive and differential are contained in the transmission casing and share the same lubricant.

24 Maintenance and inspection

Note: *Scrupulous cleanliness is essential when working on the automatic transmission. Introduction of dirt or foreign matter into the transmission fluid may cause expensive damage.*

1 At every major service interval, or whenever leakage or malfunction is suspected, check the fluid level as follows. The car must be parked on level ground.

2 With the transmission in P and the bonnet open, start the engine and allow it to idle for one minute. Withdraw the transmission dipstick, wipe it on a clean lint-free rag, push the dipstick home again, then withdraw it and read it. This must be done within two minutes.

3 There are two sets of calibrations on the dipstick. The side marked '+20°C' should be used when the transmission is cold (fluid temperature below 35°C/95°F); the quantity of fluid required to raise the level from 5 mm (0.2 in) below MAX to MAX is approximately 0.25 litre (0.44 pint).

4 The dipstick side marked '+94°C' should be used when the transmission is at operating temperature (after at least 13 miles/20 km driving). The amount of fluid required to raise the level from MIN to MAX is approximately 0.5 litre (0.88 pint).

5 If topping-up is necessary, do so via the dipstick tube. Use only clean ATF of the specified type. Be careful not to overfill and not to introduce dirt. A regular need for topping-up indicates that there is a leak somewhere, which should be found and rectified.

6 When the fluid level is correct, refit the dipstick in its tube and switch off the engine.

7 At every fourth major service, or more frequently if the vehicle is operated under arduous conditions (eg taxi work, full-time towing or extremes of climate), the transmission fluid should be renewed as follows.

8 Allow the transmission to cool down if the vehicle has just been run, as the transmission fluid can be hot enough to cause severe scalding.

9 Position a suitable container under the fluid pan. Remove all the fluid pan screws except the two shown (Fig. 6.33). Slacken the two remaining screws by a few turns and carefully tip the pan so that the fluid pours into the container. When most of the fluid has drained, remove the screws and tip out the rest of the fluid. Recover the fluid pan gasket.

10 Clean the sealing surfaces of the transmission and the fluid pan, being careful not to damage them.

11 Common sense suggests that the opportunity should be taken to clean the fluid pick-up filter mesh and to renew the pick-up O-ring seal.

12 Refit the fluid pan, using a new gasket. Tighten the screws progressively in criss-cross sequence to the specified torque.

13 Fill the transmission with fresh ATF of the specified type via the dipstick tube. When the quantity of fluid poured in approaches the amount specified, check the fluid level on the 'cold' side of the dipstick, as described earlier in this Section. Check for leaks around the fluid pan gasket after the transmission has warmed up, then recheck the fluid level.

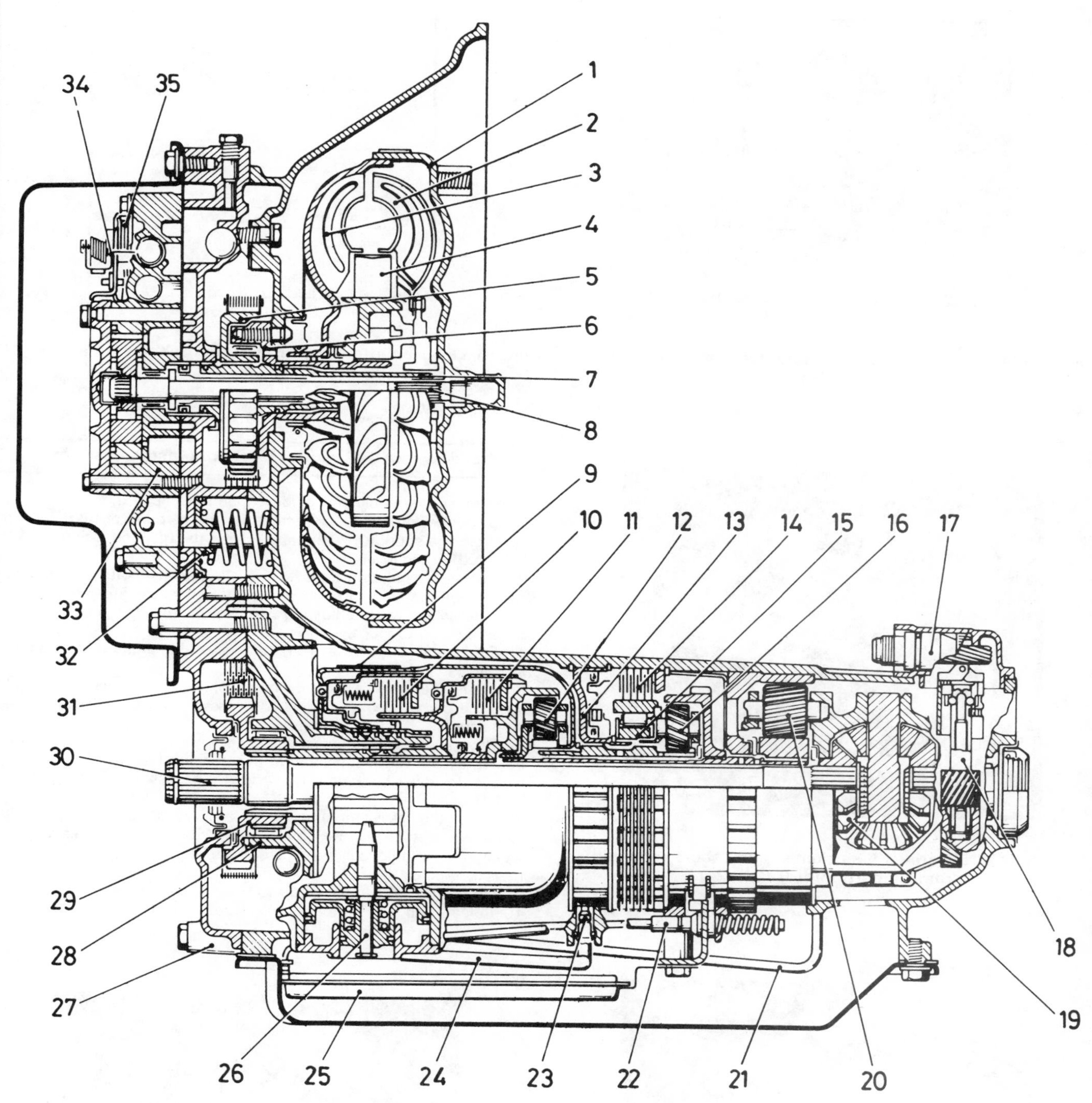

Fig. 6.30 Sectional view of 125 THM automatic transmission (Sec 23)

1 Torque converter
2 Turbine wheel
3 Pump wheel
4 Guide wheel
5 Drive sprocket
6 Drive sprocket carrier
7 Turbine shaft
8 Oil pump shaft
9 Brake band
10 Direct clutch
11 Forward clutch
12 Input planet carrier
13 Clutch housing
14 Low and reverse clutch
15 Freewheel
16 Reaction planetary set
17 Speedometer drive pinion
18 Governor
19 Differential
20 Axle drive
21 Governor fluid line
22 Parking lock actuation
23 Seal
24 Fluid line
25 Fluid filter
26 Brake band servo unit
27 Casing
28 Driven sprocket carrier
29 Driven sprocket
30 Axleshaft
31 Chain drive
32 Accumulator
33 Valve and pump assembly
34 Throttle valve kickdown actuator
35 Line boost valve

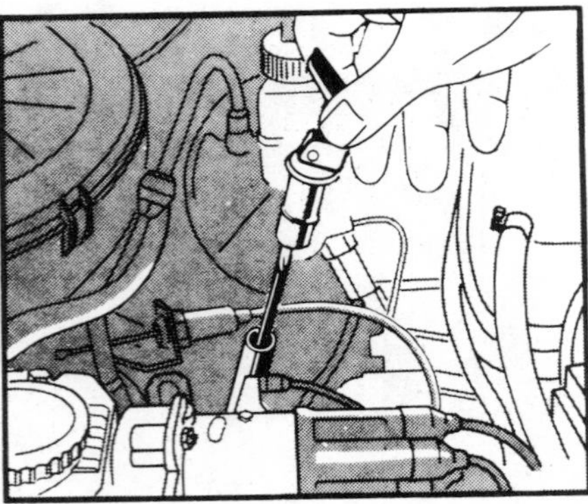

Fig. 6.31 Withdrawing the automatic transmission dipstick (Sec 24)

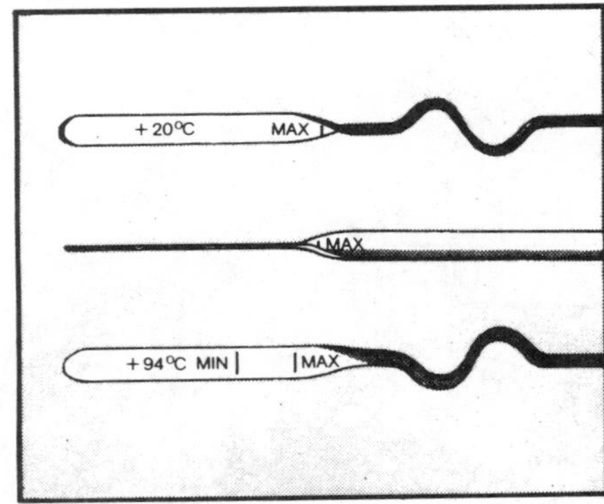

Fig. 6.32 Automatic transmission dipstick markings (Sec 24)

Fig. 6.33 With screws A slackened and others removed, drain fluid at point B (Sec 24)

25 Kickdown cable – removal, refitting and adjustment

1 Remove the air cleaner, as described in Chapter 3.

2 Disconnect the kickdown cable for the carburettor by pulling the clip from the support bracket and prising the ball end fitting from the ball-stud on the lever.

3 At the transmission end, remove the locking bolt from the cable sleeve, pull the sleeve upwards and disconnect the inner cable.

4 Release the cable adjusting mechanism from the support bracket by depressing the lugs.

5 Fit the new cable by reversing the removal operations, then adjust it as follows.

6 Check that there is a small amount of slack in the accelerator cable with the pedal released. Adjust if necessary at the accelerator pedal stop screw.

7 Have an assistant depress the accelerator pedal slowly until it just contacts the kickdown switch. In this position the throttle plate in the carburettor must be wide open. Adjust if necessary at the carburettor end of the cable.

8 Have the assistant press the accelerator pedal beyond the kickdown detent to the floor. The ratchet of the self-adjusting mechanism should be heard to operate, confirming that adjustment has taken place.

9 No further adjustment of the cable is necessary.

10 Release the accelerator pedal and refit the air cleaner.

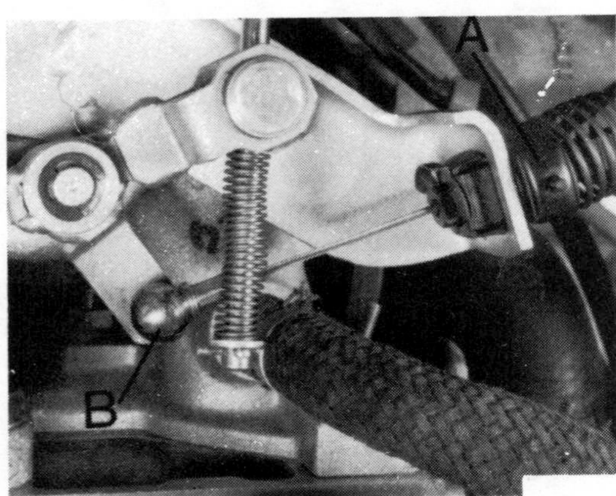

Fig. 6.34 Kickdown cable connection at carburettor (Sec 25)

A Cable adjuster *B Ball end fitting*

Fig. 6.35 Locking bolt (arrowed) secures kickdown cable to transmission (Sec 25)

Fig. 6.36 Kickdown cable adjusting mechanism release lugs (arrowed) (Sec 25)

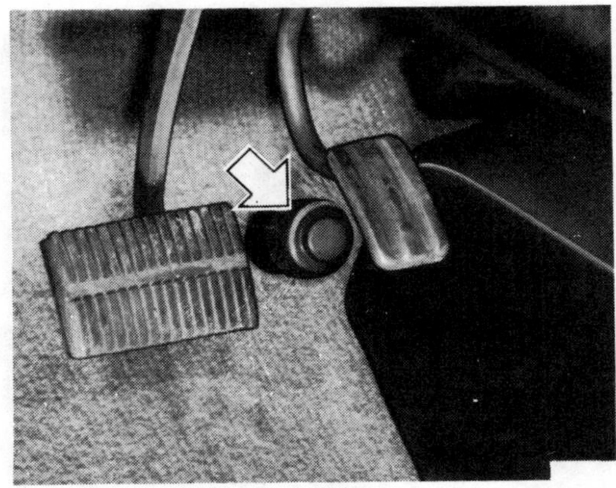

Fig. 6.37 Kickdown switch (arrowed) under accelerator pedal (Sec 25)

26 Speed selector control cable – removal, refitting and adjustment

1 Disconnect the battery earth lead.

2 Detach the selector lever surround by unscrewing and drawing back the centre console, removing the reflective strip and slot covering from the surround, and disengaging the surround from the console and the selector lever. Pull off the lamp base as the surround is withdrawn.

3 Disconnect the cable inner and outer components from the selector lever.

4 At the transmission, disconnect the cable inner by removing its retaining ring. Release the cable outer from its support.

5 Draw the cable into the engine bay and remove it. Installation of the new cable may be simplified if a piece of string is drawn out by the end of the old cable, and used in fitting the new one.

6 When fitting the new cable, set the selector lever and the lever on

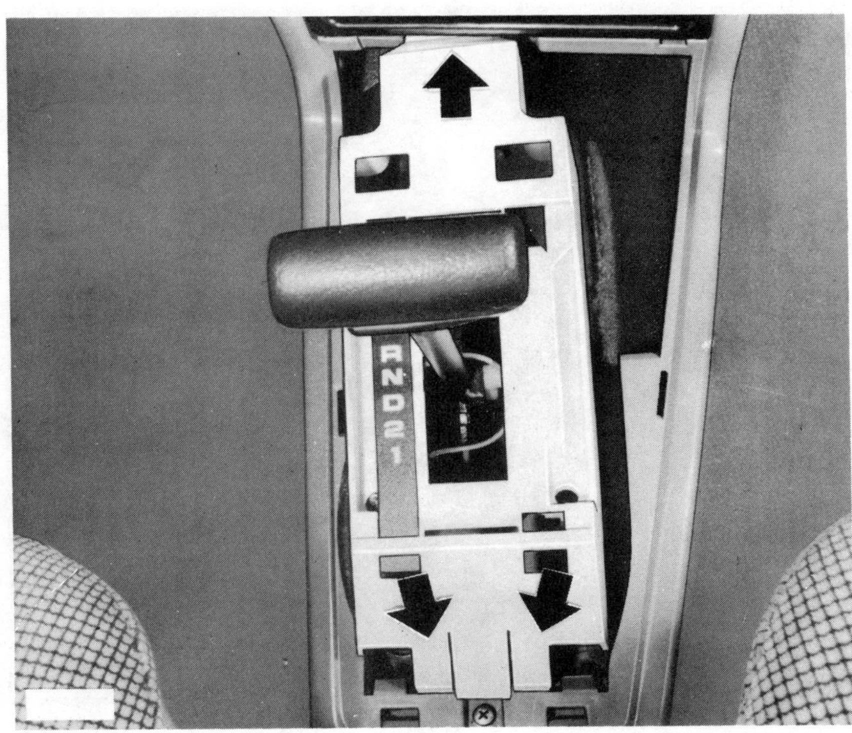

Fig. 6.38 Selector lever surround retaining lugs (arrowed) (Sec 26)

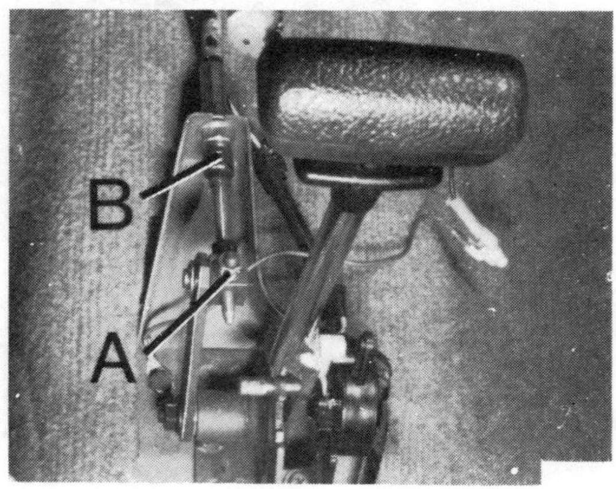

Fig. 6.39 Selector cable attachment at hand control lever (Sec 26)

A Clamp *B Sleeve*

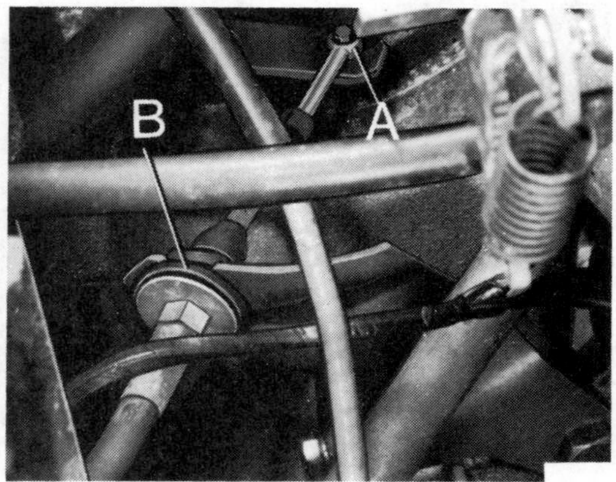

Fig. 6.40 Selector cable retaining clip (A) and support (B) (Sec 26)

the transmission in position P. Fit the cable so that it is neither taut nor slack.

7 Check that all positions can be engaged, and that the selector lever on the transmission is positively positioned in its correct detent and not under any tension in any position. Adjust if necessary at the console end.

8 Refit the remaining components in the reverse order to removal.

27 Starter inhibitor/reversing lamp switch – removal and refitting

1 Disconnect the battery earth lead.

2 Detach the selector lever surround, as described in Section 26.

3 Remove the two screws which secure the switch.

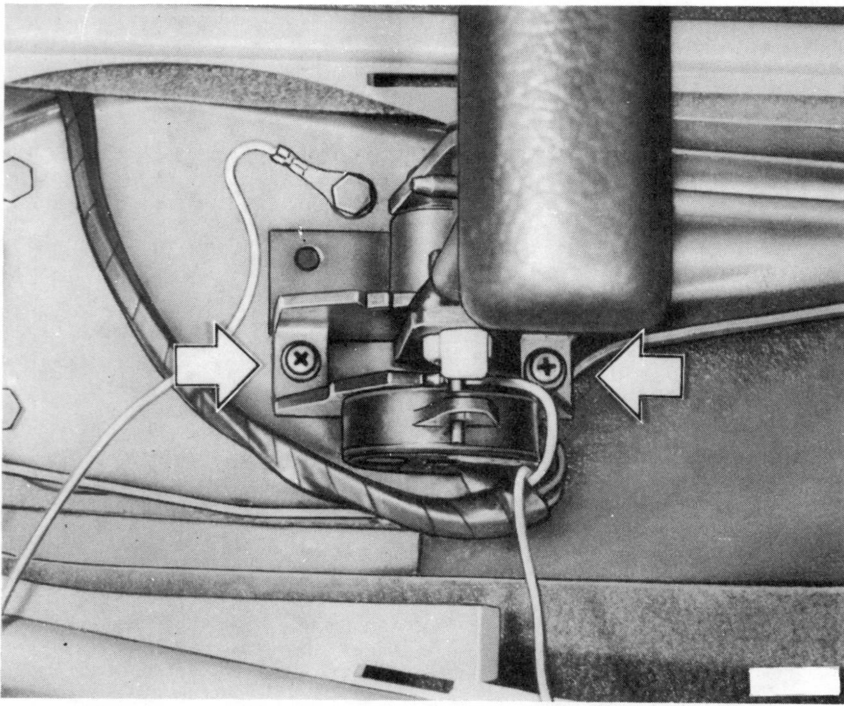

Fig. 6.41 Two screws (arrowed) secure starter inhibitor/reversing lamp switch (Sec 27)

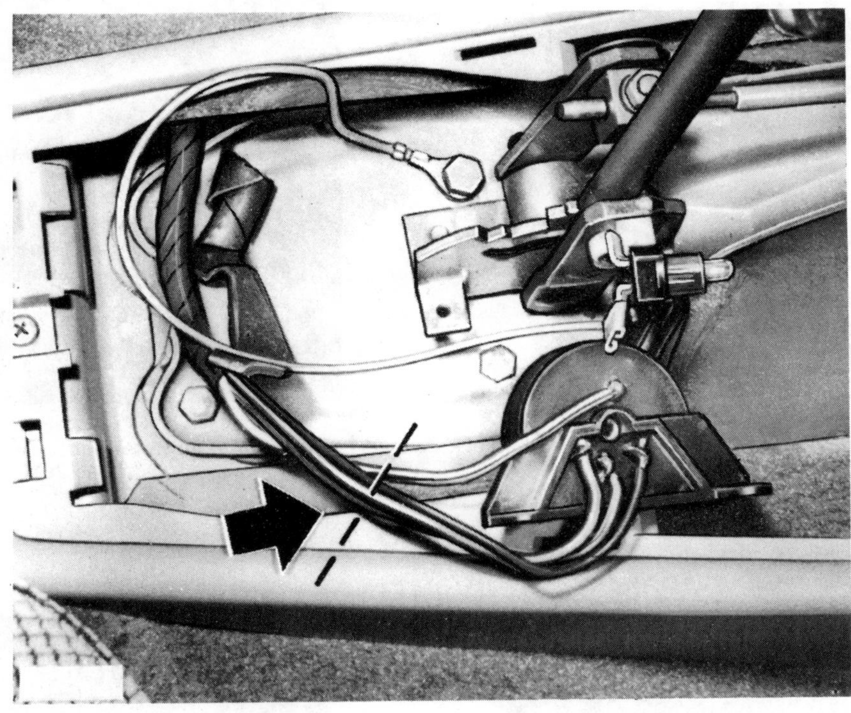

Fig. 6.42 Cut the switch wires at the point arrowed (Sec 27)

4 Detach the green/white cable from the selector illumination lamp base.

5 Strip back the wiring harness outer covering by about 10 cm (4 in), then sever the wires at the point shown (Fig. 6.42). Deal with the wiring harness or the new switch in a similar fashion.

6 Remove the old switch and fit the new one. Connect the wires using proprietary cable connectors or a terminal block, making sure that only wires of the same colour are joined together. All joints must be insulated.

7 Temporarily reconnect the battery. Switch on the ignition and check that the reversing lamps come on only in position 'R', and that the engine can be started only in position P and N. No provision is made for adjustment, but minor misalignment may be corrected by packing up one end of the switch with washers.

8 Disconnect the battery, refit the selector lever surround and reconnect the battery.

28 Automatic transmission – removal and refitting

1 Disconnect the battery earth lead.

2 Remove the air cleaner, as described in Chapter 3.

3 Disconnect the earth strap from the transmission end cover.

4 Disconnect the kickdown cable at the carburettor end, then unbolt it from the transmission – see Section 25.

5 Release the selector cable inner from the selector lever on the transmission, then unbolt the cable bracket. There is no need to remove the cable from the bracket.

6 Disconnect the speedometer cable from the transmission.

7 Remove the top three bolts which secure the transmission to the engine. Note that the centre bolt also secures a coolant pipe bracket.

8 Slacken the front wheel bolts, raise and securely support the front of the car and remove the front wheels.

9 Support the engine from above, either with a bar and adjustable hook braced across the engine bay, or with a crane or similar engine lifting tackle. Adjust the tackle to take the weight of the engine.

10 Disconnect the control arm balljoints on both sides.

11 Separate the driveshafts from the transmission, as described in Chapter 7. Be prepared for some fluid spillage. Plug the driveshaft apertures and tie the driveshafts up out of the way.

12 On models so equipped, disconnect and plug the oil cooler lines at the transmission. Be prepared for fluid spillage.

13 Remove the cover from the bottom of the torque converter housing.

14 Remove the screws which secure the torque converter to the flexplate, turning the engine as necessary to bring the screws into view.

15 Remove the remaining transmission-to-engine bolts.

16 Unbolt the engine/transmission rear mounting from the body. Also unbolt the exhaust bracket.

17 Support the transmission with a trolley jack, preferably using a cradle to spread the load and to stop it falling.

18 Remove the engine/transmission left-hand mounting completely.

19 Remove the two bolts which hold the transmission to the engine mounting bracket.

20 Carefully move the transmission away from the engine, lower it and withdraw it from below the vehicle. If the dipstick/oil filler tube gets in the way, it can be removed before the transmission is withdrawn, but be prepared to catch the considerable amount of fluid which will be released.

21 If the transmission is to be renewed, remember to salvage the mounting brackets and the oil cooler unions.

22 Refit the transmission in the reverse order to removal, observing the following points.

23 Before offering the transmission to the engine, check that the torque converter is correctly meshed with the oil pump. To do this, measure dimension A (Fig. 6.50). This should be between 9.00 and 10.00 mm (0.35 and 0.39 in). If it is not, rotate the converter, at the same time applying hand pressure, until it meshes with the pump.

24 Apply a smear of molybdenum disulphide paste, or other 'dry' lubricant, to the torque converter pilot spigot and to the corresponding recess in the tail of the crankshaft.

25 When bolting the torque converter to the flexplate, align the coloured spot on the converter as closely as possible with the white spot on the flexplate. Note that there will be a small clearance (0.4 to 1.5 mm/0.016 to 0.059 in) between the converter and the flexplate

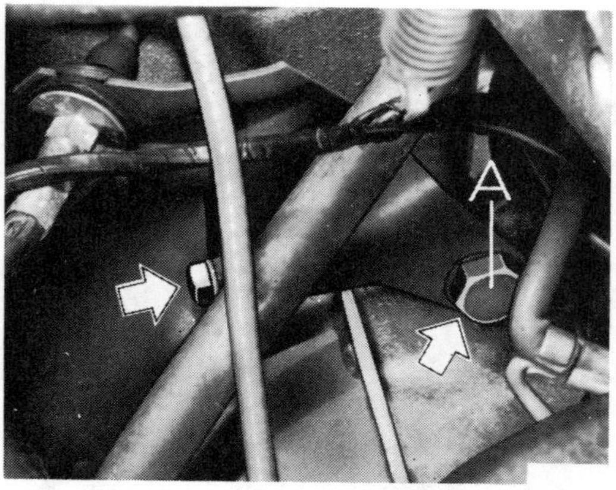

Fig. 6.43 Selector cable support bracket bolts (arrowed) Bolt A is also a transmission-to-engine bolt (Sec 28)

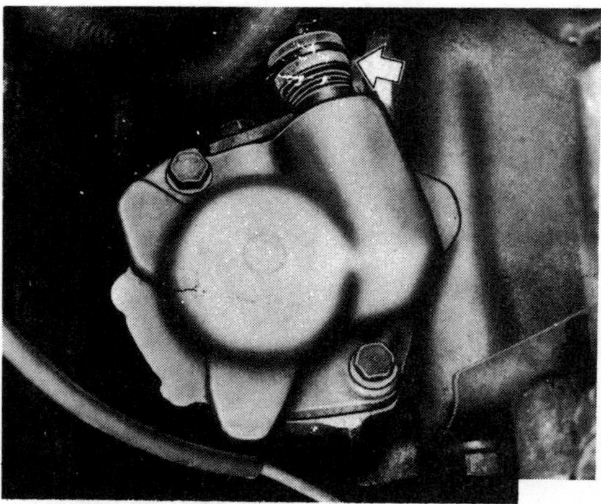

Fig. 6.44 Speedometer cable connection (arrowed) (Sec 28)

Fig. 6.45 Top three transmission-to-engine bolts (arrowed) (Sec 28)

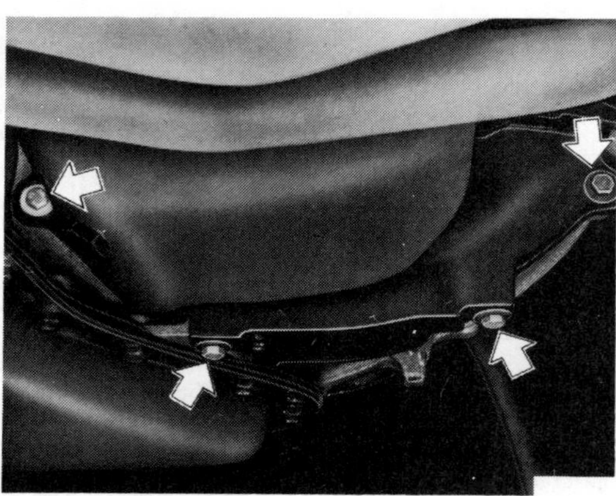

Fig. 6.46 Torque converter cover plate bolts (arrowed) (Sec 28)

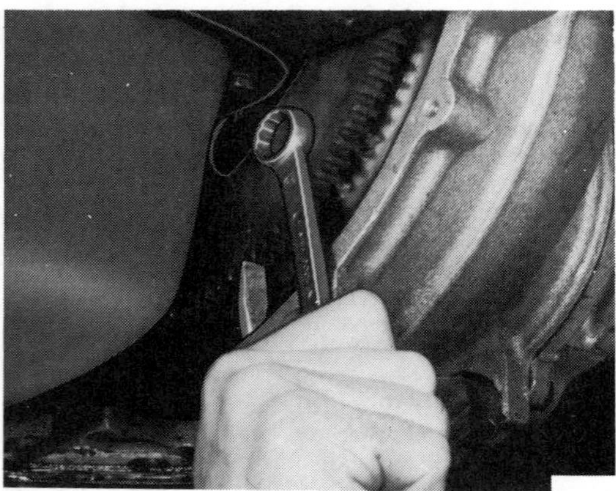

Fig. 6.47 Undoing a torque converter-to-flexplate bolt (Sec 28)

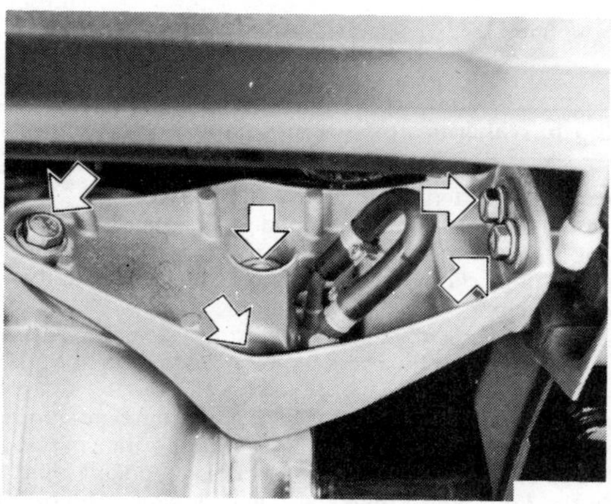

Fig. 6.48 Left-hand mounting bolts (arrowed). Hose loop in centre is bridging cooler connections (Sec 28)

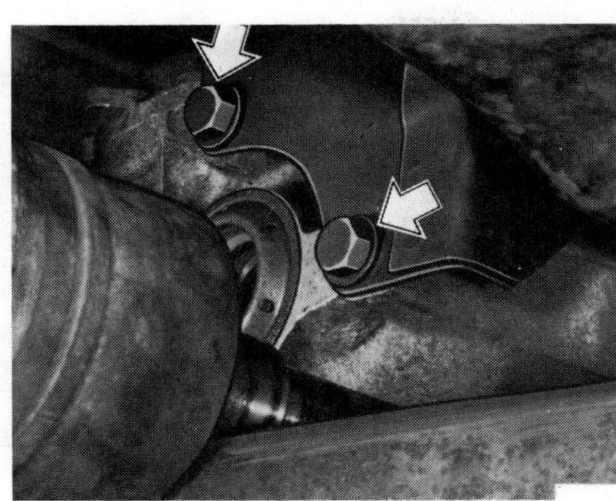

Fig. 6.49 Two bolts (arrowed) hold the transmission to the engine mounting bracket (Sec 28)

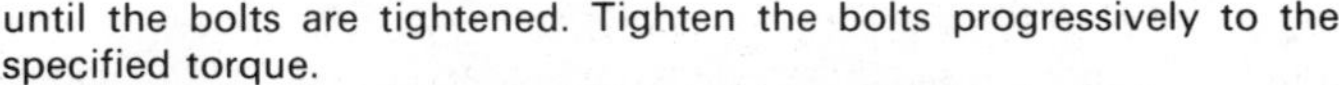

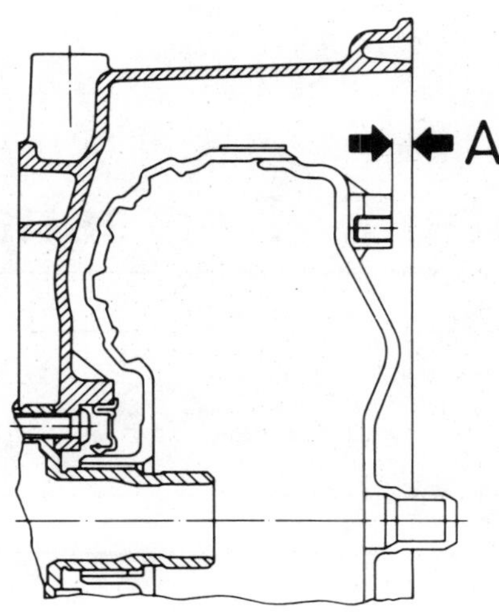

Fig. 6.50 Torque converter engagement check. For A see text (Sec 28)

until the bolts are tightened. Tighten the bolts progressively to the specified torque.

26 Transmissions with codes EF and EK are not intended to have an oil cooler connected; do not attempt to uncap the cooler connection points.

27 Adjust the speed selector and kickdown cables, as described in Sections 26 and 25.

28 Refill the transmission with fluid, as described in Section 24. If a new transmission and torque converter are being fitted, the quantity of ATF required will be greater than after fluid changing – see Specification.

29 Fault diagnosis – automatic transmission

1 Without special test equipment, the DIY mechanic should not attempt any more than the adjustments and checks described in the preceding Sections.

2 Any fault not attributable to low fluid level or cable maladjustment should be referred to a GM dealer or other competent specialist.

3 Before removing the transmission for repair, make sure that the repairer does not wish to perform diagnostic tests with the transmission installed.

Chapter 7 Driveshafts

Contents

Specifications

General

Type	Open shafts with constant velocity joint at each end
Identification	Bead on RH shaft, groove on LH shaft

Torque wrench settings

	Nm	lbf ft
Driveshaft nut:		
Stage 1	100	74
Slacken, then Stage 2	20	15
Stage 3	Tighten through further 90°; slacken if necessary to align split pin holes	
Damper weight (RH shaft)	10	7
Control arm balljoint pin nut	70	52

1 General description

Open tubular driveshafts are fitted. Each shaft has a constant velocity (CV) joint at each end to allow steering and suspension movements to occur without affecting the quality of the drive.

The right-hand shaft is considerably longer than the left, and may carry a damper weight to reduce resonant vibrations.

Although the shafts appear identical to those fitted to earlier GM front-wheel-drive cars, they are not, in fact, interchangeable. Shafts are identified by a bead on the right-hand shaft and a groove on the left-hand shaft.

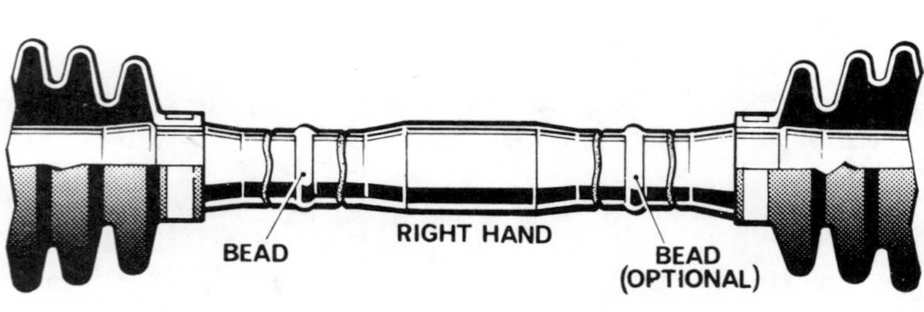

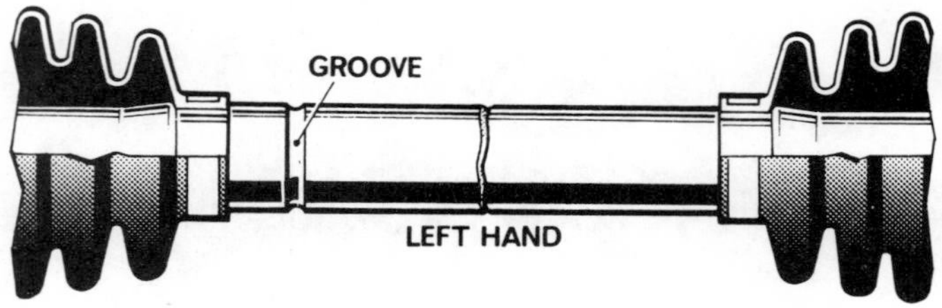

Fig. 7.1 Identification of right-hand and left-hand driveshafts (Sec 1)

2 Maintenance and inspection

1 At every major service interval, and more frequently if the time can be spared, inspect the rubber bellows which protect the inner and outer CV joints. If they are torn, split or perished they should be renewed as a matter of urgency, as described in Section 4. Rapid wear of the CV joint, due to loss of lubricant and entry of water and grit, will occur if damaged bellows are not renewed.
2 Wear in the outer CV joints is detected as a regular knocking when accelerating from rest with the steering on full lock. In severe cases it is only necessary to turn the steering slightly for the noise to begin. Wear in the inner joints may be felt as a vibration when accelerating hard in a straight line.
3 The CV joints are lubricated and sealed during manufacture. Provided that the rubber bellows remain intact, no further lubrication is necessary. Worn joints cannot be repaired, but must be renewed complete.

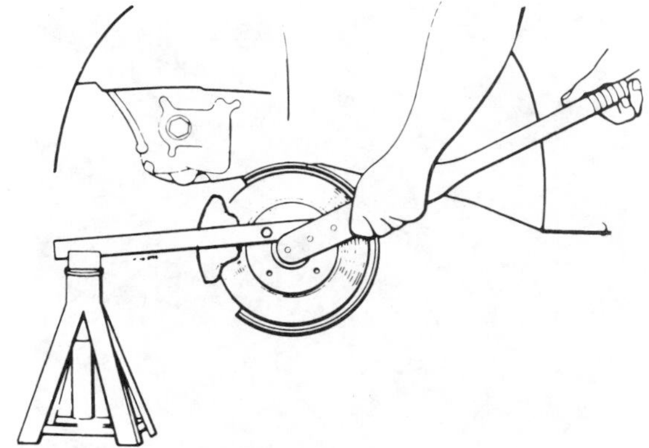

Fig. 7.2 Undoing a driveshaft nut (Sec 3)

3 Driveshaft – removal and refitting

1 Slacken the front wheel bolts on the side concerned, raise and support the front of the vehicle and remove the roadwheel.
2 Extract the split pin from the driveshaft retaining nut, then unscrew the nut using a socket and bar. Prevent the driveshaft from turning by having an assistant apply the footbrake hard, or by bolting a suitably drilled steel bar to the hub. Remove the nut and retrieve the washer.
3 Separate the control arm balljoint, as described in Chapter 10.
4 The driveshaft must now be released from the transmission. The makers specify a variety of tools for the different transmissions: they are wide metal forks with a good chamfer on the leading edge. A similarly chamfered bar, a tyre lever or even a large blunt screwdriver may serve instead (photo). Drive the tool into the gap between the joint and the casing to release the circlip from the differential side gear (photo). A good blow will be needed to jar the circlip out of its groove. In exceptionally difficult cases it will be necessary to remove the differential cover plate and apply a flat chisel to the inboard end of the shaft.
5 On automatic transmission models only, the right-hand driveshaft should be released by means of a non-ferrous (soft metal) drift applied to the joint casing.
6 Once the circlip has been released, pull the joint out of the transmission by hand. Some oil or ATF will be spilt, so have a container handy. If possible, plug the hole to keep dirt out.
7 It should now be possible to push the outboard end of the shaft out of the splines in the hub (photo). If this cannot be done by hand, it is best to use a screw or hydraulic pusher bolted to the hub. Blows from a

Fig. 7.3 Releasing a driveshaft from the transmission with the maker's tool (Sec 3)

3.4A Home made tool for releasing driveshafts

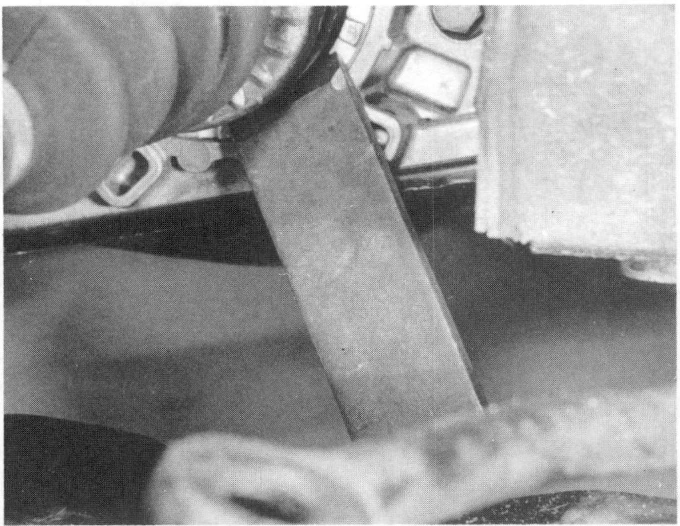

3.4B Releasing a driveshaft from the differential

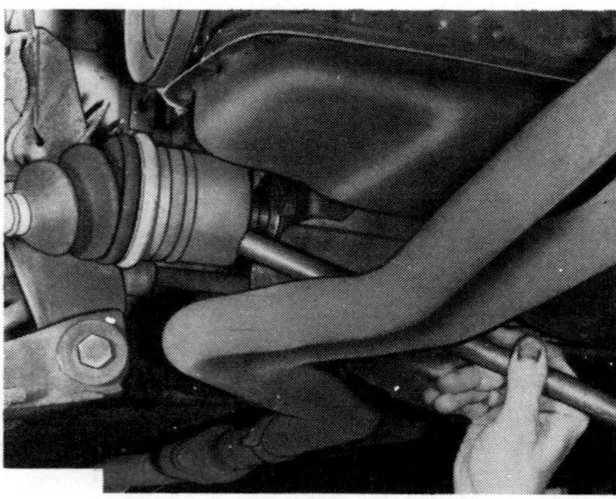

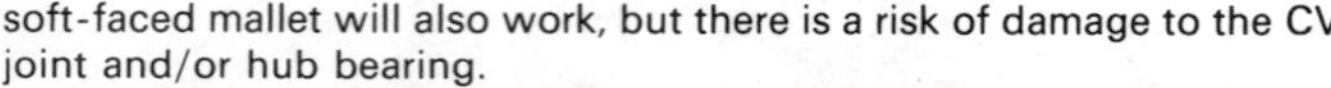

Fig. 7.4 Releasing the right-hand driveshaft – automatic transmission models (Sec 3)

3.7 Removing the driveshaft from the hub

soft-faced mallet will also work, but there is a risk of damage to the CV joint and/or hub bearing.

8 Note that, with the driveshaft removed from the hub, the two halves of the hub bearing are no longer positively located. **The vehicle must not be moved on its wheels in this state, or the bearing will be damaged.** If it is essential to move the vehicle without the driveshaft fitted, clamp the bearing with a dummy shaft or some stout studding, nuts and washers.

9 Do not allow a serviceable driveshaft to rest on its bellows for long periods, or they may become permanently distorted.

10 Before refitting the driveshaft, make sure that the contact faces of the outer CV joint and the hub bearing are perfectly clean. Check the condition of the circlip on the differential end of the shaft and renew it if its condition is suspect (photo).

11 Lubricate the shaft splines at the hub end with gear oil and insert the shaft into the hub. Fit a new washer and a new nut. Only tighten the nut finger tight at this stage.

12 Insert the inner end of the shaft in the transmission. Push it in by hand as far as it will go. Drive the joint home using a screwdriver or drift applied to the bead of the weld around the joint (**not** to the metal cover) until the circlip snaps into place. Check that the circlip is home by pulling on the outer part of the CV joint. It is not possible to check for secure engagement by pulling on the shaft.

13 Reconnect the control arm balljoint, tighten its nut to the specified torque and secure with a new split pin.

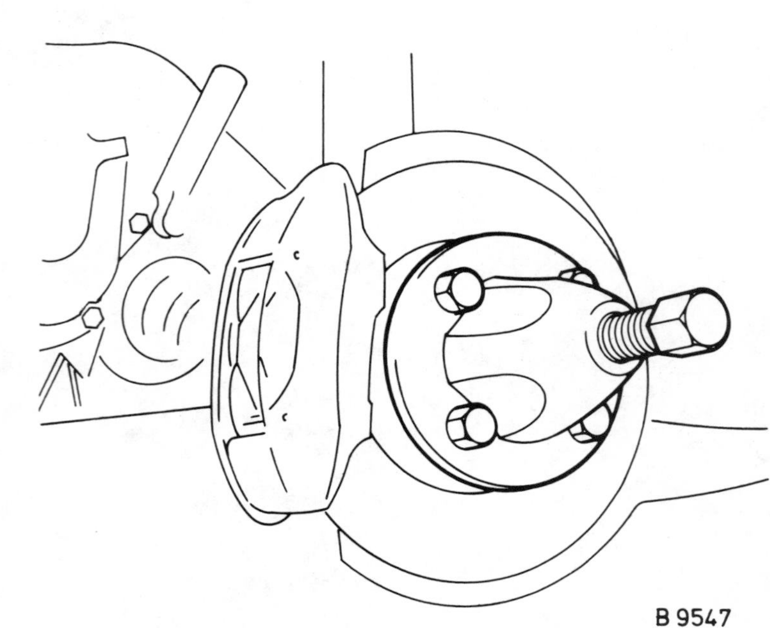

Fig. 7.5 Using a screw pusher to press the driveshaft out of the hub (Sec 3)

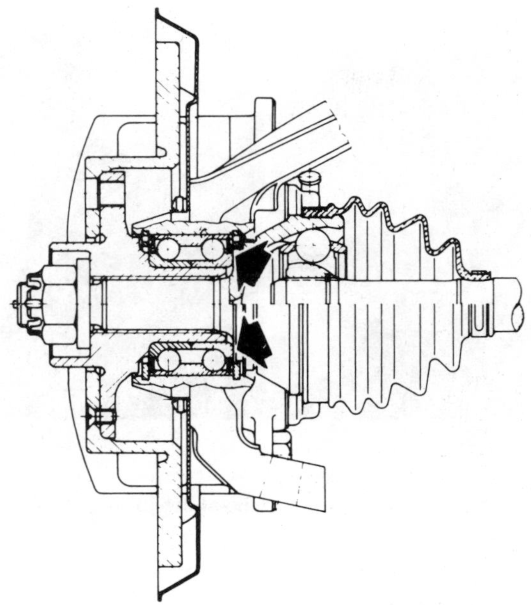

Fig. 7.6 Sectional view of hub and driveshaft. Contact faces (arrowed) must be clean (Sec 3)

14 Tighten the driveshaft nut to the Stage 1 specified torque. Back it off and retighten to the Stage 2 torque. Tighten the nut further through the angle specified for Stage 3.
15 Secure the nut with a new split pin. If the split pin holes are not aligned, **back off** the nut until they are – **do not** tighten it further to align.
16 If the damper weight on the right-hand shaft has been disturbed, make sure it is secured at the correct distance from the outboard bellows (Fig. 7.7).
17 Refit the roadwheels, lower the car and tighten the wheel bolts. Check the transmission oil level and top up as necessary (Chapter 6, Section 2 or 24).

3.10 Driveshaft circlip (arrowed) at differential end

4 Driveshaft joint – bellows renewal

1 Remove the driveshaft from the car, as described in the previous Section.

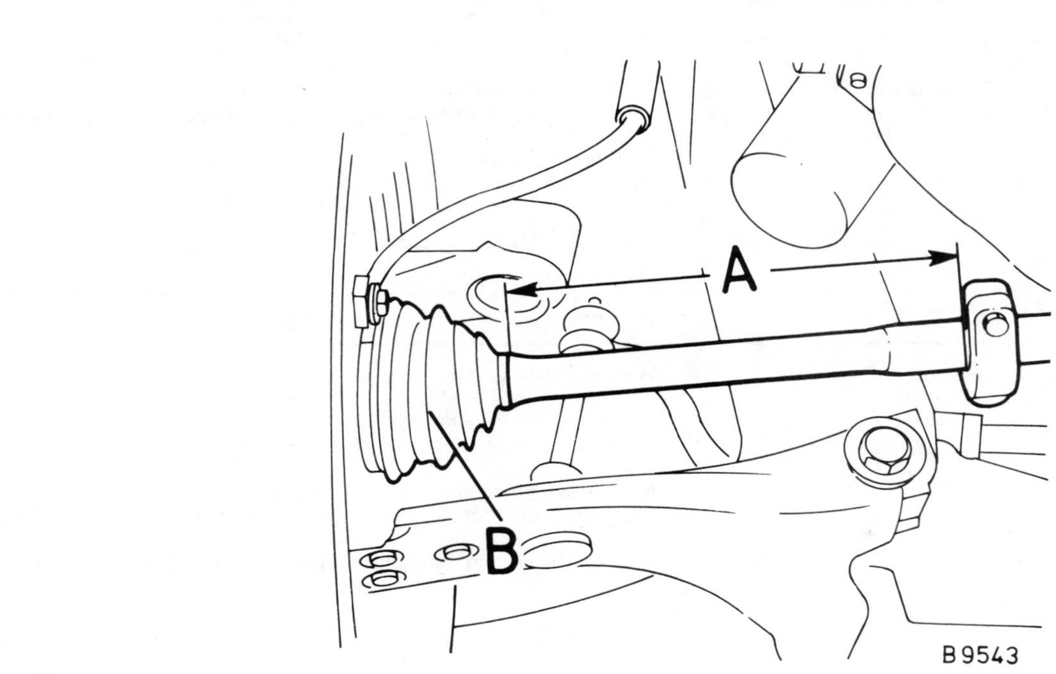

Fig. 7.7 Driveshaft damper weight distance from end of bellows (B) (Sec 3)

A = 260 mm (10.24 in)

Fig. 7.8 Driveshaft joint retaining circlip (arrowed) (Sec 4)

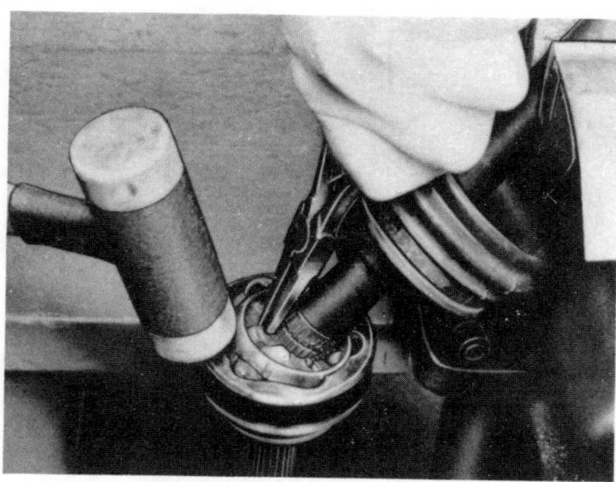

Fig. 7.9 Removing a driveshaft joint (Sec 4)

2 Remove the metal clips securing the bellows to the driveshaft and constant velocity joint. Fold the bellows back and slide it along the driveshaft to expose the external components of the joint.
3 Secure the driveshaft in a vice, spread the retaining circlip with circlip pliers and tap the joint off the shaft using a soft-faced mallet.
4 With the constant velocity joint removed, the bellows can now be slid off the end of the driveshaft. If both are to be removed, the other one can be withdrawn from the same end of the driveshaft without having to remove the other joint.
5 Thoroughly clean away all traces of the old grease from the constant velocity joint using paraffin or a suitable solvent. Obtain new bellows, new retaining clips and a suitable quantity of the special lubricating grease from a GM dealer.
6 Slide the bellows onto the shaft until the smaller diameter engages with the groove on the shaft.
7 Wrap the small metal clip around the bellows and, pulling the clip as tight as possible, engage the lug on the end of the clip with one of the slots. Use a screwdriver if necessary to push the clip as tight as possible before engaging the lug and slot. Now finally tighten the clip by compressing the raised square portion of the clip with pincers or pliers.
8 Fold the bellows back and engage the constant velocity joint with the driveshaft splines. Using a soft-faced mallet, tap the joint onto the shaft until the circlip engages with its groove.
9 Fill all the spaces in the joint with the special lubricating grease, moving the joint around at the same time. Apply a liberal quantity of grease and make sure it enters all the spaces and cavities between the joint members.
10 Fold the bellows back over the joint, making sure the larger diameter fits over the retaining clip groove in the joint outer diameter.
11 Expel all air from the bellows and then fit the large retaining clip using the same procedure as for the small one.
12 The driveshaft can now be refitted to the car, as described in Section 3.

5 Driveshaft joint – removal and refitting

1 All the information for joint renewal will be found in the preceding Section. A worn joint cannot be repaired, but must be renewed complete.
2 When renewing a joint it is wise to renew the bellows at the same time.

6 Fault diagnosis – driveshafts

Symptom	Reason(s)
Knocking noise when accelerating with steering on lock	Worn constant velocity outer joints
Vibration	Worn constant velocity inner joints Damaged or distorted driveshaft
Knock or clunk when taking up drive	Incorrectly tightened driveshaft retaining nut Worn splines on constant velocity joint, hub flange or differential side gear Wear in suspension components, joints or attachments (see Chapter 10)

Chapter 8 Steering

Contents

Specifications

General

Type	Rack and pinion; power assistance optionally available on some models
Ratio:	
Without power assistance	22 : 1 or 24.5 : 1
With power assistance	18 : 1

Power steering

Fluid type	Dexron ® II type ATF
Fluid capacity	1 litre (1.8 pints) approx
Drivebelt tension (with special gauge):	
New	450 N (101 lbf)
Used	250 to 300 N (56 to 68 lbf)

Toe setting (laden)*

All models	1 mm (0.04 in) toe-out to 1 mm (0.04 in) toe-in

** Vehicle laden with 70 kg (154 lb) in each front seat, and fuel tank half full*

Torque wrench settings

	Nm	lbf ft
Adjuster screw locknut	60	44
Flexible coupling clamp bolts	22	16
Steering wheel nut	25	18
Steering gear mountings	15	11
Pinion nut	40	30
Steering damper mounting (pinion end)	12	9
Steering damper mounting (moving end)	See text	
Tie-rod to rack	110	81
Tie-rod balljoint nut	60	44
Tie-rod and balljoint clamp bolts	20	15
Steering column support to bulkhead	22	16
Steering column bracket self-locking nut	15	11

Torque wrench settings

	Nm	lbf ft
Power steering fittings:		
Hydraulic unions on rack	37	27
Hydraulic unions on pump	28	21
Union nut – flexible hose to high pressure pipe	42	31
Pump support to block	40	30
Pump brackets to support	15	11
Tensioner strap to pump	40	30
Tensioner strap to support	15	11
Tensioner locknuts	40	30

1 General description

The steering gear is of rack and pinion type. A collapsible steering column is fitted; on some models the top part of the column is adjustable to provide different steering wheel positions.

A steering damper is fitted to certain models without power assistance to reduce the feedback of shocks to the steering wheel.

Power assistance is available as an option on the larger-engined models. Assistance is by hydraulic pressure, generated in a pump driven from the crankshaft pulley.

2 Maintenance and inspection

1 At every major service interval the following work should be performed.
2 Carefully inspect the rubber bellows which protect the steering gear. If they are cut, split or otherwise damaged they should be renewed, as described in Section 9. Neglect of damaged bellows may lead to damage to the steering gear itself.
3 Observe the tie-rod balljoints while an assistant turns the steering wheel back and forth through an arc of about 20°. If there is any side to side movement of the balljoints as the steering is turned they should be renewed, as described in Section 8. Renewal is also necessary if the rubber dust covers around the balljoints are split, or damaged, or show any signs of deterioration.
4 Also inspect the condition of the flexible rubber coupling at the base of the steering column and renew this component if the rubber shows signs of deterioration or swelling, or if any cracks or splits are apparent. Full details will be found in Section 6.
5 On models with power steering, carry out the following additional work.
6 Check the power steering fluid level, using the dipstick built into the reservoir cap. With the fluid cold (approx 20°C/68°F) the level should be up to the lower mark on the dipstick; with the fluid hot (80°C/176°F) the level should be at the upper mark. Top up if necessary with clean fluid of the specified type. A regular need for topping-up can only be due to a leak, which should be found and rectified. Under no circumstances must the pump be allowed to run dry.
7 Check the condition and tension of the steering pump drivebelt, as described in Section 15.
8 On all models, have the front wheel toe setting checked at alternate service intervals, or sooner if abnormal tyre wear is noticed. See Section 18 for details.

3 Steering wheel – removal and refitting

1 Disconnect the battery earth lead.
2 Prise off the central cap from the steering wheel. Disconnect the horn contact wires and remove the cap (photo).
3 Set the steering in the straight-ahead position.
4 Relieve the locktabs and undo the central retaining nut (photo).
5 Depending on the work to be done, it may ease refitting to mark the relationship of the wheel centre to the shaft splines.
6 Pull the wheel off the shaft splines. If pulling by hand, be careful not to injure yourself if the wheel suddenly comes free. Use a puller if it is tight. **Do not** use a hammer: damage to the column may result.
7 If wished, the horn contact ring can now be unclipped. Note that the direction indicator return segment on the ring points to the left.
8 Before refitting, make sure that the washer and spring are in place on the shaft. Fit the steering wheel onto the splines, making sure it is correctly aligned.
9 Fit a new lockwasher and refit the nut. Tighten the nut to the specified torque and bend up the lockwasher tabs.
10 Reconnect the horn contact wires and press the central cap into place.
11 Reconnect the battery earth lead.

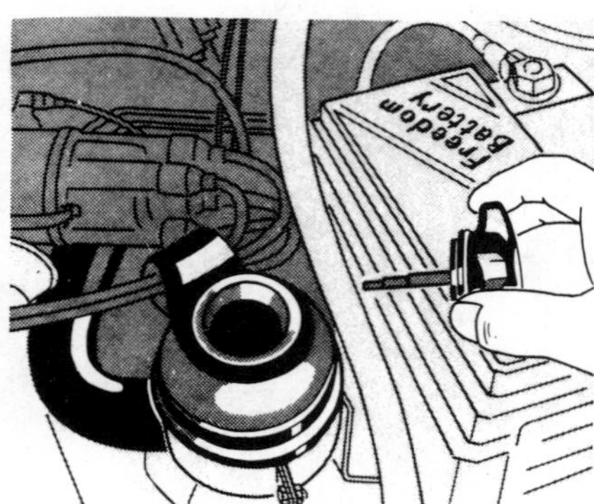

Fig. 8.1 Power steering fluid level dipstick screws into fluid reservoir cap (Sec 2)

3.2 Removing the steering wheel central cap

3.4 Steering wheel retaining nut and locktabs (arrowed)

4 Steering column – removal and refitting

1 Disconnect the battery earth lead.
2 Although not strictly necessary, access will be improved if the steering wheel is removed. See Section 3.
3 Remove the upper and lower switch shrouds. These are secured by eight screws with the fixed steering wheel, or five screws with the adjustable wheel (photos).
4 Remove the steering lock cylinder, as described in Section 7.
5 Disconnect the ignition switch multi-plug.
6 Remove the multi-function switches by depressing their retaining clips. With the adjustable wheel it may be necessary to undo the switch housing screws and draw the housing away from the dashboard to provide sufficient clearance.
7 Make sure that the steering is in the straight-ahead position, then remove the flexible coupling clamp bolt from the base of the column. Unbolt the column support from the bulkhead and recover the washer.
8 Remove the column upper mounting bracket nut and bolt. The bolt is of the shear-head type: drill it and extract it with a proprietary stud extractor, or it may be possible to unscrew the bolt by driving its head round with a chisel or punch. The nut is a self-locking type and should be renewed.
9 Withdraw the column slightly to free it from the flexible coupling, then remove it from the vehicle. Avoid knocking or dropping it as this could damage the collapsible section.
10 If a new column assembly is to be fitted, a large plastic washer will be found at the base of the column tube. This is to centre the shaft in the tube and should be removed when fitting is complete.
11 Commence refitting by making sure that the roadwheels are still in the straight-ahead position, and that the flexible coupling is positioned so that the column clamp bolt will be horizontal and on top.
12 Offer the column assembly to its mountings, inserting the base of the shaft into the coupling. Insert the mounting nuts and bolts, but only tighten them finger tight at this stage. Do not try to force the column into position or damage may result.
13 Tighten the column bulkhead support bolt to the specified torque. Make sure the washer is in place.
14 Tighten the upper mounting bracket fastenings: the shear-head bolt should be tightened until its head breaks off. The new self-locking nut should be tightened to the specified torque.
15 Pull the shaft upwards as far as it will go and tighten the flexible coupling clamp bolt to the specified torque.
16 Prise out the plastic washer from the base of the column tube. It can stay on the shaft.
17 Reconnect the ignition switch and refit the multi-function switches.
18 Refit the remaining components in the reverse order to removal.

5 Steering column – dismantling and reassembly

Unless stated otherwise, there is no need to remove the steering column for these operations.

Fixed steering wheel

1 If not already done, remove the steering wheel, the switch shrouds, the steering lock cylinder and the multi-function switches. See Sections 3, 4 and 7.
2 Prise out the switch housing safety plugs (Fig. 8.3). Turn the housing anti-clockwise and pull it to withdraw it.
3 The ball-bearing may be removed from the housing by prising apart the two bearing fixing catches and pressing out the bearing with a piece of tube. When pressing in the new bearing, make sure that the thrust washer and contact springs are in position (Fig. 8.4).
4 The ignition/starter switch is secured to the steering lock housing by two grub screws. Remove the screws to extract the switch. It is

4.3A Removing an upper shroud securing screw

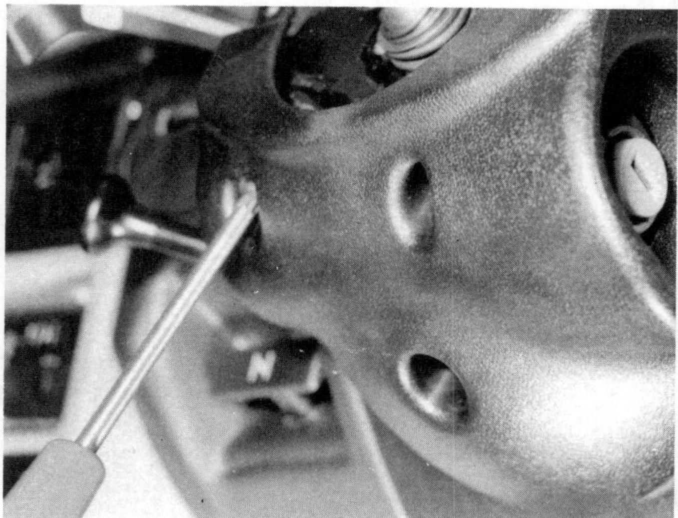
4.3B Removing a lower shroud securing screw – adjustable wheel

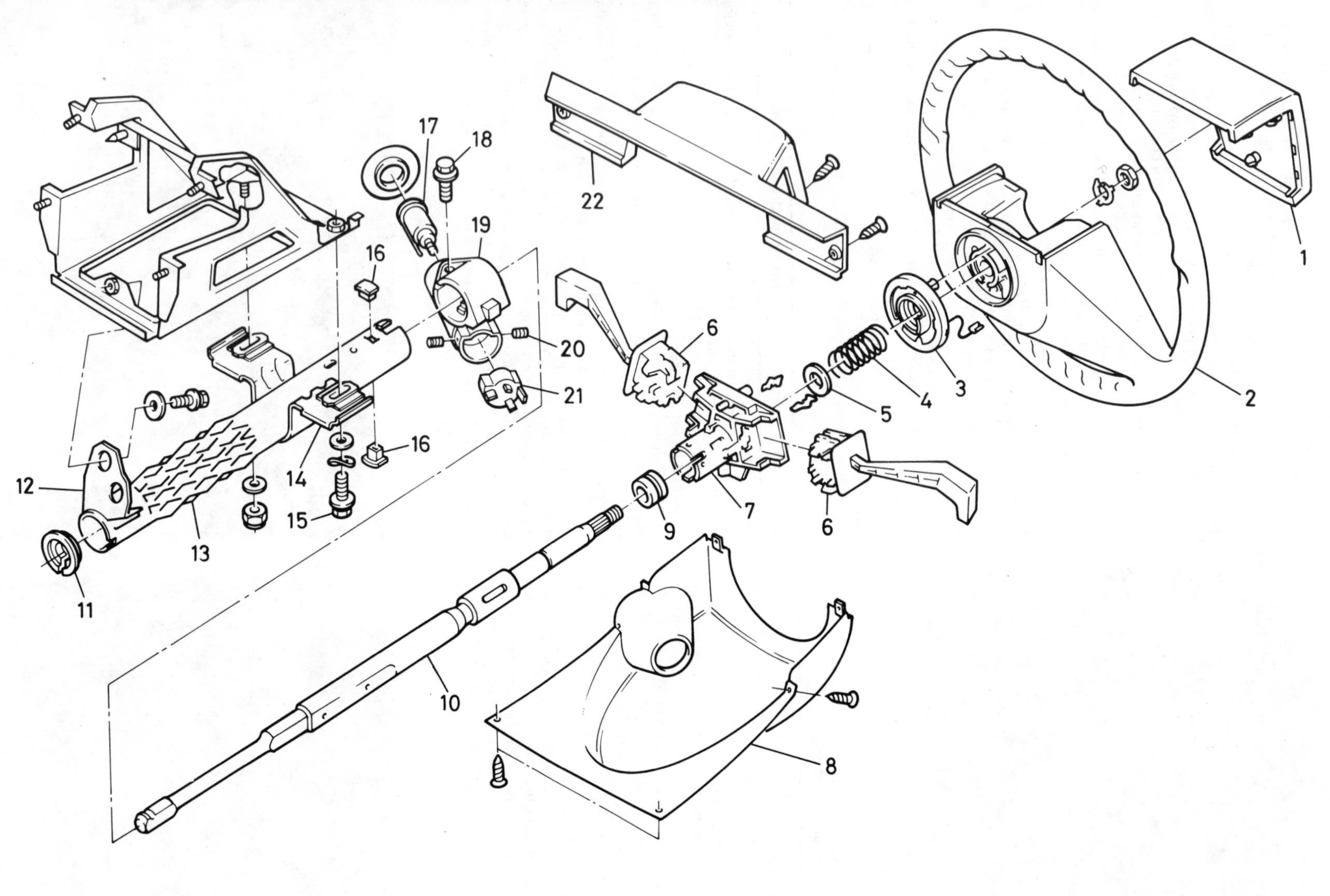

Fig. 8.2 Exploded view of fixed type steering column components (Sec 5)

1 Central cap
2 Steering wheel
3 Horn contact ring
4 Spring
5 Washer
6 Multi-function switches
7 Switch housing
8 Lower shroud
9 Bearing
10 Shaft
11 Centering washer
12 Bulkhead mounting
13 Collapsible section
14 Upper mounting
15 Shear-head bolt
16 Safety plugs
17 Ignition/steering lock barrel
18 Shear-head bolt
19 Ignition switch/steering lock housing
20 Grub screws
21 Ignition/starter switch
22 Upper shroud

Fig. 8.3 Switch housing safety plugs (arrowed) (Sec 5)

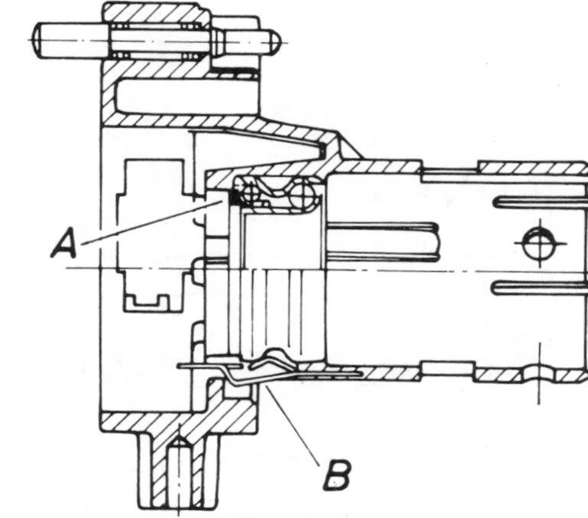

Fig. 8.4 Sectional view of steering column switch housing (Sec 5)

A Thrust washer B Contact spring

recommended that the switch and the lock barrel are not both removed at the same time so that their mutual alignment is not lost.
5 The ignition switch/steering lock housing can only be removed after removing the column assembly. It is secured by a shear-head bolt.
6 Reassembly by reversing the dismantling procedure.

Adjustable steering wheel

7 If not already done, remove the steering wheel, the switch shrouds and the steering lock cylinder. See Sections 3, 4 and 7.
8 Unscrew the wheel tilt adjuster knob.
9 Undo the two securing screws with a splined key and remove the switch housing, complete with switches (photo). Either unclip the switches and let them hang, or unplug their connectors to remove them completely.
10 The column upper and lower surrounds may be removed after undoing the six retaining screws.
11 The tilt adjuster spring may be removed by simply prising it free with a screwdriver; be careful lest it flies out (photo).
12 The ignition/starter switch is secured to the lock housing by two grub screws (photo). In the workshop it was not found possible to

5.9 Undoing a switch housing securing screw

5.11 Removing the tilt adjuster spring

5.12 One of the ignition/starter switch grub screws (arrowed); other one is on opposite side

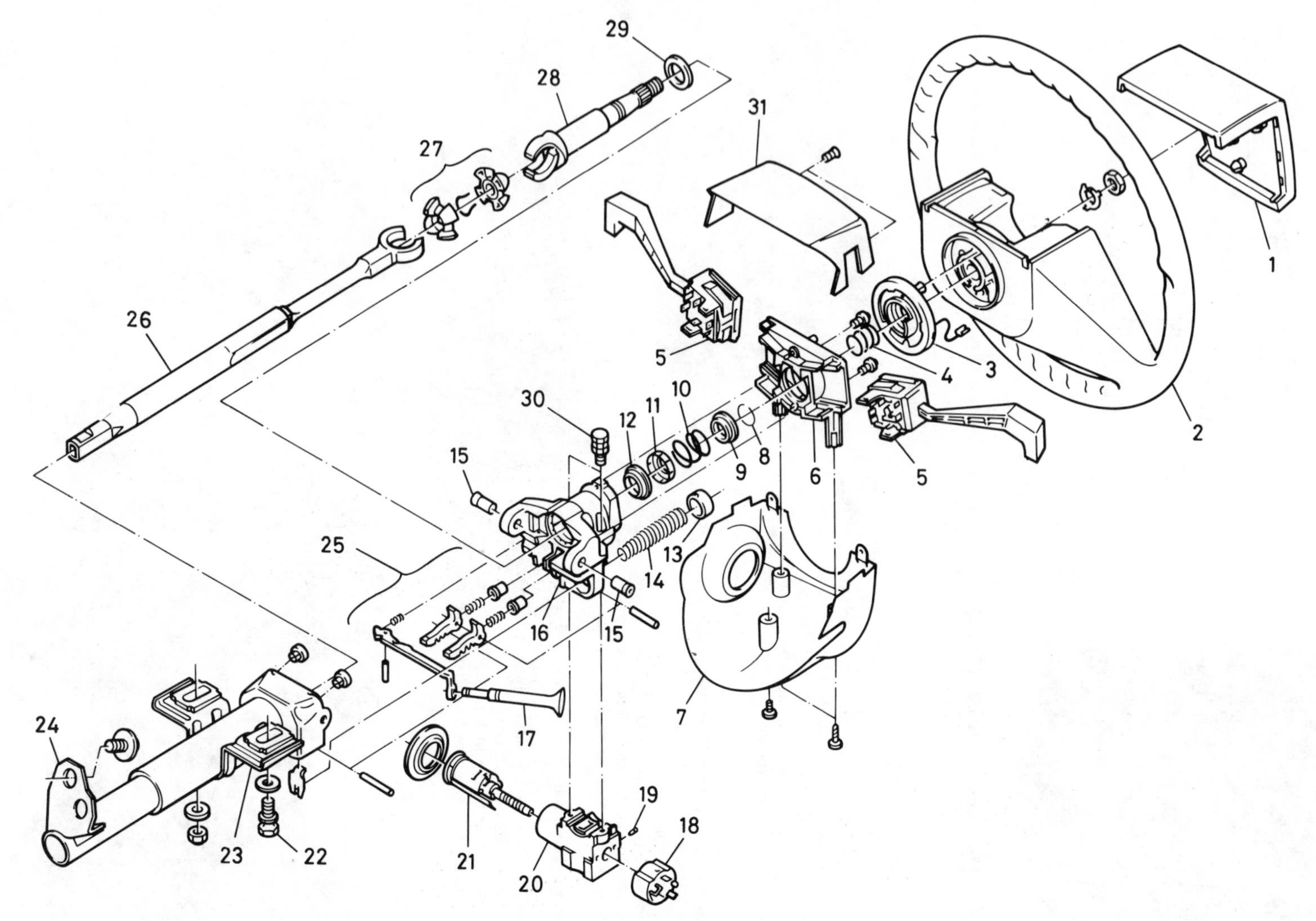

Fig. 8.5 Exploded view of adjustable type steering column components (Sec 5)

1 Central cap
2 Steering wheel
3 Horn contact ring
4 Spring
5 Multi-function switches
6 Switch housing
7 Lower shroud
8 Retaining ring
9 Pressure ring
10 Spring
11 Pressure ring
12 Bearing upper race
13 Spring cup
14 Adjuster spring
15 Fulcrum pins
16 Bearing housing
17 Tilt knob
18 Ignition/starter switch
19 Grub screw
20 Ignition/steering lock housing
21 Ignition/steering lock barrel
22 Shear-head bolt
23 Upper mounting
24 Bulkhead mounting
25 Detent components
26 Lower shaft
27 Universal joint
28 Upper shaft
29 Bearing lower race
30 Shear-head bolt (2 fitted)
31 Upper shroud

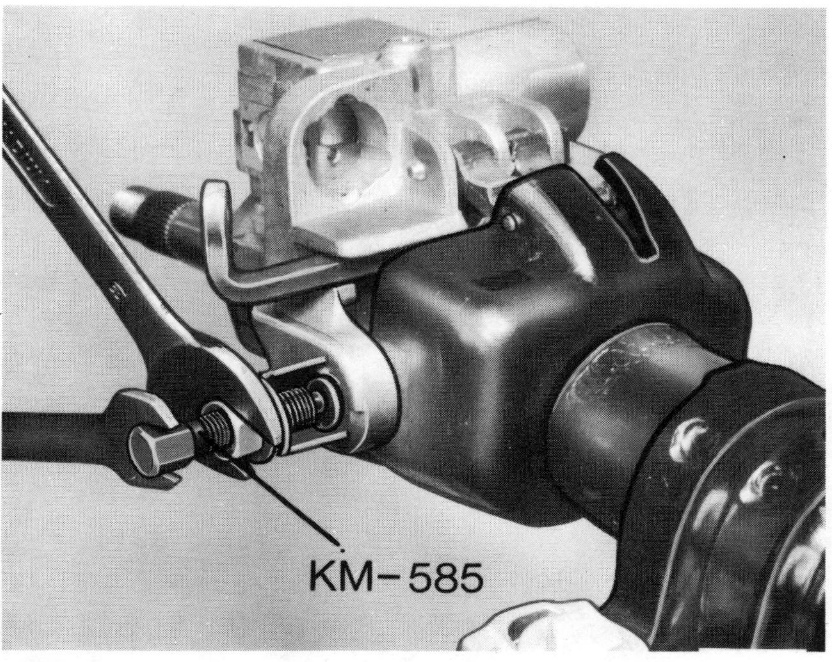

Fig. 8.6 Extracting the fulcrum pins with tool KM-585 (Sec 5)

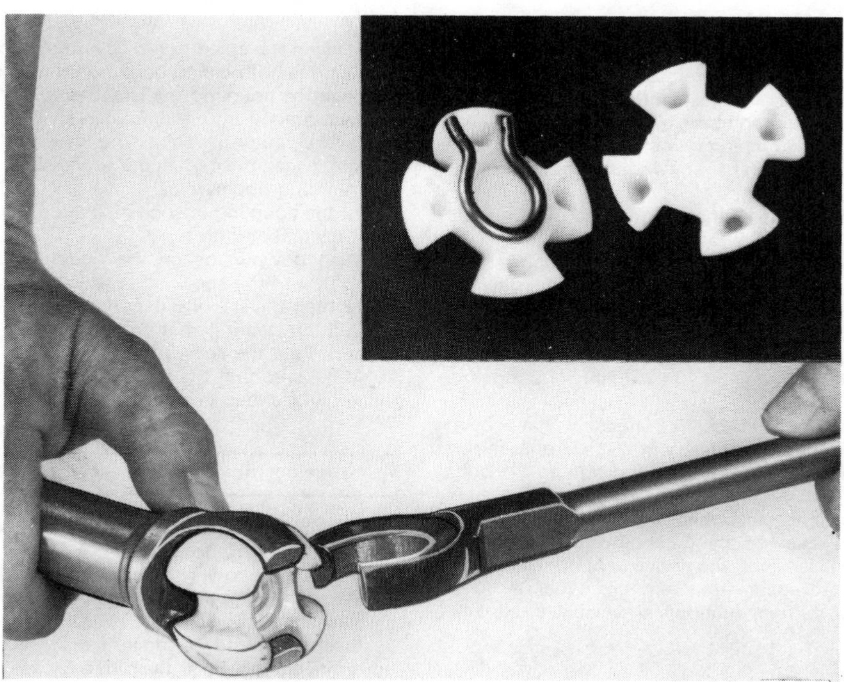

Fig. 8.7 Shaft universal joint – note spring clip location (inset) (Sec 5)

Fig. 8.8 Checking the gap between the bearing housing and a buffer (Sec 5)

reach the 'hidden' grub screw with the column installed. For this and further dismantling the column must therefore be removed – see Section 4. Check parts availability before dismantling.
13 The steering lock housing is secured to the bearing housing by two shear-head bolts which must be extracted in order to separate the two.
14 The column bearing upper race can be renewed after removing the retaining ring, pressure rings and spring.
15 To remove the bearing housing from the column, the fulcrum pins must be extracted using extractor KM-585 or its equivalent.
16 The column bearing lower race can be driven off the upper shaft and a new race pressed on. The bearings themselves can only be renewed complete with housing.
17 The shaft universal joint and the tilt mechanism detent components can be dismantled for component renewal if necessary.
18 Reassemble in the reverse order to dismantling, noting the following points.
19 If the steering lock housing and bearing housing have been separated, clean out the securing bolt holes with a tap. Apply thread locking compound to the new shear-head bolts and tighten the bolts until their heads break off.
20 After refitting the fulcrum pipe, stake them in three places.
21 If the bearings have been renewed, the gaps between the bearing housing and the buffers which limit the movement in the upper position should be checked to ensure that they are equal. A kit of different thicknesses of buffer, with instructions, is available if required.

6 Steering column flexible coupling – removal and refitting

1 Position the steering in the straight-ahead position.
2 Slacken the steering rack mountings on the bulkhead.
3 Remove both clamp bolts from the coupling.
4 Push the coupling upwards, remove it from the pinion shaft, tilt it and withdraw it from the column shaft.
5 Before refitting, make sure that the roadwheels are still in the straight-ahead position and that the steering wheel spokes are centred and pointing downwards.
6 Fit the coupling in such a position that the column clamp bolt will be horizontal and on top.
7 Push downwards on the coupling and tighten the pinion side clamp bolt to the specified torque.
8 Tighten the steering gear mountings to the specified torque.
9 Pull the steering shaft upwards as far as it will go and tighten the clamp bolt to the specified torque.
10 Make sure that the roadwheels and the steering wheel are still in the straight-ahead position.

7 Steering lock cylinder – removal and refitting

1 Disconnect the battery earth lead. Insert the ignition key into the lock and turn it to position II.
2 Remove the lower switch shroud. Note that it shares two securing screws with the upper shroud. Turn the steering wheel as necessary to gain access to the screws.
3 Insert a thin rod – a small Allen key is fine – into the hole in the lock housing (photo). Press the rod to release the detent spring and pull the lock cylinder out using the key.
4 To refit the lock cylinder, remove the rod and push the cylinder in until it clicks into place. It will only fit in one way.
5 Refit the switch shroud and remove the ignition key.
6 Reconnect the battery.

Fig. 8.9 Steering column coupling clamp bolts (arrowed) (Sec 6)

7.3 Releasing the steering lock detent spring with an Allen key (arrowed)

8.2 Tie-rod balljoint separator in use. It is better practice to leave the balljoint nut loosely fitted

8 Tie-rod balljoints – removal and refitting

1 Remove the roadwheel on the side concerned.
2 Slacken the balljoint nut, release the ball-pin using a balljoint separator and remove the nut. Extract the balljoint from the steering arm (photo).
3 Slacken the clamp bolt which secures the balljoint to the threaded adjustment pin. Mark the position of the balljoint on the adjustment pin with paint or tape, then unscrew the balljoint from the pin.
4 Note that the balljoints are handed. The right-hand balljoint is marked R; the left-hand balljoint has no marking.
5 Screw in the new balljoint onto the adjustment pin to approximately the same position as was occupied by the old one. Secure it with the clamp bolt.
6 Connect the balljoint to the steering arm. Secure it with a new self-locking nut, tightened to the specified torque.
7 Refit the roadwheel, lower the vehicle and tighten the wheel bolts.
8 Check the front wheel alignment, as described in Section 18, and adjust if necessary. No harm will result from driving the vehicle a short distance to have the alignment checked.

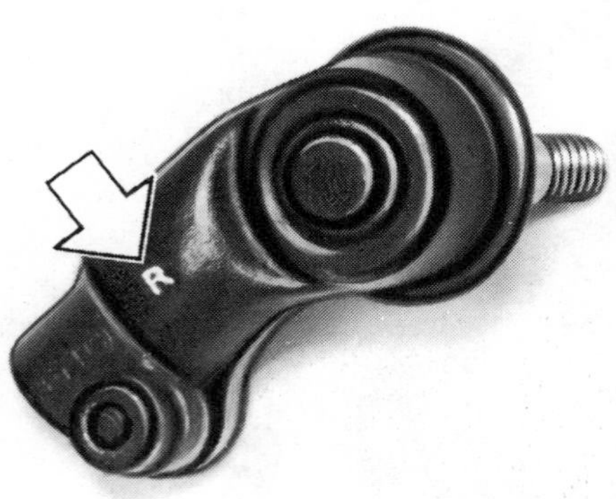

Fig. 8.10 Right-hand balljoint identification mark (arrowed) (Sec 8)

Fig. 8.11 Mounting bracket and pinion sealing cap correctly installed – location aids arrowed (Sec 9)

9 Steering rack bellows – removal and refitting

1 Remove the steering gear, as described in Section 11.
2 Remove the mounting bracket and rubber insulator from the end of the rack furthest from the pinion.
3 On power-assisted racks, disconnect the hydraulic pipe union adjacent to the end of the bellows.
4 Remove the clamping wires and slide both bellows and the connecting tube off the rack. Separate the bellows from the tube.
5 Fit the new bellows and the tube to the rack. Secure the bellows with new wire clips, positioned so that when the rack is in the car the ends of the clips will point upwards. Make sure that the bellows are not twisted.
6 On power-assisted only, reconnect the hydraulic pipe union using new sealing rings. Tighten the union to the specified torque.
7 Refit the rubber insulator and mounting bracket. The concave end of the mounting bracket flange must point downwards when the rack is fitted.
8 If the pinion sealing cap has been disturbed, make sure it is refitted with its notch engaged with the rib on the pinion housing.
9 Refit the steering gear, as described in Section 11.

10 Steering damper – removal and refitting

1 When fitted, the steering damper is removed as follows.
2 Remove the securing nut at the moving end of the damper (photo). Recover the washer.
3 Unbolt the damper from the bracket at the pinion end and remove it.
4 When refitting, secure the pinion end of the damper first and tighten its mounting bolt to the specified torque.
5 Tighten the securing nut at the moving end of the damper to obtain a dimension A as shown in Fig. 8.12.

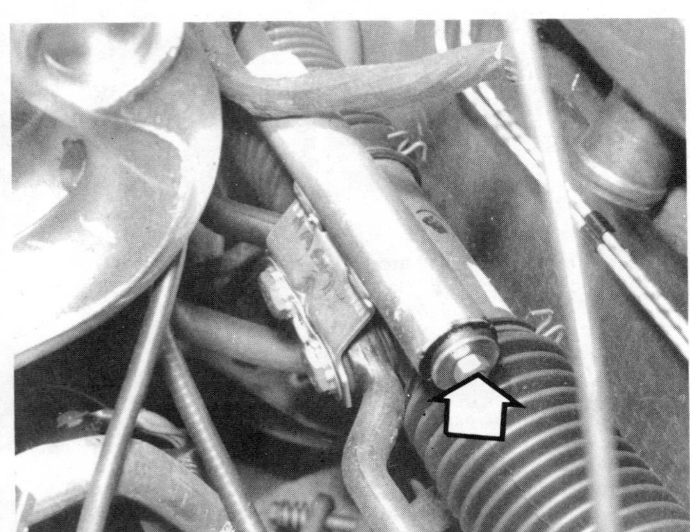

10.2 Steering damper securing nut (arrowed)

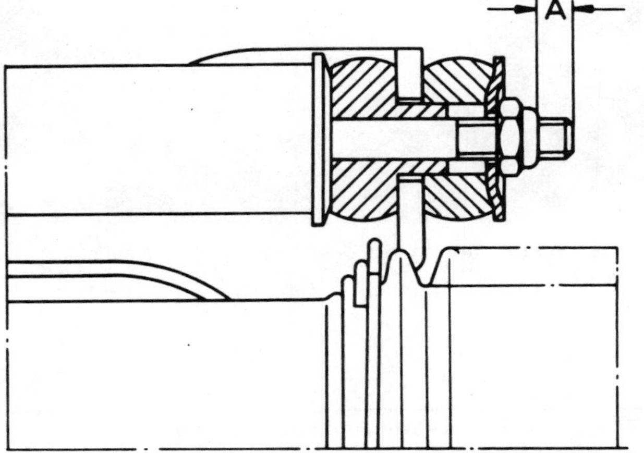

Fig. 8.12 Steering damper securing nut setting (Sec 10)

A = 6 mm (0.24 in)

11 Steering gear – removal and refitting

Manual steering

1 Disconnect the battery earth lead.
2 On carburettor models only, remove the air cleaner, as described in Chapter 3.
3 On LHD models with a headlamp washer system, release the fluid reservoir and move it to one side.
4 Remove both tie-rod bolts from the centre of the rack (photo). Recover the bolt locks, the spacer plate and the washers.
5 If a steering damper is fitted, unbolt it at the pinion end and remove it, complete with the moving end tube and bracket.
6 Set the steering in the straight-ahead position.
7 Slacken both clamp bolts on the flexible coupling. Push the coupling upwards as far as it will go.
8 Remove the front left-hand roadwheel (RHD models – for LHD, the right-hand wheel).
9 Unbolt the steering gear mounting brackets from the bulkhead. Make sure that the pinion is free of the coupling, then withdraw the steering gear through the wheel arch.
10 Commence refitting by fastening the steering gear to the bulkhead. Tighten the mounting bracket bolts to the specified torque. Use new self-locking nuts on the mounting studs.
11 Before connecting the flexible coupling make sure the steering gear is in the straight-ahead position (Fig. 8.13).
12 Reconnect the flexible coupling as described in Section 6.
13 Reconnect the tie-rods to the rack, remembering to fit the washers under the rod ends. (Note that the tie-rods are handed: they are fitted correctly when their clamp bolts are fitted from below). Fit the spacer plate or damper bracket and tighten the bolts to the specified torque, using new lockplates.
14 Refit the remaining components in the reverse order to removal.

Power steering

15 The operations are similar to those just described, but additionally the flow and return pipes must be disconnected from the pinion housing.
16 Allow the fluid to drain from the open unions, then plug the holes to keep dirt out. Introduction of dirt may seriously damage the hydraulic system.
17 Top up and bleed the system on completion, as described in Section 14.

11.4 Tie-rod connection to steering rack

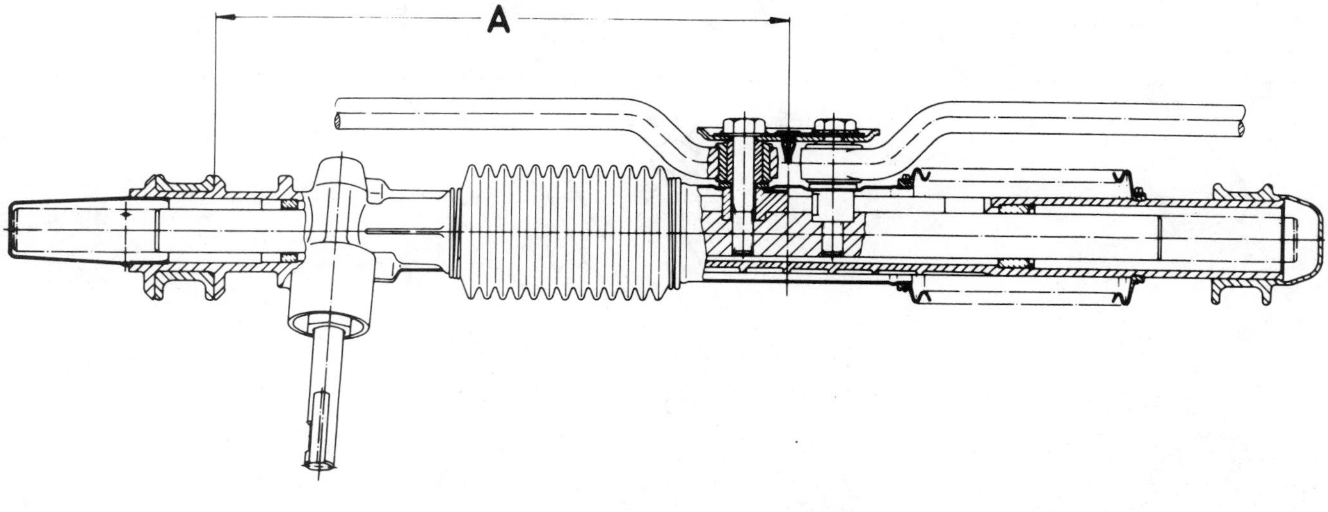

A

Fig. 8.13 Steering gear centralising diagram – LHD shown (Sec 11)

A = 325 mm (12.8 in)

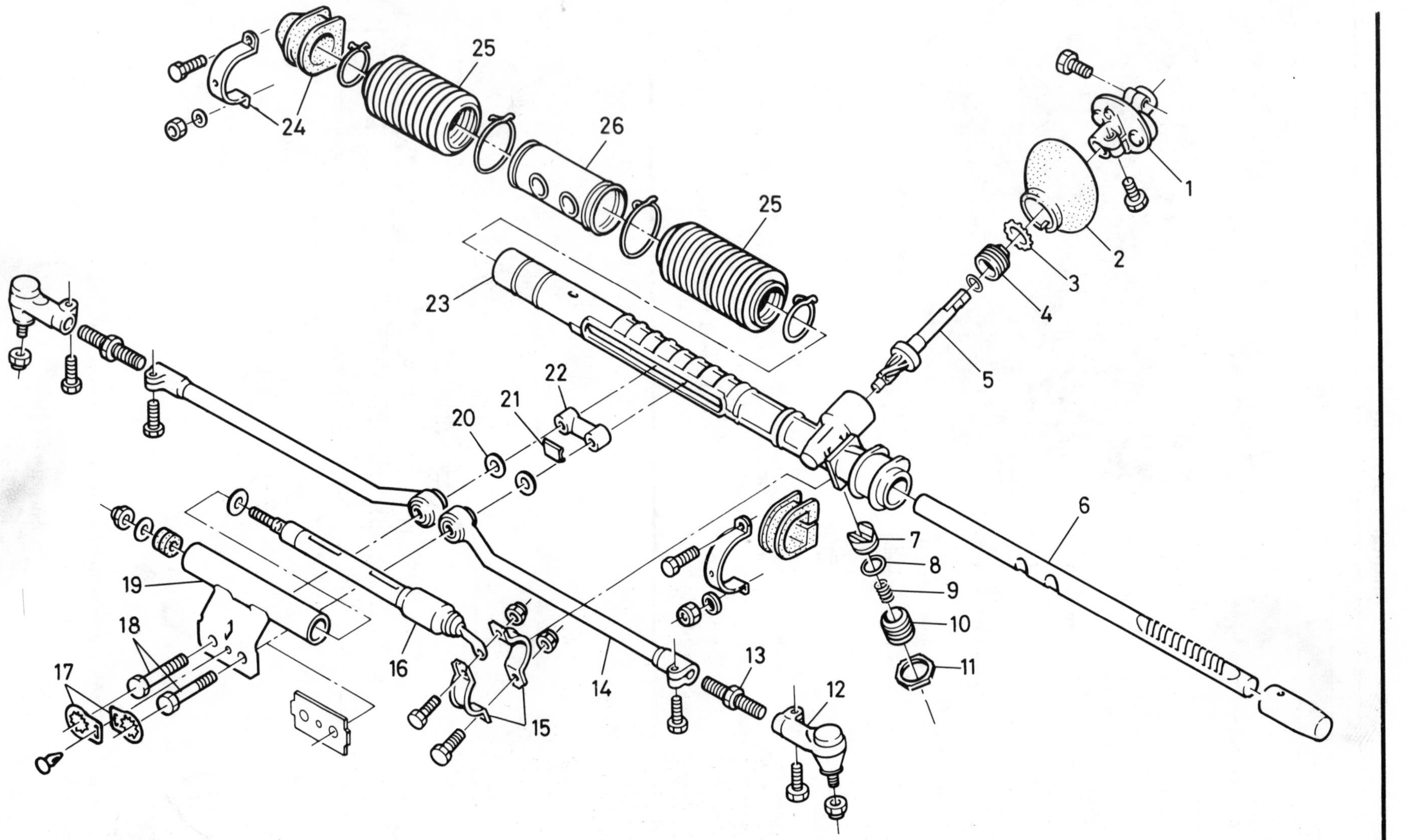

Fig. 8.14 Exploded view of manual steering gear – LHD shown (Sec 11)

1 *Flexible coupling*
2 *Boot*
3 *Locking ring*
4 *Pinion nut*
5 *Pinion/bearing/shaft assembly*
6 *Rack*
7 *Damper slipper*
8 *Seal*
9 *Spring*
10 *Adjuster screw*
11 *Adjuster locknut*
12 *Tie-rod balljoint*
13 *Adjustment pin*
14 *Tie-rod*
15 *Damper clamp*
16 *Damper (when fitted)*
17 *Lockplates*
18 *Tie-rod bolts*
19 *Damper tube*
20 *Washer*
21 *Guide piece*
22 *Slide*
23 *Rack housing*
24 *Mounting bracket and rubber*
25 *Bellows*
26 *Tube*

12 Steering gear (manual steering) – overhaul

1 Remove the steering gear from the vehicle, as previously described.
2 Clean away external dirt.
3 Remove the bellows and housing sleeve.
4 Remove the slide and guide piece from the rack.
5 Release the locknut from the rack adjuster setscrew.
6 Unscrew and remove the setscrew and extract the coil spring, seal and damper slipper.
7 Extract the locking ring from around the pinion nut, unscrew the nut and extract the seal.
8 Withdraw the rack and the pinion.
9 Push out the cap from the end of the housing using a long rod.
10 Further dismantling is not possible. If the rack bushes or pinion needle bearing are worn, renew the housing complete. The pinion can only be renewed complete with the ball-bearing.
11 Note that two different ratios of steering gear are fitted; components are not interchangeable between the two. The pinion shaft for 22:1 steering had no identification groove, and the corresponding rack has 28 teeth. The pinion shaft for 24.5:1 steering has one identification groove, and the rack has 32 teeth.
12 Clean away old lubricant. Apply grease (to GM spec 19 48 588) to all moving components, and insert a further 50 g (2 oz approx) of the grease between the rack bushes on the inside of the housing.
13 Fit the rack into the housing so that the end furthest from the pinion is positioned at the correct distance from the end of the housing. Fit the pinion so that, when meshed, its cut-out is positioned as shown (Fig. 8.18).

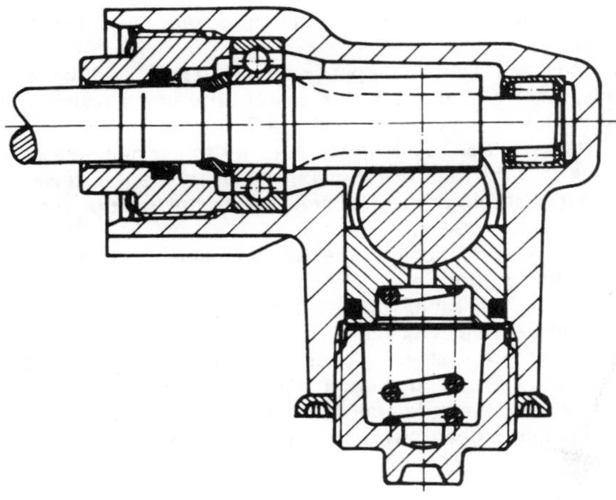

Fig. 8.15 Sectional view of pinion and rack damper (Sec 12)

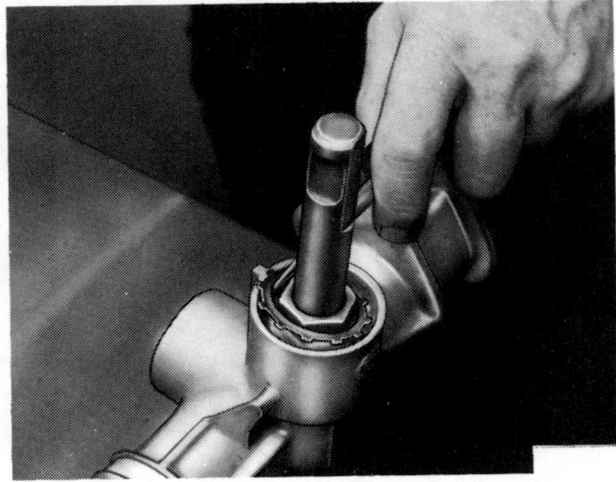

Fig. 8.16 Removing the pinion nut locking ring (Sec 12)

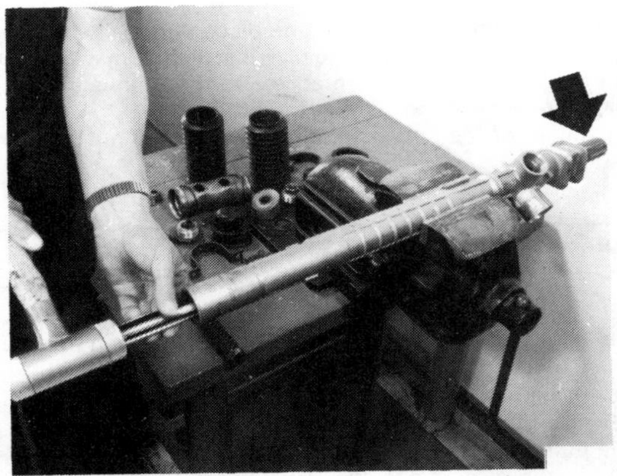

Fig. 8.17 Driving out the rack housing end cap (arrowed) (Sec 12)

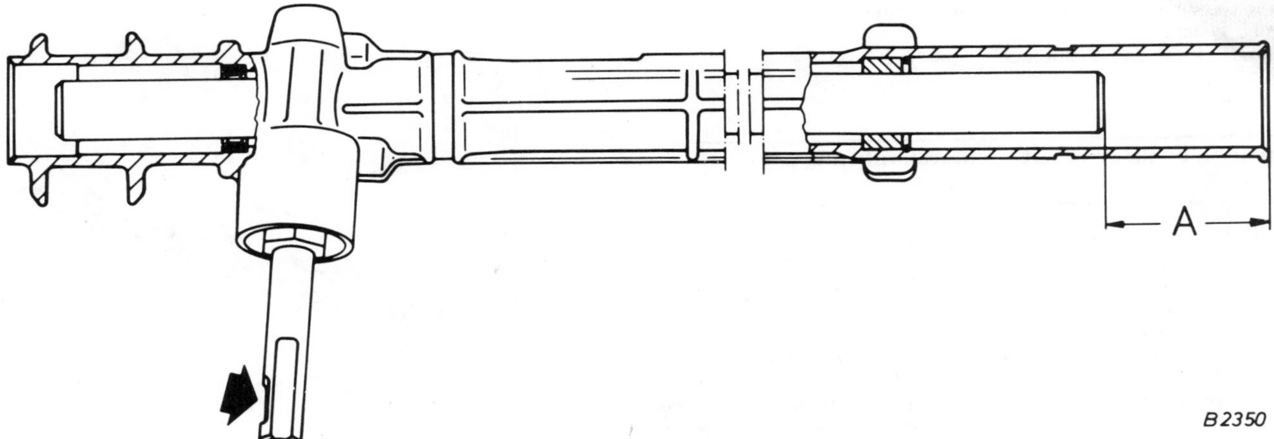

Fig. 8.18 Correct positioning of pinion cut-out (arrowed) (Sec 12)

A = 61 mm (2.4 in)

14 Apply grease to the pinion ball-bearing. Screw in the pinion nut and tighten it to the specified torque. Fit a new locking ring, driving it home with a piece of tube.
15 The steering gear must now be adjusted. Make up two tubular distance pieces to the dimensions shown in Fig. 8.19. Using the tie-rod securing bolts, secure the slide, guide piece and distance pieces to the rack.
16 Insert the rack damper slipper (with a new seal) and the spring into their hole. Screw in the adjuster screw until some resistance is felt (turning torque approximately 5 Nm/3.7 lbf ft).
17 From this position, back off the adjuster screw by between 20° and 40°. Check that the rack will move freely over its entire travel.
18 Without disturbing the adjuster screw, fit the locknut and tighten it to the specified torque.
19 Tap a new end cap into the housing and remove the distance pieces and tie-rod bolts.
20 Fit the bellows, tube, mounting components and pinion sealing cap. Refer to Section 9 for details.
21 After refitting the steering gear, carry out a test drive on a route having curves. The steering should show a well-defined self-centering action: if not, the rack damper has been over-adjusted and must be reset. The steering gear must be removed again for this.

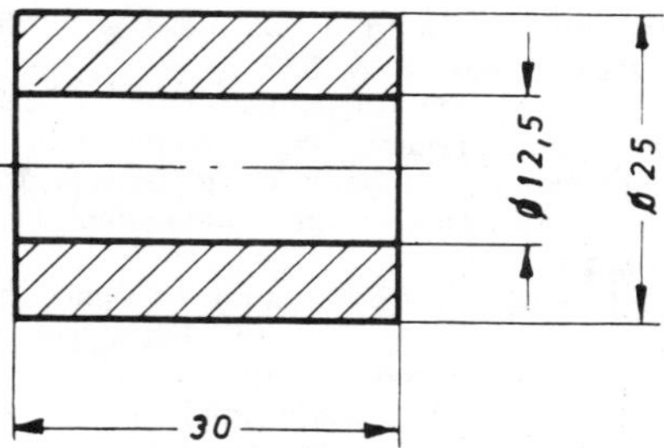

Fig. 8.19 Distance piece for rack adjustment – dimensions in mm (Sec 12)

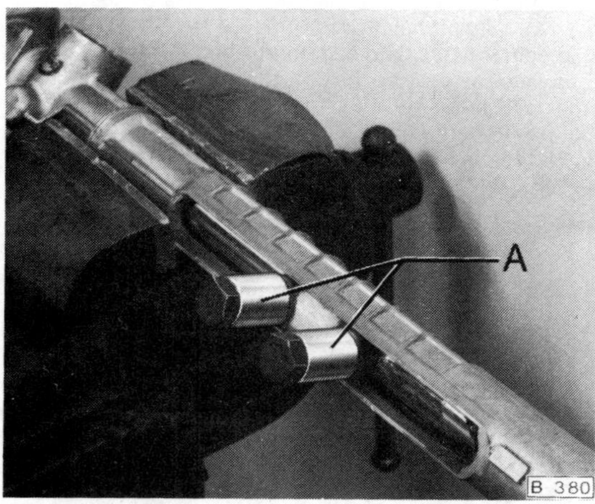

Fig. 8.20 Distance pieces (A) bolted to rack (Sec 12)

13 Steering gear (power-assisted) – overhaul

1 Overhaul of the power steering gear is not undertaken by GM dealer, so it is certainly not recommended that the DIY mechanic attempt ot.
2 Fluid leaks from the hydraulic unions can normally be corrected by renewing the union seals with the rack installed. It may be necessary to displace the brake servo to gain access to the unions at that end.
3 Bellows renewal is covered in Section 9.
4 Adjustment of the power steering gear should not be attempted.

14 Power-assisted steering – bleeding

1 After any of the hydraulic unions has been disturbed, or if the fluid level has been allowed to fall so low that air has been introduced into the system, bleeding should be carried out as follows.
2 Top up the reeservoir with fresh clean fluid of the specified type. Fluid drained from the system must not be re-used.
3 If the pump is dry, start the engine momentarily and then switch it off. Top up the reservoir to the lower mark on the dipstick, run the engine briefly again and repeat the process until the fluid level stabilises. It is important that the pump is not allowed to run dry.
4 With the engine running at idle speed, turn the steering wheel approximately 45° to left and right of centre, then from lock to lock. Do not hold the wheel on either lock, as this improves some strain on the hydraulic system.
5 Switch off the engine and correct the fluid level.

15 Steering pump drivebelt – removal, refitting and tensioning

1 To remove the pump drivebelt, just slacken the pump pivot and tensioner strap nuts and bolts.
2 Move the tensioner strap locknuts to reduce the belt tension until the belt can be slipped off the pulleys.
3 Fit the new belt and tension it as follows.
4 Nip up the pump and strap nuts and bolts so that the pump is just free to move.
5 Act on the tensioner strap locknuts until the correct belt tension is achieved. Ideally a belt tension gauge should be used; otherwise an intelligent guess must be made. If in doubt, err on the slack side – a new belt is cheaper than a new pump. See also Chapter 2, Section 9.
6 Tighten the pump and tensioner fastening to their specified torques.
7 Recheck the tension of a new belt after a few hundred miles.

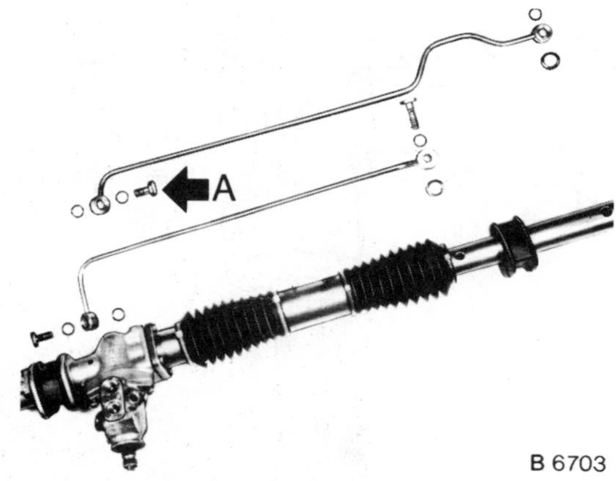

Fig. 8.21 Power steering gear, hydraulic pipes and unions – LHD shown (Sec 13)

A Inaccessible union

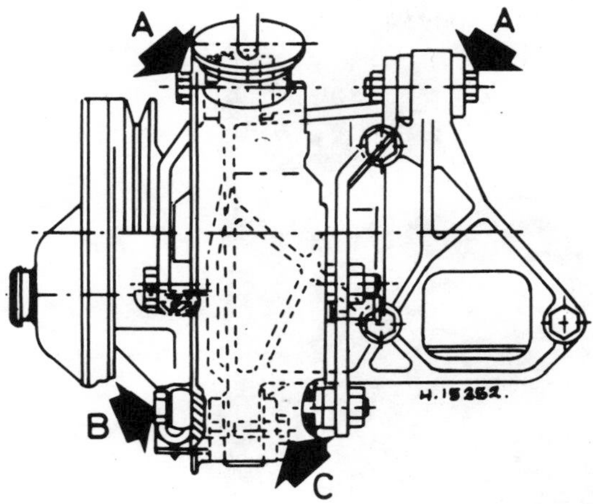

Fig. 8.22 Steering pump drivebelt adjustment (Sec 15)

A Pump pivot bolts
B Tensioner strap pivot bolt
C Tensioner strap mounting bolt

Fig. 8.23 Steering pump tensioner locknuts (arrowed) (Sec 15)

16 Steering pump – removal and refitting

1 Remove the pump drivebelt, as previously described.
2 Disconnect the fluid feed and return hoses from the pump. Be prepared for fluid spillage. Plug the openings; being careful not to introduce dirt.
3 Unbolt and remove the pump.
4 A defective pump must be renewed: no spares are available.
5 Refit in the reverse order to removal. Tension the drivebelt, as previously described, before tightening the pump mountings.
6 Bleed the system, as described in Section 14. Pay particular attention to the procedure required to prime the pump if a new pump has been fitted.

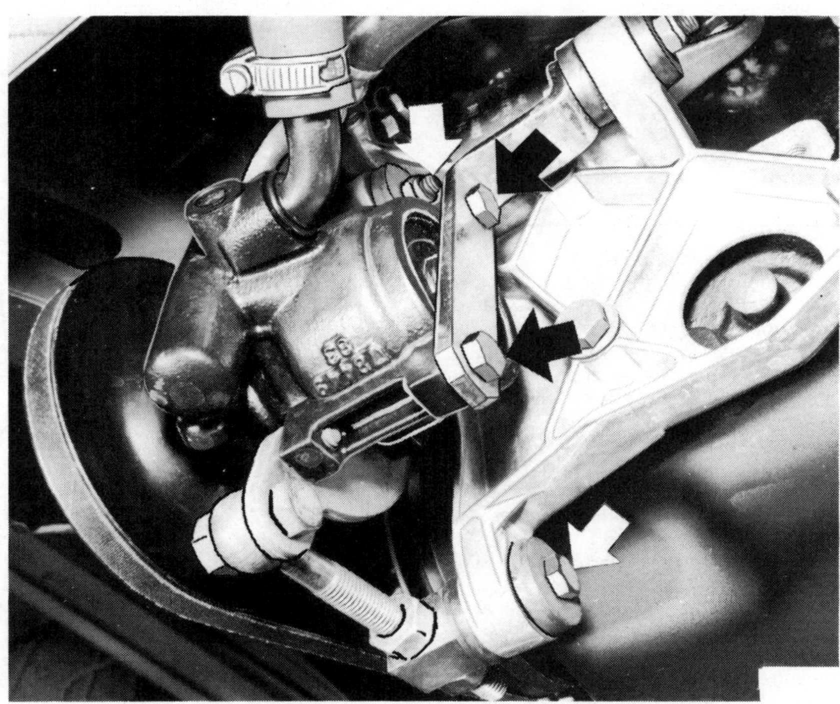

Fig. 8.24 Steering pump mounting nuts and bolts (arrowed) (Sec 16)

Fig. 8.25 Fluid reservoir mounting bolt and hose unions (arrowed) (Sec 17)

17 Power steering fluid reservoir – removal and refitting

1 Slacken the reservoir clamp bolt.
2 Disconnect both hoses from the reservoir. Be prepared for fluid spillage. Remove the reservoir.
3 Refit in the reverse order to removal. Bleed the system on completion, as described in Section 14.

18 Front wheel alignment (all models) – checking and adjusting

1 Accurate front wheel alignment is essential for precise steering and handling, and for even tyre wear. Before carrying out any checking or adjusting operations, make sure that the tyres are correctly inflated, that all steering and suspension joints and linkages are in sound condition and that the wheels are not buckled or distorted, particularly around the rims. It will also be necessary to have the car positioned on flat level ground with enough space to push the car backwards and forwards through about half its length.
2 Front wheel alignment consists of four factors:

Camber is the angle at which the roadwheels are set from the vertical when viewed from the front or rear of the vehicle. Positive camber is the angle (in degrees) that the wheels are tilted outwards at the top from the vertical.

Castor is the angle between the steering axis and a vertical line when viewed from each side of the vehicle. Positive castor is indicated when the steering axis is inclined towards the rear of the vehicle at its upper end.

Steering axis inclination is the angle, when viewed from the front or rear of the vehicle, between the vertical and an imaginary line drawn between the upper and lower front suspension strut mountings.

Toe setting is the amount by which the distance between the front inside edges of the roadwheel differs from that between the rear inside edges, when measured at hub height. If the distance betwen the front edges is less that that at the rear, the wheels are said to toe-in. If it is greater than at the rear, the wheels toe-out.

3 Camber, castor and steering axis inclination are set during manufacture and are not adjustable. Unless the vehicle has suffered accident damage, or there is gross wear in the suspension mountings or joints, it can be assumed that these settings are correct. If for any reason it is believed that they are not correct, the task of checking them should be left to a GM dealer who will have the necessary special equipment needed to measure the small angles involved.

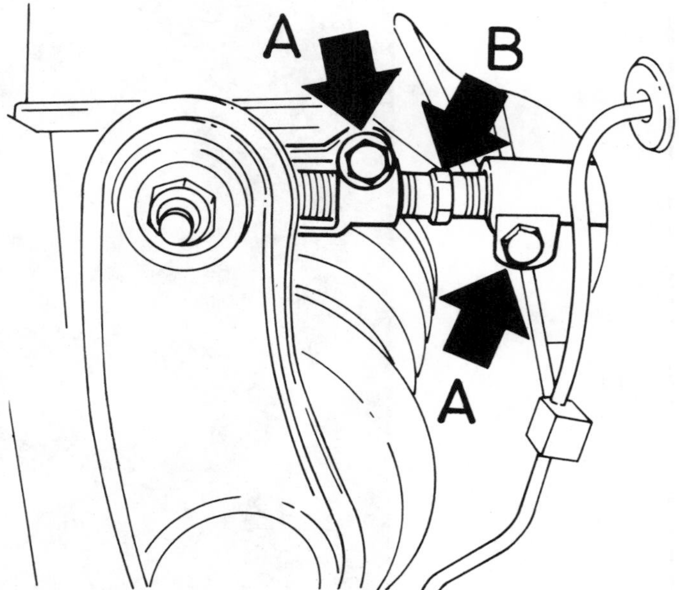

Fig. 8.26 Toe adjustment points (only one side shown) (Sec 18)

A Clamp bolts *B Adjustment pin*

4 It is, however, within the scope of the home mechanic to check and adjust the front wheel toe setting. To do this a tracking gauge must first be obtained. Two types of gauges are available and can be obtained from motor accessory shops. The first type measures the distance between the front and rear inside edges of the roadwheels, as previously described, with the car stationary. The second type, known as a scuff plate, measures the actual position of the contact surface of the tyre, in relation to the road surface, with the vehicle in motion. This is doen by pushing or driving the front tyre over a plate which then moves slightly according to the scuff of the tyre and shows this movement on a scale. Both types have their advantages and disadvantages, but either can give satisfactory results if used correctly and carefully.
5 Many tyre specialists will also check toe settings free or for a nominal charge.
6 Make sure that the steering is in the straight-ahead position when making measurements.
7 If adjustment is found to be necessary, clean the ends of the tie-rods in the area of the adjustment pin and clamp bolts.
8 Slacken the clamp bolts (one on each tie-rod balljoint and one on each tie-rod) and turn the adjustment pin on each tie-rod by the same amount in the same direction. Only turn each pin by a quarter turn at a time before rechecking.
9 When adjustment is correct, tighten the clamp bolts to the specified torque. Check that the tie-rod lengths are equal to within 5 mm (0.2 in) and that the steering wheel spokes are in the correct straight-ahead position.

19 Fault diagnosis – steering

Symptom	Reason(s)
Steering stiff or heavy	Low tyre pressures Incorrect front wheel alignment Damaged, distorted or unlubricated rack or balljoints Lack of power assistance (see below)
Excessive play at wheel	Wear in rack-and-pinion Wear in balljoints Worn flexible coupling Worn column UJ (when applicable)
Steering wander	Incorrect tyre pressures Incorrect wheel alignment Wear in balljoints Wear in suspension components
Wheel wobble or vibration	Wheels out of balance Wheel damaged (out of true) Worn or damaged driveshaft joint Worn hub bearings
Lack of power assistance	Low fluid level (check for leaks) Drivebelt slack or broken Pump defective* Steering gear defective*
Noisy operation	Air in system Low fluid level Drivebelt slack Internal wear in pump or steering gear*

** Have the system tested by a GM dealer to find out where the fault lies*

Chapter 9 Braking system

Contents

Specifications

General

System type	Discs front, drums rear
Actuation:	
Footbrake	Dual hydraulic circuit with servo assistance
Handbrake	Mechanical to rear wheels
Adjustment	Automatic in normal use

Servo

Type	Single diaphragm, vacuum operated
Diameter	203 mm (8 in) nominal

Front (disc) brakes

Disc diameter	236 mm (9.3 in)
Disc thickness – new:	
1.2 and 1.3	10.0 mm (0.39 in)
1.6	12.7 mm (0.50 in)
1.8	20.0 mm (0.79 in)
Disc thickness – regrinding limit	1.0 mm (0.04 in) off new thickness
Disc thickness – wear limit	2.0 mm (0.08 in) off new thickness
Disc thickness variation	0.01 mm (0.0004 in) max
Disc run-out (installed)	0.1 mm (0.004 in) max
Disc scoring depth	0.4 mm (0.016 in) max
Pad thickness (lining and backplate):	
New	15.5 to 15.9 mm (0.61 to 0.63 in)
Wear limit	7 mm (0.28 in)

Rear (drum) brakes

Drum internal diameter – new:	
All Hatchbacks, and 1.3 Estates with manual transmission	200 mm (7.88 in)
All other Estates and Vans	230 mm (9.06 in)
Drum internal diameter – refinishing limit	1 mm (0.04 in) greater than new diameter
Drum out-of-round	0.1 mm (0.004 in) max
Lining wear limit	0.5 mm (0.02 in) above rivet heads

Hydraulic system

Fluid specification	FMVSS 571, 116 DOT 3/DOT 4, SAE J1703, or equivalent

Torque wrench settings

	Nm	lbf ft
Caliper mounting bolts	95	70
Caliper-to-bracket bolts (GMF)	95	70
Caliper hydraulic union	25	18
Wheel cylinder mounting bolt	9	7
Master cylinder mounting nuts	18	13
Wheel cylinder hydraulic union	11	8
Bleed screws	9	7
Pressure regulating valve:		
On rear axle (Estate and Van)	20	15
On master cylinder (GMF)	40	30
On master cylinder (ATE)	12	9
Servo to bracket	18	13
Servo bracket to bulkhead	18	13
Master cylinder stop screw (ATE)	6	4
Rear brake backplate bolts	28	21
Handbrake lever bolts	20	15

1 General description

The footbrake operates on all four wheels. Disc brakes are fitted at the front and self-adjusting drums at the rear. Actuation is hydraulic with servo assistance. The handbrake is cable-operated and acts on the rear wheels only.

The hydraulic system is split into two circuits, each circuit acting on one front and one diagonally opposite rear brake. In the event of rupture of the hydraulic system in one circuit, the remaining circuit will still function so that some braking capability remains. In such a case the pedal travel will increase and greater effort will be needed.

The hydraulic supply to the rear brakes is regulated so that the front brakes always lock first under heavy braking. On Hatchback models the regulation is by pressure-sensitive valves screwed into the master cylinder; on Estate and Van models the valve is load-sensitive and is located near the rear axle, by whose movement it is modulated.

The brake servo is of the direct-acting type, fitted between the pedal and the master cylinder. It is powered by vacuum developed in the inlet manifold. Should the servo fail, the brakes will still operate, but increased pedal pressure will be required.

Depending on operating territory and equipment level, warning lights may be fitted to indicate low brake fluid level, handbrake application and brake pad wear. Sometimes one warning light has a dual function: refer to the owner's handbook for details.

2 Maintenance and inspection

1 Even though warning lights are provided for various braking system functions, the conscientious owner will not rely on these but will verify the condition of components visually.

2 Weekly, or before a long journey, check the brake fluid level in the master cylinder reservoir. The reservoir is translucent so the level can be seen without removing the cap. A slow fall in level as the pads wear is normal, and as long as the level stays above the MIN mark there is no need to top up to compensate for this. If topping-up is necessary, use only fresh hydraulic fluid of the specified type (photo). A regular need for topping-up indicates that there is a leak somewhere, which must be found and rectified without delay.

3 At every major service interval, or sooner if prompted by abnormal operation or illumination of a warning light, inspect the front brake pads for wear and renew them if necessary. See Section 3 for details.

4 At the same intervals the handbrake linkage and cables should be inspected, lubricated and adjusted if necessary. See Sections 22 and 23 for further information.

5 At the same time inspect the hydraulic pipes and hoses, and renew as necessary. Refer to Section 16. On Estate/Van models, check the pressure regulating valve also – see Section 15.

6 At alternate service intervals, inspect the rear brake shoes for lining wear and renew if necessary – see Section 8. Take the opportunity to check the wheel cylinders for leaks and the brake drums for scoring or other damage (Section 11).

7 It is advisable to check the operation of the warning lights from time to time. The 'handbrake applied' warning light should illuminate every time the handbrake is applied with the ignition on. The 'low fluid level' warning may be checked by releasing the handbrake (check the wheels) and, with the ignition on, having an assistant remove the master cylinder reservoir cap. The warning light should illuminate as the float is lifted clear of the fluid. The 'pads worn' light (when fitted) may be checked by earthing the sensor wire with the ignition on. The sensor itself is rubber-covered and it is unwise to strip the covering off simply for test purposes.

2.2 Topping-up the brake hydraulic reservoir

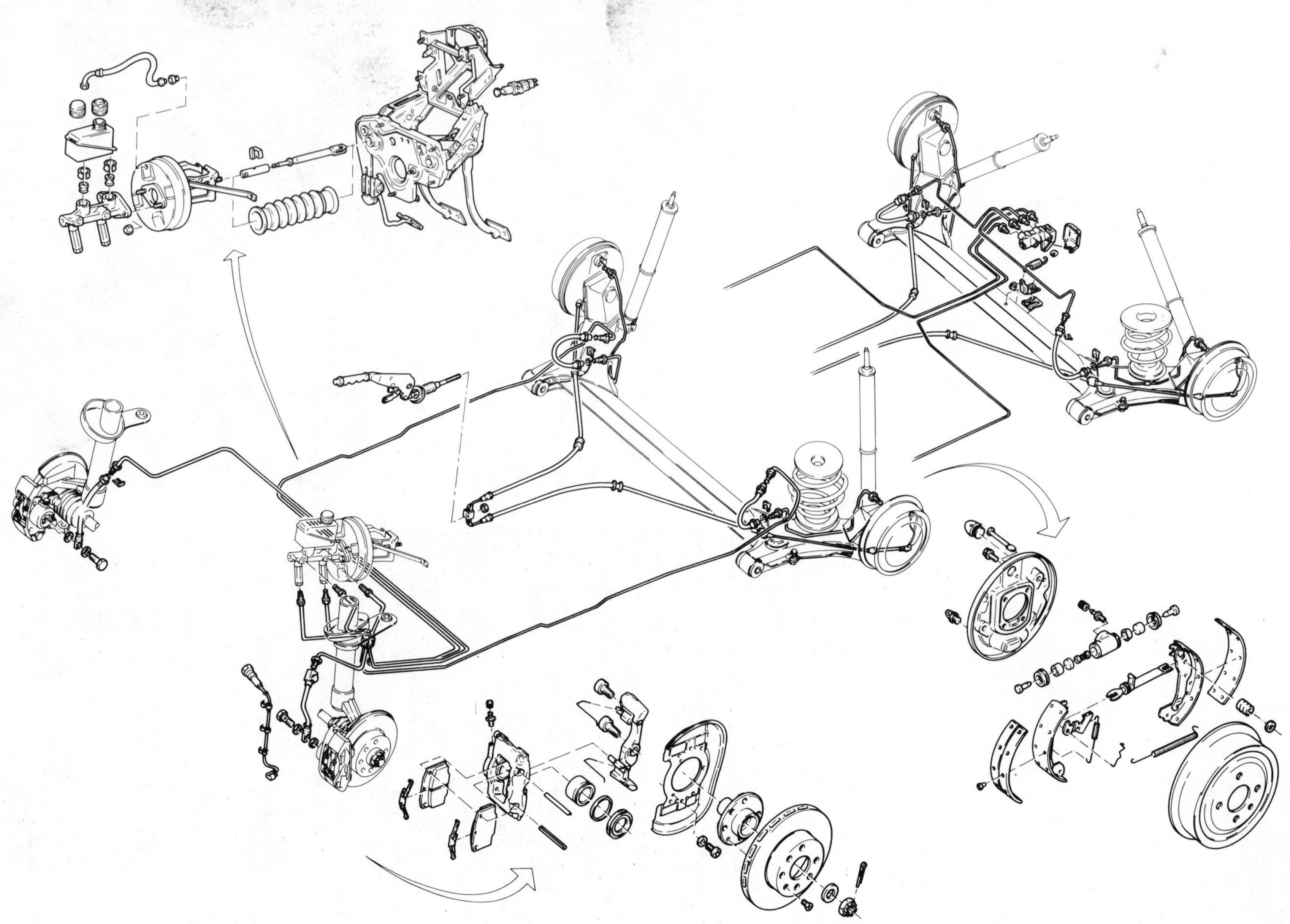

Fig. 9.1 Braking system components – LHD shown, RHD similar (Sec 1)

8 Annually, regardless of mileage, renew the brake fluid by bleeding, as described in Section 17.
9 Although not specified by the makers, it is advisable to renew the flexible hoses, and the rubber seals in the calipers, wheel cylinders and master cylinder, after 54 000 miles or 3 years, whichever comes first. Details will be found in the appropriate Sections of this Chapter.
10 It is strongly advised that only the maker's spare parts, or reputable equivalents, be used in the braking system.

3 Front brake pads – inspection and renewal

1 Slacken the front wheel bolts, raise and support the front of the vehicle and remove the front wheels.
2 Inspect the thickness of the friction material on each pad, visible through the front of the caliper. If any one pad is at or below the minimum thickness given in the Specifications, all four must be renewed.
3 Drive out the pad retaining pins by applying a hammer and punch to their inboard ends. Recover the springs (photo).
4 On models so equipped, disconnect the wear warning sensor from the pad (photo). The sensor and its cable must be renewed whenever new pads are fitted.
5 Withdraw the outboard pad, using a pair of pliers if necessary (photo).
6 Push the inboard pad away from the disc slightly to free it, then remove it (photo). Do not press the brake pedal while the pads are removed.
7 Take the opportunity to inspect the disc, as described in Section 6.
8 Clean the brake caliper with a soft wire brush. *Be careful not to inhale the dust, which may contain asbestos.* If there are any signs of hydraulic fluid leakage, or if the pads were very unevenly worn, the caliper should be removed for overhaul, as described in Section 4 or 5.
9 To accommodate the thickness of the new pads, the caliper piston must be pushed back into its bore using a tyre lever, a strip of wood or some similar blunt instrument. Do not lever against the disc when doing this. As the piston is pushed back, the fluid level in the master cylinder reservoir will rise; syphon some out if necessary with an old (clean) battery hydrometer or similar.
10 Apply a little disc brake anti-seize or anti-squeal compound to the backs of the new pads – be careful not to contaminate the friction surfaces. Insert the pads into the caliper with the friction linings towards the disc.
11 Apply some anti-seize compound to the pad retaining pins. Drive in the lower pin, fit the anti-rattle springs with their long ends nearest the disc, and secure them with the upper retaining pin (photo).

Fig. 9.2 Driving out a pad retaining pin (Sec 3)

3.3 Removing an anti-rattle spring

3.4 Wear warning sensor clipped to pad

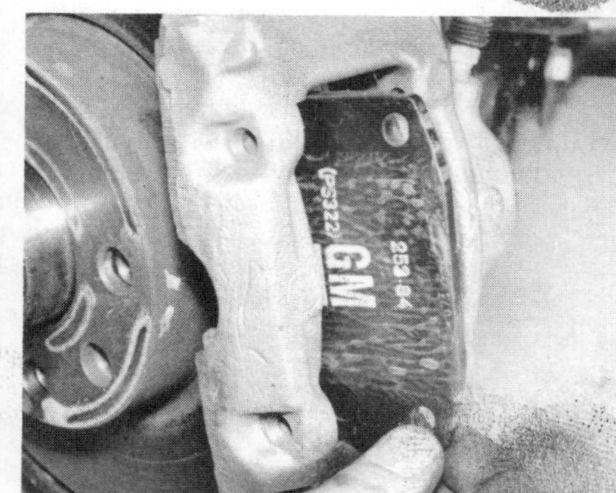

3.5 Removing the outboard pad

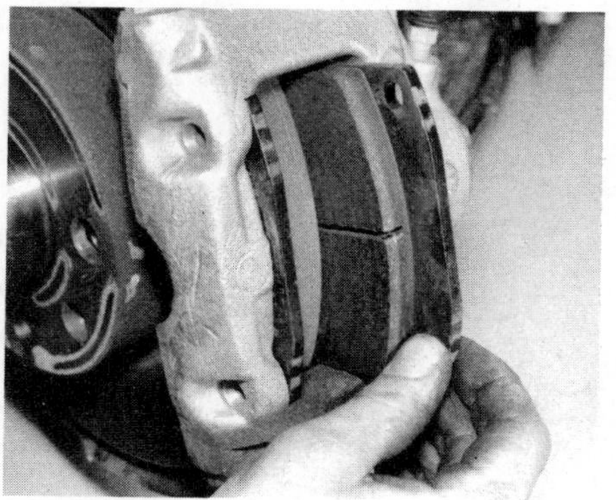

3.6 Removing the inboard pad

3.11 Pad retaining pins and anti-rattle springs correctly fitted

12 Fit the new wear warning sensor, when applicable. Secure its harness to the caliper flexible hose and plug in its connector in the engine bay.
13 Repeat the operations on the other front brake.
14 Refit the roadwheels, lower the vehicle and tighten the wheel bolts.
15 Press the brake pedal several times to bring the new pads up to the disc.
16 Check the brake fluid level and top up to the MAX mark if necessary.
17 Avoid harsh braking as far as possible for the first hundred miles or so until the new linings have bedded in.

4 Brake caliper (ATE) – removal, overhaul and refitting

1 Raise and support the front of the vehicle and remove the roadwheel.
2 Disconnect the pad wear warning sensor, when fitted.
3 Unscrew and remove the hydraulic union bolt from the inboard side of the caliper. Clamp the hose or plug the union to minimise fluid leakage, or allow the fluid to drain into a suitable container.
4 Use an Allen key to remove the two caliper mounting bolts. Thread locking compound was applied during assembly so they will be tight.
5 Clean the caliper and clamp it in a vice. Remove the pins, anti-rattle springs and pads, as described in Section 3.
6 Separate the caliper body from the bracket by sliding it off the pins. Remove the springs from the bracket.
7 Prise off the piston dust excluder retaining ring with a screwdriver, then remove the dust excluder.
8 Place a piece of wood in front of the piston and apply low air pressure – eg from a foot pump – to the hydraulic union to eject the piston from its bore.
9 Pick out the seal from the groove in the cylinder using a plastic or wooden instrument.
10 Inspect the surfaces of the piston and cylinder bore for scoring or evidence of metal-to-metal rubbing. If evident, renew the caliper complete.
11 If these components are in good condition, discard the rubber seal and dust excluder and obtain a repair kit which will contain all the necessary replaceable items.
12 Clean the piston and cylinder bore with brake hydraulic fluid or methylated spirit – nothing else!
13 Commence reassembly by fitting the seal into the cylinder groove.
14 Locate the dust excluder in its groove in the piston. Dip the piston in clean brake fluid, or apply rubber grease to its external surface, and insert it squarely into the cylinder. Check that the piston step is positioned as shown (photo).
15 When the piston has been partially depressed, engage the dust excluder with the rim of the cylinder and fit the retaining clip.
16 Depress the piston fully into its cylinder bore.
17 Secure the caliper bracket in a vice and install the guide springs.
18 Slide the caliper body into the bracket until the body and bracket are flush with the guide pin sleeves resting against the bracket.
19 Before refitting the caliper to the steering knuckle, clean the thread locking compound out of the mounting bolt holes using a tap or an old bolt with a slot cut in it.
20 Refit the caliper, using new bolts coated with thread locking compound. Tighten the bolts to the specified torque.
21 Connect the hydraulic union, using a new hollow screw and new seals. Tighten the screw to the specified torque.
22 Fit the brake pads and their securing components, as described in Section 3. Reconnect the wear warning sensor, if fitted.
23 Bleed the hydraulic system, as described in Section 17.
24 Refit the roadwheel, lower the vehicle and tighten the wheel bolts.

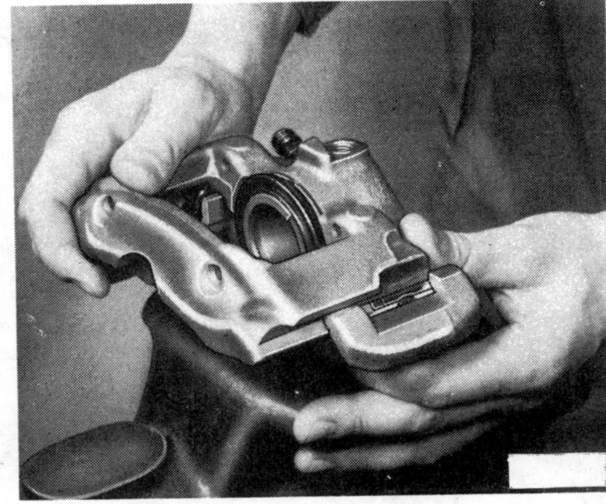

Fig. 9.3 Separating ATE caliper body and bracket (Sec 4)

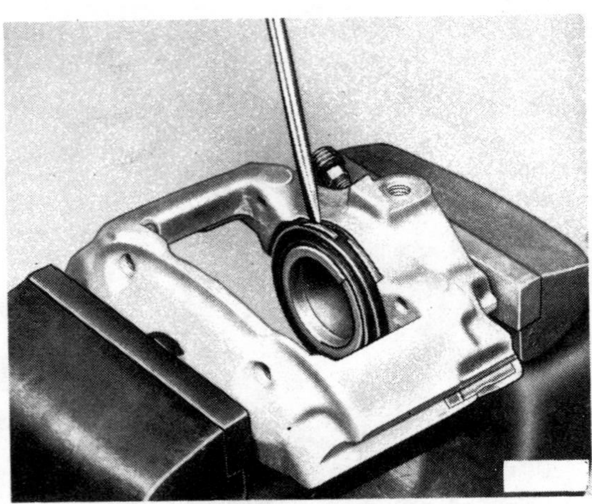

Fig. 9.4 Prising off the dust excluder retaining ring – ATE (Sec 4)

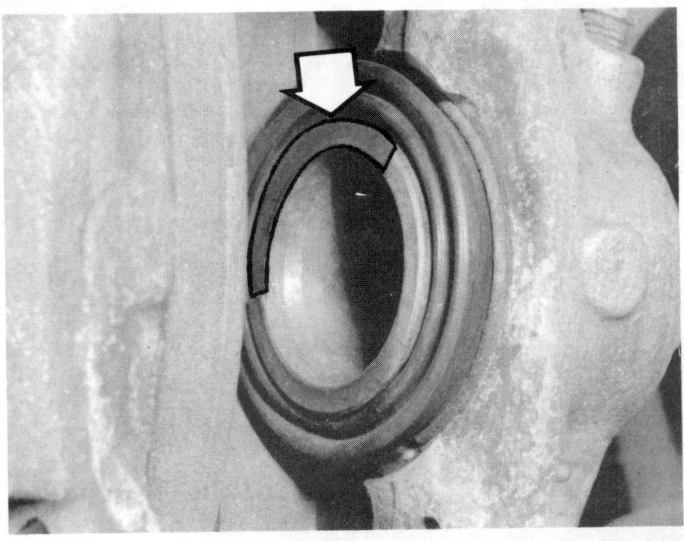

4.14 Correct positioning of recessed part of caliper piston (arrowed)

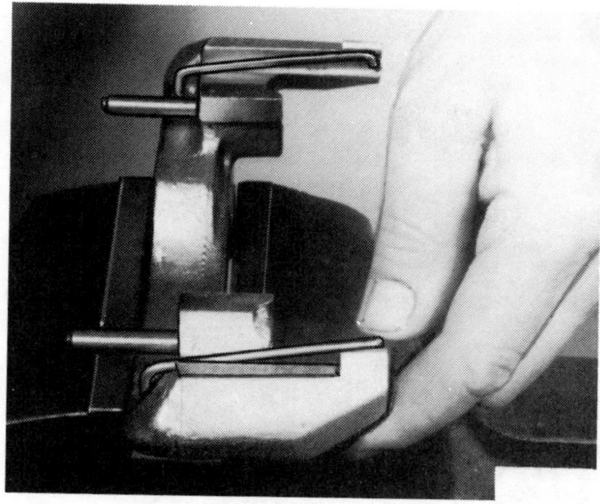

Fig. 9.5 Fitting the bracket guide springs – ATE (Sec 4)

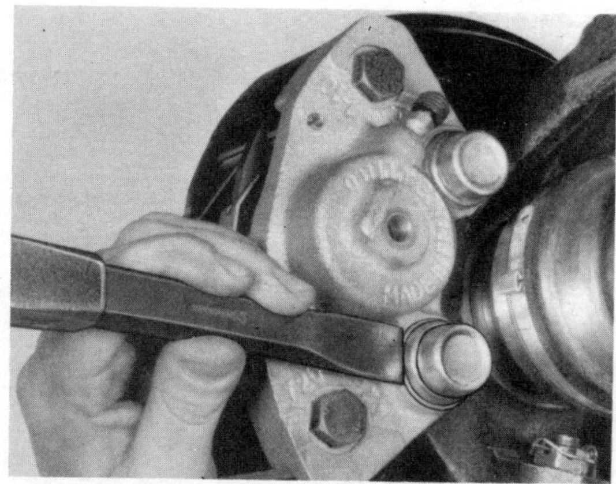

Fig. 9.6 Removing the caliper mounting bolt caps – GMF (Sec 5)

5 Brake caliper (GMF) – removal, overhaul and refitting

1 Raise and support the front of the vehicle and remove the roadwheel.
2 Remove the pad wear warning sensor, when fitted.
3 Unscrew and remove the hydraulic union bolt from the inboard side of the caliper. Clamp the hose or plug the union to minimise fluid leakage, or allow the fluid to drain into a suitable container.
4 Remove the mounting bolt protective caps with a chisel, then use an Allen key to unscrew the mounting bolts. They will be tight. Do not unscrew the two hexagon-headed bolts which connect the caliper body and bracket.
5 Remove the caliper from the vehicle.
6 Clean the caliper, mount it in a vice and remove the pins, pads and anti-rattle springs, as described in Section 3.
7 Using a chisel, release the sliding sleeve inboard dust caps from the housing.
8 Lever off the piston dust excluder.
9 Press the sliding sleeves inwards slightly and remove their dust caps, then press the sleeves out of the housing.
10 Remove the piston, as described in Section 4, paragraph 8.
11 Undo the two hexagon-headed bolts and separate the caliper from the bracket.
12 Prise the piston seal out of the bore with a wooden or plastic instrument.
13 Inspect and clean the components, as described in Section 4, paragraphs 10 to 12.
14 Lubricate the new seal with brake fluid or brake rubber grease and fit it to its recess in the bore.
15 Coat the piston with brake fluid or brake rubber grease and carefully insert it part way into the bore.
16 Engage the new dust excluder with the groove on the piston. Press the piston home, then seat the dust excluder with a mallet and a piece of tubing.
17 Refit the caliper to the bracket and tighten the retaining bolts to the specified torque.
18 Remove the old sealing rings from the sliding sleeves. Coat the sleeves with the special grease provided in the repair kit and fit the new seals in the grooves.
19 Insert the sliding sleeves into their holes, with the dust cap grooves on the piston side. Do not push them home yet.
20 Fit the new dust caps to the sleeve grooves, then seat the caps in the housing grooves using a mallet and a piece of tubing. Push the sleeves home.
21 Refit the caliper, pads etc, as described in Section 4, paragraphs 19 to 23. Also fit new protective caps over the mounting bolts and seat them with a mallet and tube.
22 Refit the roadwheel, lower the vehicle and tighten the wheel bolts.

Fig. 9.7 Releasing the sliding sleeve inner dust caps (Sec 5)

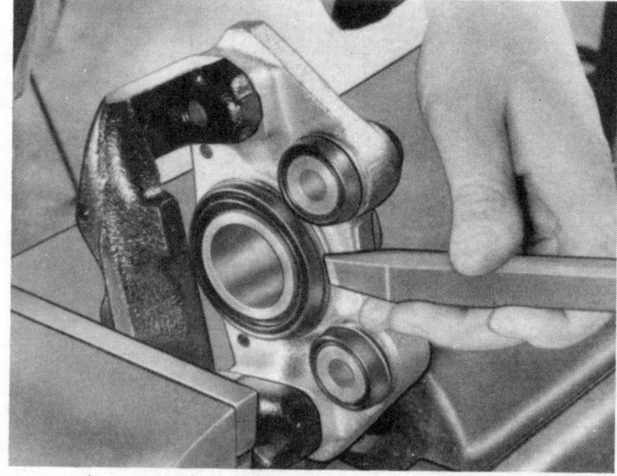

Fig. 9.8 Releasing the piston dust excluder from the housing (Sec 5)

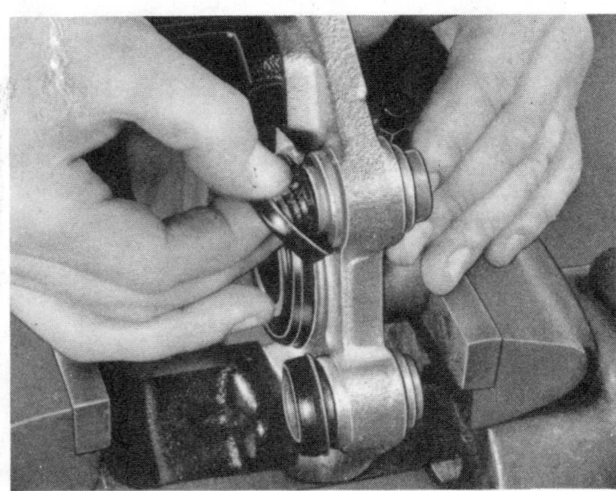

Fig. 9.9 Removing the dust caps from the sliding sleeves (Sec 5)

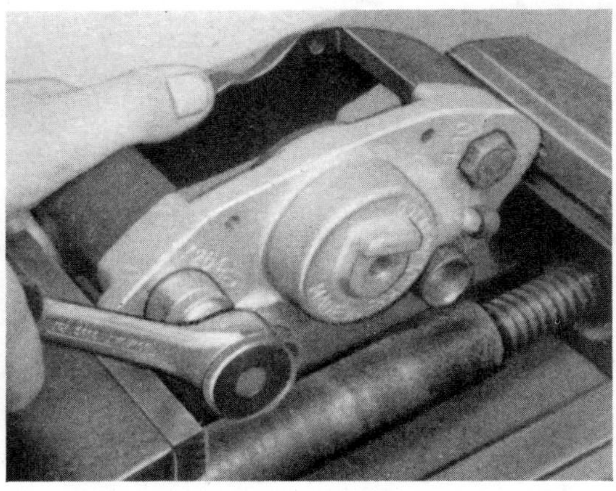

Fig. 9.10 Undoing a caliper-to-bracket bolt (Sec 5)

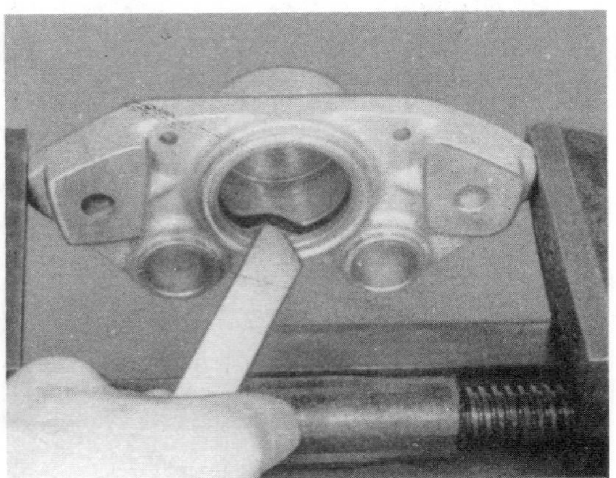

Fig. 9.11 Prising the piston seal out of the bore using a blunt instrument (Sec 5)

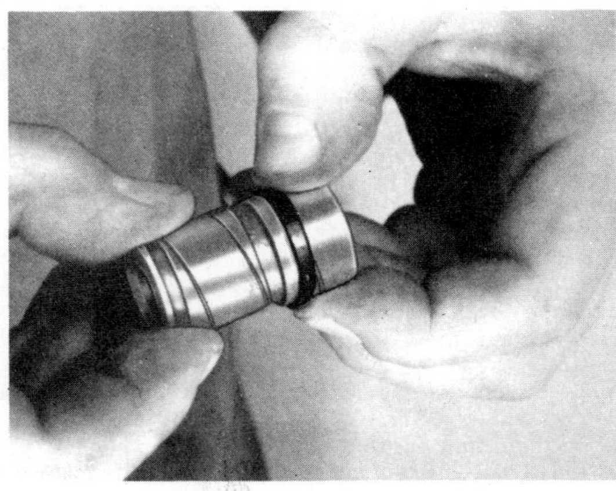

Fig. 9.12 Fitting new seals to the sliding sleeves (Sec 5)

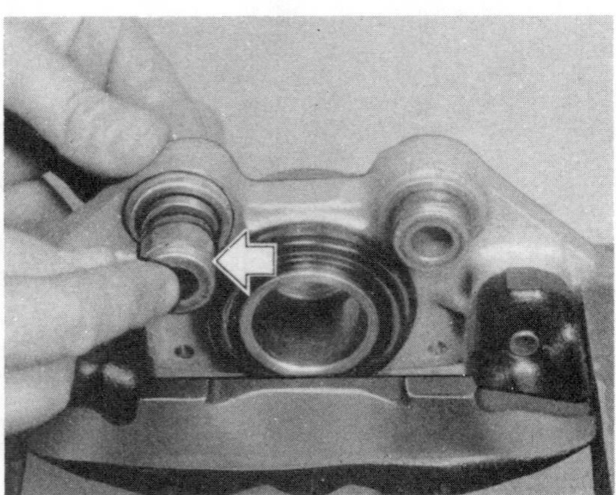

Fig. 9.13 Fit the sliding sleeves with the dust cap grooves (arrowed) on the piston side (Sec 5)

6 Brake disc – inspection, removal and refitting

1 Remove the wheel trim, slacken the wheel bolts and jack up the front of the car. Support the car on axle stands and remove the roadwheel.

2 Rotate the disc by hand and examine it for deep scoring, grooving or cracks. Light scoring is normal, but if excessive the disc must be, refinished or renewed.

3 If it is thought that the disc is distorted, check it for run-out using a dial gauge or using feeler blades between the disc and a fixed point as the disc is rotated. If the run-out exceeds the tolerance shown in the Specifications, refinishing or renewal is necessary. Bolt the disc to the hub using wheel bolts for this operation.

4 To remove a brake disc, first remove the brake pads, as described in Section 3.

5 On models fitted with alloy roadwheels, remove the protective shield from around the disc centre hub.

6 Undo the small screw securing the disc to the hub, tilt the disc slightly and remove it from the hub and caliper. If necessary pull the caliper outwards slightly to provide extra clearance.

7 If the disc has been removed for renewal or machining, it is

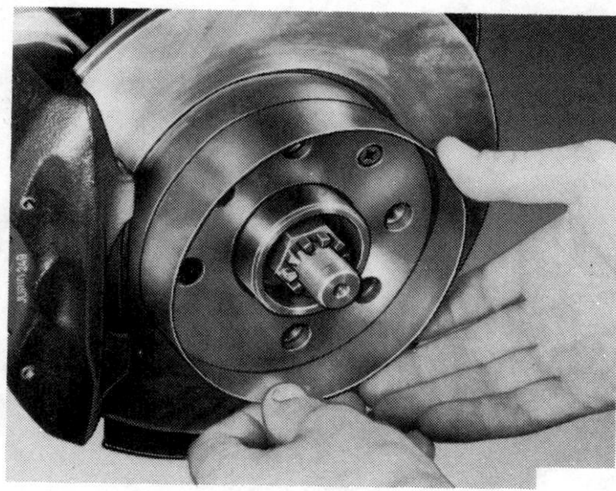

Fig. 9.14 Removing the protective shield found with alloy wheels (Sec 6)

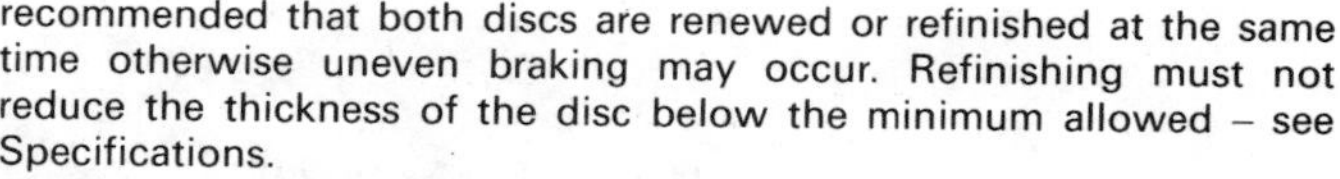

recommended that both discs are renewed or refinished at the same time otherwise uneven braking may occur. Refinishing must not reduce the thickness of the disc below the minimum allowed – see Specifications.
8 Refit in the reverse order to removal.

7 Disc shield – removal and refitting

1 Remove the brake caliper, as described in Section 4 or 5, but without disconnecting the hydraulic union. Hang the caliper up using wire or string – do not allow it to hang on its hose.
2 Remove the brake disc after removing the screw which secured it to the hub.
3 Use a screwdriver through the holes in the hub flange to undo the disc shield screws.

Fig. 9.15 Removing the disc securing screw (Sec 6)

4 Cut off the shield connecting web with tin snips and remove the shield.
5 Similarly cut the web off the new shield before fitting. Paint over the cut edges to prevent corrosion.
6 Refit in the reverse order to removal, using new caliper mounting bolts etc, as necessary.

8 Rear brake shoes – inspection, removal and refitting

1 An inspection hole is provided in each brake backplate; with the plug removed from the hole, the thickness of the leading shoe lining can be seen. This is a somewhat perfunctory check; for a thorough inspection the drum must be removed, as follows.
2 Chock the front wheels and engage a gear. Slacken the rear wheel bolts, raise and support the rear of the car and remove the rear wheels.

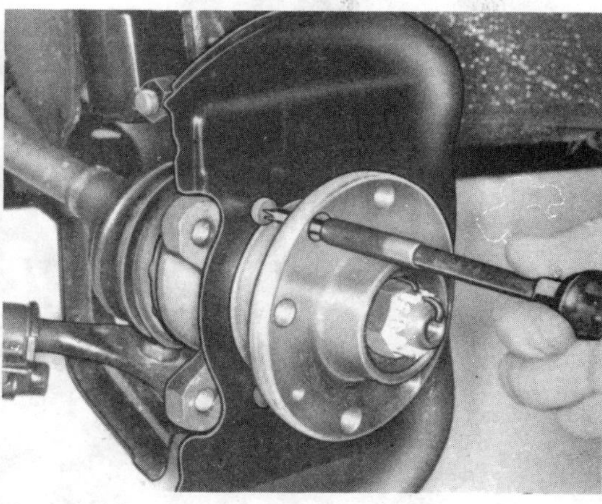

Fig. 9.16 Undoing a disc shield retaining screw (Sec 7)

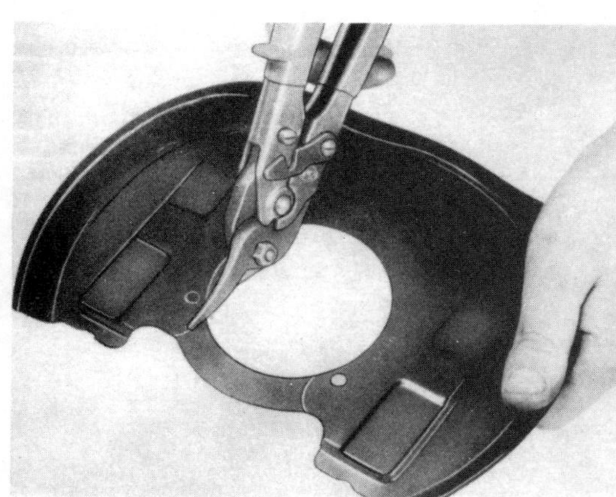

Fig. 9.17 Cut off the web before fitting the new shield (Sec 7)

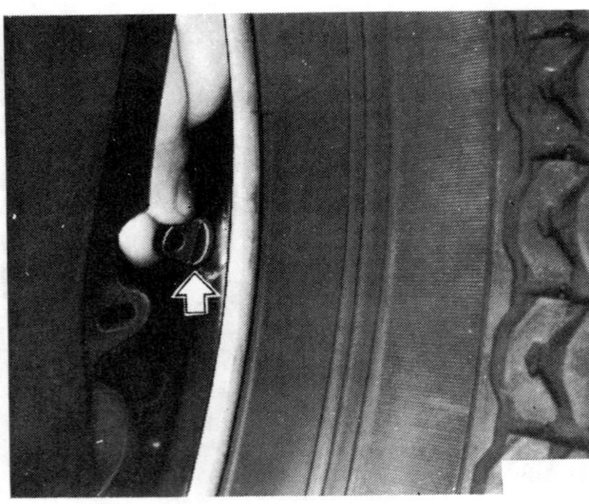

Fig. 9.18 Brake shoe inspection plug (arrowed) on backplate (Sec 8)

8.3 Removing a brake drum securing screw

Release the handbrake and slacken the handbrake cable adjuster (see Section 22).

3 Remove the brake drum securing screw and pull off the drum (photo). If it is stuck, release the brake shoes by inserting a screwdriver into the hole in the backplate and pushing the handbrake lever back towards its shoe (Fig. 9.19).

4 Clean the dust from the drum and shoes using a damp cloth or paintbrush. *Take care not to inhale the dust or disperse it into the air.* (Original equipment linings are asbestos-free, but this may not apply to replacement linings.)

5 If any of the linings are worn down to the specified minimum, or are contaminated, torn or otherwise damaged, all four must be renewed as follows. (If the linings are in good condition, refit the drum and proceed to paragraph 23.)

6 Remove the steady pins, springs and washers by depressing the washers and turning them anti-clockwise. Renew them if they are damaged (photo).

7 Disconnect the handbrake cable from the operating lever (photo). If there is insufficient slack at the cable, disconnect it at the equaliser yoke.

Fig. 9.19 Pushing back the handbrake lever (Sec 8)

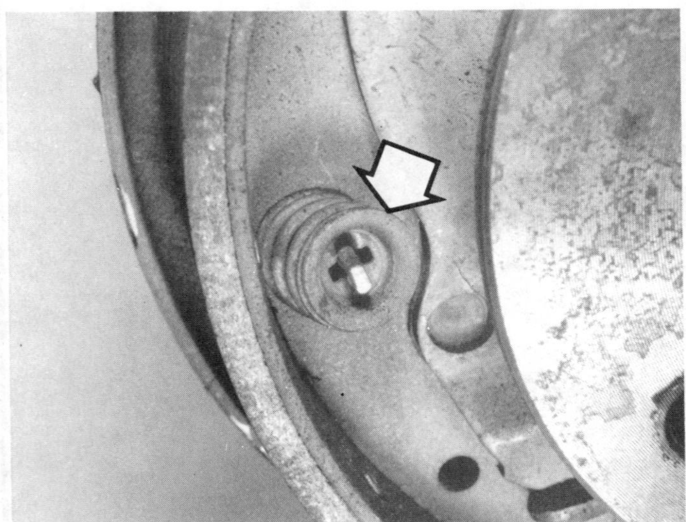

8.6 Brake shoe steady pin and washer (arrowed)

8.7 Handbrake cable attachment to operating lever (arrowed)

8 The return springs may be unhooked now and the shoes removed separately, or the assembly of shoes, strut and springs may be removed together. The second course is particularly easy if the hub is removed (see Chapter 10), as has been done for some of the photographs. Be careful not to damage the wheel cylinder rubber boots.
9 If the shoes are to be removed for some time, secure the wheel cylinder pistons with a stout rubber band or a spring clip. In any event, do not press the brake pedal while the drum is removed.
10 Clean the brake backplate, again *being careful not to inhale the dust or to disperse it into the air.*
11 Apply a smear of copper-based anti-seize compound to the shoe rubbing areas on the backplate.
12 Investigate and rectify any source of contamination of the linings (wheel cylinder or hub bearing oil seal leaking).
13 Unusually, linings are still available separately for these brake shoes. Renewal of the shoes complete with linings is to be preferred, however, unless the reader has the necessary skills and equipment to fit new linings to the old shoes.
14 Dismantle the shoes, strut and springs. Note how the springs are fitted, and which way round the strut goes. Be careful not to interchange left-hand and right-hand adjuster components; the threaded rod is marked L or R, and the other 'handed' components are colour-coded: black for the left-hand side, and silver for the right (photo).

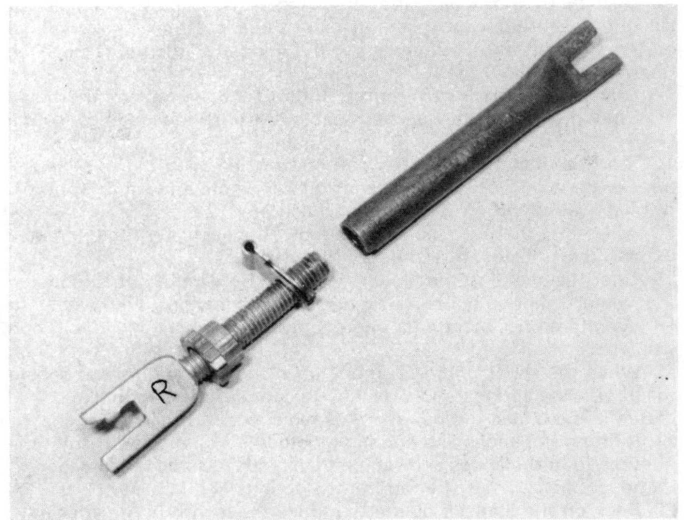

8.14 Self-adjusting strut components – right-hand side

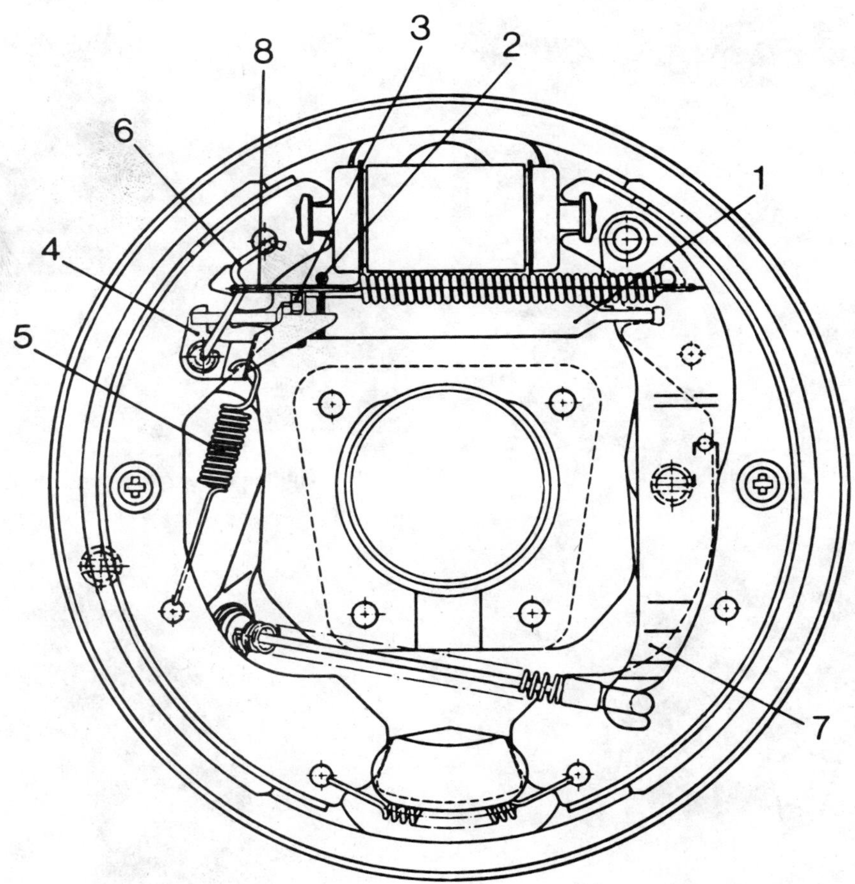

Fig. 9.20 Rear brake components with drum removed (Sec 8)

1 Strut
2 Thermoclip
3 Adjuster pinion
4 Adjuster lever
5 Adjuster lever spring
6 Adjuster lever bracket
7 Handbrake lever
8 Upper return spring

15 Dismantle and clean the adjusting strut. Apply a smear of silicone-based lubricant to the adjuster threads. If new brake linings are being fitted, the thermoclip (in the middle of the strut) must be renewed too.
16 Examine the shoe return springs. If they are distorted or if they have seen much service, renewal is advisable. Weak springs may cause the brakes to bind.
17 If a new handbrake lever was not supplied with the new shoes, transfer the old lever. It may be secured with a pin and circlip (photo), or by a rivet which will have to be drilled out.
18 Assemble the new shoes, springs and adjuster components. Expand the adjuster strut to ease fitting (photos).
19 Offer the shoes to the brake backplate. Be careful not to damage the wheel cylinder boots or to displace the pistons. Remember to remove the rubber band or spring clip from the wheel cylinder, if one was used.
20 When the shoes are in position, insert the steady pins and secure them with the springs and washers. Reconnect the handbrake cable, and refit and adjust the hub if it was removed.
21 If fitting the shoes and springs together is found too difficult, it is possible to fit the shoes and secure them with the steady pins, then to introduce the adjuster strut and fit the springs and adjuster.
22 Back off the adjuster pinion to reduce the length of the strut until

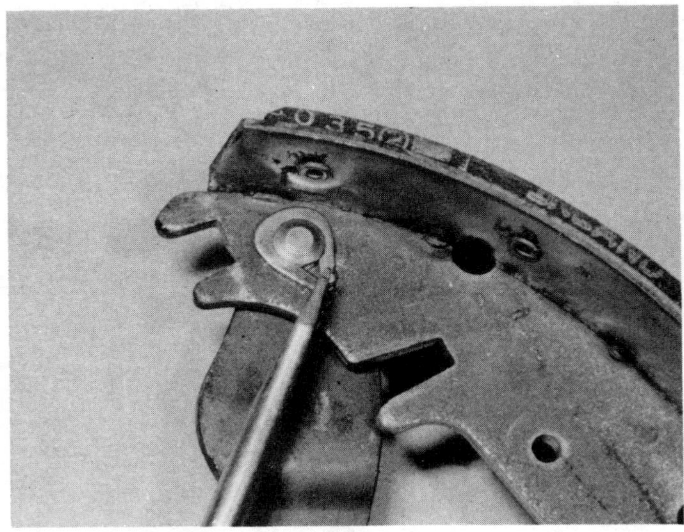

8.17 Handbrake lever secured by pin and circlip

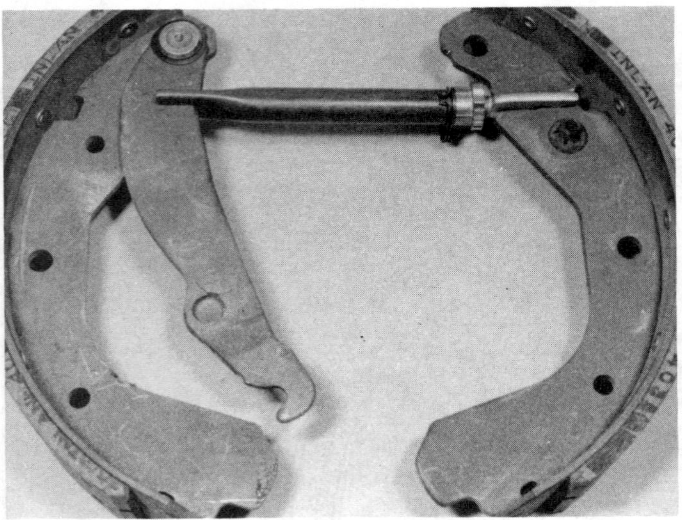

8.18A Self-adjusting strut correctly fitted

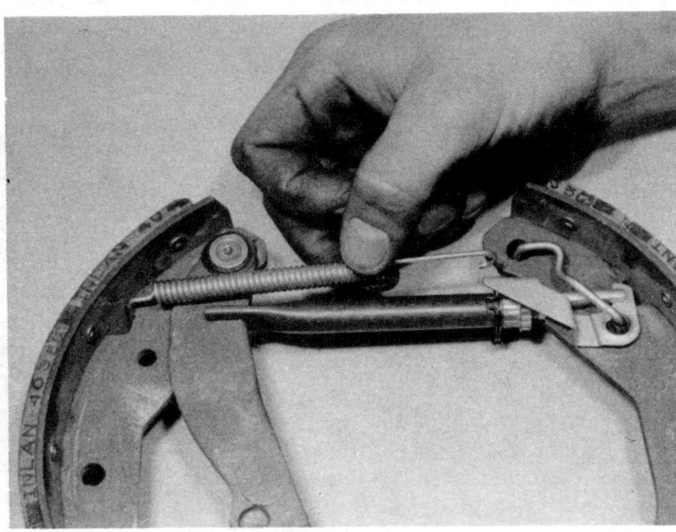

8.18B Fitting the upper return spring to the adjuster lever bracket

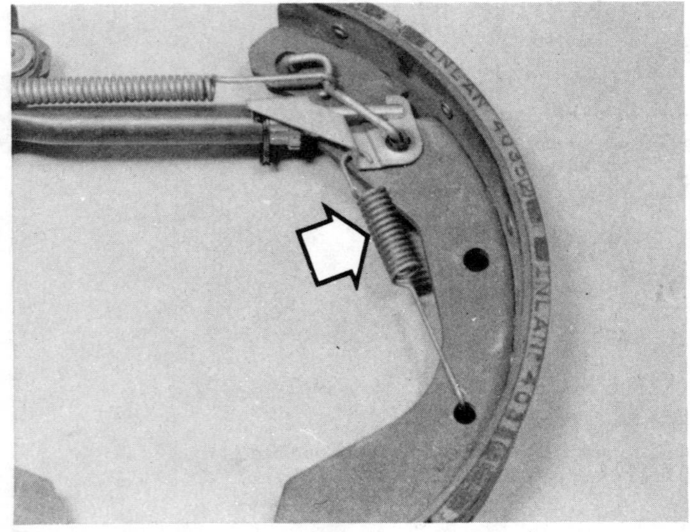

8.18C Adjuster lever spring (arrowed) fitted

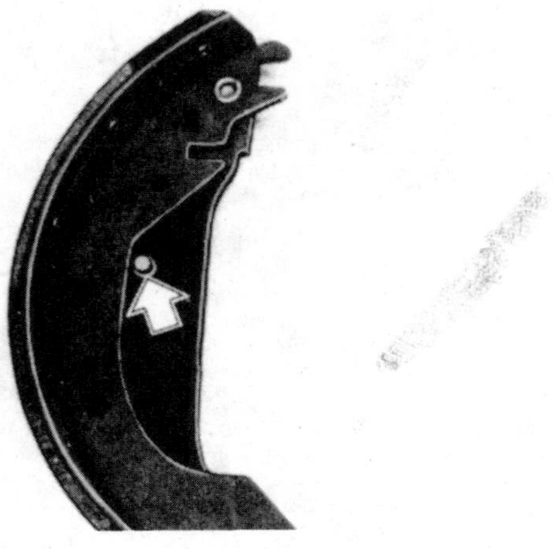

Fig. 9.21 Handbrake lever pin (arrowed) should rest against brake shoe web during assembly (Sec 8)

the brake drum will pass over the new linings. Make sure that the handbrake lever is correctly positioned (pin on the edge of the shoe web, not riding on top of it). Refit and secure the brake drum.
23 Repeat the operations on the other rear brake, then adjust the brakes by operating the footbrake at least 10 times. A clicking noise will be heard at the drums as the automatic adjusters operate; when the clicking stops, adjustment is complete.
24 Check the handbrake adjustment and correct it if necessary (Section 22).
25 When new linings have been fitted, avoid harsh braking as far as possible for the first hundred miles or so to allow the linings to bed in.

9 Rear wheel cylinder – removal, overhaul and refitting

1 Remove the brake drum, as described in the previous Section.
2 Disconnect the shoe upper return spring using a pair of pliers. Be careful, the spring is under considerable tension.

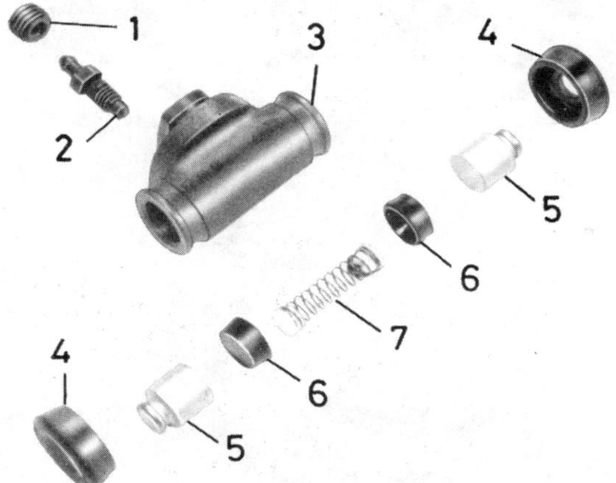

Fig. 9.22 Exploded view of a rear wheel cylinder (Sec 9)

1 Dust cap
2 Bleed screw
3 Cylinder body
4 Dust excluder
5 Piston
6 Seal
7 Spring

3 Move the brake shoes outwards slightly so that their upper ends clear the wheel cylinder. Be careful not to displace the adjuster strut.
4 Clean the rear of the backplate around the wheel cylinder attachment. Unscrew the hydraulic union, being prepared for some fluid spillage. Cap the pipe (eg with a bleed nipple dust cap) to reduce fluid loss.
5 Unbolt and remove the wheel cylinders.
6 Clean away external dirt and pull off the rubber dust excluders from the cylinder body.
7 The pistons will normally be ejected by pressure of the coil spring, but if they are not, tap the end of the cylinder on a piece of hardwood or apply low air pressure from a tyre foot pump at the pipeline connection.
8 Inspect the surfaces of the piston and the cylinder bore for scoring or metal-to-metal rubbed areas. If these are evident, renew the wheel cylinder complete.
9 If these components are in good order, discard the seals and dust excluders and obtain a repair kit which will contain all the renewable items.
10 Fit the piston seals (using the fingers only to manipulate them into position, so that the spring is between them. Dip the pistons in clean hydraulic fluid and insert them into the cylinder.
11 Fit the dust excluders.
12 Refit the wheel cylinder to the backplate. Tighten the mounting bolt and the hydraulic union to the specified torque.
13 Refit the upper return spring to the brake shoes.
14 Refit and secure the brake drum.
15 Bleed the hydraulic system, as described in Section 17.
16 Operate the footbrake at least 10 times to settle the adjuster strut, then check the handbrake adjustment (Section 22).

10 Rear brake backplate – removal and refitting

1 Remove the brake drum, as described in Section 8.
2 Remove the rear hub, as described in Chapter 10, Section 11.
3 Remove the brake shoes, as described in Section 8.
4 Remove the wheel cylinder, as described in Section 9.
5 Remove the handbrake cable from the backplate by releasing its retainer.
6 Unbolt and remove the backplate. Recover the gasket.
7 When refitting, use a new gasket between the backplate and the stub axle. Tighten the mounting bolts to the specified torque.
8 Refit the remaining components in the reverse order to removal. Adjust the rear hub, as described in Chapter 10, Section 10. Bleed the hydraulic system, as described in Section 17, and adjust the brakes, as described in Section 8.

11 Brake drum – inspection and renovation

1 Whenever the brake drum is removed, inspect the lining rubbing surface. If deep grooves or scores are present, it is possible to have the drum skimmed as long as the internal diameter is not increased above the maximum specified. Light grooving is normal and requires no attention.
2 In theory, it is necessary to fit thicker brake linings after the drum has been skimmed in order to match the increased radius more precisely. Consult a GM dealer to determine the availability of oversize linings.
3 A drum which is cracked or out-of-round must be renewed.
4 Brake drums should be reconditioned or renewed in pairs to maintain even braking effort on both sides of the vehicle.

12 Master cylinder – removal and refitting

1 Disconnect the low fluid level switch wires from the master cylinder cap (photo). Remove the cap.
2 Syphon out as much brake fluid as possible from the reservoir in order to minimise spillage later. Do not syphon by mouth, as brake fluid is poisonous: use an old poultry baster or similar item. Do not drip brake fluid onto the paintwork, or it will quickly strip it. Discard the evacuated fluid.

12.1 Disconnecting the low fluid level warning switch

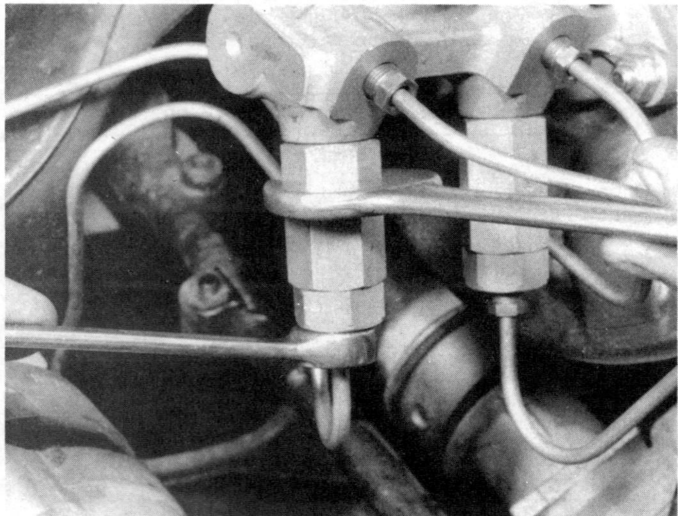

12.3 Slackening the hydraulic pipe union at the pressure regulating valve

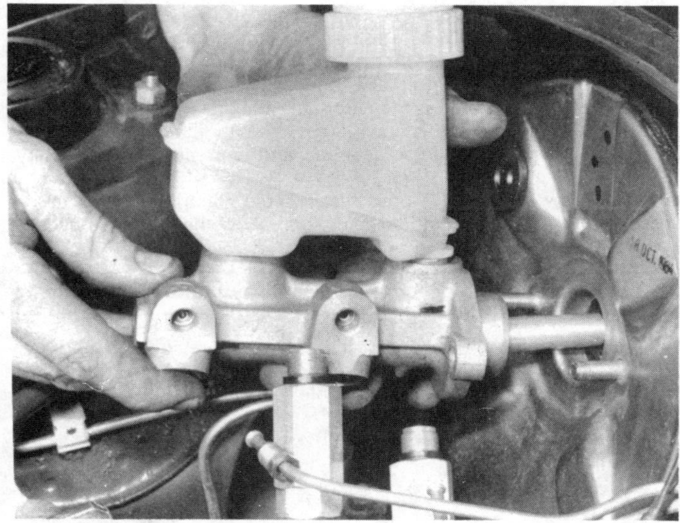

12.4 Removing the master cylinder

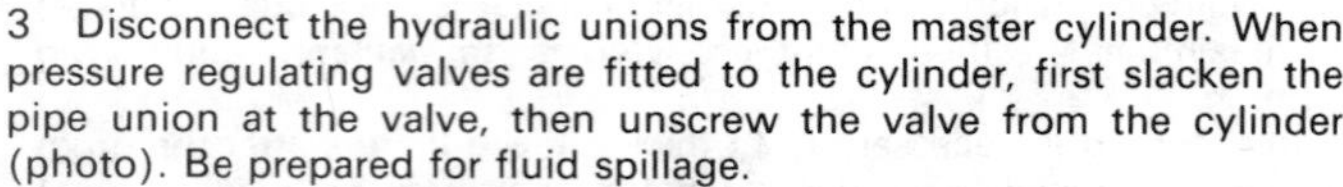

3 Disconnect the hydraulic unions from the master cylinder. When pressure regulating valves are fitted to the cylinder, first slacken the pipe union at the valve, then unscrew the valve from the cylinder (photo). Be prepared for fluid spillage.
4 Remove the nuts which secure the master cylinder to the servo and withdraw the cylinder from the servo (photo). Recover the pushrod if it is loose.
5 Refit in the reverse order to removal. Tighten the mounting nuts and hydraulic unions to the specified torque, and bleed the hydraulic system, as described in Section 17.

13 Master cylinder (ATE) – overhaul

1 With the master cylinder removed, clean away all external dirt.
2 Prise the fluid reservoir from the cylinder body.
3 Depress the primary (rear) piston slightly and remove its retaining circlip.
4 Withdraw the primary piston. Make sure that the stop washers do not catch in the circlip groove.
5 Depress the secondary (front) piston with a suitable rod and remove the stop screw from the cylinder body.
6 Shake or tap out the secondary piston.
7 Clean all the parts in brake fluid or methylated spirit. Examine the pistons and the cylinder bore for scoring, rust, or evidence of metal-to-metal contact; if found, renew the cylinder complete. Strip the seals from the primary piston if it is to be re-used noting which way round they are fitted.
8 The makers do not supply a seal kit alone, but provide a repair kit consisting of a complete secondary piston and the other necessary seals, springs, washers etc in a special assembly tube. Should a proprietary seal kit be available, fit new seals using the fingers only, and make sure that the new seals are fitted the same way round as the old ones. The remainder of this Section describes the fitting of the maker's repair kit.
9 Lubricate the cylinder bore with brake fluid or brake rubber grease.
10 Clamp the cylinder in a soft-jawed vice with the bore more or less horizontal. Screw in the stop screw a little way, but not so far that it protrudes into the bore.
11 Remove the large plug from the assembly tube. Remove all the components from the short part of the tube and push the short part into the long part until they are flush.
12 Insert the assembly tube into the cylinder bore as far as the collar on the short sleeve. Use a blunt rod to push the secondary piston into the bore until it contacts the end of the cylinder. Nip up the stop screw, withdraw the rod and sleeve and tighten the stop screw fully.
13 Reposition the master cylinder in the vice with the bore opening facing upwards.

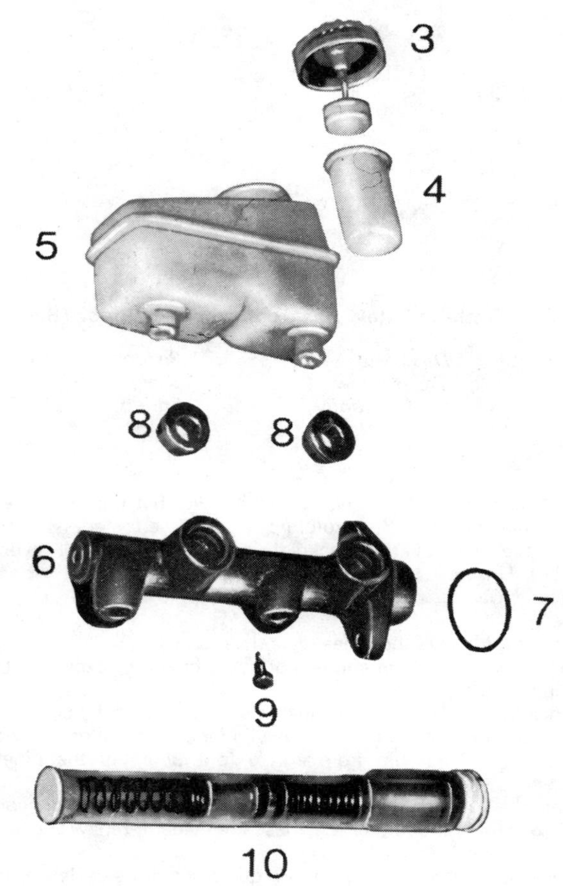

Fig. 9.23 Exploded view of ATE master cylinder (Sec 13)

3 Reservoir cap/low level switch
4 Float guide sleeve
5 Reservoir
6 Cylinder body
7 O-ring
8 Seals
9 Stop screw
10 Repair kit in assembly tube

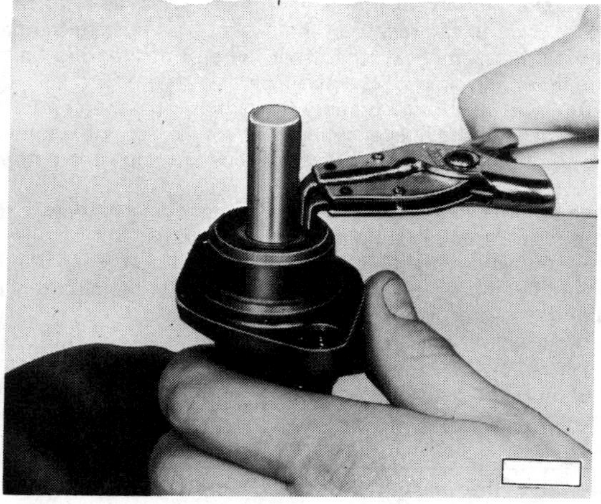

Fig. 9.24 Extracting the primary piston circlip – ATE (Sec 13)

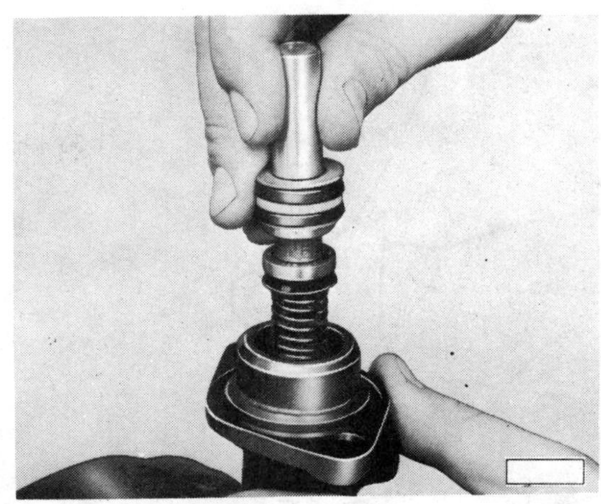

Fig. 9.25 Removing the primary piston – ATE (Sec 13)

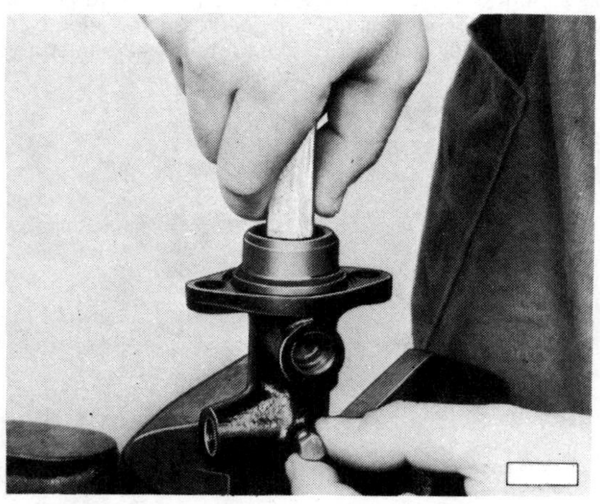

Fig. 9.26 Depressing the secondary piston and removing the stop screw – ATE (Sec 13)

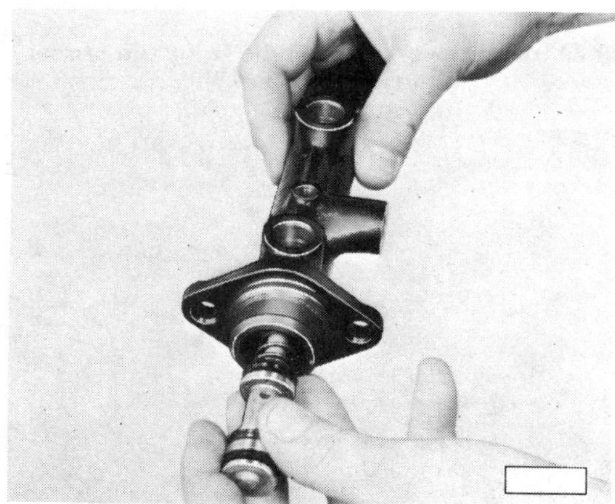

Fig. 9.27 Removing the secondary piston – ATE (Sec 13)

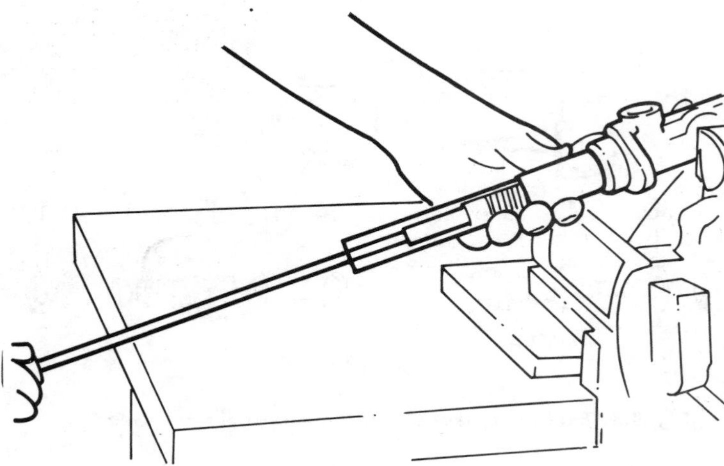

Fig. 9.28 Using a rod and the assembly tube to insert the secondary piston – ATE (Sec 13)

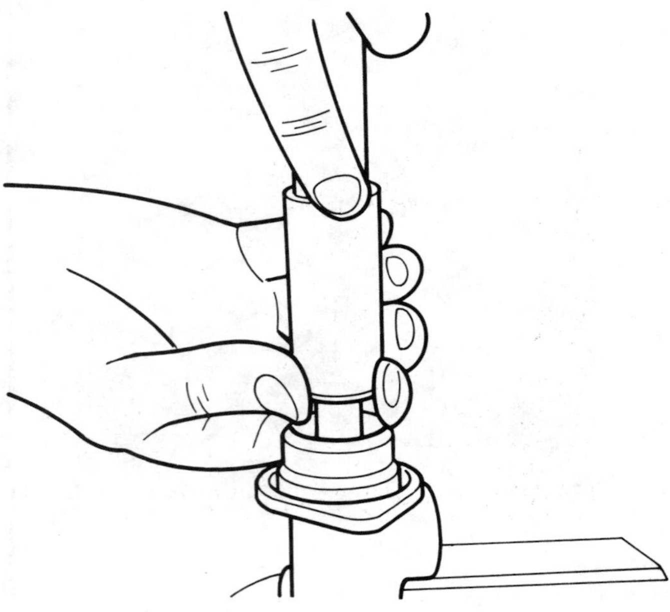

Fig. 9.29 Using the assembly tube to fit the primary piston – ATE (Sec 13)

14 Smear the primary piston skirt and seal grooves with the special grease provided in the repair kit. Fit the stop washer to the piston.
15 Adjust the assembly tube so that the end of the long part is flush with the inner shoulder of the short part.
16 Fit the front seal to the primary piston with the open end of the seal facing the front of the master cylinder. Place the assembly tube over the cylinder to compress the seal, insert the piston and tube part way into the bore and withdraw the tube.
17 Place the intermediate ring on the primary piston, then fit the other seal using the assembly tube in a similar manner.
18 Place the end washer on the primary piston, then depress the piston slightly and fit the circlip. Make sure that the circlip is properly seated and that the piston is free to move.
19 Fit new sealing rings and press the fluid reservoir into position.
20 Prime the cylinder by pouring clean brake fluid into the reservoir and working the pistons with a rod until fluid is ejected from all orifices.

14 Master cylinder (GMF) – overhaul

1 With the master cylinder removed, clean off all external dirt.
2 Prise the fluid reservoir from its location.
3 Clamp the cylinder in a soft-jawed vice, rear end uppermost, and prise out the pushrod seal.
4 Use a blunt rod to depress the primary (rear) piston by 10 mm (0.4 in) or so until it can be retained in the depressed position by inserting a smooth rod (eg a knitting needle) onto the primary inlet hole.

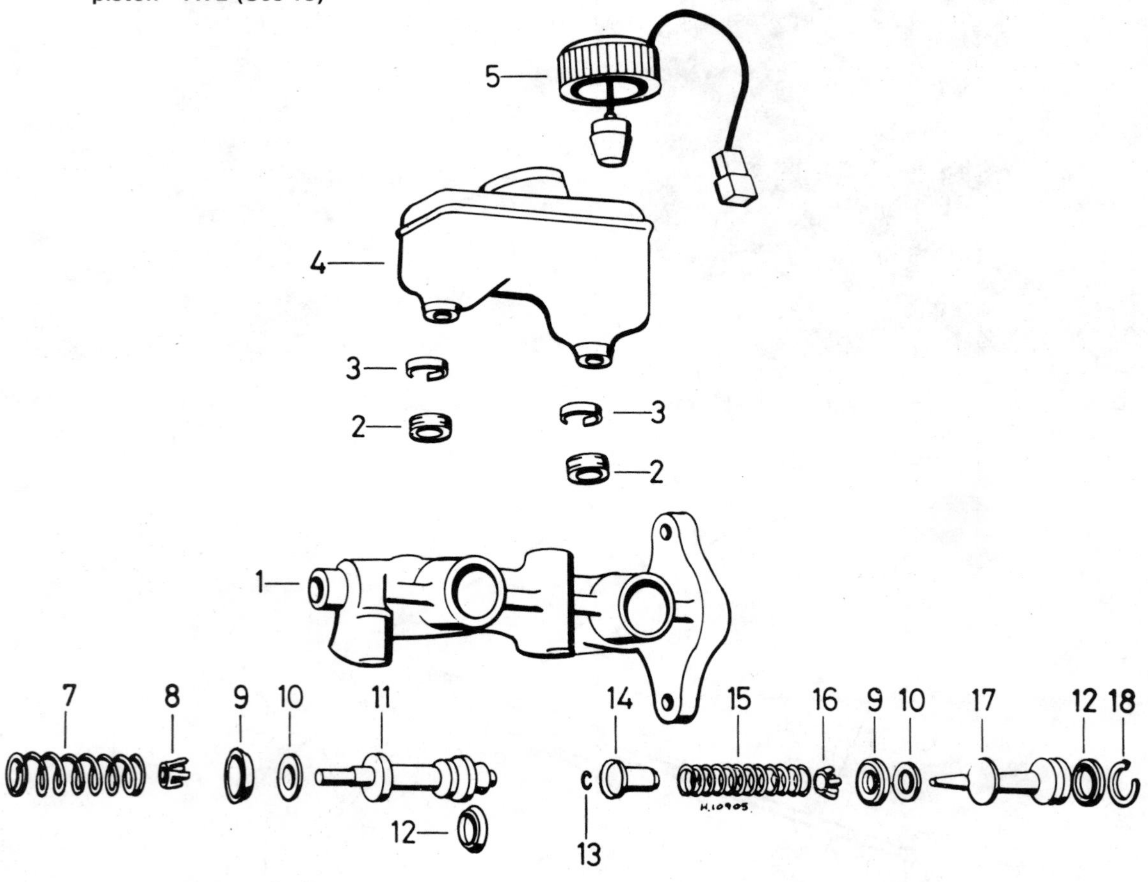

Fig. 9.30 Exploded view of GMF master cylinder (Sec 14)

1 *Body*
2 *Seals*
3 *Circlips*
4 *Reservoir*
5 *Reservoir cap/low level switch*
7 *Spring*
8 *Spring retainer*
9 *Secondary seals*
10 *Shims*
11 *Secondary piston*
12 *Primary seals*
13 *Circlip*
14 *Spring sleeve*
15 *Spring*
16 *Spring retainer*
17 *Primary piston*
18 *Circlip*

5 Carefully extract the circlip from the end of the cylinder by prising it out with a screwdriver.
6 Knock, shake or blow the pistons out of the cylinder.
7 Clean all parts with brake fluid or methylated spirit. Examine the pistons and the cylinder bore for scoring, rust or evidence of metal-to-metal contact; if found, renew the cylinder complete.
8 The makers do not supply a kit of seals alone, but provide a repair kit consisting of both pistons in a special assembly tube. Should a proprietary seal kit be obtained, note the direction of fitting of the seals before removing them from the pistons.
9 Lubricate the cylinder bore with brake fluid or brake rubber grease. Clamp the cylinder with the bore horizontal.
10 Remove the plug from the assembly tube and insert the short part of the tube into the cylinder bore as far as the shoulder on the tube. Use a blunt rod to push the piston out of the tube and into the bore; retain the pistons in the bore with the smooth rod or needle used when dismantling. Withdraw the rod and the tube.
11 Fit a new circlip to the end of the cylinder. Depress the primary piston and withdraw the retaining rod or needle. Make sure that the circlip is properly seated and that the pistons are free to move.
12 Fit new sealing rings and press the reservoir into position.
13 Prime the cylinder, as described for the ATE type (Section 13).

Fig. 9.31 Extracting the primary piston circlip – GMF (Sec 14)

15 Pressure regulating valves – testing, removal and refitting

1 Accurate testing of either type of pressure regulating valve (master cylinder mounted or underbody mounted) is not possible without special equipment. Malfunction may be suspected if the rear brakes lock prematurely in heavy braking, or if they seem not to be functioning at all.
2 A quick check of the underbody mounted valve fitted to Estate and Van models may be made by observing the valve whilst an assistant makes sharp applications of the brake pedal. (The weight of the vehicle must be on its wheels.) The lever on the valve must be seen to move as the pedal is depressed and released; if not, the valve is certainly defective.
3 Removal and refitting procedures are as follows.

Hatchback

4 Empty the master cylinder reservoir, as described in Section 12.
5 Slacken the pipe unions at the pressure regulating valves, unscrew the valves from the master cylinder and then release them from the pipe unions. Be prepared for fluid spillage.
6 Make sure that both new valves are of the same type and are stamped with the same numbers (indicating their calibration). The valves must always be renewed in pairs, even if only one seems to be defective.
7 Screw the new valves loosely onto the pipe unions, then screw them into the master cylinder. Tighten the valves and then the hydraulic unions to their specified torques.
8 Bleed the hydraulic system, as described in Section 17.

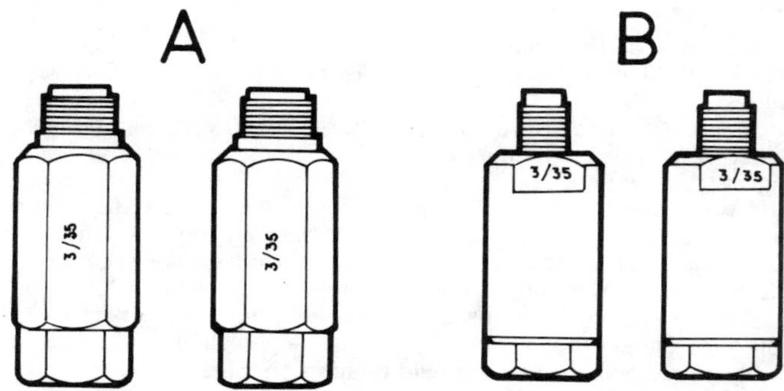

Fig. 9.32 Two types of pressure regulating valve (Sec 15)

A GMF *B ATE*

Estate and Van

9 Raise and securely support the rear of the vehicle.
10 Slacken the valve spring bracket, push the bracket rearwards and unhook the spring from it (photo).
11 Clean around the hydraulic unions. Identify the unions with tape or dabs of paint, then unscrew them from the valve. Be prepared for fluid spillage.
12 Unbolt and remove the valve.
13 Transfer the stone guard to the new valve.
14 Bolt the new valve to the underbody and tighten the mounting bolts to the specified torque.
15 Secure the hydraulic unions to the valve.
16 Bleed the hydraulic system, as described in Section 17.
17 Attach the spring to the valve and to the spring bracket. Adjust the position of the spring bracket so that the spring is neither taut nor slack, then secure the bracket.
18 Lower the vehicle. Perform a road test to confirm that rear brake operation is satisfactory. Note that increasing the spring tension increases the pressure to the rear brakes, and *vice versa*.

15.10 Load-dependent pressure regulating valve, spring and bracket

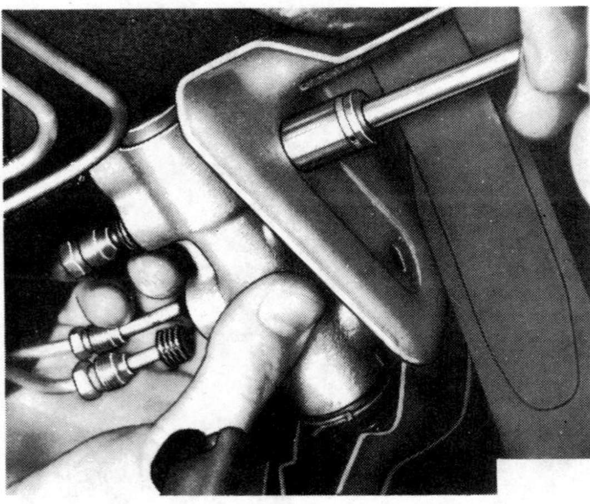

Fig. 9.33 Removing a pressure regulating valve – Estate or Van (Sec 15)

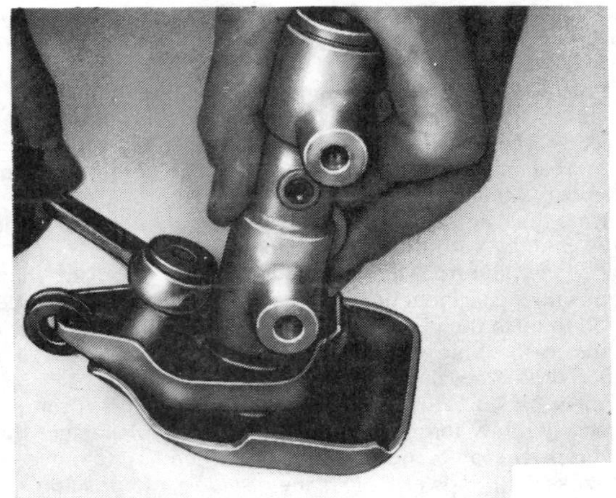

Fig. 9.34 Unbolting the stone guard from the pressure regulating valve – Estate or Van (Sec 15)

16 Hydraulic pipes and hoses – inspection and renewal

1 At the specified intervals, or whenever leakage is suspected, examine the hydraulic pipes and hoses, hose connections and pipe unions.
2 Check the condition of the four hoses: if they appear swollen, chafed or cracked they must be renewed. Bend the hoses with the fingers to show up cracks.
3 Always unscrew the rigid pipe from the flexible hose first, then release the end of the hose from its support bracket. The left-hand front hose is secured to its bracket by a bolt; the others are secured by retaining clips which must be pulled out with pliers (photos).
4 The hose can now be unscrewed from its caliper or connector. On calipers a banjo type connector is used: new sealing washers, and ideally a new hollow screw, should be used on reassembly.
5 On vehicles with a pad wear warning system, the warning sensor cable must be unclipped from the front hoses before removing them.
6 After refitting a flexible hose, check that it will not rub against a tyre or other moving component. If necessary one end or the other can be repositioned to give the hose the required 'set', but the total movement should not exceed a quarter turn, otherwise twisting will be excessive.
7 Wipe the rigid brake pipes clean and inspect them for signs of corrosion or other damage.
8 Make sure that the pipes are a snug fit in their securing clips; bend the clips if necessary to achieve this.
9 Any pipe which is touching adjacent components should be carefully bent out of the way, or chafing will occur.
10 Any section of pipe which is rusty or damaged should be renewed. Pipes are available made up to the correct length and with unions fitted from most dealers; many accessory shops can also supply ready-made pipes and some can make them up to order. Pipes are also available in materials other than steel: obviously such pipes will not rust, but they may be subject to other problems (eg fatigue fractures if inadequately supported).
11 When fitting a new pipe, use the old one as a guide to bending. Do not make any bends sharper than necessary. With non-steel pipes, follow the maker's instructions concerning bending and the provision of support clips.
12 Bleed the hydraulic system on completion, as described in Section 17.

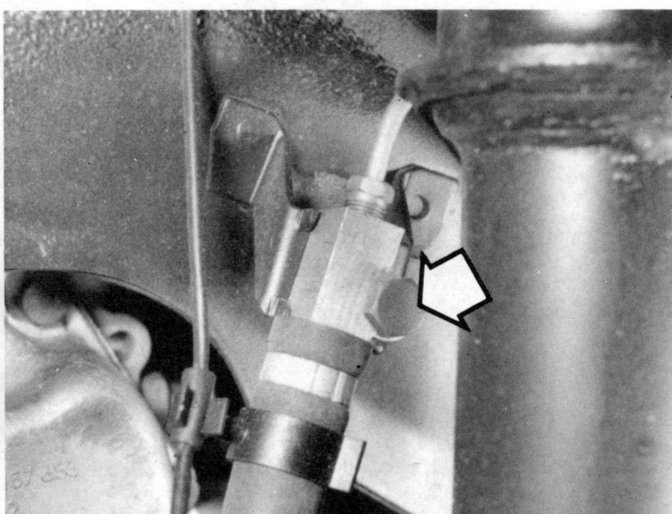

16.3A Left-hand front hose securing bolt (arrowed)

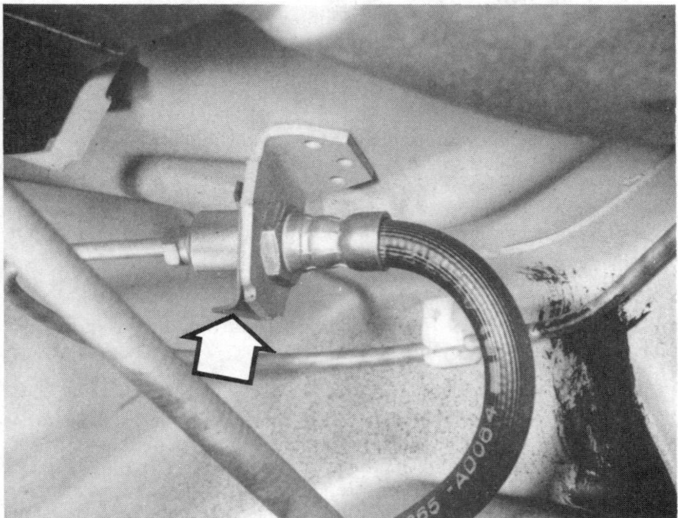

16.3B Hose-to-bracket retaining clip (arrowed)

17 Hydraulic system – bleeding

1 Whenever the brake hydraulic system has been dismantled to renew a pipe or hose (or if any other component has been disconnected in any way), air will be introduced into the system. The system will therefore require 'bleeding' in order to remove this air and restore the system's effectiveness. The design of the braking system is such that two entirely separate hydraulic circuits are used, each operating one front and one diagonally opposite rear brake. Therefore unless the master cylinder has been removed or the fluid is being changed at the annual renewal period, it will usually only be necessary to bleed one circuit if a component or pipe has been disconnected.
2 There are a variety of do-it-yourself brake bleeding kits available from motor accessory shops and it is recommended that one of these kits is used wherever possible as they greatly simplify the bleeding operation. If one of these kits is being used, follow the manufacturer's instructions in conjunction with the following procedure.
3 On Estate and Van models, the pressure regulating valve spring must be removed, and the valve operating lever be secured in the fully forwards position with string or wire, before bleeding commences. On completion, refit the spring; setting it free of tension, as described in Section 15.
4 During the bleeding operation, the level of hydraulic fluid in the master cylinder reservoir must be maintained at least half-full and only clean, unused fluid of an approved type should be used for topping-up. *Never re-use fluid bled from the system.*
5 Before starting, check that all pipes and hoses are secure, unions tight and all bleed screws closed. Take great care not to allow brake fluid to come into contact with the car paintwork, otherwise the finish will be seriously damaged. Wash off any spilt fluid immediately with cold water.
6 If a brake bleeding kit is not being used, gather together a clean jar, a suitable length of plastic or rubber tubing which is a tight fit over the bleed screws and a new tin of brake fluid.
7 Clean the area around the bleed screw on one of the front brake calipers and remove the dust cap. Connect one end of the tubing to the bleed screw and immerse the other end in the jar containing sufficient brake fluid to keep the end of the rubber submerged.
8 Open the bleed screw half a turn and have an assistant depress the brake pedal to the floor and then slowly release it. Tighten the bleed screw at the end of each downstroke to prevent the expelled air and fluid from being drawn back into the system. Continue this procedure until clean brake fluid, free from air bubbles, can be seen flowing into the jar, and then finally tighten the bleed screw.
9 Remove the tube, refit the dust cap and repeat this procedure on the diagonally opposite rear wheel and then if necessary on the front and rear wheels of the other circuit.
10 When bleeding is complete, top up the fluid level in the master cylinder reservoir and refit the cap.

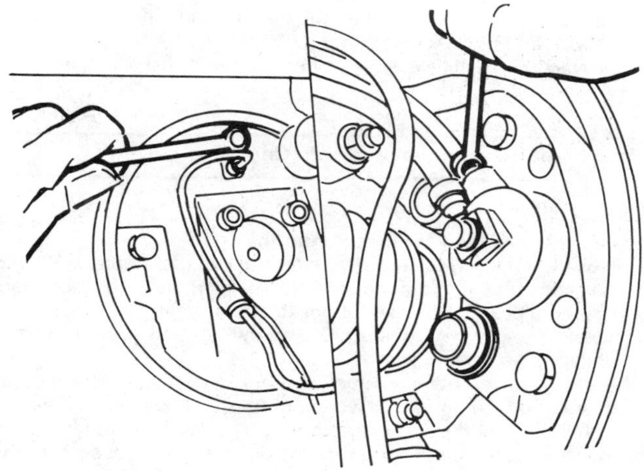

Fig. 9.35 Rear wheel cylinder and front caliper bleed screw locations (Sec 17)

18.2 Brake servo vacuum connection at inlet manifold (fuel injection model)

18 Brake servo vacuum hose and non-return valve – renewal

1 The plastic hose fitted as original equipment cannot be re-used; to renew the valve, the hose must therefore be renewed as well. A serviceable valve can, however, be transferred to the new hose.
2 Unscrew the hose union nut at the inlet manifold (photo).
3 Pull or prise the elbow connector out of the servo (photo).
4 Cut the hose off the non-return valve, the elbow and the manifold connectors.
5 Cut the new hose to length – it is sold by the yard – and secure it to the valve and fittings using hose clips. Make sure that the arrows on the valve point towards the manifold.
6 Refit the connectors to the manifold and to the servo.

19 Brake servo – testing

1 To establish whether or not the servo is operating, proceed as follows.
2 With the engine not running, apply the brake pedal several times to exhaust any residual vacuum.

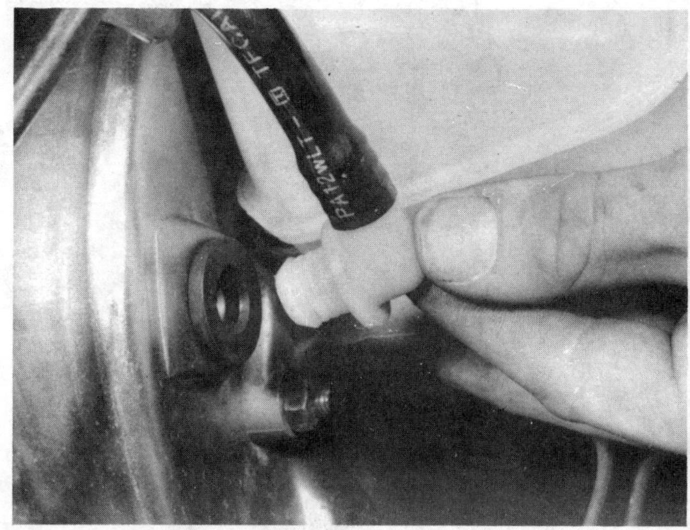

18.3 Brake servo vacuum connection at servo

3 Hold the brake pedal depressed and start the engine. The pedal should be felt to move down when the engine starts. If not, check the vacuum hose and non-return valve.
4 If the vacuum system is satisfactory, the servo itself is faulty and must be renewed.

20 Brake servo – removal and refitting

Right-hand drive

1 Remove the vacuum connector from the servo.
2 Remove the nuts which secure the master cylinder to the servo and draw the cylinder away from the servo. There is no need to disconnect the hydraulic pipes, but be careful not to strain them.
3 Inside the car, remove the stop-lamp switch and disconnect the brake pedal clevis – see Section 21.
4 The servo must now be removed from its bracket. The recommended method is to undo the two 6 mm Allen screws which hold the bracket halves together. Access to these screws is obtained by removing the wiper arms, wind deflector and water deflector; the screws are then accessible through two holes which may have rubber plugs in them. The screws are extremely tight, and without doubt a well-fitting key and square drive adaptor will be needed (photo).
5 If the Allen screws cannot be undone, it is possible to reach behind the servo and undo the four nuts which hold it to the bracket (photo). Small hands, some dexterity and a good deal of patience will be needed. The nuts are of the self-locking type and resist removal all the way.
6 With the screws or nuts removed, the servo can be removed from the car.
7 If a new servo is to be fitted, transfer the clevis and locknut to it. Measure the fitted position of the clevis on the old servo pushrod and fit it in the same position on the new one.
8 Refit in the reverse order to removal, noting the following points:

(a) Use sealing compound on the bracket halves if they were separated (photo)
(b) Make sure the vacuum connection point is in the correct position (photo)
(c) Use thread locking compound or new self-locking nuts, as appropriate

20.4 Removing a servo bracket screw

20.5 Three of the four servo-to-bracket nuts (arrowed) – servo and bracket removed for clarity

20.8A Servo mounting bracket lower half remains on bulkhead

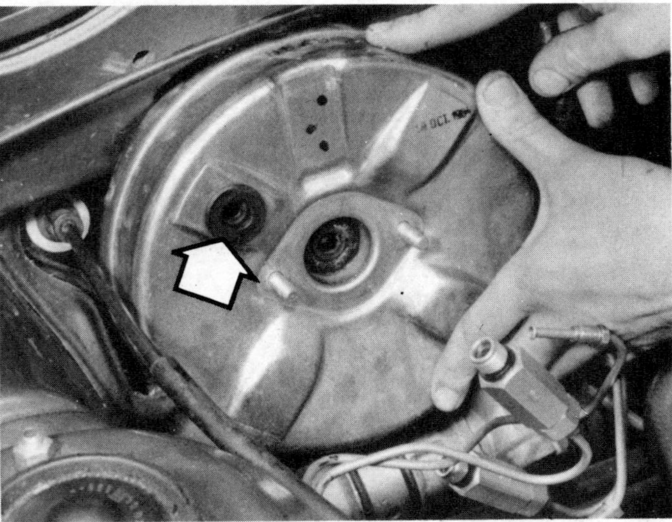

20.8B Fit the servo with the vacuum connector (arrowed) positioned as shown

Fig. 9.36 Three servo mounting nuts (arrowed) – LHD (Sec 20)

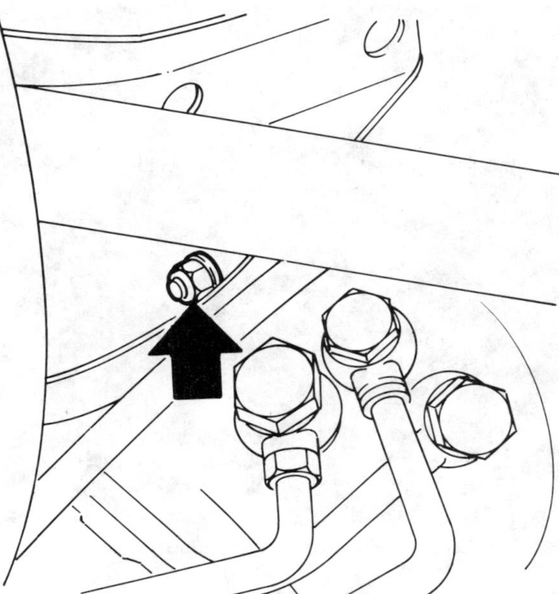

Fig. 9.37 Servo mounting nut (arrowed) obscured by steering gear – LHD (Sec 20)

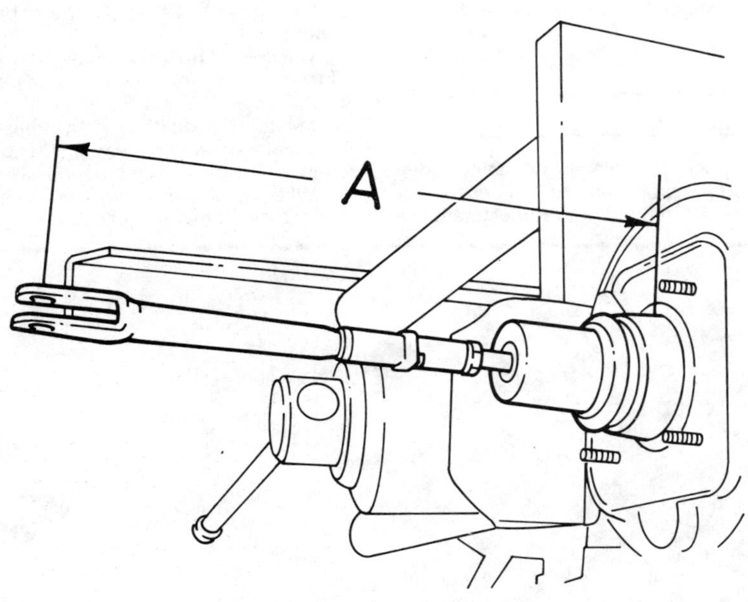

Fig. 9.38 Servo clevis adjustment – LHD (Sec 20)

A = 278.5 mm (10.97 in)

Left-hand drive

9 The procedure is similar to that just described, but access to the servo bracket fastenings is much easier (Fig. 9.36). If power steering is fitted, a flexible head socket drive will be needed to reach the lower nut without disturbing the steering gear. On all models it will be necessary to remove thé windscreen washer reservoir.

10 When transferring the clevis and threaded sleeve to the new servo, set the clevis-to-servo distance as shown in Fig. 9.38.

21 Brake pedal – removal and refitting

1 Remove the stop-lamp switch by turning it 90° left or right and withdrawing it from its bracket (photo).

2 Unhook the pedal return spring.

3 Detach the clevis from the brake pedal by removing the clevis pin retainer (split pin or spring clip) and pushing the pin out.

21.1 Stop-lamp switch 'keyhole' mounting (arrowed)

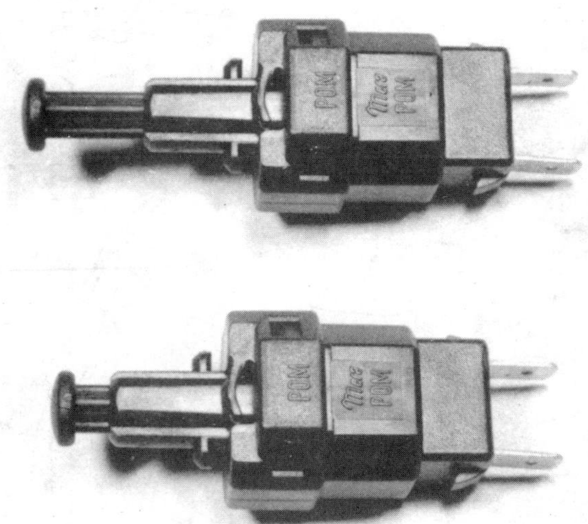

21.6 Stop-lamp switch plunger in extended position (top) and after fitting (bottom)

4 Remove the split pin from the end of the brake pedal shaft. Undo the shaft nut, remove the washer and push the shaft out towards the steering column. The pedal can now be removed.
5 Refit in the reverse order to removal, using new split pins or other safety securing devices.
6 Before fitting the stop-lamp switch, pull its plunger out as far as it will go. The switch will adjust itself once it is fitted (photo).

22 Handbrake – adjustment

1 Normal adjustment of the handbrake takes place automatically due to the self-adjusting mechanism of the rear brakes. To compensate for cable stretch, or after a new cable has been fitted or the adjustment has otherwise been disturbed, proceed as follows.
2 Chock the front wheels, release the handbrake and raise and support the rear of the vehicle so that the rear wheels are clear of the ground.
3 Tighten the nut on the handbrake cable yoke until the rear wheels start to become stiff to turn, then back it off until they are free again (photo).
4 Check that the handbrake starts to take effect at the second notch of lever movement, and is fully applied by the fourth or fifth notch.
5 A further check may be made by removing the plug in the brake backplate (Fig. 9.39). When adjustment is correct, the pin on the handbrake operating lever is clear of the shoe web by approximately 3 mm (0.12 in) with the handbrake released.
6 When adjustment is correct, lower the vehicle, apply the handbrake and remove the wheel chocks.

22.3 Handbrake cable adjusting nut (arrowed) on yoke

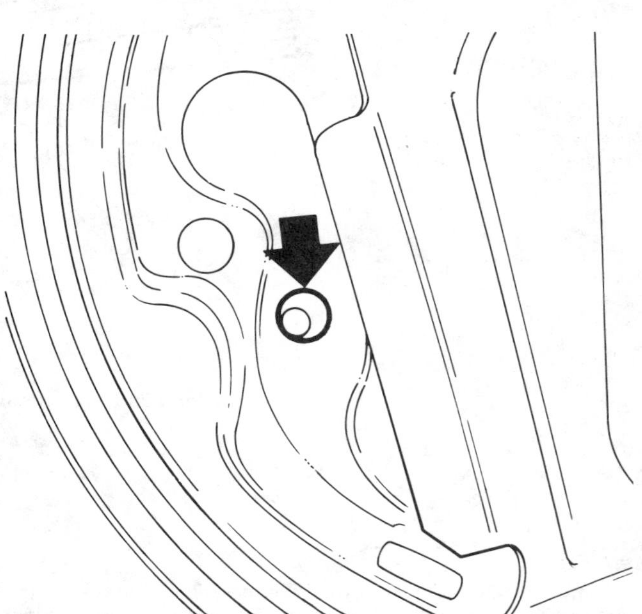

Fig. 9.39 Handbrake lever pin (arrowed) visible through inspection hole (Sec 22)

23 Handbrake cable – removal and refitting

1 Unscrew the yoke adjustment nut completely and remove the yoke.
2 Remove the brake drums, as described in Section 8.
3 Free the cable from the brackets on the underbody, fuel tank and rear axle.
4 Unhook the ends of the inner cable from the operating levers on the rear brakes.
5 Prise out the retaining ring and free the plastic sleeve from each brake backplate.
6 Withdraw the cable from the backplates and remove it.
7 Refit in the reverse order to removal. Note that the dark cable guide is fitted uppermost at the yoke.
8 Adjust the rear brakes by repeated applications of the footbrake – see Section 8 – then adjust the handbrake, as described in Section 22.

24 Handbrake lever – removal and refitting

1 Unscrew the yoke adjustment nut completely and remove the yoke. Also remove the rubber boot from the pull-rod.
2 Remove the front passenger seat (RHD) or driver's seat (LHD) by unbolting its rails from the floor.
3 Free the centre console by removing its single securing screw, which is concealed by a plastic plug. Remove the electric window and/or electric mirror switches, when fitted, then slide the console rearwards to free it and lift it off the handbrake lever.
4 Cut the carpet, as shown in Fig. 9.40.
5 Remove the two securing bolts and withdraw the handbrake lever (photo).
6 The handbrake warning switch can be unbolted from the lever. The ratchet pawl and segment can be renewed if facilities exist for removing and refitting their fastening bushes and rivets.
7 Commence refitting by bolting the handbrake lever in place. Tighten the bolts to the specified torque.

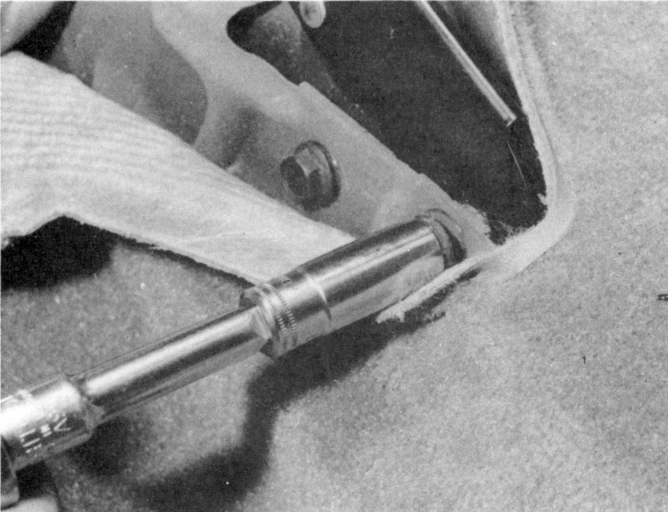

24.5 Unbolting the handbrake lever

8 Secure the carpet with glue and/or sticky tape. (The cut area will be covered by the console.)
9 Refit and secure the console, and its switches when applicable.
10 Refit and secure the front seat.
11 Refit the rubber boot and yoke. Adjust the handbrake, as described in Section 22.

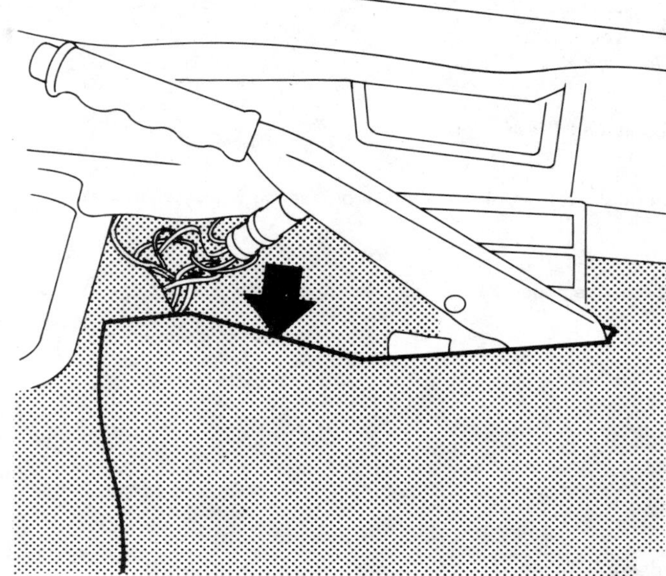

Fig. 9.40 Cut the carpet at the area arrowed (Sec 24)

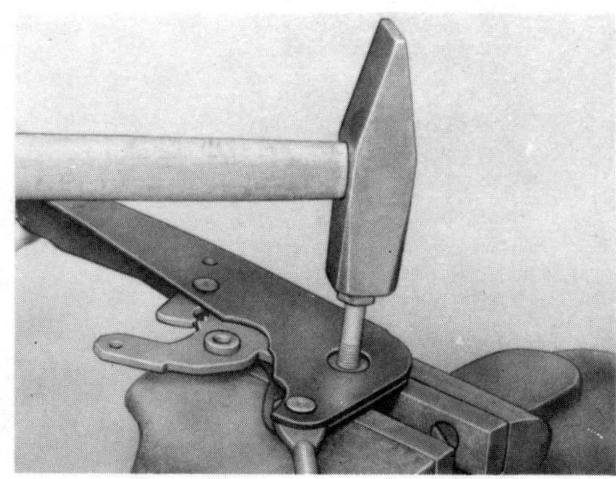

Fig. 9.41 Removing the handbrake lever pivot sleeve (Sec 24)

Fault diagnosis overleaf

25 Fault diagnosis – braking system

Before diagnosing faults from the following chart, check that braking irregularities are not caused by:

Uneven and incorrect tyre pressures
Wear in the steering mechanism
Defects in the suspension or shock absorbers

Symptom	Reason(s)
Excessive pedal travel	Rear brake self-adjusters faulty Air in hydraulic system Faulty master cylinder
Brake pedal feels spongy	Air in hydraulic system Faulty master cylinder
Judder felt through brake pedal or steering wheel when braking	Excessive run-out or distortion of front discs or rear drums Brake pads or linings worn Brake backplate or disc caliper loose
Excessive pedal pressure required to stop car	Faulty servo unit, disconnected or damaged vacuum hose Brake pads or linings worn or contaminated Brake shoes incorrectly fitted Incorrect grade of pads or linings fitted Failure of one hydraulic circuit
Brakes pull to one side	Brake pads or linings worn or contaminated Wheel cylinder or caliper piston seized Brake caliper seized on sliding sleeves Brake pads or linings renewed on one side only Brake disc or drum refinished or renewed on one side only
Brakes binding	Brake shoe return springs weak or broken Incorrect handbrake adjustment Wheel cylinder or caliper piston seized Faulty master cylinder
Rear wheels locking under normal braking	Rear brake linings contaminated Faulty pressure regulating valve(s)
Brakes squeal	Pads or shoes badly worn Non-original pads or shoes fitted

Chapter 10 Suspension

For modifications, and information applicable to later models, see Supplement at end of manual

Contents

Specifications

General

Front suspension type	Independent, MacPherson strut, with anti-roll bar on most models
Rear suspension type	Semi-independent, trailing link with coil springs and telescopic shock absorbers. Level control system optional; anti-roll bar on some models
Vehicle condition for 'laden' measurements	70 kg (154 lb) in each front seat, fuel tank roughly half full, level control system (when fitted) inflated to 1 bar (14.5 lbf/in^2)

Front wheel alignment

Toe	See Chapter 8 Specifications
Camber (non-adjustable):	
Laden value	−1° 15′ + 0° 15′
Difference between sides	1° max
Castor (non-adjustable):	
Laden value – Hatchback	+0° 45′ to +2° 45′
Laden value – Estate	0° 00′ to +2° 00′
Difference between sides	1° max

Rear wheel alignment

Camber (non-adjustable):	
Laden value	0° to −1°
Difference between sides	0° 30′ max
Toe (non-adjustable):	
Laden value	0° to 0° 40′ (0 to 4 mm) toe-in
Difference between sides	0° 15′ max

Wheels and tyres

Wheel size	$4^1/_2$J x 13, 5J x 13, $5^1/_2$J x 13 or $5^1/_2$J x 14
Tyre sizes:	
$4^1/_2$J x 13	145 SR 13-74S
5J x 13	155 SR 13-78S or 155 TR 13-78T
$5^1/_2$J x 13	155 SR 13-78 S, 155 TR 13-78 T, 175/70 SR 13-80 S, 175/70 TR 13-80 T, or 175/70 HR 13-80 H
$5^1/_2$J x 14	175/65 TR 14-81 T, or 185/60 HR 14-82 H

Tyre pressures

Pressures for cold tyres in bar (lbf/in²). These figures are taken from the maker's latest technical data and may differ from those given in the driver's handbook.

Hatchback – up to 3 passengers:	**Front**	**Rear**
1200/1300, 145 SR 13	1.9 (28)	1.7 (25)
1200/1300, 155 SR 13	1.8 (26)	1.6 (23)
1200/1300, 165 SR 13	1.7 (25)	1.7 (25)
1200/1300, 175/70 SR 13	1.8 (26)	1.6 (23)
1600 (all tyre sizes)	2.0 (29)	1.8 (26)
1800 (all tyre sizes)	2.1 (31)	1.9 (28)
Hatchback – full load:	**Front**	**Rear**
1200/1300, 145 SR 13	2.0 (29)	2.3 (33)
1200/1300, 155 SR 13	1.9 (28)	2.1 (31)
1200/1300, 165 SR 13	1.8 (26)	2.0 (29)
1200/1300, 175/70 SR 13	1.9 (28)	2.1 (31)
1600 (all tyre sizes)	2.1 (31)	2.3 (33)
1800 (all tyre sizes)	2.2 (32)	2.4 (35)
Estate and Van – up to 3 passengers:	**Front**	**Rear**
1300 (all tyre sizes)	1.8 (26)	1.8 (26)
1600 (all tyre sizes)	2.0 (29)	2.0 (29)
Estate and Van – up to 4 passengers plus 60 kg (132 lb), or equivalent	**Front**	**Rear**
1300 (all tyre sizes)	1.9 (28)	2.3 (33)
1600 (all tyre sizes)	2.1 (31)	2.5 (36)
Estate and Van – full load:	**Front**	**Rear**
1300 (all tyre sizes)	2.0 (29)	2.8 (41)
1600 (all tyre sizes)	2.1 (31)	3.0 (44)

Torque wrench settings

	Nm	lbf ft
Front suspension		
Control arm pivot bolt	140	103
Control arm clamp bolts	70	52
Control arm balljoint pin nut	70	52
Control arm balljoint securing nuts	65	48
Suspension strut top mounting nuts	30	22
Suspension strut piston rod nut	55	41
Suspension strut ring nut	200	148
Steering tie-rod balljoint nut	60	44
Anti-roll bar brackets	40	30
Rear suspension		
Axle arm mountings to underbody	105	77
Rear anti-roll to rear axle	80	59
Shock absorber lower mountings:		
Hatchback	70	52
Estate	10	7
Shock absorber top mountings:		
Hatchback	See text	
Estate	10	7
Rear hub bearing nut:		
Stage 1	25	18
Stage 2	See text	
Wheels		
Wheel bolts	90	66

1 General description

The front suspension is fully independent. It consists of MacPherson struts; the coil springs surrounding the shock absorbers. An anti-roll bar is fitted to most models.

Rear suspension is by axle tube and twin trailing arms. Coil springs and telescopic shock absorbers are used, mounted independently of each other. Again, an anti-roll bar is fitted to most models.

A driver-operated level control system is available as an option on some models. The system enables the vehicle ride height and attitude to be maintained regardless of loading.

Steel roadwheels are standard equipment, with light alloy wheels available as an option. Radial tyres are standard fitting on all models.

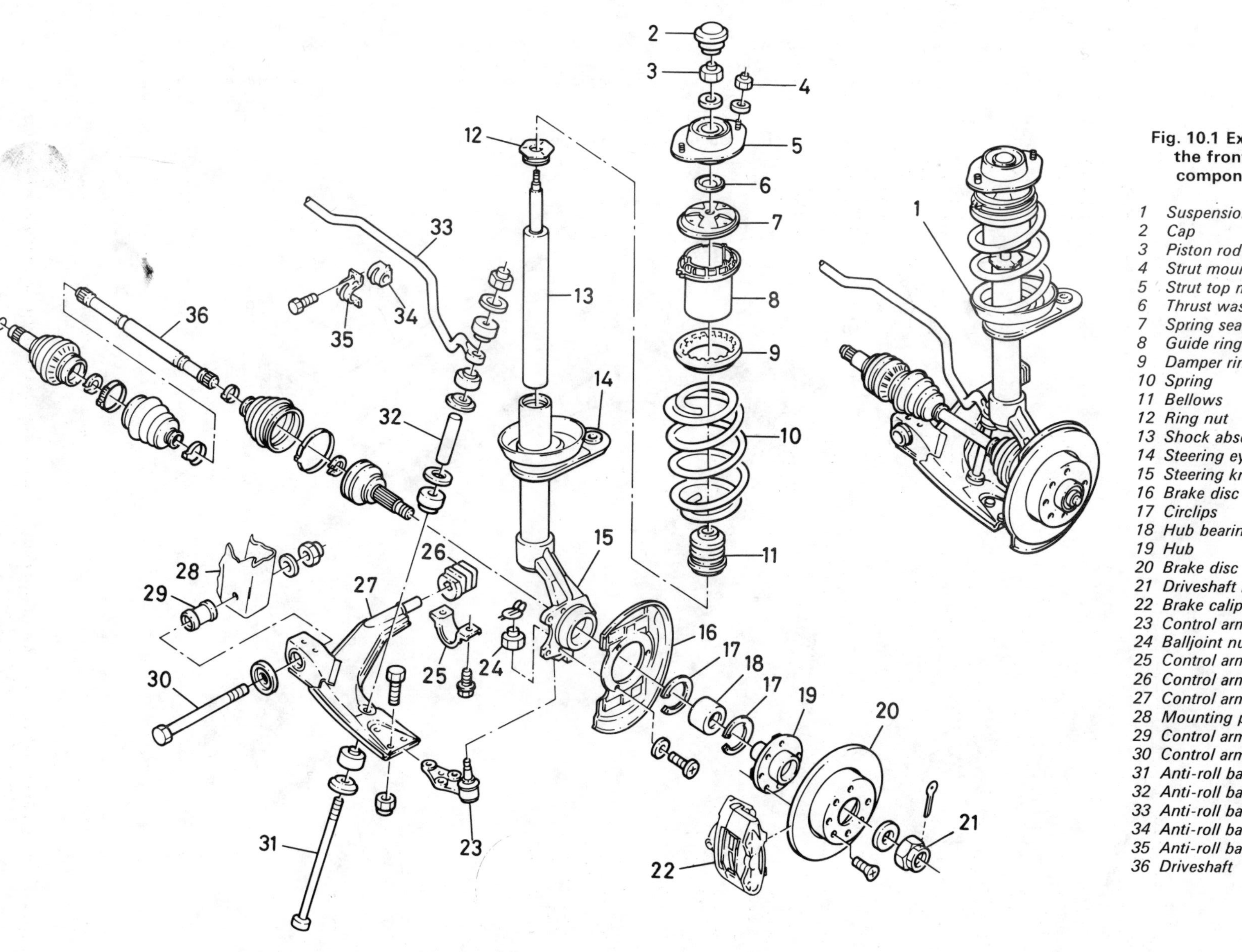

Fig. 10.1 Exploded view of the front suspension components (Sec 1)

1 Suspension assembly (LH)
2 Cap
3 Piston rod nut
4 Strut mounting nut
5 Strut top mounting
6 Thrust washer
7 Spring seat
8 Guide ring
9 Damper ring
10 Spring
11 Bellows
12 Ring nut
13 Shock absorber cartridge
14 Steering eye
15 Steering knuckle
16 Brake disc shield
17 Circlips
18 Hub bearing
19 Hub
20 Brake disc
21 Driveshaft nut
22 Brake caliper
23 Control arm balljoint
24 Balljoint nut
25 Control arm clamp
26 Control arm rear bush
27 Control arm
28 Mounting point
29 Control arm pivot bush
30 Control arm pivot bolt
31 Anti-roll bar link bolt
32 Anti-roll bar link
33 Anti-roll bar
34 Anti-roll bar mounting
35 Anti-roll bar clamp
36 Driveshaft

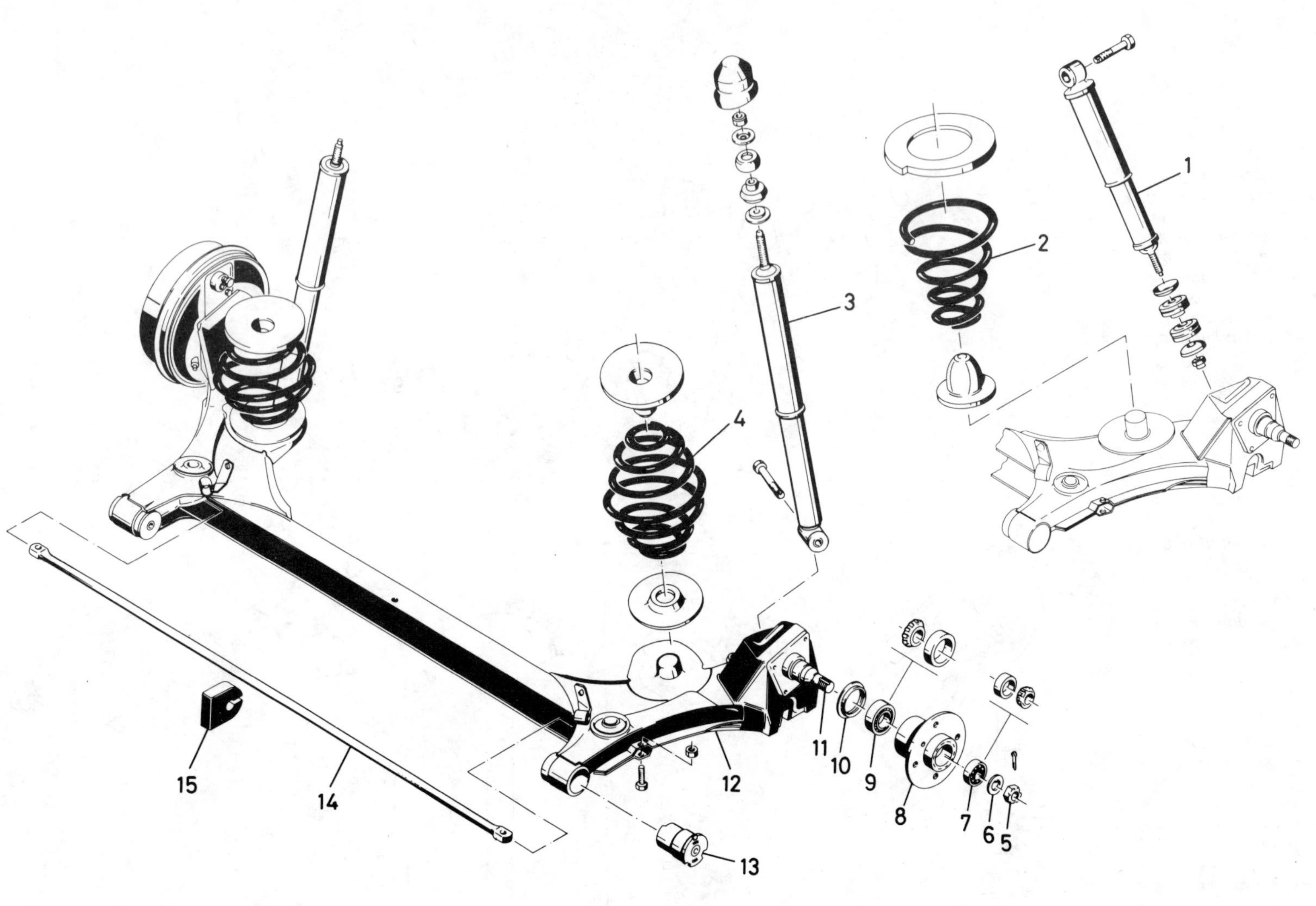

Fig. 10.2 Exploded view of rear suspension components (Sec 1)

1 *Shock absorber (Estate)*
2 *Spring (Estate)*
3 *Shock absorber (Hatchback)*
4 *Spring (Hatchback)*
5 *Hub nut*
6 *Thrust washer*
7 *Outer bearing*
8 *Hub*
9 *Inner bearing*
10 *Oil seal*
11 *Stub axle*
12 *Axle arm*
13 *Axle arm bush*
14 *Anti-roll bar*
15 *Rubber damper*

2 Maintenance and inspection

1 Weekly, or before a long journey, the tyre pressures should be checked and corrected if necessary. Investigate regular or substantial pressure loss without delay. For more details see Section 18.
2 At every major service interval, make a thorough inspection of the front and rear suspension, using the following as a guide.

Front suspension

3 Raise and securely support the front of the car.
4 Visually inspect the control arm balljoint dust covers for splits or deterioration and renew the balljoint assembly, as described in Section 8, if any damage is apparent.
5 Grasp the roadwheel at the 12 o'clock and 6 o'clock positions and try to rock it. Very slight free play may be felt, but if the movement is appreciable further investigation is necessary to determine the source. Continue rocking the wheel while an assistant depresses the footbrake. If the movement is now eliminated or significantly reduced, it is likely that the hub bearings are at fault. If the free play is still evident with the footbrake depressed, then there is wear in the suspension joints or mountings. Pay close attention to the control arm balljoint and control arm inner mounting. Renew any worn components, as described in the appropriate Sections of this Chapter.
6 Using a large screwdriver or flat bar, check for wear in the anti-roll bar mountings (where fitted) and control arm inner mountings by carefully levering against these components. Some movement is to be expected as the mountings are made of rubber, but excessive wear should be obvious. Renew any bushes that are worn.

Rear suspension

7 Jack up the rear of the car and securely support it on axle stands. Release the handbrake.
8 Visually inspect the rear suspension components, attachments and linkages for any obvious signs of wear or damage.
9 Grasp the roadwheel at the 12 o'clock and 6 o'clock positions and try to rock it. Any excess movement here indicates incorrect adjustment or wear in the rear hub bearings. Wear may also be accompanied by a rumbling sound when the wheel is spun, or a noticeable roughness if the wheel is turned slowly. Adjustment and repair procedures are described in Sections 10 and 11.

Wheels and tyres

10 Carefully inspect each tyre, including the spare, for signs of uneven wear, lumps, bulges or damage to the sidewalls or tread face. Refer to Section 18 for further details.
11 Check the wheel rims for distortion, damage and excessive run-out. Also make sure that the balance weights are secure with no obvious signs that any are missing.
12 Check the tightness of the wheel bolts by slackening each one in turn and immediately retightening it to the specified torque. This ensures not only that the bolts are tight, but that they can be undone in the event of a puncture.

Shock absorbers

13 Check for any signs of fluid leakage around the front suspension strut or rear shock absorber body. Should any fluid be noticed the shock abssorber or strut is defective internally and renewal is necessary.
14 The efficiency of the shock absorber may be checked by bouncing the car at each corner. Generally speaking the body will return to its normal position and stop after being depressed. If it rises and returns on a rebound, the shock absorber or suspension strut is probably suspect. Examine also the upper and lower mountings for any sign of wear. Refer to the appropriate Sections of this Chapter for renewal procedures.

Level control system

15 Refer to Section 17.

3 Front suspension strut – removal and refitting

1 Slacken the front wheel bolts, raise and support the vehicle and remove the front wheel.
2 Remove the split pin and undo the driveshaft retaining nut. Refer to Chapter 7, Section 3 for details. Remove the nut and washer.
3 Unbolt the brake caliper and tie it up out of the way so that the hydraulic hose is not strained. Refer to Chapter 9, Section 4 or 5, for details.
4 Disconnect the tie-rod and control arm balljoints using a proprietary balljoint separator.
5 Push the driveshaft out of the hub and tie it up out of the way. If difficulty is experienced, refer to Chapter 7, Section 3. Remember that the vehicle must not be moved on its wheels without the hub bearing being clamped.
6 Undo the two securing nuts from the suspension turret and remove the strut downwards.
7 Commence refitting by offering the strut to the turret. Secure it with new self-locking nuts, tightened to the specified torque.
8 Lubricate the driveshaft splines and pass the driveshaft into the hub. Fit a new washer and castellated nut, but only tighten the nut finger tight at this stage.
9 Reconnect the control arm balljoint. Tighten the pin nut to the specified torque and secure it with a new split pin.
10 Reconnect the tie-rod balljoint. Fit a new self-locking nut and tighten it to the specified torque.
11 Clean out the brake caliper mounting bolt holes, then refit the caliper and secure with new bolts coated with thread locking compound. Tighten the bolts to the specified torque – see Chapter 9 Specifications. On GMF calipers, fit new bolt caps.
12 Tighten the driveshaft nut, as described in Chapter 7, Section 3.
13 Refit the roadwheel, lower the vehicle and tighten the wheel bolts.

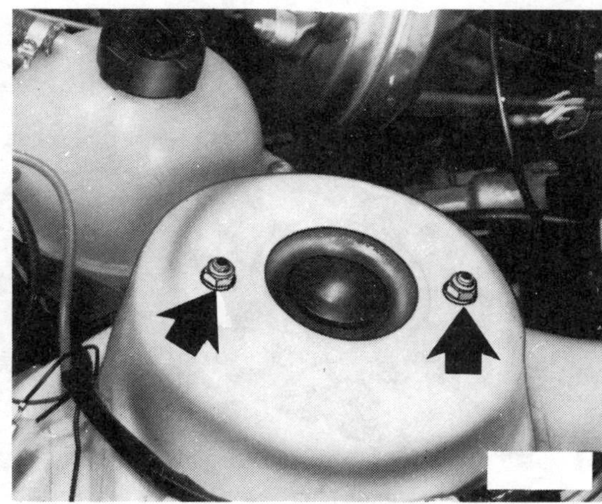

Fig. 10.3 Suspension strut securing nuts (arrowed) (Sec 3)

4 Front hub bearings – renewal

1 Remove the front suspension strut, as described in the previous Section.
2 Remove the securing screw and take off the brake disc.
3 Support the steering knuckle and press or drive out the hub. Alternatively, draw off the hub by screwing two wheel bolts onto progressively thicker packing pieces (photos).
4 Remove the brake disc shield.
5 Remove the two circlips (photo) and press or drive the bearing outer races out of the steering knuckle.
6 If the bearing inner race stayed on the hub, press or pull it off.
7 Fit the outboard circlip to its groove in the steering knuckle so that the ends of the circlip will point downwards when the strut is installed.
8 Press the new bearing into position, acting only on the outer race, until it contacts the outboard circlip.
9 Fit the inboard circlip, again with the ends pointing downwards.
10 Refit the brake disc shield.

4.3A Removing the hub from the carrier

4.3B Hub removed from carrier

4.5 Removing a hub bearing circlip

11 Support the bearing inner race with a tube and press the hub into position.
12 Refit and secure the brake disc.
13 Refit the suspension strut.

5 Front suspension strut – overhaul

Note: *A spring compressor of sound construction is essential for this work. Use of makeshift or unsuitable tools may result in injury.*
1 Remove the strut, as described in Section 3.
2 Clamp the strut in a vice. Fit the spring compressor and tighten it to unload the pressure on the upper seat.
3 Hold the flats on the piston rod to stop it rotating and unscrew the piston rod nut. A 19 mm ring spanner with a deep offset will be needed.
4 Remove the top mounting and ball-bearing.
5 Carefully release the spring compressor. Remove the spring seat, guide ring, damper ring and bellows, followed by the spring itself.

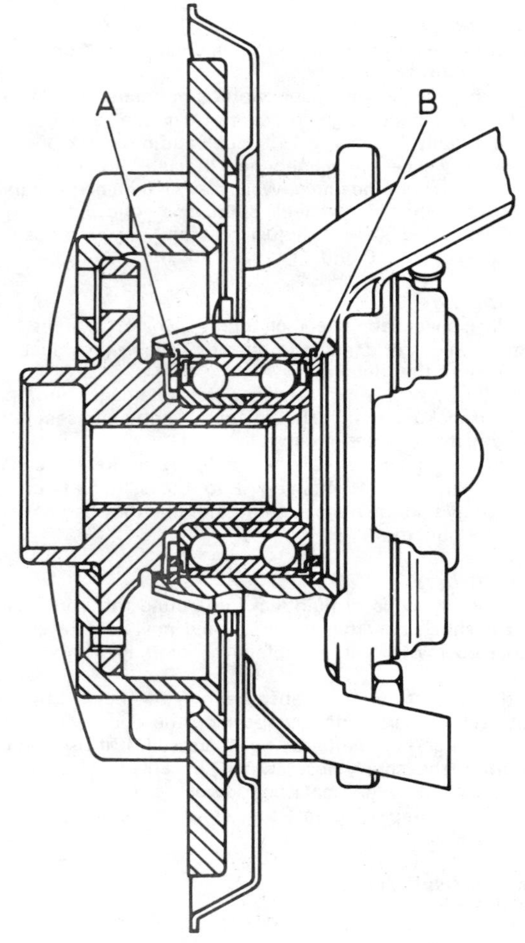

Fig. 10.4 Sectional view of front hub (Sec 4)

A Outboard circlip *B Inboard circlip*

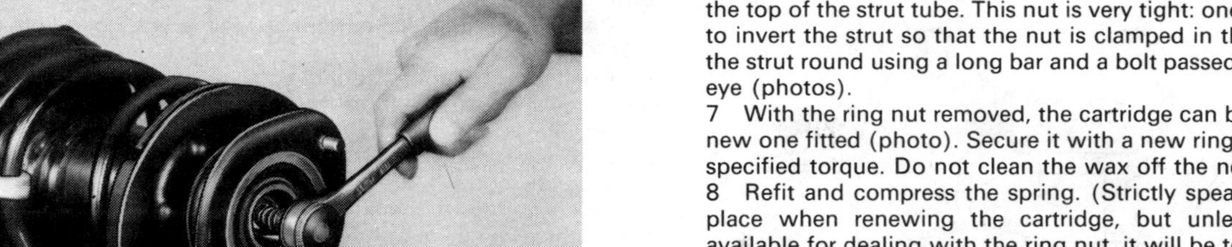

Fig. 10.5 Unscrewing the piston rod nut (Sec 5)

6 To remove the shock absorber cartridge, unscrew the ring nut from the top of the strut tube. This nut is very tight: one way of undoing it is to invert the strut so that the nut is clamped in the vice, then levering the strut round using a long bar and a bolt passed through the steering eye (photos).

7 With the ring nut removed, the cartridge can be withdrawn and the new one fitted (photo). Secure it with a new ring nut, tightened to the specified torque. Do not clean the wax off the new nut.

8 Refit and compress the spring. (Strictly speaking it can be left in place when renewing the cartridge, but unless special tools are available for dealing with the ring nut, it will be too much in the way.)

9 Fit the bellows, damper ring, guide ring and spring seat. Note that the lug on the spring seat points forwards (in the installed position) on the left-hand strut, and backwards on the right-hand strut.

10 Lubricate the top mounting ball-bearing with grease to GM spec 19 41 574. (The bearing cannot be renewed independently of the mounting).

11 Fit the top mounting to the strut piston rod, making sure that the lower thrust washer is fitted with the raised edge upwards (Fig. 10.7). Hold the piston rod still and fit a new self-locking nut; tighten the nut to the specified torque.

5.6A One method of unscrewing the strut ring nut

5.6B Removing the strut ring nut

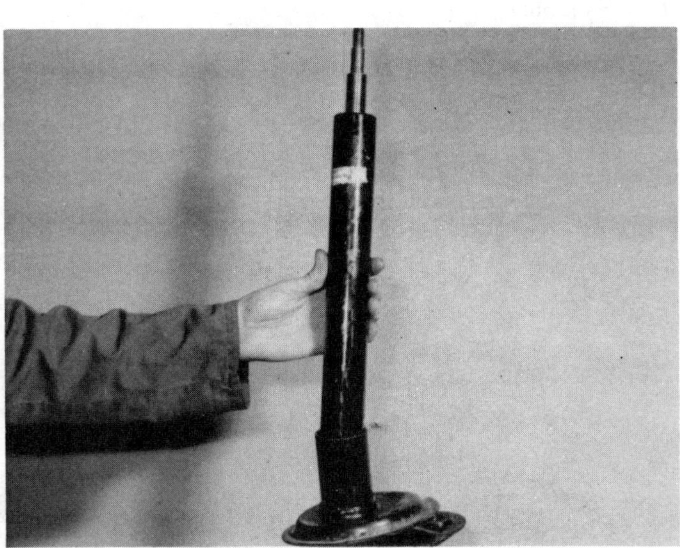

5.7 Removing the shock absorber cartridge

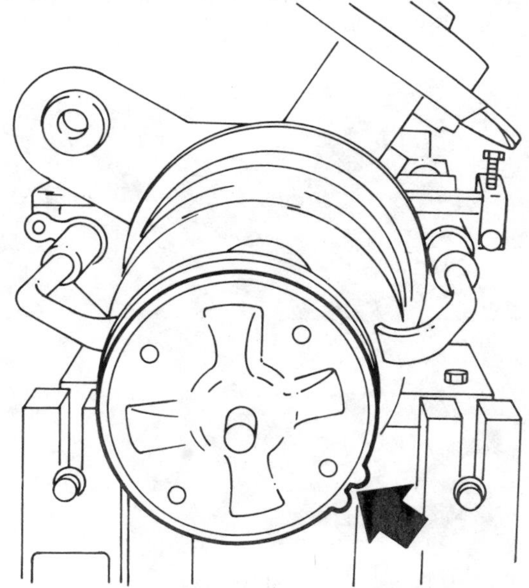

Fig. 10.6 Lug on spring seat (arrowed) points forwards on LH strut, rearwards on RH strut (Sec 5)

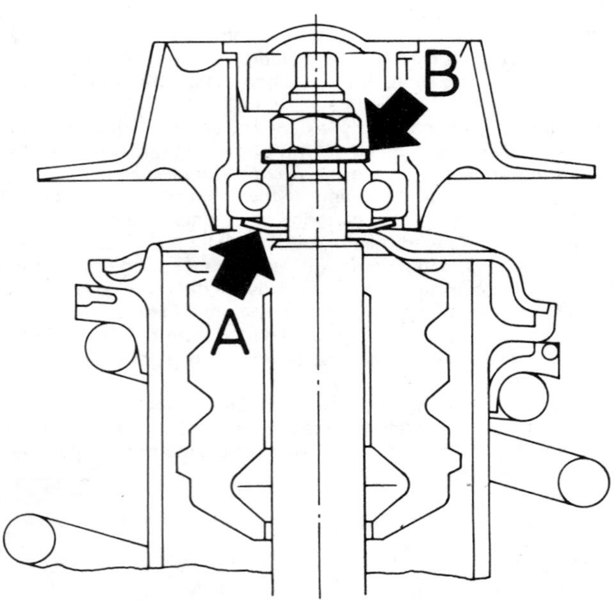

Fig. 10.7 Sectional view of strut top mounting (Sec 5)

A Lower thrust washer *B Upper thrust washer*

12 Release the spring compressor. Make sure that the ends of the springs are correctly seated.
13 Release the strut from the vice and refit it to the vehicle, as described in Section 3.
14 If new springs or shock absorbers are being fitted, it is good practice to fit new components to both sides. A great variety of springs is available: consult your GM dealer to be sure of obtaining the correct ones.

6 Front suspension control arm – removal and refitting

1 Slacken the front wheel bolts, raise and support the vehicle and remove the front wheel.
2 When fitted, unbolt the anti-roll bar from the control arm.
3 Remove the split pin and slacken the control arm balljoint nut (photo). Separate the balljoint with a proprietary separator and remove the nut.

6.3 Control arm balljoint nut (arrowed)

4 Unscrew the clamp bolts and the pivot bolts from the inboard end of the arm (photo). Withdraw the arm.
5 Before refitting, clean out out the clamp bolt holes with a tap or a bolt with a slot cut in it.
6 Commence refitting by bolting the arm loosely into position. Fit the pivot bolt with its head facing towards the front of the vehicle and use a new self-locking nut.
7 Use new clamp bolts and coat their threads with locking compound.
8 Jack up under the control arm so that it is more or less horizontal, then tighten the pivot bolt to the specified torque.
9 Tighten the clamp bolts to the specified torque. Lower the jack under the control arm.
10 Tighten the balljoint pin nut to the specified torque and secure with a new split pin.
11 Reconnect the anti-roll bar (if applicable). Refer to Section 9 for tightening procedure.
12 Refit the roadwheel, lower the vehicle and tighten the wheel bolts.

7 Control arm bushes – renewal

1 Remove the control arm, as described in the previous Section.
2 Press out the front bush using suitable pieces of tube and a vice or a long bolt and washers. The bush should be removed from front to rear.
3 Fit the new front bush in the same direction (front to rear), using liquid detergent as a lubricant. The inner sleeve collar faces rearwards. When correctly fitted, the bush should overhang equally on both sides.
4 Support the front of the rear bush. Note which way round it is fitted, then press the arm out of it.
5 Lubricate the rear spigot with liquid detergent, then press on the new rear bush, making sure it is the right way round (flattened surface towards balljoint pin).
6 Refit the control arm, as described in Section 6.

8 Control arm balljoint – renewal

1 Remove the control arm, as described in Section 6.
2 Drill out the rivets which secure the old balljoint. Use a pillar drill with a 12 mm bit, and drill accurately into a centre punch mark on each rivet head. Have this work done professionally if need be: sloppy drilling will render the arm scrap.
3 Fit the new balljoint and secure it with the bolts and self-locking nuts provided. The nuts should be fitted on the underside of the arm. Tighten the nuts to the specified torque.
4 Refit the control arm, as described in Section 6.

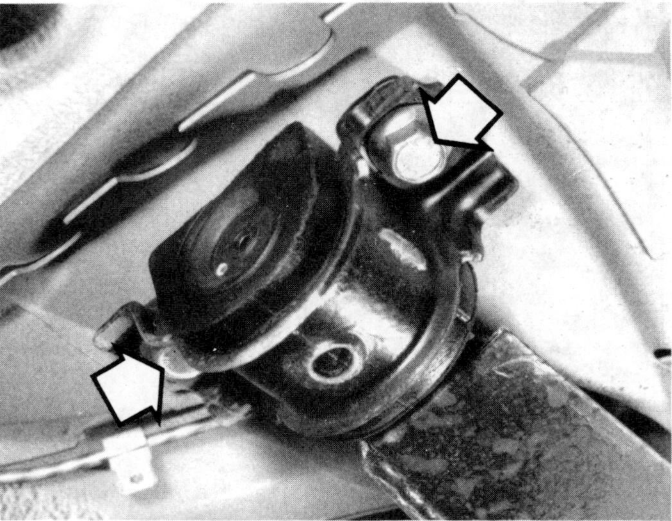

6.4 Control arm clamp bolts (arrowed)

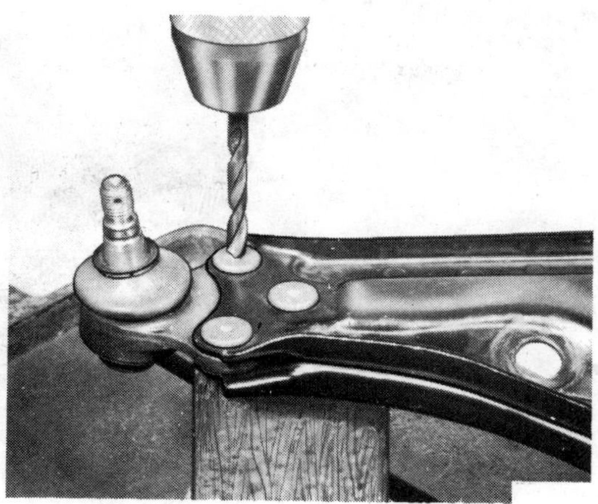

Fig. 10.8 Drilling out the control arm balljoint rivets (Sec 8)

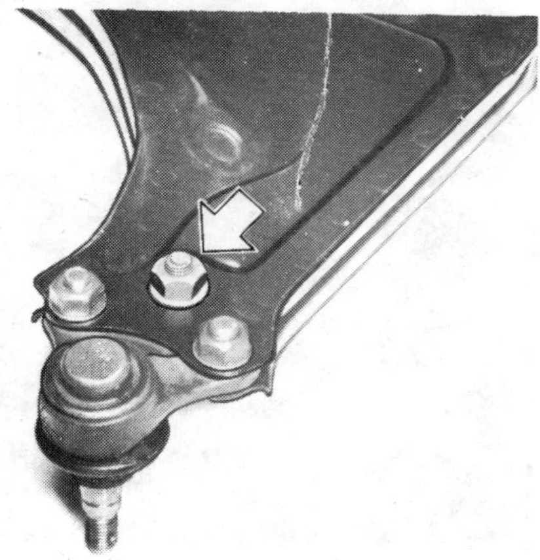

Fig. 10.9 Repair kit balljoint securing nuts (arrowed) on underside of arm (Sec 8)

9.2 Front anti-roll bar end link

9 Front anti-roll bar – removal and refitting

1 Raise and support the front of the vehicle.
2 Unbolt both ends of the anti-roll bar from the control arms (photo).
3 Unbolt the two brackets from the bulkhead.
4 Remove the anti-roll bar through one of the wheel arches, turning the steering wheel as necessary to obtain sufficient clearance.
5 Renew the rubber mountings as necessary. Use a silicone-based lubricant on the bulkhead bracket bushes.
6 When refitting, fasten the two brackets first; tightening their bolts to the specified torque.
7 Tighten the end mountings to achieve a dimension A, as shown in Fig. 10.10, using new self-locking nuts.
8 Lower the vehicle when the anti-roll bar is secured.

10 Rear hub bearings – adjustment

1 Chock the front wheels, engage a gear (or P) amd release the handbrake.

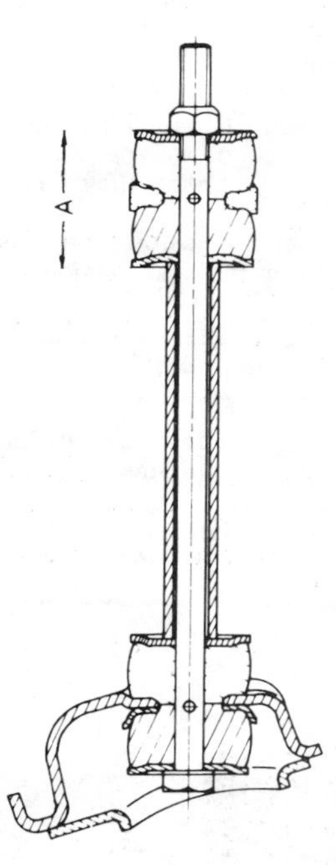

Fig. 10.10 Anti-roll bar link cushion setting (Sec 9)

A = 38 mm (1.5 in)

2 Remove the wheel trim. If the roadwheels have no central hole, slacken the wheel bolts.
3 Raise and support the rear of the vehicle so that the wheel is free to turn. If it has no central hole, remove it.
4 Prise off the hub grease cap using a stout screwdriver.
5 Remove the split pin from the hub nut. Tighten the nut to 25 Nm (18 lbf ft), at the same time turning the wheel or brake drum, in order to settle the bearings.
6 Slacken the hub nut until the thrust washer behind the nut can just be moved by poking it with a screwdriver. Do not lever or twist against the hub nut or brake drum when testing the washer for freedom of movement.
7 Insert a new split pin to secure the hub nut. If the split pin holes are not aligned, tighten the nut to align the nearest holes, temporarily insert the split pin and check to see if the washer can still be moved. If it

Fig. 10.11 Prising off the rear hub grease cap (Sec 10)

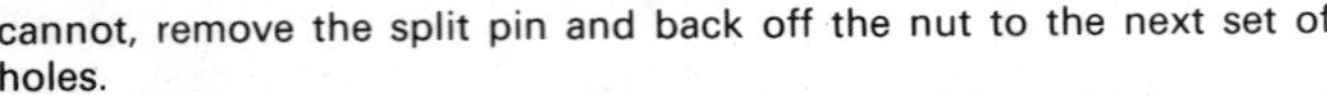

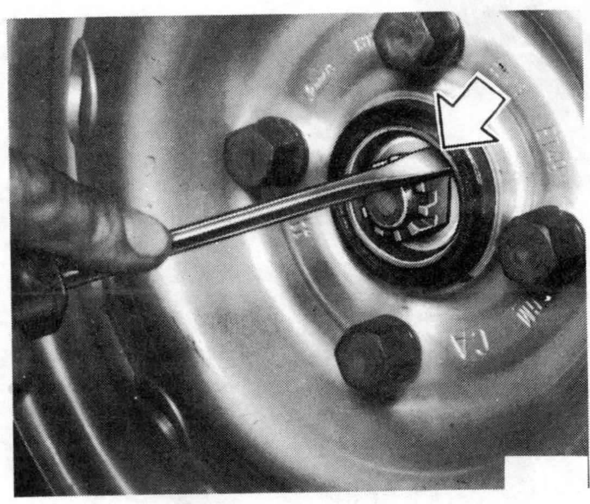

Fig. 10.12 Using a screwdriver (arrowed) to check for thrust washer free movement (Sec 10)

cannot, remove the split pin and back off the nut to the next set of holes.

8 When adjustment is correct, spread the legs of the split pin around the nut. Refit the grease cap, and the roadwheel is removed, and lower the vehicle. Tighten the wheel bolts if they were disturbed and refit the wheel trim.

9 If adjustment fails to cure noise or roughness, the bearings should be renewed, as described in the next Section.

11 Rear hub bearings – renewal

1 Remove the brake drum, as described in Chapter 9, Section 8.

2 Prise off the hub grease cap, remove the split pin and undo the hub nut (photo).

3 Pull the hub off the stub axle. Catch the thrust washer and the outer bearing race, which will be displaced.

4 Prise the oil seal out of the inboard side of the hub.

5 Extract the inner bearing race, then press or drive the bearing outer tracks from the hub.

6 Clean out the old grease from the hub cavity. Make sure the bearing seats are undamaged, then press or drive the new tracks squarely into the hub.

7 Generously grease the bearing races, the new oil seal and the bearing tracks. Half fill the space between the tracks with grease.

8 Fit the inner race and then the oil seal; lips inwards. Tap the seal into place with a tube or a piece of wood.

9 Fit the hub to the stub axle, being careful not to damage the oil seal. Fit the outer bearing race, the thrust washer and the castellated nut (photos).

10 Tighten the nut finger tight, then refit the brake drum, as described in Chapter 9, Section 8.

11 Adjust the bearings, as described in the previous Section.

Fig. 10.13 Removing the rear hub (Sec 11)

Fig. 10.14 Prising out the rear hub oil seal (Sec 11)

11.2 Rear hub nut split pin

11.9A Fit the outer bearing race ...

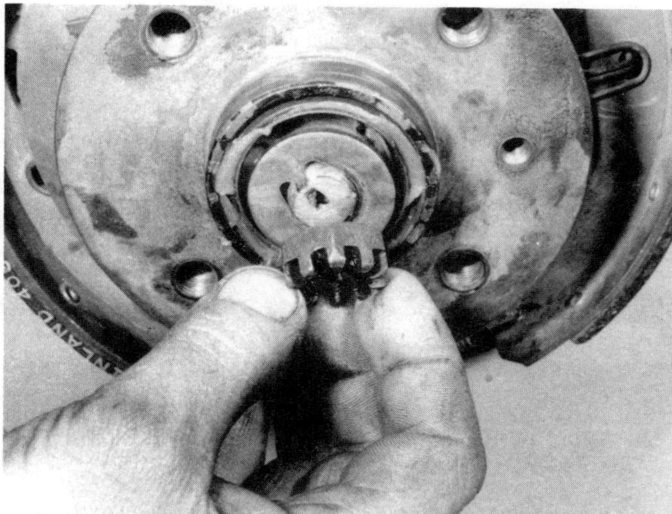

11.9B ... the washer and the castellated nut

12 Rear shock absorbers – removal and refitting

Hatchback

1 Shock absorbers should be renewed in pairs, but they should only be removed from one side at a time.

2 Inside the vehicle, remove the cap from the shock absorber top mounting. Grip the flats on the piston rod with pliers or a small spanner and unscrew the top mounting nut. Remove the nut, washer and rubber buffer (photo).

3 Raise and support the rear of the vehicle.

4 On vehicles with the level control system disconnect the pressure line from the shock absorber by undoing the union nut.

5 Unbolt the shock absorber lower mounting (photo). Free the shock absorber from the bracket and remove it from the vehicle.

6 Commence refitting by introducing the shock absorber to the lower mounting bracket. Use a plastic or wooden mallet if need be.

7 Wedge the shock absorber so that the lower mounting hole is aligned. Fit the lower mounting bolt, tapping it gently through the shock absorber eye, and tighten it to the specified torque.

8 Partly lower the vehicle, guiding the top of the shock absorber into position. Make sure that the washer and rubber buffer for the underside of the top mounting are in position.

12.2 Rear shock absorber upper mounting – Hatchback

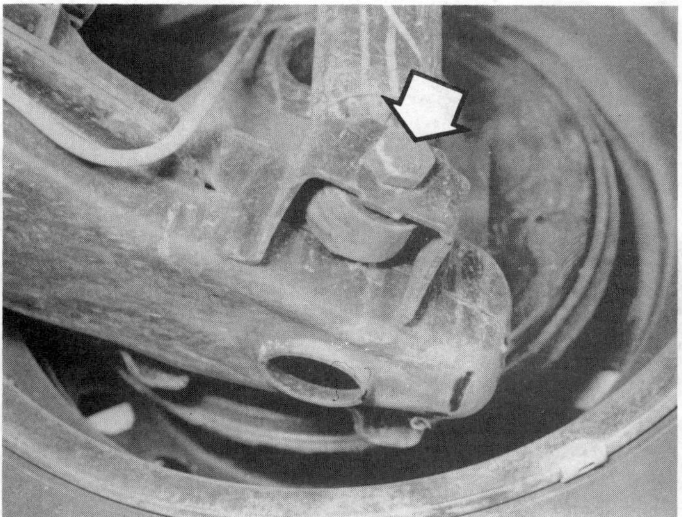

12.5 Rear shock absorber lower mounting bolt (arrowed) – Hatchback

Fig. 10.15 Prising the rear shock absorber out of its bracket (Sec 12)

9 Lower the vehicle to the ground. Fit the top mounting rubber buffer and washer. Tighten the mounting nut or nuts to achieve an exposed piston rod length as given in Fig. 10.16. Refit the cap.
10 Repeat the operations on the other side of the vehicle.

Estate and Van
11 Raise and support the rear of the vehicle.
12 On vehicles with the level control system, disconnect the pressure line from the shock absorber by undoing the union nut.
13 Unload the shock absorber mounting by jacking up under the axle arm. Remove the lower mounting nut, washer and rubber buffer (photo). Lower the jack.
14 Remove the top mounting bolt (photo) and extract the shock absorber from its mountings.
15 Commence refitting by securing the top end of the shock absorber, but only tighten the bolt loosely at first.
16 Secure the bottom mounting, making sure that the rubber buffers and washers are in position, and tighten the cap nut to the specified torque.
17 Tighten the top mounting to the specified torque.
18 Repeat the operations on the other side of the vehicle, then lower it to the ground.

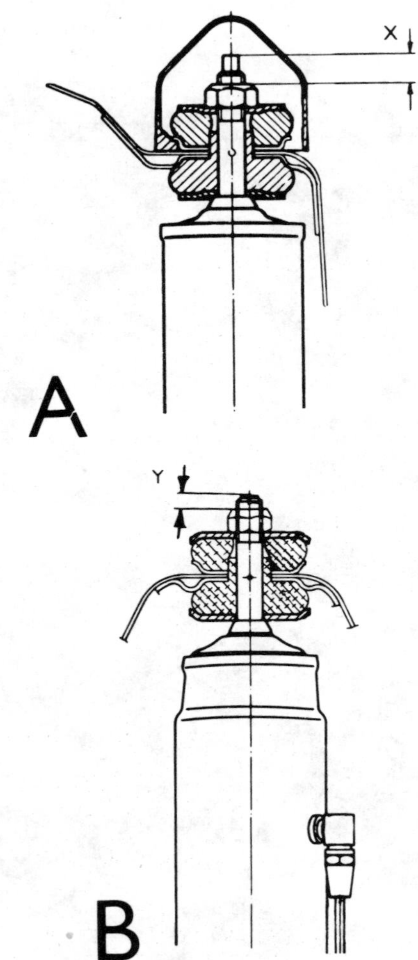

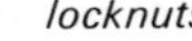

Fig. 10.16 Rear shock absorber top mounting setting (Sec 12)

A Without level control — *X = 9 mm (0.35 in)*
B With level control or two locknuts — *Y = 6 mm (0.24 in)*

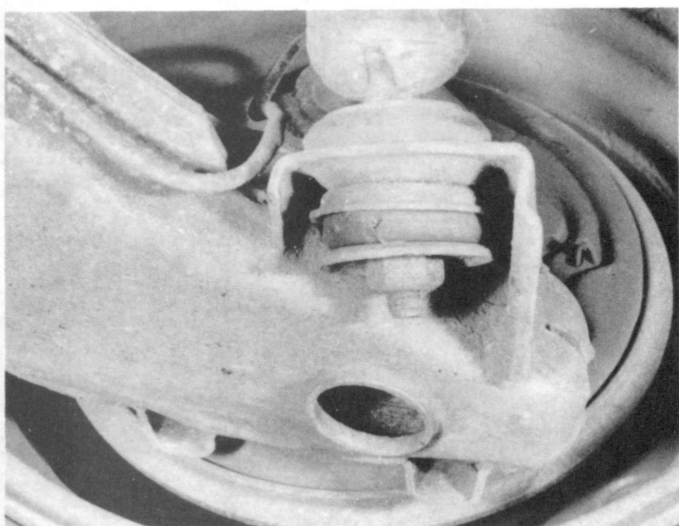

12.13 Rear shock absorber lower mounting – Estate

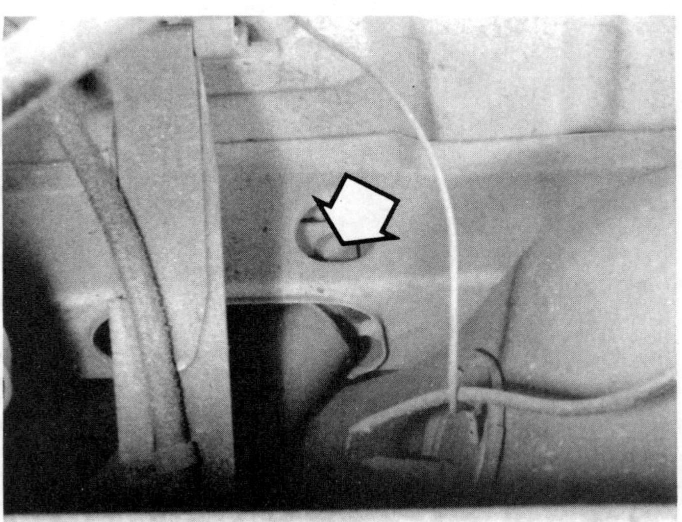

12.14 Rear shock absorber top mounting bolt (arrowed) – Estate

All models with level control

19 Reconnect the pressure line unions and inflate the system to 0.8 bar (11.6 lbf/in²).

13 Rear anti-roll bar – removal and refitting

1 Slacken the rear wheel bolts on one side only. Raise and support the rear of the vehicle and remove the roadwheel.
2 Remove the mounting nut and bolt from both ends of the anti-roll bar (photo).
3 Remove the rubber damper from the centre of the axle.
4 Remove the anti-roll bar from the side on which the wheel was removed. If it is reluctant to move, drive it from the other side.
5 Refit in the reverse order to removal. Use liquid detergent as a lubricant when fitting the rubber damper. Tighten the anti-roll bar mountings to the specified torque.

14 Rear springs – removal and refitting

1 Rear springs should be renewed in pairs.
2 On vehicles with a level control system, depressurize it at the filling valve.
3 Raise and support the rear of the vehicle.

Hatchback

4 Unload the shock absorber mounting on one side by jacking up under the axle arm. A tool made up to the dimensions shown in Fig. 10.18 is useful for this.
5 Unbolt the shock absorber lower mounting. Free the lower end of the shock absorber from its bracket.
6 Lower the jack and remove the spring and rubber dampers. Lever the axle arm downwards slightly if necessary to remove the spring.
7 If the spring is to be renewed, it is sound policy to renew the rubber dampers also.

13.2 Rear anti-roll bar mounting nut and bolt (arrowed)

Fig. 10.17 Removing the rear anti-roll bar (Sec 13)

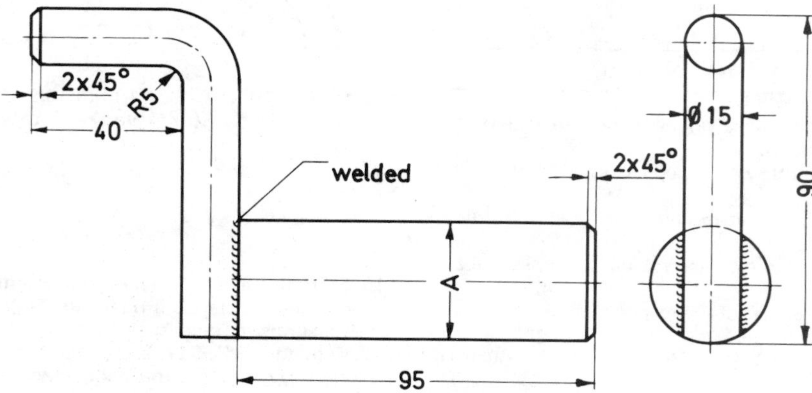

Fig. 10.18 Rear axle arm jacking adaptor. All dimensions in mm; diameter A to suit jack (Sec 14)

Fig. 10.19 Removing a rear spring (Sec 14)

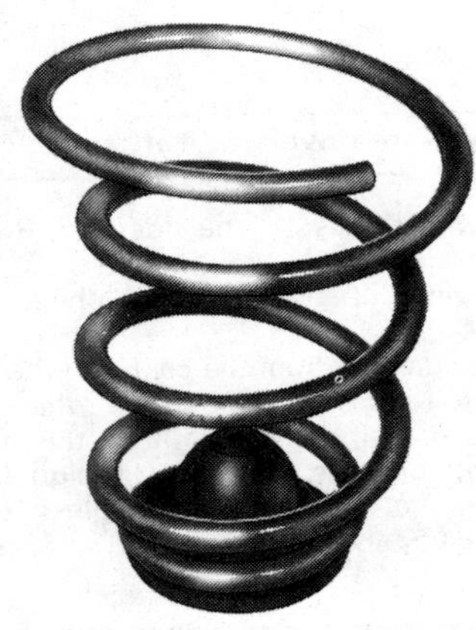

Fig. 10.20 Rear spring and lower damper – Estate (Sec 14)

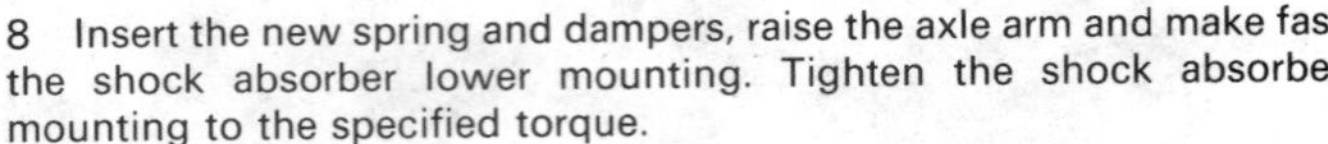

8 Insert the new spring and dampers, raise the axle arm and make fast the shock absorber lower mounting. Tighten the shock absorber mounting to the specified torque.
9 Repeat the operations on the other side of the vehicle.

Estate and Van

10 Jack up under one axle arm (see Fig. 10.78) and unbolt the shock absorber lower mounting. Lower the jack and repeat the operation on the other side, leaving the jack in place.
11 Remove the springs and lower dampers, lowering the jack as necessary.
12 If renewing the sprung upper dampers, glue them in position with impact adhesive to aid fitting.
13 Fit the new spring and dampers. The spring ends must be correctly positioned in the upper seats (Fig. 10.21).
14 Raise the jack and reconnect the shock absorber lower mounting on that side, then transfer the jack to the other side and secure the other shock absorber.
15 Tighten the shock absorber lower mountings to the specified torque.

All models

16 Lower the vehicle. When fitted, inflate the level control system to 0.8 bar (11.6 lbf/in²).

15 Rear axle assembly – removal and refitting

1 Slacken the rear wheel bolts, raise and support the rear of the vehicle and remove the rear wheels.
2 On vehicles with a level control system, depressurize it at the filling valve.
3 Disconnect the handbrake cable at the equaliser yoke and free it from the underbody guides.
4 Unhook the rear part of the exhaust system from its rubber mountings.
5 Disconnect the brake flexible hose at the rear axle brackets. Plug or cap the hoses to reduce fluid spillage.
6 On Estate and Van models, unbolt the brake pressure regulating valve spring bracket.
7 Remove the rear springs, as described in Section 14.
8 Support the centre of the rear axle with a jack and a block of wood or a cradle. Unhook the axle arm mountings from the underbody (photo) and lower the jack. An assistant should steady the assembly whilst it is being unbolted and lowered.
9 Pass the handbrake cable over the exhaust system and remove the axle assembly.

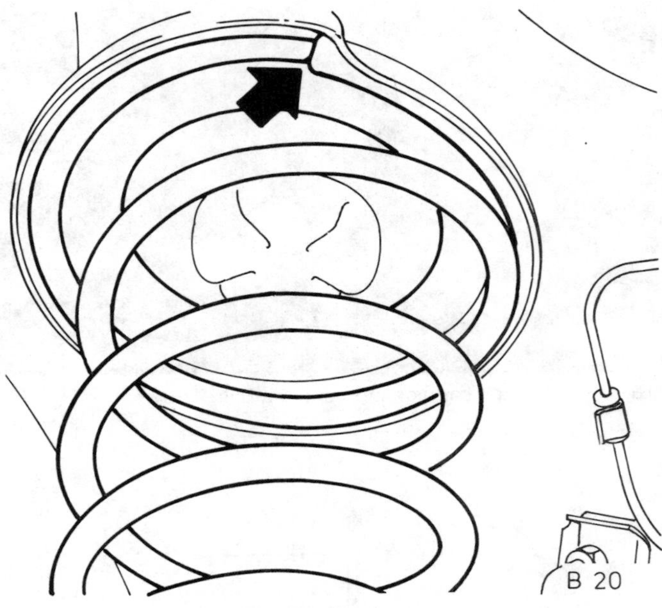

Fig. 10.21 Correct location of upper end of spring (arrowed) – Estate (Sec 14)

10 Strip the axle of brake components, hubs, anti-roll bar etc, if needed for transfer to a new axle. Refer to the appropriate Chapters and Sections for details.
11 With the aid of an assistant, offer the new axle to the vehicle, remembering to pass the handbrake cable over the exhaust system. Insert the axle arm mounting bolts, but do not tighten them yet.
12 Fit the springs and secure the shock absorbers, as described in Section 14.
13 Reconnect the brake flexible hoses, then bleed the hydraulic system, as described in Section 17 of Chapter 9.
14 On Estate and Van models, secure the brake pressure regulating valve spring bracket, as described in Section 15 of Chapter 9.

15.8 Axle arm mounting nut and bolt (arrowed)

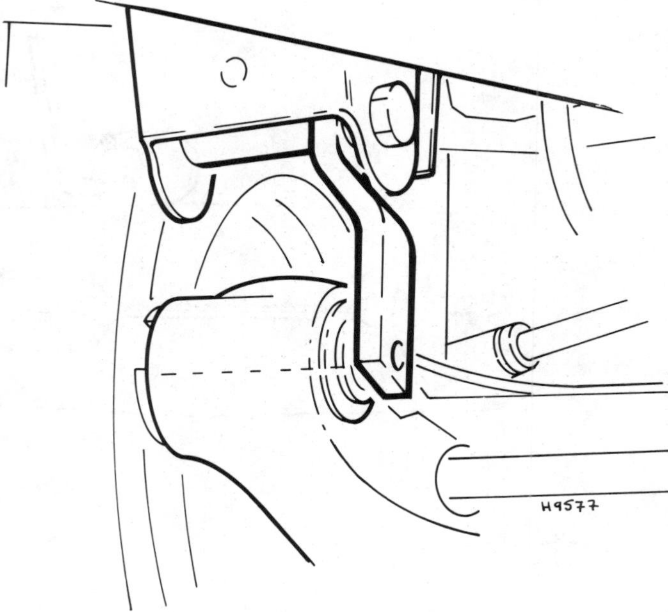

Fig. 10.22 Cranked link used to support axle arm (Sec 16)

15 Secure the exhaust system to its mountings.
16 Secure the handbrake cable to its guides and to the yoke.
17 Adjust the rear wheel bearings, as described in Section 10.
18 Adjust the brakes by making at least 10 applications of the brake pedal, then adjust the handbrake, as described in Chapter 9, Section 22.
19 Fit the roadwheels, lower the vehicle and tighten the wheel bolts.
20 Load the vehicle by having two assistants sit in the front seats, then tighten the axle arm mounting bolts to the specified torque.
21 When a level control system is fitted, inflate it to 0.8 bar (11.6 lbf/in²).

16 Rear axle mounting bushes – renewal

1 The mounting bushes must always be renewed in pairs. Without doubt the opportunity should be taken to renew them if the axle is removed for some other reason. They can be renewed with the axle *in situ* as follows.
2 Depressurize the level control system, when fitted.
3 Remove the rear springs, as described in Section 14, then reattach the shock absorber lower mountings.
4 On Estate and Van models, unbolt the brake pressure regulating valve spring bracket.
5 Unclip the brake flexible hose from the brackets on the underbody. If care is taken there is no need to disconnect the hoses.
6 Support the axle centrally with a hydraulic jack and a block of wood or a cradle.
7 Remove the axle arm mounting bolts and carefully lower the axle until the bushes are accessible. Bend the brake pipes slightly if necessary to avoid straining the flexible hoses.
8 Cut or chisel the flange from the outboard face of one bush. In order to restrain the axle from moving during this operation, the makers specify the use of a cranked link, one end of which bolts to the axle arm mounting, the other end carrying a pin which locates in the inner side of the bush (Fig. 10.22). Be careful not to knock the axle off the jack: provide additional supports if possible.
9 Draw the old bush out from the inboard side to the outboard, using suitable tubes, bolts and washers. (The maker's special tool set for this job, consisting of the tubes etc plus the cranked link, is numbered KM-452-A.) Removal of the bush will be easier if the axle arm around it is heated to 50° to 70°C (122° to 158°F) using hot air, steam or a soldering iron. **Do not** use a naked flame: the fuel tank is not far away.
10 Coat the new bush with liquid detergent and draw it into place, observing the correct orientation (Fig. 10.24), until the flange rests against the edge of the axle arm.

Fig. 10.23 Parts of tool KM-452-A being used to draw out an axle arm bush (Sec 16)

11 Repeat the operations on the other side of the vehicle.
12 Raise and secure the axle, but do not tighten the axle arm bolts yet.
13 Secure the brake flexible hose to their brackets.
14 Refit the springs, as described in Section 14.
15 On Estate and Van models, refit the pressure regulating valve spring bracket, as described in Chapter 9, Section 15.
16 Lower the vehicle onto its wheels, have two assistants sit in the front seats and tighten the axle arm mounting bolts to the specified torque.
17 When fitted, pressurize the level control system to 0.8 bar (11.6 lbf/in²).

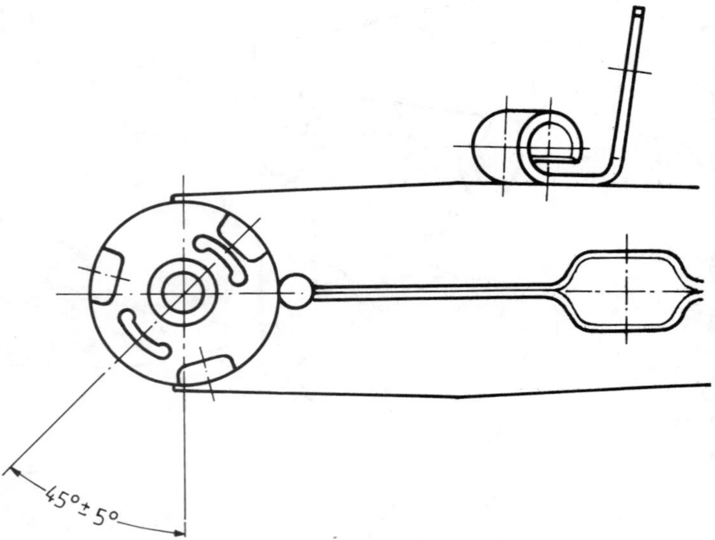

Fig. 10.24 Correct orientation of rear axle arm bush (Sec 16)

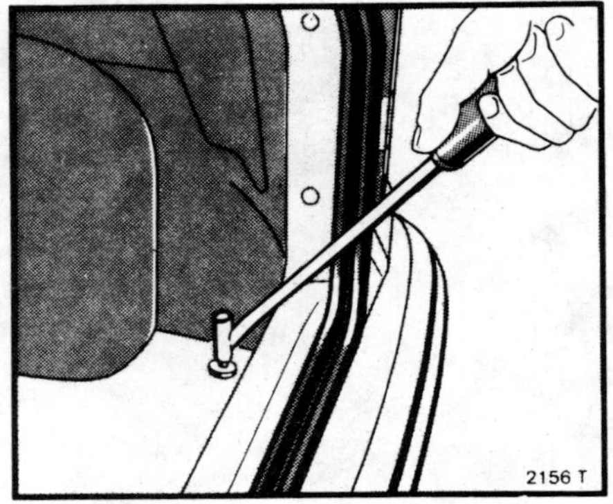

Fig. 10.25 Inflating the level control system (Sec 17)

Fig. 10.26 Measuring the rear ride height (Sec 17)

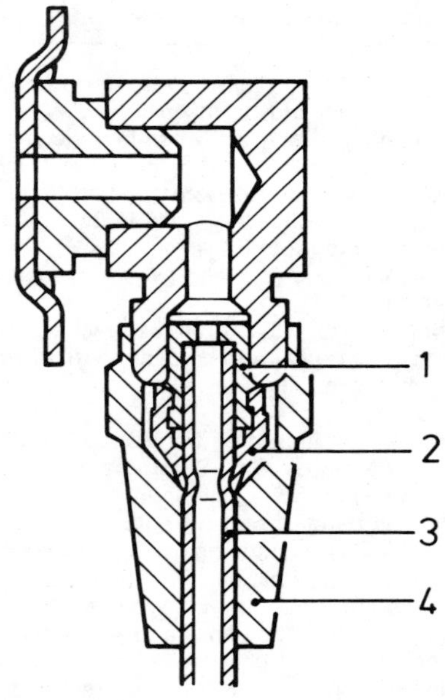

Fig. 10.27 Sectional view of a level control system pressure union (Sec 17)

1 Seal
2 Sleeve
3 Pressure line
4 Union nut

17 Level control system – description and maintenance

1 On vehicles equipped with this system ride height can be controlled by pressurizing the rear shock absorbers with air. The shock absorbers are connected to each other, and to the filling valve, by a high pressure pipeline. The filling valve is similar to a tyre inflation valve; it is located on the right-hand side of the load area.
2 For normal (unladen) running, the system should be pressurized to 0.8 bar (11.6 lbf/in^2). Before loading the vehicle, measure the ride height between the rear bumper and the ground. After loading, restore the ride height by increasing the system pressure using tyre inflation equipment. Do not exceed 5 bar (72.5 lbf/in^2).
3 Do not drive the veicle unladen with a high pressure in the system, nor inflate the system to the maximum pressure before loading.
4 Maintenance consists of checking the pressure lines and unions for security and good condition.

18 Wheels and tyres – general care and maintenance

Wheels and tyres should give no real problems in use provided that a close eye is kept on them with regard to excessive wear or damage. To this end, the following points should be noted.

Ensure that tyre pressures are checked regularly and maintained correctly. Checking should be carried out with the tyres cold and not immediately after the vehicle has been in use. If the pressures are checked with the tyres hot, an apparently high reading will be obtained owing to heat expansion. Under no circumstances should an attempt be made to reduce the pressures to the quoted cold reading in this instance, or effective underinflation will result.

Underinflation will cause overheating of the tyre owing to excessive flexing of the casing, and the tread will not sit correctly on the road surface. This will cause a consequent loss of adhesion and excessive wear, not to mention the danger of sudden tyre failure due to heat build-up.

Overinflation will cause rapid wear of the centre part of the tyre tread coupled with reduced adhesion, harsher ride, and the danger of shock damage occurring in the tyre casing.

Regularly check the tyres for damage in the form of cuts or bulges, especially in the sidewalls. Remove any nails or stones embedded in the tread before they penetrate the tyre to cause deflation. If removal of a nail *does* reveal that the tyre has been punctured, refit the nail so that its point of penetration is marked. Then immediately change the wheel and have the tyre repaired by a tyre dealer. Do *not* drive on a tyre in such a condition. In many cases a puncture can be simply repaired by the use of an inner tube of the correct size and type. If in any doubt as to the possible consequences of any damage found, consult your local tyre dealer for advice.

Periodically remove the wheels and clean any dirt or mud from the inside and outside surfaces. Examine the wheel rims for signs of rusting, corrosion or other damage. Light alloy wheels are easily damaged by 'kerbing' whilst parking, and similarly steel wheels may become dented or buckled. Renewal of the wheel is very often the only course of remedial action possible.

The balance of each wheel and tyre assembly should be maintained to avoid excessive wear, not only to the tyres but also to the steering and suspension components. Wheel imbalance is normally signified by vibration through the vehicle's bodyshell, although in many cases it is particularly noticeable through the steering wheel. Conversely, it should be noted that wear or damage in suspension or steering components may cause excessive tyre wear. Out-of-round or out-of-true tyres, damaged wheels and wheel bearing wear/maladjustment also fall into this category. Balancing will not usually cure vibration caused by such wear.

Wheel balancing may be carried out with the wheel either on or off the vehicle. If balanced on the vehicle, ensure that the wheel-to-hub relationship is marked in some way prior to subsequent wheel removal so that it may be refitted in its original position.

General tyre wear is influenced to a large degree by driving style – harsh braking and acceleration or fast cornering will all produce more rapid tyre wear. Interchanging of tyres may result in more even wear, but this should only be carried out where there is no mix of tyre types on the vehicle. However, it is worth bearing in mind that if this is completely effective, the added expense of replacing a complete set of tyres simultaneously is incurred, which may prove financially restrictive for many owners.

Front tyres may wear unevenly as a result of wheel misalignment. The front wheels should always be correctly aligned according to the settings specified by the vehicle manufacturer.

Legal restrictions apply to the mixing of tyre types on a vehicle. Basically this means that a vehicle must not have tyres of differing construction on the same axle. Although it is not recommended to mix tyre types between front axle and rear axle, the only legally permissible combination is crossply at the front and radial at the rear. When mixing radial ply tyres, textile braced radials must always go on the front axle, with steel braced radials at the rear. An obvious disadvantage of such mixing is the necessity to carry two spare tyres to avoid contravening the law in the event of a puncture.

In the UK, the Motor Vehicles Construction and Use Regulations apply to many aspects of tyre fitting and usage. It is suggested that a copy of these regulations is obtained from your local police if in doubt as to the current legal requirements with regard to tyre condition, minimum tread depth, etc.

19 Suspension geometry and wheel alignment – general

With the exception of the front wheel toe setting, all the front and rear suspension angles are set during manufacture and are not adjustable. Unless the vehicle has suffered accident damage, or there is gross wear in the suspension mountings or joints, it can be assumed that these settings are correct. If for any reason it is believed tht they are not correct, the task of checking them should be left to a GM dealer who will have the necessary special equipment needed to measure the small angles involved.

Front wheel toe setting adjustment procedures and further information on front wheel alignment will be found in Chapter 8. For reference purposes the front and rear suspension angles are given in the Specifications at the beginning of this Chapter.

20 Fault diagnosis – suspension

Note: *Before diagnosing suspension faults, be sure that the trouble is not due to incorrect tyre pressures, a mixture of tyre types or binding brakes*

Symptom	Reason(s)
Vehicle pulls to one side	Incorrect front or rear wheel alignment Accident damage to steering or suspension components
Vehicle wanders	Excessive wear in suspension mountings, joints or components Incorrect front or rear wheel alignment Wear in steering components (see Chapter 8)
Wheel wobble or vibration	Roadwheels out of balance Roadwheels buckled Lump or bulge in tyre Excessive wear in suspension mountings, joints or components Fault shock absorbers or front struts
Excessive pitching or rolling on corners or during braking	Faulty shock absorbers or front struts Worn anti-roll bar rubber bushes or loose mounting clamps

Chapter 11 Bodywork and fittings

For modifications, and information applicable to later models, see Supplement at end of manual

Contents

Specifications

Torque wrench settings

	Nm	lbf ft
Bonnet hinges	20	15
Tailgate hinges	20	15
Tailgate lock striker	20	15
Front and rear trim panel nuts	12	9
Tailgate strut attachments	20	15
Seat belt mountings	35	26
Rear crossmember-to-lock bolts	55	41
Rear body panel-to-lock bolts	20	15
Front seat mountings	20	15
Front seat back-to-frame bolts	30	22

1 General description

The main body structure is a welded construction of individually shaped panels which make up a 'monocoque' bodyshell, without a separate chassis. Various areas are strengthened to provide for suspension, steering and engine attachments and load distribution. The whole shell is very srong and rigid for its weight.

The front wings are bolted in position and can be renewed without special equipment.

Interior fittings are of an extremely high standard, even on basic models.

2 Maintenance – bodywork and underframe

The general condition of a vehicle's bodywork is the one thing that significantly affects its value. Maintenance is easy but needs to be regular. Neglect, particularly after minor damage, can lead quickly to further deterioration and costly repair bills. It is important also to keep watch on those parts of the vehicle not immediately visible, for instance the underside, inside all the wheel arches and the lower part of the engine compartment.

The basic maintenance routine for the bodywork is washing – preferably with a lot of water, from a hose. This will remove all the loose solids which may have stuck to the vehicle. It is important to flush these off in such a way as to prevent grit from scratching the finish. The wheel arches and underframe need washing in the same way to remove any accumulated mud which will retain moisture and tend to encourage rust. Paradoxically enough, the best time to clean the underframe and wheel arches is in wet weather when the mud is thoroughly wet and soft. In very wet weather the underframe is usually cleaned of large accumulations automatically and this is a good time for inspection.

Periodically, except on vehicles with a wax-based underbody protective coating, it is a good idea to have the whole of the underframe of the vehicle steam cleaned, engine compartment included, so that a thorough inspection can be carried out to see what minor repairs and renovations are necessary. Steam cleaning is available at many garages and is necessary for removal of the accumulation of oily grime which sometimes is allowed to become thick in certain areas. If steam cleaning facilities are not available, there are one or two excellent grease solvents available which can be brush applied. The dirt can then be simply hosed off. Note that these methods should not be used on vehicles with wax-based underbody protective coating or the coating will be removed. Such vehicles should be inspected annually, preferably just prior to winter, when the underbody should be washed down and any damage to the wax coating repaired. Ideally, a completely fresh coat should be applied. It would also be worth considering the use of such wax-based protection for injection into door panels, sills, box sections, etc, as an additional safeguard against rust damage.

After washing paintwork, wipe off with a chamois leather to give an unspotted clear finish. A coat of clear protective wax polish will give added protection against chemical pollutants in the air. If the paintwork sheen has dulled or oxidised, use a cleaner/polisher combination to restore the brilliance of the shine. This requires a little effort, but such dulling is usually caused because regular washing has been neglected. Care needs to be taken with metallic paintwork, as special non-abrasive cleaner/polisher is required to avoid damage to the finish. Always check that the door and ventilator opening drain holes and pipes are completely clear so that water can be drained out (photos). Bright work should be treated in the same way as paint work. Windscreens and windows can be kept clear of the smeary film which often appears by the use of a proprietary glass cleaner. Never use any form of wax or other body or chromium polish on glass.

3 Maintenance – upholstery and carpets

Mats and carpets should be brushed or vacuum cleaned regularly to keep them free of grit. If they are badly stained remove them from the vehicle for scrubbing or sponging and make quite sure they are dry before refitting. Seats and interior trim panels can be kept clean by wiping with a damp cloth. If they do become stained (which can be more apparent on light coloured upholstery) use a little liquid detergent and a soft nail brush to scour the grime out of the grain of the material. Do not forget to keep the headlining clean in the same way as the upholstery. When using liquid cleaners inside the vehicle do not over-wet the surfaces being cleaned. Excessive damp could get into the seams and padded interior causing stains, offensive odours or even rot. If the inside of the vehicle gets wet accidentally it is worthwhile taking some trouble to dry it out properly, particularly where carpets are involved. *Do not leave oil or electric heaters inside the vehicle for this purpose.*

4 Minor body damage – repair

The photographic sequences on pages 246 and 247 illustrate the operations detailed in the following sub-sections.

Note: *For more detailed information about bodywork repair, the Haynes Publishing Group publish a book by Lindsay Porter called The Car Bodywork Repair Manual. This incorporates information on such aspects as rust treatment, painting and glass fibre repairs, as well as details on more ambitious repairs involving welding and panel beating.*

2.0A Door drain holes

2.0B Clearing a sill drain hole

Repair of minor scratches in bodywork

If the scratch is very superficial, and does not penetrate to the metal of the bodywork, repair is very simple. Lightly rub the area of the scratch with a paintwork renovator, or a very fine cutting paste, to remove loose paint from the scratch and to clear the surrounding bodywork of wax polish. Rinse the area with clean water.

Apply touch-up paint to the scratch using a fine paint brush; continue to apply fine layers of paint until the surface of the paint in the scratch is level with the surrounding paintwork. Allow the new paint at least two weeks to harden: then blend it into the surrounding paintwork by rubbing the scratch area with a paintwork renovator or a very fine cutting paste. Finally, apply wax polish.

Where the scratch has penetrated right through to the metal of the bodywork, causing the metal to rust, a different repair technique is required. Remove any loose rust from the bottom of the scratch with a penknife, then apply rust inhibiting paint to prevent the formation of rust in the future. Using a rubber or nylon applicator fill the scratch with bodystopper paste. If required, this paste can be mixed with cellulose thinners to provide a very thin paste which is ideal for filling narrow scratches. Before the stopper-paste in the scratch hardens, wrap a piece of smooth cotton rag around the top of a finger. Dip the finger in cellulose thinners and then quickly sweep it across the surface of the stopper-paste in the scratch; this will ensure that the surface of the stopper-paste is slightly hollowed. The scratch can now be painted over as described earlier in this Section.

Repair of dents in bodywork

When deep denting of the vehicle's bodywork has taken place, the first task is to pull the dent out, until the affected bodywork almost attains its original shape. There is little point in trying to restore the original shape completely, as the metal in the damaged area will have stretched on impact and cannot be reshaped fully to its original contour. It is better to bring the level of the dent up to a point which is about ⅛ in (3 mm) below the level of the surrounding bodywork. In cases where the dent is very shallow anyway, it is not worth trying to pull it out at all. If the underside of the dent is accessible, it can be hammered out gently from behind, using a mallet with a wooden or plastic head. Whilst doing this, hold a suitable block of wood firmly against the outside of the panel to absorb the impact from the hammer blows and thus prevent a large area of the bodywork from being 'belled-out'.

Should the dent be in a section of the bodywork which has a double skin or some other factor making it inaccessible from behind, a different technique is called for. Drill several small holes through the metal inside the area – particularly in the deeper section. Then screw long self-tapping screws into the holes just sufficiently for them to gain a good purchase in the metal. Now the dent can be pulled out by pulling on the protruding heads of the screws with a pair of pliers.

The next stage of the repair is the removal of the paint from the damaged area, and from an inch or so of the surrounding 'sound' bodywork. This is accomplished most easily by using a wire brush or abrasive pad on a power drill, although it can be done just as effectively by hand using sheets of abrasive paper. To complete the preparation for filling, score the surface of the bare metal with a screwdriver or the tang of a file, or alternatively, drill small holes in the affected area. This will provide a really good 'key' for the filler paste.

To complete the repair see the Section on filling and re-spraying.

Repair of rust holes or gashes in bodywork

Remove all paint from the affected area and from an inch or so of the surrounding 'sound' bodywork, using an abrasive pad or a wire brush on a power drill. If these are not available a few sheets of abrasive paper will do the job just as effectively. With the paint removed you will be able to gauge the severity of the corrosion and therefore decide whether to renew the whole panel (if this is possible) or to repair the affected area. New body panels are not as expensive as most people think and it is often quicker and more satisfactory to fit a new panel than to attempt to repair large areas of corrosion.

Remove all fittings from the affected area except those which will act as a guide to the original shape of the damaged bodywork (eg headlamp shells etc). Then, using tin snips or a hacksaw blade, remove all loose metal and any other metal badly affected by corrosion. Hammer the edges of the hole inwards in order to create a slight depression for the filler paste.

Wire brush the affected area to remove the powdery rust from the surface of the remaining metal. Paint the affected area with rust inhibiting paint; if the back of the rusted area is accessible treat this also.

Before filling can take place it will be necessary to block the hole in some way. This can be achieved by the use of aluminium or plastic mesh, or aluminium tape.

Aluminium or plastic mesh is probably the best material to use for a large hole. Cut a piece to the approximate size and shape of the hole to be filled, then position it in the hole so that its edges are below the level of the surrounding bodywork. It can be retained in position by several blobs of filler paste around its periphery.

Aluminium tape should be used for small or very narrow holes. Pull a piece off the roll and trim it to the approximate size and shape required, then pull off the backing paper (if used) and stick the tape over the hole; it can be overlapped if the thickness of one piece is insufficient. Burnish down the edges of the tape with the handle of a screwdriver or similar, to ensure that the tape is securely attached to the metal underneath.

Bodywork repairs – filling and re-spraying

Before using this Section, see the Sections on dent, deep scratch, rust holes and gash repairs.

Many types of bodyfiller are available, but generally speaking those proprietary kits which contain a tin of filler paste and a tube of resin hardener are best for this type of repair. A wide, flexible plastic or nylon applicator will be found invaluable for imparting a smooth and well contoured finish to the surface of the filler.

Mix up a little filler on a clean piece of card or board – measure the hardener carefully (follow the maker's instructions on the pack) otherwise the filler will set too rapidly or too slowly. Using the applicator apply the filler paste to the prepared area; draw the applicator across the surface of the filler to achieve the correct contour and to level the filler surface. As soon as a contour that approximates to the correct one is achieved, stop working the paste – if you carry on too long the paste will become sticky and begin to 'pick up' on the applicator. Continue to add thin layers of filler paste at twenty-minute intervals until the level of the filler is just proud of the surrounding bodywork.

Once the filler has hardened, excess can be removed using a metal plane or file. From then on, progressively finer grades of abrasive paper should be used, starting with a 40 grade production paper and finishing with 400 grade wet-and-dry paper. Always wrap the abrasive paper around a flat rubber, cork, or wooden block – otherwise the surface of the filler will not be completely flat. During the smoothing of the filler surface the wet-and-dry paper should be periodically rinsed in water. This will ensure that a very smooth finish is imparted to the filler at the final stage.

At this stage the 'dent' should be surrounded by a ring of bare metal, which in turn should be encircled by the finely 'feathered' edge of the good paintwork. Rinse the repair area with clean water, until all of the dust produced by the rubbing-down operation has gone.

Spray the whole repair area with a light coat of primer – this will show up any imperfections in the surface of the filler. Repair these imperfections with fresh filler paste or bodystopper, and once more smooth the surface with abrasive paper. If bodystopper is used, it can be mixed with cellulose thinners to form a really thin paste which is ideal for filling small holes. Repeat this spray and repair procedure until you are satisfied that the surface of the filler, and the feathered edge of the paintwork are perfect. Clean the repair area with clean water and allow to dry fully.

The repair area is now ready for final spraying. Paint spraying must be carried out in a warm, dry, windless and dust free atmosphere. This condition can be created artificially if you have access to a large indoor working area, but if you are forced to work in the open, you will have to pick your day very carefully. If you are working indoors, dousing the floor in the work area with water will help to settle the dust which would otherwise be in the atmosphere. If the repair area is confined to one body panel, mask off the surrounding panels; this will help to minimise the effects of a slight mis-match in paint colours. Bodywork fittings (eg chrome strips, door handles etc) will also need to be masked off. Use genuine masking tape and several thicknesses of newspaper for the masking operations.

Before commencing to spray, agitate the aerosol can thoroughly, then spray a test area (an old tin, or similar) until the technique is mastered. Cover the repair area with a thick coat of primer; the thickness should be built up using several thin layers of paint rather than one thick one. Using 400 grade wet-and-dry paper, rub down the surface of the primer until it is really smooth. While doing this, the work area should be thoroughly doused with water, and the wet-and-dry paper periodically rinsed in water. Allow to dry before spraying on more paint.

Spray on the top coat, again building up the thickness by using several thin layers of paint. Start spraying in the centre of the repair area and then, using a circular motion, work outwards until the whole repair area and about 2 inches of the surrounding original paintwork is covered. Remove all masking material 10 to 15 minutes after spraying on the final coat of paint.

Allow the new paint at least two weeks to harden, then, using a paintwork renovator or a very fine cutting paste, blend the edges of the paint into the existing paintwork. Finally, apply wax polish.

5 Major body damage – repair

Major impact or rust damage should only be repaired by a GM dealer or other competent specialist. Alignment jigs are needed for successful completion of such work; superficially effective repairs may leave dangerous weaknesses in the structure. Unrectified distortion can also impose severe stresses on steering and suspension components, with consequent premature failure.

6 Maintenance – hinges and locks

1 Periodically oil the door, bonnet and tailgate hinges using a couple of drops of light machine oil or clean engine oil. A good time to do this is after the car has been washed.
2 At the same time, oil the bonnet release catch and the safety catch pivot pin.
3 Do not over-lubricate door locks and catches: excess lubricant may end up on clothing or upholstery. A little light oil on the lock dovetail, and a smear of grease on the striker, should be sufficient.

7 Bonnet – removal and refitting

1 Open and prop the bonnet.
2 When an under-bonnet light is fitted, disconnect its electrical lead.
3 Mark around the hinge bolts with a soft lead pencil as a guide for refitting. Have an assistant support the bonnet, then remove the hinge bolts from each side (photo).

7.3 Removing a bonnet hinge bolt

4 Lift away the bonnet. If it is to be re-used, rest it carefully on rags or cardboard. If a new bonnet is to be fitted, transfer serviceable items (rubber buffers, lock striker etc) to it.
5 Refit in the reverse order to removal, using the hinge bolt alignment marks for guidance when applicable.
6 If the lock striker was disturbed, adjust it to the dimension shown in Fig. 11.1 before tightening its locknut.
7 Adjust the hinge bolts and front buffers until a good fit is obtained with the bonnet closed.

8 Bonnet release cable – removal and refitting

1 If the release cable is broken, the bonnet lock can be released by reaching up from under the front panel and operating the lock by hand.
2 Unbolt the cable clip from the rear of the bonnet lock platform.
3 Prise the cable and fitting out of the release slide, using a screwdriver against the spring tension.

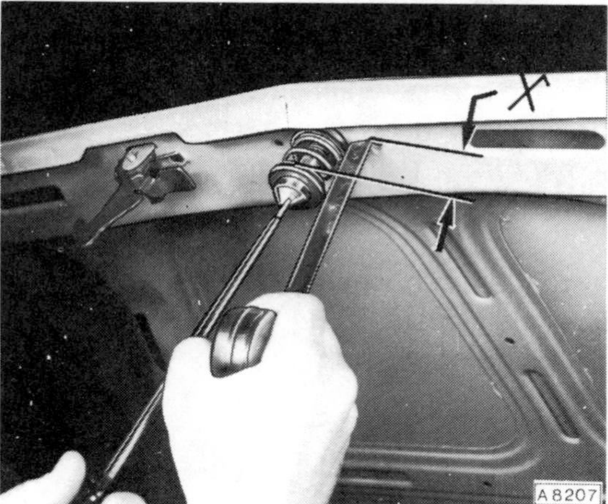

Fig. 11.1 Adjusting the bonnet lock striker projection (Sec 7)

X = 40 to 45 mm (1.6 to 1.8 in)

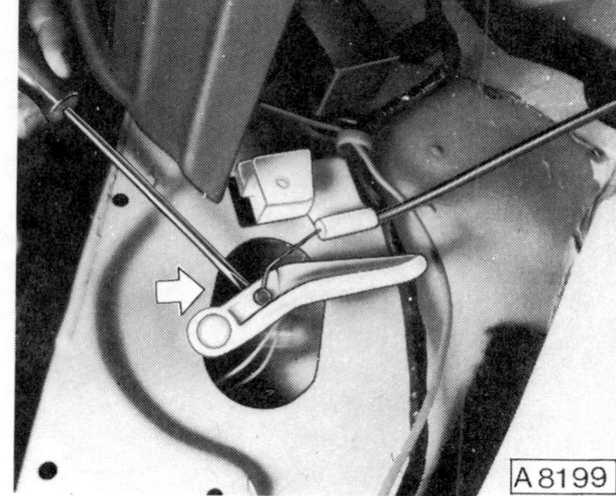

Fig. 11.2 Disconnecting bonnet release cable from handle (Sec 8)

4 Inside the car, free the cable from the release lever and bracket.
5 Release the grommet from the bulkhead and withdraw the cable from under the bonnet.
6 Fit the new cable in the reverse order to removal. Adjust the position of the cable under the front panel clip so that, with the release lever at rest, the inner cable is just slack. Check that the release slide moves when an assistant operates the release lever, then close the bonnet and check for correct operation.

9 Front trim panel – removal and refitting

1 The front trim panel incorporates the radiator grille and the front bumper.
2 Remove the three screws which secure the panel to the bonnet lock platform (photo).
3 From under the vehicle remove the two nuts which secure the lower part of the panel (photo).
4 Pull the panel forwards so that it slides off the side mountings. If front foglights are fitted, disconnect them as the panel is withdrawm. Also disconnect the headlamp washer pipes (when fitted).
5 Refit in the reverse order to removal. The side mountings are riveted in position and can be renewed if wished after drilling out the rivets.

9.2 Undoing a front trim panel screw

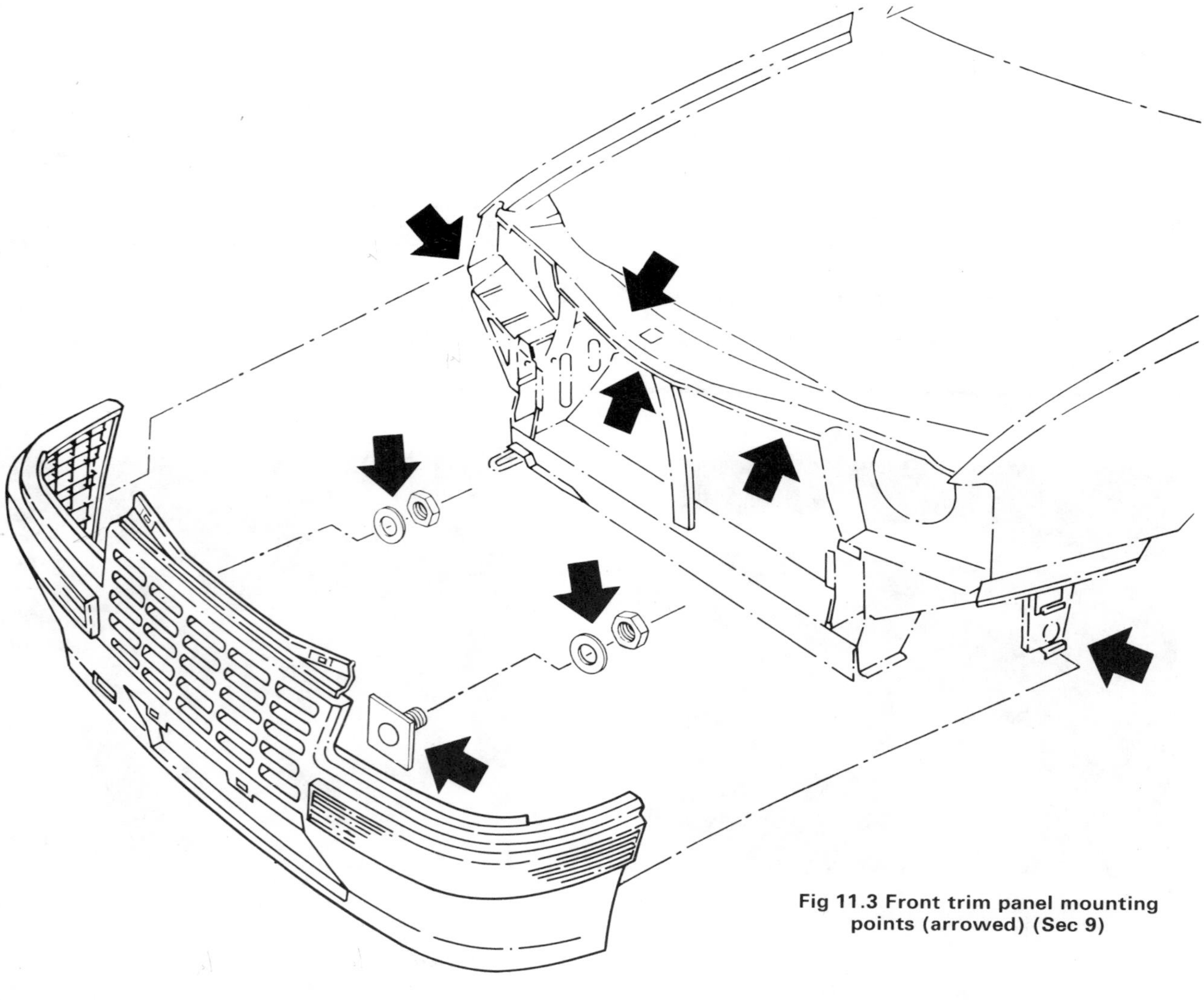

Fig 11.3 Front trim panel mounting points (arrowed) (Sec 9)

9.3 Front trim panel securing nut (arrowed)

10.2 Rear trim panel securing nut

10.3 Freeing one end of the rear trim panel – screw holes arrowed

10 Rear trim panel – removal and refitting

1 Remove the number plate lamps (see Chapter 12, Section 36).
2 Inside the car, free the soft trim from the rear panel to expose the two securing nuts (photo). Remove the nuts.
3 Remove the two screws from inside each wheel arch to free the ends of the rear trim panel (photo). Withdraw the panel, disconnecting the rear foglight wires as it is withdrawn.
4 Refit in the reverse order to removal.

11 Front wing – removal and refitting

1 Remove the front trim panel, as described in Secion 9.
2 Remove the direction indicator lamp unit (see Chapter 12, Section 37).
3 Remove the wheel arch protective panelling by pushing the centres out of the plastic rivets and unclipping it from the edge of the wing. Remove the headlamp washer reservoir, when fitted.
4 Remove the twelve bolts which secure the wing to the car. Free the wing from the sealing compound on its flanges and remove it.
5 Clean all sealant away from the body flange; commence refitting by applying a thick bead of new sealant.
6 Offer the wing to the vehicle and bolt it loosely into position. When it is corectly aligned with the surrounding bodywork, fully tighten the bolts.
7 Coat the inside of the wing with protective wax or similar compound; when necessary, paint the outside of the wing to match the rest of the car.
8 Refit the headlamp washer reservoir, when applicable.
9 Refit the wheel and protective panelling, using new plastic rivets or other proprietary fasteners.
10 Refit the direction indicator lamp and the front trim panel.

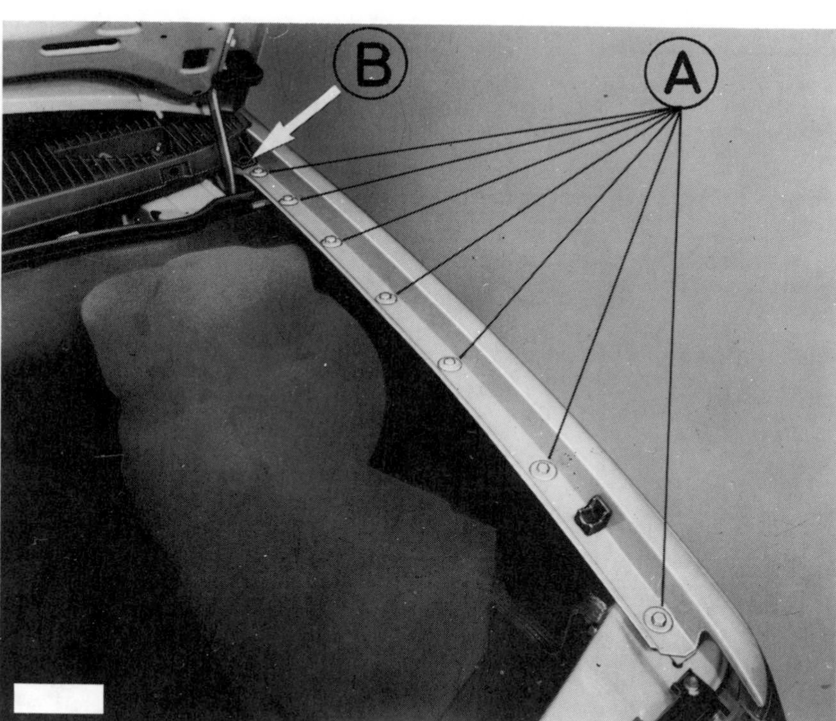

Fig 11.4 Front wing attaching bolts (Sec 11)

A Along edge of engine bay
B By wind deflector

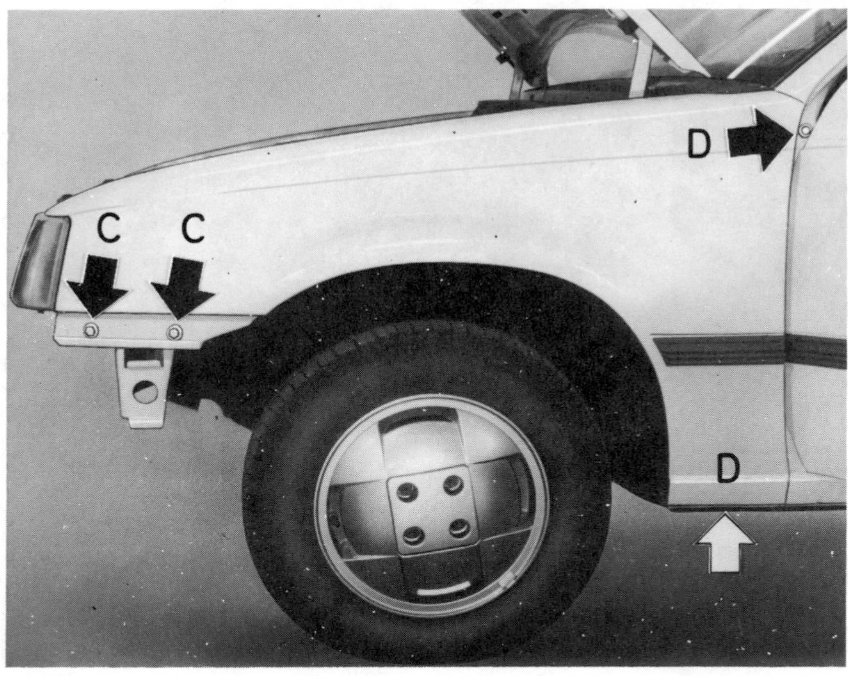

Fig. 11.5 More front wing attaching bolts (Sec 11)

C On wheel housing bracket
D On A-pillar

12 Wind deflector – removal and refitting

1 The wind deflector fills the gap between the rear of the bonnet and the base of the windscreen.
2 Remove both windscreen wiper arms (see Chapter 12).
3 Remove the wind deflector securing screws (photo).
4 Free the wind deflector from its clips and remove it. Disconnect the windscreen washer hoses as it is withdrawn.
5 The two halves of the wind deflector can be separated if wished by pulling them apart. Each half may also be removed individually, leaving the other in place.
6 Refit in the reverse order to removal.

12.3A Wind deflector screw at the wing

12.3B Wind deflector screw near the wiper

13 Door inner trim panel – removal and refitting

1 The procedure is described for a front door; rear doors are similar, except where noted.

2 Except on models with electric windows, the window winder handle must first be removed. In the absence of special tool KM-317-A, release the handle securing clip by introducing a strip of rag between the handle and the door trim panel and working it back and forth to pick up the ends of the clip. Remove the handle, clip and trim plate (photo).

3 Prise the surround from the remote control handle (photo).

4 Unscrew the interior lock button (photo).

5 When a door pocket is fitted, prise out the screw cover, extract the securing screw and remove the pocket (photo). On rear doors, unclip the ashtray housing.

6 Remove the armrest. Precise details of fixing will vary with trim level, but usually there are two Torx screws at the fore end (photo). Some armrests also have an ordinary self-tapping screw at the rear end.

7 With some trim levels there is a self-tapping screw securing the trim to the door shut face. Remove this if present (photo).

8 Uncap the retaining clips with a broad-bladed screwdriver or a pallette knife and remove the panel. The degree of force needed to release the clips is not far off that which will break them: obtain new clips for refitting if necessary.

9 Free the plastic sheets from the door or trim panel as appropriate.

10 Refit in the reverse order to removal. make sure that the plastic sheet is intact and securely glued round the bottom and sides on the door: if it is broken or detached, rainwater may leak into the vehicle or damage the door trim.

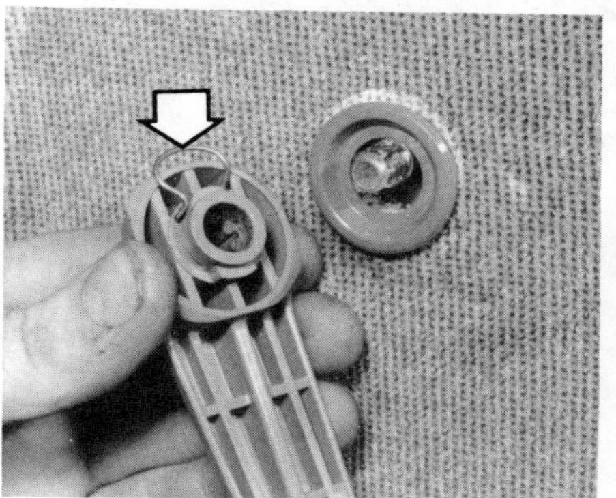

13.2 Window winder handle spring clip (arrowed)

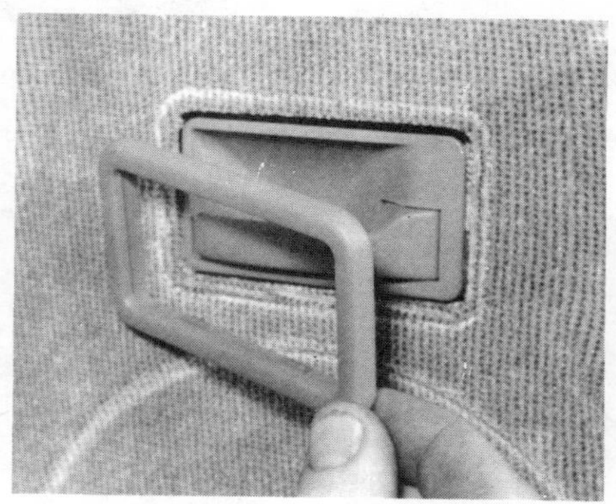

13.3 Removing the surround from the remote control handle

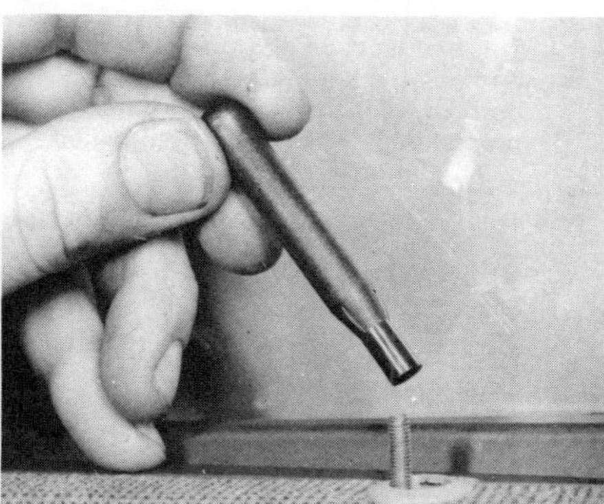

13.4 Unscrewing the lock button

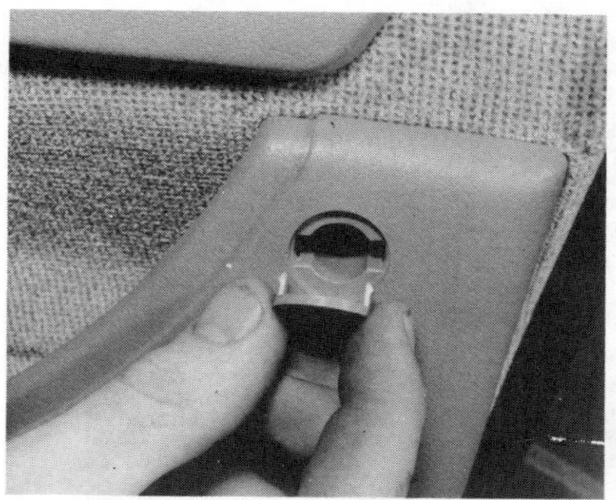

13.5A Door pocket screw cover

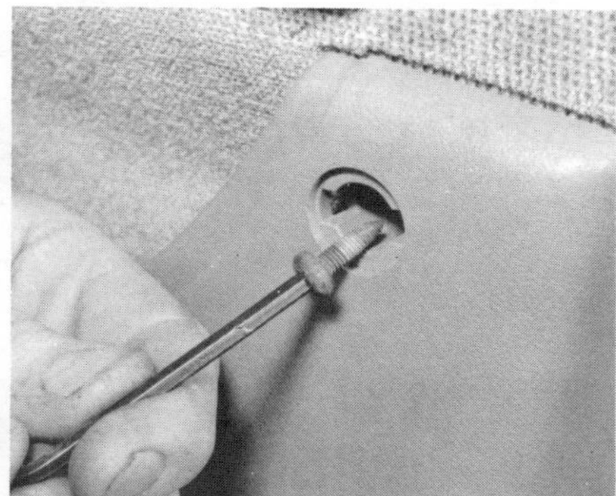

13.5B Removing a door pocket screw

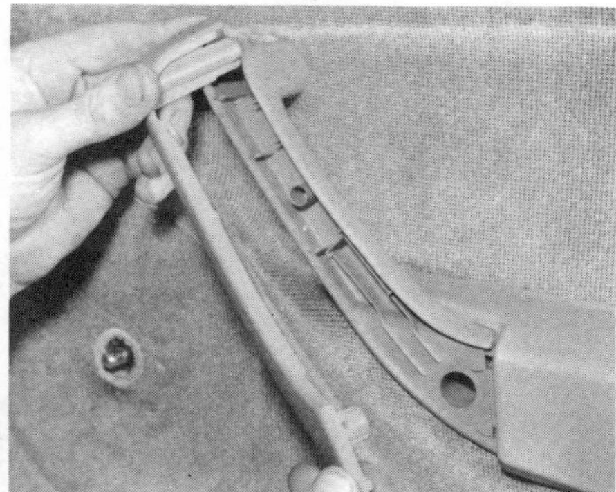

13.6A Removing the armrest screw cover

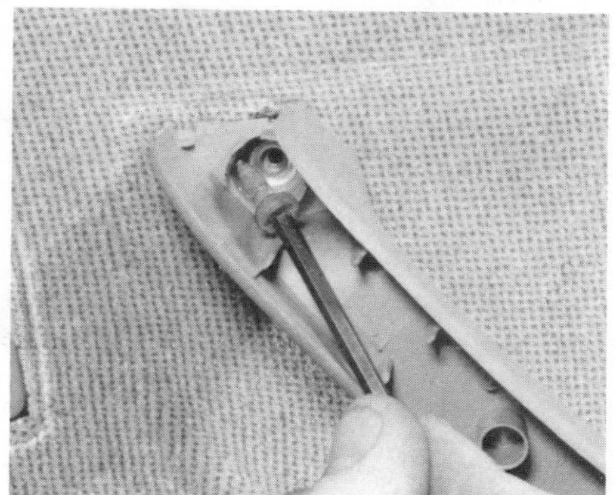

13.6B Removing an armrest screw

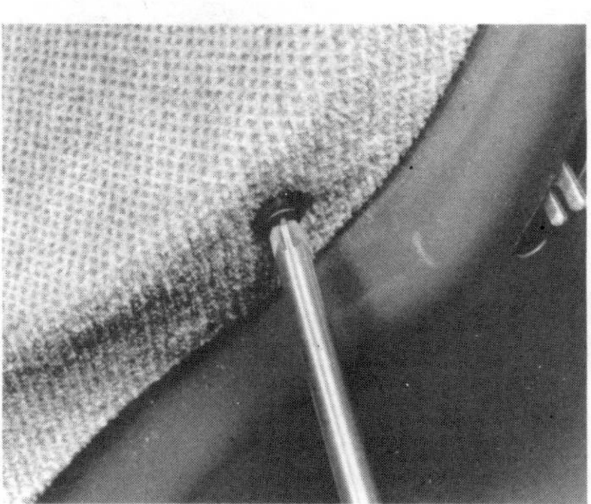

13.7 Trim securing screw on the door shut face – rear door shown

This sequence of photographs deals with the repair of the dent and paintwork damage shown in this photo. The procedure will be similar for the repair of a hole. It should be noted that the procedures given here are simplified – more explicit instructions will be found in the text

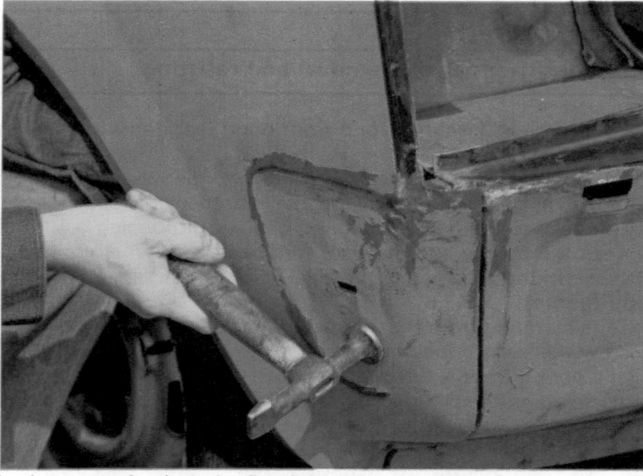

In the case of a dent the first job – after removing surrounding trim – is to hammer out the dent where access is possible. This will minimise filling. Here, the large dent having been hammered out, the damaged area is being made slightly concave

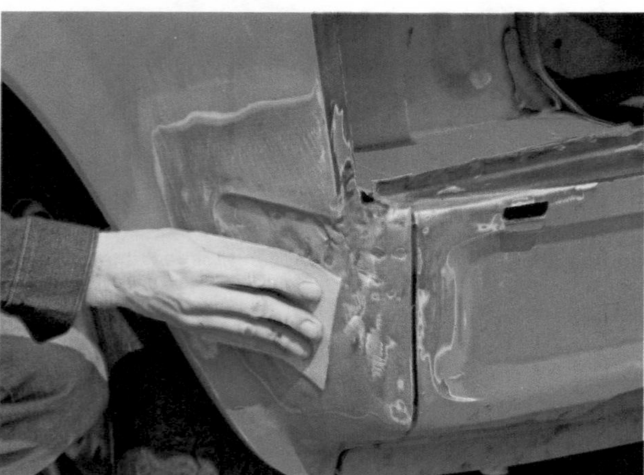

Now all paint must be removed from the damaged area, by rubbing with coarse abrasive paper. Alternatively, a wire brush or abrasive pad can be used in a power drill. Where the repair area meets good paintwork, the edge of the paintwork should be 'feathered', using a finer grade of abrasive paper

In the case of a hole caused by rusting, all damaged sheet-metal should be cut away before proceeding to this stage. Here, the damaged area is being treated with rust remover and inhibitor before being filled

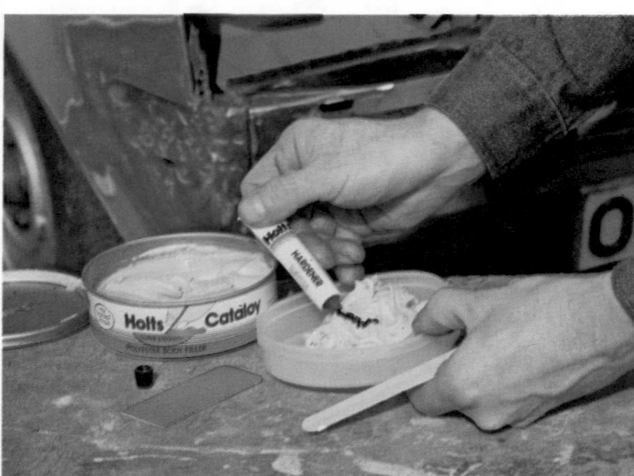

Mix the body filler according to its manufacturer's instructions. In the case of corrosion damage, it will be necessary to block off any large holes before filling – this can be done with aluminium or plastic mesh, or aluminium tape. Make sure the area is absolutely clean before ...

... applying the filler. Filler should be applied with a flexible applicator, as shown, for best results; the wooden spatula being used for confined areas. Apply thin layers of filler at 20-minute intervals, until the surface of the filler is slightly proud of the surrounding bodywork

Initial shaping can be done with a Surform plane or Dreadnought file. Then, using progressively finer grades of wet-and-dry paper, wrapped around a sanding block, and copious amounts of clean water, rub down the filler until really smooth and flat. Again, feather the edges of adjoining paintwork

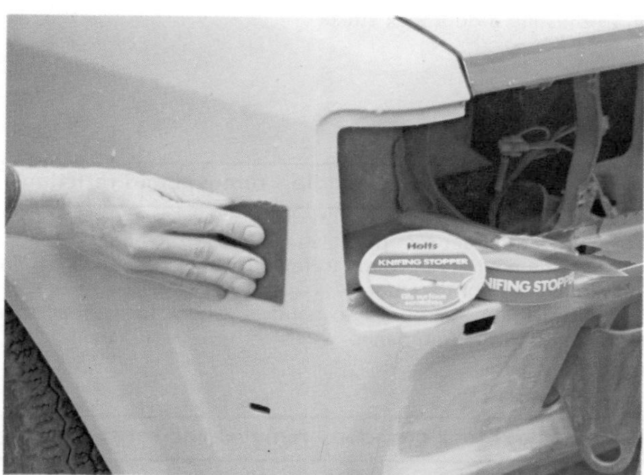

Again, using plenty of water, rub down the primer with a fine grade wet-and-dry paper (400 grade is probably best) until it is really smooth and well blended into the surrounding paintwork. Any remaining imperfections can now be filled by carefully applied knifing stopper paste

The top coat can now be applied. When working out of doors, pick a dry, warm and wind-free day. Ensure surrounding areas are protected from over-spray. Agitate the aerosol thoroughly, then spray the centre of the repair area, working outwards with a circular motion. Apply the paint as several thin coats

The whole repair area can now be sprayed or brush-painted with primer. If spraying, ensure adjoining areas are protected from over-spray. Note that at least one inch of the surrounding sound paintwork should be coated with primer. Primer has a 'thick' consistency, so will find small imperfections

When the stopper has hardened, rub down the repair area again before applying the final coat of primer. Before rubbing down this last coat of primer, ensure the repair area is blemish-free – use more stopper if necessary. To ensure that the surface of the primer is really smooth use some finishing compound

After a period of about two weeks, which the paint needs to harden fully, the surface of the repaired area can be 'cut' with a mild cutting compound prior to wax polishing. When carrying out bodywork repairs, remember that the quality of the finished job is proportional to the time and effort expended

14 Door – removal and refitting

1 The door hinges are welded onto the door and onto the hinge pillar. The only remedy for worn hinges, unless oversize pins can be procured, is to renew the door and/or pillar.
2 To remove a door, open it fully and support its lower edge with well-padded blocks. Disconnect any door component wiring harness (mirrors, windows, central locking etc).
3 Disconnect the check strap and have an assistant support the door whilst the hinge pins are extracted. The pins should be extracted upwards, using a slide hammer, after removing their caps.
4 Refit the door in the reverse order to removal, using new hinge pins. Gross adjustment of the door position is possible by bending the hinges or hinge eyes. Fine adjustment to obtain satisfactory shutting is made by turning the socket-headed lock striker (photo).

14.4 Adjusting a door lock striker

15 Door lock – removal and refitting

1 Remove the door trim panel, as described in Section 13.
2 Remove the three screws which secure the lock to the door shut face (photo).
3 Disconnect the control rods and remove the lock. (In the case of the front door, do not disconnect the interior lock button rod, but withdraw the lock and rod complete.)
4 Refit in the reverse order to removal. When refitting the front door lock, make sure that the tongue on the lock engages with the slot in the cylinder arm (photo).
5 Check for correct operation before refitting the door trim panel.
6 Central locking system components are considered in Chapter 12, Sections 41 and 42.

16 Door exterior handle – removal and refitting

1 Remove the door trim panel, as described in Section 13.
2 Wind up the window fully.
3 Unclip the handle-to-lock rod from the lock.
4 Unbolt the handle from inside the door and remove it. Some manipulation will be needed to get the goose-neck and the operating rod through the hole.
5 Refit in the reverse order to removal. Check for correct operation before refitting the trim panel.

17 Door remote control handle – removal and refitting

1 Remove the door trim panel, as desribed in Section 13.
2 Slide the handle rearwards to free it (photo). Unhook the link rod and remove it from the door.
3 Refit in the reverse order to removal. Check for correct operation before refitting the trim panel.

18 Front door lock cylinder – removal and refitting

1 Remove the door trim panel, as described in Section 13.
2 Release the lock cylinder retaining clip by prising it forwards. Withdraw the cylinder and associated components from the outside of the door.

15.2 Door lock securing screws (arrowed)

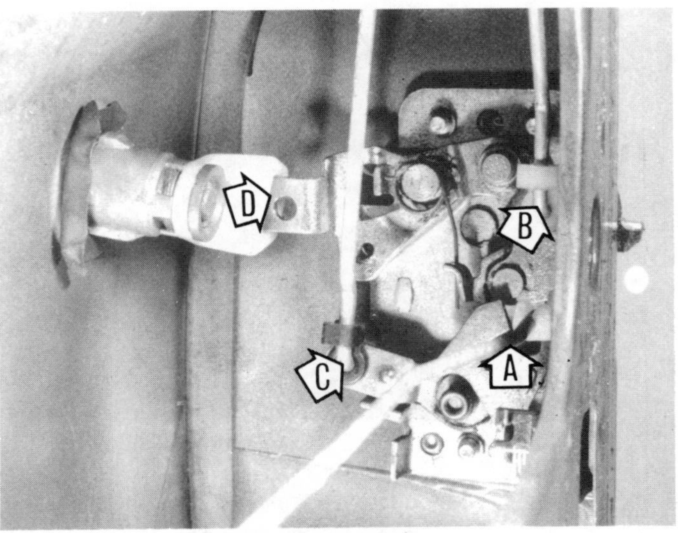

15.4 Door lock attachments inside the door
A Remote control handle rod — *C Exterior handle rod*
B Lock button rod — *D Lock cylinder arm*

Fig. 11.6 Door exterior handle retaining nuts (arrowed) (Sec 16)

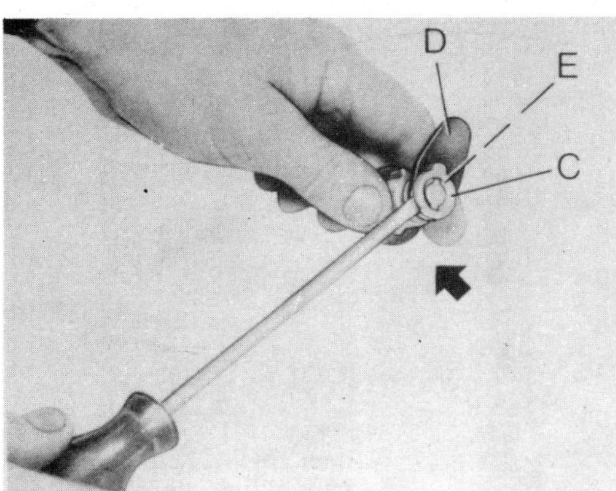

Fig. 11.7 Separating the lock cylinder from its housing (Sec 18)

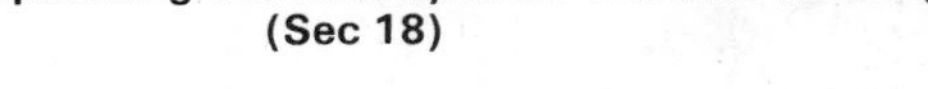

C End piece
D Arm
E Circlip

3 The cylinder may be separated from the other items by inserting the key in the slot, then using a screwdriver to prise off the end piece and arm. Withdraw the cylinder from the housing and recover the circlip.
4 Reassemble in the reverse order, noting the position of the spring legs and their relationship to the arm (Figs. 11.9 and 11.10).
5 Refit in the reverse order to removal. Check for correct operation before refitting the trim panel.

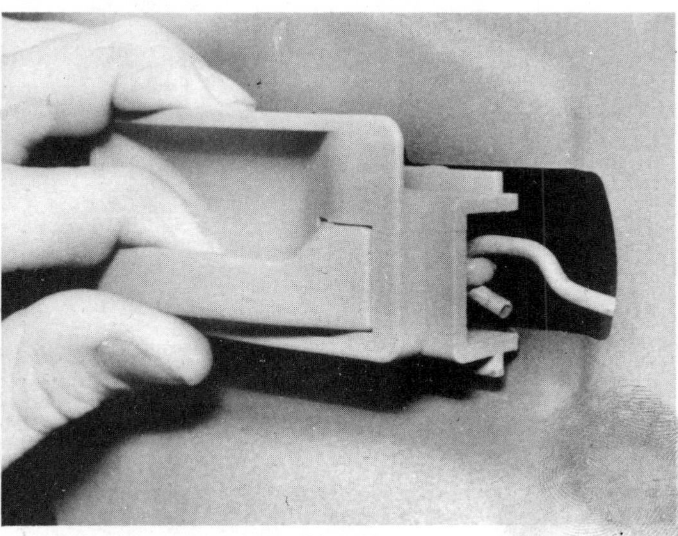

17.2 Removing a remote control handle

Fig. 11.8 Front door lock cylinder and associated components (Sec 18)

1 Ignition key
2 Lock cylinder
3 Circlip
4 Housing
5 Seal
6 Spring
7 Arm
8 End piece

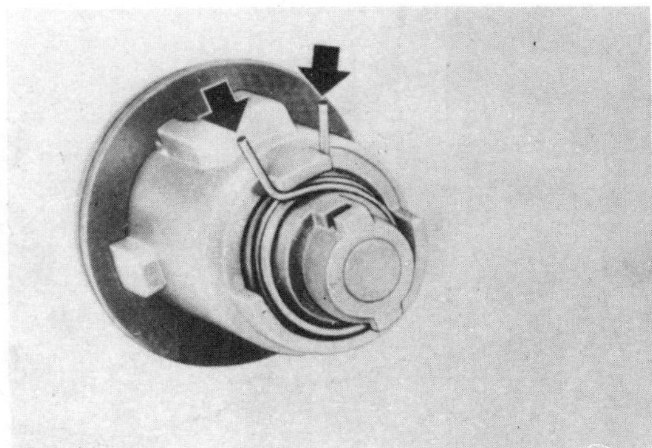

Fig. 11.9 Lock cylinder spring legs (arrowed) correctly positioned (Sec 18)

Fig. 11.10 Relationship of lock cylinder arm to housing (Sec 18)

7 Arm *8 End piece*

19 Window lifting mechanism – removal and refitting

1 Remove the door trim panel, as described in Section 13.
2 Various types of mechanism may be fitted: scissors or cable, manual or electric. In all cases the principles of removal are similar. The electric motors cannot be repaired, though sometimes they can be renewed separately from the lifting mechanism.
3 Lower the window to the halfway position and wedge it securely.
4 Disconnect the wiring harness from the electrically-operated mechanism.
5 Drill the heads off the rivets and remove the mechanism from the door. The cable mechanism lifter must also be unbolted from the window channel (photo).
6 Refit in the reverse order to removal, using new blind rivets. Lubricate the sliders and channel of the scissor type mechanism with silicone grease (photo). Tension the cable on the electric mechanism by turning the adjusters through 90° (Fig. 11.12).
7 Check for correct operation before refitting the door trim.

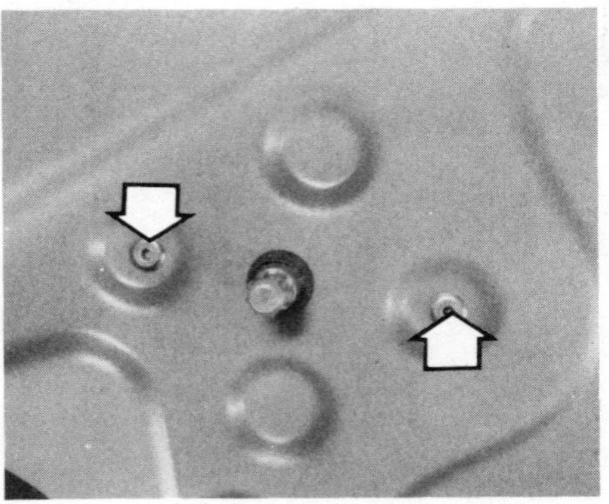

19.5A Two window lifting mechanism securing rivets (arrowed)

19.5B Window lifting channel bolts (arrowed)

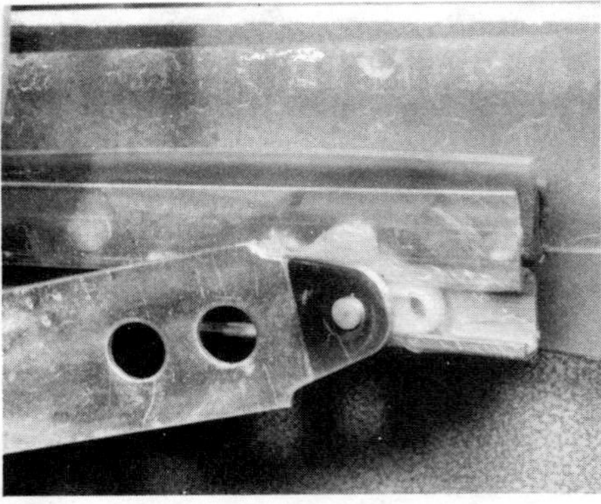

19.6 Scissor lifting mechanism slider

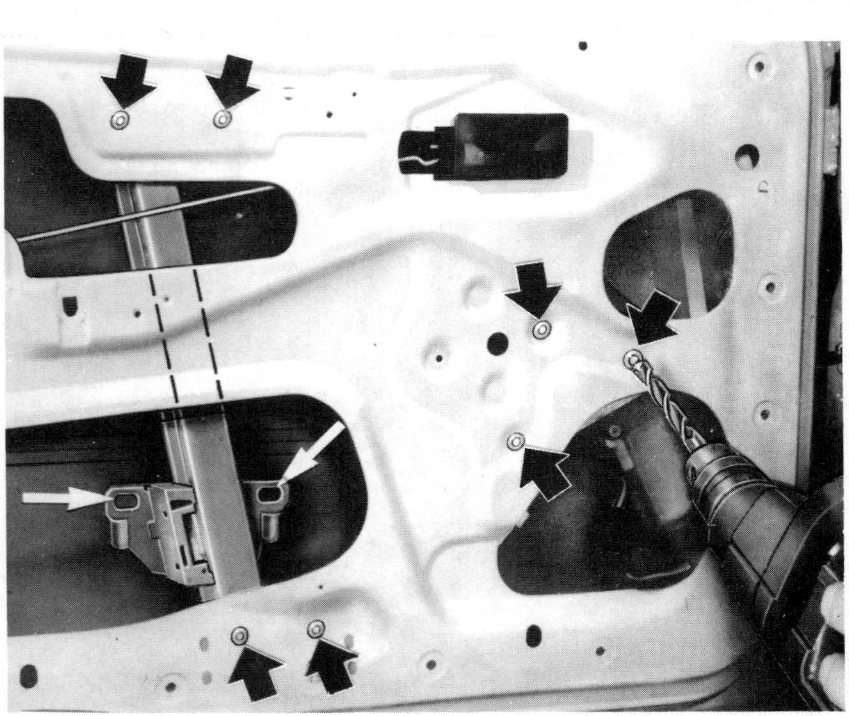

Fig. 11.11 Window lifting mechanism rivets and window channel bolts (arrowed) – front door, cable mechanism, electric drive (Sec 19)

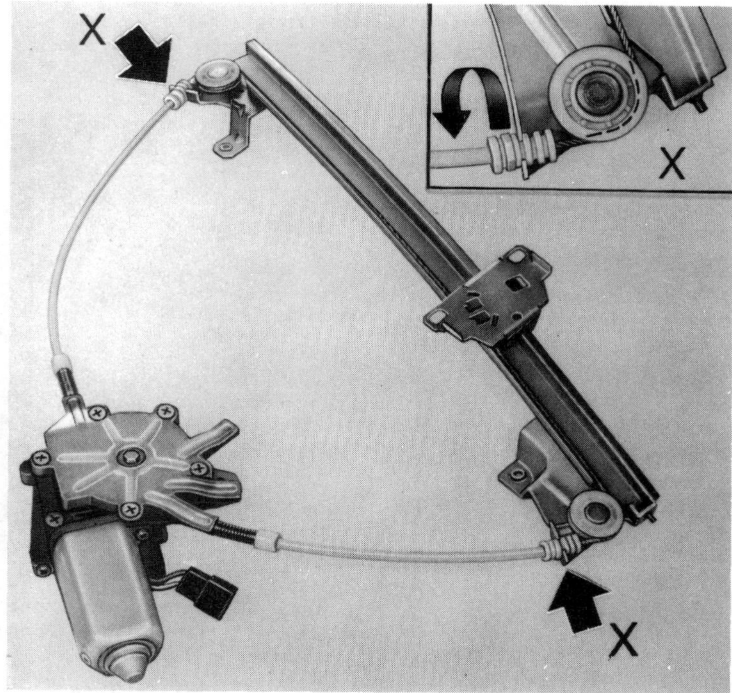

Fig. 11.12 Cable tensioning adjusters (X) – electric drive (Sec 19)

20 Door window – removal and refitting

1 Remove the door trim panel, as described in Section 13.
2 Remove the window weatherstrip from the top of the opening in the door.
3 In the case of the rear door, unbolt and remove the rear guide rail, then remove the fixed part of the window complete with seal.
4 If a scissor type lifter is fitted to the front door, remove the rear guide rail. If a cable type lifter is fitted, unbolt the lifter from the glass channel.

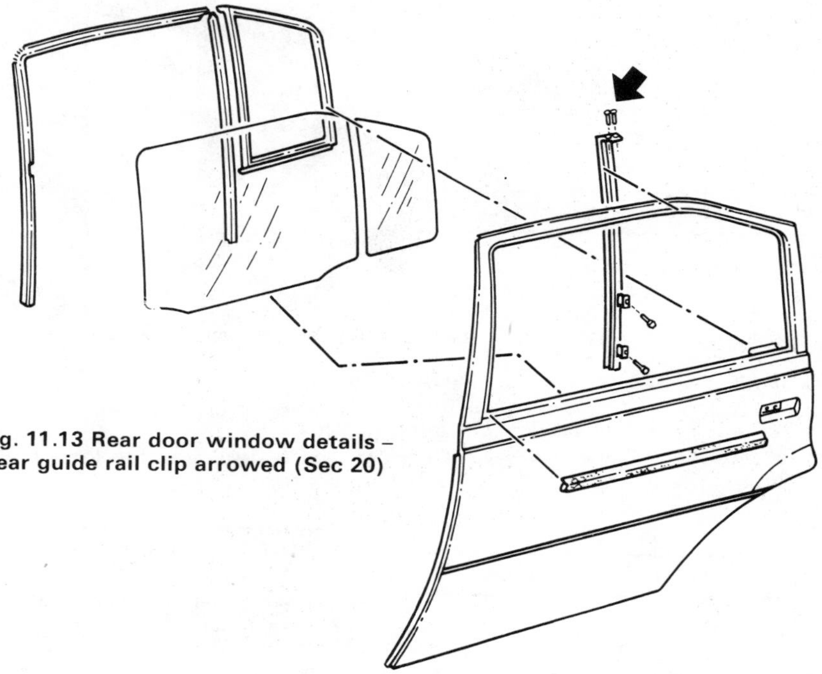

Fig. 11.13 Rear door window details – rear guide rail clip arrowed (Sec 20)

20.6 Adjusting the rear window guide rail. There is another locknut behind the panel

5 Carefully lift the window out through its opening in the door. It will have to be tilted at a considerable angle.
6 Refit in the reverse order to removal. Adjust the angle of the rear door window guide rail by means of the adjustment screw and locknuts until smooth operation is achieved (photo). Note that there are two locknuts, one on each side of the panel.

21 Tailgate – removal and refitting

1 Open the tailgate and have an assistant support it.
2 Disconnect the rear screen washer tube and any wiring that enters the tailgate – this will vary according to model and equipment. Remove the tailgate trim panel if necessary to carry out the disconnections.
3 Disconnect the struts from the tailgate – see Section 23.
4 Extract the hinge pin circlips and press or drive out the hinge pins (photo). Lift away the tailgate.
5 Refit in the reverse order to removal. Note that the circlip ends of the hinge pins face outwards. Lubricate the pins before fitting.

22 Tailgate hinge – removal and refitting

1 Open the tailgate and have an assistant support it.
2 Disconnect the strut on the side being worked on – see Section 23.
3 Extract the circlip and press or drive out the hinge pin.
4 Unclip the roof trim panels and loosen the headlining to gain access to the hinge screws.
5 Undo the two screws with an offset screwdriver and remove the hinge, seal and screw plate.
6 Refit in the reverse order to removal. Tighten the hinge screws to the specified torque. Lubricate the hinge pin before fitting; fit the pin with its circlip end facing outwards.

23 Tailgate strut – removal and refitting

1 Open the tailgate and have an assistant support it.
2 Release the strut from its mounting balljoints by prising the spring clips a little way out and pulling the strut off the balljoints (photo). If the strut is to be re-used, do not remove the spring clips completely, nor prise them out further than 6 mm (0.24 in).

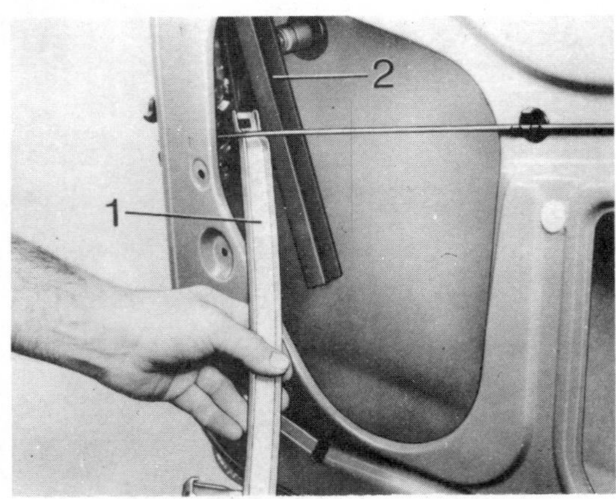

Fig 11.14 Removing the front door window rear guide rail (Sec 20)

1 Guide rail *2 Seal*

21.4 Tailgate hinge showing circlip (arrowed)

3 Dispose of used struts carefully, since they contain gas under pressure.
4 Refit in the reverse order to removal.

24 Tailgate lock – removal and refitting

1 Remove the tailgate trim panel by releasing its retaining clips.
2 Remove the retaining screws from the lock (photo). There are three retaining screws on the Hatchback, four on the Estate and Van.
3 Unhook the operating rod from the lock cylinder arm (photo). It may be necessary to unbolt the lock cylinder in order to disengage the rod. Remove the lock and rod together.

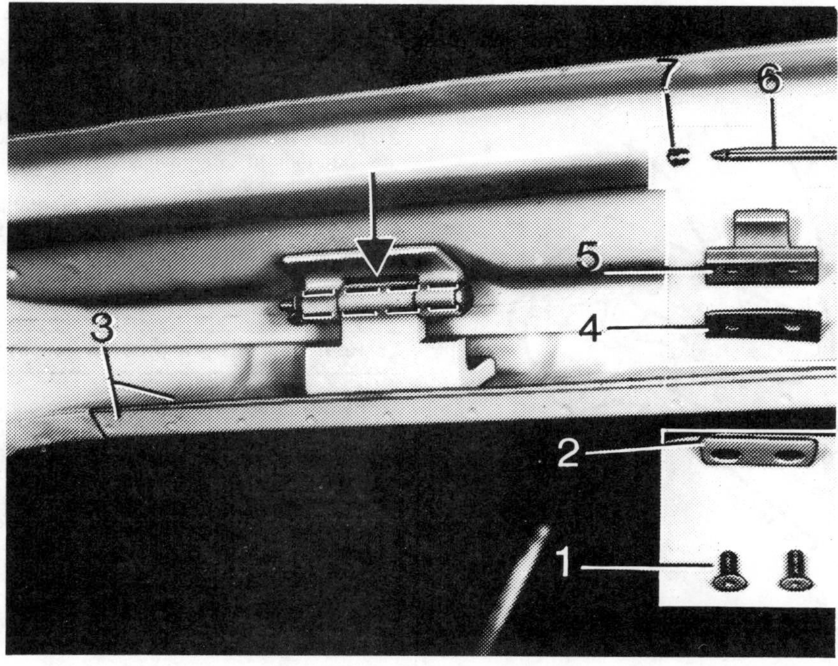

Fig. 11.15 Tailgate hinge components (Sec 22)

1 Screw
2 Screw plate
3 Roof panel
4 Seal
5 Hinge
6 Hinge pin
7 Circlip

23.2 Releasing a tailgate strut spring clip

24.2 Tailgate lock retaining screws (arrowed) – Hatchback

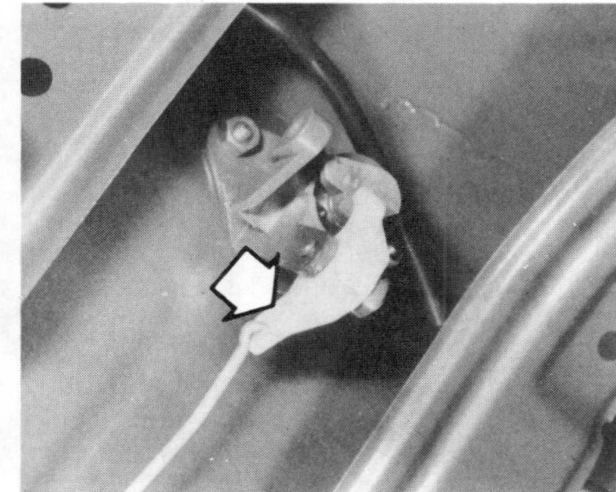

24.3 Lock operating rod connection to arm (arrowed)

4 If a new lock is being fitted, transfer the spring and rod to it.
5 Refit in the reverse order to removal. Check for correct operation before refitting the trim panel.

25 Tailgate lock cylinder – removal and refitting

1 Remove the tailgate trim panel by releasing its retaining clips.
2 Remove the two retaining nuts, disengage the lock operating rod and remove the lock cylinder, complete with housing.
3 Remove the lock cylinder from the housing by driving out the roll pin, moving aside the catch and extracting the circlip. Remove the cylinder with the key inserted.
4 Fit the new cylinder and secure with the circlip and roll pin.
5 Refitting is a reversal of the removal procedure. Check for correct operation before refitting the trim panel.

26 Windscreen and other fixed glass – removal and refitting

1 With the exception of the small fixed windows in the rear passenger door, whose removal is covered in Section 20, the fixed glass is glued in position with special adhesive.
2 Special tools, equipment and expertise are required for successful removal and refitting of glass fixed by this method. The work must therefore be left to a GM dealer, a windscreen specialist or other competent professional.
3 The same remarks apply if sealing of the windscreen or other glass surround is necessary.

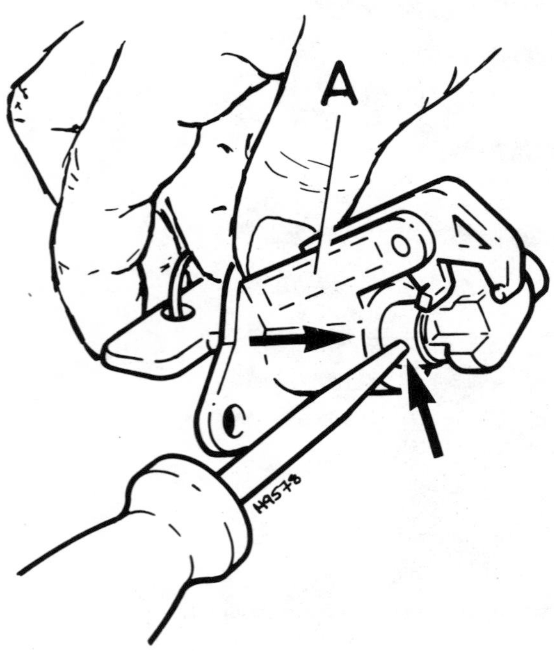

Fig. 11.16 Tailgate lock cylinder removal – roll pin and circlip arrowed (Sec 25)

A Key number

27 Rear quarterlight (opening type) – removal and refitting

1 Unclip the interior trim panels from around the quarterlight.
2 Remove the three screws which secure the catch to the body.
3 Unscrew the two special nuts which hold the hinges to the front of the quarterlight. Remove the quarterlight and recover the hinge securing components.
4 Transfer the catch to the new quarterlight, if applicable, by drilling out the connecting pin and unscrewing the glass fitting. Use a new connecting pin on reassembly.
5 Refit in the reverse order to removal.

28 Rear quarterlight (opening type) – weatherstrip renewal

1 Remove the quarterlight, as described in the previous Section.
2 Cut the old weatherstrip and rubber mount from the body flange. Clean up the flange, but do not remove the old adhesive completely.
3 Clean the mating face of the new weatherstrip with petrol or other suitable solvent, taking appropriate precautions.
4 Apply a 6 mm (0.24 in) bead of polyurethane-based glass adhesive on top of the remains of the old adhesive.
5 Fit the new weatherstrip, refit the quarterlight and keep it closed for at least four hours (or as advised by the makers of the adhesive) to allow the adhesive to set.

29 Interior rear view mirror and mounting – removal and refitting

1 The mirror is secured to its mounting plate by an Allen screw. Remove the screw to detach the mirror.
2 The mounting plate is glued to the windscreen with special adhesive. It is not intended that it should be removed.

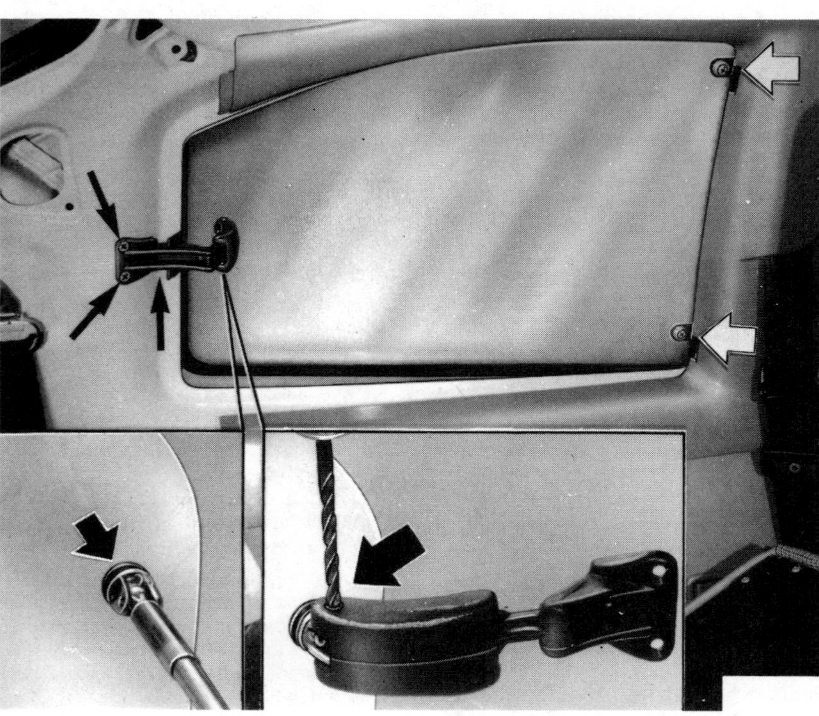

Fig. 11.17 Opening quarterlight fixings (top) and catch removal (Sec 27)

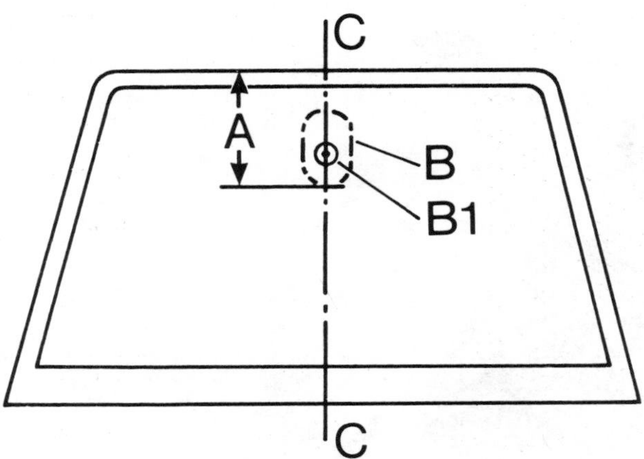

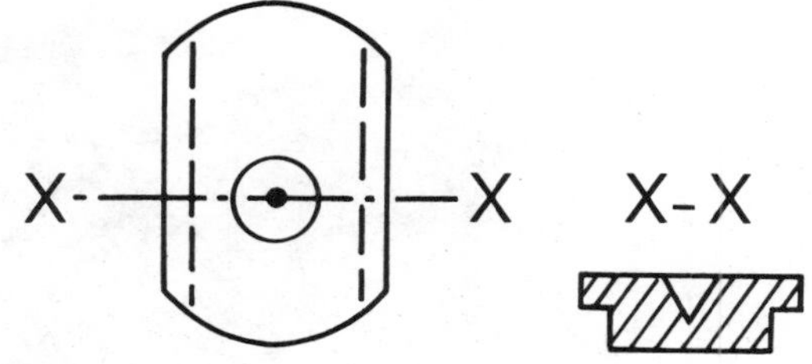

Fig. 11.18 Interior rear view mirror mounting positioning diagram (Sec 29)

A = 110 mm (4.33 in) *B1 Screw hole*
B Mounting plate *C Screen centre-line*

3 If refitting an accidentally detached mounting plate, or fitting a new mounting to a new screen, use a proprietary adhesive suitable for glass in accordance with its maker's instructions. Make sure that the hole for the Allen screw is correctly positioned.

30 Exterior rear view mirror – repair, removal and refitting

1 The door-mounted rear view mirrors may be manually or electrically adjusted; the electric units also incorporate a glass heating element.
2 On all types, the mirror glass may be renewed separately. Prise out the old glass (if intact) with a wooden wedge, (photo) and when applicable disconnect the electrical cables. Engage the new glass with the linkage, connect the wires if applicable and snap the glass home (photo). Be careful when pressing the glass home: the sudden movement as the ball enters its socket may cause the glass to break.
3 To renew an electric mirror motor, prise out the glass as just described, undo the motor securing screws and disconnect its multi-plug. Fit the new motor in the reverse order to removal.
4 To remove a manually adjusted mirror, pull off the adjuster handle and unclip the corner trim. Undo the three retaining screws and remove the mirror (photo).
5 Removal of the electrically adjusted mirror is similar, but instead of pulling off the handle, the wiring harness must be disconnected. The harness connector is located inside the door cavity.
6 Refitting of all types of mirror is a reversal of the removal procedure.

30.2A Remove the glass by levering with a wooden wedge

30.2B Engage the linkage and press the ball into the socket (arrowed)

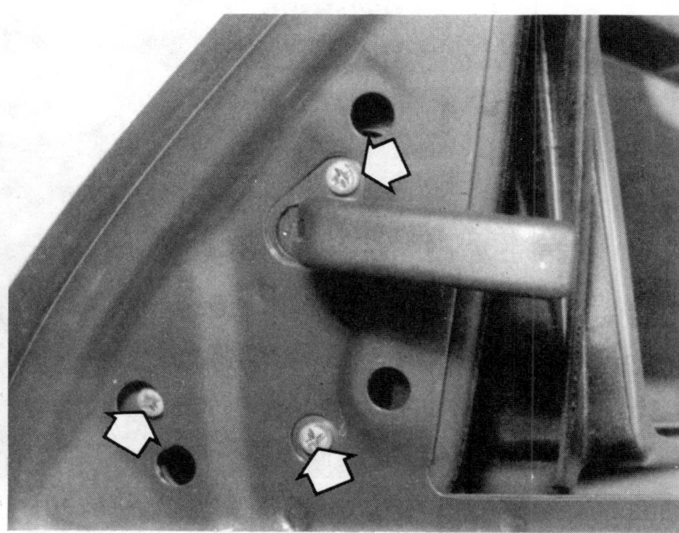

30.4 Mirror retaining screws (arrowed)

Fig. 11.19 Mirror heating wire connectors (arrowed) (Sec 30)

Fig. 11.20 Mirror motor securing screws (arrowed) (Sec 30)

31.1 Seat rail trim removal

31.2A Seat rail front retaining bolt (one of two)

31.2B Seat rail rear retaining bolt (one of two)

31 Front seat – removal and refitting

1 Remove the trim which covers the seat outboard rail. This trim is secured by a single self-tapping screw at the front (photo).
2 Remove the four bolts which secure the seat rails to the floor (photo). Remove the seat, complete with rails; disconnecting the seat heating wires (when fitted).
3 The seat can be separated from the rails if wished, for example if attention to the adjustment mechanisms is necessary.
4 Refit in the reverse order to removal, but observe the following tightening sequence for the rail bolts:

(a) Nip up the rear bolts
(b) Tighten the front bolts to the specified torque
(c) Tighten the outboard rear bolt to the specified torque
(d) Tighten the inboard rear bolt to the specified torque

5 Refit the seat rail trim.

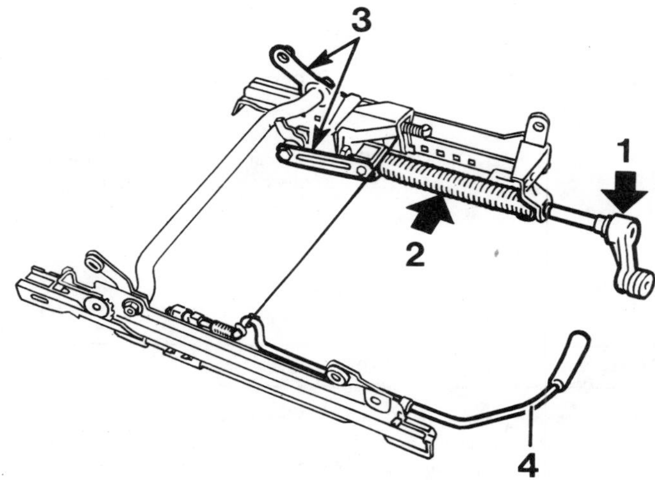

Fig. 11.21 Seat rails and adjustment mechanisms (Sec 31)

1 Crank handle
2 Spring
3 Height adjuster
4 Release lever

32 Head restraints – removal and refitting

1 Both front and rear head restraints are removed in the same way.
2 Pull the head restraint up as far as it will go.
3 Release the catch spring by pushing it rearwards and remove the head restraint. The catch springs are located on the left-hand side on front seats and on the right-hand side on rear seats.
4 The guide sleeves can be removed if necessary by releasing the retaining lugs with a screwdriver and pulling them upwards.
5 Refit in the reverse order to removal.

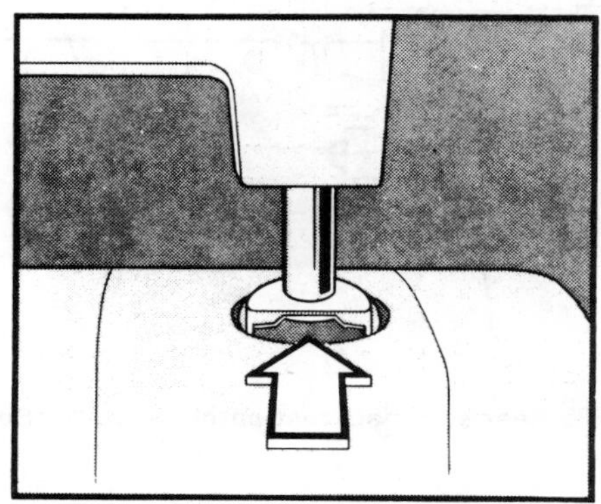
Fig. 11.22 Head restraint catch spring (arrowed) (Sec 32)

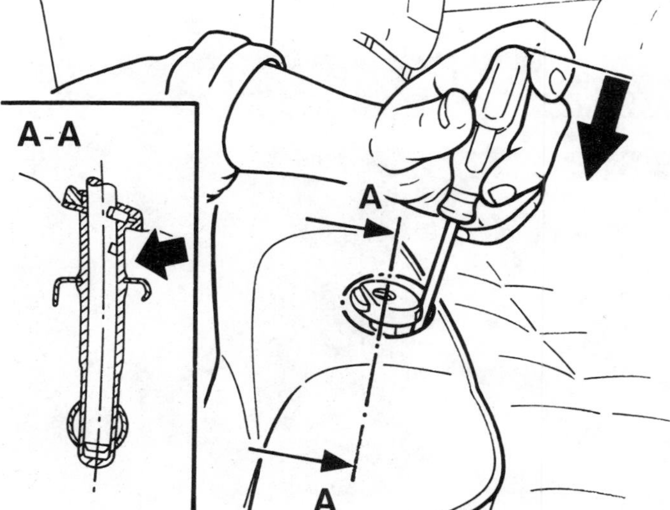

Fig. 11.23 Removing a head restraint guide sleeve – push down with screwdriver to release retaining lugs (arrowed) (Sec 32)

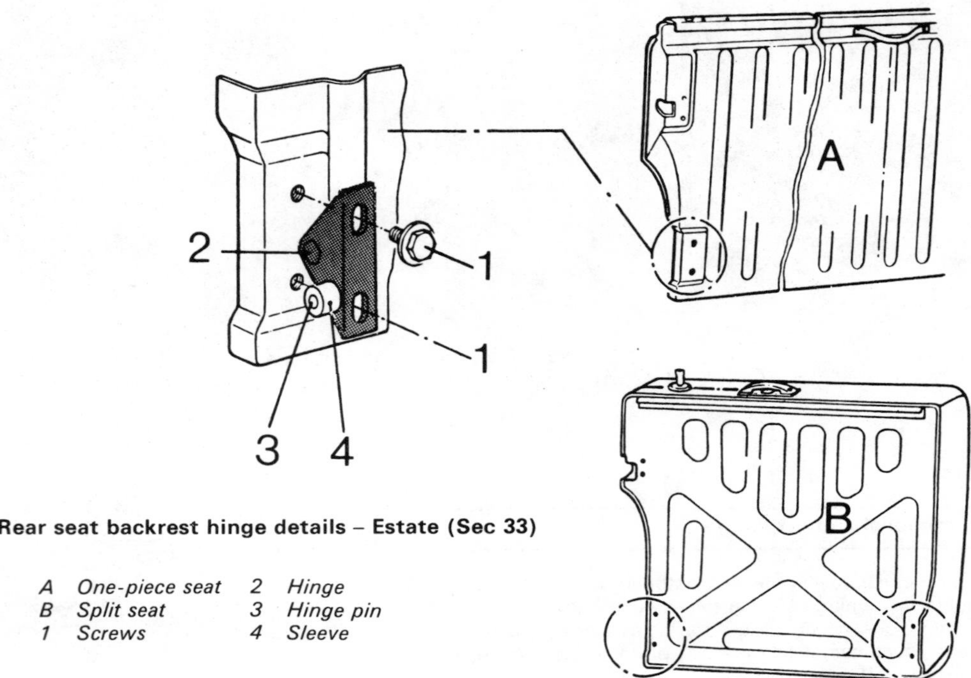

Fig. 11.24 Rear seat backrest hinge details – Estate (Sec 33)

A One-piece seat
B Split seat
1 Screws
2 Hinge
3 Hinge pin
4 Sleeve

33 Rear seat – removal and refitting

1 Uncover the hinges at the front of the seat. Free them by extracting the circlips and removing the hinge pins (photo). The bench section(s) of the seat can now be removed if wished.
2 Unclip the carpet from the backrest (photo).
3 Free the backrest from its catches, unscrew the side hinges and remove the backrest. If a split seat is fitted, also separate the centre bearing (photos).
4 Refit in the reverse order to removal. When securing the split type backrest, start at the centre and work outwards.

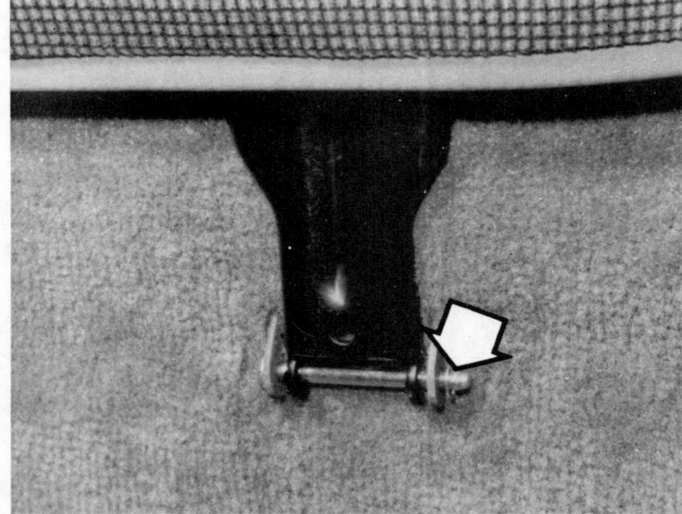

33.1 Rear seat front hinge – circlip arrowed

5 If adjustment of the catch striker is necessary, slacken the nut at the back of the striker pin, engage the seat backrest and then tighten the nut (photo). This applies to Hatchback models. No procedure is laid down for Estate models; Fig. 11.25 gives details of the catch construction.

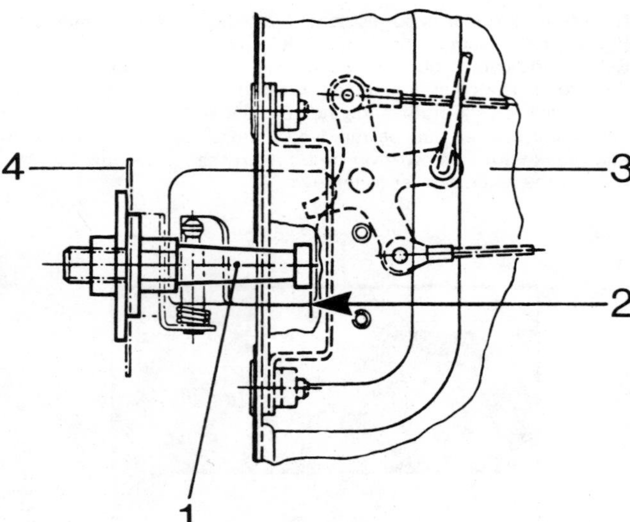

Fig. 11.25 Rear seat backrest catch – Estate (Sec 33)

1 Striker
2 Distance to other striker = 1162 ± 2.5 mm (45.78 ± 0.10 in)
3 Backrest
4 Rear quarter panel

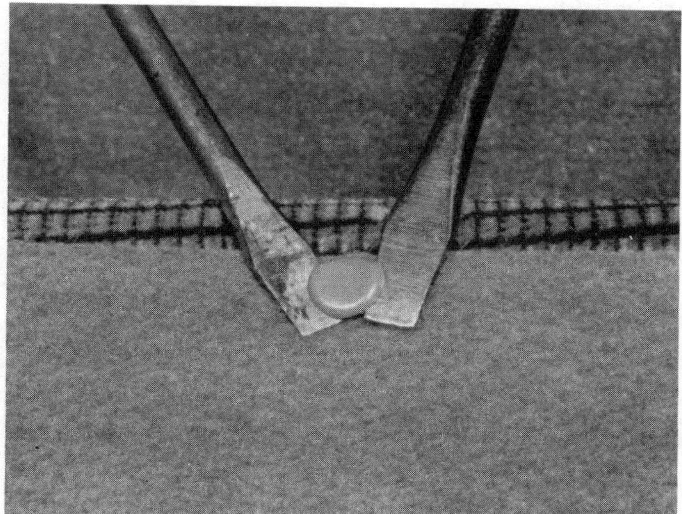
33.2 Removing a carpet securing plug

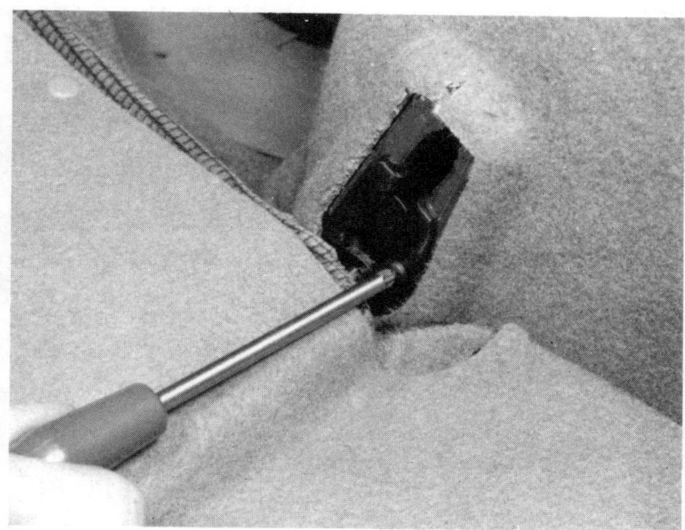
33.3A Unscrewing the side hinge plate

33.3B Seat pivot lifts out of hinge

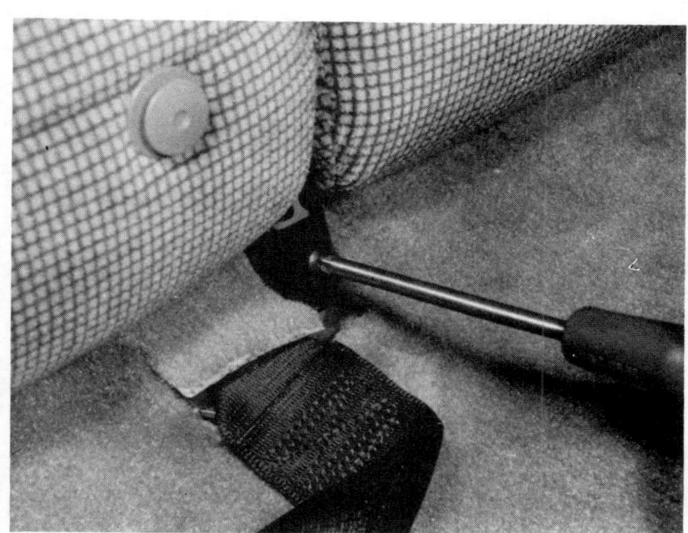
33.3C Unscrewing the centre hinge cover

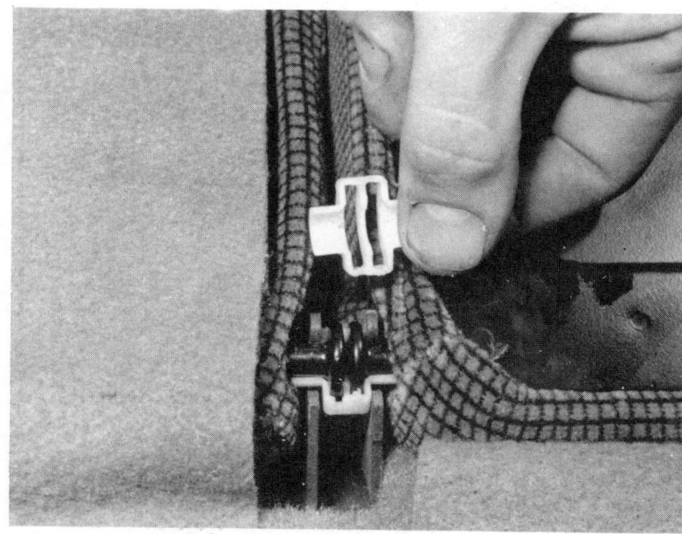
33.3D Centre hinge top half bearing

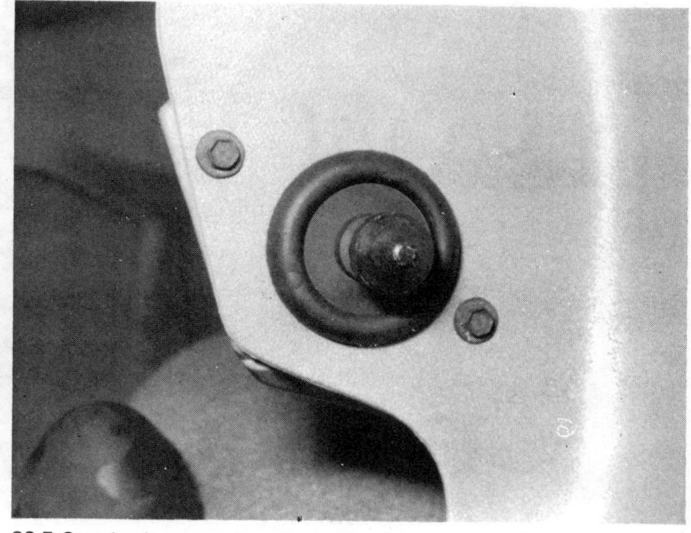
33.5 Seat backrest catch striker – Hatchback

34.2 Removing a luggage area side panel

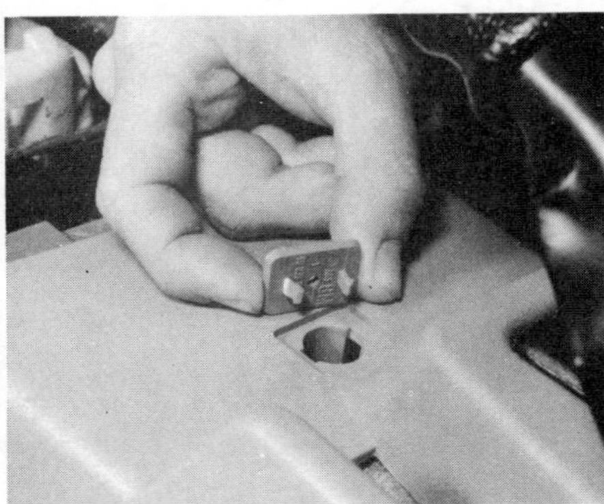

35.2A Centre console rear half screw cover

35.2B Removing the centre console rear half screw

34 Luggage area trim panels – removal and refitting

1 The 'soft' trim panels and carpets are mostly retained by plastic plugs. These can be levered out, but sometimes break. Where more frequent removal is envisaged, eg for access to the spare wheel and tools, the plugs are of a different design and incorporate pulling straps.
2 The side covers may be removed by unbolting them and (when applicable) disconnecting the loudspeaker wires (photo). They carry the rear parcel shelf catches on some models; the catches can be removed simply by pulling them towards the centre of the vehicle.
3 Other 'hard' trim panels are either clipped or screwed into position.

35 Centre console – removal and refitting

1 The centre console is in two parts: the rear half, surrounding the handbrake lever, and the front half, which sits below the heater controls.
2 Commence removal with the rear half. Prise out the screw cover and remove the securing screw (photos).
3 Slide the console rearwards to free it. Removal of the front half may proceed without further disturbing the rear; to remove the rear half completely, disconnect or remove any switches from it and lift it over the handbrake lever.
4 Unclip the cover from around the base of the gear lever. There is no need to remove the gear lever boot itself. Undo the two screws to front and rear of the gear lever (photos). On automatic transmission versions, remove the selector lever cover.
5 Release the two retaining clips and remove the oddments box from below the heater control panel.
6 Remove the two screws which secure the console to the heater control panel (photo). Withdraw the console.
7 Refit in the reverse order to removal.

Fig. 11.26 Releasing the oddments box retaining clips (Sec 35)

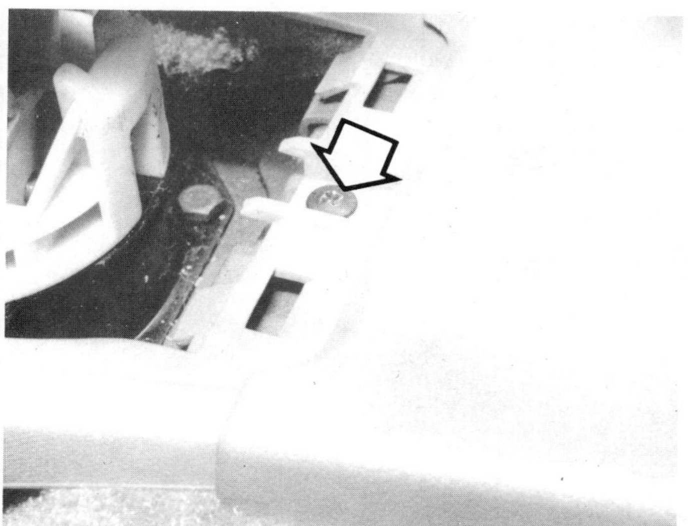

35.4A Centre console screw (arrowed) to rear of gear lever

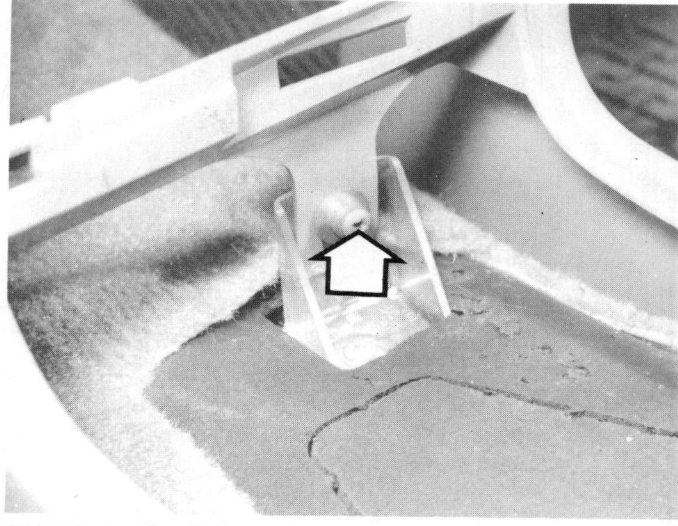

35.4B Centre console screw (arrowed) in front of gear lever

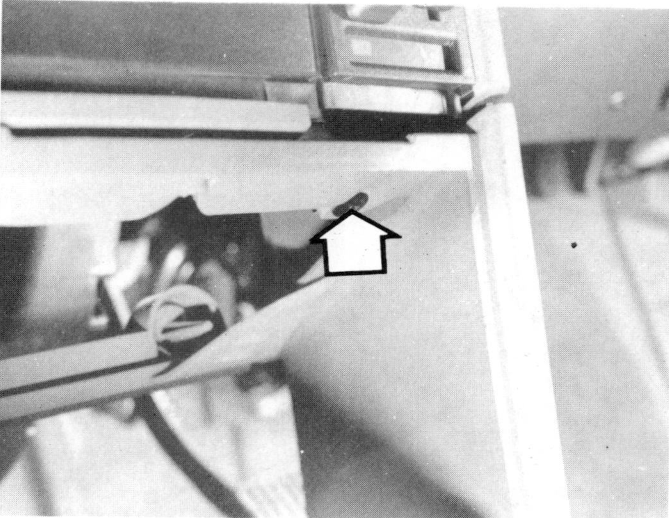

35.6 Centre console screw (arrowed) below heater control panel

36 Glovebox – removal and refitting

1 Open the glovebox and prise out the two check strap plugs (photo).
2 Support the glovebox and remove the two hinge bolts (photo). The gearbox can now be removed.
3 Refit in the reverse order to removal. Note that the hinge bolt holes are slotted to allow for fine adjustment when fitting.

37 Heater – description

The heater operates by passing fresh air, drawn in from the area at the base of the windscreen, through a matrix which is heated by engine coolant.

Temperature regulation is achieved by mixing hot and cold air. Flap valves are used for this; other flap valves direct the air to the windscreen, floor or side outlets.

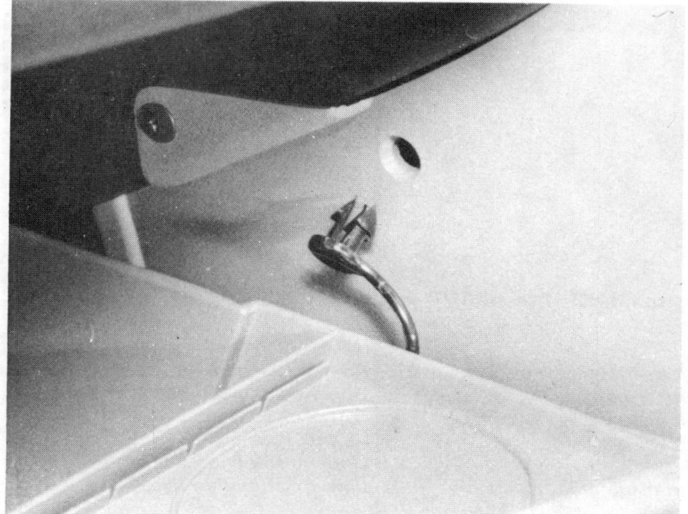

36.1 Glovebox check strap disconnected

36.2 Glovebox hinge bolt

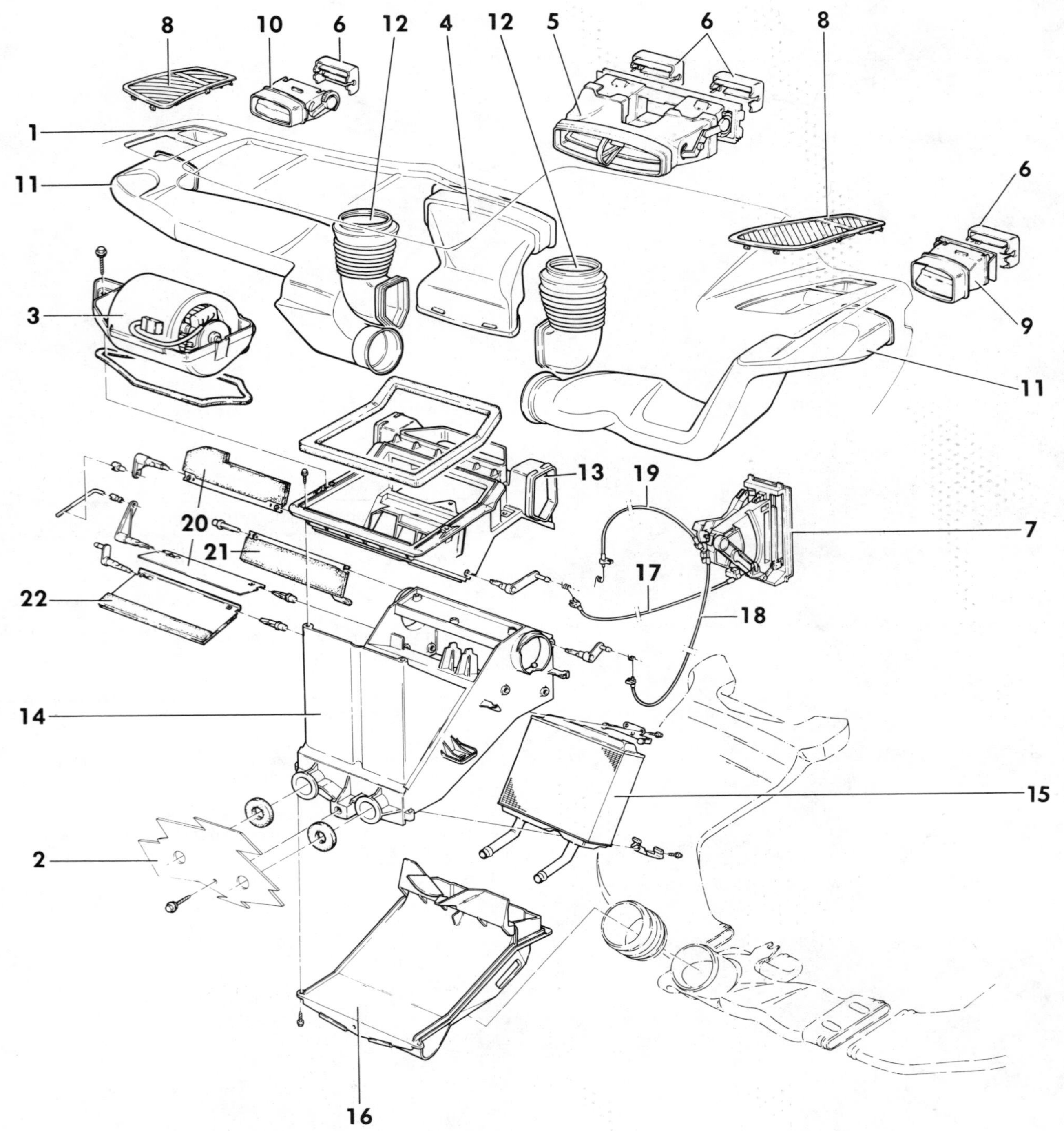

Fig. 11.27 Exploded view of heater components. LHD shown, RHD similar (Sec 37)

1 *Facia panel*
2 *Bulkhead*
3 *Blower motor*
4 *Centre duct*
5 *Centre vent housing*
6 *Swivelling vents*
7 *Controls*
8 *Side grilles*
9 *Side vent housing*
10 *Side vent housing*
11 *Side ducts*
12 *Windscreen ducts*
13 *Air distribution housing (upper half)*
14 *Air distribution housing (lower half)*
15 *Heater matrix*
16 *Air distribution housing cover*
17 *Air mix (temperature) cable*
18 *Upper distribution cable*
19 *Lower distribution cable*
20 *Air mix flaps*
21 *Upper distribution flap*
22 *Lower distribution flap*

An electric fan is used to boost airflow through the heater when the normal ram airflow is insufficient, or in extreme climatic conditions.

Fresh air is available at the centre vents, regardless of the heater settings. Stale air is exhausted through grilles towards the rear of the vehicle.

38 Heater components – removal and refitting

Control panel

1 Remove the front half of the centre console, as described in Section 35.

2 Remove the radio (if fitted) and its surround, as described in Chapter 12, Section 52. If a radio is not fitted, remove the blanking plate.

3 Detach the three control cables from the air distribution housing, noting their locations for refitting. Their sleeves are colour-coded as follows:

Brown	*Foot level distribution*
White	*Hot/Cold air mix*
Black	*Screen level distribution*

4 Remove the two screws from the top of the radio aperture and the two side screws, one on each side (photos).

5 Draw the control panel away (photo). To remove it completely, disconnect the wires from the blower switch and (when fitted) the cigarette lighter.

6 Refit in the reverse order to removal. No adjustment of the cable is required: correct length is achieved by the precise location of the cable outer clamps.

38.4A Removing a screw from the top of the radio aperture

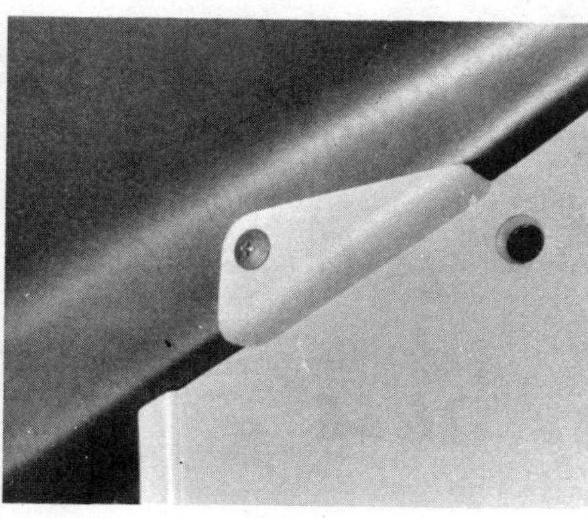

38.4B Heater control panel side screw

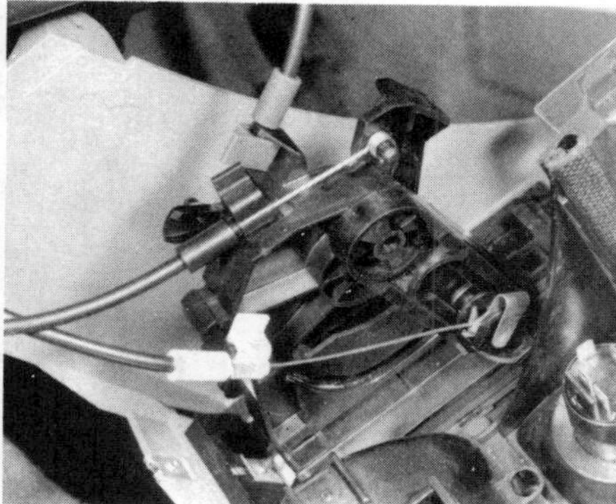

38.5 Removing the heater control panel

Fig. 11.28 Five nuts (arrowed) securing facia panel to bulkhead. LHD shown, RHD similar (Sec 38)

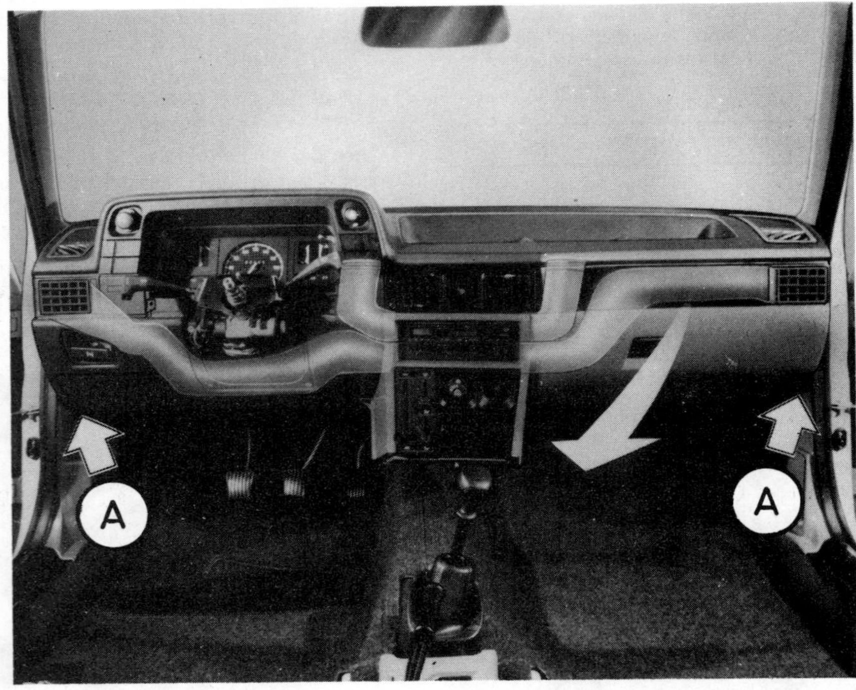

Fig. 11.29 Remove two remaining screws (A) and withdraw facia – LHD shown, RHD similar (Sec 38)

Blower motor

7 Remove the wind deflector, as described in Section 12.

8 Remove the water deflector by freeing it from under the rubber seal and extracting its securing clip (photos). It may also be necessary to slacken or remove one of the wiper spindle nuts.

9 Disconnect the multi-plug, remove the two securing nuts and remove the motor (photo).

10 If the housing halves are unclipped, the motor and ballast resistor can be removed by undoing the two screws at the resistor end (photo). Spares for the meter are not available, but a competent auto-electrician may be able to repair certain types of fault.

11 Refit in the reverse order to removal.

Heater matrix

12 Remove the front half of the centre console, as described in Section 35.

13 Disconnect the control cables from the air distribution housing. Removal of the heater control panel is recommended, as described earlier in this Section, to improve access.

14 Under the bonnet, clamp the coolant hoses at the heater matrix stubs (below the steering rack) and disconnect them. Be prepared for coolant spillage.

15 Remove the four screws which secure the air distribution housing cover (photos). The carpet will have to be turned back to get at the lower ones.

16 Disconnect the rear heating duct bellows, when fitted, and remove the air distirbutor housing cover.

17 Remove the three screws which secure the heater matrix (photo). The air mix flap will have to be moved in order to get at the top two screws. Remove the matrix brackets.

18 Withdraw the matrix into the car, keeping it as flat as possible to minimise coolant spillage.

19 Refit in the reverse order to removal; top up the cooling system on completion (Chapter 2).

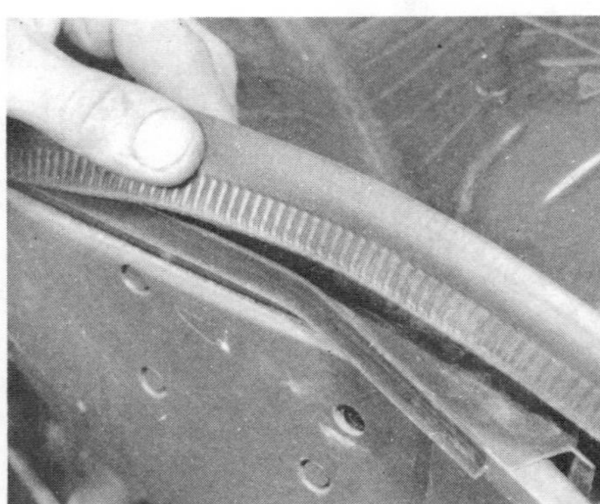

38.8A Lift the rubber seal to free the water deflector

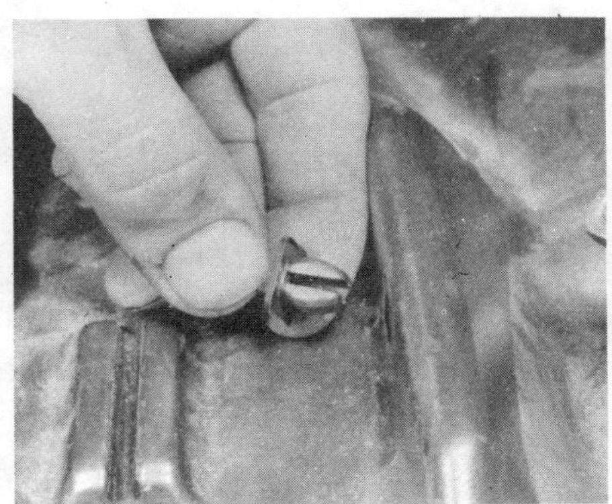

38.8B Water deflector clip

38.9 Removing a blower motor securing nut

38.10 Blower motor-to-housing screws (arrowed)

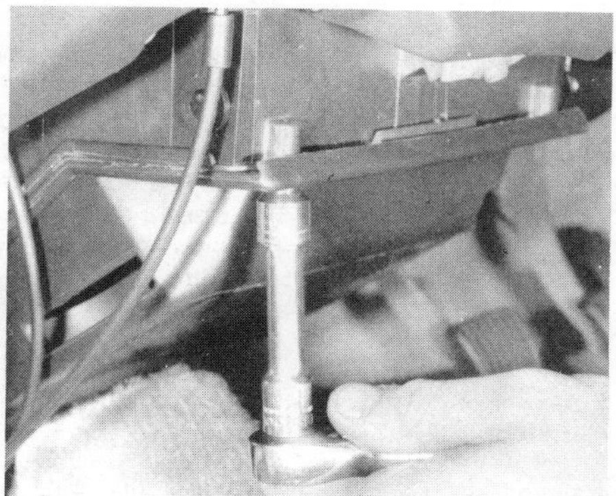
38.15A Removing an air distribution housing upper screw

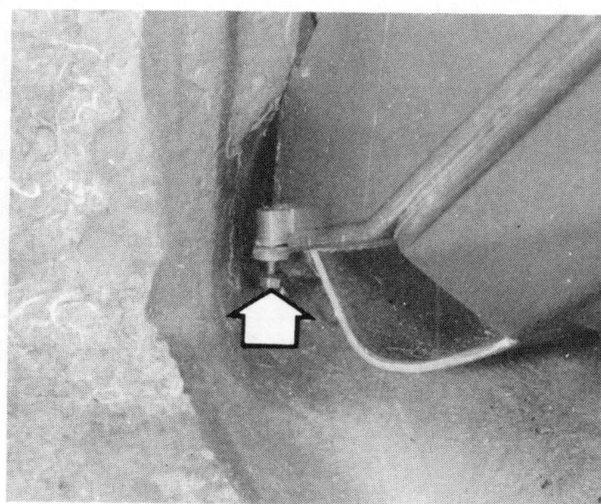
38.15B Air distribution housing lower screw (arrowed)

38.17A Removing the heater matrix lower screw

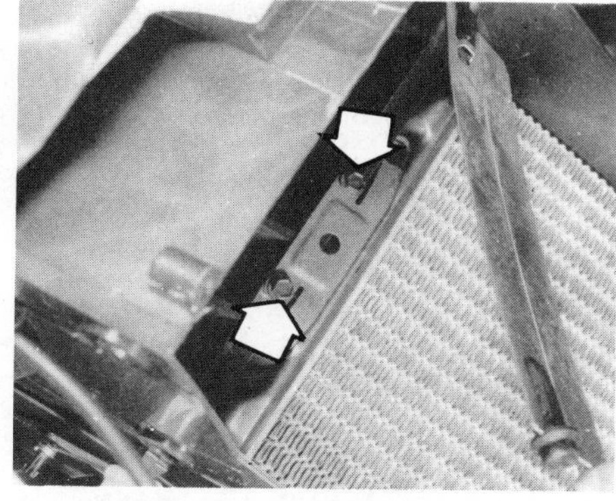
38.17B Heater matrix upper securing screws (arrowed)

Air distribution housing

20 Remove the blower motor and the heater matrix, both as described earlier in this Section.

21 Remove the five nuts which secure the facia panel and the pedal bracket to the bulkhead.

22 Remove the steering column switch shrouds. On models with an adjustable column, also remove the adjuster knob and the column lower cover. Refer to Chapter 8 if necessary.

23 Disconnect the hoses and ducts which connect the air distribution housing to the facia panel ducts.

24 Remove the two remaining screws, one at each end, which secure the facia panel. Pull the facia panel away on the passenger side and have an assistant withdraw the air distribution housing, also towards the passenger side.

25 Refit in the reverse order to removal. Use new self-locking nuts when securing the facia panel and pedal bracket to the bulkhead.

26 Top up the cooling system on completion.

39 Vents and grilles – removal and refitting

1 The flat grilles at each end of the facia simply unclip. According to equipment level they may also cover a loudspeaker (photo).

2 The swivelling vents can be unclipped after swivelling them downwards as far as possible. The side vent housings are secured by a single screw and clips (photo); the clips will probably be destroyed during removal.

3 The centre vent housing is secured by four screws, two above and two below (photo). The lower screws also secure the radio surround.

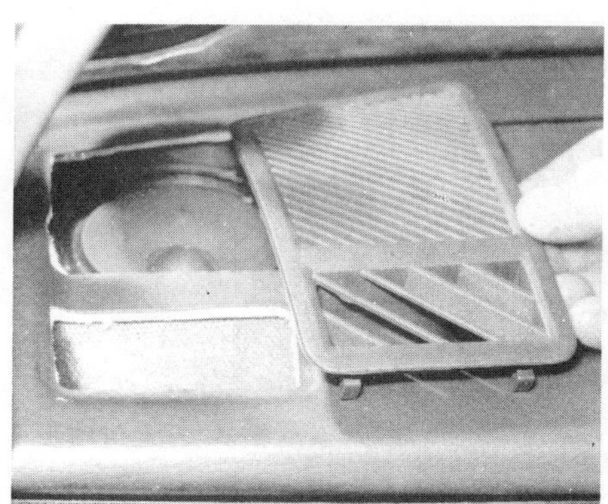
39.1 Removing an end grille and speaker cover

39.2 Removing a swivelling vent housing securing screw

39.3 Removing a centre vent housing screw

This housing also carries the clock, when fitted, which must be disconnected when removing the housing.

4 The air extraction grilles on the outside of the vehicle can be carefully prised out of their locations with a wooden or plastic wedge, being careful not to damage the paintwork.

5 All these components can be refitted by simply clipping and/or screwing them back into position.

40 Gutter covers – removal and refitting

1 The main gutters are covered by a strip with opening slots to accommodate a roof rack (photo).

2 The cover strip can be unclipped if wished by tugging sharply to free it from its clips.

3 When refitting, start at the back of the vehicle and work towards the front. Make sure that the clips engage between the notches on the gutter cover (Fig. 11.30).

41 Seat belts – general

1 Inertia reel front seat belts are fitted to all models. According to trim level, these may have adjustable upper mountings. Rear seat belts are available as an optional extra at time of purchase, or as a kit for aftermarket fitting.

2 Keep the belts untwisted so that they retract into their reels when not in use. Occasionally check the function of the inertia reel units by braking sharply from 5 mph (traffic permitting): the belts should lock. A defective unit must be renewed.

3 Only use soap and water to clean the belts. Strong detergents, bleaches or dyes may weaken the webbing. After cleaning, keep the belts extended until they are dry.

4 Belts which have been subject to impact loads must be renewed.

5 When renewing a belt, note carefully the fitted sequence of mounting washers and spacers. Use new mounting components when these are supplied, and tighten the mountings to the specified torque (photo).

6 Access to the adjustable top mounting is not immediately obvious. It is necessary to remove the floor level trim strip, then free the door seal from the pillar. The pillar trim can then be pulled inwards to free its top and centre mountings, then slid downwards to release the bottom lip. Notice how the belt feeds through the pillar trim (photo).

40.1 Roof rack opening slot in gutter

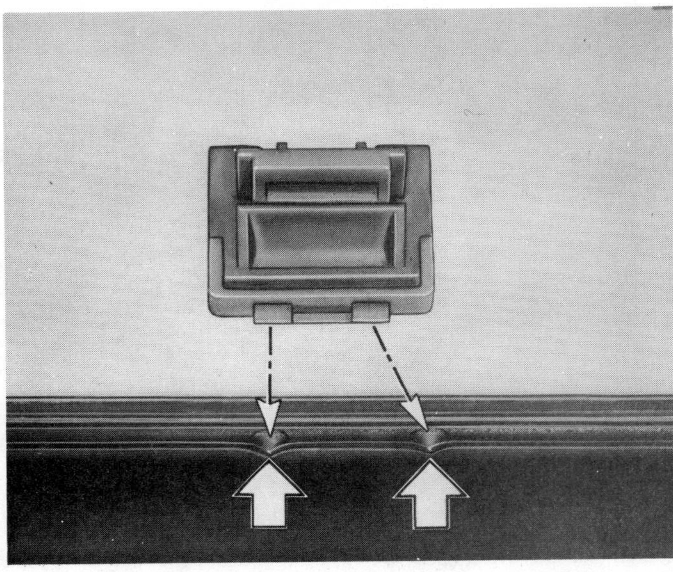

Fig. 11.30 Gutter clips must engage between notches (arrowed) (Sec 40)

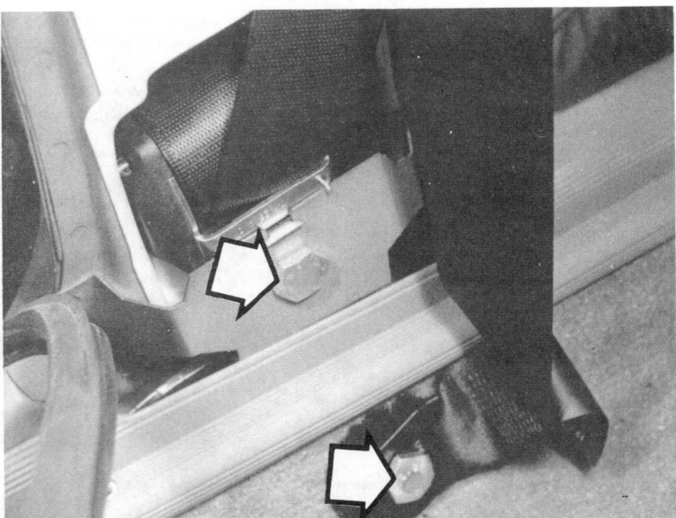

41.5 Front seat belt inertia reel and lower mounting bolts (arrowed)

41.6A Front seat belt adjustable top mounting

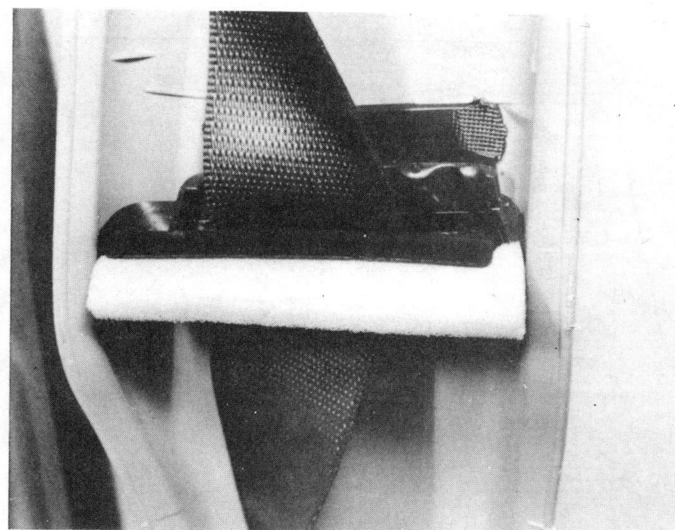

41.6B Belt feeds through guide in pillar trim

41.7A Rear seat belt inertia reel

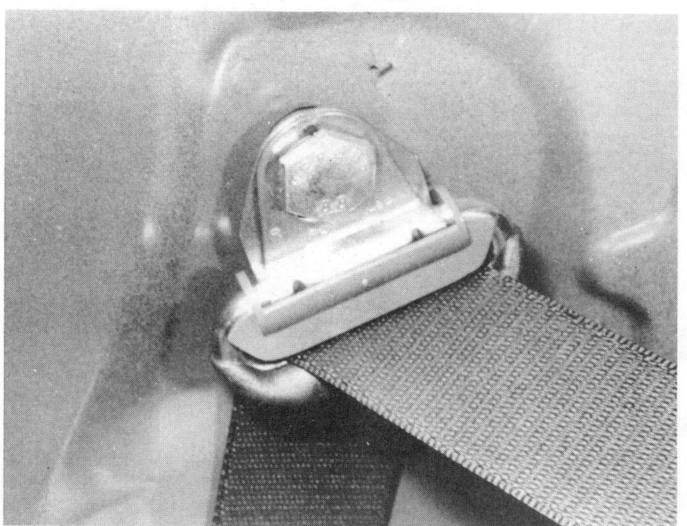

41.7B Rear seat belt upper mounting

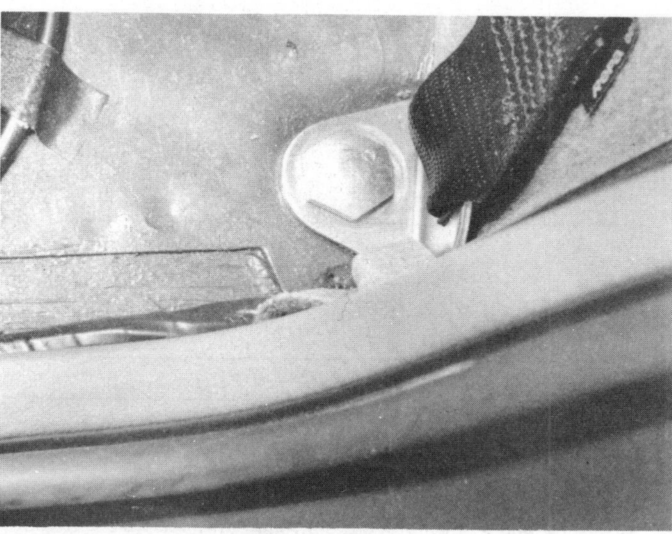

41.7C Rear seat belt floorpan mounting

7 Access to the rear inertia reel is gained by removing most of the rear quarter trim panels; on 5-door models the door seal will have to be disturbed to remove the panels. Access to the floor mountings is gained by folding the seat forwards (photos).

42 Sunroof – operation and maintenance

1 A slide-and-tilt glass panel sunroof is available as an optional extra on most models. It is operated by a crank handle. After depressing the release button, turning the handle anti-clockwise open the roof. Turning the handle clockwise when the roof is closed causes its rear end to tilt up for ventilation.
2 A louvred panel, known as a sunshade, can be drawn out under the glass. This should only be done when the glass is closed or in the 'tilt' position.
3 Maintenance is confined to checking periodically that the drain hoses are not blocked at their lower ends (Fig. 11.32).
4 No lubrication or other maintenance is specified.

Fig 11.31 Sunroof crank handle – release button arrowed (Sec 42)

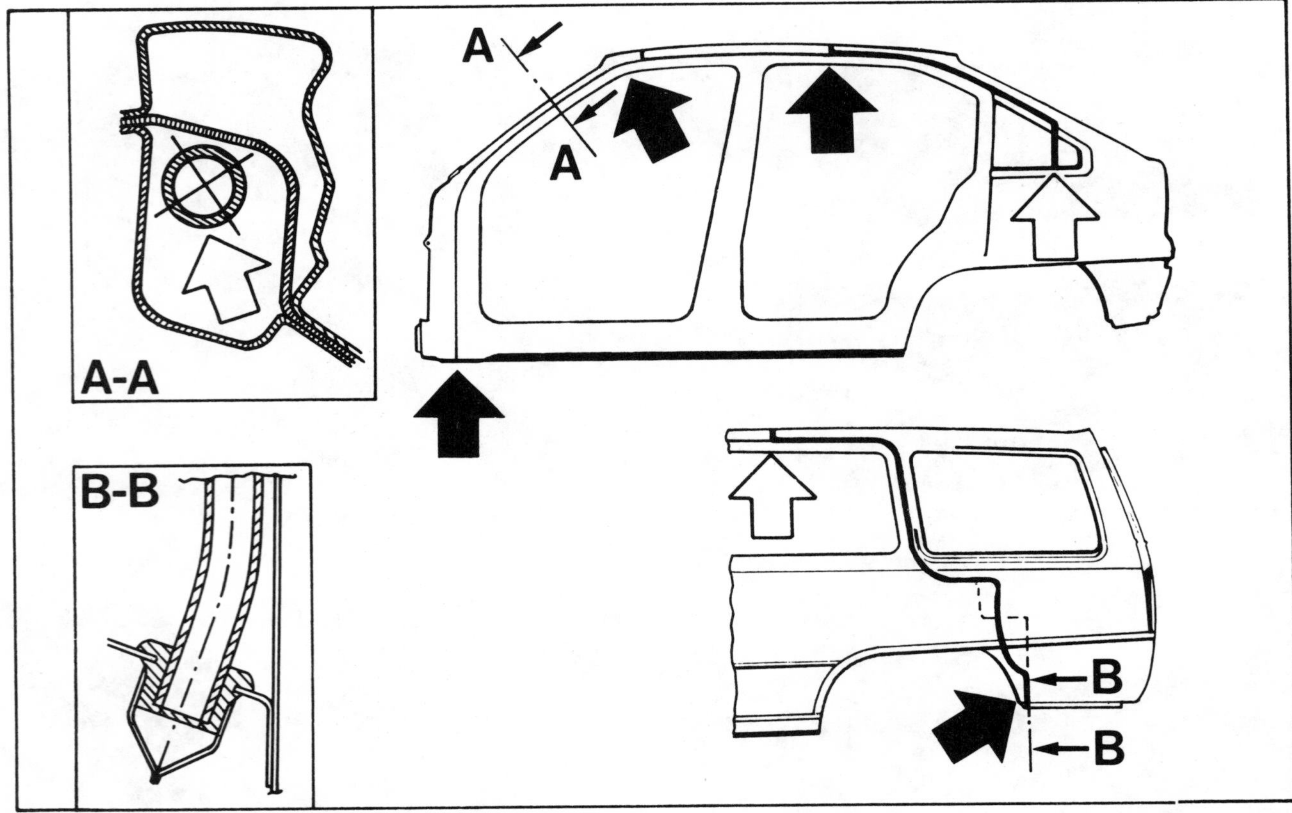

Fig. 11.32 Sunroof drain hose ends (arrowed) (Sec 42)

43 Sunroof – component renewal *in situ*

1 The operations in this Section do not require the complete sunroof to be removed from the vehicle.

Glass panel

2 Close the panel and push the sunshade fully rearwards. Remove the clips from the slide block guides.
3 Unscrew the panel from the slide block guides on both sides and remove it.
4 Before refitting a new panel, measure the distance between the attaching flanges. Bend the flanges if necessary to achieve the desired dimension (Fig. 11.35).
5 Remove the protective sheet from the new panel and fit it with the chequered edge forwards. Raise the panel into the 'tilt' position and fit it loosely to the slide block guides.
6 Before tightening the slide block guide screws, close the panel and adjust its position as shown in Fig. 11.36, then tighten the screws.

Controlled gap seal

7 The 'controlled gap seal' is the seal which surrounds the glass panel.
8 Remove the glass panel, as previsouly described.
9 Strip off the seal and clean off old sealing compound, being careful not to damage the glass.
10 Apply sealant (GM 90140944, or equivalent) all around the edge of the glass panel.
11 Fit the new seal, starting at the middle of the left-hand edge and working round. Immediately refit the panel and check that the seal fits properly in the closed position. If the specified sealant has been used, it will not set for an hour or so, during which time the position of the seal can be altered slightly to provide a good fit. Make sure that the panel height adjustment is correct (paragraph 6).

Gutter

12 Remove the glass panel, as previously described.
13 Remove the two Torx screws which secure the gutter. Lift the gutter out of the cut-out in the roof.
14 Refit the gutter to the cut-out at an angle, pushing it up to the stop on both sides so that the retaining lugs are forced into the gutter guides.
15 Refit and tighten the Torx screws.
16 Refit and adjust the glass panel.

Sunshade

17 Remove the gutter, as just described.
18 Carefully prise the four sunshade springs out of the roof guides, using a plastic implement to avoid damage. Withdraw the sunshade from the guides.
19 Refit in the reverse order to removal. Make sure that all the spring ends enter the guides.

Crank drive

20 Remove the central securing screw from the handle – the screw head is concealed by a plastic cover. Pull off the handle and unclip its recessed backplate, being careful not to damage the headlining.
21 Remove the two securing screws and withdraw the crank drive mechanism.
22 When fitting a new crank drive mechanism, adjust it as follows.
23 If the sunroof is open, temporarily refit the crank drive and close the roof, then remove the crank drive again.
24 Turn the drive pinion by hand – **not** with the handle – until the stop pin emerges from the housing.
25 Refit and secure the crank drive with the stop pin facing forwards. Refit the backplate and handle.

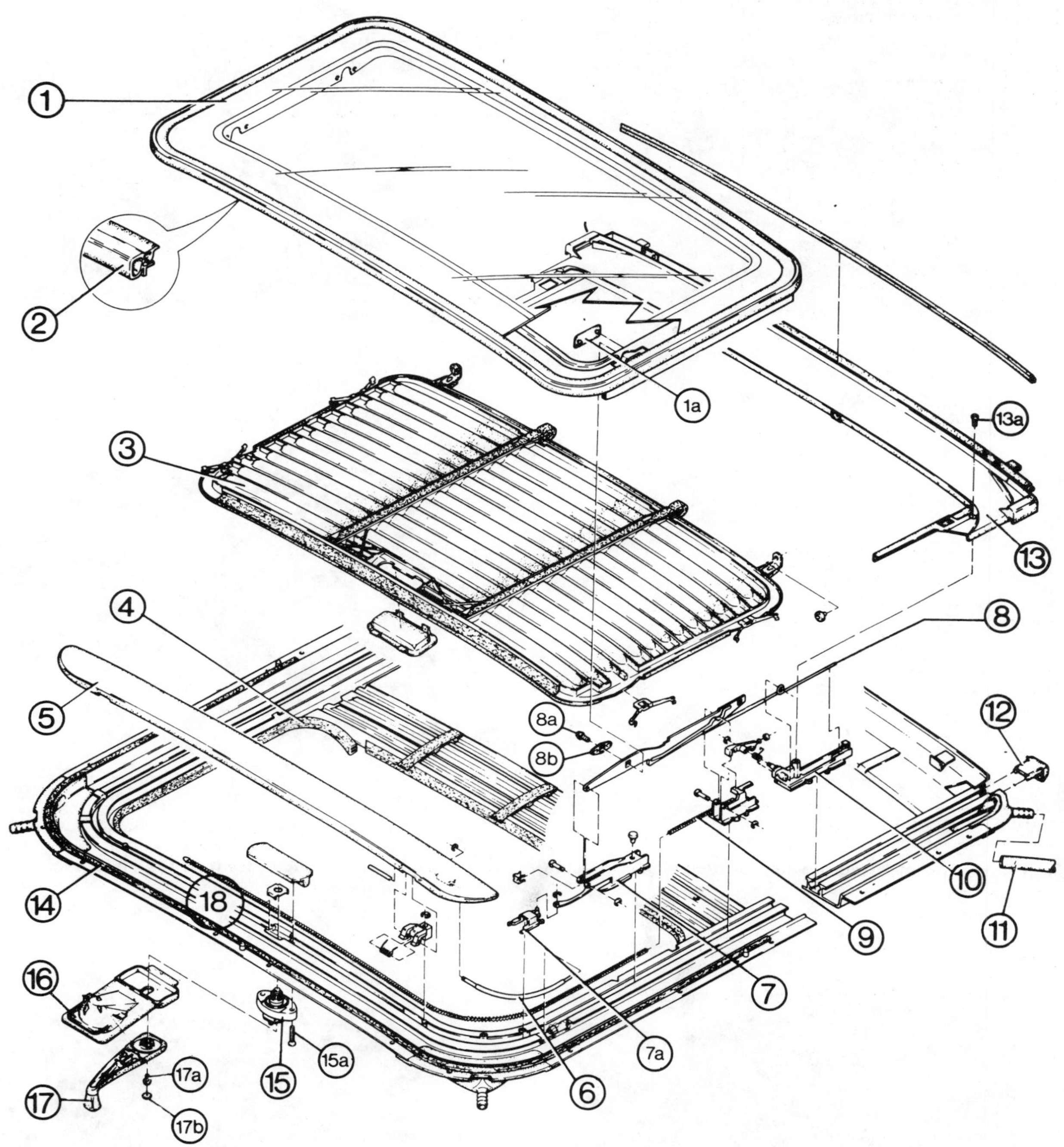

Fig. 11.33 Exploded view of sunroof components (Sec 43)

1	Glass panel	7	Front guide	11	Drain hose	15a	Screw
1a	Clip	7a	Slide block	12	Roof guide plug	16	Handle backplate
2	Controlled gap seal	8	Slide block guide	13	Gutter	17	Crank handle
3	Sunshade	8a	Screw	13a	Gutter screw	17a	Screw
4	Seal	8b	Lockplate	14	Seal	17b	Scew cover
5	Wind deflector	9	Cable	15	Crank drive	18	Frame
6	Lifter	10	Gutter guide				

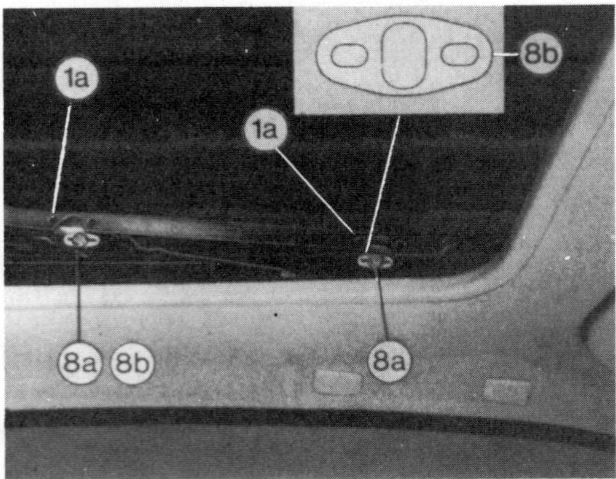

Fig. 11.34 Glass panel fixings (Sec 43)

1a Clip locations *8b Lockplate*
8a Screws

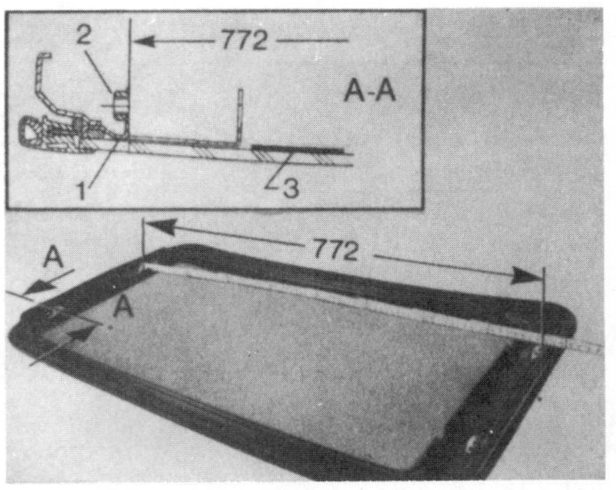

Fig. 11.35 Panel attaching flange distance (in mm) (Sec 43)

1 Flange *3 Protective sheet (new panel)*
2 Nut

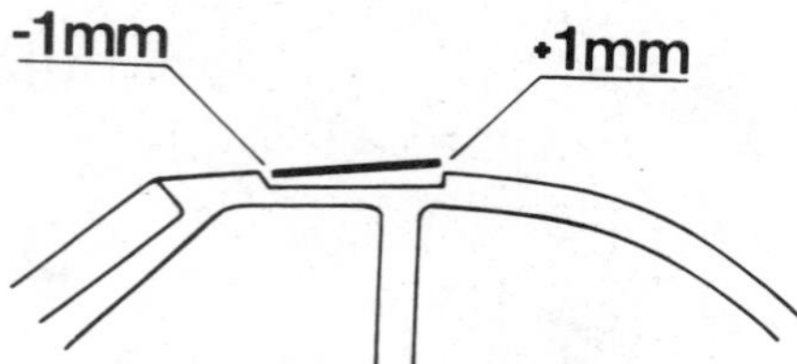

Fig. 11.36 Correct fitted position of glass panel (Sec 43)

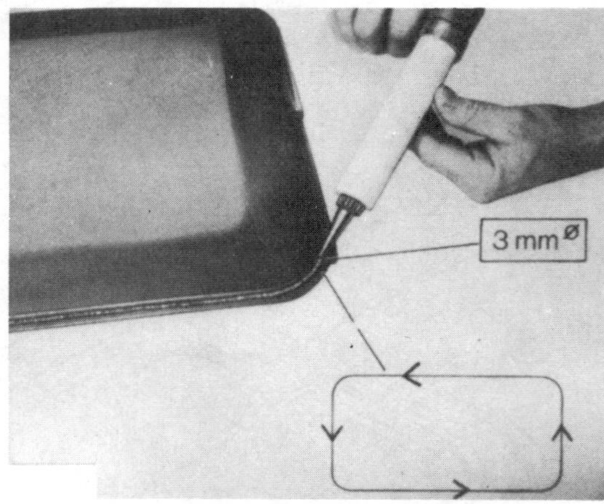

Fig. 11.37 Applying sealant to the glass panel (Sec 43)

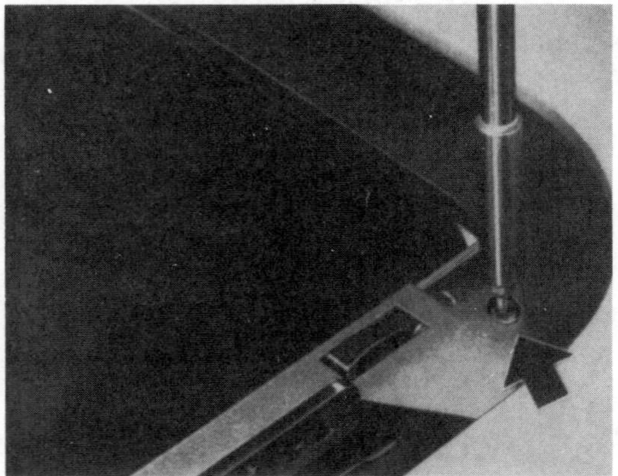

Fig. 11.38 Removing a gutter retaining screw (arrowed) (Sec 43)

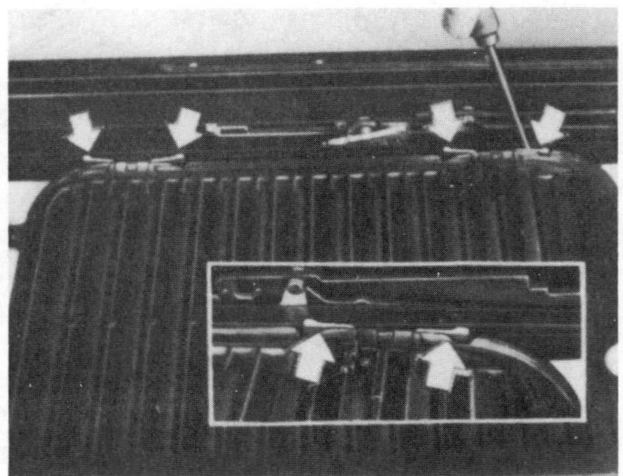

Fig. 11.39 Prising the sunshade spring ends (arrowed) out of the roof guides (Sec 43)

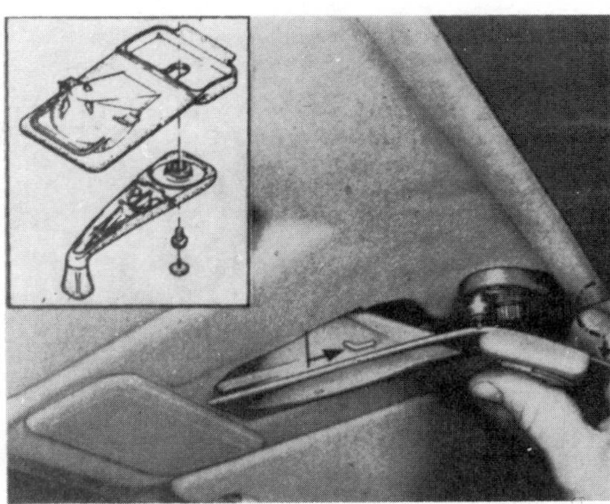

Fig. 11.40 Removing the crank handle and its backplate (Sec 43)

Fig. 11.41 Turn the drive pinion (bottom arrow) until the stop pin emerges (top arrow) (Sec 43)

Fig. 11.42 Refitting the crank drive – stop pin (large arrow) faces forwards. Small arrows show retaining screws (Sec 43)

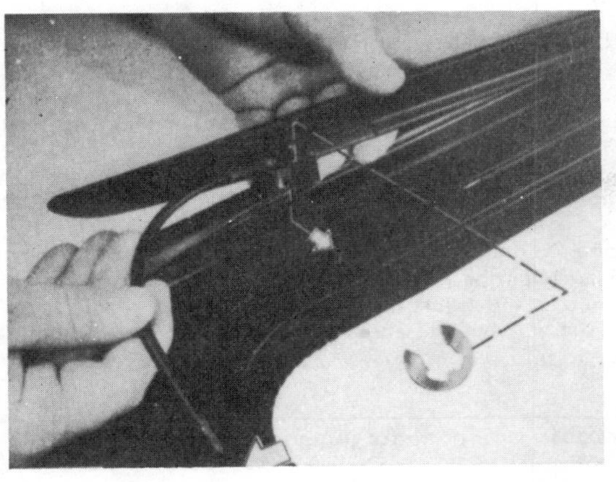

Fig. 11.43 Securing a lifter and bearing block to the wind deflector (Sec 43)

Wind deflector

26 Remove the glass panel, as previously described.

27 Crank the handle to move the slide blocks rearwards until the wind deflector can be raised and removed.

28 Transfer the lifters and bearing blocks to the new deflector; secure them with circlips.

29 Fit the new deflector, bring the slide blocks back to the closed position and refit the glass panel.

44 Sunroof assembly – removal and refitting (complete)

1 Disconnect the battery earth lead.

2 Remove the glass panel, as previously described.

3 Remove the crank handle and its backplate.

4 Remove the interior lamp and grab handles. Loosen the door seals at their top edges. Remove or loosen all interior trim panels which abut the headlining, then open the tailgate and slide the headlining out rearwards, freeing it from the rear of the roof frame.

5 Disconnect the four drain hoses from the corners of the sunroof frame.

Fig. 11.44 Removing the headlining (Sec 44)

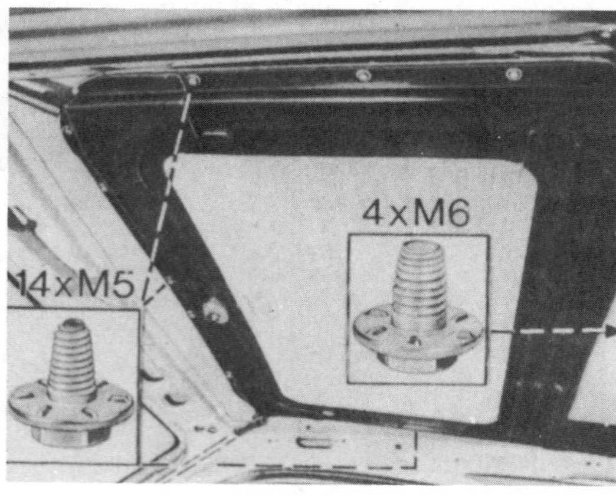

Fig. 11.45 Sunroof frame fixing screws (Sec 44)

6 With the help of an assistant, remove the sunroof frame securing screws and withdraw the unit through the tailgate.
7 Before refitting, check the adjustment of the unit by turning the crank handle as far as its stop. In this position, the cable guide pin should be aligned with the notch in the roof guide (Fig. 11.46). If this is not so, remove the crank drive and adjust it, as described in Section 43, paragraph 24. Align the guide pin with the notch and refit the crank drive.
8 Secure the unit to the roof – the M6 screws must be renewed, but the M5 ones can be re-used. Refit the headlining and the displaced trim, then refit and adjust the glass panel.
9 Refit the grab handles and interior light, then reconnect the battery earth lead.

45 Sunroof – components renewal (unit removed)

1 The sunroof must be removed, as described in the previous Section, before the items in this Section can be renewed.

Operating cables

2 The operating cables must always be renewed in pairs, even if only one is broken.
3 With the sunroof removed, unscrew the gutter securing screws and remove the gutter. Also remove the crank drive unit.
4 Pull the plugs out of the rear ends of the roof guides.
5 Pull the cables out of the roof guides. Separate them from the slide block guides.
6 Offer the new cables to the roof guides. Fit the slide block guides and secure them with the guide pins and circlips. The circlips go on the outboard sides of the guides.
7 Push the cable guides forwards until their pins are aligned, as shown in Fig. 11.46. Adjust the crank drive, as desribed in Section 43, paragraph 24, then refit it.
8 Refit the roof guide plugs and the gutter.

Gutter guide

9 Unscrew the gutter securing screws and remove the gutter. Also remove the crank drive unit and the roof guide end plugs.
10 Partly withdraw the cables until the gutter guide and connecting rod can be withdrawn from the slide block guide.
11 Fit the new guide and connecting rod. Push the slide block guide and gutter guide forwards until the lever engages in the roof guide recess.
12 Adjust the cable guides and crank drive, as described in paragraph 7, then refit the crank drive.
13 Refit the roof guide plugs and the gutter.

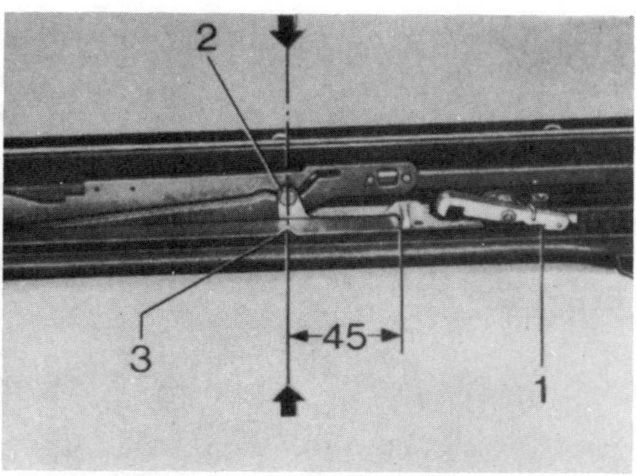

Fig 11.46 Cable guide pin (2) aligned with notch (3) – distance in mm (Secs 44 and 45)

1 Gutter guide lever

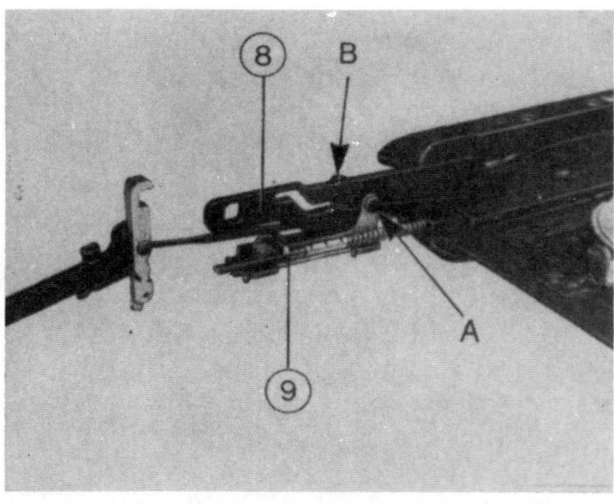

Fig. 11.47 Removing an operating cable (Sec 45)

A Guide pin
B Circlip
8 Slide block guide
9 Cable (with guide piece)

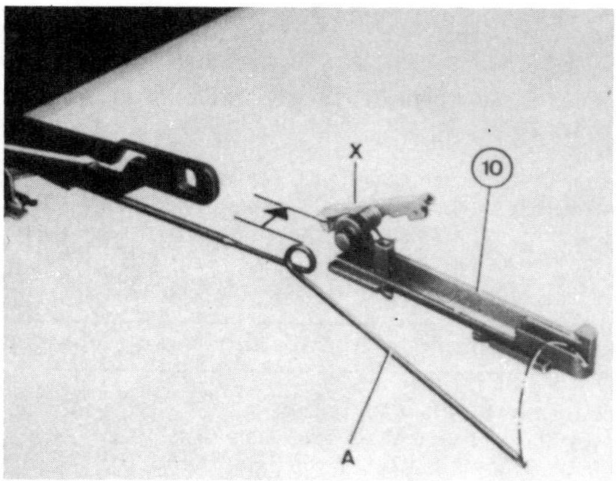

Fig. 11.48 Fitting a gutter guide (Sec 45)

A Connecting rod
X Catch lever
10 Gutter guide

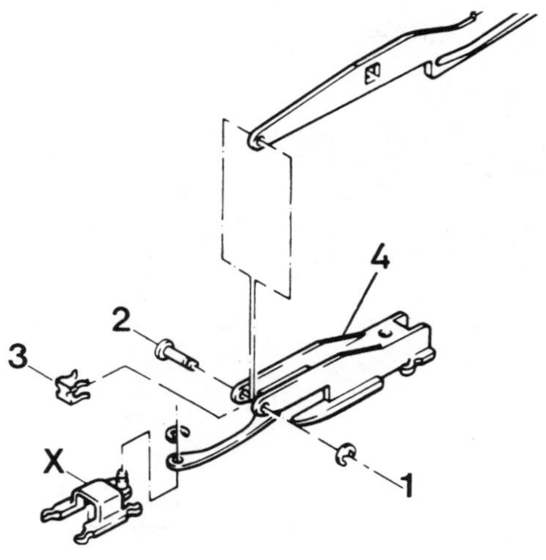

Fig. 11.49 Front guide securing details (Sec 45)

1 Circlip
2 Pin
3 Spring clip
4 Front guide
X Slide block

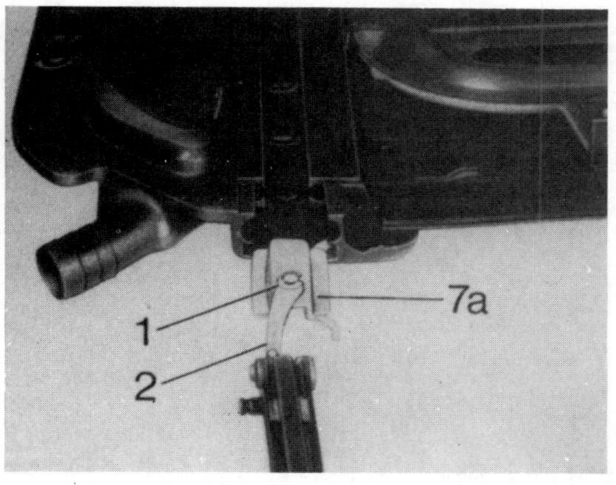

Fig. 11.50 Slide block removed (Sec 45)

1 Clip
2 Connecting link
7a Slide block

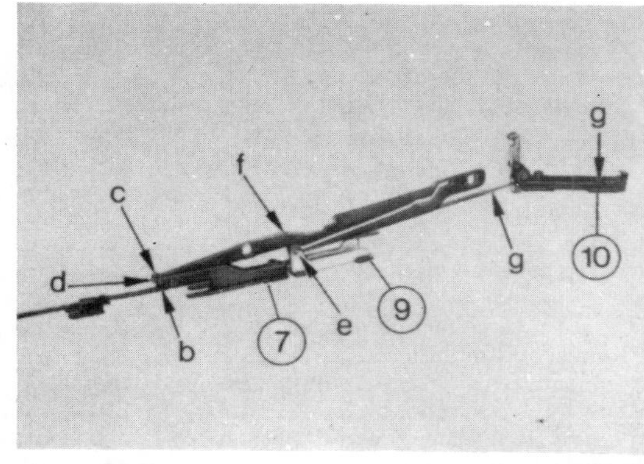

Fig. 11.51 Slide block guide assembly details (Sec 45)

b Circlip
c Pin
d Spring washer
e Circlip
f Bolt (sic)
g Connecting rod
7 Front guide
8 Slide block guide
9 Cable guide
10 Gutter guide

Front guide

14 The procedure is similar to that for gutter guide renewal. The front guide is attached to the slide block guide (Fig. 11.49).
15 Lightly grease the surfaces of the slide block when refitting. Adjust the cable guides and crank drive, as previously described.

Slide block

16 Proceed as for cable renewal until the slide block guide is accessible. Remove the circlip and separate the slide block from the slide block guide.
17 Fit the new slide block and secure with a new circlip. Lightly grease the surfaces of the slide block.
18 Reassemble in the reverse order to dismantling; adjusting the cable guides and crank drive as previously described.

Slide block guide

19 Again, the procedure is similar to that for cable renewal. Refer to Fig. 11.57 for assembly details.

Chapter 12 Electrical system

For modifications, and information applicable to later models, see Supplement at end of manual

Contents

Specifications

General

System type ..... 12 volt, negative earth

Battery

Type (original equipment) ..... Lead acid, maintenance-free
Capacity ..... 36 to 66 Ah depending on model and territory

Alternator

Make ..... Bosch or Delco-Remy
Type ..... Rotating field, integral voltage regulator
Output voltage (nominal):
  Bosch 14.0V
  Delco 13.6V
Output current (max) ..... 45 to 65 A according to model
Brush wear limit:
  Bosch ..... 5 mm (0.20 in) protrusion
  Delco ..... 11 mm (0.43 in) overall length

Starter motor

Make	Bosch or Delco-Remy
Type	Pre-engaged
Brush wear limit:	
Bosch type DF	11.5 mm (0.45 in) overall length
Bosch type EF	13.0 mm (0.51 in) overall length
Delco	5.0 mm (0.20 in) overall length
Commutator minimum diameter:	
Bosch type DF	31.2 mm (1.23 in)
Bosch type EF	33.5 mm (1.32 in)
Delco	37.0 mm (1.46 in)

Fuses (typical)

Fuse No	Rating (A)	Circuit(s) protected
1	10	LH side and tail lamps
2	10	RH side and tail lamps, instrument and engine bay illumination
3	10	LH main beam
4	10	RH main beam
5	10	LH dipped beam
6	10	RH dipped beam
7	10	Spare
8	10	Direction indicators, stop-lamps, foglamp relay
9	30	Wipers and washers
10	10	Rear foglamp
11	30	Horn, radiator fan
12	20	Heater blower
13	20	Reversing lamps, cigarette lighter, carburettor preheating, electric mirrors, glovebox lamp
14	20	Trailer feed (terminal 30)
15	20	Interior lights, hazard warning flasher, clock, radio
16	20	Fuel injection control unit, or spare
17	20	Front foglamps
18	20	Heated rear window

Bulbs (typical)

Function	Designation	Wattage
Headlamp	H4	60/55
Front side (parking) lamp	HL	4
Front foglamp	YC	55
Direction indicator lamp	P25-1	21
Interior lamps	K	10
Glovebox lamp	L	5
Number plate lamp	G	10
Rear foglamp	P25-1	21
Reversing lamp	P25-1	21
Stop and tail lamp	P25-2	21/5
Instrument panel illumination	T5	2
Warning and pilot lamps	W55/1.2	1.2
Ashtray lamp	–	0.5
Automatic transmission selector lamp	–	0.5
Rear foglamp pilot	Integral with switch	
Front foglamp pilot	Integral with switch	

Torque wrench settings

	Nm	lbf ft
Starter motor mounting bolts:		
1.2	Not specified	Not specified
1.3	25	18
1.6 and 1.8	45	33
Alternator bracket to cylinder block:		
1.2	Not specified	Not specified
1,3, 1.6 and 1.8	40	30
Alternator pulley nut:		
Bosch	35 to 45	26 to 33
Delco	66	49
Alternator housing bolts:		
Bosch	35 to 55	26 to 41
Delco	5	4
Windscreen wiper arm to shaft	11	8

1 General description

The electrical system is of the usual 12 volt, negative earth type. Electrical power is produced by an alternator, belt-driven from the crankshaft pulley. A lead-acid battery provides a reserve of power for starting the engine and for periods when the electrical load exceeds the alternator's output.

As is normal practice in car electrical systems, most components only receive a live feed, earth return being made via the bodywork or other metal structure instead of by means of a wire. This should be borne in mind when investigating faults: loose or corroded component mountings can have the same effect as a broken feed wire.

The reader whose competence or interest extends beyond the items covered in this Chapter may wish to study the Automobile Electrical Manual; available from the publishers of this book.

2 Electrical system – precautions

It is necessary to take extra care when working on the electrical system to avoid damage to semiconductor devices (diodes and transistors) and to avoid the risk of personal injury. In addition to the precautions given in Safety First! at the beginning of this manual, observe the following when working on the system.

1 Always remove rings, watches, etc before working on the electrical system. Even with the battery disconnected, capacitive discharge could occur if a component live terminal is earthed through a metal object. This could cause a shock or nasty burn.

2 Do not reverse the battery connections. Components such as the alternator or any other having semiconductor circuitry could be irreparably damaged.

3 Never disconnect the battery terminals, or alternator wiring connections, when the engine is running.

4 The battery leads and alternator connections must be disconnected before carrying out any electric welding on the car.

5 Never use an ohmmeter of the type incorporating a hand-cranked generator for circuit or continuity testing.

3 Maintenance and inspection

1 Weekly, or before a long journey, check the operation of all the electrical accessories (wipers, washers, lights, indicators, horn etc). Refer to the appropriate Section of this Chapter if any components are found to be inoperative.

2 At every major service interval a more thorough inspection should be made, as follows.

3 Visually check all accessible wiring connectors, harnesses and retaining clips for security, or signs of chafing or damage. Rectify any problems encountered.

4 Check the alternator drivebelt for cracks, fraying or damage. Renew the belt if worn or, if satisfactory, check and adjust the belt tension (photo). These procedures are covered in Chapter 2.

5 Check the condition of the wiper blades and, if they are cracked or show signs of deterioration, renew them, as described in Section 45. Check the operation of the windscreen and tailgate washers and adjust the nozzles if necessary.

6 Check the battery terminals and, if there is any sign of corrosion, disconnect and clean them thoroughly. Smear the terminals and battery posts with petroleum jelly before refitting. If there is any sign of corrosion on the battery tray, remove the battery, clean the deposits away and treat the affected metal with an anti-rust preparation. Repaint the tray in the original colour after treatment.

7 The battery fitted by the makers is (apart from the terminals) maintenance-free. A replacement battery may have detachable cell covers: if so, check that the plates in the cells are covered with electrolyte. Top up with distilled water if necessary. Do not fill the cells to the brim: if no correct level is marked, top up so that the plates are covered by approximately 6 mm (0.24 in) of electrolyte.

8 Top up the windscreen and tailgate washer reservoir and check the security of the pump wires and water pipes (photo).

9 It is advisable to have the headlight aim adjusted using optical beam setting equipment.

10 While carrying out a road test, check the operation of all the instruments and warning lights, and the operation of the direction indicator self-cancelling mechanism.

4 Battery – removal and refitting

1 The battery is located on the left-hand side of the engine bay.

2 Slacken the clamp nut and bolt on the negative (–) terminal clamp (photo). Lift the clamp off the terminal post. If the clamp is stuck to the

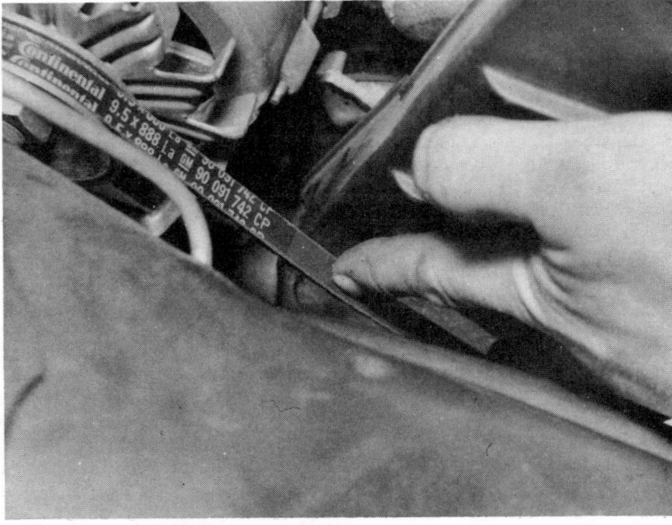

3.4 Checking the alternator drivebelt tension

3.8 Topping-up the windscreen washer reservoir

4.2 Disconnect the battery negative terminal first

post, beware of using force to free it as the post may be broken. Warm water will usually do the trick.

3 Similarly disconnect the positive (+) terminal; this may be protected by a plastic cover.

4 Undo the clamp bolt at the base of the battery and lift out the battery. Be careful, it is heavy. Keep it upright and do not drop it.

5 Refit in the reverse order to removal, connecting the earth (negative) lead last. Use a little proprietary anti-corrosion compound, or petroleum jelly, on the terminal posts. Do not overtighten the clamp bolt or the terminal clamps.

5 Battery – charging

1 In normal use the battery should be kept charged by the alternator. Except in extremely adverse conditions a regular need to charge the battery from an external source suggests that the battery or alternator is faulty, or that a short-circuit is draining the battery.

2 Charging from an external source may be useful to temporarily revive a flagging battery. A battery which is not in use should be given a refresher charge every six to eight weeks.

3 The state of charge of the battery fitted as original equipment is shown by a 'magic eye' indicator on the top face of the battery (Fig. 12.1). If the indicator is dark with a green dot, the battery is charged. If

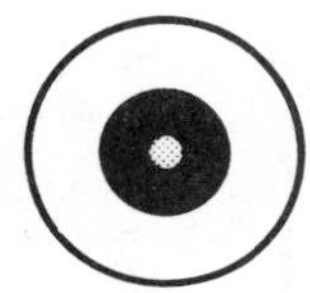
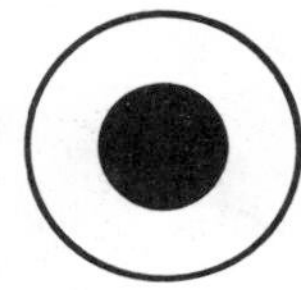
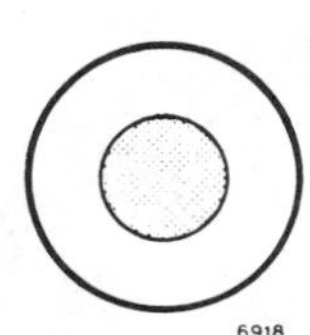

Fig. 12.1 Battery charge indicator (Sec 5)

the indicator is dark with no dot, the charge is low but the battery is probably serviceable. If the indicator is light or bright yellow, the battery is almost certainly unfit for service: consult a GM dealer or battery specialist.

4 Disconnect the battery from the car, preferably remove it completely, before connecting a mains charger.

5 As a rule of thumb, the charging rate (in amps) should not exceed one tenth of the battery capacity (in amp-hours). This suggests a rate of between four and six amps, which is about the output of most domestic battery chargers. Make sure that dual voltage equipment is set to 12 volts.

6 Connect the charger to the battery, observing correct polarity (+ to + and – to –), then switch on the mains. Switch off the mains **before** disconnecting the charger. Ensure adequate ventilation during charging. If using the 'magic eyes' indicator to determine the state of charge, shake the battery gently occasionally to encourage the indicator to move.

7 Rapid or 'boost' charging should be avoided except under expertly supervised conditions. With the sealed type of battery there is a risk of explosion due to rapid build-up of gas during charging. Any battery can be ruined by overheating caused by over-fast charging.

6 Alternator – general description

Cars covered by this manual are fitted with either a Bosch or a Delco-Remy alternator; the two types are similar in construction and in output. The alternator generates alternating current (ac) which is rectified by diodes into direct current (dc) as this is the current needed for charging the battery.

The alternator is of the rotating field, ventilated design and comprises principally a laminated stator on which is wound the output winding, a rotor carrying the field winding, and a diode rectifier. A votage regulator is incorporated in the Delco-Remy alternator, but on the Bosch machine it is separately mounted at the rear. The alternator generates its current in the stator windings and the rotor carries the field. The field brushes therefore are only required to carry a light current and as they run on simple slip rings they have a relatively long life. This design makes the alternator a reliable machine requiring little servicing.

The rotor is belt-driven from the crankshaft pulley through a pulley keyed to the rotor shaft. A fan adjacent to the pulley draws cooling air through the unit. Rotation is clockwise when viewed from the drive end.

7 Alternator – removal and refitting

1 Disconnect the battery earth (negative) lead.

2 Make a note of the electrical connections at the rear of the alternator, then disconnect the multi-plug, spade terminals or other connectors as appropriate.

3 Remove the alternator strap bolts, noting the short earth lead which links the alternator to the engine. Slacken the pivot bolt, swing the alternator towards the engine and remove the drivebelt.

4 Remove the pivot bolt and lift off the alternator. On one car examined, the pivot bolt had been inserted from the 'wrong' side so that it could not be withdrawn far enough to release the alternator: in this case it is necessary to unbolt the alternator mounting from the block.

5 Take care not to knock or drop the alternator.

6 Refit in the reverse order to removal; tension the drivebelt as described in Chapter 2, Section 9.

8 Alternator – testing in the car

1 Should it appear that the alternator is not charging the battery, check first that the drivebelt is intact and in good condition and that its tension is correct (Chapter 2). Also check the condition and security of the alternator electrical connections and the battery leads.

2 Accurate assessment of alternator output requires special equipment and a degree of skill. A rough idea of whether output is adequate can be gained by using a voltmeter (range 0 to 15 or 0 to 20 volts) as follows.

3 Connect the voltmeter across the battery terminals. Switch on the headlights and note the voltage reading: it should be between 12 and 13 volts.

4 Start the engine and run it at a fast idle (approx 1500 rpm). Read the voltmeter: it should indicate 13 to 14 volts.

5 With the engine still running at a fast idle, switch on as many electrical consumers as possible (heated rear window, heater blower etc). The voltage at the battery should be maintained at 13 to 14 volts. Increase the engine speed slightly if necessary to keep the voltage up.

6 If alternator output is low or zero, check the brushes, as described in one of the following Sections. If the brushes are OK, seek expert advice.

7 Occasionally the condition may arise where the alternator output is excessive. Clues to this condition are constantly blowing bulbs; brightness of lights varying considerably with engine speed; overheating of alternator and battery, possibly with steam or fumes coming from the battery. This condition is almost certainly due to a defective voltage regulator, but expert advice should be sought.

9 Alternator brushes (Delco-Remy) – inspection and renewal

1 Remove the alternator from the engine, as described in Section 7.

2 Scribe a line across the drive end housing and slip ring end housing to ensure correct location when refitting.

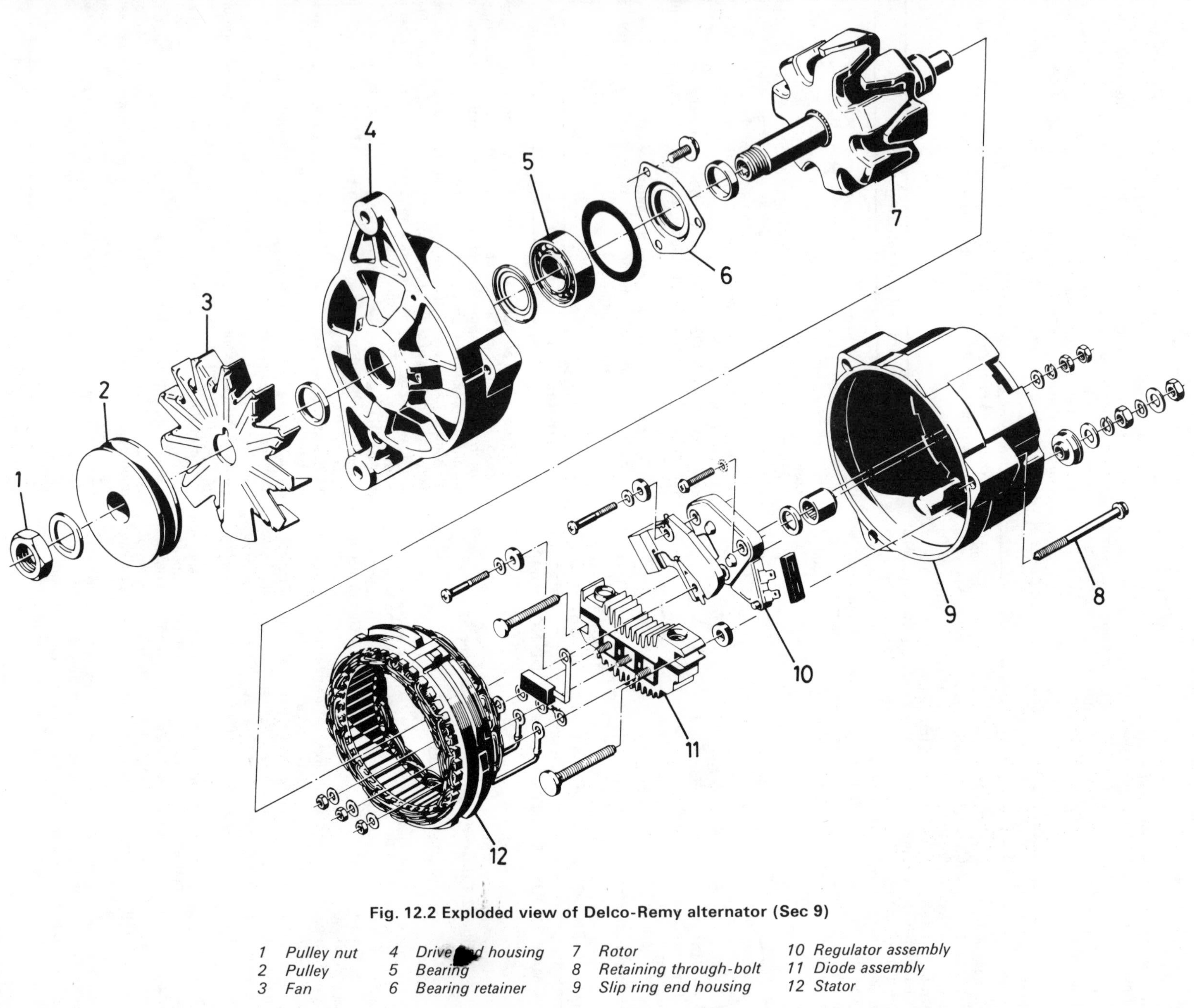

Fig. 12.2 Exploded view of Delco-Remy alternator (Sec 9)

1 Pulley nut
2 Pulley
3 Fan
4 Drive end housing
5 Bearing
6 Bearing retainer
7 Rotor
8 Retaining through-bolt
9 Slip ring end housing
10 Regulator assembly
11 Diode assembly
12 Stator

9.3A Separating the alternator housings

9.3B Check the condition of the slip rings (arrowed)

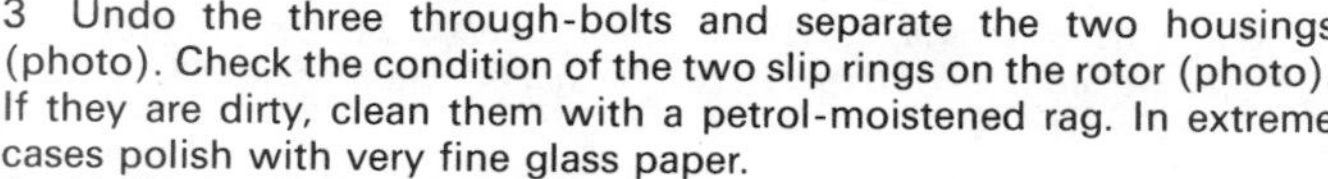

3 Undo the three through-bolts and separate the two housings (photo). Check the condition of the two slip rings on the rotor (photo). If they are dirty, clean them with a petrol-moistened rag. In extreme cases polish with very fine glass paper.
4 Undo the three nuts and washers securing the stator leads to the rectifier and lift away the stator assembly (photo). Remove the terminal screw and lift out the diode bracket.
5 Undo the two screws retaining the brush holder and voltage regulator to the end housing and remove the brush holder assembly. Note insulation washers under the screw heads.
6 Check that the brushes move freely in the guides and that the length is greater than the limit given in the Specifications. If any doubt exists regarding the condition of the brushes the best policy is to renew them.
7 To fit new brushes, unsolder the old brush leads from the brush holder and solder on the new leads in exactly the same place.
8 Check that the new brushes move freely in the guides. If they bind, lightly polish with a very fine file.
9 Before refitting the brush holder assembly, retain the brushes in the retracted position using a piece of stiff wire or a small twist drill (photo).
10 Refit the brush holder so that the stiff wire or twist drill protrudes through the small slot in the end housing (photo).

9.4 Starter lead retaining nuts (A) and brush holder securing screws (B)

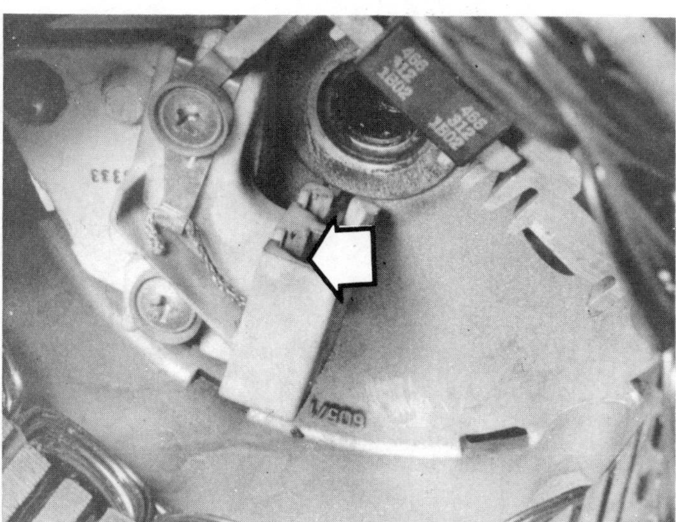

9.9 Alternator brushes held retracted with a small twist drill (arrowed)

9.10 With the brush holder fitted, the twist drill protrudes through the slot in the housing

11 Refit the diode bracket and stator to the end housing, making sure the stator leads are in their correct positions.
12 Assemble the two housings, ensuring that the scribe marks are aligned. Insert the three through-bolts and tighten fully.
13 Now carefully pull the stiff wire or twist drill out of the slot in the housing so that the brushes drop onto the rotor slip ring.
14 The alternator can now be refitted to the car and tested.
15 It should be remembered that is an alternator is being changed for a new or reconditioned unit then the pulley/fan assembly will be required from the original alternator. To release the pulley nut, hold the rotor shaft with an Allen key while the nut is unscrewed (photo).

9.15 Removing the alternator pulley nut

10 Alternator brushes (Bosch) – inspection and renewal

1 Undo and remove the two screws, spring and plain washers that secure the brush box to the rear of the slip ring end housing. Lift away the brush box and voltage regulator.
2 Check that the carbon brushes are able to slide smoothly in their guides without any sign of binding.
3 Measure the length of the brushes. If they have worn below the specified limit, they must be renewed.
4 Hold the brush wire with a pair of engineer's pliers and unsolder it from the brush box. Lift away the two brushes.
5 Insert the new brushes and check to make sure that they are free to move in their guides. If they bind, lightly polish with a very fine file.
6 Solder the brush wire ends to the brush box taking care that solder is not allowed to pass to the stranded wire.
7 Whenever new brushes are fitted, new springs should also be fitted.
8 Refitting the brush box is the reverse sequence to removal.

11 Starter motor – general description

The starter motor is mounted on the rear face of the crankcase and may be of either Delco-Remy or Bosch manufacture. Both makes are of the pre-engaged type, ie the drive pinion is brought into mesh with the starer ring gear on the flywheel before the main current is applied.

When the starter switch is operated, current flows from the battery to the solenoid which is mounted on the starter body. The plunger in the solenoid moves inwards, so causing a centrally pivoted lever to push the drive pinion into mesh with the starter ring gear. When the solenoid plunger reaches the end of its travel, it closes an internal contact and full starting current flows to the starter field coils. The armature is then able to rotate the crankshaft, so starting the engine.

A special freewheel clutch is fitted to the starter drive pinion so that as soon as the engine fires and starts to operate on its own it does not drive the starter motor.

When the starter switch is released, the solenoid is de-energised and a spring moves the plunger back to its rest position. This operates the pivoted lever to withdraw the drive pinion from engagement with the starter ring.

The construction of the two makes of starter motor is quite similar and the removal, refitting, dismantling, inspection and reassembly procedures detailed here will serve for both motors. Significant differences will be noted.

12 Starter motor – testing in the car

1 If the starter motor fails to turn the engine when the switch is operated, provided that engine seizure is not the problem, there are five or six possible causes:

(a) *The battery is faulty*
(b) *The electrical connections between the switch, solenoid, battery and starter motor are somewhere failing to pass the necessary current from the battery through the starter to earth*
(c) *The solenoid switch is faulty*
(d) *The starter motor is mechanically or electrically defective*
(e) *The starter motor pinion and/or flywheel ring gear is badly worn and in need of replacement*
(f) *On automatic transmission models, the starter inhibitor switch may be defective or maladjusted. See Chapter 6, Section 27*

2 To check the battery, switch on the headlights. If they dim after a few seconds the battery is in a discharged state. If the lights glow brightly, operate the starter switch and see what happens to the lights. If they dim then you know that power is reaching the starter motor but failing to turn it. If the starter turns slowly when switched on, proceed to the next check.
3 If, when the starter switch is operated, the lights stay bright, then insufficient power is reaching the motor. Remove the battery connections, starter/solenoid power connections and the engine earth strap and thorougly clean them and refit them. Smear petroleum jelly around the battery connections to prevent corrosion. Corroded connections are the most frequent cause of electric system malfunctions.
4 When the above checks and cleaning tasks have been carried out, but without success, you will possibly have heard a clicking noise each time the starter switch was operated. This was the solenoid switch

Fig. 12.3 Brush holder/regulator retaining screws (arrowed) – Bosch alternator (Sec 10)

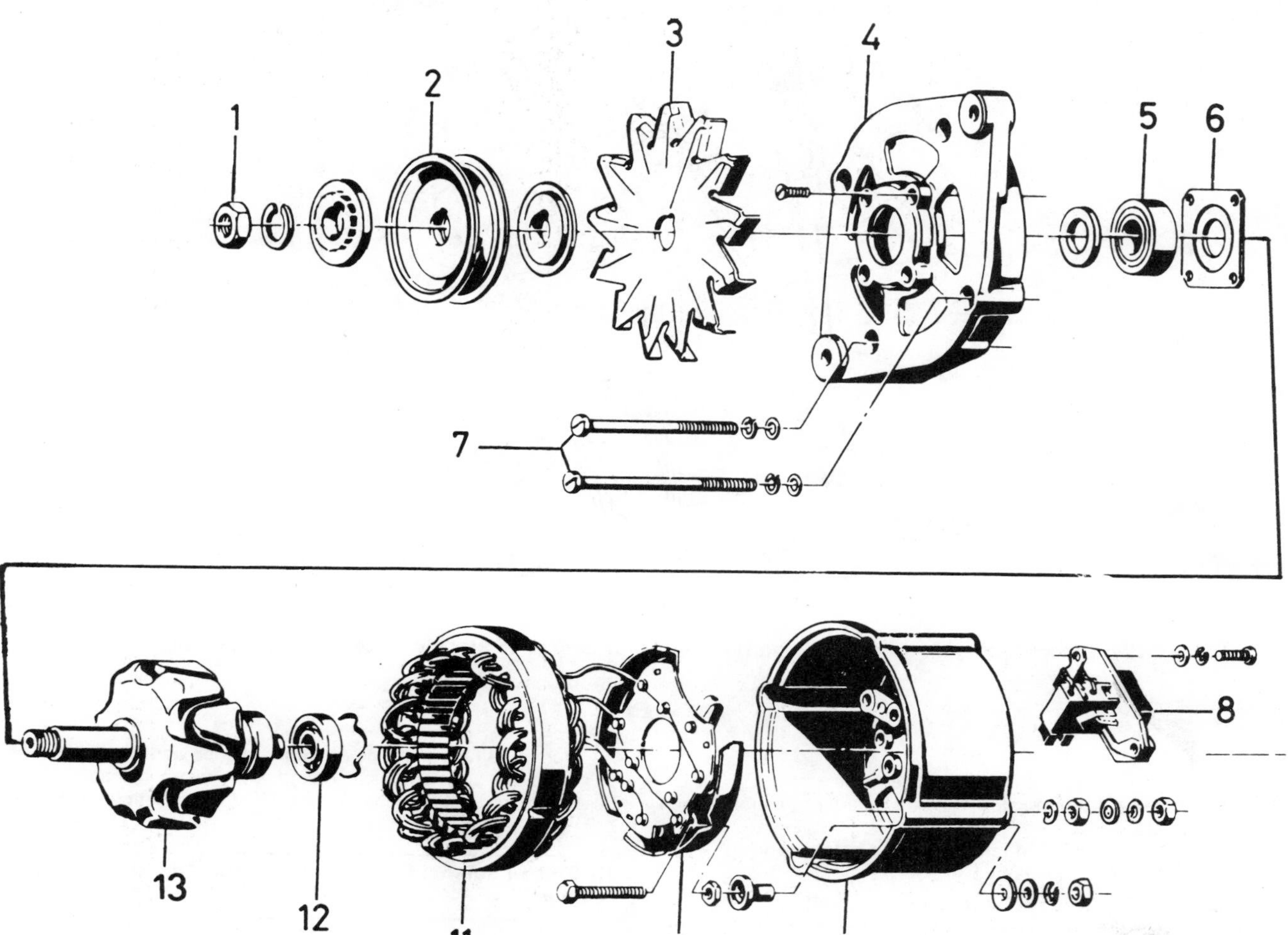

Fig. 12.4 Exploded view of Bosch alternator (Sec 10)

1 Pulley nut
2 Pulley
3 Fan
4 Drive end housing
5 Bearing
6 Bearing retainer
7 Through-bolts
8 Brush holder/regulator
9 Slip ring end housing
10 Collector ring endplate
11 Stator
12 Bearing
13 Rotor

operating, but it does not necessarily follow that the main contacts were closing properly (if no clicking has been heard from the solenoid, it is certainly defective). The solenoid contact can be checked by putting a voltmeter or bulb across the main cable connection on the starter side of the solenoid and earth. When the switch is operated, there should be a reading or lighted bulb. If there is no reading or lighted bulb, the solenoid unit is faulty and should be renewed.

5 If the starter motor operates but doesn't turn the engine then it is most probable that the starter pinion and/or flywheel ring gear are badly worn, in which case the starter motor will normally be noisy in operation.

6 Finally, if it is established that the solenoid is not faulty and 12 volts are getting to the starter, then the motor is faulty and should be removed for inspection.

13 Starter motor – removal and refitting

1 Disconnect the battery earth lead.

OHV engine

2 Disconnect the battery positive leads; separate the starter motor lead from the other. Also disconnect the positive lead from the alternator.

3 Separate the gearshift linkage to improve access. Unbolt and remove the starter motor from above, disconnecting the solenoid command lead.

4 If a new starter motor is being fitted, transfer the electrical lead to it.

5 Refit in the reverse order to removal.

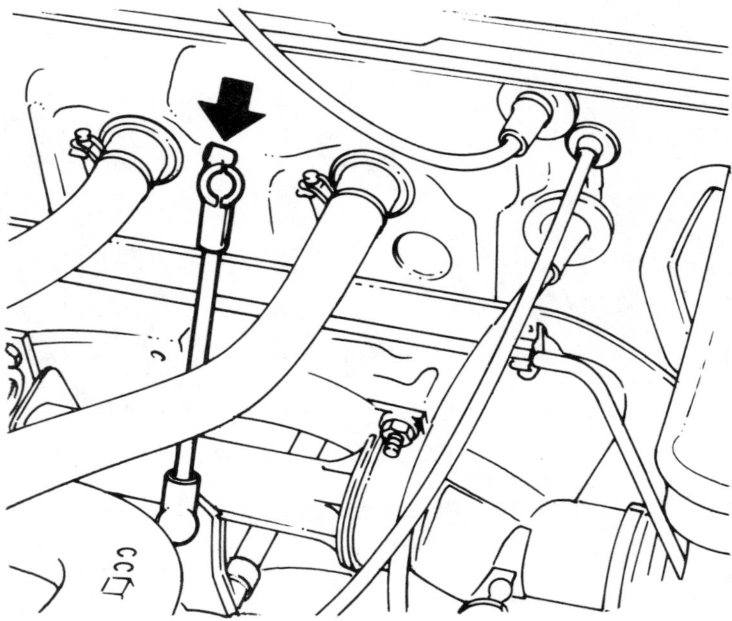

Fig. 12.5 Disconnect gearchange linkage (arrowed) for access to starter motor on OHV engine (Sec 13)

OHC engine

6 Raise and support the front of the vehicle.
7 Note the electrical connections to the starter solenoid, then disconnect them.
8 Unbolt the starter motor and remove it from below (photo).
9 Refit in the reverse order to removal.

14 Starter motor overhaul – general

1 Before embarking on a comprehensive overhaul of a well worn motor, compare the cost of the proposed repairs with the cost of a new or reconditioned motor. The difference may not be very great.

13.8 Starter motor mounting bolts (arrowed) – engine removed for clarity

2 Premature failure of one component such as the solenoid, brushes or pinion can be economically rectified by removing the motor, as just described, and dismantling, as described in the following Sections.

15 Starter solenoid – removal and refitting (starter motor removal)

1 At the rear of the solenoid, undo the retaining nut and washer and slip the electrical feed wire off the terminal stud.
2 Remove the two or three screws which secure the solenoid to the starter drive end housing.
3 Withdraw the solenoid switch housing, spring and armature; unhook the armature from the pinion actuating arm.
4 A defective solenoid must be renewed.
5 Refit in the reverse order to removal.

16 Starter motor brushes – inspection and renewal

Bosch

1 With the starter removed from the engine and on a clean bench, begin by removing the armature end cap which is secured by two small screws on the end of the motor (photo). Remove the armature retaining clip, washers and the rubber sealing ring which were exposed (photo). Undo and remove the two long bolts which hold the motor assembly together (photo). The end cover can now be removed to reveal the brushes and mounting plate (photos).
2 Take the brushes from the holder and slip the holder off the armature shaft. Retrieve the spacer washers between the brush plate and the armature block, where fitted.
3 Inspect the brushes: if they are worn down to less than the minimum length given in Specifications, they should be renewed. Cut off the old brushes and solder on the new ones; hold the lead on the brush side with pliers to stop solder running up it.
4 Wipe the starter motor armature and commutator with a non-fluffy rag wetted with petrol.
5 Reassemble the brushes into the holder (photo) and refit the holder over the armature shaft, remembering to fit the two washers between the holder and armature, where fitted.

Fig. 12.6 Removing the starter motor solenoid – Bosch (Sec 15)

Fig. 12.7 Removing the starter motor solenoid – Delco-Remy (Sec 15)

16.1A Remove the armature end cap ...

16.1B ... followed by the retaining clip, washers and sealing ring

16.1C Undo and remove the two long through-bolts ...

16.1D ... and lift off the end cover

16.1E Commutator and field coil brushes

16.5 Brush holder with earth brushes fitted – field coil brushes are fitted during assembly

Fig. 12.8 Soldering a new brush to the field winding – Bosch (Sec 16)

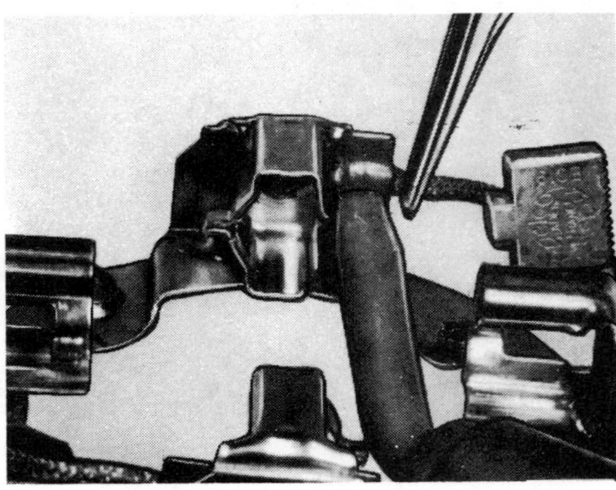

Fig. 12. 9 Soldering a new brush to the brush holder – Delco-Remy (Sec 16)

6 Refit the motor end cover and secure with two long bolts.
7 Refit the armature shaft end cap after fitting the rubber sealing ring, washer and shaft clip.

Delco-Remy

8 With the motor removed from the engine and on a clean bench, begin by undoing and removing the two long bolts which hold the motor assembly together. Punch mark the relative positions of the end cover and the yoke to ensure correct relocation on assembly.
9 Undo the two small screws which secure the end cover to the brush holder plate and lift off the end cover.
10 Lift the brush springs to remove the positive brushes and then remove the brush holder plate from the motor.
11 If the brushes are worn to less than the minimum length given in the Specifications, they should be renewed.
12 When soldering new positive brushes, hold the connecting wires in a pair of pliers to prevent the solder from running into the wire strands and reducing its flexibility. Use a 12 to 15 watt pencil soldering iron.
13 Clean the motor armature and commutator with a non-fluffy rag moistened with petrol.
14 Position the brushes in the brush holder plate and place this assembly over the commutator.
15 Relocate the end cover, aligning the relevant marks, and refit the brush holder securing screws and the two long through-bolts.

17 Starter motor – dismantling and reassembly

1 The complete overhaul of a starter motor is beyond the resources of the average home mechanic as special tools and equipment for testing are necessary, but if the appropriate spares can be obtained repairs can be made by renewing parts. With the starter on the bench proceed as follows.

Bosch

2 Undo the two screws and remove the end cap from the commutator cover.
3 Prise the clip off the end of the armature and, after carefully noting the sequence of assembly, remove the washers and rubber sealing ring from the armature.

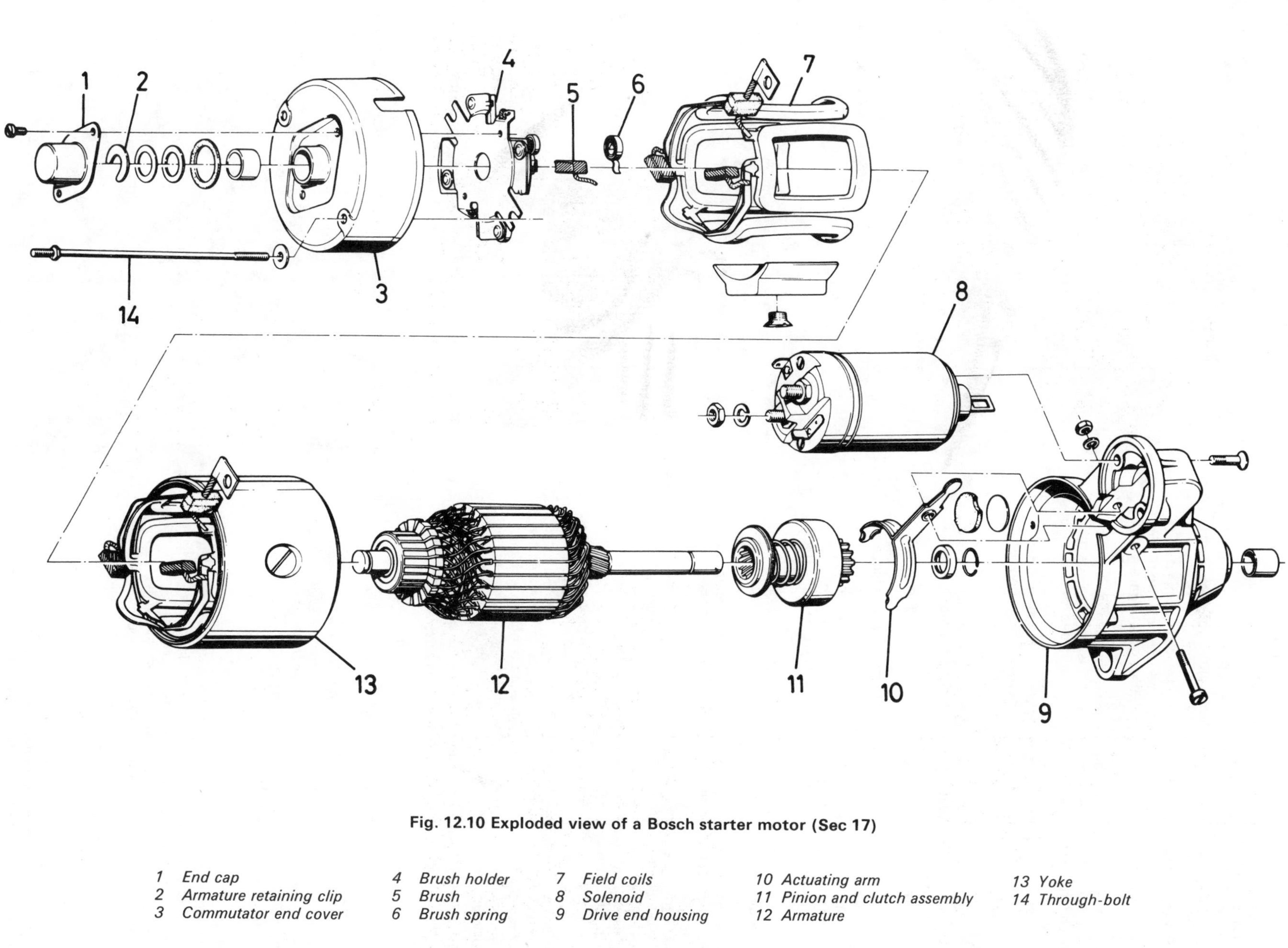

Fig. 12.10 Exploded view of a Bosch starter motor (Sec 17)

1 End cap
2 Armature retaining clip
3 Commutator end cover
4 Brush holder
5 Brush
6 Brush spring
7 Field coils
8 Solenoid
9 Drive end housing
10 Actuating arm
11 Pinion and clutch assembly
12 Armature
13 Yoke
14 Through-bolt

4 Mark the commutator cover relative to the starter yoke and then remove the two long bolts which bold the assembly together. Remove the commutator cover.
5 Lift the brush springs to remove the positive brushes and then remove the brushplate from the assembly. Note and remove any shims that may be fitted.
6 Disconnect the field winding lead from the solenoid terminal and then undo the retaining screws to release the solenoid from the assembly. As the solenoid is removed, unhook the end fitting from the actuating arm.
7 Unscrew and remove the actuating arm pivot and then remove the drive end housing from the yoke assembly. As this is done remove the rubber plug and the actuating arm. Slide the armature out of the casing.
8 If it is required to remove the pinion or the clutch from the armature, press the retaining ring back on the shaft to enable the snap-ring to be removed. Then slide the components off the shaft.
9 With the starter motor dismantled, the various components can be cleaned and inspected for general wear and/or signs of damage. Use a petrol-damped cloth for cleaning, but avoid wetting electrical components. Dry thoroughly with a fluff-free cloth.
10 Renew worn or damaged carbon brushes as explained in Section 16.
11 If the starter motor has shown a tendency to jam or a reluctance to disengage then the starter pinion is almost certainly the culprit. Dirt accumulation on the shaft or on the pinion could cause this. After cleaning off any such dirt, check that the pinion can move freely in a spiral movement along the shaft. If it still tends to bind or stick, or if it is defective in any way, renew the pinion.
12 A badly worn or burnt commutator will need skimming on a lathe, but if it is only dirty or lightly marked, clean it up with a piece of fine grade glass paper wrapped round. If the commutator has to be skimmed have the job done by a specialist, but make sure that the minimum diameter, as listed in the Specifications, is maintained. After skimming, the separators should be undercut using a piece of old hacksaw blade ground down to the same thickness as the separators. Undercut to a depth of about 0.5 to 0.8 mm (0.02 to 0.03 in) and then clean up with fine grade glass cloth. Do not use emery on the commutator as abrasive particles could get embedded in the copper and cause rapid brush wear.
13 An armature with a bent shaft or other signs of damage must be renewed. Electrical checks should be undertaken by an auto-electrician with special equipment. Although simple continuity checks are possible with a lamp and low power source, more extensive checking is needed which is beyond the scope of the home mechanic.
14 Reassembly of the starter motor is a straightforward reversal of the dismantling sequence, but the following points should be noted:

(a) *After assembling the clutch and pinion to the armature shaft, fit the retaining ring using a new snap-ring and then reposition the retainer*
(b) *Make sure that all shims and washers are fitted in the correct order*
(c) *Align the locating key and slot when assembling the yoke to the end housing*
(d) *Make sure that the carbon brushes slide freely in their boxes*
(e) *Lightly oil all sliding parts including the armature spiral spline, the actuating arm sliding surfaces, the clutch bearing surfaces and armature bearings. Of course, no oil must contaminate the commutator or brushes*

Delco-Remy

15 Mark the commutator end cover and the drive end housing relative to the yoke to ensure correct reassembly, and then disconnect the field winding connection from the lower stud on the solenoid.
16 Undo and remove the two long bolts which hold the motor assembly together (photo). Punch mark the relative positions of the end cover and the yoke to ensure correct relocation on assembly.
17 Undo the two small screws which secure the end cover to the brush holder plate and lift off the end cover (photos).
18 Lift the brush springs to remove the positive brushes and then remove the brush holder plate from the motor (photo).
19 Undo the retaining screws and remove the solenoid and its spring from the drive end housing (photo). Extract the clip from the actuating arm spindle (photo) and tap the spindle out of the housing (photo). This will allow the armature and the actuating arm to be removed

Fig. 12.11 Driving the pinion retaining ring back – Bosch (Sec 17)

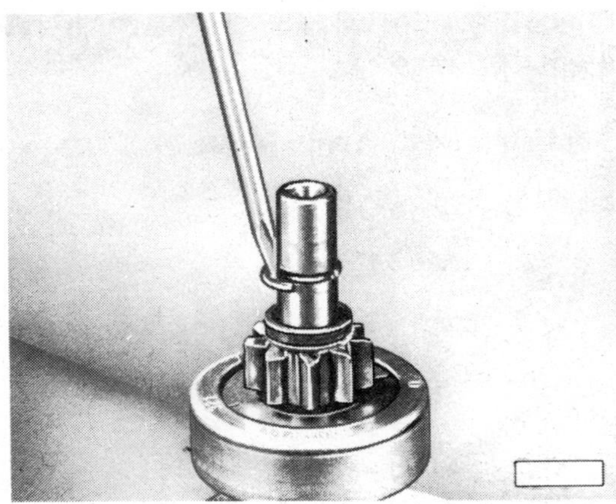

Fig. 12.12 Removing the pinion retaining snap-ring – Bosch (Sec 17)

17.16 Removing the starter motor through-bolts

17.17A Remove the small screws ...

17.17B ... and lift off the end cover

17.18 Withdraw the brush holder

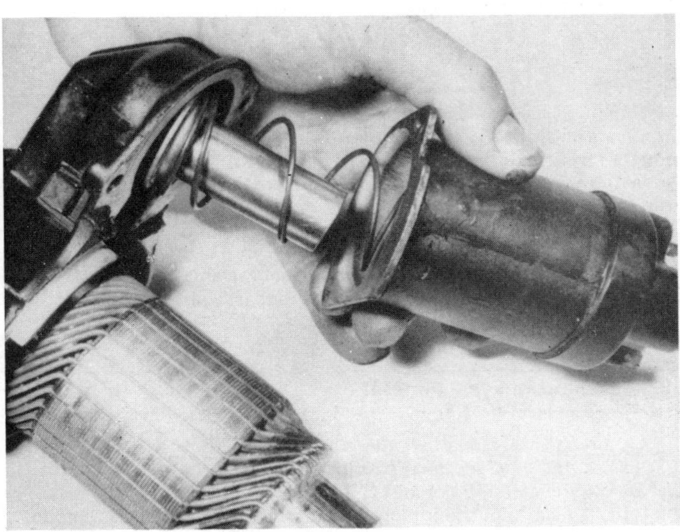
17.19A Removing the solenoid and spring

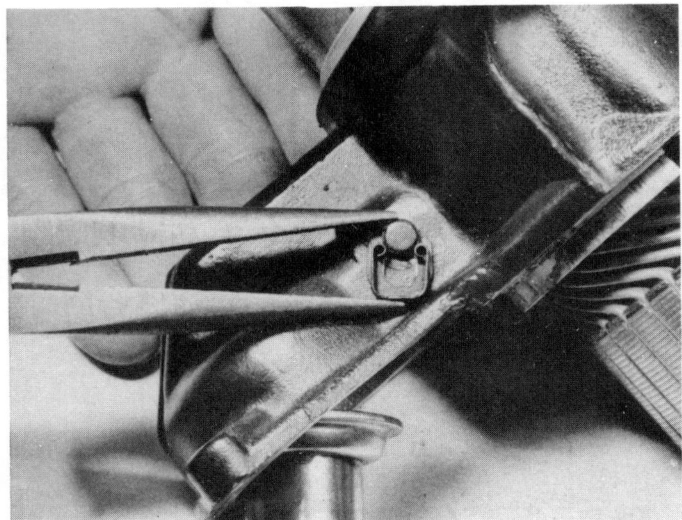
17.19B Extracting the actuating arm spindle clip ...

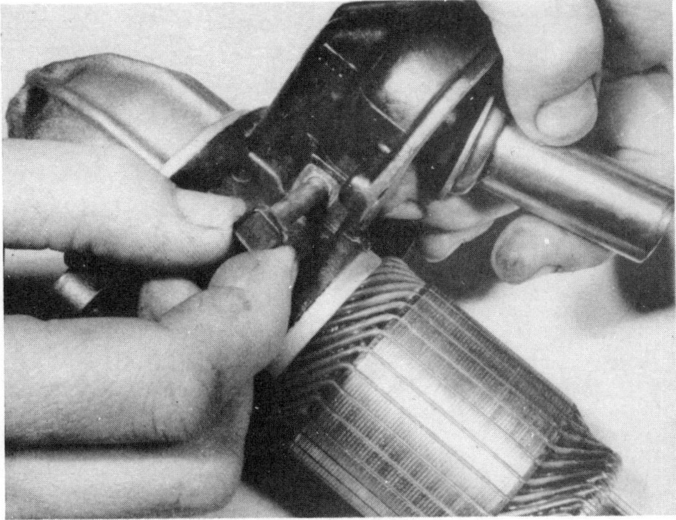
17.19C ... and the actuating arm spindle

17.19D Removing the armature and actuating arm from the drive end housing

together (photo). The actuating arm can then be removed from the armature assembly (photo).

20 With the exception of the above, the remainder of the dismantling and reassembly procedures for this starter are the same as those described in paragraphs 8 to 14, to which reference should now be made. When the solenoid has been refitted to the drive end housing, use a little plastic sealing compound to seal the slot in the housing to prevent water entering. Then continue the reassembly as described.

18 Fuses and relays – general

1 All the car's electrical circuits are protected by fuses; most of the fuses are found in a fuse/relay box located under a cover to the right of and below the steering column (photo).

2 Typical fuse applications are given in the Specifications; model-specific information will be found printed on the fuse/relay box lid.

3 The fuses are of the 'blade' type. Their ratings are printed on their backs and additionally they are colour-coded. A blown fuse may be recognized by its melted or missing wire link.

18.1 Removing the cover from the fuse/relay box

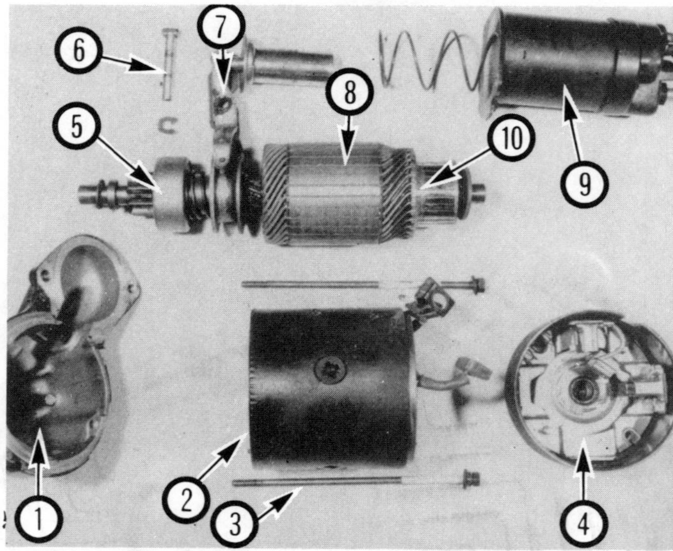

17.19E Exploded view of the Delco-Remy starter motor

1 Drive end housing
2 Yoke
3 Through-bolt
4 End cover and brush holder
5 Pinion and clutch
6 Actuating arm spindle
7 Actuating arm
8 Armature
9 Solenoid
10 Commutator

4 When renewing a fuse, switch off the circuit(s) concerned first. If the new fuse blows immediately when switching on, find and rectify the cause. The most usual cause of a blown fuse if a short-circuit to earth somewhere along the wire feeding the component concerned. The wire may be disconnected, trapped or frayed. Pay special attention to wire runs through grommets, under carpets etc.

5 Where a blown fuse serves more than one component, the defective circuit can be traced by switching on each component in turn until the replacement fuse blows.

6 **Never** attempt to bypass a fuse with silver foil or wire, nor fit a fuse of a higher rating than specified. Serious damage, or even fire, may result.

7 Models with a full range of optional equipment may carry one or two fuses on the other side of the fuse/relay box. When a headlamp washer system is fitted, its fuse and relay are mounted under the bonnet on the left-hand suspension turret (photos).

8 All models have some relays on the accessible side of the fuse/relay box; according to equipment level, some other relays may be found on the reverse side. Unclip the box to gain access. For relay identification see Figs. 12.14 and 12.15.

9 A relay is essentially an electrically-operated switch. If a circuit served by a relay becomes inoperative, remember that the relay could be at fault. Test by substitution of a known good relay.

Fig. 12.13 Blade type fuse – wire link (arrowed) must be intact (Sec 18)

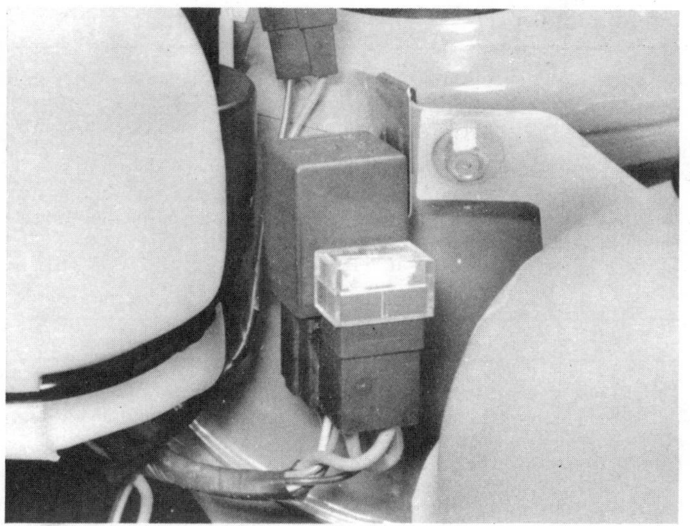

18.7A Headlamp washer relay and fuse

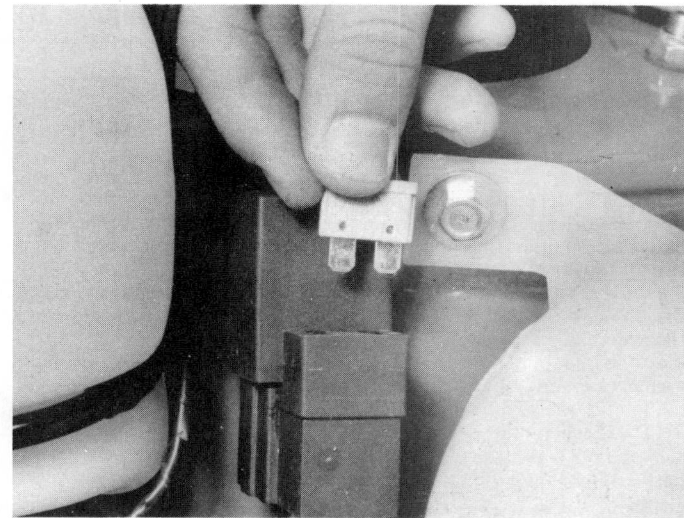

18.7B Removing the headlamp washer fuse

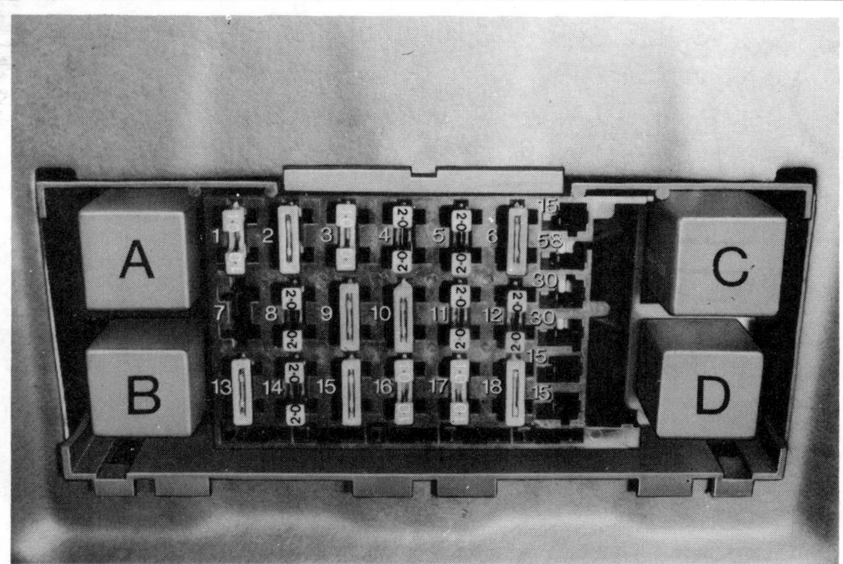

Fig. 12.14 Relay identification – accessible side. For fuse identification see Specifications (Sec 18)

A Flasher unit
B Heated rear window relay
C Windscreen wiper relay/delay unit
D Front foglamp relay

Fig. 12.15 Fuse and relay identification – reverse side (Sec 18)

E Trip computer relay
F Rear wiper relay (not GTE)
G Day running lamp relay (not UK)
H Headlamp cut-out (not UK)
I Headlamp warning buzzer
19 Central locking fuse
20 Electric window winder fuse

19 Direction indicator and hazard warning systems – general

1 Should the direction indicators become faulty in operation, check the bulbs for security and make sure that the contact surfaces (including bulb holder earthing points) are not corroded. If one bulb blows, or is not making good contact, the system will not flash on that side of the car.
2 If the direction indicators operate on one side, but not on the other, the problem is likely to be the bulbs, the wiring on that side or the steering column switch.
3 If the direction indicators do not work at all, but the hazard warning system functions, check for a blown fuse in position 8. If the fuse is OK, the fault is likely to be in the flasher unit.
4 The flasher unit is located in the fuse/relay box. Testing is by substitution of a known good unit: no repair is possible. To remove a flasher unit, simply unplug it.

20 Facia switches – removal and refitting

1 Before removing any switch, disconnect the battery earth lead; reconnect it after refitting the switch.

Lighting master switch

2 Release the spring clips at the side of the switch by pressing them with a bent screwdriver or similar tool. Draw the switch out of the facia, disconnect its wiring plug and remove it (photo). If the switch cannot be released, remove the instrument panel surround, as described in Section 32.
3 To refit, connect the wiring plug to the switch and press the switch home until the clips snap into place.

Hazard warning switch

4 This is removed and refitted in the same way as the lighting master switch.

Foglamp switch

5 Carefully prise the switch from its location, disconnect its wires and withdraw it (photo).
6 Refit in the reverse order to removal.

Instrument illumination control

7 Remove the instrument panel surround, as described in Section 32.
8 Slacken the securing screw and remove the illumination control (photo).
9 Refit in the reverse order to removal.

Heater blower/heated rear window switch

10 This switch is released in a similar way to the lighting master switch. If the switch cannot be relased, withdraw the heater control panel, as described in Chapter 11, Section 38.
11 Refit in the reverse order to removal.

21 Steering column switches – removal and refitting

1 Disconnect the battery earth lead.
2 Although not strictly necessary, access will be improved if the steering wheel is removed, as described in Chapter 8, Section 3. Otherwise, remove the wheel centre trim.
3 Remove the upper and lower switch shrouds. These are held in

20.2 Removing the lighting master switch – one of the spring clips is arrowed

20.5 Removing a foglamp switch

20.8 Removing the instrument illumination control

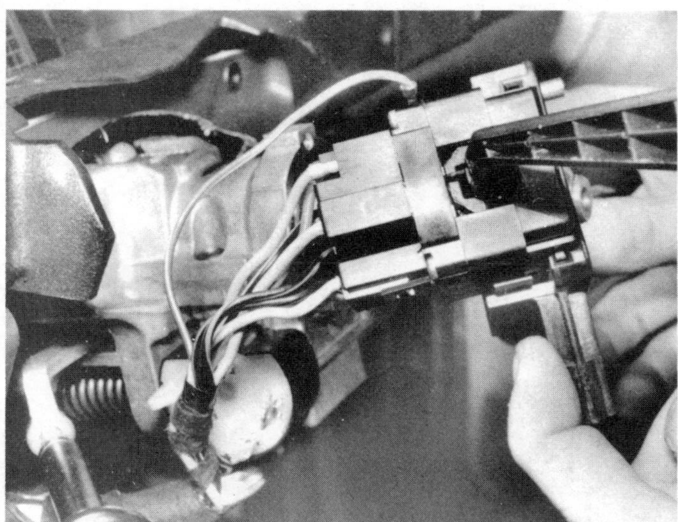

21.4A Drawing the steering column switches up the column

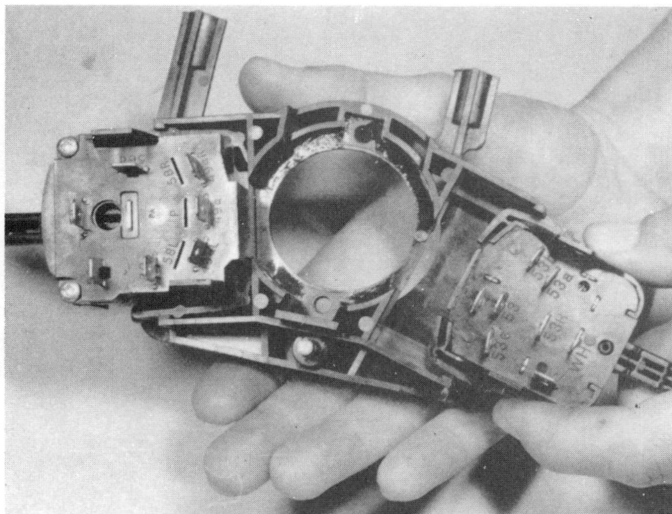

21.4B Unclipping a steering column switch – assembly removed for clarity

place by eight screws with the fixed type steering wheel, or five screws with the adjustable wheel.

4 In theory it is now possible to unclip and withdraw either of the multi-function switches. In practice it was found necessary, when the adjustable wheel was fitted, to undo the two switch housing screws and draw the switch assembly up the column slightly. The switch in question can then be unplugged, unclipped and removed (photos).

5 Refit in the reverse order to removal.

22 Ignition/starter switch – removal and refitting

1 Refer to Chapter 8, Section 5.

23 Reversing lamp switch – removal and refitting

Manual transmission

1 The switch is located on the front of the transmission, below the clutch release lever.

2 Disconnect the wires from the switch, unscrew it and remove it.

3 Refit in the reverse order to removal.

Automatic transmission

4 See Chapter 6, Section 27.

24 Stop-lamp switch – removal and refitting

1 Refer to Chapter 9, Section 21, paragraphs 1 and 6.

25 Handbrake warning switch – removal and refitting

1 Proceed as described in Chapter 9, Section 24, but without disconnecting the handbrake lever from the yoke.

26 Electric mirror switch – removal and refitting

1 Free the rear half of the centre console, as described in Chapter 11, Section 35.

2 Disconnect and unclip the switch.

3 Refit in the reverse order to removal.

27 Electric window winder switch – removal and refitting

1 Proceed as described for the electric mirror switch (Section 26).

28 Interior light switches – removal and refitting

1 The main interior light is operated by door plunger switches. Similar switches control the luggage area and glovebox light, when fitted.

2 Removal is similar in every case. After displacing any trim which may be in the way, the switch is unscrewed or unclipped and withdrawn from its location (photos). The electrical lead(s) can then be unplugged and the switch removed. Tape the wires if necessary to avoid losing them inside the switch hole.

3 Refit in the reverse order to removal. Check for correct operation before refitting any trim.

28.2A Glovebox light switch unclipped from its location

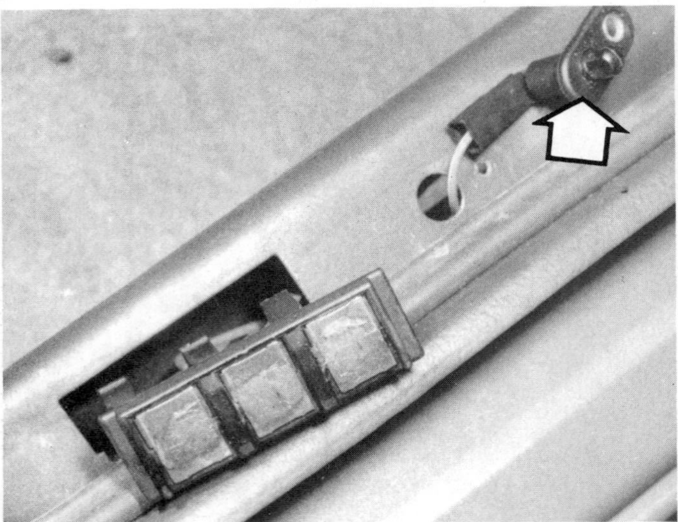

28.2B Luggage area light switch (arrowed) next to contact plate on tailgate sill

29.2 Horn contact pin (arrowed)

29 Horn and switch – removal and refitting

1 The horn switch is incorporated in the steering wheel centre trim. This may be unclipped and removed, as described in Chapter 8, Section 3.
2 The horn contact ring can be renewed after removing the steering wheel. The contact ring bears on a spring-loaded pin in the middle of the steering column switch housing (photo).
3 The horn itself is located in front of the radiator, unless an oil cooler is fitted, when it is located behind the battery. Disconnect and unbolt the horn to remove it; remove the front trim panel if necessary for access.
4 If the horn does not work, check with a 12 volt test lamp that voltage is present at the horn terminals when the horn push is operated. If the horn itself is defective it must be renewed.
5 Refit all components in the reverse order to removal.

30 Clock – removal and refitting

1 Disconenct the battery earth lead.
2 Carefully pull the clock from its location. Disconnect the supply and illumination leads from the clock and remove it (photo).
3 Refit in the reverse order to removal.

31 Cigarette lighter – removal and refitting

1 Disconnect the battery earth lead.
2 Extract the heater element from the lighter socket.
3 Carefully prise the lighter socket out of the illuminating ring. Unplug the socket and remove it.
4 Refit in the reverse order to removal. When inserting the socket into the illuminating ring, make sure that the ring lugs pass over a smooth part of the socket; twist the socket clockwise when home to engage the lugs.

32 Instrument panel – removal and refitting

1 Disconnect the battery earth lead.
2 Remove the horn push from the steering wheel.

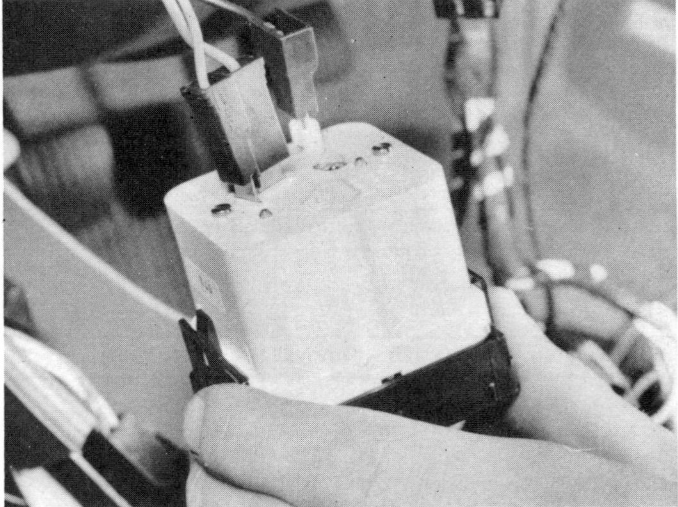

30.2 Removing the clock

3 Remove the steering column switch upper shroud, which is secured by four screws. Unlock the steering and turn the wheel as necessary to gain access to two of the screws.
4 Remove the four screws which secure the instrument panel surround and bottom trim strip. There are two screws at the top and one in each bottom corner; they may be covered by cosmetic caps (photo).
5 Withdraw the instrument panel surround, disconnecting the wires from the various switches (photo).
6 Except on the LCD instrument panel, disconnect the speedometer cable by depressing its retaining clip and pulling it away from the speedo.
7 Remove the single securing screw and withdraw the instrument panel (photos). Disconnect the electrical leads if the panel is to be removed completely, making notes if there is any possibility of confusion later. When an econometer is fitted, disconnect the vacuum hose.
8 Refiit in the reverse order to removal.

Fig. 12.16 Fitting the cigarette lighter socket into the illuminating ring (Sec 31)

32.4 Removing an instrument panel surround screw

32.5 Withdrawing the instrument panel surround

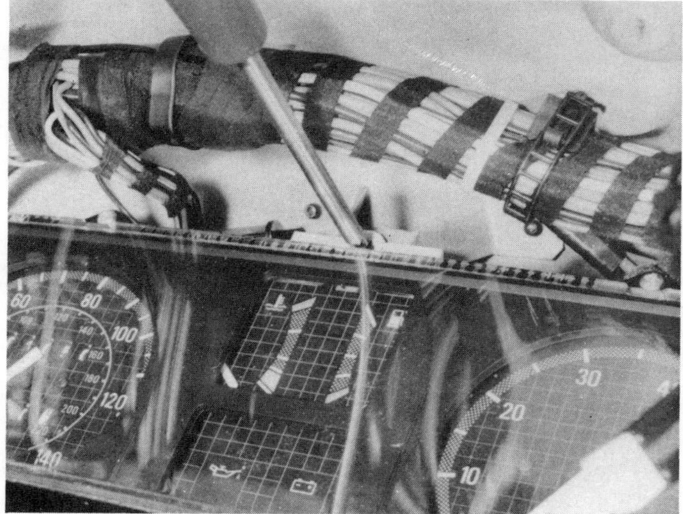

32.7A Removing the instrument panel securing screw

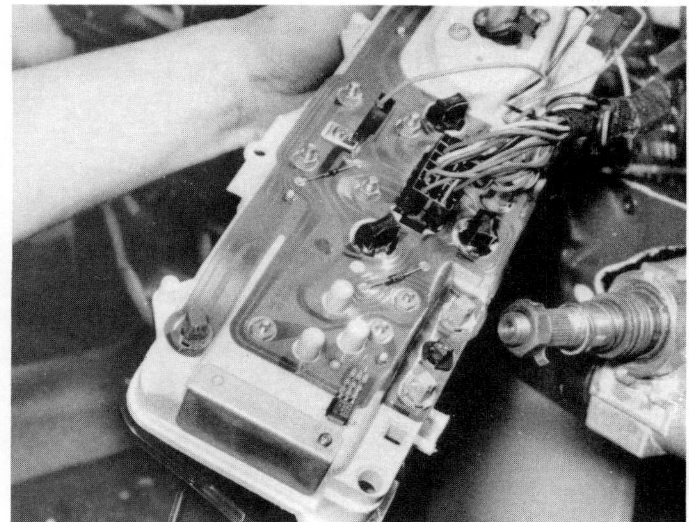

32.7B Withdrawing the instrument panel

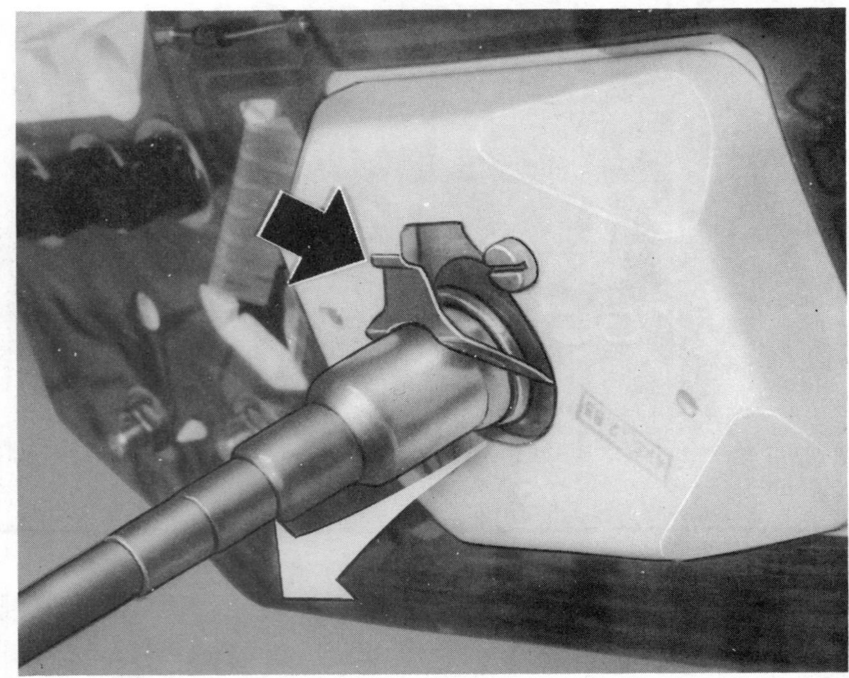

Fig. 12.17 Depress clip (arrowed) to release speedometer cable (Sec 32)

33 Instrument panel – dismantling and reassembly

1 No attempt must be made to dismantle the LCD type instrument panel: its bulbs can be renewed, but that is all. Consult a GM dealer if an instrument fault is suspected: special test equipment is required for accurate diagnosis.

2 Individual instruments can be removed from the conventional instrument panel after removing the cover, which is secured by two screws at the top and three lugs at the bottom. The instruments are secured by screws or nuts (photo).

3 Illumination and warning lamp bulbs can be removed by turning the combined bulb and holder anti-clockwise and withdrawing it from the rear of the panel (photo). There is no need to remove the instrument panel completely to do this – just withdraw it far enough to gain access to the printed circuit.

4 The printed circuit can be renewed if all the instruments etc are transferred from the old one.

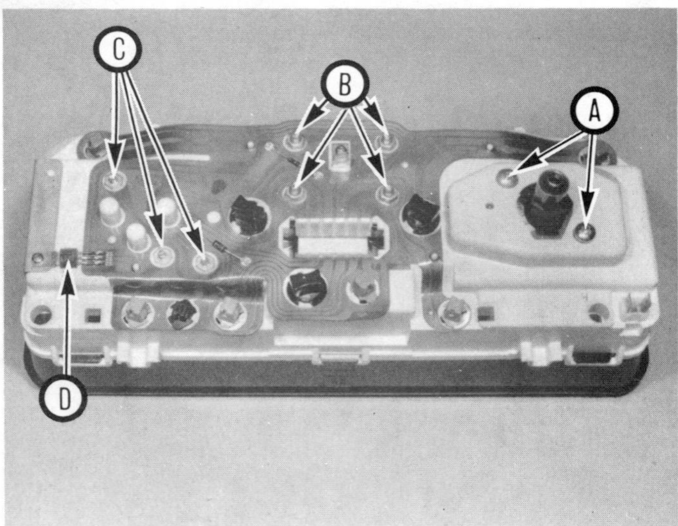

33.2 Instrument panel rear view (typical)
A Speedometer retaining screws
B Fuel/temperature gauge retaining nuts
C Tachometer retaining nuts
D Instrument voltage stabiliser

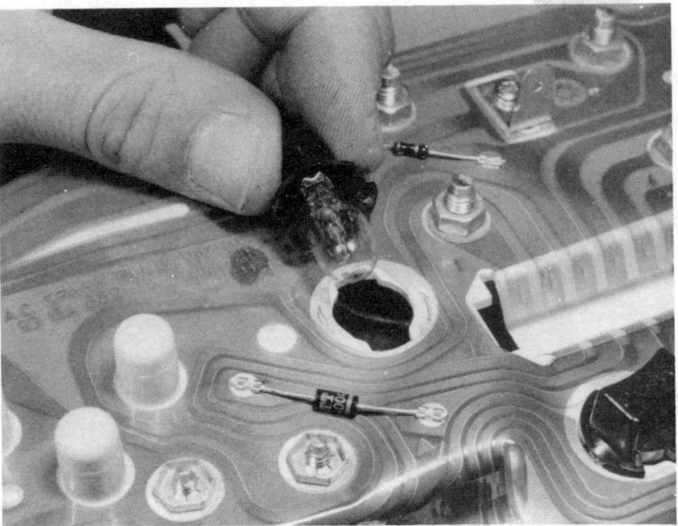

33.3 Removing an instrument panel bulb

34 Speedometer cable – renewal

1 A mechanical cable is not used with the LCD instrument panel; the electrical sender bolts onto the gearbox in the same position as the conventional cable.
2 To renew a mechanical cable, first disconnect it from the speedometer head. If it is not possible to reach up behind the instrument panel, partly withdraw it, as described in Section 32 (photo).
3 Working under the bonnet, free the cable grommet from the bulkhead and draw the cable into the engine bay. Recover the grommet.
4 Undo the knurled nut which secures the cable to the transmission (or trip computer speed sender, when fitted). Remove the cable.
5 Refit in the reverse order to removal. The cable must not be kinked or made to bend sharply. If lubricant is applied to the inner cable, do not put any on the top 15 cm (6 in) or so, in case it gets into the speedometer head.

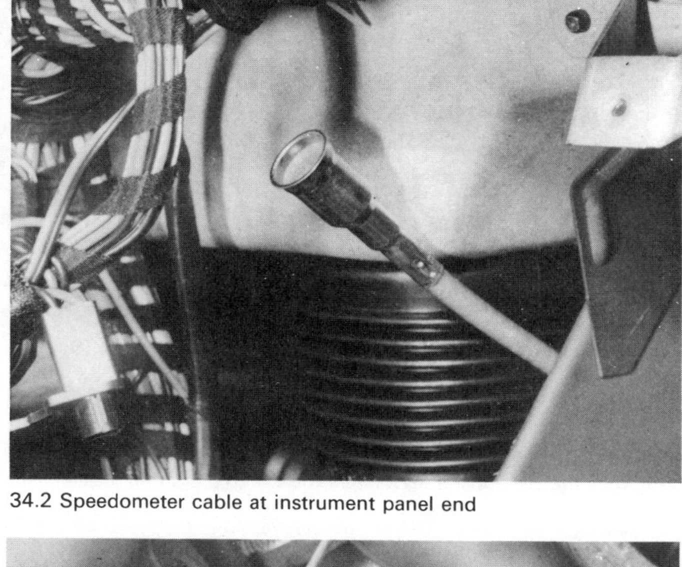
34.2 Speedometer cable at instrument panel end

35 Oil pressure gauge sender – renewal

1 When fitted, the oil pressure gauge sender is screwed into the oil filter carrier, in the position otherwise occupied by the low oil pressure warning switch (photo).
2 To remove the sender, disconnect its wires and unscrew it. Be prepared for a little oil spillage.
3 Refit in the reverse order to removal, using a new sealing ring.

35.7 Oil pressure gauge sender wires (arrowed)

36 Bulbs – renewal

Headlamp

1 Open the bonnet and disconnect the wiring plug from the rear of the headlamp unit (photo).
2 Remove the rubber cover to expose the spring clip which secures the bulb (photo).
3 Release the spring clip and withdraw the bulb (photo). Be careful if it has just been in use, it may be very hot.
4 Do not touch the bulb glass with the fingers: traces of grease can blacken the glass and shorten bulb life. Use a clean cloth moistened with methylated spirit to clean a bulb which has been accidentally touched.
5 Fit the new bulb in the reverse order to removal. Make sure that the lugs on the bulb engage in the recesses in the bulb holder.

36.1 Disconnecting the headlamp wiring plug

36.2 Rubber cover removed to expose the spring clip

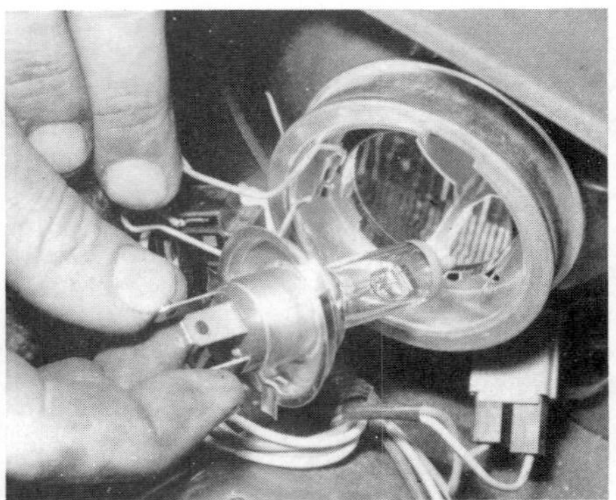

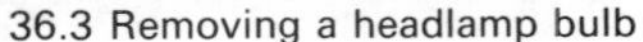

36.3 Removing a headlamp bulb

36.7 Removing a sidelamp bulb and holder

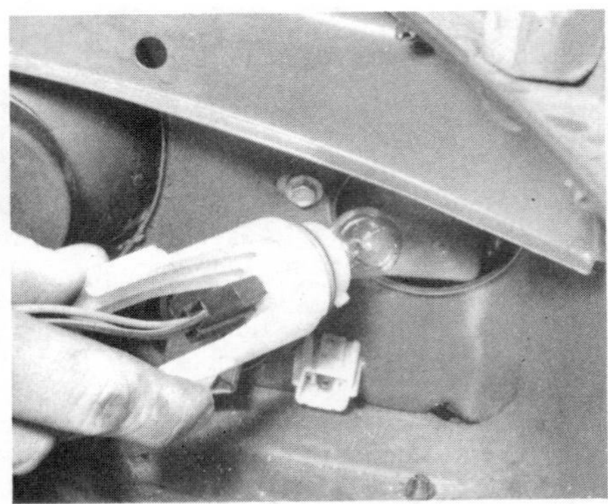

36.9 Removing a direction indicator bulb and holder

Sidelamp (front parking lamp)

6 Open the bonnet and disconnect the wiring plug from the sidelamp bulb holder.

7 Remove the bulb holder by depressing it and twisting it anti-clockwise (photo).

8 Extract the old bulb from the holder and insert the new one. Refit and reconnect the bulb holder.

Front direction indicator

9 Open the bonnet. Remove the bulb holder by squeezing its legs together and twisting it anti-clockwise (photo).

10 Fit the new bulb and refit the bulb holder.

Front foglamp

11 Working under the front bumper, remove the rear cover from the lamp unit by twisting it anti-clockwise.

12 Unclip and remove the bulb, separating its electrical connector at the first junction, not at the bulb itself.

13 Do not touch the bulb glass: see paragraph 4.

14 Connect the new bulb, secure it and refit the lamp cover.

Rear lamp cluster

15 Remove the trim panel or access cover from the area of the rear lamp cluster.

16 Disconnect the wiring plug, depress the bulb holder retaining lug and withdraw the bulb holder (photos).

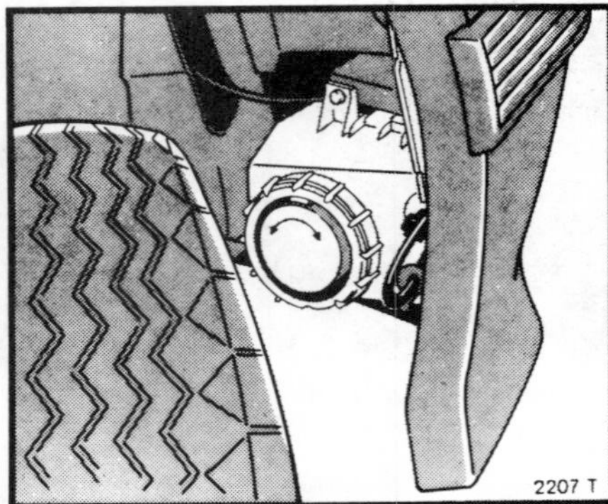

Fig. 12.18 Front foglamp rear cover is removed by twisting (Sec 36)

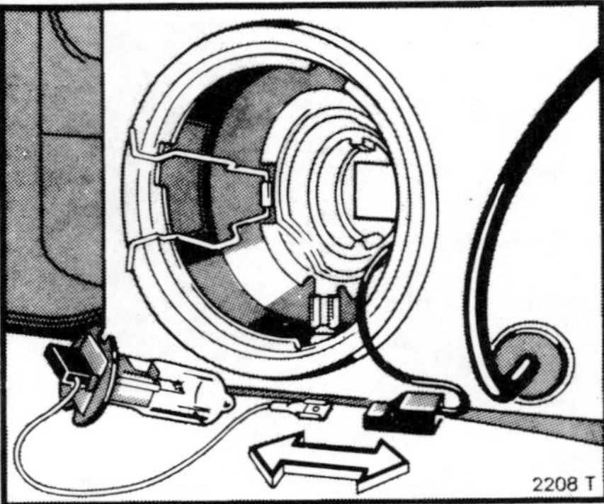

Fig. 12.19 Separating the front foglamp wiring connector (Sec 36)

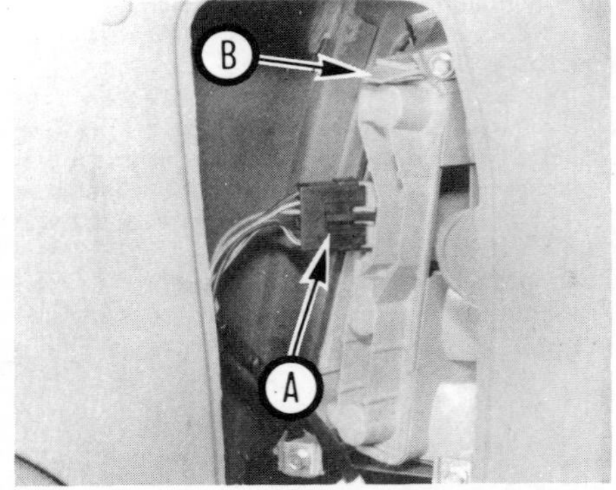

36.16A Rear lamp cluster wiring plug (A) and retaining lug (B)

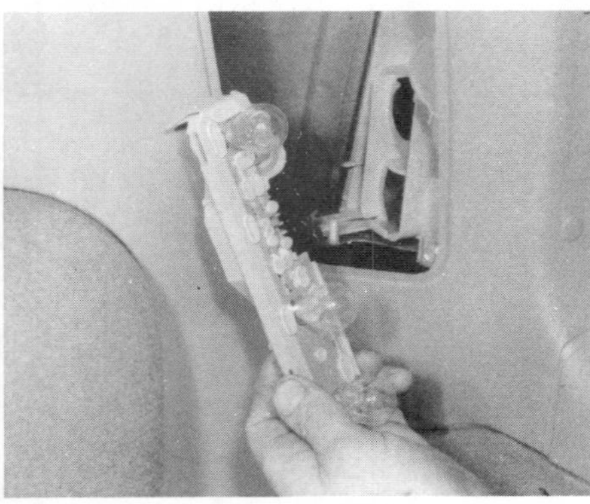

36.16B Rear lamp cluster bulbs and holder

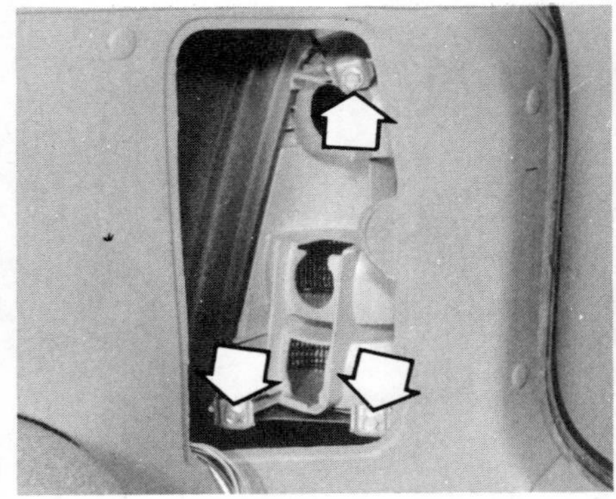

36.17A Rear lamp unit retaining screws (arrowed) – Hatchback

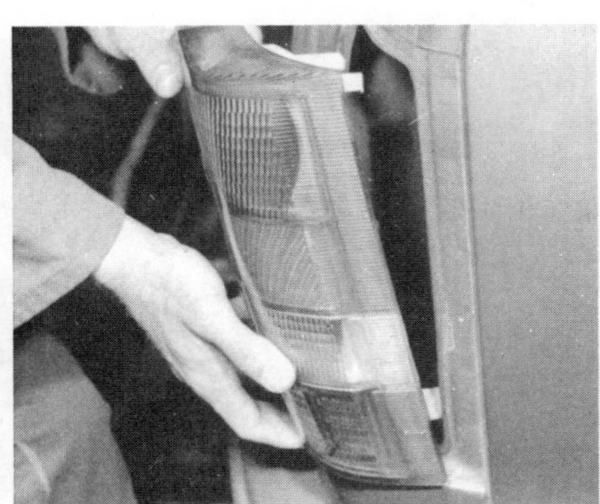

36.17B Removing a rear lamp lens

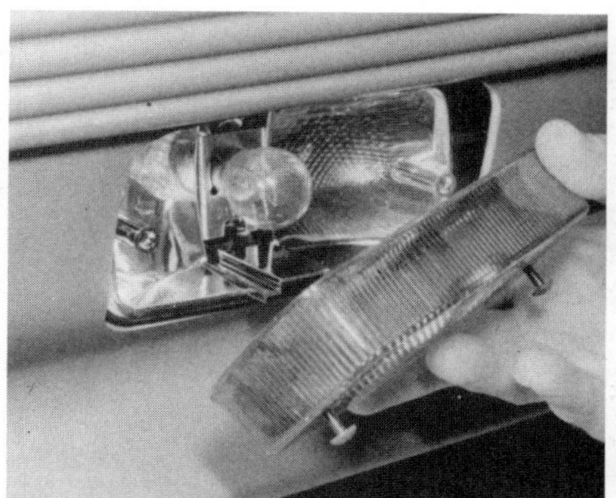
36.19 Removing a rear foglamp lens

36.22 Prising out the number plate lamp

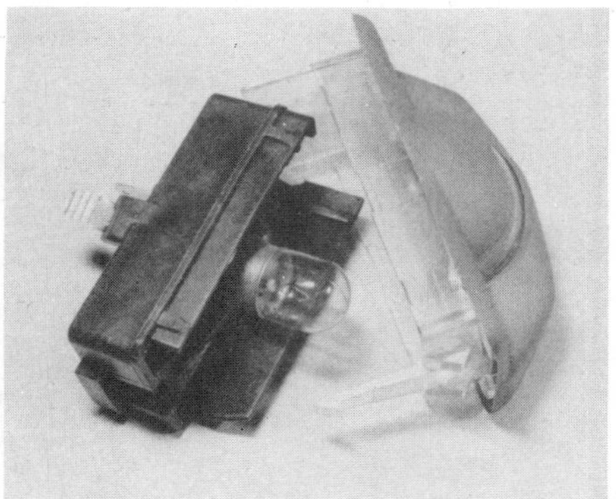
36.23 Number plate lamp bulb holder and lens separated

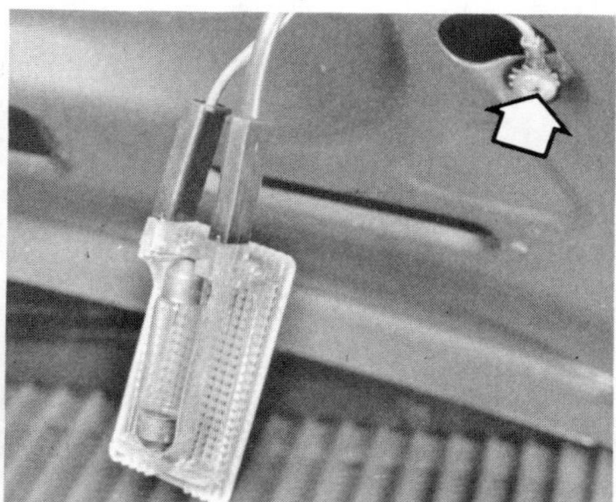
36.25A Under-bonnet lamp unclipped – note earth screw (arrowed)

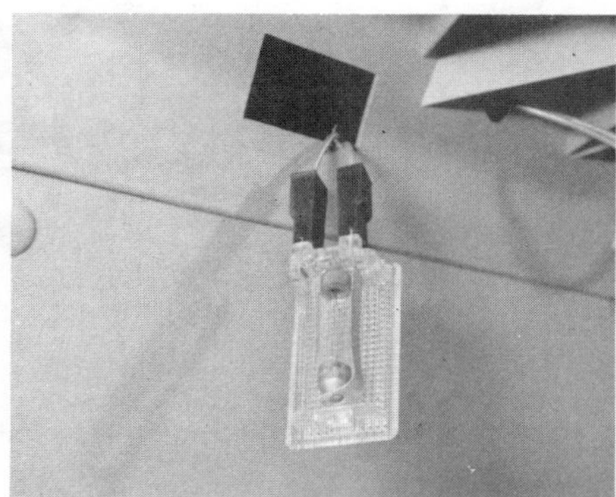
36.25B Luggage area lamp unclipped

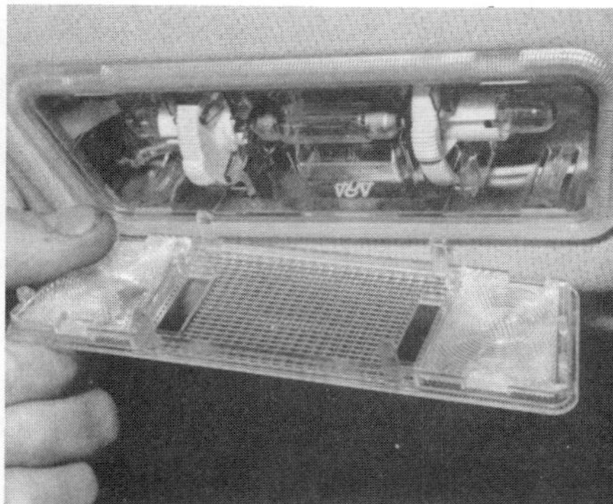
36.25C Removing the cover from the main interior lamp

17 The rear lamp unit itself can be removed after undoing the three retaining screws (two on Estates) (photos).
18 Refit in the reverse order to removal. If the lamp unit has been removed, make sure its retaining plates are correctly fitted before tightening the retaining screws.

Rear foglamp

19 Remove the lens from the foglamp by undoing its two retaining screws (photo).
20 Extract the bayonet fitting bulb and fit the new one.
21 Refit and secure the lens.

Number plate lamp

22 Prise the lamp unit out of the rear bumper and disconnect its wiring plug (photo).
23 Unclip the two halves of the lamp unit to gain access to the bulb (photo).
24 Refit in the reverse order to removal.

Interior lamps

25 Bulb renewal is similar for all types of interior lamp, and for the under-bonnet lamp (when fitted). Either unclip the lamp cover, or carefully prise the lamp unit from its location (photos).
26 Extract the old bulb, fit the new one and refit the lamp or cover.

Instrument panel and switch illumination lamps

27 Renewal of instrument panel bulbs is considered in Section 33.
28 Switches such as the lighting master switch and the heated rear window/heater blower control are illuminated by bulbs which can be renewed after removal of the switch (photo).
29 The pilot illumination in switches such as that controlling the foglamps is integral with the switch and cannot be renewed separately.

Check control display lamps

30 Carefully prise the check control unit from its location. The bulb holders are accessible from below.
31 Refit in the reverse order to removal.

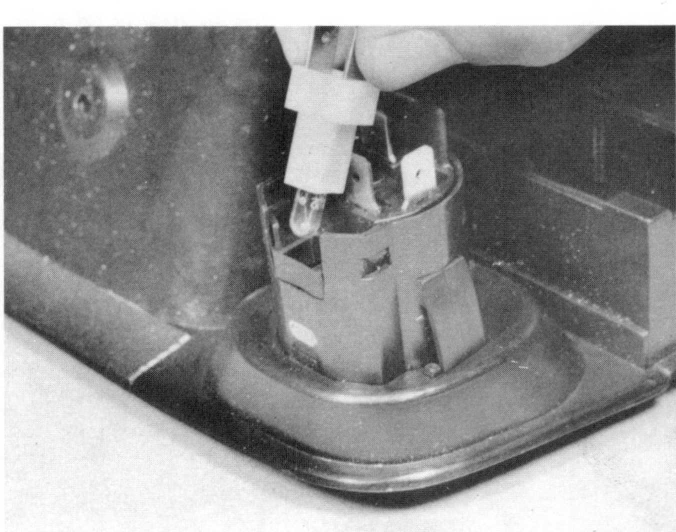
36.28 Removing a switch illumination bulb

Fig. 12.20 Check control bulb holder identification (Sec 36)

1	*Bulb failure*	*3*	*Engine oil level*	*5*	*Brake pad wear*
2	*Stop-lamp circuit*	*4*	*Brake fluid level*	*6*	*Screen washer fluid*

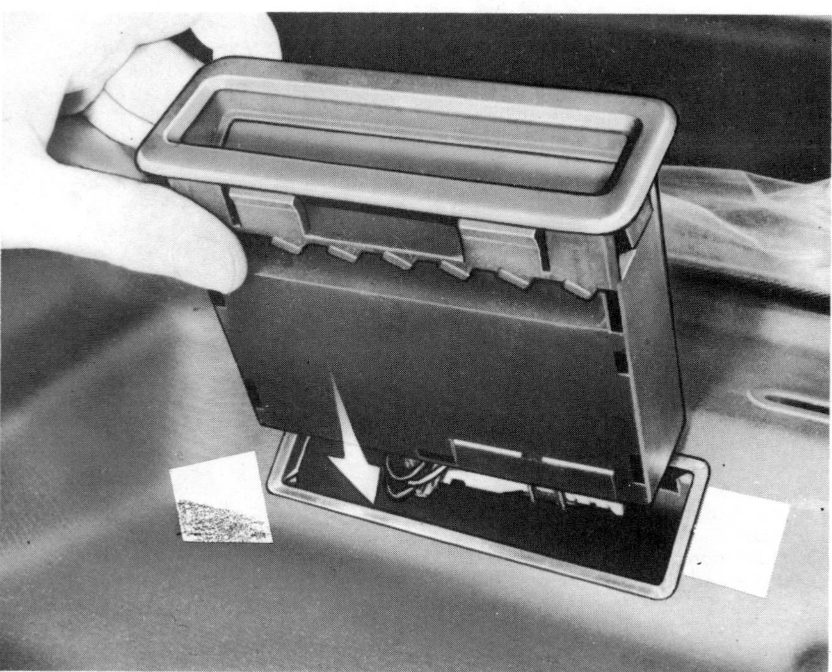

Fig. 12.21 Refitting the check control display unit (Sec 36)

37 Headlamp/direction indicator lens assembly – removal and refitting

1 Remove the direction indicator, headlamp and sidelamp bulbs, as previously described (Section 36).
2 Undo the securing screw and withdraw the direction indicator lens (photos).
3 Remove the two screws which secure the headlamp unit, free it from its clips and withdraw it (photos). Do not disturb the alignment adjusting screws.
4 Refit in the reverse order to removal. Make sure that the front panel sealing lip aligns with the headlamp; use sealing tape if necessary.
5 If a new unit has been fitted, or if the headlamp alignment has been otherwise disturbed, have the alignment checked and adjusted (see Section 38).

38 Headlamp beam alignment

1 Correct alignment of the headlamp beams is most important, not only to ensure good vision for the driver but also to protect other

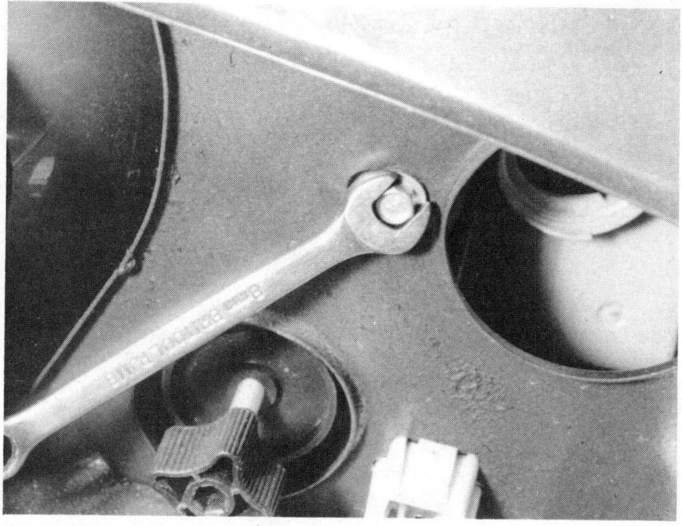

37.2A Undoing a direction indicator lens screw

37.2B Removing a direction indicator lens

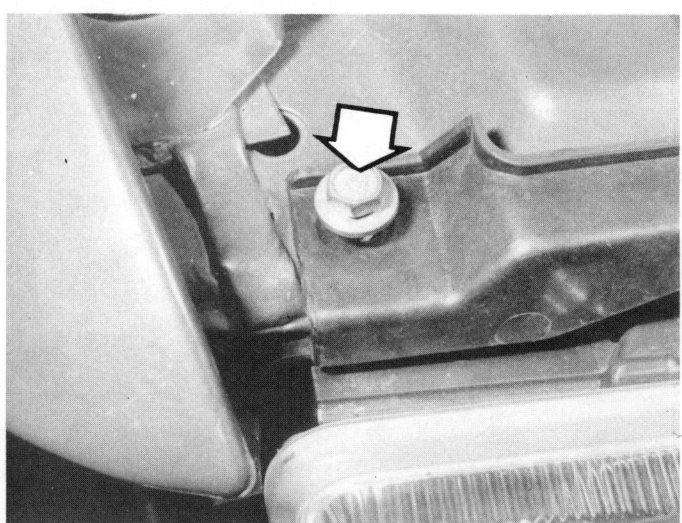

37.3A Headlamp lens outboard securing screw (arrowed)

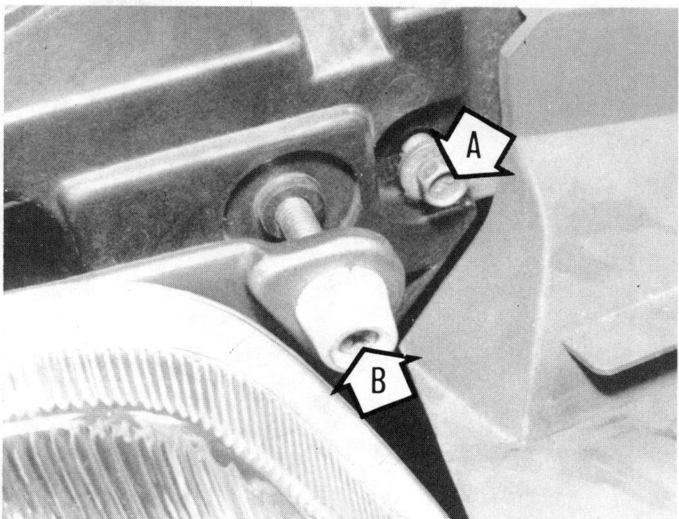

37.3B Headlamp lens inboard securing screw (A). Do not disturb alignment adjusting screw (B)

37.3C Removing a headlamp lens

drivers from being dazzled. Accurate alignment is quickly achieved using the optical setting equipment installed at most garages, to whom the work should be entrusted.
2 In an emergency, adjustments can be made on a 'trial and error' basis. The vertical adjustment screws are accessible from under the bonnet (photo). The lateral adjustment screws are positioned as shown in photo 37.3B.

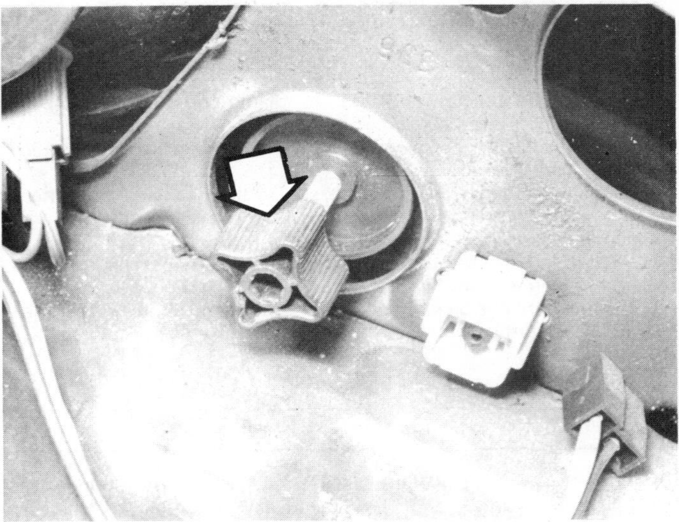

38.2 Headlamp beam vertical adjustment screw (arrowed)

39 Trip computer – general

1 A trip computer is fitted to some top line models. The computer collects fuel consumption and distance data and integrates them with respect to time. In this way it can provide estimates of fuel consumption (both instantaneous and average), average speed and range on fuel remaining. Normal time clock and stopwatch functions are available, and an external temperature sensor is also provided.
2 For detailed operating instructions, refer to the owner's handbook supplied with the vehicle.
3 Testing of the computer and its satellite components is beyond the scope of the average DIY mechanic, but there is no reason why defective components should not be renewed, as described in the next Section.

40 Trip computer – component renewal

Temperature sensor

1 Separate the temperature sensor lead at the multi-plug near the left-hand headlamp.
2 Pull the temperature sensor from the front bumper, unclip its lead and remove it.
3 Refit in the reverse order to removal.

Distance sender

4 The distance sender is located on the speedo cable take-off point on the transmission; except with LCD instruments the speedo cable screws into the sender.
5 Separate the sender multi-plug, then unclip the sender unit from the transmission.
6 Unscrew the speedometer cable (when fitted) from the sender and remove the sender.
7 Refit in the reverse order to removal.

Fuel flow meter

8 The fuel flow meter is located on the wheel housing.
9 Disconnect the battery earth lead.
10 Disconnect the fuel flow meter multi-plug.
11 Identify the fuel hoses, then disconnect and plug them. Be prepared for fuel spillage.

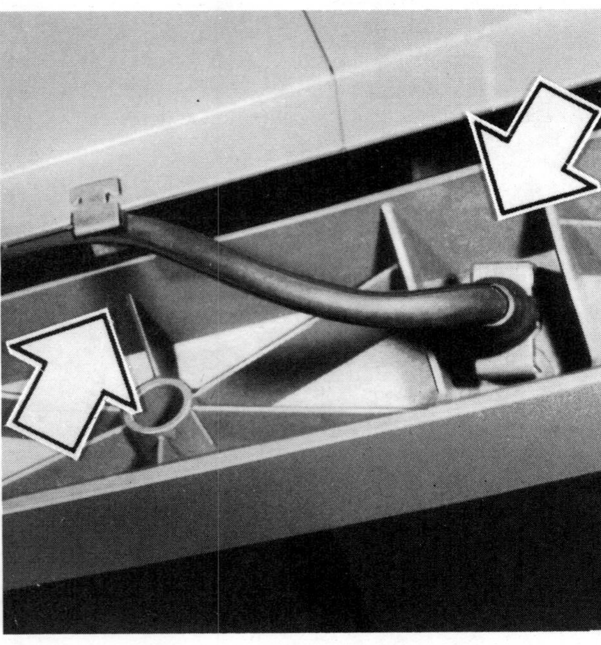

Fig. 12.22 Temperature sensor retaining clamps (arrowed) (Sec 40)

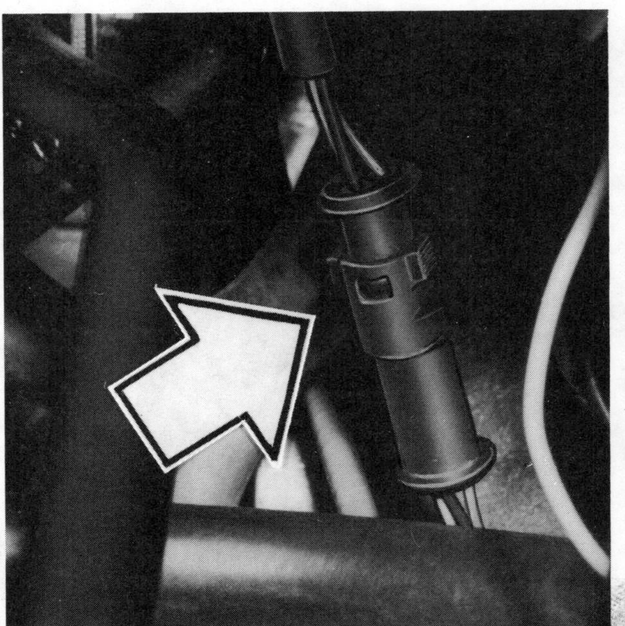

Fig. 12.23 Distance sender multi-plug (arrowed) (Sec 40)

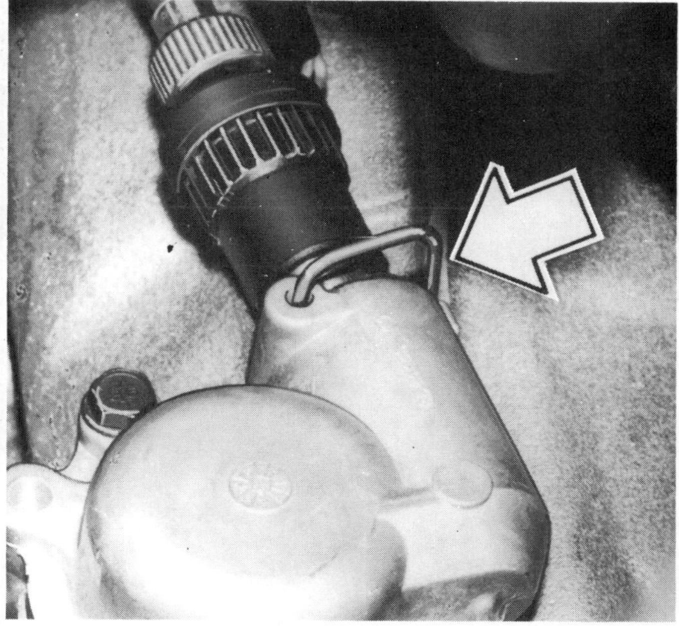

Fig. 12.24 Distance sender retaining clip (arrowed) (Sec 40)

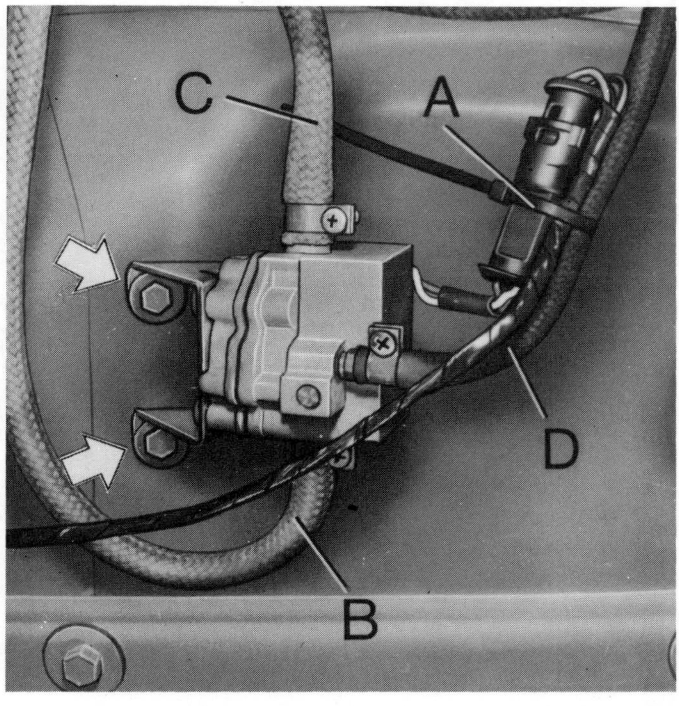

Fig. 12.25 Fuel flow meter connection (Sec 40)

A Multi-plug *C To carburettor*
B From pump *D Return line*

12 Unbolt and remove the fuel flow meter.
13 Refit in the reverse order to removal.

Computer unit

14 Disconnect the battery earth lead.
15 Remove the radio, as described in Section 52.
16 Carefully press the computer out of its location. Unplug its electrical connector and remove it.
17 Refit in the reverse order to removal. A new computer will have to be calibrated on the vehicle; this should be done by a GM dealer.

Computer display lighting

18 Remove the computer, as just described.
19 Grip the bulb holder carefully with pliers and twist it to remove it. The capless bulb can then be extracted and renewed.
20 Refit in the reverse order to removal.

Fig. 12.26 Removing the trip computer – electrical connector arrowed (Sec 40)

Fig 12.27 Removing the trip computer bulb holder (Sec 40)

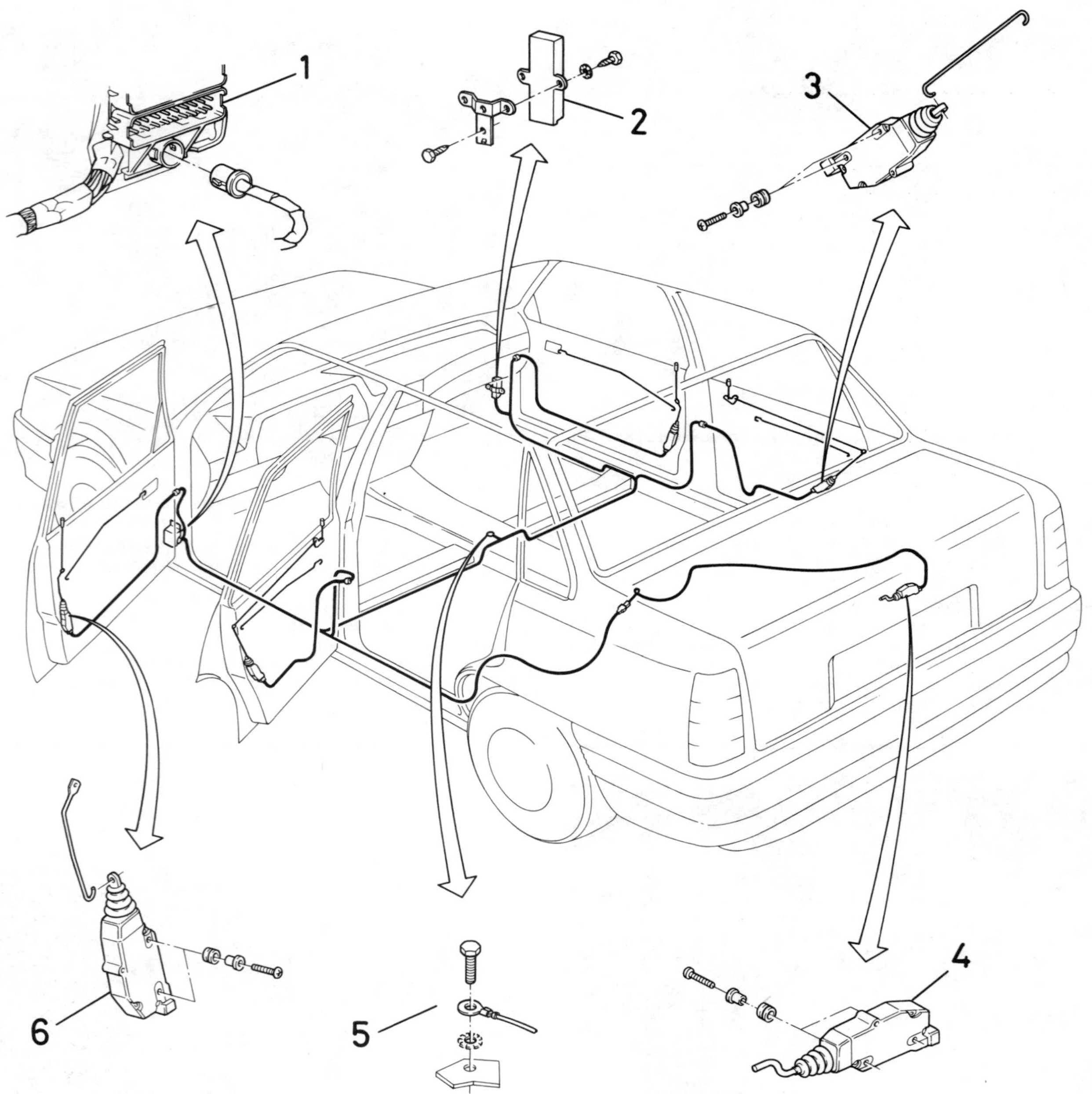

Fig. 12.28 Central locking system components. LHD shown, RHD similar (Sec 41)

1 Central plug connector
2 Electronic control unit
3 Servo motor (passenger door)
4 Servo motor (boot lid/tailgate)
5 Earth point
6 Driver's door switch

41 Central locking system – general

1 On models so equipped, electric servo motors cause all the passenger door locks and the tailgate lock to follow the position of the driver's door lock. The major components of the system are shown in Fig. 12.28.
2 An electronic control unit, located in the passenger footwell, generates the electrical pulses needed to operate the lock motors.

42 Central locking system – component renewal

Driver's door switch
1 Remove the door inner trim panel, as described in Chapter 11, Section 13. Peel away the waterproof sheet in the area of the switch.
2 Remove the two securing screws, disconnect the switch plug and unhook the switch from the lock actuating rod. Remove the switch.
3 Refit in the reverse order to removal; make sure that the electrical

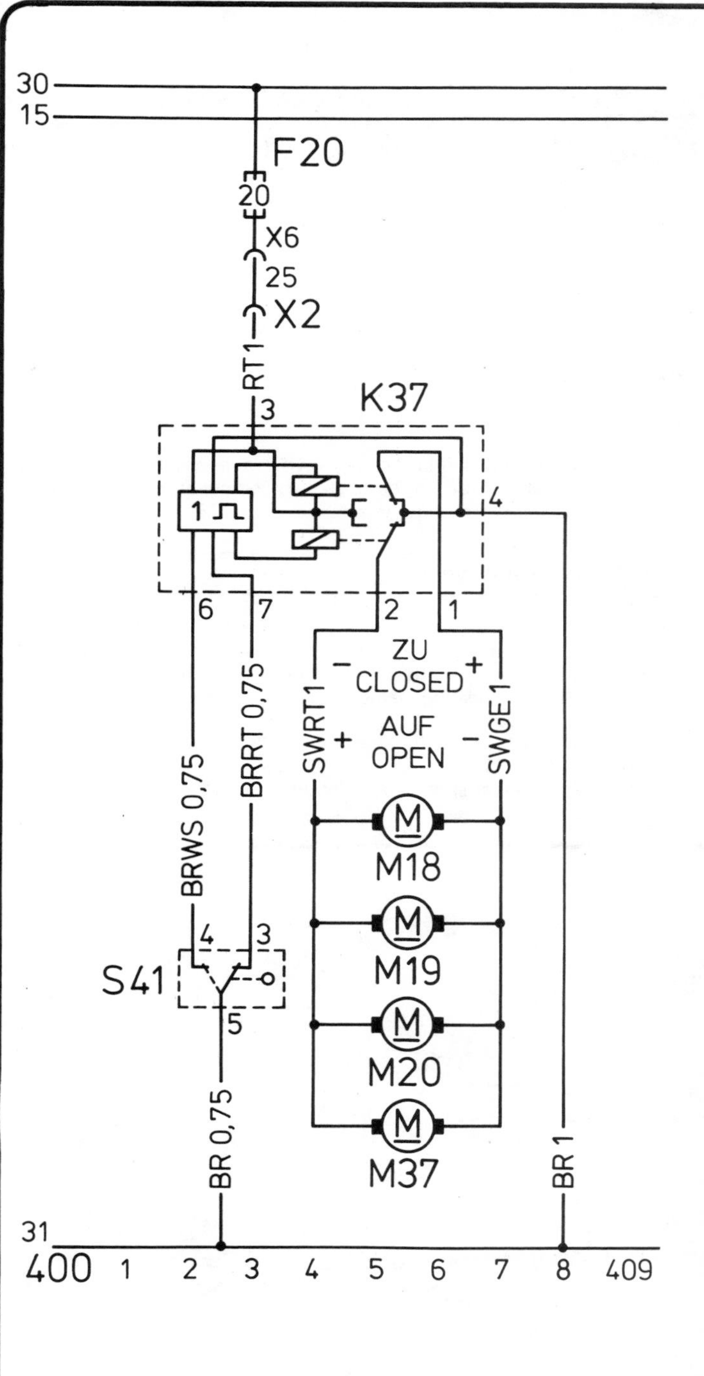

Fig. 12.29 Circuit diagram for central locking system. For colour codes etc see main wiring diagram (Sec 41)

F20	*Fuse*
K37	*Control unit*
M18	*Front passenger door motor*
M19	*LH rear door motor*
M20	*RH rear door motor*
M37	*Tailgate motor*
S41	*Driver's door switch*
X2	*Auxiliary connector plug*
X6	*Wiring harness plug*

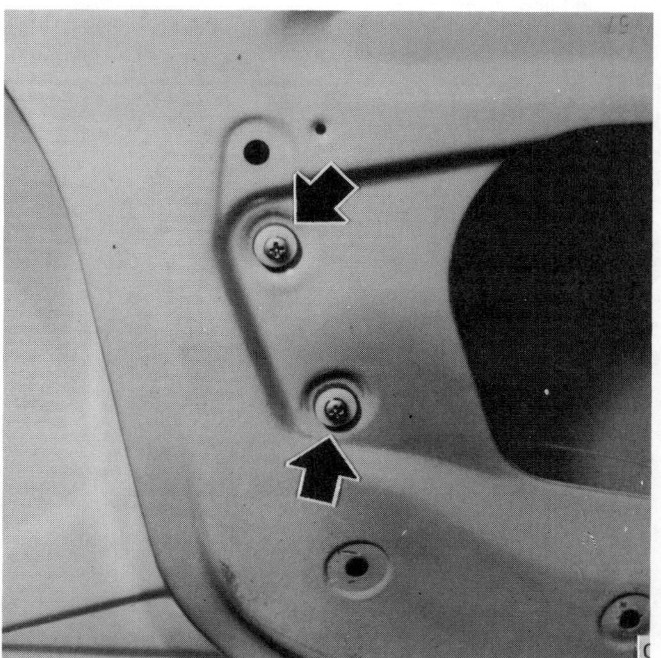

Fig. 12.30 Central locking switch retaining screws (arrowed) (Sec 42)

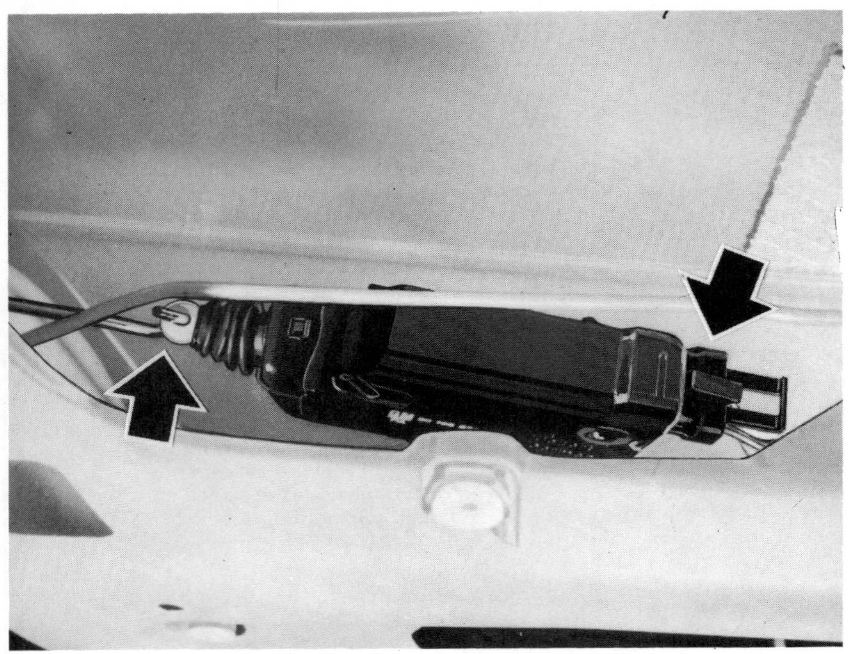

Fig. 12.31 Central locking switch wiring plug (arrowed, right) and lock actuating rod (arrowed, left) (Sec 42)

plug is connected the right way round. Renew the rubber mountings if necessary.

Passenger door and tailgate servo motors

4 Proceed as just described for the driver's door switch. Removal of the tailgate trim panel is achieved by carefully releasing its retaining clips.

Control unit

5 Remove the trim panel from the passenger side footwell.
6 On fuel injection models, release and move aside the fuel injection control unit and its bracket.
7 Remove the single screw which secures the control unit bracket to the A-pillar.
8 Extract the control unit and bracket. Disconnect the electrical plug and unscrew the unit from the bracket to remove it completely.
9 Refit in the reverse order to removal.

43 Heated seats – general

1 In some territories, electric heating elements for the front seats can be specified as an option. The heating elements are controlled by facia-mounted switches; they also incorporate a thermostatic control.
2 Do not use the heating elements when the engine is not running, or the battery will quickly be discharged.
3 In the event of malfunction, first check the wiring runs and connectors (Fig. 12.34).
4 Element renewal should be referred to a GM dealer or upholstery specialist.

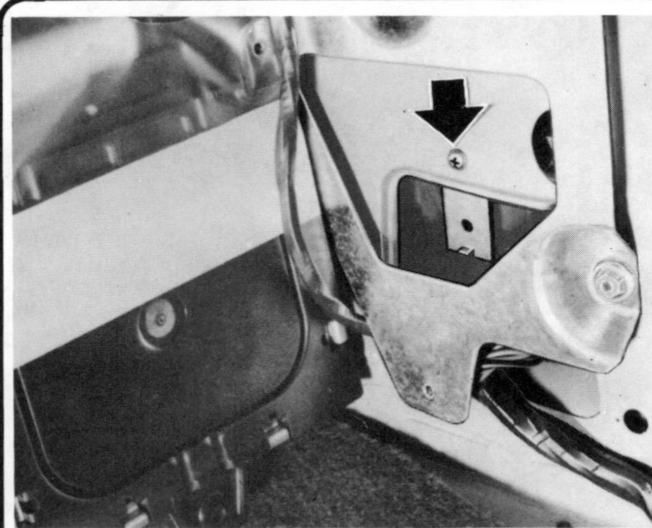

Fig. 12.32 Control unit securing screw (arrowed) in A-pillar (Sec 42)

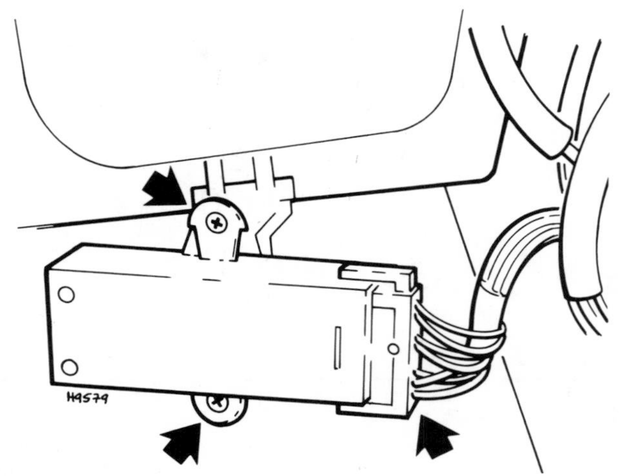

Fig. 12.33 Control unit-to-bracket screws and multi-plug (arrowed) (Sec 42)

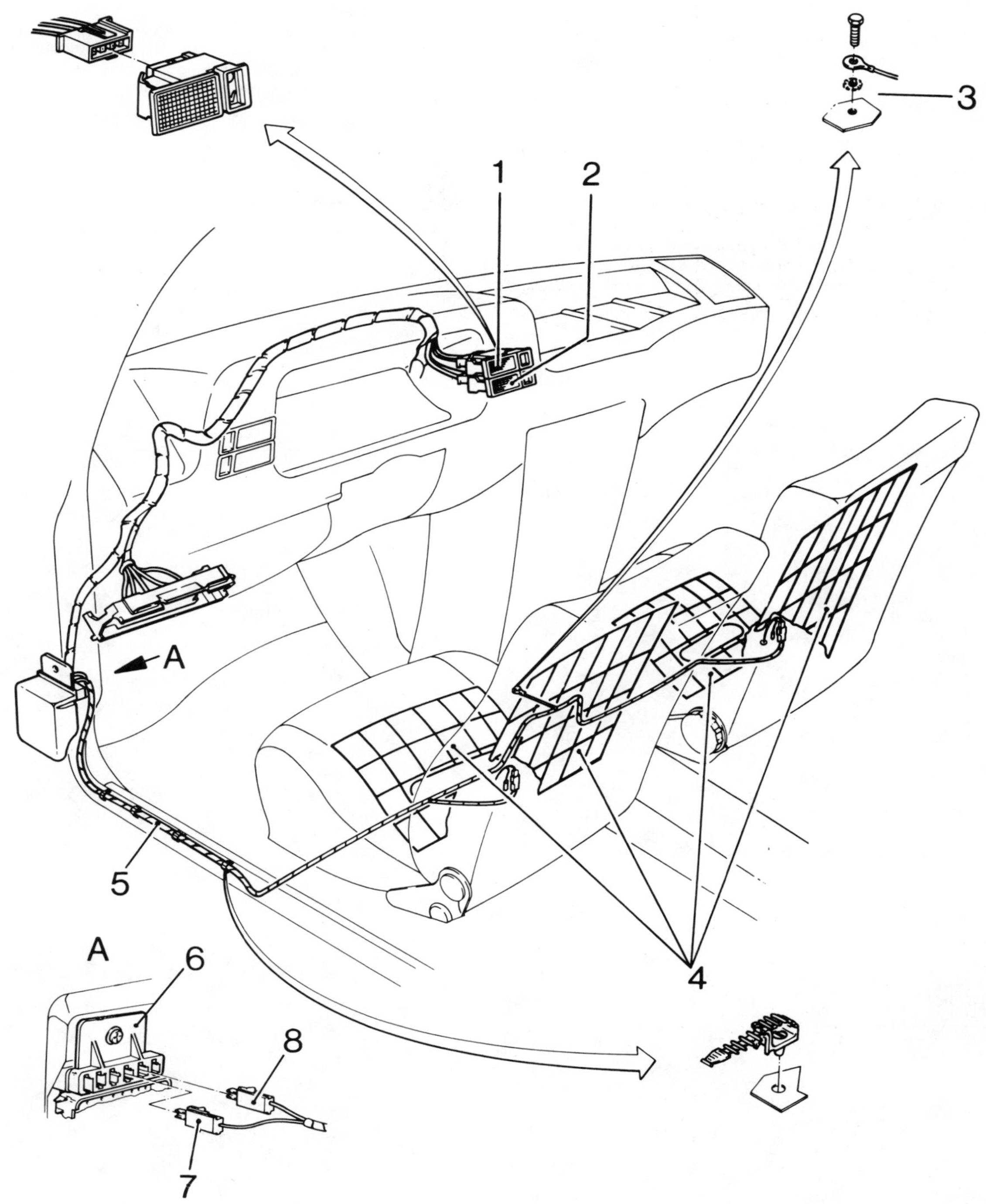

Fig. 12.34 Seat heating components. LHD shown, RHD similar (Sec 43)

1 Driver's seat switch
2 Passenger's seat switch
3 Earth point
4 Heating elements
5 Wiring harness
6 Central connector
7 RH seat plug (green)
8 LH seat plug (orange)

44 Tailgate contact pins and plate – removal and refitting

1 A three-pole contact unit transfers electrical power for the tailgate units (heated window, wiper motor) when the tailgate is shut. The unit consists of a contact plate in the load area sill and spring-loaded pins in the tailgate.
2 To remove the plate or the pins, first disconnect the battery earth lead.
3 Remove the tailgate trim or rear sill trim, as appropriate. Unclip the contact plate or pins from its location and disconnect the wire (photo).
4 Refit in the reverse order to removal. The component mountings are inhibited to prevent incorrect fitting.

45 Wiper blades and arms – removal and refitting

1 To remove a wiper blade, lift the wiper arm away from the glass. Swivel the blade on the arm, depress the catch on the U-shaped retainer and slide the blade off the arm (photo).
2 Before removing a wiper arm, make sure that the motor is in its parked position. Mark the position of the blade on the screen with sticky tape or wax crayon as a guide to refitting.
3 Lift up the cover and unscrew the arm retaining nut (photo).
4 Pull the arm off the splined shaft. If it has not been moved for a long time it will be tight: apply some penetrating fluid.
5 Refit in the reverse order to removal.

46 Windscreen wiper motor and linkage – removal and refitting

1 Remove the windscreen wiper arms, as described in the previous Section.
2 Disconnect the battery earth lead.
3 Remove the four screws and take off both halves of the wind deflector panel. See Chapter 11, Section 12.
4 Remove the clamp nuts from both wiper spindles (photo).

44.3 Removing the tailgate contact pins

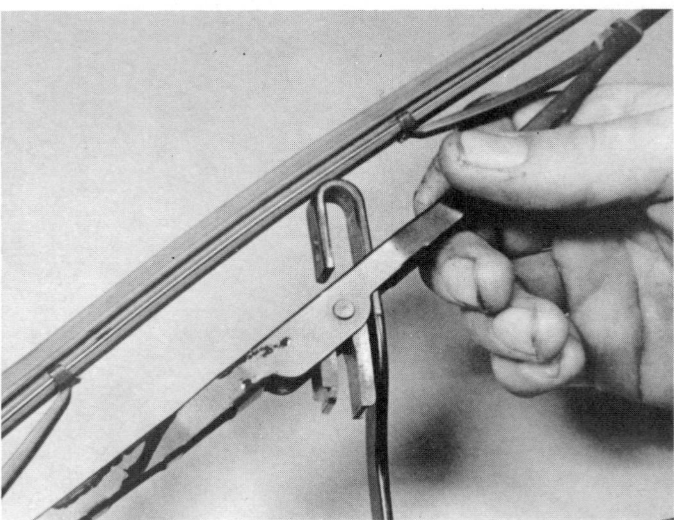

45.1 Removing a wiper blade from its arm

45.3 Wiper arm retaining nut

46.4 Wiper spindle clamp nut (arrowed)

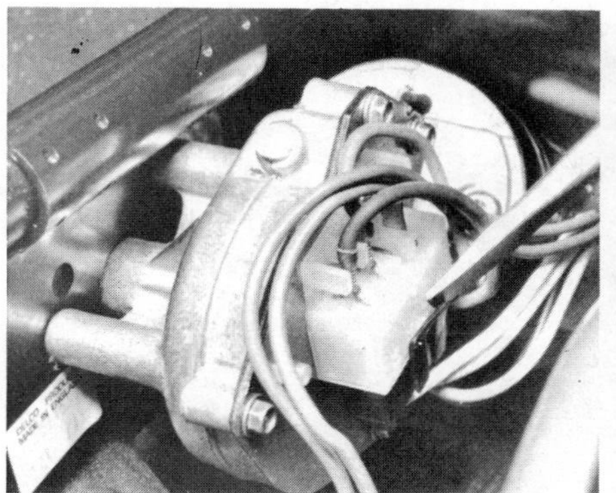
46.6 Releasing the wiper motor electrical plug

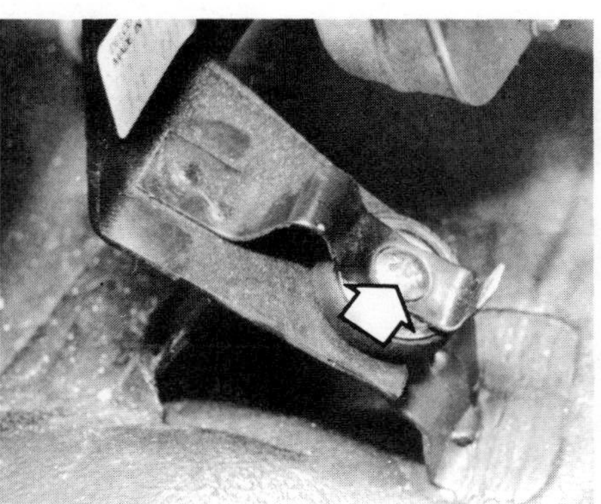
46.7 Wiper motor securing screw (arrowed)

46.8A Wiper motor spindle nut (arrowed)

46.8B Undoing the wiper motor securing screws

46.9 Choice of wiper motor mounting holes – RHD arrowed

5 Free the bulkhead rubber seal, remove the single securing screw and take off the water deflector.
6 Release the retainer and disconnect the electrical multi-plug from the motor (photo).
7 Undo the single securing screw and remove the motor and linkage (photo).
8 The motor may be separated from the linkage by undoing the spindle nut. To remove the motor from its bracket, also remove the three securing screws (photos).
9 Refit in the reverse order to removal. Note that two sets of motor mounting holes are provided, apparently to provide for different sweep and parking requirements for RHD and LHD cars (photo).

47 Rear window wiper motor – removal and refitting

1 Disconnect the battery earth lead.
2 Remove the wiper arm, as described in Section 45.
3 Remove the clamp nut from the wiper spindle.
4 Remove the tailgate inner trim panel.
5 Remove the contact pin nut (see Section 44) and disconnect the wiper motor wire from it. (On Estate models, simply disconnect the motor from the tailgate harness.)
6 Remove the two securing screws and carefully withdraw the motor and its wiring (photo).
7 Refit in the reverse order to removal, but check for correct operation before refitting the trim panel.

48 Windscreen/rear window washer system – general

1 All models are fitted with an electrically-operated windscreen washer. The reservoir is mounted on the rear left-hand side of the engine bay; the pump is a push fit into a grommet in the base of the reservoir.
2 When a rear window washer is fitted, this uses a second pump which shares the same reservoir. A small bore tube carries the water through the car to the tailgate.
3 To renew a pump, first drain the reservoir (if necessary). Disconnect the electrical plug from the pump and rock the pump out of

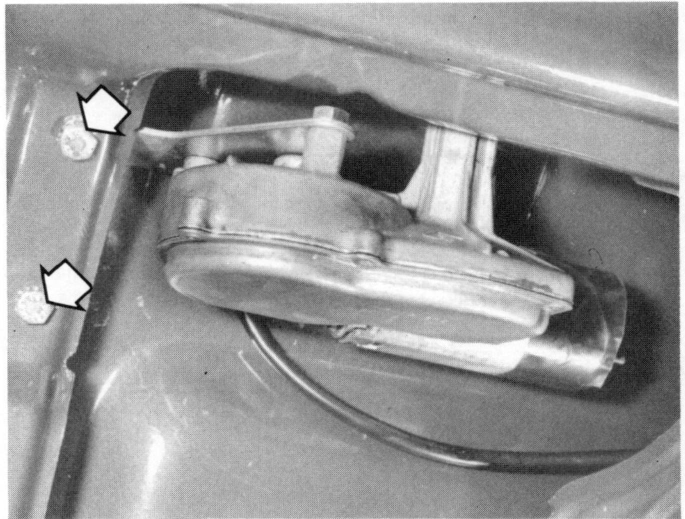
47.6 Rear wiper motor securing screws (arrowed)

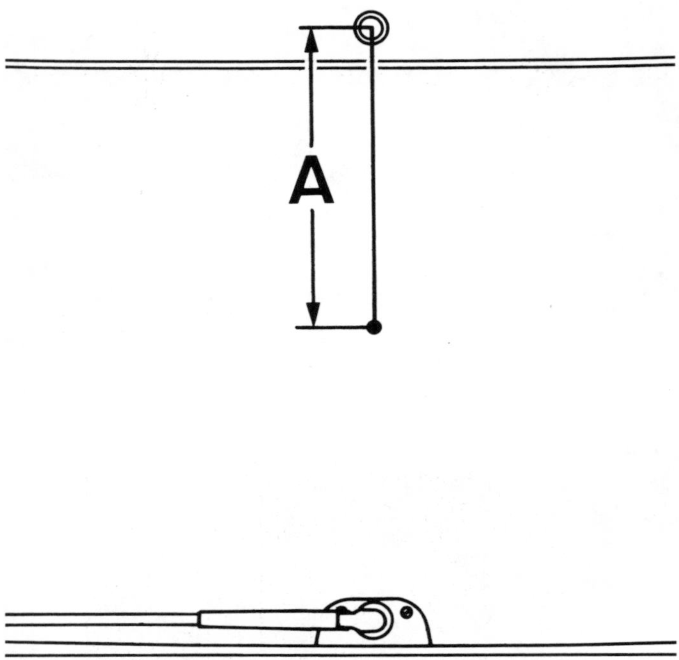

Fig. 12.35 Rear washer jet aiming point (Sec 48)

A (Hatchback, except GTE) = 223 ± 50 mm (8.8 ± 2.0 in)
A (GTE and Estate) = 300 ± 50 mm (11.8 ± 2.0 in)

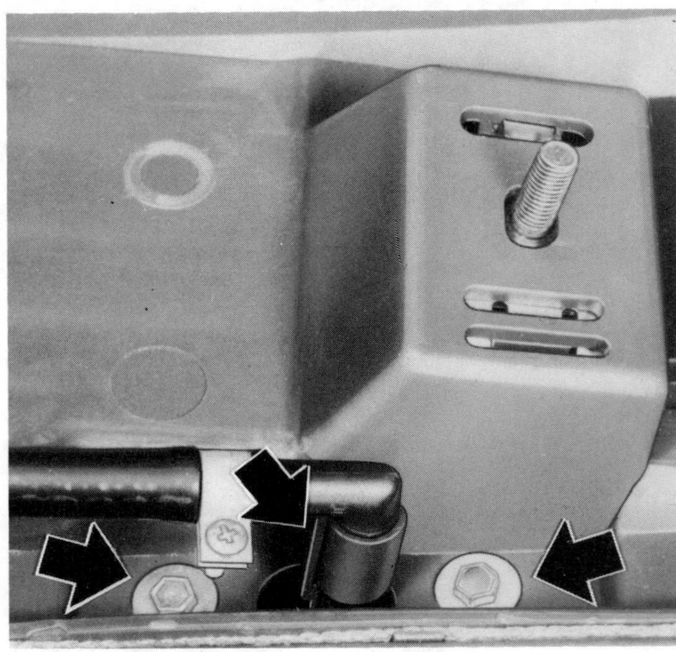

Fig. 12.36 Headlamp washer jet retaining screws and pipe connector (arrowed) (Sec 49)

its grommet. Cut the tube off as close as possible to the pump outlet stub.
4 Use a new grommet when fitting a new pump. A short length of rubber hose should be used to connect the tube to the pump, as the tube is too stiff to pass over the outlet stub easily.
5 Washer jet aim can be adjusted by inserting a pin or similar item and carefully moving the jet.

49 Headlamp washer system – general

1 When fitted, the headlamp washer system has its own reservoir and high pressure pump. The reservoir is located in the engine bay, except on models with fuel injection and/or a trip computer, when it is located under the left-hand wheel arch.
2 A relay controls the headlamp washer pump so that it operates when the windscreen washer is in use and the headlamps are on.
3 The washer jets are located in the bumper overriders. They can only be renewed as an assembly; the front trim panel must be removed first (Chapter 11, Section 9).
4 Pump renewal is similar to that of the windscreen and rear window washer pumps (Section 48). To remove the wheel arch protective panelling, press the centres out of the plastic rivets; use new rivets or clips on reassembly. The reservoir can be removed from under the wing after unscrewing its filler neck and removing the securing screw.

50 Washer fluid – general

1 Washer reservoirs should only be filled with clean water and a proprietary screen wash additive. The use of household detergents may clog the pump or jets and smear the glass.
2 In freezing conditions use an additive with antifreeze properties. **Never** use cooling system antifreeze as this will attack rubber components and damage the paintwork. A small quantity (up to 10%) of methylated spirit is effective in providing protection against freezing.

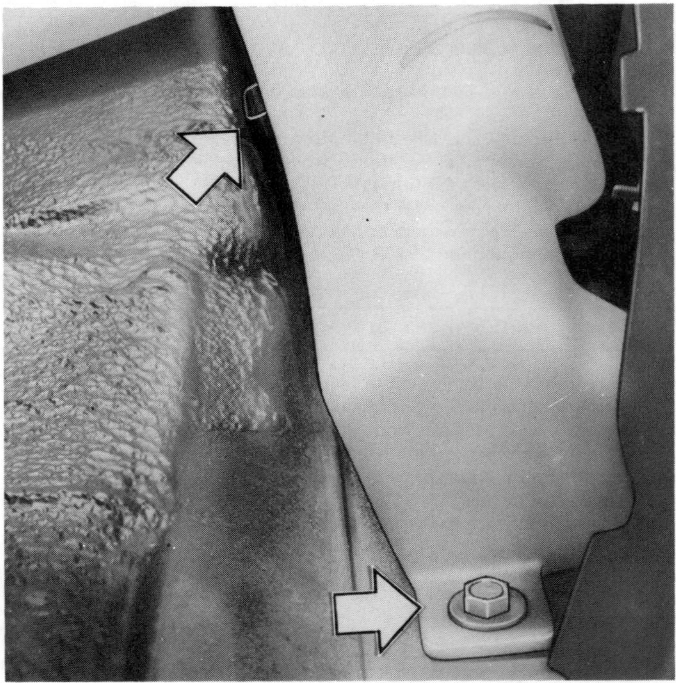

Fig. 12.37 Headlamp washer reservoir securing screw and clip (arrowed) (Sec 49)

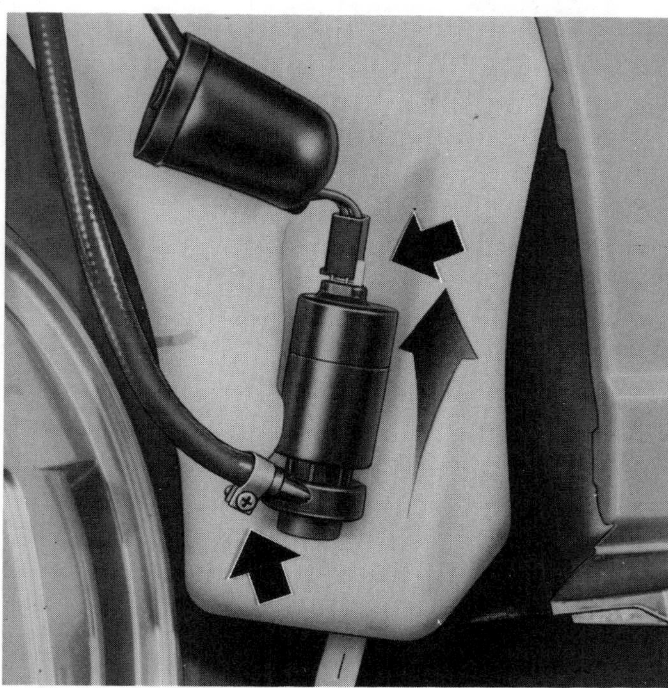

Fig. 12.38 Headlamp washer pump electrical plug and hose clamp screw (arrowed) (Sec 49)

Fig. 12.39 Slacken bulb failure monitor securing screws (arrowed) to release it (Sec 51)

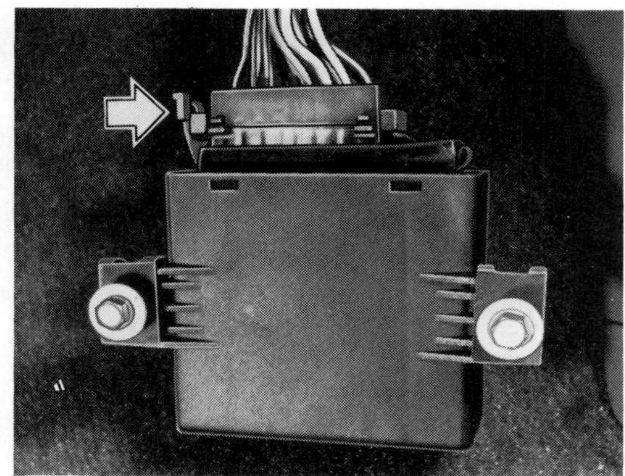

Fig. 12.40 Bulb failure monitor removal – multi-plug catch arrowed (Sec 51)

51 Check control system – general

1 Fitted to some higher specifications models, the check control system monitors important fluid levels, brake pad wear and bulb failure. A bank of six or seven warning lights to the left of the instrument panel conveys the information to the driver.

2 All the warning lights should come on for a few seconds when the ignition is first switched on; they should then all go out, except for the stop-lamp warning light, which will go out once the brake pedal is operated. If any warning light stays on, or comes on during operation, the components or system indicated should be checked.

3 The main bulb failure indicator light monitors dipped headlights and tail lights; the stop-lamp indicator light monitors the stop-lamps and stop-lamp switch.

4 The bulb failure monitor unit is located under the facia panel on the passenger side. It is secured by two screws which are accessible after removing the trim and opening the glovebox.

5 The oil level warning light receives information from a special engine oil dipstick (photo). This dipstick is fragile. Obviously a correct reading will only be obtained if the car is parked on level ground.

6 The brake fluid level warning light is controlled by a float switch in the master cylinder reservoir.

7 Brake pad wear is detected by wear sensors incorporated into the pads. This warning light will illuminate during braking if attention is required.

8 Screen washer fluid level is monitored by a float switch in the reservoir.

9 Renewal of the check control warning light bulbs is covered in Section 36.

10 Note that fitting bulbs of incorrect wattage may cause the bulb failure unit to give false alarms. For the same reason, the advice of a GM dealer should be sought if it is proposed to wire in a trailer socket.

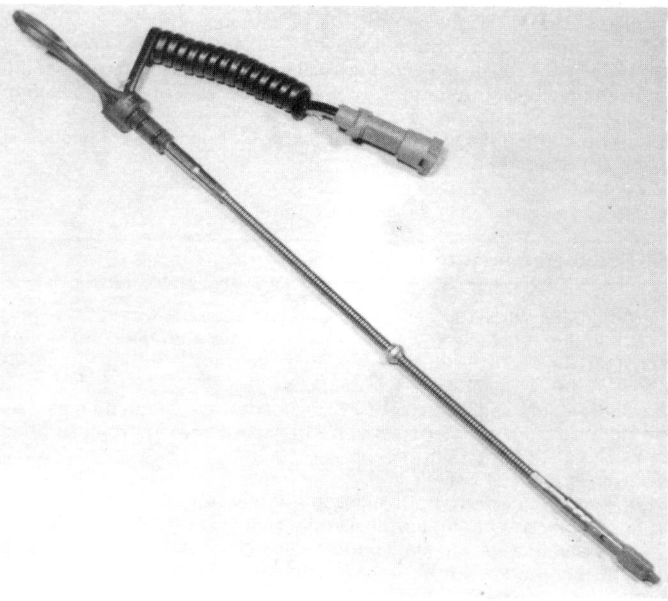

51.5 Special dipstick used with check control system

52.2A Inserting the special clips for radio removal

52.2B Removing the radio from its aperture

52.4 Removing the radio surround

52 Radio equipment (factory-fitted) – removal and refitting

1 All models are fitted with at least a radio, and most leave the factory with a combined radio/cassette player. This Section outlines removal and refitting procedures for the commonly found equipment.

2 Radio/cassette units are to the latest DIN standard; they are released by inserting two special clips into the holes on each side of the unit. The clips are pressed in until they snap into place, then used to pull the radio out of its aperture. The various plugs can then be removed from the rear of the radio (photos).

3 The special clips used to release the radio should have been supplied with the car; if not, they can be obtained from a car entertainment specialist.

4 With the radio removed, its surround can be removed if necessary by unclipping it (photo).

5 To refit the radio, reconnect its plugs and push it home until the retaining springs click into place.

6 Loudspeakers are positioned one at each end of the facia panel, and (on some models) one at each end of the parcel shelf or in the tailgate. Removal and refitting are self-explanatory once the appropriate trim has been removed – see Chapter 11.

7 The radio aerial is mounted on the right-hand front wing. To remove it, first remove the wheel arch protective panelling by pressing out the centres of the plastic rivets. The aerial can then be released from its bracket and the top mounting nut be undone.

8 If the aerial cable (and motor cables, when applicable) cannot be disconnected at the aerial end, they will have to be disconnected at the radio and fed back through the inner wing. Removal of some facia trim may be necessary to gain adequate access.

9 When refitting the aerial, make sure that a good earth connection is made at the mounting bracket.

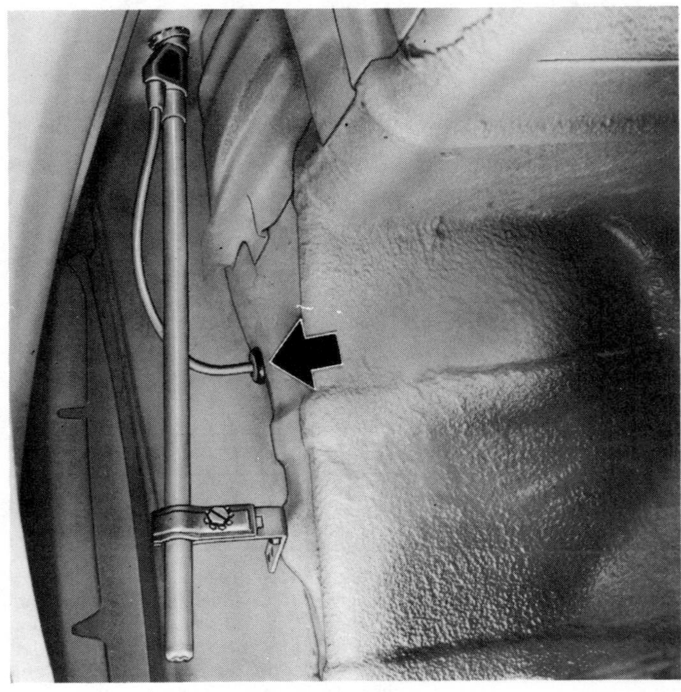
Fig. 12.41 Radio aerial mounting under wing – cable grommet arrowed (Sec 52)

53 Radio equipment – suppression of interference

1 Adequate radio interference suppression equipment is fitted during manufacture. If vehicle-generated interference is a problem, make sure first that the radio is properly trimmed (see manufacturer's instructions) and that the aerial is well earthed.

2 Radio equipment which is fitted instead of the original items may be more sensitive to interference. If not already present, the use of an in-line choke in the radio power supply, as close as possible to the receiver, is often of benefit.

3 If interference from the windscreen wiper motor is a problem, an in-line choke can be fitted to its supply leads (Fig. 12.43). Make sure that the choke is of adequate current carrying capacity.

4 The ignition system is already suppressed and no further attempt should be made in that direction.

5 Consult a GM dealer or car entertainment specialist for further advice if necessary.

54 Wiring diagram – general

1 The wiring diagrams are of the current flow type. Each circuit is shown in the simplest possible fashion. The bottom line of the diagram represents the 'earth' or negative connection; the numbers below this line are track numbers, which enable circuits and components to be located using the key.

2 The lines at the top of the diagram represent 'live' or positive connection points. The line labelled '30' is live at all times, whilst that labelled '15' is live only when the ignition is on.

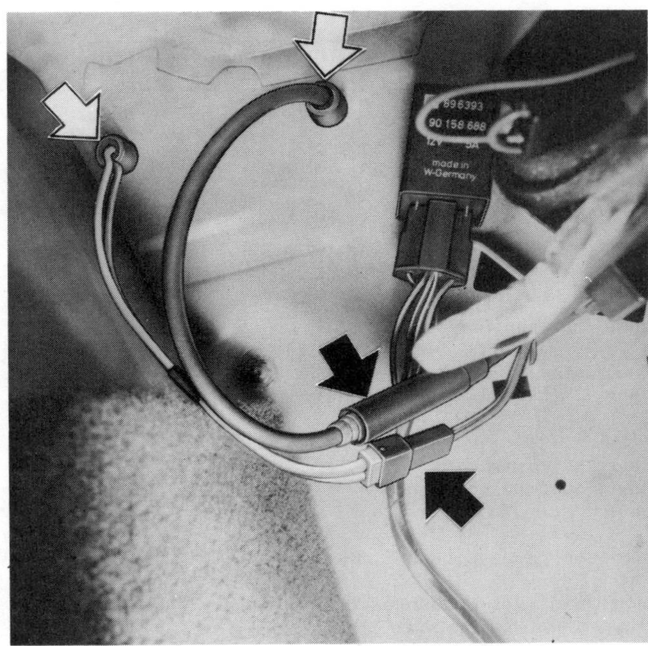

Fig. 12.42 Motorised aerial cable connectors (black arrows) and grommets (white arrows) (Sec 52)

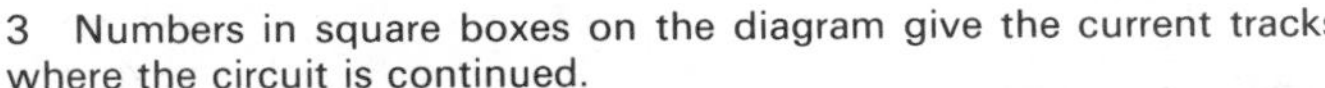

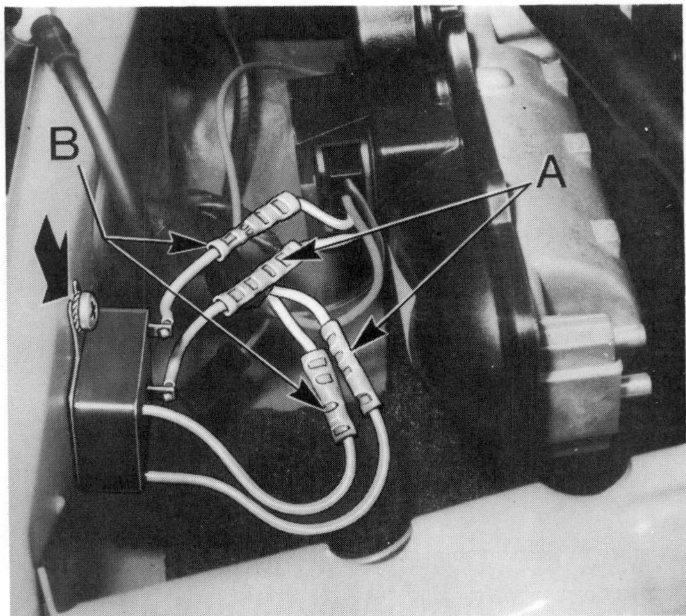

Fig. 12.43 In-line choke connections for wiper motor interference suppression. Choke securing screw is arrowed (Sec 53)

A White cable (terminal 53B) *B Yellow cable (terminal 53)*

3 Numbers in square boxes on the diagram give the current tracks where the circuit is continued.

4 As an example of how to use the diagrams, trace the heated rear window circuit (around track 202 in the 1985 model year diagrams) with the help of the following text.

5 Starting at the top of track 202, the supply for the window heating element comes from line '30' (permanently live). It proceeds via fuse F18 (20 amps) to terminal 30 of relay K1, using a red wire of cross-section 1.5 mm² – this is what 'RT 1.5' along the wire path means. From terminal 87 of the relay the circuit goes via terminal 24 of connector X6 to the element itself (E19); from the connector to the element the wire is coloured black. A further black wire completes the circuit by joining the element to earth. In this case the 'earth' wire simply attaches the component to the nearest piece of metal bodywork (photo); in other cases earthing is achieved by the component mounting and no wire is used.

6 It is also necessary to see how the heated rear window relay (K1) is energised if a fault is being traced. The heated rear window switch S3 earths the relay coil in the 'on' position by means of the brown/white wire from terminal 85 of K1 (track 201) to S3 (track 203), then from S3 to earth as a brown wire in track 204. Following the blue/white wire from the 'live' side of the relay coil (terminal 86), this finishes in a square box labelled '114'. Referring to track 114 as instructed, the box labelled '201' shows where the circuit continues; it is evident from track 113 that the relay will only be energised when the alternator (G2) is producing a voltage. This ingenious arrangement means that the battery cannot be discharged by using the heated rear window when the engine is not running.

7 The main wiring harness connectors are located behind the trim in the front passenger footwell (photo).

54.5 Heated rear window earth wire

54.7 Wiring harness main connectors

55 Fault diagnosis – electrical system

Symptom	Reason(s)
Starter motor does not turn – no voltage at motor	Battery terminals loose or corroded Battery discharged or defective Starter motor connections loose or broken Starter switch or solenoid faulty
Starter motor does not turn – voltage at motor	Starter motor internal defect
Starter motor turns very slowly	Battery nearly discharged or defective Battery terminals loose or corroded Starter motor internal defect
Starter motor noisy or rough	Mounting bolts loose Pinion or flywheel ring gear teeth damaged or worn
Alternator not charging battery	Drivebelt slipping or broken Alternator brushes worn Alternator connections loose or broken Alternator internal defect
Alternator overcharging battery	Alternator voltage regulator faulty
Battery will not hold charge	Short-circuit causing continual drain on battery Battery defective internally Battery case dirty and damp
Fuel or temperature gauge gives no reading	Sender unit defective Wire discontinued or broken Fuse blown Gauge faulty Instrument voltage stabiliser faulty (will affect all instruments)
Fuel or temperature gauge reads too high	Sender unit defective Wire earthed Gauge faulty Instrument voltage stabiliser faulty
Horn operates continuously	Horn push stuck down Cable to horn push earthed
Horn does not operate	Fuse blown Cable or connector broken or loose Horn contact ring dirty or corroded
Lights do not come on	Battery discharged Fuse(s) blown Light switch faulty Bulbs blown
Lights give poor illumination	Lenses or reflectors dirty Bulbs blackened Incorrect wattage bulbs fitted
Wiper motor fails to work	Fuse blown Connections loose or broken Relay defective Switch defective Motor defective
Wiper motor works slowly and draws little current	Brushes badly worn Commutator dirty or burnt
Wiper motor works slowly and draws heavy current	Linkage seized or otherwise damaged Motor internal gault
Wiper motor works, but blades do not move	Linkage broken or disconnected Motor gearbox badly worn
Defect in any other components	Fuse blown Relay faulty (when applicable) Supply wire broken or disconnected Switch faulty (when applicable) Earth return faulty (check for loose or corroded mountings) Component itself faulty

Wiring diagrams commence overleaf

Key to Fig. 12.44. Not all items are fitted to all models

Refer to Section 54 for general information

No	Description	Track
E1	RH sidelamp	235
E2	RH tail lamp	237, 440
E3	Number plate lamp	238, 451
E4	LH sidelamp	231
E5	LH tail lamp	232, 438
E6	Engine bay lamp	240
E7	RH main beam	246
E8	LH main beam	245
E9	RH dipped beam	249, 444
E10	LH dipped beam	248, 442
E11	Instrument illumination	242
E12	Auto transmission selector lamp	346
E13	Luggage area lamp	285
E14	Interior lamp	291
E15	Glovebox lamp	339
E16	Cigarette lighter lamp	338
E17	RH reversing lamp	336
E18	LH reversing lamp	335
E19	Heated rear window	202
E20	LH front foglamp	257
E21	RH front foglamp	258
E24	Rear foglamp	253
E25	LH seat heater	368
E30	RH seat heater	372
E32	Clock illumination	297
E33	Ashtray lamp	347
E34	Heater control lamp	242
E38	Computer illumination	355
E39	Rear foglamp	254
E40	Number plate lamp (Estate)	239,452
E41	Interior lamp with delay unit	287, 289
E42	Radio illumination	431, 433
F1 to F20	Fuses	Various
F22	Fuse (mixture preheating)	164
F25	Instrument voltage stabiliser	213
G1	Battery	101
G2	Alternator	113
H1	Radio	429, 431
H2	Horn	211
H3	Direction indicator repeater	279
H4	Oil pressure warning lamp	221
H5	Brake fluid level warning lamp	219
H6	Hazard warning repeater	276
H7	No charge warning lamp	113
H8	Main beam pilot lamp	247
H9	RH stop-lamp	269, 448
H10	LH stop-lamp	268, 446
H11	RH front direction indicator	281
H12	RH rear direction indicator	282
H13	LH front direction indicator	277
H14	LH rear direction indicator	278
H16	Glow plug light (Diesel)	195
H17	Trailer direction indicator repeater	273
H19	Buzzer (headlamps on)	293
H20	Choke warning lamp	340
H21	Handbrake warning lamp	218
H23	Radio receiver (with automatic aerial)	432, 433
H25	Mirror heating pilot light	383, 392
K1	Heated rear window relay	201, 202
K2	Flasher unit	274
K5	Front foglamp relay	258, 259
K8	Wiper delay relay	305 to 308
K9	Headlamp washer relay	312 to 314
K10	Trailer flasher unit	273, 274
K15	Fuel injection control module	173 to 183
K20	Ignition module (electronic ignition)	118, 119
K25	Preheater relay (Diesel)	195 to 198

No	Description	Track
K28	Day running light relay (not UK)	421, 422
K30	Rear window wiper relay	319 to 321
K31	Fuel pump relay (fuel injection)	169 to 171
K35	Mirror heating timer	397, 399
K36	Computer relay	360 to 362
K37	Central locking relay	402 to 408
K39	Dashpot relay (not UK)	160, 162
K45	Preheater relay (not UK)	164 to 166
K46	Ignition timing control (not UK)	145 to 150
K52	Ignition module (not UK)	142, 143
K53	Ignition timing control (not UK)	134 to 139
L1	Ignition coil (contact breaker system)	109
L2	Ignition coil (electronic system)	117,126,143
L3	Ignition coil (not UK)	136
M1	Starter motor	105 to 107
M2	Windscreen wiper motor	303 to 306
M5	Heater blower motor	205 to 207
M4	Radiator cooling fan	210
M3	Windscreen washer pump	302
M8	Rear window wiper motor (except GTE)	317 to 319
M9	Rear window washer pump	322, 330
M12	Starter motor (Diesel)	193, 194
M14	LH front window motor	411
M15	RH front window motor	417
M16	LH rear window motor	413
M17	RH rear window motor	415
M18	Front passenger door lock actuator	404, 407
M19	LH rear door lock actuator	404, 407
M20	RH rear door lock actuator	404, 407
M21	Fuel pump (fuel injection)	169
M24	Headlamp washer pump	314
M26	Radio aerial motor	433, 434
M30	LH electric mirror	368 to 381, 387 to 390
M31	RH electric mirror	394 to 397
M36	Rear window wiper motor (GTE only)	327 to 330
M37	Tailgate lock actuator	404, 407
P1	Fuel gauge	214
P2	Temperature gauge	206
P3	Clock	296
P4	Fuel gauge sender	214, 471
P5	Temperature gauge sender	216, 481
P7	Tachometer	225
P10	Oil pressure sensor	488
P11	Airflow meter (fuel injection)	188 to 190
P12	Temperature sensor (fuel injection)	188 to 190
P13	Temperature sensor (ambient air)	360
P14	Distance recorder	133, 134, 156, 157 351, 352, 492, 493
P15	Fuel flow meter	353, 354
P23	Vacuum sensor (not UK)	135 to 137
P24	Temperature sensor (not UK)	138, 139
P25	Bulb failure sensor	438 to 448
P26	Engine oil level sensor	457, 458
P27	LH brake pad wear sensor	460
P28	RH brake pad wear sensor	461
R1	Ballast resistor (contact breaker ignition)	109
R2	Carburettor heater	341
R3	Cigarette lighter	337
R5	Glow plugs (Diesel)	188 to 190
R7	Mixture preheating	164
R11	Instrument illumination rheostat	475
R12	Automatic choke heater	343

Key to Fig. 12.44. Not all items are fitted to all models (continued)

No	Description	Track
S1	Ignition/starter switch	106,107
S2.1	Main lighting switch	239,240 439, 440
S2.2	Interior light switch	289
S3	Heater blower/heated rear window switch	203 to 207
S5.2	Dipswitch	247,248,444
S5.3	Direction indicator switch	280, 281
S5.5	Horn switch	211
S6	Distributor (contact breaker type)	109, 111
S7	Reversing lamp switch	335
S8	Stop-lamp switch	268, 446
S9.2	Windscreen wiper switch	302 to 306
S9.3	Rear window wiper switch (except GTE)	320, 321
S9.4	Rear window wiper switch (GTE only)	329, 330
S10	Starter inhibitor switch (automatic transmission)	107
S11	Brake fluid level switch	219
S13	Handbrake switch	218, 484
S14	Oil pressure switch	221, 486
S15	Luggage area light switch	285
S16	RH door switch	290
S17	LH door switch	291
S18	Glovebox lamp switch	339
S21	Front foglamp switch	260, 262
S22	Rear foglamp switch	253, 255
S29	Radiator fan thermoswitch	210
S30	LH seat heating switch	368, 370
S37	Window switches	410 to 418
S41	Central locking switch	402, 403
S44	Throttle valve switch (fuel injection)	188 to 190
S47	Door switch (with headlamp buzzer)	292, 293
S50	Choke warning switch	340
S52	Hazard warning switch	274 to 278
S55	RH seat heating switch	372 to 374
S60	Clutch pedal switch (not UK)	159
S66	Vacuum switch (not UK)	148
S68.1	Mirror adjustment switch	377 to 380, 385 to 389
S68.2	Mirror heating switch	383, 392
S68.3	Mirror changeover switch	386 to 390
S73	Mixture preheating switch	165
S74	Engine temperature switch (not UK)	151
S75	Oil temperature switch (not UK)	151
S77	Distance switch (not UK)	153 to 156
S81	Brake fluid level switch	459
S82	Washer fluid level switch	462
U1	Day running light transformer (not UK)	422 to 426
U3	Computer board	352 to 361
U3.1	Clock priority switch	359
U3.2	Function select switch	359
U3.3	Reset/adjust switch	359
U5	Check control display	454 to 462
U5.1	Bulb failure warning lamp	454
U5.2	Stop-lamp failure warning lamp	456
U5.3	Oil level warning lamp	457
U5.4	Brake fluid level warning lamp	458
U5.5	Brake pad wear warning lamp	460
U5.6	Washer fluid level warning lamp	461
U6	LCD instrument panel	469 to 492
U6.1	No charge warning symbol	469
U6.2	Voltmeter	470 to 472
U6.3	Fuel gauge	471
U6.4	Oil pressure warning symbol	486
U6.5	Oil pressure gauge	488
U6.6	Temperature gauge	481
U6.7	Running lights pilot lamp	478
U6.8	Speedometer	491, 492
U6.9	Main beam pilot lamp	482
U6.10	Direction indicator repeater (LH)	486
U6.11	Direction indicator repeater (RH)	488
U6.13	Handbrake warning lamp	484
U6.14	Tachometer	484
U6.15	Trailer direction indicator repeater	480
U6.21	Relay (display lighting)	474 to 476
U6.22	Display lighting	475, 476
U6.23	Speedometer illumination	491
U6.24	Miles/km changeover switch	493
U6.25	Calibration switch	478
V4	Blocking diode (rear foglamps)	253
V5	Blocking diode (rear foglamps)	257
V6	Blocking diode (parking lights, not UK)	240
X1	Trailer socket	Various
X2	Auxiliary connectors	Various
X5	Engine wiring harness connector	Various
X6	Rear wiring harness connector	Various
X7	Front wiring harness connector	Various
X8	LCD instrument connector (26-way)	469 to 492
X9	LCD instrument connector (16-way)	476 to 490
X10	Ignition timing connector (not UK)	138 to 140
Y5	Solenoid valve (Diesel)	199
Y6	Auxiliary air valve (fuel injectors)	188 to 190
Y7	Fuel injectors	188 to 190
Y10	Distributor (with Hall sensor)	122
Y11	Hall sensor	108, 109 145 to 147
Y14	Inductive sensor (not UK)	135 to 137
Y15	Inductive sensor with ignition module	125, 126
Y17	Idle cut-off solenoid	342
Y18	Dashpot solenoid (not UK)	159
Y22	Distributor (not UK)	147
Y23	Distributor (with inductive sensor)	129
Y24	Distributor (not UK)	139

Colour code

BL	Blue	LI	Lilac
BR	Brown	RT	Red
GE	Yellow	SW	Black
GN	Green	VI	Violet
GR	Grey	WS	White
HBL	Light blue		

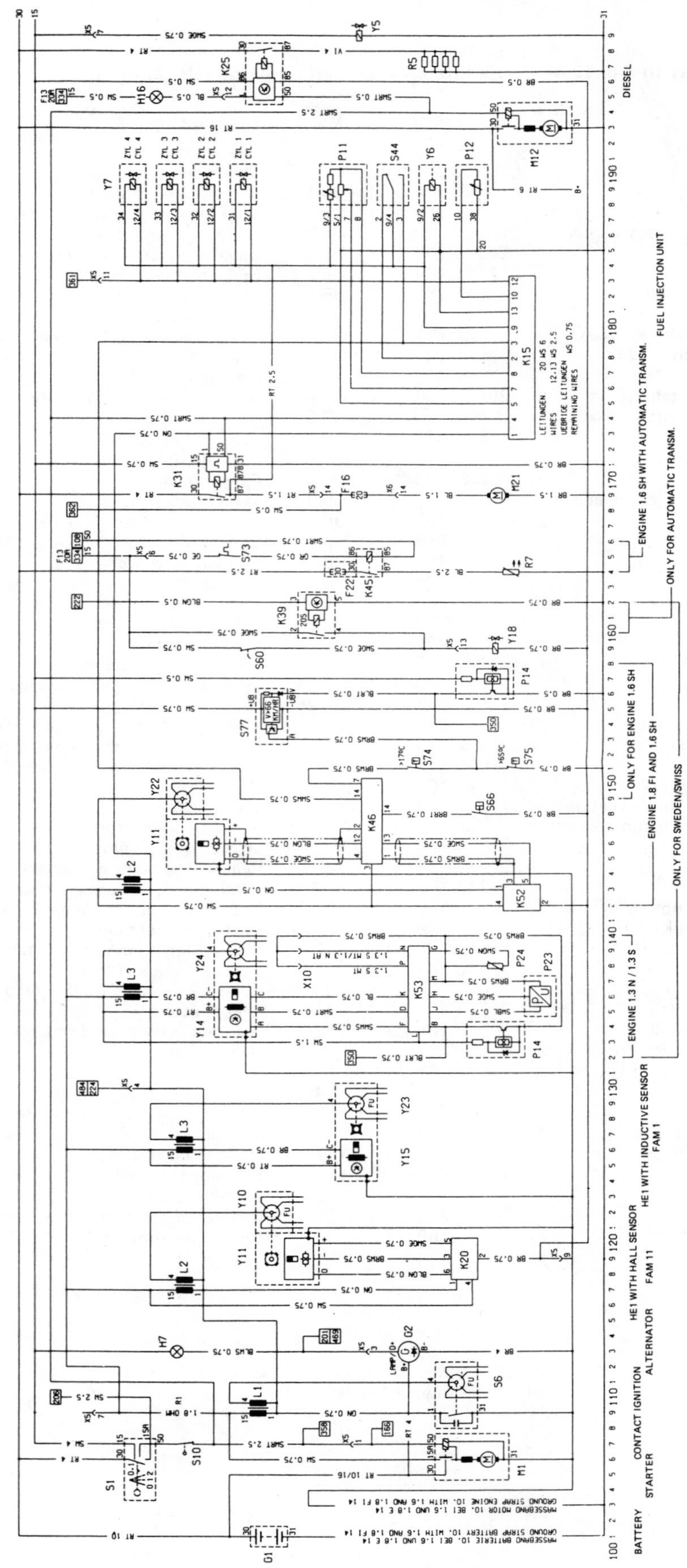

Fig. 12.44 Wiring diagram up to 1986. For key see pages 314 and 315

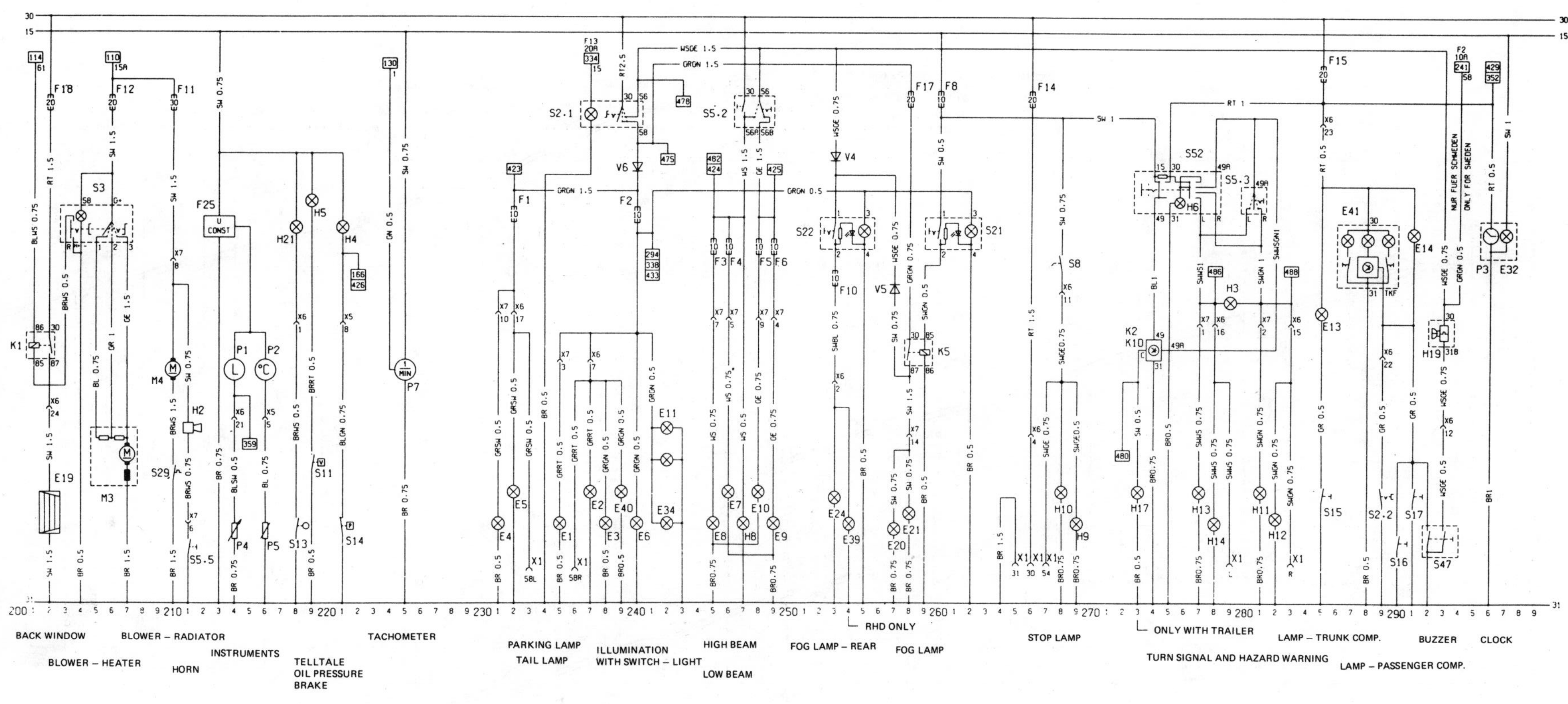

Fig. 12.44 Wiring diagram up to 1986 (continued). For key see pages 314 and 315

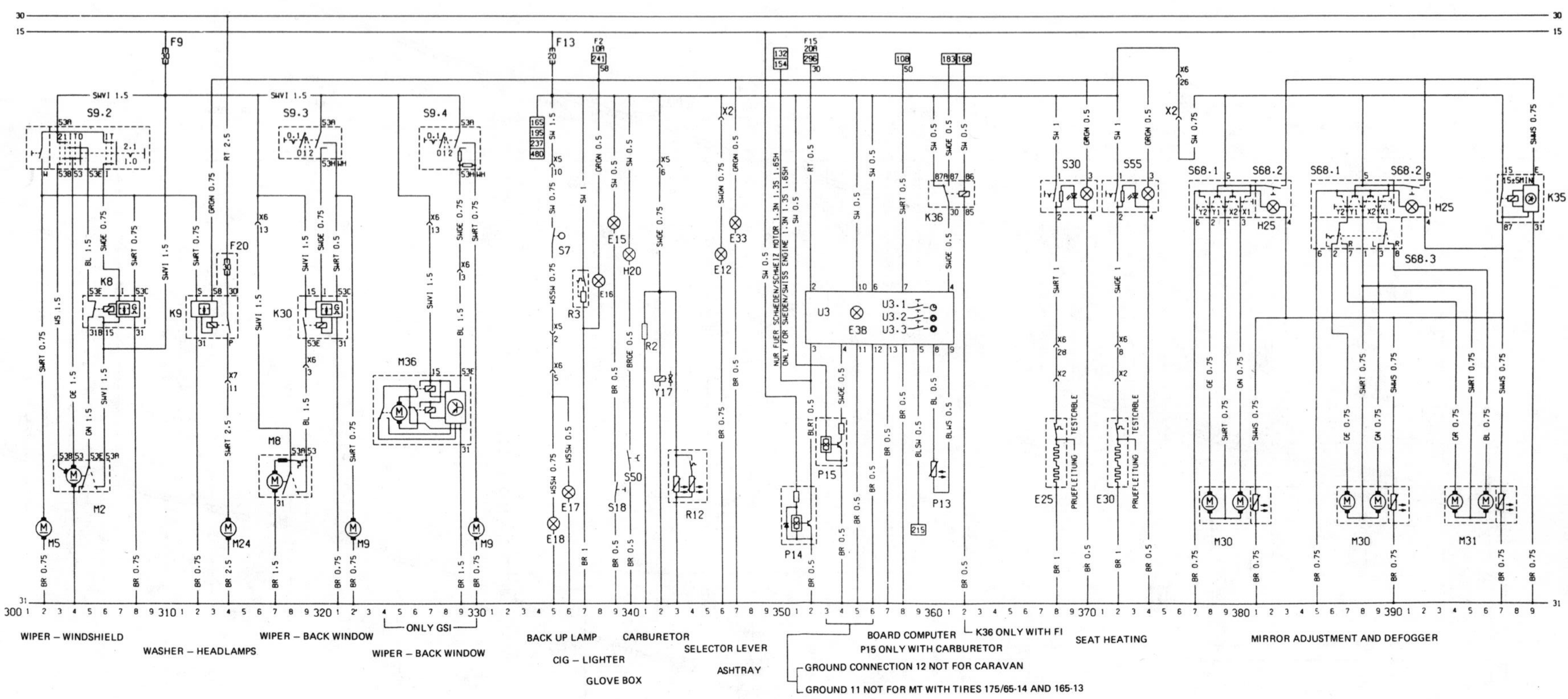

Fig. 12.44 Wiring diagram up to 1986 (continued). For key see pages 314 and 315

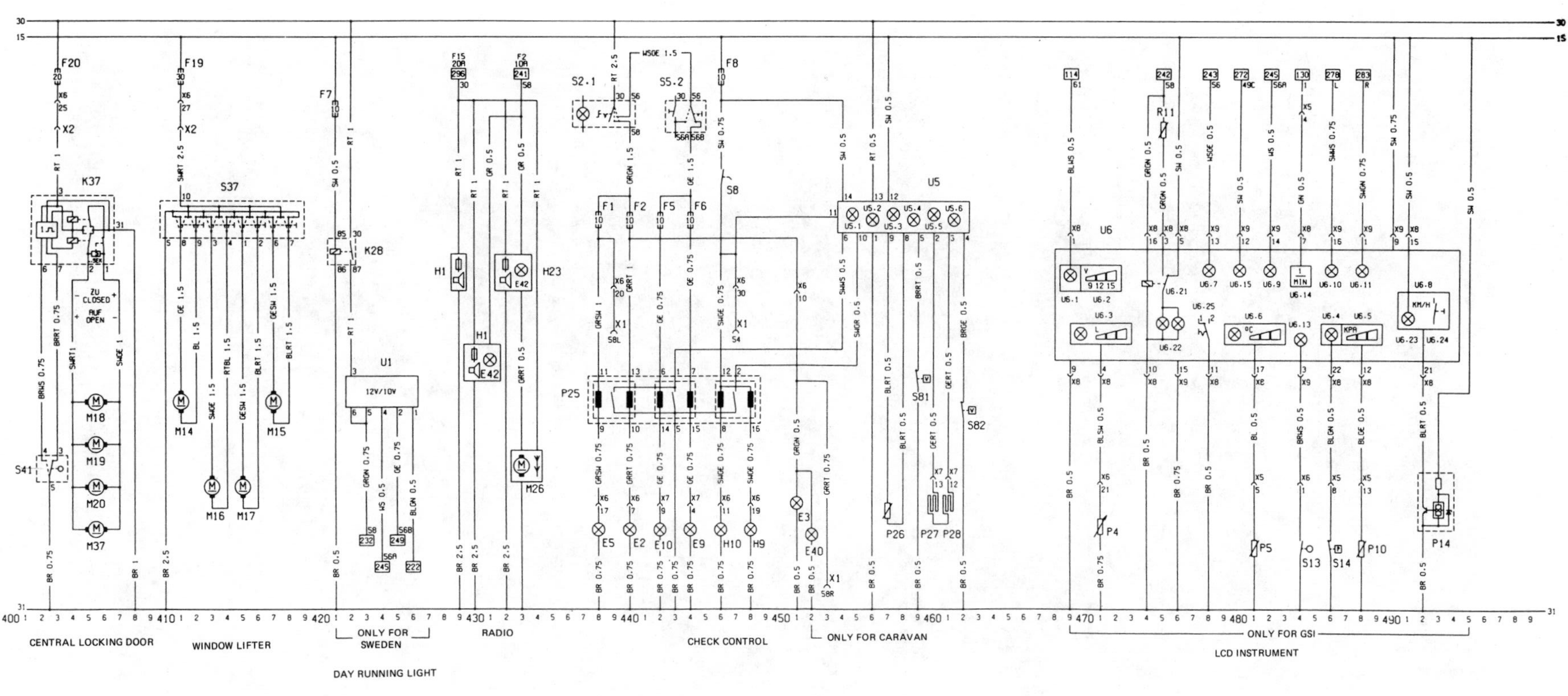

Fig. 12.44 Wiring diagram up to 1986 (continued). For key see pages 314 and 315

Vauxhall Belmont

Chapter 13 Supplement: Revisions and information on later models

Contents

1 Introduction

This Supplement contains information which is additional to, or a revision of, material in the first twelve Chapters.

Most of the information deals with the bodywork changes involved with the introduction of the Belmont Saloon. The Belmont is mechanically identical to the Astra Hatchback; using the same engines, transmissions, steering and suspension. The information in the first twelve Chapters covers both the Astra and Belmont model range.

The Sections in the Supplement follow the same order as the Chapters to which they relate. The Specifications are all grouped together for convenience, but they too, follow Chapter order.

It is recommended that before any particular operation is undertaken, reference is made to the appropriate Section(s) of the Supplement. In this way any changes to procedure or components can be noted before referring to the main Chapters.

2 Specifications

The figures given here are revisions of, or supplementary to, those appearing elsewhere in this Manual

Transmission – 1986 models

Manual transmission

Final drive ratios:
Estate and Van .... 3.74 : 1 or 3.94 : 1

Automatic transmission

Final drive ratios:
1.3 .... 3.74 : 1
1.6 .... 3.43 : 1
1.8 .... 3.43 : 1

Suspension (Astramax)

Wheels and tyres

Wheel size .... 5J x 13 or 5 1/2 J x 14
Tyre size .... 155 R 13-78 S, 165 R 13-86 R or 165 R 14-84

Tyre pressures (cold)

	Front	Rear
Up to 2 passengers and 100 kg (220 lb) luggage:		
155 R 13	2.0 bar (29 lbf/in²)	2.2 bar (32 lbf/in²)
165 R 13 and 165 R 14	1.8 bar (26 lbf/in²)	2.2 bar (32 lbf/in²)
Full load:		
155 R 13	2.1 bar (31 lbf/in²)	3.0 bar (44 lbf/in²)
165 R 13 and 165 R 14	1.8 bar (26 lbf/in²)	3.0 bar (44 lbf/in²)

Torque wrench settings

	Nm	lbf ft
U-bolt nuts	45	33
Bump stop cup nut	20	15
Shock absorber lower mounting	70	52
Brake regulating valve spring bracket	20	15
Bump stop	50	37

General dimensions, weights and capacities – 1986 models

Dimensions – Belmont

Overall height	1.400 m (55.1 in)
Overall width	1.658 m (65.3 in)
Overall length	4.218 m (166.1 in)
Wheelbase	2.520 m (99.2 in)

Weights – Belmont*

Kerb weight:	
1.3 L (manual)	890 kg (1962 lb)
1.3 L (automatic)	925 kg (2039 lb)
1.3 GL (manual)	915 kg (2017 lb)
1.3 GL (automatic)	950 kg (2094 lb)
1.6 L (manual)	955 kg (2105 lb)
1.6 L (automatic)	980 kg (2160 lb)
1.6 GL/GLS (manual)	980 kg (2160 lb)
1.6 GL/GLS (automatic)	1005 kg (2216 lb)
1.8 GLSi	985 kg (2171 lb)
Gross vehicle weight:	
1.3 L (manual)	1365 kg (3009 lb)
1.3 L (automatic)	1410 kg (3108 lb)
1.3 GL (manual)	1385 kg (3053 lb)
1.3 GL (automatic)	1410 kg (3108 lb)
1.6 L (manual)	1445 kg (3186 lb)
1.6 L (automatic)	1465 kg (3230 lb)
1.6 GL/GLS (manual)	1465 kg (3230 lb)
1.6 GL/GLS (automatic)	1485 kg (3274 lb)
1.8 GLSi	1465 kg (3230 lb)
Payload:	
Deduct kerb weight from gross vehicle weight	

* *Kerb weights are approximate and vary according to equipment fitted. Gross vehicle weight and payload may be subject to current legislation*

Capacities (approx)

Fuel tank	52 litres (11.4 gallons)
Engine oil (drain and refill, including filter):	
1.3	3.00 litres (5.3 pints)
1.6	3.25 litres (5.7 pints)
Automatic transmission (drain and refill)	7.0 litres (12.3 pints)
Headlamp washer reservoir	5.5 litres (9.7 pints)

3 Engine

Unleaded high octane petrol

1 All engines can be successfully run on unleaded high octane petrol, but the following points should be noted.

OHV engines

2 Cars with engines produced before March 1985 (engine number less than 1 031 045): after 5 tankfuls of unleaded petrol, a tankful of full leaded high octane fuel must be used.

Carburettor engines

3 If detonation (pinking or knock) occurs, the ignition timing should be retarded by up to 5° (see later in this Chapter).

Fuel injection engines

4 Using unleaded petrol can cause high speed knock which cannot be heard, but can lead to engine damage; the ignition timing **must** be retarded by 5° (see later in this Chapter).

Cylinder block core plugs – renewal

Front core plugs

5 Remove the radiator and fan assembly (Chapter 2, Section 6).
6 Remove the exhaust manifold (Chapter 3, Section 32).
7 Remove the right-hand engine mounting (Chapter 1, Section 17).
8 Remove the core plugs by hammering a screwdriver through and prising them free.
9 Fit the new core plugs by simply hammering them into position. The use of a sealant is not usually necessary.
10 Refit the disconnected ancillaries by reference to the appropriate Chapters.

Rear core plugs

11 Drain the coolant (Chapter 2, Section 3).
12 Remove the inlet manifold (Chapter 3, Section 31).
13 Remove the coolant distribution hose which runs across the rear of the engine.
14 Remove the core plugs by hammering a screwdriver through and

prising them free. Note that it may be possible to gain better access by removing the starter and alternator (Chapter 12).
15 Fit the new core plugs by simply hammering them into position. The use of a sealant is not usually necessary.
16 Refit the disconnected ancillaries by reference to the appropriate Chapters. Refill the cooling system (Chapter 2, Section 5).

4 Fuel system

Fuel tank – 1986 models

1 The fuel tank used on 1986 models is of revised capacity. The removal and refitting procedures are the same as given in Chapter 3, Section 7. Note that early and late model fuel tanks are not interchangeable.

5 Ignition system

Retarding the ignition timing (for unleaded fuel)

1 When using unleaded high octane fuel, the ignition timing may be retarded in the following way.
2 Turn the engine by means of the crankshaft pulley bolt, or by engaging top gear and pulling the car forward, until No 1 piston is at TDC on the firing stroke. This can be felt by removing No 1 spark plug and feeling for compression with your fingers as the engine is turned.
3 Make a mark on the crankshaft pulley in alignment with the timing mark, or pointer, on the engine.
4 The original pulley mark indicates 10° BTDC, and the new mark TDC; 5° ignition retardation, therefore, is central between the two.
5 Make a new timing mark on the crankshaft pulley, and adjust the ignition timing as described in Chapter 4, Section 11.
6 GM recommend the ignition timing on fuel injection engines be retarded by exactly 5° when using unleaded high octane petrol. For carburettor engines, the recommendation is up to 5° if detonation occurs; some experimentation may be worthwhile to achieve satisfactory running.

6 Suspension

Wheel trims – removal and refitting

1 Some models have a square panel covering the four wheel nuts in the centre of the wheel trim.
2 This panel is removed by gently levering it off to gain access to the wheel nuts (photo).
3 Push the panel back firmly on refitting.

Rear axle (Astramax) – removal and refitting

4 Slacken the rear wheel bolts, raise and support the rear of the vehicle and remove the rear wheels.
5 Remove the brake drum and disconnect the handbrake cable (Chapter 9, Section 8).
6 Disconnect the brake flexible hoses at the rear axle brackets. Plug or cap the hoses to reduce fluid spillage.
7 Support the centre of the rear axle with a jack and a block of wood, or a cradle.
8 Remove the shock absorber lower mounting bolt.
9 Unscrew the nut securing the bump stop cup, and remove the cup.
10 Unscrew the nuts on the U-bolts securing the rear axle to the leaf spring. Remove the tensioning plate and the U-bolts.
11 Repeat the procedure on the other side, but be prepared for the rear axle to rotate if the jack isn't central.
12 Lower the jack and remove the axle from the vehicle.
13 Strip the axle of brake components, hubs etc, if needed for transfer to a new axle. Refer to the appropriate Chapters for details.
14 Refitting is generally a reversal of removal, but note the following.
15 The hole in the tensioning plate for the bump stop cup locating lug must be towards the centre of the vehicle.
16 The exposed lengths of thread on any U-bolt must not differ by more than 3 mm (0.12 in). Tighten the nuts to the specified torque.
17 Refit the bump stop cup to the tensioning plate (locating lug towards the centre of the vehicle) and tighten the nut to the specified torque.
18 On completion, bleed the braking system and adjust the handbrake (Chapter 9).

Rear leaf spring (Astramax) – removal and refitting

19 Raise the rear of the vehicle and support it securely. Position a jack under the axle.
20 Remove the handbrake cable mounting from the spring.
21 Disconnect the brake pressure regulating valve spring from the leaf spring.
22 Unbolt the front leaf spring-to-body attachment. Remove the bolt.
23 Unbolt the rear left spring-to-shackle attachment. Remove the bolt.
24 Remove the bump stop cup nut from the tensioning plate, and remove the cup.
25 Unscrew the nuts securing the U-bolts to the tensioning plate, and remove the plate and U-bolts.
26 Remove the leaf spring from the vehicle.
27 If the spring is being renewed, unbolt and remove the brake regulating valve spring bracket.
28 If necessary, press out the existing bushes from the ends of the leaf spring. Coat new ones with detergent to facilitate fitment.
29 Refitting is generally a reversal of removal, but note that the shorter section of the leaf spring is to the front of the vehicle.
30 The U-bolts and tensioning plate should be refitted as described in paragraphs 15 and 16.
31 Attach the brake regulating valve spring to the bracket. Adjust the position of the bracket so that the spring is neither taut nor slack. Secure the bracket to the leaf spring.

Bump stop (Astramax) – removal and refitting

32 Raise the rear of the vehicle and support it securely.
33 Unscrew the bolt through the bump stop.
34 Refitting is a reversal of removal.

6.2 Levering off a wheel trim panel

7 Bodywork and fittings

Boot lid and torsion rod assemblies (Belmont) – removal and refitting

1 Open the boot lid.
2 Draw an alignment mark across both the boot lid and the hinge bracket on both sides of the vehicle.
3 Disconnect the cable to the boot lock central locking servo motor (the connector is in the left-hand corner of the boot area).
4 With an assistant helping, support both sides of the boot lid while undoing the boot lid-to-bracket bolts (photo).
5 Remove the boot lid.
6 The torsion rods are held in place by spring tension, and can be removed by unhooking them firstly from their central housing bracket (photo) and then from the hinge bracket end (photo).

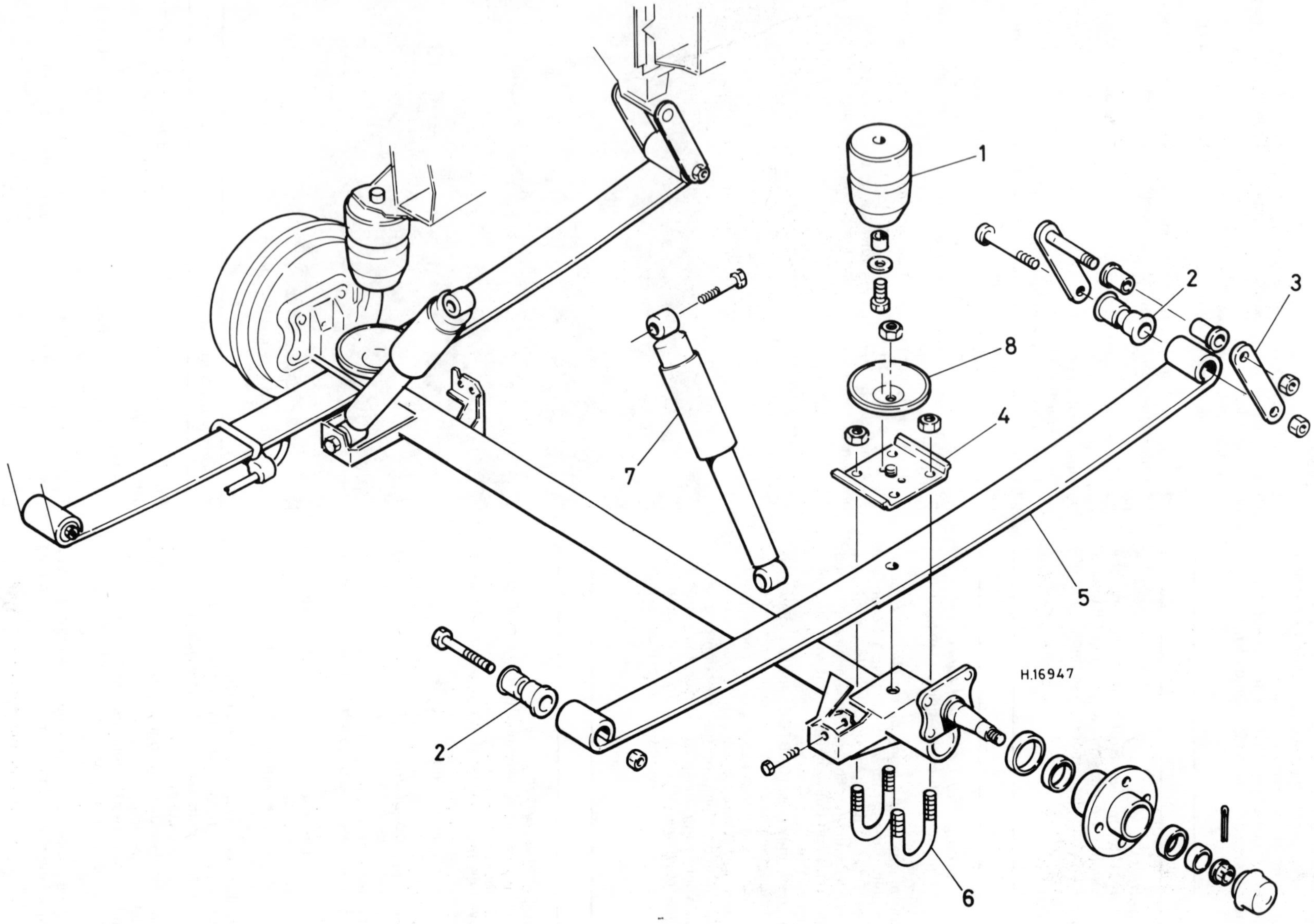

Fig. 13.1 Exploded view of the Astramax rear suspension (Sec 6)

1 *Bump stop*
2 *Bushes*
3 *Shackle*
4 *Tensioning plate*
5 *Leaf spring*
6 *U-bolt*
7 *Shock absorber*
8 *Bump stop cup*

7.4 Boot lid-to-hinge bolts

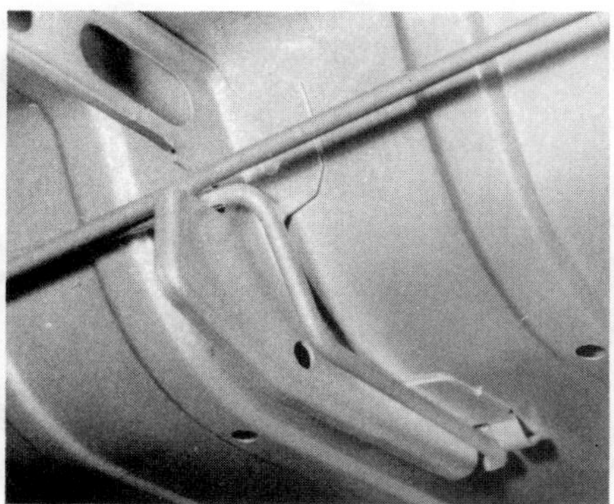
7.6A Torsion rod central housing bracket

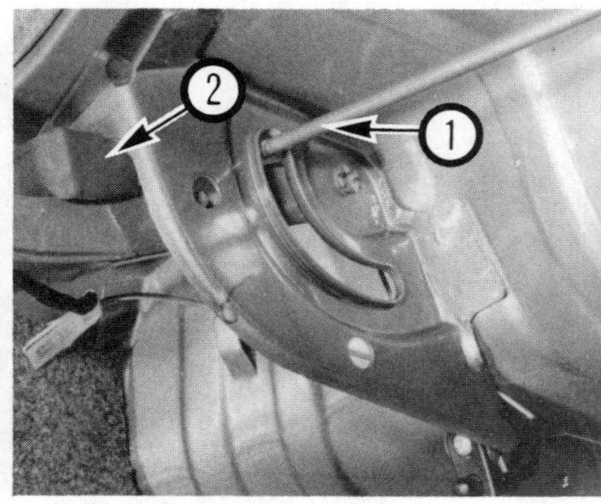

7.6B Hinge bracket assembly

1 Torsion rod   2 Rubber bump stop

7.11 Boot lid lock securing screws (arrowed)

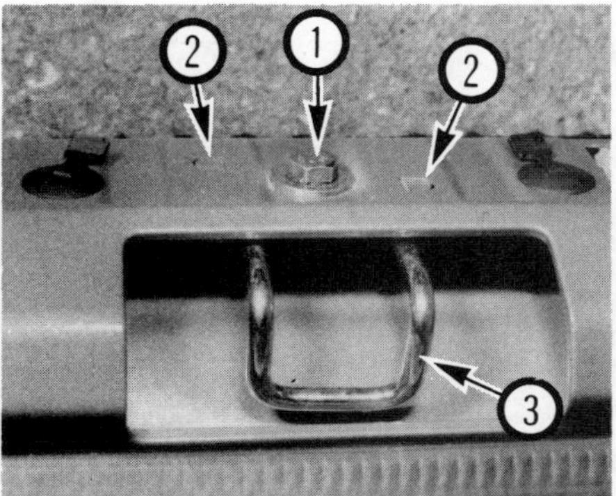

7.15 Boot lock catch

1 Retaining and adjusting bolt   3 Catch
2 Locating spigots

7.20 Spare wheel and tool kit stowage (Belmont)

7 Refitting is a reversal of removal.
8 On earlier models it may be found that despite correct alignment the boot lid may contact the rear screen at the centre of its front edge.
9 This can be remedied by the fitting of rubber bump stops which curtail the height of travel of the boot lid (see photo 7.6B).

Boot lid lock assembly (Belmont) – removal and refitting

10 Mark a line around the outer edge of the lock assembly on the boot lid.
11 Remove the securing screws (photo) and lift the lock away from the boot lid.
12 Refit in the reverse order, using the previously made line to position the lock.
13 Check the operation of the lock assembly by closing and opening the boot several times.

Boot lock catch (Belmont) – removal and refitting

14 Remove the protective trim panel from the boot lip.
15 The lock catch is retained by one bolt, and also has two locating spigots which enter cut-outs in the frame (photo).
16 The height of the catch may be adjusted by loosening the bolt and moving the catch up or down to allow the boot lid to close smoothly and be a snug fit with its edge seal.
17 Refit in the reverse order.

Boot area trim and carpeting (Belmont) – removal and refitting

18 To remove the carpet from the boot, tilt the rear seats forward.
19 The front edge of the carpet is retained in the floor by plastic 'poppers' which pull out.
20 Remove these and the carpet may be lifted out, revealing the spare wheel and tool kit (photo).
21 The carpeting trim along the sill is retained in the same way (photo) and can be removed after the boot lip protective plastic panel has been removed. This panel is held by screws (photo).
22 The boot side panels are held by screws (photo) and poppers.
23 Refit the trim in reverse order.

Boot lid handle (Belmont) – removal and refitting

24 The plastic boot lid handle fitted above the number plate is secured to the boot lid by two nuts, accessible from inside the boot lid (photo).

Folding rear seats (Belmont) – removal and refitting

25 The procedure is as described in Chapter 11, Section 33.
26 The rear seat backrest catch is secured by one central nut (photo), accessible from within the boot area.

Roof rack system – installation

27 GM market a custom-made roof rack which is designed for fitting in the roof guttering (see Chapter 11, photo 40.1).
28 The fitting of the roof rack requires special drills to accurately position the support rails, and it is recommended that this work be left to your dealer.

Plastic components

29 With the use of more and more plastic body components by the vehicle manufacturers (eg bumpers, spoilers, and in some cases major body panels), rectification of damage to such items has become a matter of either entrusting repair work to a specialist in this field, or renewing complete components. Repair by the DIY owner is not really feasible owing to the cost of the equipment and materials required for effecting such repairs. The basic technique involves making a groove

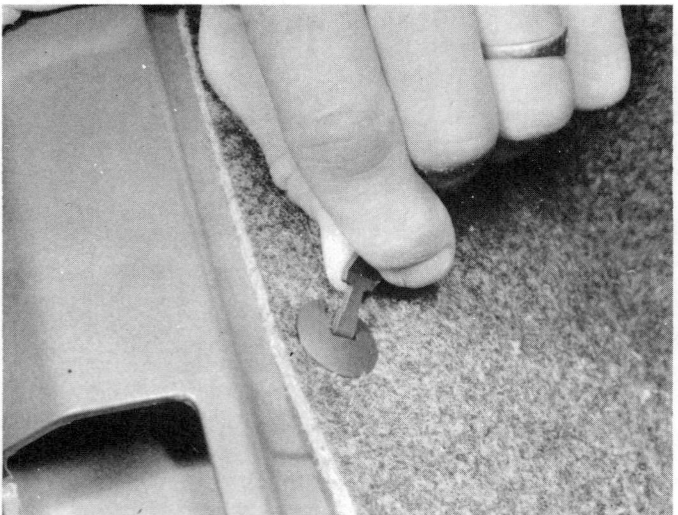

7.21A Removing a carpet retaining popper

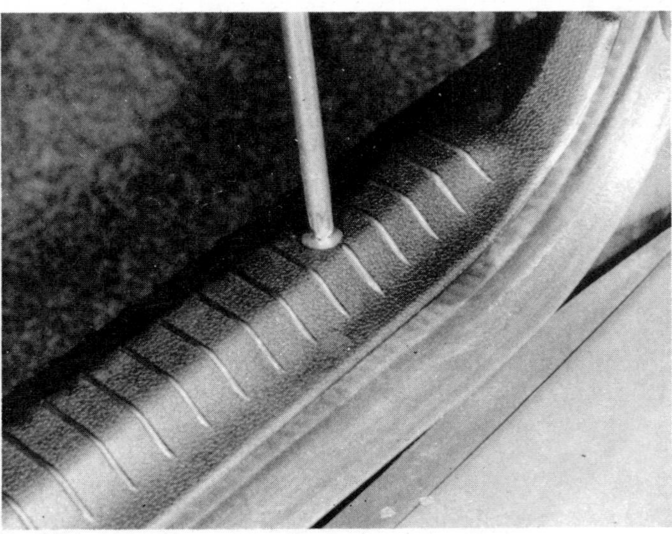

7.21B Boot lip protective panel retaining screw

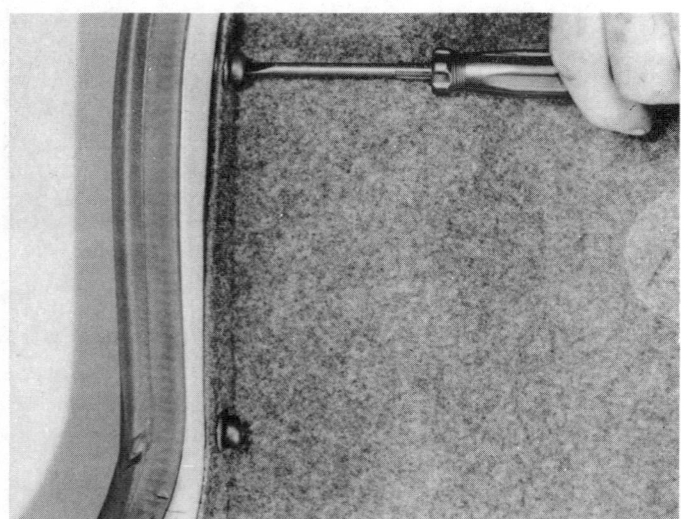

7.22 Removing a side panel retaining screw

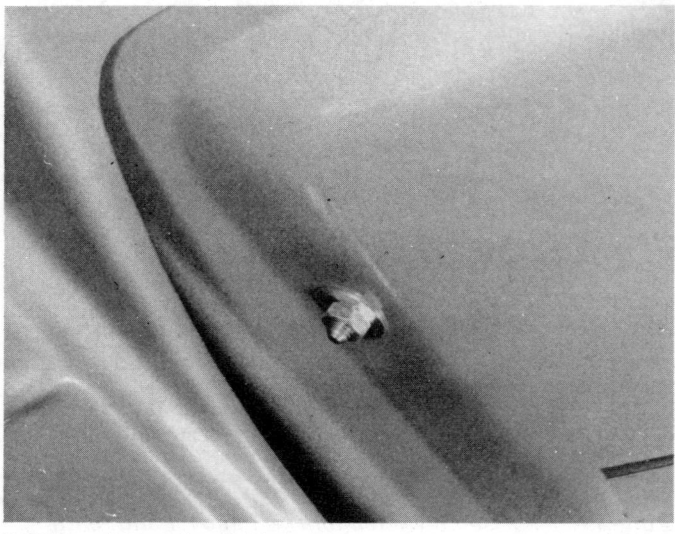

7.24 Boot lid handle retaining nut

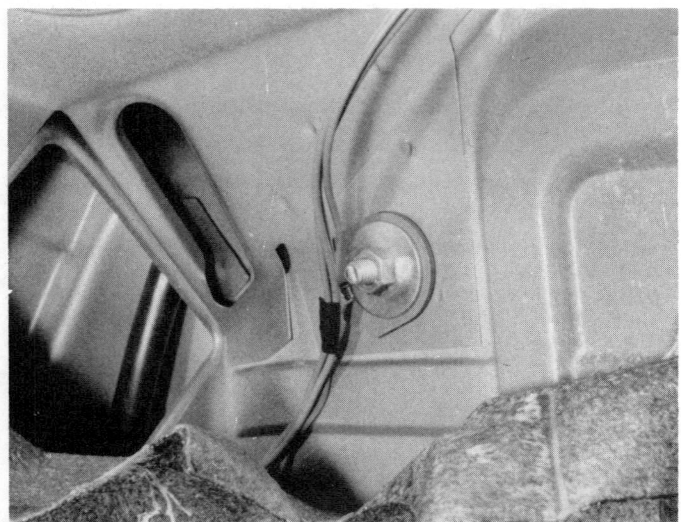

7.26 Rear seat backrest catch retaining nut

along the line of the crack in the plastic using a rotary burr in a power drill. The damaged part is then welded back together by using a hot air gun to heat up and fuse a plastic filler rod into the groove. Any excess plastic is then removed and the area rubbed down to a smooth finish. It is important that a filler rod of the correct plastic is used, as body components can be made of a variety of different types (eg polycarbonate, ABS, polypropylene).

30 If the owner is renewing a complete component himself, he will be left with the problem of finding a suitable paint for finishing which is compatible with the type of plastic used. At one time the use of a universal paint was not possible owing to the complex range of plastics encountered in body component applications. Standard paints, generally speaking, will not bond to plastic or rubber satisfactorily. However, it is now possible to obtain a plastic body parts finishing kit which consists of a pre-primer treatment, a primer and coloured top coat. Full instructions are normally supplied with a kit, but basically the method of use is to first apply the pre-primer to the componet concerned and allow it to dry for up to 30 minutes. Then the primer is applied and left to dry for about an hour before finally applying the special coloured top coat. The result is a correctly coloured component where the paint will flex with the plastic or rubber, a property that standard paint does not normally possess.

8 Electrical system

Headlamp 'on' warning buzzer – wiring connectors

1 All 1986 models have been produced with an additional black cable in the wiring loom.

2 This black cable is for use on later vehicles equipped with a warning buzzer which operates only with the ignition switched off.

3 When renewing a buzzer unit (see Fig. 12.15) on 1986 models, note the colour of the electrical connections on removal, and reconnect in the same way.

4 Do not attempt to connect the black cable.

Rear lamp cluster (Belmont) – bulb renewal

5 The rear lamp cluster is easily accessible after removal of the boot area side trim panels (photo).

6 Bulb renewal and lens removal/refitting are as detailed in Chapter 12, Section 36.

Boot area light and microswitch (Belmont) – removal and refitting

7 The boot area lamp is clipped into a housing in the side panel by the left-hand boot lid hinge (photo).

8 Bulb changing and renewal of lamp unit are self evident.

9 The operating microswitch is screwed in position on the left-hand boot lid hinge bracket (photo).

10 Again, renewal is self evident.

Boot lid central locking mechanism (Belmont) – removal and refitting

11 Open the boot lid and remove the plastic cover (photo).

12 The latch mechanism is held by two nuts and the servo motor by two screws (photo).

13 The manual release control rod can also be seen in the photo.

14 The removal and refitting procedure is as given in Chapter 12, Section 42.

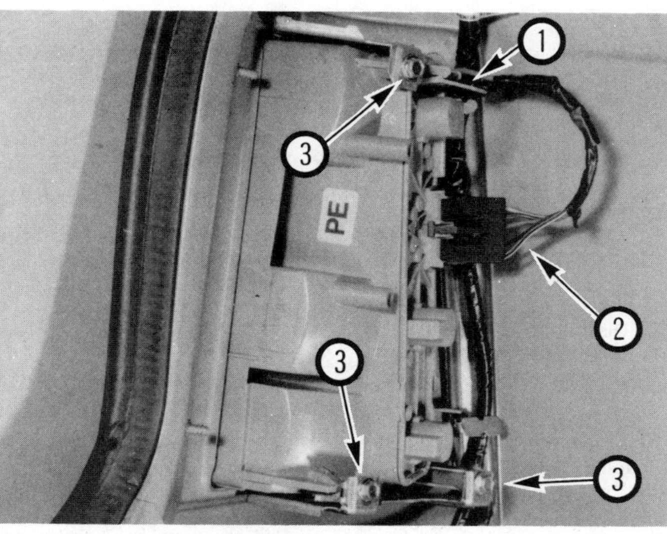

8.5 Rear lamp cluster (Belmont)

1 Retaining lug
2 Wiring plug
3 Retaining screws

8.7 Removing the boot area light

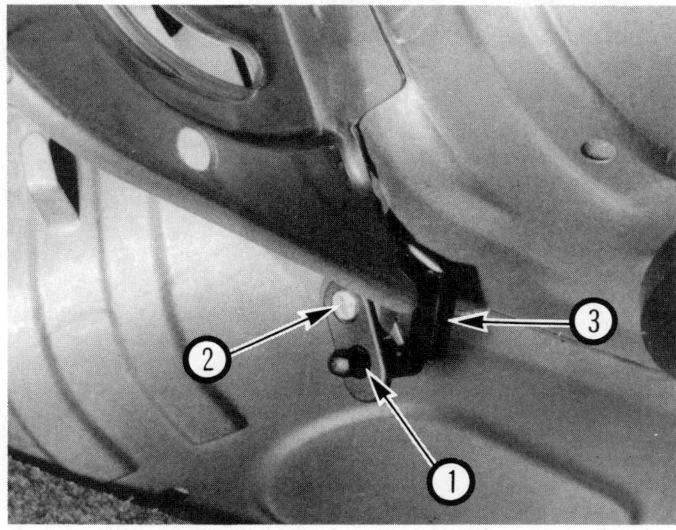

8.9 Boot light micro switch

1 Plunger
2 Retaining screw
3 Wiring plug

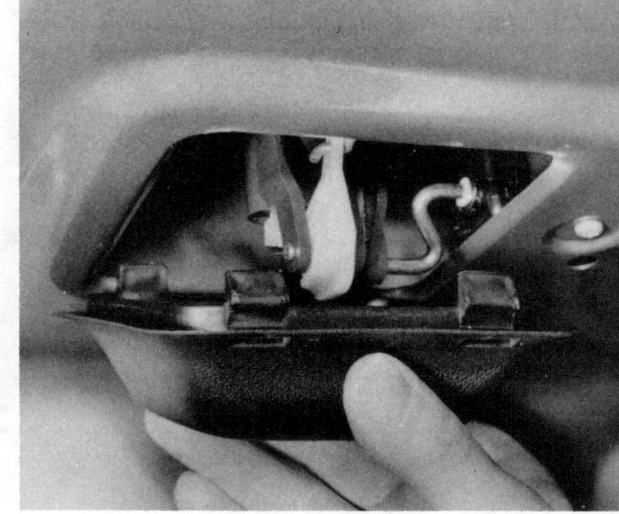

8.11 Removing the plastic cover from the central locking mechanism

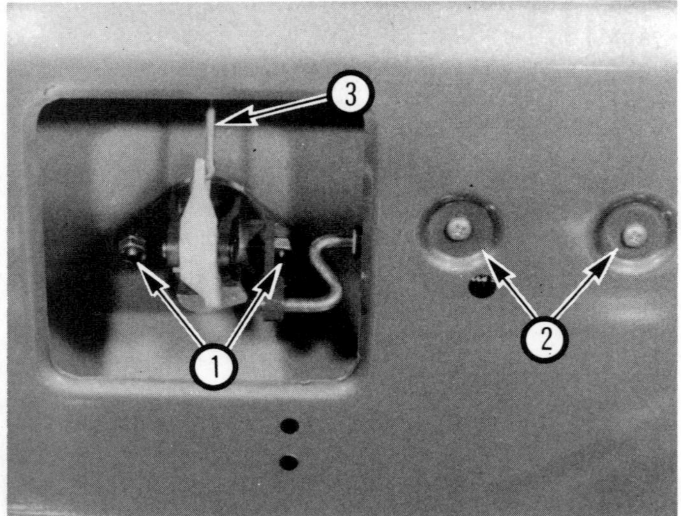

8.12 Latch mechanism and servo motor retaining screws/nuts

1 Latch mechanism nuts
2 Servo motor screws
3 Manual release control rod

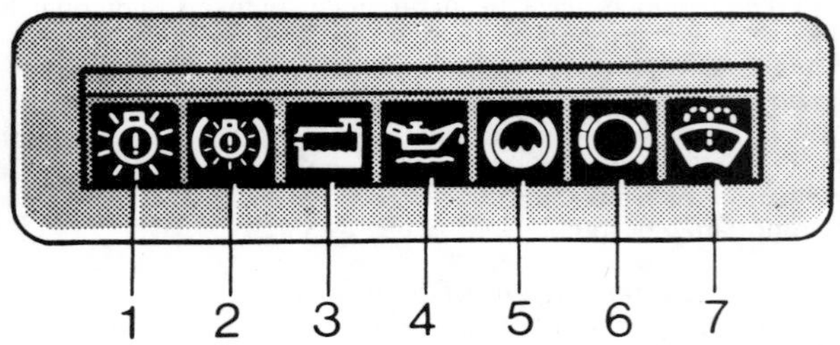

Fig. 13.2 Check control instrument housing – 1986 models (Sec 8)

1 Low beam headlamps, rear lamps
2 Brake lamps
3 Coolant level
4 Engine oil level
5 Brake fluid level
6 Brake pad thickness
7 Fluid level of windshield wash/wipe system

Check control system – 1986 models

15 The check control system fitted to 1986 models has an additional 'coolant level' function and the indicator positions have been changed.
16 The monitor switch for the 'coolant level' function is installed on the cover of the coolant expansion tank.
17 When installing a check control instrument unit incorporating a 'coolant level' indicator to a vehicle without the monitor switch fitted, remove the bulb from the 'coolant level' indicator, or the bulb will remain illuminated constantly.

Radio equipment (Belmont) – removal and refitting

18 The removal and refitting of the radio equipment is adequately covered in Chapter 12, Section 52, apart from the rear-mounted speakers.
19 These are mounted in the rear parcel shelf.
20 Access to the back of the speakers is gained from within the boot area.
21 Remove the plastic cover which clips in place (photo) then, from on top of the parcel shelf, remove the securing screws (photo).
22 Disconnect the electrical leads and lift out the speaker.
23 Refit in the reverse order.

Fault diagnosis – windscreen wipers

24 In addition to those fault diagnosis items given in Section 55 of Chapter 12, the following symptoms and reasons may be useful.
25 It is emphasised that, as the symptoms are closely related, careful fault diagnosis is required.

8.21A Removing a plastic cover from a rear speaker

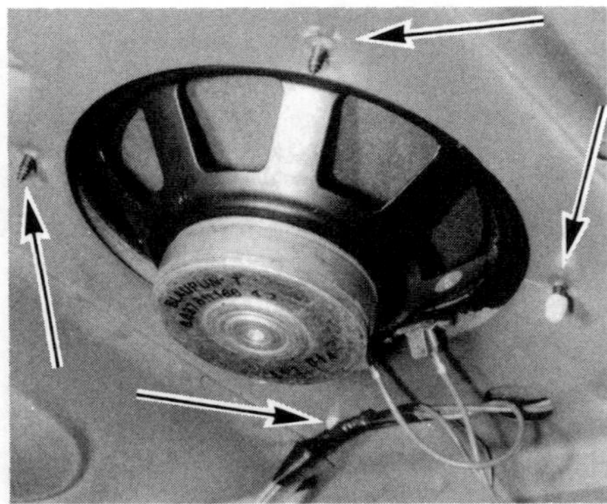

8.21B Speaker securing screws (arrowed) seen from below

Symptom	Reason(s)
Wipers do not park correctly after wash/wipe sequence	Faulty relay
No wash/wipe sequence and/or no intermittent wipe	Faulty relay
Wipers work continuously when switched to intermittent	Faulty motor
Wipers do not park correctly	Faulty motor or relay

Key to Fig. 13.3. Not all items are fitted to all models

Refer to Section 54 of Chapter 12 for general information

No	Description	Track
E1	RH sidelamp	235
E2	RH tail lamp	237, 440
E3	Number plate lamp	238, 451
E4	LH sidelamp	231
E5	LH tail lamp	232, 438
E6	Engine bay lamp	240
E7	RH main beam	246
E8	LH main beam	245
E9	RH dipped beam	249, 444
E10	LH dipped beam	248, 442
E11	Instrument illumination	242
E12	Auto transmission selector lamp	346
E13	Luggage area lamp	285
E14	Interior lamp	291
E15	Glovebox lamp	339
E16	Cigarette lighter lamp	338
E17	RH reversing lamp	336
E18	LH reversing lamp	335
E19	Heated rear window	202
E20	LH front foglamp	257
E21	RH front foglamp	258
E24	Rear foglamp	253
E25	LH seat heater	368
E26	Light switch illumination	237
E30	RH seat heater	372
E32	Clock illumination	297
E33	Ashtray lamp	347
E34	Heater control lamp	242
E38	Computer illumination	355
E39	Rear foglamp	254
E40	Number plate lamp (Estate)	239, 452
E41	Interior lamp with delay unit	287, 289
E42	Radio illumination	431, 433
F1 to F20	Fuses	Various
F22	Fuse (mixture preheating)	164
F25	Instrument voltage stabiliser	213
G1	Battery	101
G2	Alternator	113
H1	Radio	429, 431
H2	Horn	211
H3	Direction indicator repeater	278
H4	Oil pressure warning lamp	221
H5	Brake fluid level warning lamp	219
H6	Hazard warning repeater	276
H7	No charge warning lamp	223
H8	Main beam pilot lamp	247
H9	RH stop-lamp	269, 448
H10	LH stop-lamp	268, 446
H11	RH front direction indicator	281
H12	RH rear direction indicator	282
H13	LH front direction indicator	277
H14	LH rear direction indicator	278
H16	Glow plug light (Diesel)	195
H17	Trailer direction indicator repeater	273
H19	Buzzer (headlamps on)	293
H20	Choke warning lamp	340
H21	Handbrake warning lamp	218
H23	Radio receiver (with automatic aerial)	432, 433
H25	Mirror heating pilot light	383, 392
H30	Warning light (TBI)	569
H33	Auxiliary direction indicator light (left)	276
H34	Auxiliary direction indicator light (right)	280
K1	Heated rear window relay	201, 202
K2	Flasher unit	274
K5	Front foglamp relay	258, 259
K8	Wiper delay relay	305 to 308
K9	Headlamp washer relay	312 to 314
K10	Trailer flasher unit	273, 274
K15	Fuel injection control module	173 to 183, 522 to 534
K20	Ignition module (electronic ignition)	118, 119
K25	Preheater relay (Diesel)	195 to 198
K28	Day running light relay (not UK)	421, 422
K30	Rear window wiper relay	319 to 321
K31	Fuel pump relay (fuel injection)	169 to 171, 518 to 520
K35	Mirror heating timer	397, 399
K36	Computer relay	360 to 362
K37	Central locking relay	402 to 408
K39	Dashpot relay (not UK)	160, 162
K45	Preheater relay (not UK)	164 to 166
K46	Ignition timing control (not UK)	145 to 150, 507 to 514
K52	Ignition module (not UK)	142, 143, 504, 505
K53	Ignition timing control (not UK)	134 to 139
K57	Control unit (TBI)	562 to 584
K58	Fuel pump relay (TBI)	586 to 587
K59	Day running light	421 to 426
L1	Ignition coil (contact breaker system)	109
L2	Ignition coil (electronic system)	117, 143, 505
L3	Ignition coil (not UK)	126, 136, 554
M1	Starter motor	105 to 107
M2	Windscreen wiper motor	303 to 306
M3	Heater blower motor	205 to 207
M4	Radiator cooling fan	210
M5	Windscreen washer pump	302
M8	Rear window wiper motor (except GTE)	317 to 319
M9	Rear window washer pump	322, 330
M12	Starter motor (Diesel)	193, 194
M14	LH front window motor	411
M15	RH front window motor	417
M16	LH rear window motor	413
M17	RH rear window motor	415
M18	Front passenger door lock actuator	404, 407
M19	LH rear door lock actuator	404, 407
M20	RH rear door lock actuator	404, 407
M21	Fuel pump (fuel injection)	169, 518, 587
M24	Headlamp washer pump	314
M26	Radio aerial motor	433, 434
M30	LH electric mirror	368 to 381, 387 to 390
M31	RH electric mirror	394 to 397
M33	Idling power unit	571 to 574
M36	Rear window wiper motor (GTE only)	327 to 330
M37	Tailgate lock actuator	404, 407

Key to Fig. 13.3 (continued). Not all items are fitted to all models

No	Description	Track
P1	Fuel gauge	214
P2	Temperature gauge	216
P3	Clock	296
P4	Fuel gauge sender	214, 471
P5	Temperature gauge sender	216, 481
P7	Tachometer	225
P10	Oil pressure sensor	488
P11	Airflow meter (fuel injection)	188 to 190, 541
P12	Temperature sensor (fuel injection)	188 to 190, 541
P13	Temperature sensor (ambient air)	360
P14	Distance recorder	133, 134, 156, 157 351, 352, 492, 493, 561, 562
P15	Fuel flow meter	353, 354
P23	Vacuum sensor (not UK)	135 to 137, 578 to 580
P24	Temperature sensor (not UK)	138, 139
P25	Bulb failure sensor	438 to 448
P26	Engine oil level sensor	457, 458
P27	LH brake pad wear sensor	460
P28	RH brake pad wear sensor	461
P30	Coolant temperature sensor	576, 577
P32	Lambda sensor (FI)	541
P33	Lambda sensor (FI)	578
P34	Throttle valve angle sensor (FI)	581 to 583
R1	Ballast resistor (contact breaker ignition)	109
R2	Carburettor heater	341
R3	Cigarette lighter	337
R5	Glow plugs (Diesel)	197, 198
R7	Mixture preheating	164
R11	Instrument illumination rheostat	475
R12	Automatic choke heater	343
S1	Ignition/starter switch	106, 107
S2.1	Main lighting switch	239, 240, 439, 440
S2.2	Interior light switch	289
S3	Heater blower/heated rear window switch	203 to 207
S5.2	Dipswitch	247, 248, 444
S5.3	Direction indicator switch	280, 281
S5.5	Horn switch	211
S6	Distributor (contact breaker type)	109, 111
S7	Reversing lamp switch	335
S8	Stop-lamp switch	268, 446
S9.2	Windscreen wiper switch	302 to 306
S9.3	Rear window wiper switch (except GTE)	320, 321
S9.4	Rear window wiper switch (GTE only)	329, 330
S10.1	Starter inhibitor switch (automatic transmission)	107
S10.2	Reversing light switch	334
S11	Brake fluid level switch	219
S13	Handbrake switch	218, 484
S14	Oil pressure switch	221, 486
S15	Luggage area light switch	285
S16	RH door switch	290
S17	LH door switch	291
S18	Glovebox lamp switch	339
S21	Front foglamp switch	260, 262

No	Description	Track
S22	Rear foglamp switch	253, 255
S29	Radiator fan thermoswitch	210
S30	LH seat heating switch	368, 370
S37	Window switches	410 to 418
S41	Central locking switch	402, 403
S44	Throttle valve switch (fuel injection)	188 to 190, 541
S47	Door switch (with headlamp buzzer)	292, 293
S50	Choke warning switch	340
S52	Hazard warning switch	274 to 278
S55	RH seat heating switch	372 to 374
S60	Clutch pedal switch (not UK)	159
S64	Horn	211
S66	Vacuum switch (not UK)	148
S68.1	Mirror adjustment switch	377 to 380, 385 to 389
S68.2	Mirror heating switch	383, 392
S68.3	Mirror changeover switch	386 to 390
S73	Mixture preheating switch	165
S74	Engine temperature switch (not UK)	151
S75	Oil temperature switch (not UK)	151
S77	Distance switch (not UK)	153 to 156
S81	Brake fluid level switch	459
S82	Washer fluid level switch	462
S91	Oil pressure switch (TBI)	589, 590
S92	Neutral/park switch (automatic transmission)	574
S93	Coolant fluid control switch	463
U1	Day running light transformer (not UK)	422 to 426
U3	Computer board	352 to 361
U3.1	Clock priority switch	359
U3.2	Function select switch	359
U3.3	Reset/adjust switch	359
U5	Check control display	454 to 462
U5.1	Bulb failure warning lamp	454
U5.2	Stop-lamp failure warning lamp	456
U5.3	Oil level warning lamp	457
U5.4	Brake fluid level warning lamp	458
U5.5	Brake pad wear warning lamp	460
U5.6	Washer fluid level warning lamp	461
U5.7	Coolant warning lamp	463
U6	LCD instrument panel	469 to 492
U6.1	No charge warning symbol	469
U6.2	Voltmeter	470 to 472
U6.3	Fuel gauge	471
U6.4	Oil pressure warning symbol	486
U6.5	Oil pressure gauge	488
U6.6	Temperature gauge	481
U6.7	Running lights pilot lamp	478
U6.8	Speedometer	491, 492
U6.9	Main beam pilot lamp	482
U6.10	Direction indicator repeater (LH)	486
U6.11	Direction indicator repeater (RH)	488
U6.13	Handbrake warning lamp	484
U6.14	Tachometer	484
U6.15	Trailer direction indicator repeater	480
U6.21	Relay (display lighting)	474 to 476
U6.22	Display lighting	475, 476
U6.23	Speedometer illumination	491

Key to Fig. 13.3 (continued). Not all items are fitted to all models

No	Description	Track
U6.24	Miles/km changeover switch	493
U6.25	Calibration switch	478
V1	Brake fluid diode	220
V4	Blocking diode (rear foglamps)	253
V5	Blocking diode (rear foglamps)	257
V6	Blocking diode (parking lights, not UK)	240
V7	Diode (TBI)	562
X1	Trailer socket	Various
X2	Auxiliary connectors	Various
X5	Engine wiring harness connector	Various
X6	Rear wiring harness connector	Various
X7	Front wiring harness connector	Various
X8	LCD instrument connector (26-way)	469 to 492
X9	LCD instrument connector (16-way)	476 to 490
X10	Ignition timing connector (not UK)	138 to 140
X11	Wiring connector (TBI)	–
Y5	Solenoid valve (Diesel)	199
Y6	Auxiliary air valve (fuel injectors)	188 to 190, 541
Y7	Fuel injectors	188 to 190, 541
Y10	Distributor (with Hall sensor)	122, 138 to 140
Y11	Hall sensor	118 to 121, 145 to 147, 507 to 509
Y14	Inductive sensor (not UK)	135 to 137, 550 to 554
Y15	Inductive sensor with ignition module	125, 126
Y17	Idle cut-off solenoid	342
Y18	Dashpot solenoid (not UK)	159
Y22	Distributor (not UK)	147, 151
Y23	Distributor (with inductive sensor)	129
Y24	Distributor (not UK)	139, 557
Y32	Fuel injector valve (TBI)	563

Colour code

Code	Colour	Code	Colour
BL	Blue	LI	Lilac
BR	Brown	RT	Red
GE	Yellow	SW	Black
GN	Green	VI	Violet
GR	Grey	WS	White
HBL	Light blue		

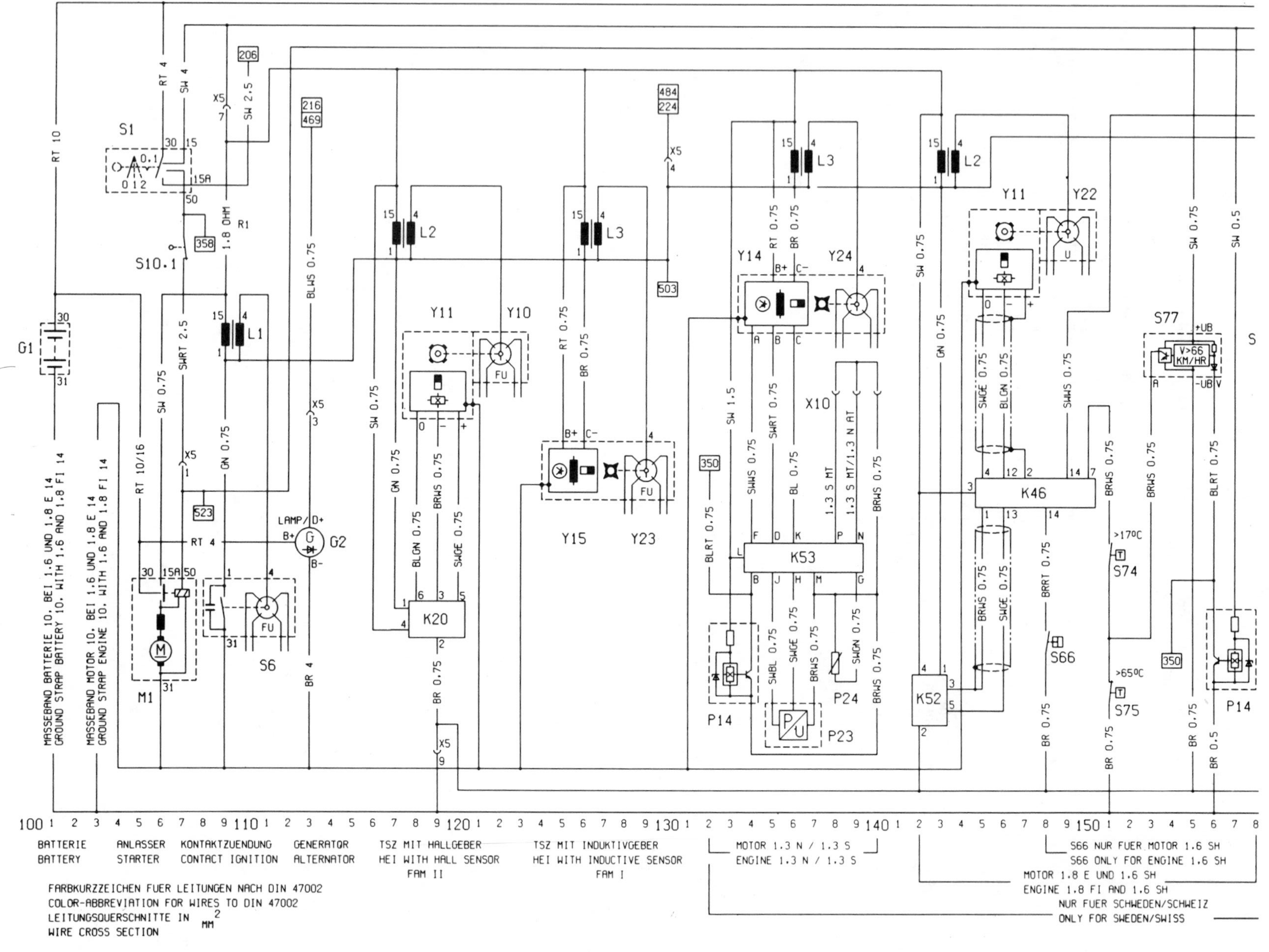

Fig. 13.3 Wiring diagram – all 1986 models

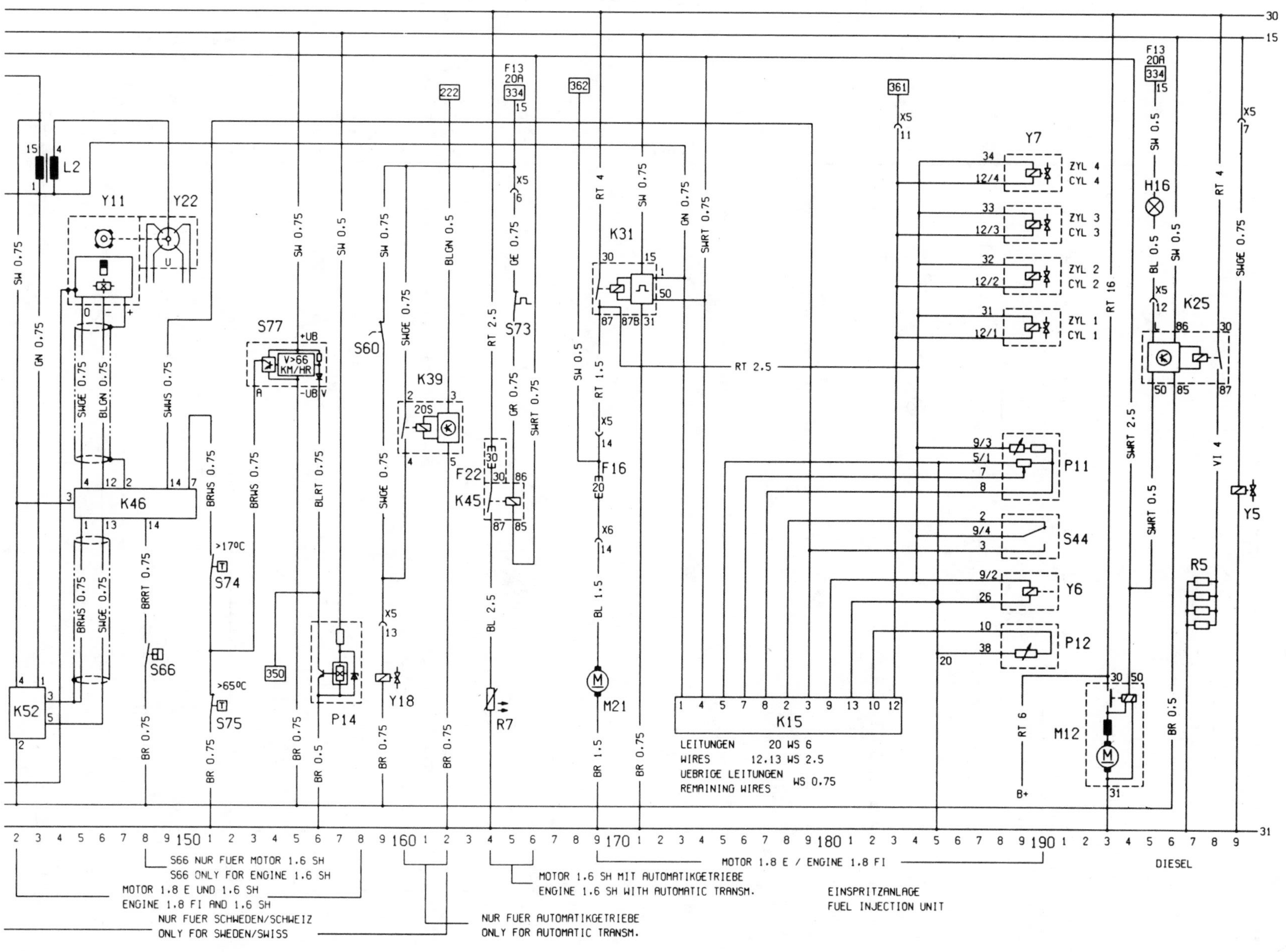

Fig. 13.3 Wiring diagram – all 1986 models (continued)

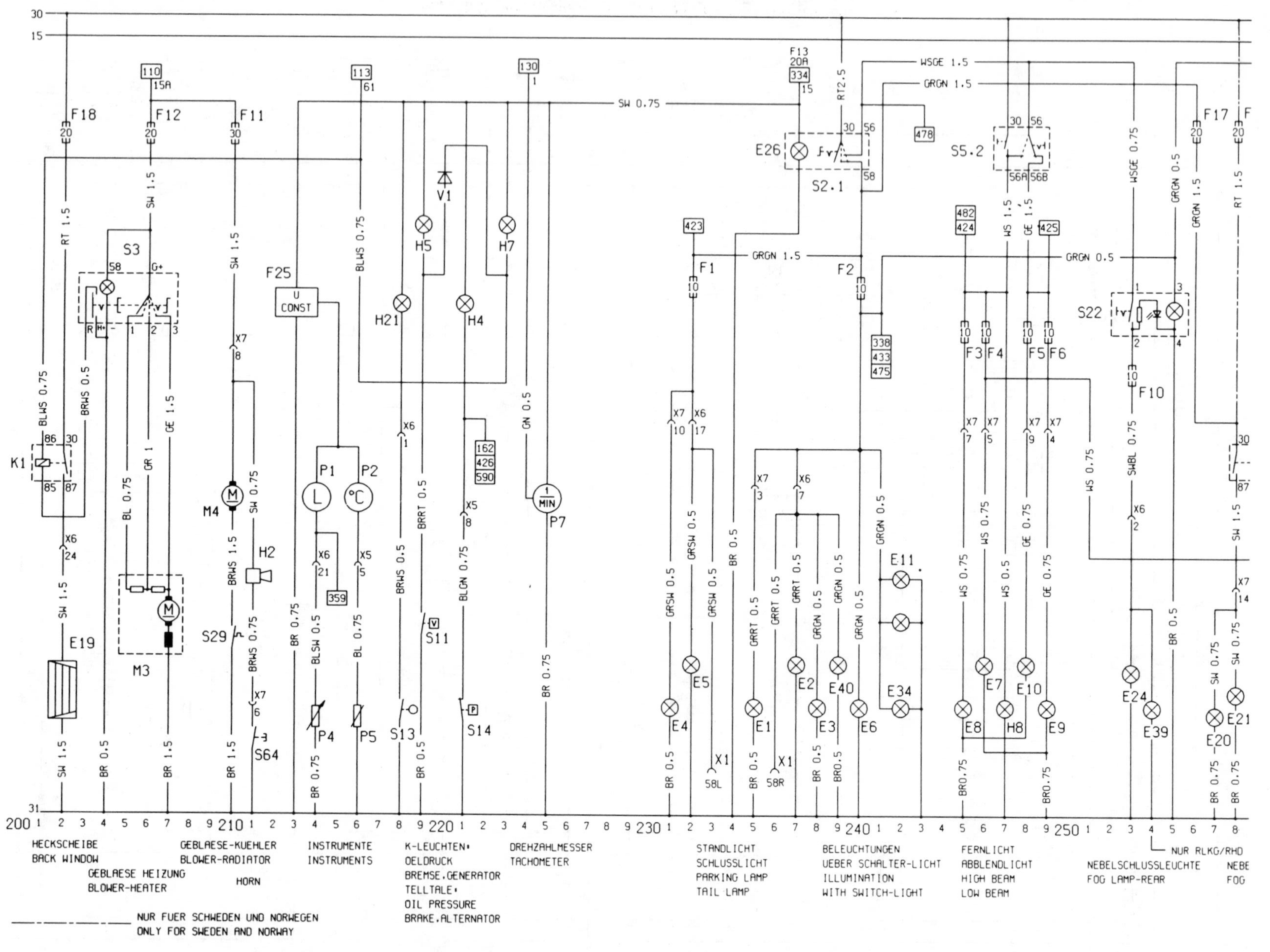

Fig. 13.3 Wiring diagram – all 1986 models (continued)

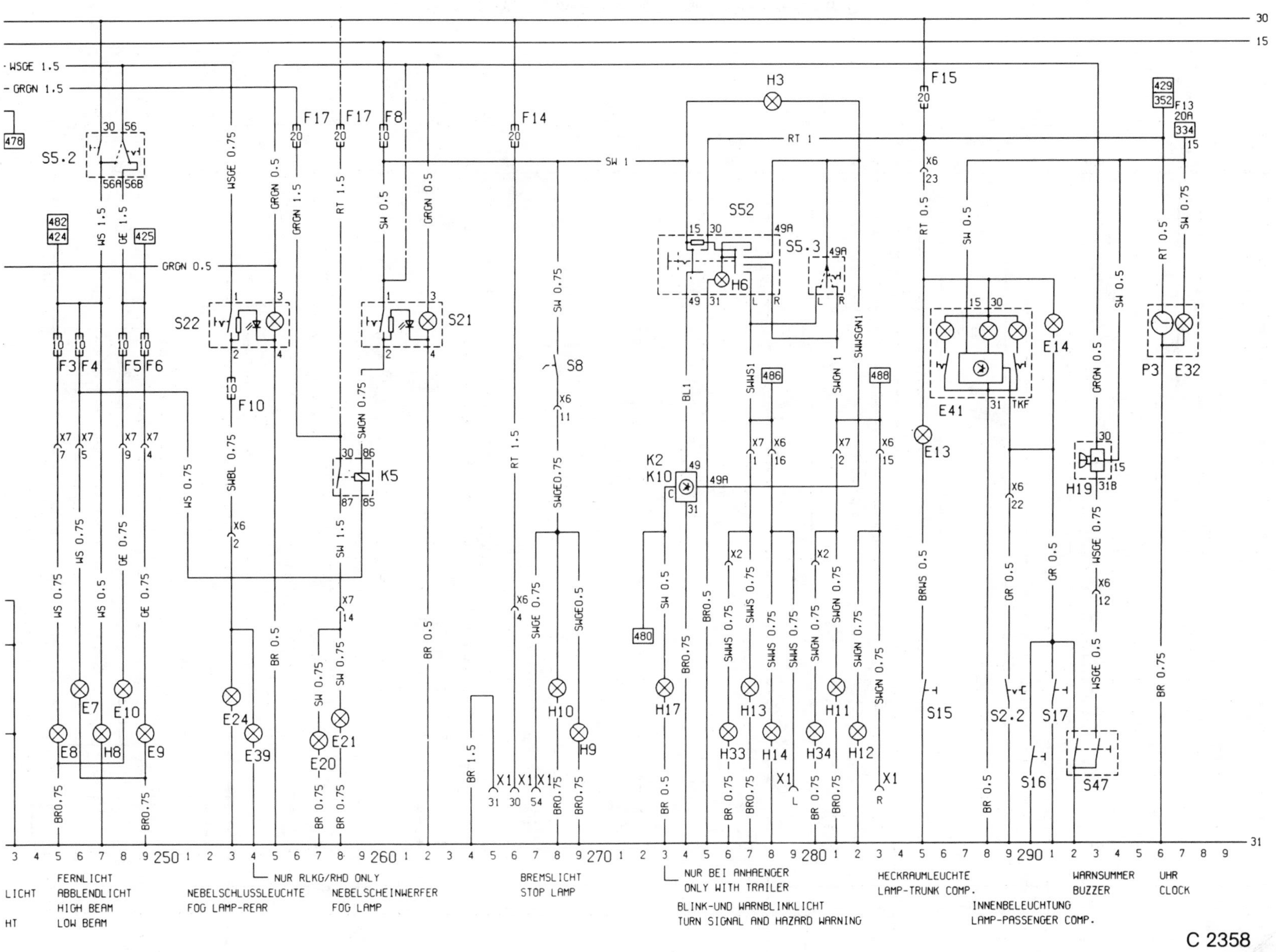

Fig. 13.3 Wiring diagram – all 1986 models (continued)

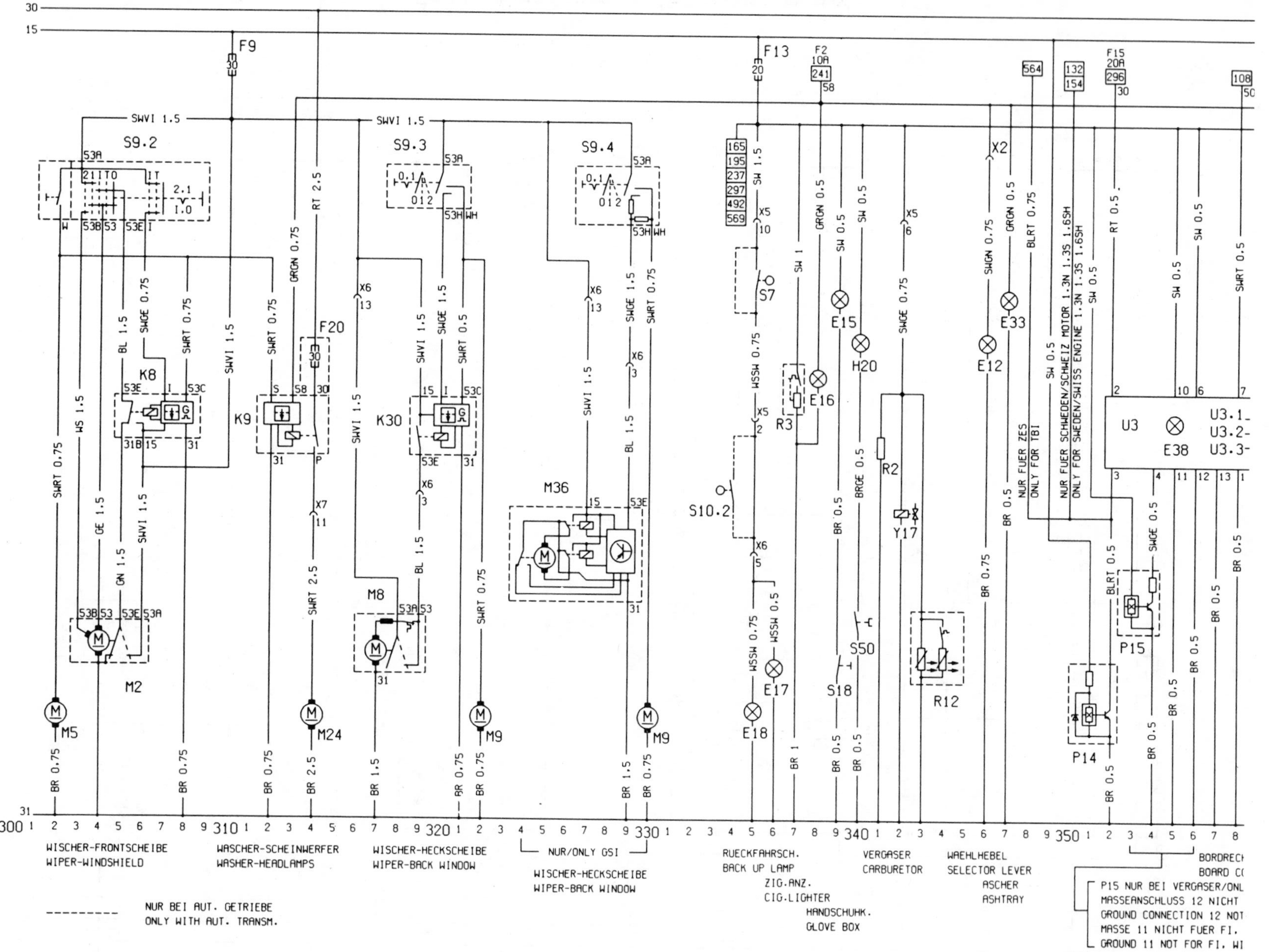

Fig. 13.3 Wiring diagram – all 1986 models (continued)

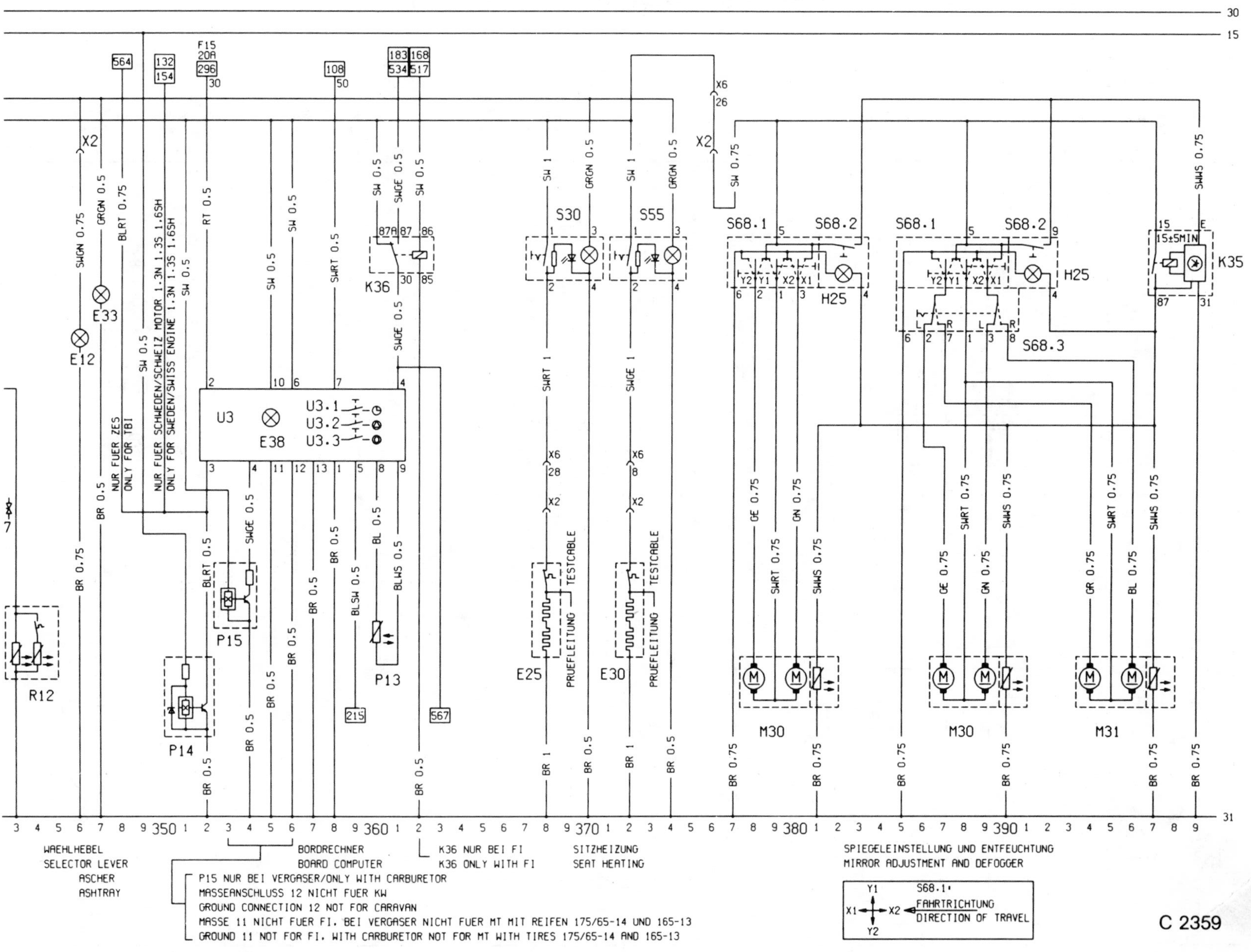

Fig. 13.3 Wiring diagram – all 1986 models (continued)

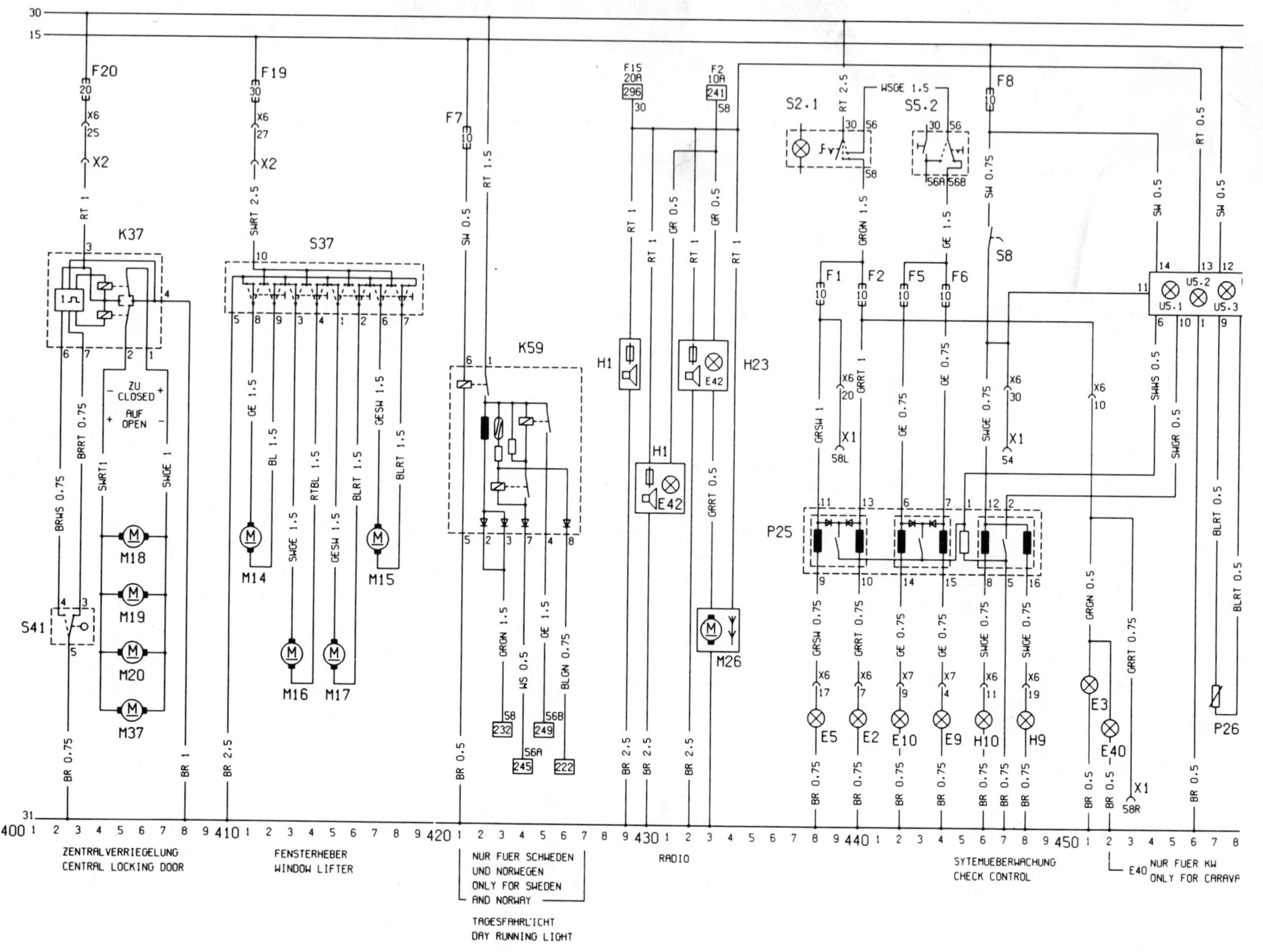

Fig. 13.3 Wiring diagram – all 1986 models (continued)

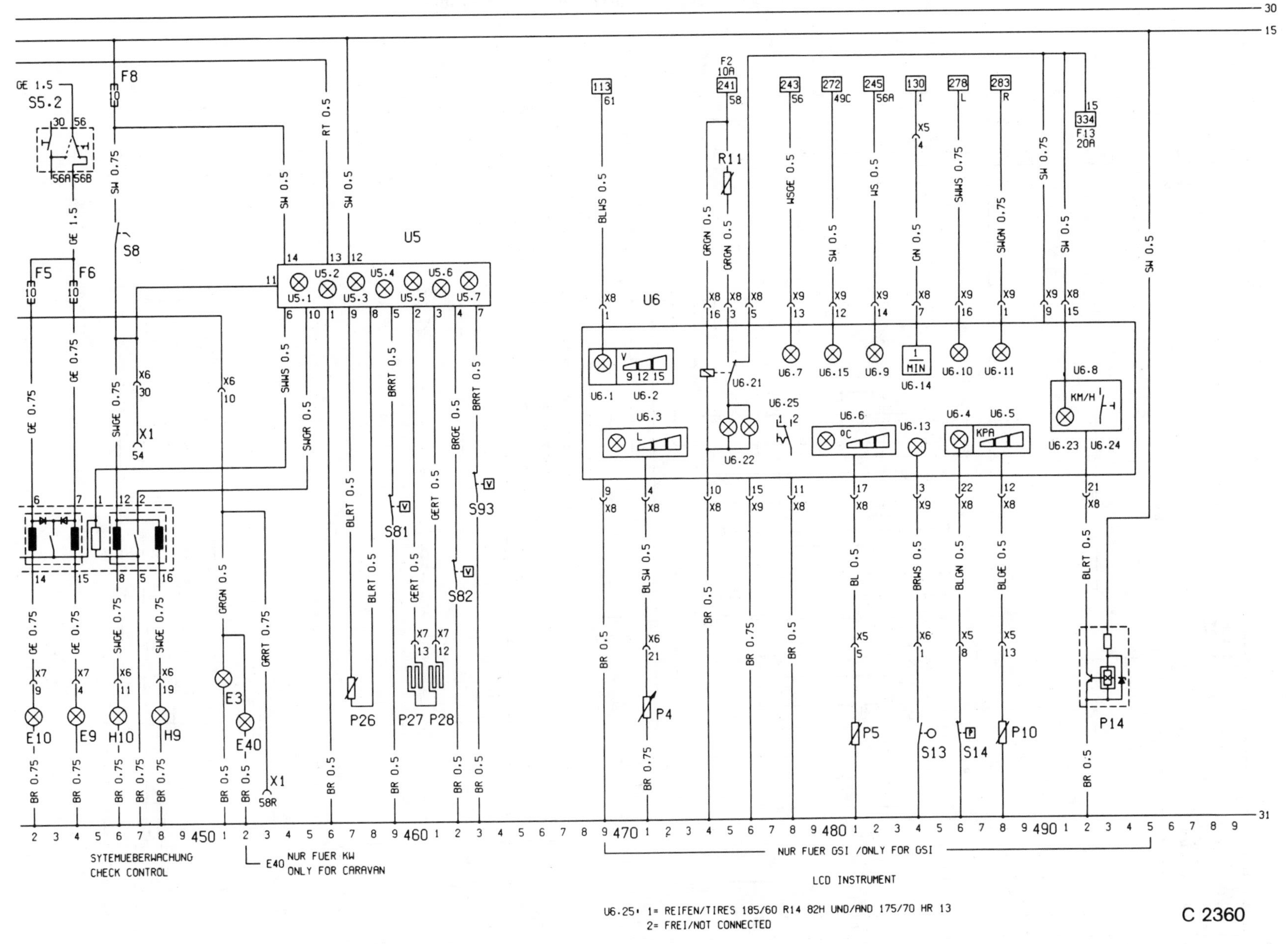

Fig. 13.3 Wiring diagram – all 1986 models (continued)

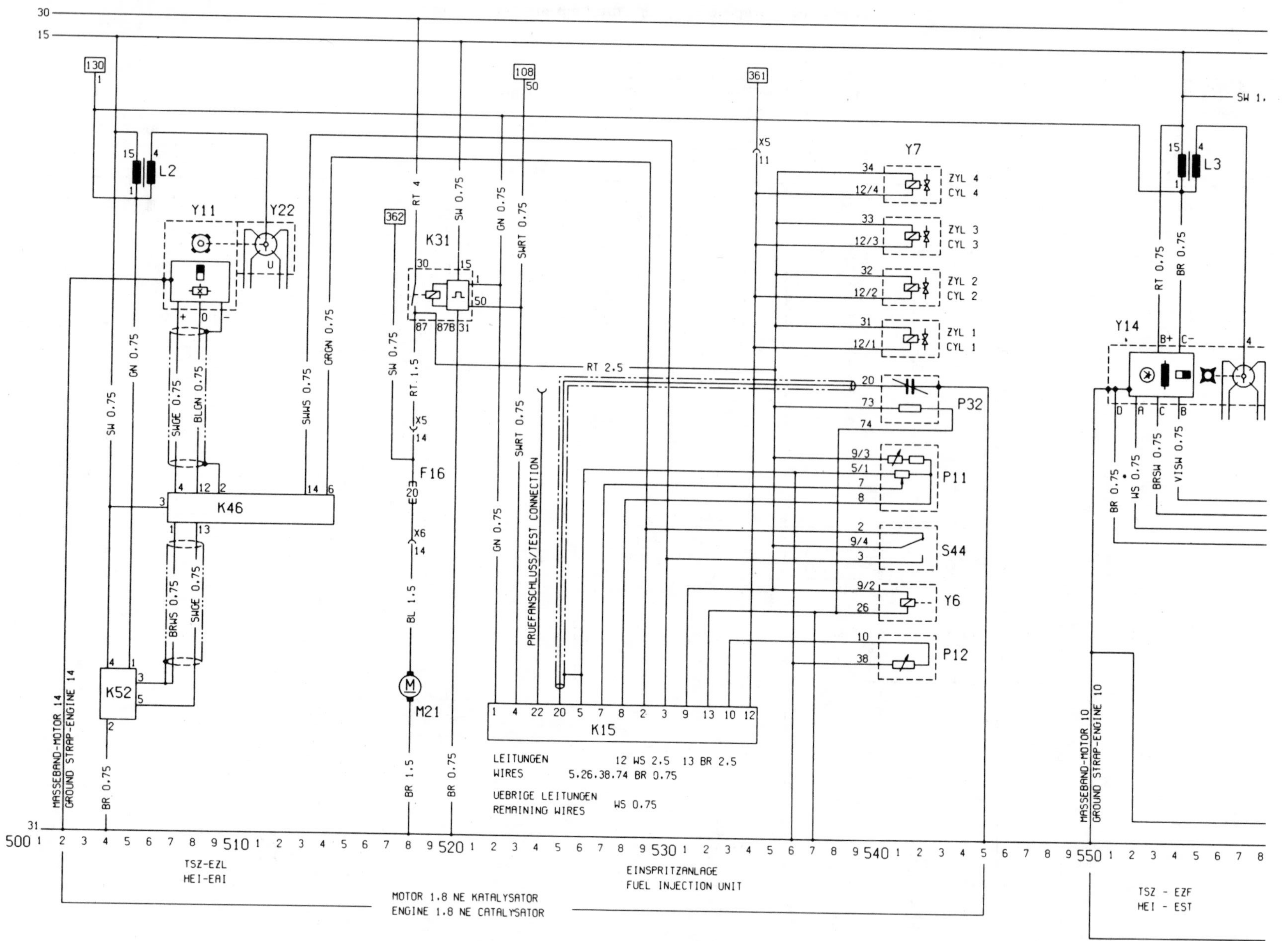

Fig. 13.3 Wiring diagram – all 1986 models (continued)

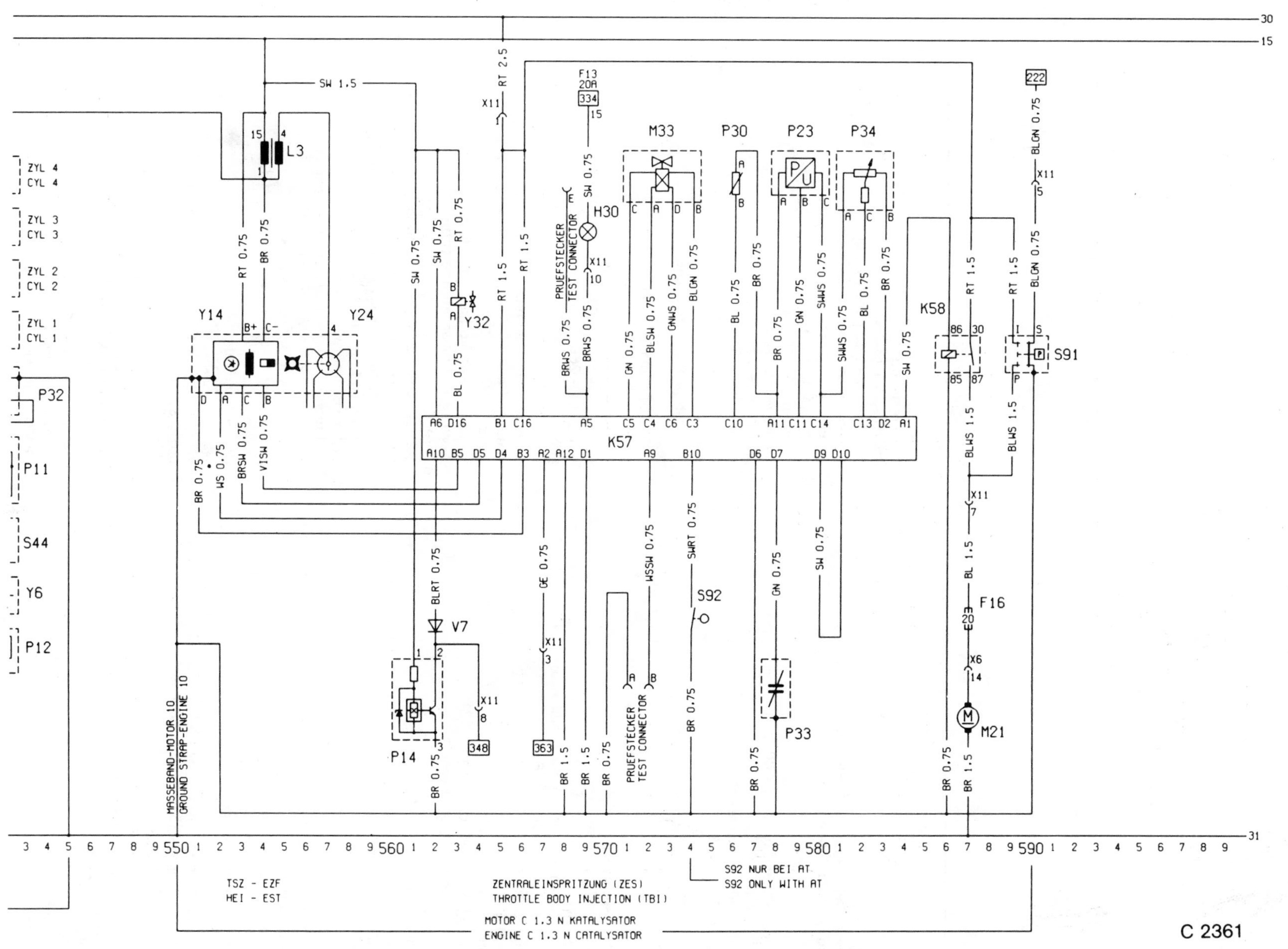

Fig. 13.3 Wiring diagram – all 1986 models (continued)

Index

C

D

O

P

R